*Foreword by*

MOEEN ALI

*Editor*

DANIEL BRIGHAM

*Compiled by*

HENRY COWEN, ED DAVIS, VITHUSHAN EHANTHARAJAH,
ED KEMP & PHIL WALKER

*Design*

JOE PROVIS & ROB WHITEHOUSE

This edition first published in the UK by All Out Cricket Ltd

© All Out Cricket Ltd 2015
www.alloutcricket.com

ISBN: 978-0-85719-477-0

This book is copyright under the Berne Convention. No reproduction without permission. All rights reserved. The publisher makes no representations, express or implied, with regard to the accuracy of the information contained in this book and cannot accept any legal responsibility for any errors or omission that may be made. A CIP Catalogue record for this book is available from the British Library.

Published by Jellyfish Publishing
www.jellyfishpublishing.co.uk

Editor: *Daniel Brigham;* Research and editorial: *Henry Cowen, Ed Davis, Vithushan Ehantharajah, Ed Kemp, Phil Walker*
Design: *Joe Provis, Rob Whitehouse;* Images: *Getty Images unless stated;*
Print: *Jellyfish Print Solutions*

Acknowledgements
The publishers would like to thank the county clubs, the Professional Cricketers' Association and the players for their assistance in helping to put together this book. Additional information has been gathered from espncricinfo.com and cricketarchive.com.

# CONTENTS

*The* Cricketers' Who's Who *2015*

OPENERS 5
FOREWORD – Moeen Ali 6
EDITOR'S NOTES – Daniel Brigham 9
THE ASHES SPIRIT – John Stern 12
A WINDOW TO THE COUNTIES – Vithushan Ehantharajah 16
THROUGH THE LOOKING GLASS – Jason Gillespie 20
KEY 24

THE TEAMS 25

COUNTY INS AND OUTS 99

THE PLAYERS 103

ENGLAND WOMEN 501

THE UMPIRES 527

ROLL OF HONOUR 555

# SUBSCRIBE TO ALLOUTCRICKET AND RECEIVE YOUR FIRST 2 ISSUES FOR JUST £2

**TAKE OUT A SUB TO AOC THIS SEASON AND YOUR FIRST TWO ISSUES WILL COST JUST A POUND APIECE!**

- **FREE DELIVERY** direct to your door
- **GREAT SAVING** on the cover price
- **COUNTY CRICKET** covered every month

Simply visit **aocsubs.com** and enter **CWW15** into the discount code box or call **0844 322 1229** and quote **CWW15**

Offer valid until September 30 2015 [open to UK residents only]. This offer is open to new subscribers only. This offer is non-refundable.

# Openers

# FOREWORD

*by Moeen Ali*

Welcome to the 2015 edition of the Cricketers' Who's Who. It is an honour to be asked to write the foreword for a publication that all county cricketers love to be a part of. It remains a privilege for all of us, and when I first came on the scene as a young county cricketer 10 years ago it was so exciting to see my name in the Who's Who, and that hasn't changed.

Now, a decade on from my first-class debut, I can look back on 2014 with very fond memories. It was a breakthrough year for me in more ways than one. It was the year when I ratified what in my mind I already knew about myself: that was I was ready for the step up to international level.

It was a year in which the national selectors showed faith in me and my ability. They handed me my international debuts in all three formats of the game and gave me the freedom to go and express myself on the field of play against the likes of Sri Lanka and India. It was a challenge I thoroughly enjoyed.

I am grateful to all those who have backed me along the way during my journey so far. Just as importantly I am also grateful to those who haven't backed me, as we all need that extra impetus to do well sometimes.

A special mention here must go to Worcestershire County Cricket Club for all the work and effort they have put in to getting the best out of me and helping me reach the pinnacle of representing my country.

My 10 seasons as a county cricketer have really been a finishing school for me. Learning my trade on the county circuit has taught me the basics and the fundamentals of the game, along with the mental aptitude needed to succeed at the highest level. I hope my story of representing my country serves as an example and indeed an inspiration to others to show that if you apply yourself there's nothing you can't achieve. Nothing is impossible.

County cricket is something I really enjoy and the camaraderie and togetherness of the boys at Worcestershire is what makes playing cricket worthwhile and satisfying. After last season's promotion to Division One of the County Championship there was a special buzz about the place, and we can't wait to get started again this summer – as I'm sure the other 17 counties can't either.

I'm really looking forward to the 2015 summer. It promises to be action-packed, with the visits of an exciting New Zealand side and, of course, Australia, as well as the county season being back in full swing again as Yorkshire, Warwickshire and Durham look to defend their titles.

The months ahead will be full of new and exciting challenges in both cricketing terms and personally, but challenges bring out the best in me and I look forward to it with real relish and enthusiasm. It is a summer not to be missed.

Finally, no review of the year would be complete without thanking my lord and creator without whom nothing is possible.

Enjoy the summer – may it be a good one!

Moeen Ali
England and Worcestershire

THE **Nightwatchman**
THE WISDEN CRICKET QUARTERLY

*"The Nightwatchman is a triumph. Left-field, laugh-out-loud funny and highly intelligent. A gem"*

ED SMITH

Order now at

**www.thenightwatchman.net**

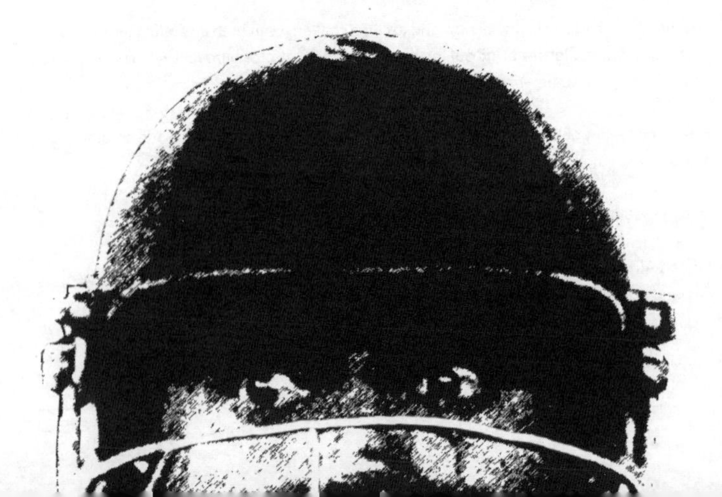

## EDITOR'S NOTES

Welcome to the 2015 Cricketers' Who's Who. England cricket fans may be forgiven for approaching the summer with a little trepidation, but there is nevertheless much to look forward to over the season.

An ignominious early World Cup exit included heavy defeats to Australia and New Zealand, the two teams England will be sparring with this summer. The Kiwis will arrive with their best – and most entertaining – side in a generation. Trent Boult and Tim Southee lead a pace attack with greater depth than their country has ever known, while Brendon McCullum captains with skill and intuition and is part of a quality batting line-up that blends flair and grit. With two Investec Test matches, five Royal London ODIs and a NatWest T20I, they will be a real force ahead of the Ashes. Australia will carry a similar level of pace threat, while in David Warner and Steve Smith they will have two of the world's most in-form batsmen as they look to win their first Ashes in England for 14 years.

Despite the fall-out from England's disastrous World Cup campaign, there are, as ever, many reasons to be cheerful. Last summer's come-from-behind Test series win over India showed a young side brimming with talent that, with the right guidance, has the potential to reinvigorate English cricket. The Test series against Sri Lanka and India also highlighted that the County Championship remains an important breeding ground for young talent. Opportunities were given to Chris Jordan, Sam Robson, Jos Buttler and Gary Ballance, while Liam Plunkett returned seven years after his previous Test. And, to the delight of anyone who has followed county cricket closely over the last few years, Moeen Ali was picked and given an extended run.

Moeen was truly the positive face of English cricket in a difficult 2014, and we are very grateful to him for agreeing to write our foreword. A brilliant maiden Test century at Headingley, 22 wickets and two ODI centuries show that the 10 seasons spent honing his skills on the domestic circuit have turned him into a classy, competitive cricketer.

As well as Moeen's foreword, this year we wanted to introduce a bit more opinion and debate into the Who's Who. So John Stern, *All Out Cricket*'s editor-at-large, tackles the nebulous Spirit of Cricket and asks whether the repercussions of Phillip Hughes' tragic death will change anything ahead of the Ashes. Meanwhile, Yorkshire's Championship-winning coach Jason Gillespie gives an Australian's opinion on what works and what doesn't about England's domestic structure, including pitches and franchises. Plus Vithushan Ehantharajah, the Christopher Martin-Jenkins Young Journalist of the Year in 2014, gives a colourful insight into life on the county circuit, from offering advice to national selectors to the dangers of Twitter.

As ever we have armed you with everything you need to know about every county and every player for the upcoming season. We've introduced a few new questions to go with the old favourites in our players' Q&As, and, as ever, they have responded with gusto (although a few may have taken the 'Pet hates' question a little too literally by nominating their least-favourite domestic animal...).

Obtaining answers from 418 county and England Women players, plus all first-class umpires, can occasionally provide a few bumps, so many thanks to all of the players and officials for their answers and to all county media officers for their invaluable assistance. Without them, this book simply wouldn't happen. Thanks must also go to the PCA for their promotion and support and to *All Out Cricket*'s magnificent editorial and design teams for getting this book onto the shelves in time for the first ball of the 2015 county season.

As ever, the players' answers kept us going through the long winter nights. We've learnt never to loan your iPhone to Kent's Ryan Davies, who has dropped five of them in the bath, that Middlesex's Nick Compton wears a pair of speedos to bat in, that Gloucestershire's Gareth Roderick would like to be Justin Bieber for a day in order to ruin his career and that Ireland's George Dockrell has never drunk a cup of tea or coffee.

For the past four years we've asked the players to nominate who they currently rate as the best player in county cricket. In 2012 and 2013 Marcus Trescothick took the honours, while Moeen Ali was the runaway winner in 2014. This year Jeetan Patel received the vast majority of picks after a stellar season in which he took 107 wickets across all formats and hit 510 Championship runs. We once again asked players to nominate their tips for the top and, among a number of youngsters to look out for, Lancashire's 18-year-old batsman Haseeb Hameed received the most plaudits.

Watching young talent emerge is always one of the joys of the season and adds to a mouthwatering summer in which England's young side take on two of the world's best teams, England Women take on Australia Women in the battle for the Ashes and Yorkshire, Durham and Warwickshire look to hold on to their titles.

Enjoy the season!

Daniel Brigham
March 2015

# CLICK IT. CRICKET.

Get online and get more from the world's best cricket magazine

alloutcricket.com

gear.alloutcricket.com

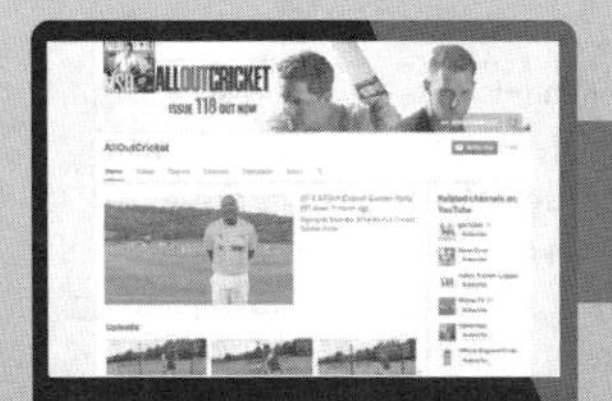


youtube.com/AllOutCricket

## COMMENT

### THE ASHES SPIRIT

*Phil Hughes' tragic death invoked debate over the spirit of cricket. Ahead of the 2015 Ashes, John Stern asks if one of sport's fiercest battles will be tamed*

It was Greg Baum, the sage of *The Age*, who quipped in the Adelaide press box that cricket's new, post-Phillip Hughes entente cordiale had lasted only three and a half days. And, inevitably, it was David Warner who punctured this bubble by goading India's fast bowler Varun Aaron after the batsman had been bowled off a no-ball.

Warner's reaction to the tragic passing of his teammate and friend, Phillip Hughes, had been intensely and publically emotional. Every milestone of his twin hundreds in Australia's first Test against India at Adelaide last December was greeted by skyward glances, fist pumps and hugs with batting partners. His press conferences were overwrought and slightly weird. But his pugilistic attitude had never disappeared. He was always fighting, as it seems he must, firstly for his "little mate" and then for himself, his team or whatever it might be that gets him going.

It is hard to reconcile that the man who told James Anderson at Brisbane in the last Ashes to "get ready for a broken f***** arm", is the same Michael Clarke who said this at Hughes's funeral: "Phillip's spirit, which is now part of the game forever, will act as a custodian of the game forever. We must listen to it, we must learn from it, we must dig in, dig in and get through to tea. And we must play on."

There was a unique emotional intensity to the Adelaide Test and a remarkable desire on the part of everyone involved, not least India's first-time Test captain Virat Kohli, to produce a spectacle worthy of Hughes' memory. The rest of the series was played out against the standard background of over-hyped aggression and storms in teacups.

This prompted an outburst from Jonathan Agnew who, in an interview with the *Radio Times*, said: "I have that Michael Clarke speech tucked away ready to throw at the Australians." The thrust of his lengthy attack on the behaviour of Clarke's team was that "cricket has gone too far".

There are three observations to make about Agnew's comments. One is that it feels desperately harsh to hold Clarke to account for an articulate, poignant eulogy made at the funeral of his close friend. Secondly, it presumes that the "spirit" of Hughes, as presented by Clarke, is precisely what Agnew takes it to mean, i.e. that players should behave better. And thirdly, it also presumes that there is some downward linear graph of player behaviour, aka the spirit of cricket.

In the modern tradition of immediate reaction and counter-reaction, Agnew's views were roundly condemned as those of an out-of-touch Pom. And certainly if one is taking players to task about their on-field attitudes then Australians cannot be the only villains here.

During the Adelaide Test Mark Nicholas, who spends half the year in Australia as the front man for Channel 9's cricket coverage, had this to say: "The spirit of the game should be the spirit of Phil Hughes. I hope that it means nothing more than a little reining in of attitudes and priorities. At large I think the modern sportsman has become very selfish and I certainly think that in Australia there has been an ugly side, at times, to the cricket. For me the spirit of cricket is about respect – for your opponent and for the game. That's all. If it brings it back to that, if it rationalises things a bit then something good can come out of it."

It's a similar view to Agnew but with a more nuanced and subtler tone. And his point about respect for opponents and the game chimes precisely with Mike Atherton's view whenever he is drawn wearily into discussing the old canard of the game's spirit.

* * *

"It was Ian Chappell who messed it all up," said David, a retired farmer from Dubbo, the central New South Wales town that was also the birthplace of Glenn McGrath. What Chappell had messed up was the change in player behaviour that occurred in the 1970s when fast bowling and overt aggression complemented each other to create the 'brand' of cricket that Australia are most closely identified with and have tried to recreate in the Lehmann-Clarke era with Mitchell Johnson as their spearhead.

David had been slightly backed into a corner by his wife Gabrielle, who said she actually enjoyed England's victory in the 2010/11 Ashes because she'd become disillusioned by the antics of the Australians. It seemed clear that she also felt a bit sorry for the Poms (never a great feeling being patronised by Australians) and she liked Alastair Cook.

David was unimpressed by this view and whatever his old-school misgivings about the post-Packer bravado, there was only one team he ever wanted to see win the Ashes and it wasn't the one in blue caps. The couple were steeped in cricket and told me they had travelled by train from Sydney to Perth for the first Test of the 1974/75 Ashes.

But Chappell didn't invent on-field aggression or the use of fast bowling as a weapon of intimidation. Sport tends to reflect the cultural mores of the times and the society in which it was played. Chappell's Aussies, like Clive Lloyd's West Indies side, were emerging shouting and screaming into a fully professional era where players were treated as something other than serfs by patrician administrators.

"The Third Test will go down in history as probably the most unpleasant ever played," is one of the great opening lines of a cricket match report. It comes from Wisden 1934 and concerns the Adelaide Test of the Bodyline series. The acrimony of Bodyline threatened not only the cricketing relations between England and Australia but the whole fabric of Empire. If the game and the Ashes can survive such a storm, then surely it can survive anything.

In the first Test of the 1948 series at Trent Bridge, Keith Miller repeatedly bounced Len Hutton and the crowd's reaction was so uproarious that the Nottinghamshire secretary had to appeal for calm. So much for post-war levity and perspective.

"The rivalry is genuine and intense, but by and large friendly," wrote Steven Lynch in his introduction to *Wisden On The Ashes*, "with the odd exception of Bodyline ... The main reason ... is the underlying comradeship of the people of England and Australia. Behind all the teasing and name-calling is a long affinity and a long friendship."

Cricket's other international rivalries might be laced with real political conflict, racial suspicion and cultural differences, but the Anglo-Australian contest is a self-contained, familial flavour. Arguments, however foul-mouthed or aggressive, are those of pent-up, petulant siblings. Occasionally unedifying but ultimately inevitable. There is a line that shouldn't be crossed and even though players know where that line is, it still gets crossed.

Like it or not, the Lehmann-Clarke axis of aggression is not based on personal enmity towards individuals. It is a tactical decision based on the premise that, allied to the fast bowling of Johnson, it can unsettle their opponents.

When Steve Waugh laid down the gauntlet to opposition captains to accept a fielder's word for disputed catches, this wasn't sportsmanship, it was gamesmanship. It was a brilliant device that managed to put mental pressure on opponents while assuming the moral high ground. It also ran contrary to the Australian cricketing principle of waiting for the umpire's decision that precludes walking.

The 2005 Ashes is remembered for many things, including the spirit in which it was played. But it wasn't all Freddie Flintoff putting his hand on Brett Lee's shoulder. What about Simon Jones and Paul Collingwood squaring up to Matthew Hayden in the T20 that preceded the series? Or England's tactical use of sub fielders that so riled Ricky Ponting? Ultimately, though, respect remained intact and both sides could acknowledge they had been part of possibly the greatest ever series. There's no better example of this than Ponting's reaction at the end of the post-match press conference in the final Test at The Oval. Under serious pressure following the result, Ponting's graciousness in defeat was actually quite moving.

The 2015 Ashes is the first since the death of Phillip Hughes and given the young batsman's connection with English county cricket, the series will undoubtedly be a vehicle for yet more tributes and memorials to his remarkable talent and character. Clarke, because he is so aware of his own image, will, I suspect, behave in a self-consciously statesmanlike way (assuming he plays). But this is the third Ashes in three years and familiarity has bred contempt. Warner will be wound up by the crowds – and by England's players. Stuart Broad will goad and chide; Jimmy Anderson will smirk.

International sport is a soap opera and sometimes the less savoury plot-lines are the ones that the casual observer latches on to. It was ever thus and it's naïve to think otherwise. But if Hughes' memory can serve one purpose, then a series played at full pelt, with a desire to entertain and to win, rather than not lose, would be a happy legacy.

*John Stern is editor-at-large of* All Out Cricket. *He tweets @JStern_Cricket*

## A WINDOW TO THE COUNTIES

*Image problem? What image problem? Vithushan Ehantharajah immersed himself in the 2014 county season and discovered a much-maligned system that continues to pump out quality players*

"He stuck around for a bit. Didn't he? Yeah?"

It sounded rhetorical, but it wasn't. It boomed out in the press dining room at The Oval, as the staff replenished the tea and coffee canteens.

Having just walked in, for the first match of the season, I steered around the two in conversation, offering a nod of 'hello' to the senior journalist involved. The question aimed at him had come from an England selector.

It was a novelty I would come to experience a handful of times that year. I spent the first innings of a Lions match in August, at Taunton, chatting to Mick Newell about the development of Alex Hales. During a rain delay at Chelmsford, Angus Fraser asked me who was the quickest bowler I had seen so far.

Back to The Oval, and the subject of the question was Zafar Ansari who, in Surrey's first innings against Glamorgan, had scored 74 off 259. Had Ansari "stuck around" for much longer, he could have claimed squatter's rights.

The selector's enquiry made it into my report later that day. It was going to be that kind of season; any sighting of a selector, coach or an England tracksuit in the club shop would merit a mention of "international presence watching on".

England's hammering in the 2013/14 Ashes tour had opened up slots in what once seemed a settled international set-up. For the first time in an age, four Test spots were up for grabs; an opening batsman, No.3, a spinner and a quick. County cricket mattered that much more.

It was my second full season covering the county circuit. As with fans, the more you watch, the greater appreciation you have for the strengths and weaknesses of each player. With every England-qualified player's performance under greater scrutiny before the first Test of the summer against Sri Lanka, hype season was open. And everyone had their horse to back, whether through fandom or hunches.

With most of my work based in the south and south-east of the country, with the occasional trip to the midlands, I was watching a lot of Sam Robson. Early season runs saw him nip ahead of the alternates and accompany Alastair Cook at the top of the order for the entire summer.

He ended up averaging just over 30, notching a century in his second Test, at Headingley. But he struggled to convince as a long-term solution as Cook's partner. As thoughts wandered to the winter tour of West Indies, talk had already turned to Yorkshire pair Adam Lyth and Alex Lees, which presented me with probably my starkest lesson.

On the domestic circuit, Robson excelled, working opening attacks in early season conditions in a manner that suggested he would succeed at a higher level. There's every chance he will go on and forge a successful Test career, but his case, in the short term, provided me with an important guide.

Robson was my first instance of tipping a player for a successful England berth (I was far from alone), having watched, essentially, the portion of his career that the England selectors were keeping tabs on, what with Robson qualifying through residency and choosing England over Australia. Time will tell whether it was the right call, and whether his exclusion from England's immediate plans will be temporary or permanent. By then, I will have probably made a few more calls.

Matt Prior's troubles with his Achilles meant the hunt for a wicketkeeper was on. While Jos Buttler was staking his claim in ODI cricket, the dearth of other young challengers saw Chris Read and James Foster touted as very capable stop-gaps.

Naturally, the sight of England wicketkeeping coach Bruce French at Chelmsford in May got Twitter chatting. However, a bigger news story overshadowed Foster that game, as Graeme Smith was ruled out of yet another Surrey season. It would be an injury that, eventually, led him to call time on his illustrious career. At the time, Surrey's director of cricket, Alec Stewart, didn't think so. We spoke on the phone – specifically, the Surrey media manager's phone – after I put in a request for clarification on some tweets Smith sent out regarding his future.

That's perhaps the most interesting change – Twitter. The day before Smith's 140-character offerings, Ashar Zaidi of Sussex had been fined for voicing his displeasure following a caught behind decision by umpire Nigel Llong, against Somerset.

"It's a coach's nightmare," Mark Robinson, Sussex head coach, had told me, with a huge sigh, after the culmination of an ill-tempered encounter at Hove between his side and Nottinghamshire had once again involved a tweet.

The flashpoint for the subsequent ire was the dismissal of Nottinghamshire's Hales, caught at first slip. After standing his ground, Hales asked Sussex's Ben Brown, the catcher, if it was a clean take. Brown confirmed that it was and may have snuck in a colourful word or two.

While the game continued on towards lunch, a freelance photographer posted a photo of the catch that seemed to show the ball grounded. Stuart Broad, on Notts duty, got hold of the snap and tweeted it out to his hundreds of thousands of followers. Soon it was everywhere.

It was petty and unnecessary, but when was the last time county cricket went viral?

There was a rumoured stand-off between Hales and Brown at lunch, and that ill-feeling did not dissipate as the game went on. Nottinghamshire's Andre Adams was seen to be exchanging some frank words with Robinson, while even members of the crowd took it upon themselves to defend their county with some jibes of their own.

Despite the tension, there were some quaint moments as the game ambled to a draw, most notably Prior and Broad sharing lifts to and from the ground because Broad was staying with Prior for the duration of the match.

As is usually the way, as centrally contracted England players both were off limits to the press. You realise very quickly on the domestic scene that a player's likeliness to speak at the end of a day's play is inversely proportional to their proximity to the national side.

The big question had been whether Prior was fit enough to retain his Test spot, especially with Buttler breathing down his neck. He looked fine, if a bit laboured, but his itinerary from the week before suggested he wanted to prove his fitness beyond reasonable doubt.

His hope of game time in the previous Championship match with Middlesex had been scuppered by rain, with all four days washed out at Merchant Taylors' School. When play was called off early on day three, he drove down to Eastbourne to take part in a 2nd XI match and kept for 30 overs. He then spent the start of day four at Hove training, before getting a call from London that there might be play after all. By the time he arrived, the match had been abandoned. A quick SOS call to French allowed him an impromptu workout session, before a drive to Cardiff for a NatWest T20 Blast match.

The miles clocked by Prior in that week was nothing out of the ordinary for the county cricketer. The new schedule, at times, meant teams were on the road for the best part of a month, jumping from format to format, on motorway to motorway, to and from their Friday-night T20s. If anything, it probably benefits the freelance journalist, who eats or starves by the empty days in their calendar, more than the players.

Many players complained about the workload and were already pushing for further modification, and changes have been mooted from 2015. The ECB's discussion document, while full of headline-grabbing suggestions, also contains smaller tweaks that could see all parties satisfied.

Many feel county cricket has an image problem. At close quarters, that doesn't seem to be the case. The changes need to be allowed time; Friday-night games produced some great crowds last year, particularly at The Oval and Lord's which boasted a few Twenty20 sell-outs. Those very crowds may find themselves drawn to other parts of the game, thanks to these new, Friday-night generation players.

Surrey's Jason Roy, Kent's Sam Billings, Essex's Tom Westley, Warwickshire's Sam Hain and Yorkshire's Lees are some of a few names that can take county cricket to a higher level in the English sporting consciousness. All have marketable characteristics, with one common factor – they're all bloody good players.

The recent successful England crop of Chris Woakes, Chris Jordan, Moeen Ali, Gary Ballance and James Taylor has ensured that some of the spotlight remains shone on the domestic game.

For all the talk of franchises and change, for those who spend their time following and covering it, it is clear the English county system continues to provide high quality.

*Vithushan Ehantharajah writes for* All Out Cricket *and* ESPNCricinfo *and in 2014 was named Christopher-Martin Jenkins Young Journalist of the Year. He tweets at @Vitu_E*

# COMMENT

## THROUGH THE LOOKING GLASS

*Fresh from leading Yorkshire to their first Championship title in 14 years, Jason Gillespie gives his verdict on English pitches, franchises and the quality of county cricket*

I am unashamedly a massive fan of county cricket.

I thoroughly enjoyed it when I was a player for Yorkshire and Glamorgan and I've really enjoyed my time here at Yorkshire as a coach; it's been wonderful. Although I don't think everything is perfect – which I'll come on to – it's important to say that the County Championship is a fantastic competition that I am honoured to have won last summer with Yorkshire. There are also a lot of really good players playing really tough cricket.

I always wanted to play county cricket in England. I had offers throughout my career, but I was focused on playing for Australia and I needed time to rest and recuperate. So I turned down a couple of opportunities while I was playing international cricket, which I don't regret because for me it was the right decision. Also, I always said I wanted to commit to a full season. I didn't want to come in for six weeks and then nick off. I wanted to immerse myself thoroughly in the experience: get to know people, get to know the place, get to know my teammates, the coaching staff; to try and be involved as much as I could and make a difference.

In my two full seasons at Yorkshire in 2006 and 2007 and my season at Glamorgan in 2008 I didn't perform as well as I would have liked. I'd love to have taken more wickets – but I had great experiences and it made me appreciate exactly what goes into being a county cricketer.

These days it is harder for an overseas player to commit to playing for a county for a full season. There is more international cricket and more demands on cricketers, while there have also been rule changes at the Home Office which means the criteria required to qualify to play in England has become more limiting. Inevitably the result is that you get fewer full-season overseas players, although this has also opened up more opportunities to give young players from county academies a chance.

Although the standard is very high, a lot of cricket is played in England and there's no doubt it's a hard workload for players. That can be good for some players and not so good for others, so you have to manage them well. The pitches can also sometimes be a problem.

For me, the absolute key for England and their domestic players to improve is to get the pitches right – to play on the best surfaces possible: good cricket wickets that offer a bit to everyone. It shouldn't need saying that all counties should be striving to play on the very best wickets to help players improve.

You want bounce and carry. That way, spinners will come into the game more – they'll get a bit of turn and get bounce. Fast bowlers will see the ball flying through and defensive edges will carry. But it also rewards good batting and it rewards positive strokeplay. So everyone benefits: fast bowlers, spin bowlers and batsmen. Everyone's a winner.

As well as improving standards you also have to remember we are in the entertainment business. Matches shouldn't be played on a low, slow dung-heap – I think back to the Test at Trent Bridge in 2014 and that was seriously boring. India made 457, England responded with 496 – even Jimmy Anderson made 81 – and India then made nearly 400 in their second innings. It was a poor surface, it didn't promote the game, it wasn't entertaining, it was dull. In this country we've got to avoid having our teams play a lot of cricket in those conditions. We want players to play on the best surfaces and we want people to come in and watch the game, and we can't entertain them on rubbish wickets like that.

That should be how we should approach Twenty20 cricket in England: the object should be to make it as entertaining as possible. The matches should be played at the best grounds with the best facilities and the best pitches in order to allow teams to play aggressive, attacking and exciting cricket. We've got some wonderful grounds in the UK and the biggest and best of them should be maximised for Twenty20. The players will love it and so will the fans.

How we structure our domestic T20 tournament is a hot topic and you can understand why. Look at what the Big Bash has done in Australia: it attracts some of the biggest players and gets huge audiences, both in terms of bums on seats at the stadiums and also on television. It's gone better than most people ever imagined, and has brought the sport to a new audience in Australia. While it used to be that people wondered what England could learn from Australia's first-class set-up, now it's more about what it can learn from the Big Bash.

Cricket Australia realised they needed to move the game forward and to align with fans' expectations. I believe the franchise model would work in England, too – as long as the profits are distributed between the counties. You're not appealing to county members, you're trying to seek new audiences; new people to welcome to the game of cricket.

Nothing should be off the table or off-limits. Boldness is needed. Two or three counties could be merged to become one team for the T20 tournament only, and you leave the County Championship with the full 18 counties as it works very well like that. It would be odd, as coach of Yorkshire, to be involved in a totally different team, but T20 is an opportunity to grow the sport and so we need to be thinking outside the box.

Although I understand why the ECB made the T20 Blast an appointment-to-view with regular Friday-night games, I think the majority of people involved in the UK would like a block of T20 cricket at the height of summer. Something about five weeks long would be ideal, as it would attract overseas stars for its entirety and also wouldn't compromise the Championship season. People say the English weather causes problems, and while that is true, you can't base all of your decisions on something you can't control.

Having England players available where possible would also be great but I'm very understanding of how much cricket they play. The international schedule is hard work so I'm conscious of that. At the end of the day you want the best players playing as often as possible so it's a balancing act. Players need to be allowed to recuperate but you also have to appreciate that the fans want to watch the top international players as well. It would also be great to have T20 matches on free-to-air TV, as they are in Australia. Sky have been brilliant for the game, but sometimes you have to think about getting the game on as many televisions as possible in order to catch the imagination of as many people as possible.

While some of the counties might feel aggrieved, if everyone is sharing from the same pot I think they'll come on board. No one's talking about changing the County Championship – which is a terrific competition and very good for producing top Test players – but there does need to be big changes to T20 cricket over here if England isn't going to be left further behind.

*Jason Gillespie is Yorkshire's head coach, played 169 times for Australia and is a columnist with* All Out Cricket*. He is a supporter of the Yorkshire Cricket Foundation, which provides cricket-based education and community programmes across Yorkshire. Visit yorkshirecricketfoundation.com to see the great work they're doing*

THE CRICKET SPECIALIST

NEW 2015 CRICKET
Available Now!

ext day delivery • Free Returns • Live Stock Updates

# KEY

## EXAMPLE

RHB LB R1 W1 MVP2

R – 1,000 or more first-class runs in an English season (the number next to 'R' denotes how many times the player has achieved this feat)
W – 50 or more first-class wickets in an English season (the number next to 'W' denotes how many times the player has achieved this feat)
MVP – Denotes a player's presence in the top 100 places of the 2014 Overall FTI MVP Rankings (the number next to 'MVP' denotes the player's specific placing)

---

* – Not out innings (e.g. 150*)
(s) – A competition has been shared between two or more winners
CB40 – Clydesdale Bank 40 (English domestic 40-over competition, 2010-2012)
CC1/CC2 – County Championship Division One/County Championship Division Two
FLt20 – Friends Life t20 (English domestic 20-over competition, 2010-2013)
LB – Leg break bowler
LF – Left-arm fast bowler
LFM – Left-arm fast-medium bowler
LHB – Left-hand batsman
LM – Left-arm medium bowler
LMF – Left-arm medium-fast bowler
MCCU – Marylebone Cricket Club University
NWT20 – NatWest T20 Blast (English domestic 20-over competition, 2014-15)
OB – Off break bowler
ODI – One-Day International
RF – Right-arm fast bowler
RFM – Right-arm fast-medium bowler
RHB – Right-hand batsman
RL50 – Royal London One-Day Cup (English domestic 50-over competition, 2014,15)
RM – Right-arm medium bowler
RMF – Right-arm medium-fast bowler
SLA – Slow left-arm orthodox bowler
SLC – Slow left-arm Chinaman bowler
T20/T20I – Twenty20/Twenty20 International
UCCE – University Centre of Cricketing Excellence
WK – Wicketkeeper
YB40 –Yorkshire Bank 40 (English domestic 40-over competition, 2013)

---

NOTES: The statistics given for a player's best batting and best bowling performances are from first-class cricket only (apart from England Women, for whom we show their best ODI performances). If a field within a player's career statistics is left blank then the record for that particular statistic is incomplete. An '-' indicates that a particular statistic is inapplicable, e.g a player has never bowled a ball in first-class cricket. All stats correct as of March 9, 2014

# *The* Teams

# DERBYSHIRE

**FORMED:** 1870
**HOME GROUND:** The 3aaa County Ground, Derby
**ONE-DAY NAME:** Derbyshire Falcons
**CAPTAIN:** Wayne Madsen
**2014 RESULTS:** CC2: 4/9; RL50: Quarter-finalists; NWT20: 9/9 in North Division
**HONOURS:** Championship: 1936; Gillette/NatWest/C&G/FP Trophy: 1981; Benson & Hedges Cup: 1993; Sunday League: 1990

## THE LOWDOWN

After the highs of 2012 and narrowly missing out on pulling off a great escape in 2013, last summer was one of consolidation for Derbyshire. Their summer was sadly overshadowed by the death of Keith Poynton, the father of wicketkeeper Tom, in a car accident just two days before the start of the season. Tom suffered serious leg injuries in the crash and missed the entire campaign, while Richard Johnson, who stepped in as wicketkeeper, soon retired after suffering with sports performance anxiety issues. In June Derbyshire had to then cope with the sudden retirement of Stephen Moore, at the time the side's leading run-scorer in the Championship. Despite all of this, they finished the season strongly and were buoyed by a first one-day quarter-final appearance in 11 years. Captain Wayne Madsen had another productive year, once again passing 1,000 four-day runs, while Mark Footitt finished with 82 Championship wickets, the most in either division. There were also encouraging signs for the future, with 23-year-old Ben Slater scoring his first and second Championship centuries in the final round of matches.

## ELITE PERFORMANCE DIRECTOR: GRAEME WELCH

Welch's first season as head coach at Derbyshire was a baptism of fire. After having to contend with the loss of Poynton, Johnson and Moore, a fourth-place finish in Division Two of the Championship is a respectable return. He has also worked his magic with Footitt, helping him to add a level of consistency to his genuine pace. Welch spent five seasons as a player at Derbyshire, including captaining the side in 2006, and went on to take the roles of Essex's and Warwickshire's bowling coach.

# COUNTY CHAMPIONSHIP AVERAGES 2014

Batting

| | Mat | Inns | NO | Runs | HS | Ave | SR | 100 | 50 | 4s | 6s |
|---|---|---|---|---|---|---|---|---|---|---|---|
| CA Pujara | 3 | 6 | 2 | 219 | 100* | 54.75 | 70.64 | 1 | 1 | 34 | 1 |
| S Chanderpaul | 7 | 12 | 2 | 496 | 92 | 49.60 | 51.61 | 0 | 6 | 56 | 3 |
| BT Slater | 7 | 14 | 0 | 646 | 119 | 46.14 | 44.49 | 2 | 3 | 83 | 0 |
| WL Madsen | 16 | 29 | 2 | 1046 | 111* | 38.74 | 48.24 | 1 | 8 | 134 | 1 |
| WJ Durston | 10 | 18 | 4 | 525 | 74* | 37.50 | 73.42 | 0 | 5 | 81 | 3 |
| SC Moore | 9 | 16 | 1 | 474 | 128 | 31.60 | 45.93 | 1 | 3 | 67 | 2 |
| DJ Wainwright | 14 | 22 | 5 | 467 | 109 | 27.47 | 44.56 | 1 | 3 | 48 | 0 |
| AL Hughes | 13 | 21 | 4 | 448 | 82 | 26.35 | 43.15 | 0 | 3 | 55 | 1 |
| BA Godleman | 9 | 17 | 1 | 418 | 104* | 26.12 | 46.59 | 1 | 3 | 40 | 3 |
| TD Groenewald | 6 | 9 | 2 | 180 | 56* | 25.71 | 68.96 | 0 | 2 | 22 | 6 |
| PM Borrington | 7 | 13 | 2 | 281 | 86* | 25.54 | 37.66 | 0 | 1 | 34 | 0 |
| SL Elstone | 6 | 9 | 0 | 199 | 63 | 22.11 | 35.40 | 0 | 1 | 20 | 0 |
| AP Palladino | 14 | 21 | 4 | 334 | 60* | 19.64 | 55.94 | 0 | 1 | 44 | 2 |
| MJ North | 5 | 8 | 0 | 148 | 44 | 18.50 | 40.54 | 0 | 0 | 23 | 1 |
| BD Cotton | 2 | 2 | 0 | 36 | 21 | 18.00 | 62.06 | 0 | 0 | 6 | 1 |
| TAI Taylor | 6 | 9 | 2 | 115 | 40 | 16.42 | 36.27 | 0 | 0 | 12 | 1 |
| MHA Footitt | 16 | 22 | 8 | 154 | 26* | 11.00 | 75.49 | 0 | 0 | 25 | 2 |
| GD Cross | 11 | 17 | 0 | 175 | 30 | 10.29 | 42.37 | 0 | 0 | 18 | 4 |
| CF Hughes | 4 | 7 | 0 | 70 | 24 | 10.00 | 31.81 | 0 | 0 | 9 | 0 |
| WA White | 4 | 6 | 0 | 56 | 38 | 9.33 | 68.29 | 0 | 0 | 6 | 3 |
| HR Hosein | 2 | 2 | 0 | 17 | 13 | 8.50 | 26.56 | 0 | 0 | 2 | 0 |
| RM Johnson | 2 | 3 | 0 | 24 | 21 | 8.00 | 30.00 | 0 | 0 | 2 | 0 |
| ML Turner | 2 | 3 | 0 | 6 | 6 | 2.00 | 20.00 | 0 | 0 | 1 | 0 |
| DM Hodgson | 1 | 2 | 0 | 1 | 1 | 0.50 | 9.09 | 0 | 0 | 0 | 0 |

Bowling

| | Overs | Mdns | Runs | Wkts | BBI | BBM | Ave | Econ | SR | 5w | 10w |
|---|---|---|---|---|---|---|---|---|---|---|---|
| BD Cotton | 39.1 | 10 | 111 | 8 | 4/20 | 5/33 | 13.87 | 2.83 | 29.3 | 0 | 0 |
| MHA Footitt | 468.2 | 96 | 1568 | 82 | 6/48 | 9/122 | 19.12 | 3.34 | 34.2 | 6 | 0 |
| SL Elstone | 30.1 | 4 | 124 | 6 | 2/8 | 2/30 | 20.66 | 4.11 | 30.1 | 0 | 0 |
| WA White | 79.0 | 17 | 229 | 11 | 4/27 | 5/55 | 20.81 | 2.89 | 43.0 | 0 | 0 |
| AP Palladino | 409.4 | 126 | 991 | 39 | 5/62 | 5/62 | 25.41 | 2.41 | 63.0 | 1 | 0 |
| WJ Durston | 166.5 | 17 | 578 | 20 | 5/19 | 7/50 | 28.90 | 3.46 | 50.0 | 1 | 0 |
| TD Groenewald | 152.0 | 40 | 464 | 16 | 5/44 | 8/106 | 29.00 | 3.05 | 57.0 | 1 | 0 |
| TAI Taylor | 142.0 | 31 | 451 | 15 | 5/58 | 6/86 | 30.06 | 3.17 | 56.8 | 1 | 0 |
| CF Hughes | 19.4 | 0 | 74 | 2 | 1/2 | 1/2 | 37.00 | 3.76 | 59.0 | 0 | 0 |
| DJ Wainwright | 334.1 | 59 | 1119 | 27 | 5/54 | 5/117 | 41.44 | 3.34 | 74.2 | 1 | 0 |
| AL Hughes | 144.4 | 33 | 440 | 10 | 4/46 | 4/75 | 44.00 | 3.04 | 86.8 | 0 | 0 |
| MJ North | 53.3 | 7 | 142 | 2 | 1/25 | 1/25 | 71.00 | 2.65 | 160.5 | 0 | 0 |
| ML Turner | 65.0 | 10 | 230 | 1 | 1/80 | 1/119 | 230.00 | 3.53 | 390.0 | 0 | 0 |
| CA Pujara | 1.0 | 0 | 6 | 0 | - | - | - | 6.00 | - | 0 | 0 |
| WL Madsen | 9.5 | 2 | 36 | 0 | - | - | - | 3.66 | - | 0 | 0 |

**Catches/Stumpings:**

34 Cross (inc 4st), 20 Madsen, 15 Hosein, 11 Durston, 9 Borrington, 7 Godleman, 6 Moore, Slater, 5 A Hughes, 4 Footitt, Palladino, Wainwright, Johnson, 3 C Hughes, North, 2 Elstone, Groenewald, 1 Taylor, Turner, Pujara, Hodgson

# ROYAL LONDON ONE-DAY CUP AVERAGES 2014

**Batting**

| | Mat | Inns | NO | Runs | HS | Ave | SR | 100 | 50 | 4s | 6s |
|---|---|---|---|---|---|---|---|---|---|---|---|
| WL Madsen | 8 | 7 | 1 | 391 | 138 | 65.16 | 99.49 | 2 | 1 | 43 | 2 |
| WJ Durston | 8 | 8 | 1 | 317 | 134 | 45.28 | 101.60 | 2 | 0 | 33 | 4 |
| BA Godleman | 8 | 8 | 1 | 264 | 96 | 37.71 | 65.34 | 0 | 1 | 23 | 1 |
| MJ North | 6 | 5 | 0 | 140 | 67 | 28.00 | 75.26 | 0 | 1 | 12 | 0 |
| AP Palladino | 8 | 4 | 2 | 56 | 28* | 28.00 | 121.73 | 0 | 0 | 4 | 3 |
| BD Cotton | 4 | 2 | 1 | 28 | 18* | 28.00 | 84.84 | 0 | 0 | 3 | 1 |
| AL Hughes | 8 | 6 | 2 | 105 | 47 | 26.25 | 69.53 | 0 | 0 | 8 | 2 |
| DJ Wainwright | 7 | 4 | 1 | 60 | 41 | 20.00 | 96.77 | 0 | 0 | 7 | 0 |
| GD Cross | 8 | 6 | 0 | 76 | 23 | 12.66 | 84.44 | 0 | 0 | 7 | 2 |
| MHA Footitt | 8 | 3 | 1 | 19 | 11* | 9.50 | 73.07 | 0 | 0 | 2 | 0 |
| SL Elstone | 8 | 7 | 1 | 50 | 37 | 8.33 | 62.50 | 0 | 0 | 2 | 0 |
| TC Knight | 1 | 1 | 0 | 0 | 0 | 0.00 | 0.00 | 0 | 0 | 0 | 0 |
| S Chanderpaul | 2 | 2 | 2 | 81 | 52* | - | 90.00 | 0 | 1 | 7 | 0 |
| TAI Taylor | 4 | - | - | - | - | - | - | - | - | - | - |

**Bowling**

| | Overs | Mdns | Runs | Wkts | BBI | Ave | Econ | SR | 4w | 5w |
|---|---|---|---|---|---|---|---|---|---|---|
| DJ Wainwright | 55.2 | 2 | 264 | 9 | 4/34 | 29.33 | 4.77 | 36.8 | 1 | 0 |
| AL Hughes | 49.0 | 0 | 242 | 3 | 2/46 | 80.66 | 4.93 | 98.0 | 0 | 0 |
| AP Palladino | 63.5 | 1 | 335 | 13 | 5/49 | 25.76 | 5.24 | 29.4 | 0 | 1 |
| TAI Taylor | 29.2 | 3 | 174 | 5 | 3/48 | 34.80 | 5.93 | 35.2 | 0 | 0 |
| BD Cotton | 30.3 | 2 | 186 | 4 | 2/42 | 46.50 | 6.09 | 45.7 | 0 | 0 |
| MJ North | 5.5 | 0 | 36 | 1 | 1/10 | 36.00 | 6.17 | 35.0 | 0 | 0 |
| WJ Durston | 32.0 | 0 | 199 | 3 | 2/47 | 66.33 | 6.21 | 64.0 | 0 | 0 |
| MHA Footitt | 64.5 | 1 | 415 | 15 | 5/59 | 27.66 | 6.40 | 25.9 | 1 | 1 |
| SL Elstone | 4.0 | 0 | 26 | 0 | - | - | 6.50 | - | 0 | 0 |

**Catches/Stumpings:**
7 Godleman, 6 Elstone, 5 Cross, 4 Durston, 3 A Hughes, Madsen, 2 Wainwright, North, Footitt, 1 Chanderpaul

# NATWEST T20 BLAST AVERAGES 2014

Batting

| | Mat | Inns | NO | Runs | HS | Ave | SR | 100 | 50 | 4s | 6s |
|---|---|---|---|---|---|---|---|---|---|---|---|
| WL Madsen | 13 | 13 | 2 | 388 | 65 | 35.27 | 146.96 | 0 | 2 | 35 | 9 |
| MJ North | 13 | 13 | 0 | 361 | 90 | 27.76 | 121.14 | 0 | 2 | 31 | 10 |
| TD Groenewald | 3 | 2 | 1 | 26 | 19* | 26.00 | 236.36 | 0 | 0 | 4 | 1 |
| WJ Durston | 11 | 11 | 0 | 278 | 89 | 25.27 | 130.51 | 0 | 2 | 27 | 10 |
| TC Knight | 7 | 6 | 2 | 96 | 44* | 24.00 | 154.83 | 0 | 0 | 1 | 8 |
| DJ Wainwright | 8 | 7 | 5 | 47 | 20* | 23.50 | 130.55 | 0 | 0 | 5 | 1 |
| SC Moore | 6 | 6 | 0 | 127 | 40 | 21.16 | 125.74 | 0 | 0 | 18 | 1 |
| GD Cross | 13 | 13 | 1 | 243 | 54 | 20.25 | 134.25 | 0 | 1 | 27 | 7 |
| BA Godleman | 4 | 4 | 0 | 78 | 39 | 19.50 | 147.16 | 0 | 0 | 6 | 4 |
| AL Hughes | 12 | 10 | 3 | 102 | 43* | 14.57 | 129.11 | 0 | 0 | 5 | 4 |
| SL Elstone | 9 | 8 | 2 | 86 | 24* | 14.33 | 130.30 | 0 | 0 | 6 | 2 |
| GTG Cork | 6 | 5 | 2 | 35 | 13* | 11.66 | 97.22 | 0 | 0 | 3 | 0 |
| CF Hughes | 9 | 9 | 0 | 96 | 30 | 10.66 | 105.49 | 0 | 0 | 11 | 2 |
| AP Palladino | 7 | 6 | 2 | 22 | 14* | 5.50 | 73.33 | 0 | 0 | 1 | 0 |
| ML Turner | 9 | 3 | 0 | 2 | 1 | 0.66 | 40.00 | 0 | 0 | 0 | 0 |
| S Chanderpaul | 1 | 1 | 0 | 0 | 0 | 0.00 | 0.00 | 0 | 0 | 0 | 0 |
| JL Clare | 1 | 1 | 1 | 5 | 5* | - | 55.55 | 0 | 0 | 0 | 0 |
| BD Cotton | 2 | - | - | - | - | - | - | - | - | - | - |
| MHA Footitt | 5 | - | - | - | - | - | - | - | - | - | - |
| M Higginbottom | 4 | - | - | - | - | - | - | - | - | - | - |

Bowling

| | Overs | Mdns | Runs | Wkts | BBI | Ave | Econ | SR | 4w | 5w |
|---|---|---|---|---|---|---|---|---|---|---|
| WJ Durston | 33.0 | 1 | 244 | 7 | 1/8 | 34.85 | 7.39 | 28.2 | 0 | 0 |
| MJ North | 21.0 | 0 | 169 | 8 | 2/25 | 21.12 | 8.04 | 15.7 | 0 | 0 |
| AP Palladino | 21.5 | 0 | 178 | 2 | 1/28 | 89.00 | 8.15 | 65.5 | 0 | 0 |
| DJ Wainwright | 24.2 | 0 | 211 | 3 | 3/26 | 70.33 | 8.67 | 48.6 | 0 | 0 |
| CF Hughes | 17.0 | 0 | 151 | 3 | 1/17 | 50.33 | 8.88 | 34.0 | 0 | 0 |
| AL Hughes | 20.0 | 0 | 180 | 2 | 1/12 | 90.00 | 9.00 | 60.0 | 0 | 0 |
| TC Knight | 5.0 | 0 | 49 | 0 | - | - | 9.80 | - | 0 | 0 |
| TD Groenewald | 11.0 | 0 | 110 | 2 | 2/38 | 55.00 | 10.00 | 33.0 | 0 | 0 |
| ML Turner | 29.4 | 0 | 313 | 9 | 3/51 | 34.77 | 10.55 | 19.7 | 0 | 0 |
| MHA Footitt | 17.0 | 0 | 181 | 7 | 2/33 | 25.85 | 10.64 | 14.5 | 0 | 0 |
| JL Clare | 4.0 | 0 | 43 | 1 | 1/43 | 43.00 | 10.75 | 24.0 | 0 | 0 |
| SL Elstone | 4.0 | 0 | 43 | 0 | - | - | 10.75 | - | 0 | 0 |
| GTG Cork | 15.0 | 0 | 168 | 5 | 2/36 | 33.60 | 11.20 | 18.0 | 0 | 0 |
| M Higginbottom | 11.0 | 0 | 127 | 2 | 1/34 | 63.50 | 11.54 | 33.0 | 0 | 0 |
| BD Cotton | 8.0 | 0 | 105 | 2 | 1/49 | 52.50 | 13.12 | 24.0 | 0 | 0 |

**Catches/Stumpings:**
5 A Hughes, 4 Turner, Higginbottom, Godleman, 3 Durston, North, Palladino, Groenewald, Elstone, Cork, Madsen, 2 Cross (inc 2st), 1 C Hughes, Knight, Chanderpaul

# DURHAM

FORMED: 1882
HOME GROUND: Emirates Durham ICG
T20 BLAST NAME: Durham Jets
CAPTAIN: Paul Collingwood (Championship), Mark Stoneman (RL50 and NWT20)
2014 RESULTS: CC1: 5/9; RL50: Winners; NWT20: 6/9 in North Division
HONOURS: Championship: (3) 2008, 2009, 2013; Gillette/NatWest/C&G/FP Trophy: 2007; Pro40/National League/CB40/YB40/RL50: 2014

## THE LOWDOWN

A season that at one point looked as if it was hovering on the brink of disaster ended with another piece of silverware for Durham. Their success in the RL Cup was the culmination of an excellent second half of the season, propelled by Ben Stokes' stunning 164 from 113 balls in the semi-final victory over Nottinghamshire. Stokes then played a sensible, unbeaten 38 in the final to bring home the Cup, their fifth title in seven seasons. Despite winning the Championship in 2013, a tightening of the budget meant they had to let go of several senior players and, as a result, spent much of the season flirting with relegation before a late-summer spurt saved them. Scott Borthwick and Mark Stoneman both passed 1,000 runs for the second successive year, while Chris Rushworth's 86 wickets across all formats went some way to making up for the loss of Graham Onions for much of the season through a series of injuries. Paul Collingwood's shrewd captaincy once again suggested England might have missed a trick, and Durham will be delighted that he's signed a new one-year contract.

## HEAD COACH: JON LEWIS

After stepping up as head coach following Geoff Cook's heart attack in June 2013, Lewis' first full season in the role was a success. Lewis joined Durham in 1997 after seven seasons at Essex. A solid opening batsman, he picked up 16 first-class centuries before retiring in 2006 to work with Durham's academy and 2nd XI.

# COUNTY CHAMPIONSHIP AVERAGES 2014

Batting

| | Mat | Inns | NO | Runs | HS | Ave | SR | 100 | 50 | 4s | 6s |
|---|---|---|---|---|---|---|---|---|---|---|---|
| KC Sangakkara | 2 | 3 | 0 | 173 | 159 | 57.66 | 56.53 | 1 | 0 | 20 | 2 |
| SG Borthwick | 15 | 27 | 1 | 1137 | 216 | 43.73 | 53.80 | 3 | 4 | 151 | 4 |
| J Harrison | 4 | 7 | 3 | 173 | 65 | 43.25 | 62.23 | 0 | 1 | 27 | 2 |
| RD Pringle | 2 | 4 | 1 | 126 | 63* | 42.00 | 56.00 | 0 | 1 | 18 | 1 |
| PD Collingwood | 16 | 28 | 5 | 864 | 101 | 37.56 | 52.71 | 2 | 5 | 94 | 10 |
| GJ Muchall | 11 | 19 | 4 | 550 | 158* | 36.66 | 65.08 | 1 | 2 | 79 | 3 |
| MD Stoneman | 16 | 28 | 0 | 1004 | 187 | 35.85 | 63.54 | 3 | 4 | 133 | 4 |
| MJ Richardson | 16 | 28 | 0 | 957 | 148 | 34.17 | 47.94 | 2 | 4 | 113 | 5 |
| P Coughlin | 5 | 7 | 1 | 191 | 85 | 31.83 | 61.41 | 0 | 1 | 22 | 1 |
| GR Breese | 4 | 6 | 0 | 174 | 62 | 29.00 | 47.02 | 0 | 1 | 22 | 0 |
| BA Stokes | 7 | 11 | 0 | 314 | 85 | 28.54 | 60.73 | 0 | 2 | 50 | 0 |
| CS MacLeod | 3 | 5 | 0 | 142 | 84 | 28.40 | 44.09 | 0 | 1 | 19 | 0 |
| JW Hastings | 8 | 14 | 1 | 337 | 83 | 25.92 | 64.55 | 0 | 3 | 39 | 10 |
| KK Jennings | 16 | 28 | 1 | 693 | 103 | 25.66 | 39.02 | 1 | 4 | 98 | 0 |
| P Mustard | 13 | 21 | 2 | 414 | 91 | 21.78 | 44.80 | 0 | 3 | 52 | 0 |
| U Arshad | 4 | 5 | 1 | 81 | 38* | 20.25 | 46.55 | 0 | 0 | 9 | 1 |
| G Onions | 5 | 7 | 2 | 71 | 23* | 14.20 | 37.36 | 0 | 0 | 9 | 0 |
| MA Wood | 7 | 11 | 2 | 127 | 20* | 14.11 | 39.31 | 0 | 0 | 19 | 0 |
| C Rushworth | 16 | 22 | 5 | 219 | 46 | 12.88 | 64.60 | 0 | 0 | 33 | 2 |
| RS Buckley | 1 | 2 | 1 | 11 | 9 | 11.00 | 22.91 | 0 | 0 | 1 | 0 |
| VR Aaron | 2 | 3 | 1 | 19 | 13 | 9.50 | 59.37 | 0 | 0 | 3 | 0 |
| PKD Chase | 3 | 5 | 3 | 7 | 4* | 3.50 | 25.92 | 0 | 0 | 0 | 0 |
| GT Main | 1 | - | - | - | - | - | - | - | - | - | - |

Bowling

| | Overs | Mdns | Runs | Wkts | BBI | BBM | Ave | Econ | SR | 5w | 10w |
|---|---|---|---|---|---|---|---|---|---|---|---|
| PKD Chase | 46.2 | 5 | 173 | 11 | 5/64 | 5/89 | 15.72 | 3.73 | 25.2 | 1 | 0 |
| JW Hastings | 272.0 | 69 | 812 | 37 | 5/94 | 8/118 | 21.94 | 2.98 | 44.1 | 1 | 0 |
| GT Main | 13.0 | 2 | 72 | 3 | 3/72 | 3/72 | 24.00 | 5.53 | 26.0 | 0 | 0 |
| C Rushworth | 488.1 | 99 | 1578 | 64 | 9/52 | 15/95 | 24.65 | 3.23 | 45.7 | 3 | 1 |
| BA Stokes | 187.4 | 23 | 756 | 30 | 7/67 | 10/121 | 25.20 | 4.02 | 37.5 | 1 | 1 |
| U Arshad | 82.1 | 18 | 309 | 12 | 4/78 | 5/114 | 25.75 | 3.76 | 41.0 | 0 | 0 |
| PD Collingwood | 85.0 | 19 | 306 | 9 | 3/26 | 3/41 | 34.00 | 3.60 | 56.6 | 0 | 0 |
| P Coughlin | 80.0 | 21 | 306 | 9 | 3/42 | 4/88 | 34.00 | 3.82 | 53.3 | 0 | 0 |
| MA Wood | 173.1 | 28 | 615 | 18 | 5/37 | 5/59 | 34.16 | 3.55 | 57.7 | 2 | 0 |
| VR Aaron | 32.3 | 7 | 108 | 3 | 2/81 | 2/81 | 36.00 | 3.32 | 65.0 | 0 | 0 |
| G Onions | 151.2 | 28 | 504 | 12 | 4/65 | 4/134 | 42.00 | 3.33 | 75.6 | 0 | 0 |
| J Harrison | 102.0 | 16 | 379 | 8 | 3/83 | 4/97 | 47.37 | 3.71 | 76.5 | 0 | 0 |
| RD Pringle | 21.3 | 1 | 108 | 2 | 2/94 | 2/95 | 54.00 | 5.02 | 64.5 | 0 | 0 |
| SG Borthwick | 183.2 | 13 | 762 | 13 | 3/70 | 3/70 | 58.61 | 4.15 | 84.6 | 0 | 0 |
| KK Jennings | 37.0 | 4 | 125 | 2 | 1/4 | 1/4 | 62.50 | 3.37 | 111.0 | 0 | 0 |
| RS Buckley | 2.0 | 0 | 9 | 0 | - | - | - | 4.50 | - | 0 | 0 |
| MD Stoneman | 21.0 | 0 | 82 | 0 | - | - | - | 3.90 | - | 0 | 0 |
| GR Breese | 45.0 | 12 | 141 | 0 | - | - | - | 3.13 | - | 0 | 0 |

**Catches/Stumpings:**

43 Mustard (inc 1st), 30 Borthwick, 16 Richardson, 11 Muchall, 9 Collingwood, 8 Breese, 5 Jennings, Stoneman, 4 MacLeod, 3 Coughlin, Sangakkara, 2 Hastings, 1 Chase, Main, Stokes

# ROYAL LONDON ONE-DAY CUP AVERAGES 2014

**Batting**

| | Mat | Inns | NO | Runs | HS | Ave | SR | 100 | 50 | 4s | 6s |
|---|---|---|---|---|---|---|---|---|---|---|---|
| BA Stokes | 7 | 7 | 1 | 410 | 164 | 68.33 | 99.75 | 2 | 1 | 47 | 10 |
| PD Collingwood | 11 | 11 | 3 | 427 | 113 | 53.37 | 103.89 | 1 | 3 | 48 | 10 |
| MD Stoneman | 11 | 11 | 1 | 435 | 102 | 43.50 | 87.00 | 1 | 4 | 52 | 6 |
| GR Breese | 11 | 7 | 4 | 107 | 34* | 35.66 | 98.16 | 0 | 0 | 15 | 1 |
| P Mustard | 11 | 11 | 0 | 362 | 89 | 32.90 | 71.25 | 0 | 2 | 43 | 3 |
| KK Jennings | 9 | 9 | 3 | 175 | 70 | 29.16 | 84.13 | 0 | 1 | 23 | 0 |
| GJ Muchall | 10 | 7 | 3 | 99 | 29* | 24.75 | 100.00 | 0 | 0 | 9 | 0 |
| SG Borthwick | 10 | 8 | 2 | 126 | 67 | 21.00 | 74.55 | 0 | 1 | 14 | 1 |
| CS MacLeod | 11 | 11 | 0 | 216 | 94 | 19.63 | 63.15 | 0 | 1 | 21 | 0 |
| JW Hastings | 10 | 7 | 1 | 59 | 16 | 9.83 | 120.40 | 0 | 0 | 8 | 1 |
| C Rushworth | 8 | 2 | 1 | 4 | 3 | 4.00 | 66.66 | 0 | 0 | 0 | 0 |
| G Onions | 6 | 1 | 0 | 3 | 3 | 3.00 | 23.07 | 0 | 0 | 0 | 0 |
| P Coughlin | 6 | 2 | 1 | 2 | 2* | 2.00 | 40.00 | 0 | 0 | 0 | 0 |

**Bowling**

| | Overs | Mdns | Runs | Wkts | BBI | Ave | Econ | SR | 4w | 5w |
|---|---|---|---|---|---|---|---|---|---|---|
| PD Collingwood | 81.1 | 6 | 320 | 14 | 4/16 | 22.85 | 3.94 | 34.7 | 1 | 0 |
| JW Hastings | 74.2 | 5 | 327 | 14 | 5/46 | 23.35 | 4.39 | 31.8 | 0 | 1 |
| P Coughlin | 38.0 | 1 | 174 | 2 | 1/34 | 87.00 | 4.57 | 114.0 | 0 | 0 |
| BA Stokes | 53.1 | 3 | 245 | 9 | 2/25 | 27.22 | 4.60 | 35.4 | 0 | 0 |
| GR Breese | 66.0 | 1 | 327 | 10 | 3/30 | 32.70 | 4.95 | 39.6 | 0 | 0 |
| C Rushworth | 69.3 | 7 | 366 | 15 | 3/23 | 24.40 | 5.26 | 27.8 | 0 | 0 |
| SG Borthwick | 39.0 | 0 | 208 | 6 | 3/51 | 34.66 | 5.33 | 39.0 | 0 | 0 |
| G Onions | 37.3 | 5 | 218 | 10 | 4/48 | 21.80 | 5.81 | 22.5 | 1 | 0 |
| CS MacLeod | 2.3 | 0 | 16 | 0 | - | - | 6.40 | - | 0 | 0 |
| KK Jennings | 10.0 | 1 | 75 | 1 | 1/9 | 75.00 | 7.50 | 60.0 | 0 | 0 |

**Catches/Stumpings:**
22 Mustard (inc 3st), 7 Muchall, 5 Stokes, MacLeod, 4 Breese, 3 Stoneman, 2 Hastings, Borthwick, Jennings, 1 Collingwood, Coughlin, Rushworth

# NATWEST T20 BLAST AVERAGES 2014

| | Mat | Inns | NO | Runs | HS | Ave | SR | 100 | 50 | 4s | 6s |
|---|---|---|---|---|---|---|---|---|---|---|---|
| JW Hastings | 8 | 5 | 1 | 184 | 80* | 46.00 | 200.00 | 0 | 2 | 9 | 14 |
| CS MacLeod | 12 | 12 | 4 | 358 | 80* | 44.75 | 130.18 | 0 | 2 | 34 | 11 |
| GJ Muchall | 13 | 12 | 6 | 228 | 43 | 38.00 | 125.27 | 0 | 0 | 16 | 4 |
| P Mustard | 13 | 13 | 0 | 297 | 54 | 22.84 | 107.60 | 0 | 1 | 36 | 4 |
| MA Wood | 3 | 2 | 1 | 21 | 12 | 21.00 | 95.45 | 0 | 0 | 1 | 0 |
| BA Stokes | 7 | 7 | 1 | 107 | 49* | 17.83 | 122.98 | 0 | 0 | 12 | 4 |
| GR Breese | 13 | 8 | 4 | 67 | 30* | 16.75 | 113.55 | 0 | 0 | 8 | 2 |
| PD Collingwood | 11 | 10 | 1 | 145 | 62 | 16.11 | 110.68 | 0 | 1 | 11 | 5 |
| MJ Richardson | 4 | 4 | 1 | 36 | 19 | 12.00 | 112.50 | 0 | 0 | 1 | 0 |
| MD Stoneman | 13 | 13 | 2 | 117 | 27* | 10.63 | 91.40 | 0 | 0 | 13 | 0 |
| RD Pringle | 9 | 5 | 1 | 34 | 17 | 8.50 | 130.76 | 0 | 0 | 3 | 1 |
| SG Borthwick | 11 | 8 | 0 | 55 | 25 | 6.87 | 78.57 | 0 | 0 | 3 | 1 |
| U Arshad | 10 | 3 | 0 | 17 | 10 | 5.66 | 80.95 | 0 | 0 | 2 | 0 |
| C Rushworth | 9 | 3 | 1 | 9 | 5 | 4.50 | 64.28 | 0 | 0 | 1 | 0 |
| KK Jennings | 4 | 1 | 1 | 0 | 0* | - | - | 0 | 0 | 0 | 0 |
| G Onions | 2 | 1 | 1 | 0 | 0* | - | - | 0 | 0 | 0 | 0 |
| P Coughlin | 1 | - | - | - | - | - | - | - | - | - | - |

Batting

| | Overs | Mdns | Runs | Wkts | BBI | Ave | Econ | SR | 4w | 5w |
|---|---|---|---|---|---|---|---|---|---|---|
| G Onions | 8.0 | 0 | 41 | 4 | 3/15 | 10.25 | 5.12 | 12.0 | 0 | 0 |
| GR Breese | 35.2 | 1 | 219 | 12 | 3/19 | 18.25 | 6.19 | 17.6 | 0 | 0 |
| PD Collingwood | 39.0 | 0 | 242 | 15 | 3/29 | 16.13 | 6.20 | 15.6 | 0 | 0 |
| BA Stokes | 14.1 | 0 | 104 | 6 | 2/20 | 17.33 | 7.34 | 14.1 | 0 | 0 |
| MA Wood | 8.0 | 0 | 62 | 2 | 1/9 | 31.00 | 7.75 | 24.0 | 0 | 0 |
| KK Jennings | 13.0 | 0 | 103 | 4 | 2/23 | 25.75 | 7.92 | 19.5 | 0 | 0 |
| JW Hastings | 25.1 | 0 | 202 | 14 | 4/26 | 14.42 | 8.02 | 10.7 | 1 | 0 |
| U Arshad | 27.1 | 2 | 222 | 8 | 2/21 | 27.75 | 8.17 | 20.3 | 0 | 0 |
| C Rushworth | 30.4 | 0 | 251 | 7 | 3/19 | 35.85 | 8.18 | 26.2 | 0 | 0 |
| SG Borthwick | 13.5 | 0 | 115 | 5 | 2/11 | 23.00 | 8.31 | 16.6 | 0 | 0 |
| P Coughlin | 3.0 | 0 | 30 | 1 | 1/30 | 30.00 | 10.00 | 18.0 | 0 | 0 |
| RD Pringle | 9.0 | 0 | 93 | 0 | - | - | 10.33 | - | 0 | 0 |

Bowling

**Catches/Stumpings:**
10 MacLeod, 9 Borthwick, 7 Mustard (inc 1st), 6 Stokes, 5 Collingwood, 4 Arshad, Muchall, Stoneman, 2 Breese, Jennings, Richardson, 1 Wood, Hastings, Rushworth

# ESSEX

**FORMED:** 1876
**HOME GROUND:** The Essex County Ground, Chelmsford
**ONE-DAY NAME:** Essex Eagles
**CAPTAIN:** James Foster (Championship), Ryan ten Doeschate (RL50 and NWT20)
**2014 RESULTS:** CC2: 3/9; RL50: Quarter-finalists; NWT20: Quarter-finalists
**HONOURS:** Championship: (6) 1979, 1983, 1984, 1986, 1991, 1992; Gillette/NatWest/C&G/FP Trophy: (3) 1985, 1997, 2008; Benson & Hedges Cup: (2) 1979, 1998; Pro40/National League/CB40/YB40/RL50: (2) 2005, 2006; Sunday League: (3) 1981, 1984, 1985

## THE LOWDOWN

It was a season of frustration for Essex. A talented squad geared towards limited-overs success found themselves knocked out at the quarter-final stages of both the T20 Blast and the RL Cup. In the County Championship they finished the season strongly, with five successive victories, but missed out on promotion by just nine points. That their 229 points was a record for a third-place finish will have been of little comfort. New Zealander Jesse Ryder was undoubtedly the star of the season. While perhaps not in the same league as the likes of former overseas players Allan Border, Mark Waugh and Saleem Malik, Ryder quickly became a fans' favourite. He surprisingly led Essex's Championship attack, with his medium-pace wobblers picking up 44 wickets. Run-scoring was again the problem, with no one passing 1,000 Championship runs, although Nick Browne did become the first Essex batsman to score two unbeaten centuries in the same match and may have a big role to play in 2015.

## HEAD COACH: PAUL GRAYSON

Now in his eighth season as Essex coach, Grayson has established a reputation for giving youth a chance. His highlight as a player was receiving a somewhat surprising call-up to the England squad for an ICC KnockOut tournament in 2000, where he played just one match before earning a recall against Zimbabwe in 2001. As a steady slow-left armer and a grafting batsman he forged a decent county career with Yorkshire and Essex before retiring in 2005. In 2008 he returned to Essex as coach.

# COUNTY CHAMPIONSHIP AVERAGES 2014

Batting

| | Mat | Inns | NO | Runs | HS | Ave | SR | 100 | 50 | 4s | 6s |
|---|---|---|---|---|---|---|---|---|---|---|---|
| AN Cook | 3 | 5 | 0 | 386 | 181 | 77.20 | 60.31 | 2 | 0 | 49 | 0 |
| NLJ Browne | 9 | 15 | 3 | 650 | 132* | 54.16 | 45.01 | 3 | 2 | 94 | 0 |
| JS Foster | 16 | 23 | 2 | 949 | 132 | 45.19 | 56.82 | 2 | 5 | 127 | 6 |
| RS Bopara | 12 | 18 | 1 | 759 | 162 | 44.64 | 44.43 | 2 | 1 | 81 | 7 |
| JD Ryder | 12 | 18 | 1 | 630 | 133 | 37.05 | 71.67 | 2 | 2 | 84 | 13 |
| RN ten Doeschate | 6 | 10 | 2 | 283 | 104* | 35.37 | 73.12 | 1 | 1 | 30 | 6 |
| T Westley | 16 | 27 | 3 | 705 | 116 | 29.37 | 51.83 | 1 | 4 | 106 | 0 |
| BT Foakes | 10 | 16 | 3 | 341 | 132* | 26.23 | 54.64 | 1 | 1 | 41 | 0 |
| ML Pettini | 4 | 7 | 0 | 181 | 71 | 25.85 | 48.91 | 0 | 2 | 24 | 0 |
| KS Velani | 4 | 5 | 1 | 98 | 29 | 24.50 | 50.51 | 0 | 0 | 18 | 0 |
| JC Mickleburgh | 9 | 14 | 1 | 312 | 67 | 24.00 | 37.63 | 0 | 1 | 35 | 0 |
| GM Smith | 11 | 17 | 1 | 348 | 85 | 21.75 | 48.94 | 0 | 2 | 47 | 2 |
| TS Mills | 6 | 7 | 4 | 64 | 30 | 21.33 | 59.25 | 0 | 0 | 9 | 1 |
| TC Moore | 4 | 4 | 2 | 27 | 17 | 13.50 | 69.23 | 0 | 0 | 2 | 1 |
| GR Napier | 11 | 15 | 0 | 195 | 62 | 13.00 | 57.86 | 0 | 1 | 28 | 2 |
| MET Salisbury | 4 | 6 | 1 | 50 | 19 | 10.00 | 34.24 | 0 | 0 | 8 | 0 |
| SI Mahmood | 2 | 4 | 1 | 30 | 17 | 10.00 | 103.44 | 0 | 0 | 6 | 0 |
| RJW Topley | 4 | 5 | 3 | 18 | 12 | 9.00 | 19.78 | 0 | 0 | 1 | 0 |
| DD Masters | 9 | 11 | 0 | 92 | 26 | 8.36 | 36.22 | 0 | 0 | 11 | 0 |
| MS Panesar | 14 | 17 | 2 | 101 | 38 | 6.73 | 58.72 | 0 | 0 | 15 | 1 |
| TJ Phillips | 2 | 3 | 0 | 17 | 12 | 5.66 | 45.94 | 0 | 0 | 3 | 0 |
| JA Porter | 3 | 3 | 2 | 5 | 5 | 5.00 | 20.00 | 0 | 0 | 0 | 0 |
| Tanveer Sikandar | 2 | 2 | 0 | 5 | 5 | 2.50 | 29.41 | 0 | 0 | 0 | 0 |
| OJ Newby | 2 | 3 | 1 | 4 | 4 | 2.00 | 21.05 | 0 | 0 | 1 | 0 |
| TR Craddock | 1 | 1 | 0 | 0 | 0 | 0.00 | 0.00 | 0 | 0 | 0 | 0 |

Bowling

| | Overs | Mdns | Runs | Wkts | BBI | BBM | Ave | Econ | SR | 5w | 10w |
|---|---|---|---|---|---|---|---|---|---|---|---|
| JD Ryder | 289.5 | 76 | 796 | 44 | 5/24 | 10/110 | 18.09 | 2.74 | 39.5 | 4 | 1 |
| GR Napier | 235.4 | 43 | 781 | 43 | 5/54 | 7/72 | 18.16 | 3.31 | 32.8 | 1 | 0 |
| DD Masters | 282.3 | 87 | 712 | 37 | 6/46 | 7/83 | 19.24 | 2.52 | 45.8 | 2 | 0 |
| JA Porter | 31.1 | 4 | 116 | 6 | 3/26 | 3/26 | 19.33 | 3.72 | 31.1 | 0 | 0 |
| RJW Topley | 150.2 | 30 | 502 | 25 | 6/41 | 10/108 | 20.08 | 3.33 | 36.0 | 2 | 1 |
| SI Mahmood | 17.0 | 0 | 76 | 3 | 3/54 | 3/54 | 25.33 | 4.47 | 34.0 | 0 | 0 |
| MS Panesar | 392.2 | 111 | 1111 | 42 | 6/111 | 11/168 | 26.45 | 2.83 | 56.0 | 4 | 1 |
| TJ Phillips | 31.0 | 1 | 119 | 4 | 2/59 | 2/41 | 29.75 | 3.83 | 46.5 | 0 | 0 |
| TS Mills | 134.0 | 27 | 442 | 13 | 4/45 | 4/45 | 34.00 | 3.29 | 61.8 | 0 | 0 |
| T Westley | 72.2 | 8 | 218 | 6 | 3/35 | 3/40 | 36.33 | 3.01 | 72.3 | 0 | 0 |
| GM Smith | 136.1 | 23 | 374 | 10 | 4/46 | 4/47 | 37.40 | 2.74 | 81.7 | 0 | 0 |
| Tanveer Sikandar | 38.0 | 6 | 117 | 3 | 2/90 | 2/90 | 39.00 | 3.07 | 76.0 | 0 | 0 |
| TC Moore | 98.0 | 19 | 328 | 8 | 4/78 | 4/105 | 41.00 | 3.34 | 73.5 | 0 | 0 |
| RN ten Doeschate | 33.2 | 1 | 176 | 4 | 2/12 | 2/12 | 44.00 | 5.28 | 50.0 | 0 | 0 |
| RS Bopara | 80.0 | 13 | 268 | 6 | 3/14 | 4/28 | 44.66 | 3.35 | 80.0 | 0 | 0 |
| TR Craddock | 11.0 | 1 | 53 | 1 | 1/30 | 1/53 | 53.00 | 4.81 | 66.0 | 0 | 0 |
| MET Salisbury | 81.0 | 12 | 296 | 5 | 4/50 | 5/117 | 59.20 | 3.65 | 97.2 | 0 | 0 |
| OJ Newby | 52.1 | 18 | 179 | 3 | 2/52 | 2/57 | 59.66 | 3.43 | 104.3 | 0 | 0 |
| BT Foakes | 1.0 | 0 | 6 | 0 | - | - | - | 6.00 | - | 0 | 0 |
| KS Velani | 4.3 | 0 | 13 | 0 | - | - | - | 2.88 | - | 0 | 0 |
| NLJ Browne | 22.0 | 4 | 94 | 0 | - | - | - | 4.27 | - | 0 | 0 |

**Catches/Stumpings:**
56 Foster (inc 3st), 20 Westley, 13 Ryder, 9 Browne, 8 Mickleburgh, 7 Smith, 6 Pettini, 5 Cook, 4 Napier, Foakes, 3 Panesar, Phillips, ten Doeschate, 2 Masters, Bopara, 1 Porter, Mahmood, Moore, Newby

# ROYAL LONDON ONE-DAY CUP AVERAGES 2014

**Batting**

| | Mat | Inns | NO | Runs | HS | Ave | SR | 100 | 50 | 4s | 6s |
|---|---|---|---|---|---|---|---|---|---|---|---|
| JD Ryder | 7 | 6 | 2 | 369 | 90 | 92.25 | 122.59 | 0 | 4 | 41 | 14 |
| T Westley | 8 | 7 | 1 | 344 | 111* | 57.33 | 93.22 | 1 | 3 | 38 | 3 |
| RN ten Doeschate | 7 | 5 | 1 | 210 | 119 | 52.50 | 103.96 | 1 | 0 | 17 | 6 |
| RS Bopara | 5 | 5 | 0 | 202 | 61 | 40.40 | 76.80 | 0 | 3 | 16 | 0 |
| ML Pettini | 8 | 7 | 1 | 232 | 102* | 38.66 | 82.56 | 1 | 1 | 20 | 2 |
| TJ Phillips | 7 | 4 | 2 | 53 | 27 | 26.50 | 74.64 | 0 | 0 | 5 | 1 |
| JS Foster | 8 | 5 | 1 | 68 | 19 | 17.00 | 73.11 | 0 | 0 | 6 | 1 |
| KS Velani | 5 | 4 | 0 | 61 | 27 | 15.25 | 107.01 | 0 | 0 | 8 | 1 |
| GM Smith | 7 | 5 | 1 | 59 | 27 | 14.75 | 78.66 | 0 | 0 | 3 | 1 |
| GR Napier | 7 | 3 | 0 | 28 | 21 | 9.33 | 71.79 | 0 | 0 | 1 | 1 |
| JC Mickleburgh | 1 | 1 | 0 | 7 | 7 | 7.00 | 58.33 | 0 | 0 | 1 | 0 |
| DD Masters | 8 | 3 | 0 | 10 | 6 | 3.33 | 35.71 | 0 | 0 | 0 | 0 |
| TS Mills | 1 | 1 | 0 | 0 | 0 | 0.00 | 0.00 | 0 | 0 | 0 | 0 |
| MET Salisbury | 5 | 1 | 1 | 5 | 5* | - | 27.77 | 0 | 0 | 1 | 0 |
| RJW Topley | 4 | 1 | 1 | 0 | 0* | - | - | 0 | 0 | 0 | 0 |

**Bowling**

| | Overs | Mdns | Runs | Wkts | BBI | Ave | Econ | SR | 4w | 5w |
|---|---|---|---|---|---|---|---|---|---|---|
| TS Mills | 2.2 | 0 | 10 | 0 | - | - | 4.28 | - | 0 | 0 |
| T Westley | 50.4 | 0 | 222 | 9 | 4/60 | 24.66 | 4.38 | 33.7 | 1 | 0 |
| DD Masters | 74.0 | 10 | 348 | 14 | 4/34 | 24.85 | 4.70 | 31.7 | 1 | 0 |
| GM Smith | 9.0 | 0 | 44 | 1 | 1/25 | 44.00 | 4.88 | 54.0 | 0 | 0 |
| TJ Phillips | 59.0 | 2 | 295 | 4 | 2/30 | 73.75 | 5.00 | 88.5 | 0 | 0 |
| JD Ryder | 8.0 | 0 | 41 | 0 | - | - | 5.12 | - | 0 | 0 |
| RS Bopara | 13.0 | 0 | 71 | 0 | - | - | 5.46 | - | 0 | 0 |
| GR Napier | 62.3 | 3 | 355 | 13 | 5/43 | 27.30 | 5.68 | 28.8 | 1 | 1 |
| RJW Topley | 29.1 | 0 | 168 | 5 | 3/56 | 33.60 | 5.76 | 35.0 | 0 | 0 |
| MET Salisbury | 22.0 | 0 | 144 | 4 | 4/55 | 36.00 | 6.54 | 33.0 | 1 | 0 |
| RN ten Doeschate | 19.0 | 0 | 140 | 3 | 1/27 | 46.66 | 7.36 | 38.0 | 0 | 0 |

**Catches/Stumpings:**

10 Foster (inc 3st), Pettini, Phillips, 2 Masters, Ryder, Napier, Topley, Salisbury, ten Doeschate, Velani, 1 Smith

# NATWEST T20 BLAST AVERAGES 2014

**Batting**

| | Mat | Inns | NO | Runs | HS | Ave | SR | 100 | 50 | 4s | 6s |
|---|---|---|---|---|---|---|---|---|---|---|---|
| RN ten Doeschate | 12 | 9 | 5 | 355 | 61* | 88.75 | 165.11 | 0 | 1 | 24 | 19 |
| TJ Phillips | 13 | 5 | 4 | 71 | 33* | 71.00 | 151.06 | 0 | 0 | 3 | 5 |
| RS Bopara | 13 | 13 | 5 | 417 | 81* | 52.12 | 143.29 | 0 | 3 | 31 | 19 |
| T Westley | 14 | 14 | 2 | 538 | 109* | 44.83 | 149.86 | 2 | 1 | 59 | 16 |
| ML Pettini | 15 | 15 | 2 | 424 | 95* | 32.61 | 134.17 | 0 | 2 | 49 | 7 |
| JS Foster | 15 | 9 | 4 | 142 | 36* | 28.40 | 149.47 | 0 | 0 | 10 | 5 |
| JD Ryder | 14 | 14 | 0 | 317 | 75 | 22.64 | 163.40 | 0 | 2 | 38 | 15 |
| AN Cook | 1 | 1 | 0 | 22 | 22 | 22.00 | 104.76 | 0 | 0 | 2 | 0 |
| BT Foakes | 13 | 9 | 2 | 149 | 46 | 21.28 | 115.50 | 0 | 0 | 9 | 1 |
| KS Velani | 3 | 2 | 0 | 36 | 34 | 18.00 | 138.46 | 0 | 0 | 6 | 1 |
| GR Napier | 9 | 1 | 0 | 17 | 17 | 17.00 | 141.66 | 0 | 0 | 2 | 1 |
| GM Smith | 8 | 3 | 1 | 26 | 25* | 13.00 | 152.94 | 0 | 0 | 1 | 2 |
| TS Mills | 4 | 1 | 0 | 0 | 0 | 0.00 | 0.00 | 0 | 0 | 0 | 0 |
| MET Salisbury | 8 | 2 | 2 | 2 | 1* | - | 100.00 | 0 | 0 | 0 | 0 |
| DD Masters | 7 | 2 | 2 | 1 | 1* | - | 100.00 | 0 | 0 | 0 | 0 |
| TC Moore | 1 | - | - | - | - | - | - | - | - | - | - |
| OJ Newby | 1 | - | - | - | - | - | - | - | - | - | - |
| MS Panesar | 2 | - | - | - | - | - | - | - | - | - | - |
| Tanveer Sikandar | 1 | - | - | - | - | - | - | - | - | - | - |
| RJW Topley | 11 | - | - | - | - | - | - | - | - | - | - |

**Bowling**

| | Overs | Mdns | Runs | Wkts | BBI | Ave | Econ | SR | 4w | 5w |
|---|---|---|---|---|---|---|---|---|---|---|
| OJ Newby | 2.0 | 0 | 12 | 1 | 1/12 | 12.00 | 6.00 | 12.0 | 0 | 0 |
| DD Masters | 27.0 | 0 | 196 | 7 | 2/17 | 28.00 | 7.25 | 23.1 | 0 | 0 |
| RS Bopara | 49.0 | 0 | 385 | 11 | 2/24 | 35.00 | 7.85 | 26.7 | 0 | 0 |
| T Westley | 6.0 | 0 | 48 | 0 | - | - | 8.00 | - | 0 | 0 |
| TJ Phillips | 42.3 | 1 | 352 | 8 | 2/35 | 44.00 | 8.28 | 31.8 | 0 | 0 |
| TS Mills | 14.0 | 0 | 122 | 6 | 3/41 | 20.33 | 8.71 | 14.0 | 0 | 0 |
| JD Ryder | 18.5 | 0 | 168 | 7 | 5/27 | 24.00 | 8.92 | 16.1 | 0 | 1 |
| MET Salisbury | 28.4 | 1 | 256 | 10 | 2/19 | 25.60 | 8.93 | 17.2 | 0 | 0 |
| RJW Topley | 43.0 | 2 | 386 | 9 | 3/26 | 42.88 | 8.97 | 28.6 | 0 | 0 |
| GR Napier | 34.3 | 0 | 313 | 8 | 2/32 | 39.12 | 9.07 | 25.8 | 0 | 0 |
| RN ten Doeschate | 7.0 | 0 | 68 | 2 | 1/8 | 34.00 | 9.71 | 21.0 | 0 | 0 |
| TC Moore | 1.0 | 0 | 10 | 0 | - | - | 10.00 | - | 0 | 0 |
| MS Panesar | 5.0 | 0 | 58 | 0 | - | - | 11.60 | - | 0 | 0 |
| GM Smith | 8.2 | 0 | 106 | 0 | - | - | 12.72 | - | 0 | 0 |
| Tanveer Sikandar | 2.0 | 0 | 29 | 0 | - | - | 14.50 | - | 0 | 0 |

**Catches/Stumpings:**
8 ten Doechate, 6 Foster (in 2st), 5 Bopara, Foakes, Phillips, 3 Topley, Pettini, 2 Salisbury, 1 Newby, Napier, Smith, Tanveer Sikandar

# GLAMORGAN

**FORMED:** 1888
**HOME GROUND:** SWALEC Stadium, Cardiff
**CAPTAIN:** Jacques Rudolph
**2014 RESULTS:** CC2: 8/9; RL50: 5/9 Group B; NWT20: Quarter-finalists
**HONOURS:** Championship: (3) 1948, 1969, 1997; Pro40/National League/ CB40/YB40/RL50: (2) 2002, 2004; Sunday League: 1993

---

### THE LOWDOWN

Glamorgan's trio of Southern Hemisphere stalwarts were again the stand-outs in a poor season. Aussies Michael Hogan and Jim Allenby and South African Jacques Rudolph were consistent performers across all formats, with Rudolph blasting the most runs in the RL Cup despite Glamorgan failing to get out of their group. Hogan passed 60 Championship wickets for the second successive season but he could do very little about Glamorgan's late-season slump which saw them losing five of their last seven matches and once again finishing above only perennial wooden-spoonists Leicestershire. Murray Goodwin's runs were very much missed as he struggled for consistency throughout the summer before bringing his 20-year career to a close by announcing his retirement, while Allenby has moved to Somerset. With Glamorgan over-reliant on players over 30, the likes of youngsters Dewi Jones, Aneurin Donald and Kieran Bull were blooded last season and provide hope for a new generation of talent to emerge this summer.

---

### HEAD COACH: TOBY RADFORD

Caerphilly-born Radford had a tricky first season as head coach at Glamorgan under chief executive Hugh Morris but has more than enough success on his CV to suggest a turnaround of fortunes may not be too far away. After a first-class career with Middlesex and Sussex, Radford moved into coaching with Berkshire before beginning a two-year stint as an ECB National Coach in 2001. In 2008 he led Middlesex to the Twenty20 Cup, before moving to the Caribbean to become director of the West Indies High Performance Centre and then being promoted to assistant coach of the national side, where he helped them to win the 2012 World Twenty20.

---

# COUNTY CHAMPIONSHIP AVERAGES 2014

## Batting

| | Mat | Inns | NO | Runs | HS | Ave | SR | 100 | 50 | 4s | 6s |
|---|---|---|---|---|---|---|---|---|---|---|---|
| CB Cooke | 12 | 20 | 1 | 807 | 171 | 42.47 | 54.23 | 1 | 7 | 91 | 1 |
| GG Wagg | 12 | 21 | 5 | 572 | 116* | 35.75 | 63.62 | 1 | 5 | 72 | 10 |
| J Allenby | 16 | 28 | 1 | 923 | 100 | 34.18 | 61.86 | 1 | 5 | 124 | 12 |
| WD Bragg | 16 | 29 | 2 | 899 | 93 | 33.29 | 41.62 | 0 | 6 | 114 | 1 |
| JA Rudolph | 15 | 27 | 0 | 857 | 139 | 31.74 | 49.45 | 2 | 5 | 115 | 2 |
| AHT Donald | 1 | 2 | 0 | 63 | 59 | 31.50 | 82.89 | 0 | 1 | 7 | 2 |
| SJ Walters | 5 | 9 | 1 | 213 | 57* | 26.62 | 53.78 | 0 | 1 | 25 | 1 |
| JC Glover | 1 | 2 | 1 | 25 | 19* | 25.00 | 35.21 | 0 | 0 | 1 | 0 |
| MA Wallace | 16 | 28 | 2 | 647 | 82 | 24.88 | 50.19 | 0 | 4 | 71 | 1 |
| GP Rees | 7 | 14 | 1 | 313 | 81 | 24.07 | 43.59 | 0 | 3 | 38 | 2 |
| WT Owen | 5 | 7 | 3 | 93 | 37* | 23.25 | 75.00 | 0 | 0 | 15 | 0 |
| MW Goodwin | 8 | 15 | 0 | 347 | 50 | 23.13 | 50.95 | 0 | 1 | 47 | 1 |
| BJ Wright | 7 | 11 | 0 | 254 | 123 | 23.09 | 58.93 | 1 | 0 | 44 | 1 |
| DA Cosker | 16 | 27 | 7 | 279 | 45 | 13.95 | 42.08 | 0 | 0 | 31 | 0 |
| DL Lloyd | 3 | 6 | 0 | 82 | 41 | 13.66 | 44.80 | 0 | 0 | 13 | 0 |
| AG Salter | 4 | 6 | 1 | 67 | 25* | 13.40 | 32.21 | 0 | 0 | 6 | 0 |
| MG Hogan | 13 | 21 | 7 | 183 | 36 | 13.07 | 68.53 | 0 | 0 | 25 | 3 |
| JAR Harris | 2 | 4 | 0 | 51 | 22 | 12.75 | 34.45 | 0 | 0 | 8 | 0 |
| RAJ Smith | 7 | 11 | 1 | 105 | 57* | 10.50 | 36.84 | 0 | 1 | 12 | 1 |
| TG Helm | 4 | 5 | 2 | 25 | 17 | 8.33 | 21.36 | 0 | 0 | 3 | 0 |
| KA Bull | 3 | 6 | 2 | 31 | 12 | 7.75 | 24.21 | 0 | 0 | 5 | 0 |
| TJ Lancefield | 3 | 5 | 0 | 24 | 19 | 4.80 | 32.00 | 0 | 0 | 1 | 0 |

## Bowling

| | Overs | Mdns | Runs | Wkts | BBI | BBM | Ave | Econ | SR | 5w | 10w |
|---|---|---|---|---|---|---|---|---|---|---|---|
| GP Rees | 1.0 | 0 | 6 | 1 | 1/6 | 1/6 | 6.00 | 6.00 | 6.0 | 0 | 0 |
| MG Hogan | 444.5 | 106 | 1232 | 63 | 5/58 | 10/125 | 19.55 | 2.76 | 42.3 | 3 | 1 |
| J Allenby | 442.4 | 119 | 1107 | 52 | 6/54 | 10/128 | 21.28 | 2.50 | 51.0 | 2 | 1 |
| KA Bull | 44.3 | 6 | 168 | 7 | 4/62 | 4/62 | 24.00 | 3.77 | 38.1 | 0 | 0 |
| JAR Harris | 47.0 | 10 | 138 | 5 | 2/34 | 3/62 | 27.60 | 2.93 | 56.4 | 0 | 0 |
| DA Cosker | 414.1 | 108 | 1175 | 40 | 5/39 | 9/133 | 29.37 | 2.83 | 62.1 | 3 | 0 |
| GG Wagg | 367.4 | 77 | 1258 | 41 | 6/29 | 8/172 | 30.68 | 3.42 | 53.8 | 1 | 0 |
| DL Lloyd | 29.0 | 1 | 110 | 3 | 2/22 | 2/22 | 36.66 | 3.79 | 58.0 | 0 | 0 |
| TG Helm | 84.0 | 15 | 276 | 7 | 2/9 | 4/44 | 39.42 | 3.28 | 72.0 | 0 | 0 |
| RAJ Smith | 157.4 | 21 | 630 | 12 | 3/38 | 4/139 | 52.50 | 3.99 | 78.8 | 0 | 0 |
| JA Rudolph | 14.3 | 2 | 54 | 1 | 1/25 | 1/25 | 54.00 | 3.72 | 87.0 | 0 | 0 |
| WT Owen | 113.0 | 18 | 495 | 8 | 3/42 | 3/69 | 61.87 | 4.38 | 84.7 | 0 | 0 |
| JC Glover | 17.0 | 1 | 82 | 1 | 1/82 | 1/82 | 82.00 | 4.82 | 102.0 | 0 | 0 |
| AG Salter | 83.0 | 14 | 332 | 4 | 2/54 | 3/118 | 83.00 | 4.00 | 124.5 | 0 | 0 |
| TJ Lancefield | 1.0 | 0 | 6 | 0 | - | - | - | 6.00 | - | 0 | 0 |
| WD Bragg | 19.3 | 2 | 76 | 0 | - | - | - | 3.89 | - | 0 | 0 |

**Catches/Stumpings:**

68 Wallace (inc 3st), 15 Allenby, 13 Rudolph, 11 Cosker, 9 Walters, 6 Hogan, Bragg, Goodwin, 4 Wagg, 3 Cooke, Wright, 2 Lloyd, Smith, Salter, 1 Rees, Harris, Helm, Owen, Lancefield, Donald

# ROYAL LONDON ONE-DAY CUP AVERAGES 2014

## GLAMORGAN

**Batting**

| | Mat | Inns | NO | Runs | HS | Ave | SR | 100 | 50 | 4s | 6s |
|---|---|---|---|---|---|---|---|---|---|---|---|
| JA Rudolph | 8 | 8 | 1 | 575 | 169* | 82.14 | 83.94 | 3 | 3 | 67 | 3 |
| AG Salter | 7 | 5 | 4 | 66 | 36* | 66.00 | 115.78 | 0 | 0 | 10 | 0 |
| MW Goodwin | 8 | 8 | 0 | 307 | 74 | 38.37 | 101.32 | 0 | 4 | 36 | 5 |
| CB Cooke | 8 | 8 | 2 | 199 | 73 | 33.16 | 79.91 | 0 | 2 | 17 | 1 |
| GP Rees | 2 | 2 | 0 | 64 | 60 | 32.00 | 81.01 | 0 | 1 | 5 | 0 |
| WD Bragg | 5 | 5 | 0 | 152 | 88 | 30.40 | 72.72 | 0 | 1 | 14 | 1 |
| MA Wallace | 8 | 7 | 3 | 95 | 21* | 23.75 | 76.00 | 0 | 0 | 9 | 0 |
| J Allenby | 7 | 7 | 0 | 154 | 70 | 22.00 | 83.69 | 0 | 1 | 24 | 0 |
| JAR Harris | 3 | 1 | 0 | 17 | 17 | 17.00 | 51.51 | 0 | 0 | 1 | 0 |
| GG Wagg | 7 | 6 | 1 | 79 | 37* | 15.80 | 75.96 | 0 | 0 | 9 | 0 |
| DL Lloyd | 7 | 5 | 0 | 53 | 32 | 10.60 | 73.61 | 0 | 0 | 5 | 0 |
| DA Cosker | 8 | 3 | 1 | 15 | 11* | 7.50 | 65.21 | 0 | 0 | 1 | 0 |
| BJ Wright | 2 | 1 | 0 | 0 | 0 | 0.00 | 0.00 | 0 | 0 | 0 | 0 |
| MG Hogan | 7 | 2 | 2 | 9 | 8* | - | 50.00 | 0 | 0 | 2 | 0 |
| D Penrhyn Jones | 1 | - | - | - | - | - | - | - | - | - | - |

**Bowling**

| | Overs | Mdns | Runs | Wkts | BBI | Ave | Econ | SR | 4w | 5w |
|---|---|---|---|---|---|---|---|---|---|---|
| J Allenby | 53.0 | 2 | 223 | 2 | 1/35 | 111.50 | 4.20 | 159.0 | 0 | 0 |
| AG Salter | 37.4 | 1 | 172 | 3 | 1/28 | 57.33 | 4.56 | 75.3 | 0 | 0 |
| DA Cosker | 68.0 | 3 | 313 | 14 | 3/33 | 22.35 | 4.60 | 29.1 | 0 | 0 |
| MG Hogan | 56.0 | 8 | 266 | 14 | 3/19 | 19.00 | 4.75 | 24.0 | 0 | 0 |
| DL Lloyd | 31.0 | 2 | 149 | 8 | 4/10 | 18.62 | 4.80 | 23.2 | 1 | 0 |
| JAR Harris | 26.0 | 0 | 153 | 3 | 2/42 | 51.00 | 5.88 | 52.0 | 0 | 0 |
| GG Wagg | 50.0 | 2 | 300 | 4 | 2/47 | 75.00 | 6.00 | 75.0 | 0 | 0 |
| WD Bragg | 2.0 | 0 | 14 | 0 | - | - | 7.00 | - | 0 | 0 |
| JA Rudolph | 7.0 | 0 | 51 | 1 | 1/32 | 51.00 | 7.28 | 42.0 | 0 | 0 |
| D Penrhyn Jones | 3.0 | 0 | 22 | 1 | 1/22 | 22.00 | 7.33 | 18.0 | 0 | 0 |

**Catches/Stumpings:**
11 Wallace, 6 Allenby, 4 Wagg, 3 Goodwin, 2 Salter, Hogan, 1 Lloyd, Rudolph, Cooke

# NATWEST T20 BLAST AVERAGES 2014

## GLAMORGAN

**Batting**

| | Mat | Inns | NO | Runs | HS | Ave | SR | 100 | 50 | 4s | 6s |
|---|---|---|---|---|---|---|---|---|---|---|---|
| JA Rudolph | 15 | 13 | 4 | 543 | 75* | 60.33 | 123.40 | 0 | 6 | 61 | 2 |
| J Allenby | 15 | 13 | 1 | 548 | 105 | 45.66 | 137.68 | 1 | 4 | 63 | 14 |
| AG Salter | 12 | 7 | 6 | 35 | 10 | 35.00 | 112.90 | 0 | 0 | 5 | 0 |
| MW Goodwin | 12 | 8 | 2 | 203 | 71 | 33.83 | 141.95 | 0 | 1 | 18 | 6 |
| CB Cooke | 15 | 11 | 3 | 246 | 65* | 30.75 | 158.70 | 0 | 1 | 25 | 8 |
| DJG Sammy | 6 | 5 | 2 | 58 | 28 | 19.33 | 118.36 | 0 | 0 | 4 | 3 |
| SJ Walters | 10 | 7 | 1 | 105 | 36 | 17.50 | 125.00 | 0 | 0 | 8 | 2 |
| MA Wallace | 15 | 11 | 0 | 166 | 38 | 15.09 | 138.33 | 0 | 0 | 16 | 5 |
| GG Wagg | 9 | 5 | 2 | 45 | 21* | 15.00 | 107.14 | 0 | 0 | 2 | 1 |
| BJ Wright | 12 | 8 | 1 | 44 | 15 | 6.28 | 110.00 | 0 | 0 | 1 | 3 |
| RAJ Smith | 2 | 1 | 0 | 2 | 2 | 2.00 | 50.00 | 0 | 0 | 0 | 0 |
| DL Lloyd | 3 | 2 | 0 | 3 | 3 | 1.50 | 42.85 | 0 | 0 | 0 | 0 |
| DA Cosker | 15 | 2 | 2 | 9 | 6* | - | 128.57 | 0 | 0 | 0 | 0 |
| MG Hogan | 14 | 1 | 1 | 0 | 0* | - | - | 0 | 0 | 0 | 0 |
| WT Owen | 10 | - | - | - | - | - | - | - | - | - | - |

**Bowling**

| | Overs | Mdns | Runs | Wkts | BBI | Ave | Econ | SR | 4w | 5w |
|---|---|---|---|---|---|---|---|---|---|---|
| J Allenby | 41.4 | 0 | 321 | 7 | 2/16 | 45.85 | 7.70 | 35.7 | 0 | 0 |
| JA Rudolph | 12.0 | 0 | 93 | 1 | 1/13 | 93.00 | 7.75 | 72.0 | 0 | 0 |
| AG Salter | 36.0 | 0 | 280 | 9 | 2/19 | 31.11 | 7.77 | 24.0 | 0 | 0 |
| MG Hogan | 51.0 | 0 | 410 | 21 | 3/30 | 19.52 | 8.03 | 14.5 | 0 | 0 |
| DJG Sammy | 23.0 | 0 | 191 | 4 | 2/29 | 47.75 | 8.30 | 34.5 | 0 | 0 |
| DA Cosker | 52.0 | 0 | 444 | 7 | 2/25 | 63.42 | 8.53 | 44.5 | 0 | 0 |
| GG Wagg | 32.0 | 0 | 274 | 13 | 3/28 | 21.07 | 8.56 | 14.7 | 0 | 0 |
| WT Owen | 28.3 | 0 | 289 | 9 | 3/32 | 32.11 | 10.14 | 19.0 | 0 | 0 |

**Catches/Stumpings:**
10 Wallace (inc 3st), 7 Hogan, 6 Cosker, Cooke, Walters, 4 Salter, 3 Allenby, Rudolph, 2 Wagg, Owen, Goodwin, Wright

# GLOUCESTERSHIRE

FORMED: 1871
HOME GROUND: Bristol County Ground
CAPTAIN: Geraint Jones (Championship), Michael Klinger (RL50 and NWT20)
2014 RESULTS: CC2: 7/9; RL50: Quarter-finalists; NWT20: 8/9 South Division
HONOURS: Gillette/NatWest/C&G/FP Trophy: (5) 1973, 1999, 2000, 2003, 2004; Benson & Hedges Cup: (3) 1977, 1999, 2000; Pro40/National League/CB40/YB40/RL50: 2000

THE LOWDOWN

A rather humdrum season – a quarter-final appearance in the RL Cup was as good as it got – was improved by the emergence of some very bright young players but offset by the loss of the Gidman brothers. Will, who has joined Nottinghamshire, and Alex, who has moved to Worcestershire, scored over 2,000 Championship runs between them last season and leave a big hole in the Gloucestershire squad as they depart for the lure of Division One cricket. Will Tavaré started to fulfil his promise with four Championship hundreds and with the Gidman departures he will need to repeat that success this season, while Gareth Roderick and Chris Dent have demonstrated enough fight to show they can offer good support. Gloucestershire often struggled for wickets but there was promise shown by young fast bowlers Liam Norwell and Craig Miles – who also put on a county record 137-run partnership for the 10th wicket against Worcestershire at Cheltenham. Geraint Jones, who spent a month on loan at Gloucestershire in 2014, has joined as Championship captain while Michael Klinger looks after the shorter formats.

HEAD COACH: RICHARD DAWSON

John Bracewell's second spell as director of cricket at Gloucestershire wasn't anywhere near as successful as his first stint, with the playing budget hit by the rebuilding of Nevil Road, and he stepped down in early 2015. Dawson comes in as head coach after spending a year as 2nd XI coach at Yorkshire. The former offspinner played seven Tests for England and took 30 wickets in 2001 as Yorkshire won their first County Championship title for 33 years, before finishing his playing career at Gloucestershire.

# COUNTY CHAMPIONSHIP AVERAGES 2014

## Batting

| | Mat | Inns | NO | Runs | HS | Ave | SR | 100 | 50 | 4s | 6s |
|---|---|---|---|---|---|---|---|---|---|---|---|
| GH Roderick | 4 | 8 | 0 | 470 | 171 | 58.75 | 71.10 | 1 | 3 | 57 | 2 |
| WRS Gidman | 13 | 20 | 5 | 826 | 125 | 55.06 | 55.51 | 3 | 2 | 109 | 4 |
| APR Gidman | 16 | 29 | 2 | 1277 | 264 | 47.29 | 66.68 | 4 | 3 | 178 | 7 |
| GO Jones | 3 | 4 | 1 | 136 | 93 | 45.33 | 78.61 | 0 | 1 | 19 | 3 |
| WA Tavaré | 15 | 26 | 1 | 953 | 139 | 38.12 | 45.79 | 4 | 3 | 135 | 4 |
| HJH Marshall | 16 | 27 | 3 | 821 | 118 | 34.20 | 48.92 | 2 | 3 | 88 | 4 |
| DA Payne | 7 | 10 | 4 | 189 | 54* | 31.50 | 60.77 | 0 | 1 | 20 | 5 |
| TMJ Smith | 13 | 19 | 4 | 453 | 80 | 30.20 | 46.89 | 0 | 1 | 57 | 1 |
| IA Cockbain | 9 | 16 | 1 | 443 | 151* | 29.53 | 32.98 | 1 | 2 | 53 | 0 |
| M Klinger | 10 | 18 | 1 | 490 | 129* | 28.82 | 52.97 | 2 | 1 | 64 | 4 |
| CN Miles | 4 | 7 | 1 | 170 | 62* | 28.33 | 54.48 | 0 | 1 | 31 | 0 |
| BAC Howell | 11 | 17 | 3 | 360 | 78* | 25.71 | 64.05 | 0 | 2 | 32 | 10 |
| LC Norwell | 10 | 12 | 5 | 173 | 78 | 24.71 | 55.80 | 0 | 1 | 24 | 2 |
| CDJ Dent | 13 | 22 | 0 | 436 | 61 | 19.81 | 50.63 | 0 | 4 | 70 | 1 |
| AP Rouse | 4 | 7 | 0 | 124 | 49 | 17.71 | 42.46 | 0 | 0 | 16 | 0 |
| MD Taylor | 9 | 12 | 5 | 118 | 32* | 16.85 | 38.06 | 0 | 0 | 12 | 0 |
| JK Fuller | 6 | 7 | 1 | 88 | 28 | 14.66 | 59.45 | 0 | 0 | 14 | 0 |
| JMR Taylor | 2 | 4 | 0 | 57 | 40 | 14.25 | 64.04 | 0 | 0 | 10 | 0 |
| DM Housego | 1 | 2 | 0 | 27 | 27 | 13.50 | 62.79 | 0 | 0 | 6 | 0 |
| PJ Grieshaber | 1 | 1 | 0 | 10 | 10 | 10.00 | 22.72 | 0 | 0 | 2 | 0 |
| GJ McCarter | 2 | 3 | 0 | 24 | 20 | 8.00 | 63.15 | 0 | 0 | 2 | 1 |
| ID Saxelby | 2 | 3 | 0 | 24 | 20 | 8.00 | 52.17 | 0 | 0 | 2 | 0 |
| CL Herring | 4 | 6 | 0 | 46 | 22 | 7.66 | 30.87 | 0 | 0 | 7 | 0 |
| MD Craig | 1 | 1 | 0 | 7 | 7 | 7.00 | 25.92 | 0 | 0 | 0 | 0 |

## Bowling

| | Overs | Mdns | Runs | Wkts | BBI | BBM | Ave | Econ | SR | 5w | 10w |
|---|---|---|---|---|---|---|---|---|---|---|---|
| CN Miles | 93.0 | 16 | 358 | 18 | 5/90 | 5/47 | 19.88 | 3.84 | 31.0 | 1 | 0 |
| ID Saxelby | 20.1 | 5 | 71 | 3 | 3/71 | 3/71 | 23.66 | 3.52 | 40.3 | 0 | 0 |
| GJ McCarter | 43.3 | 7 | 144 | 6 | 3/64 | 3/64 | 24.00 | 3.31 | 43.5 | 0 | 0 |
| WRS Gidman | 357.3 | 97 | 943 | 39 | 6/50 | 9/84 | 24.17 | 2.63 | 55.0 | 2 | 0 |
| BAC Howell | 250.2 | 59 | 714 | 23 | 4/60 | 4/60 | 31.04 | 2.85 | 65.3 | 0 | 0 |
| JK Fuller | 159.4 | 27 | 581 | 18 | 6/47 | 7/129 | 32.27 | 3.63 | 53.2 | 1 | 0 |
| HJH Marshall | 25.0 | 6 | 66 | 2 | 1/21 | 1/21 | 33.00 | 2.64 | 75.0 | 0 | 0 |
| JMR Taylor | 70.1 | 9 | 267 | 7 | 4/125 | 4/129 | 38.14 | 3.80 | 60.1 | 0 | 0 |
| LC Norwell | 304.4 | 51 | 1166 | 29 | 4/69 | 7/114 | 40.20 | 3.82 | 63.0 | 0 | 0 |
| TMJ Smith | 388.3 | 60 | 1294 | 32 | 4/35 | 5/92 | 40.43 | 3.33 | 72.8 | 0 | 0 |
| MD Taylor | 216.2 | 35 | 905 | 21 | 5/75 | 6/101 | 43.09 | 4.18 | 61.8 | 1 | 0 |
| MD Craig | 25.0 | 3 | 105 | 2 | 2/85 | 2/105 | 52.50 | 4.20 | 75.0 | 0 | 0 |
| DA Payne | 185.0 | 41 | 594 | 11 | 3/29 | 3/29 | 54.00 | 3.21 | 100.9 | 0 | 0 |
| CDJ Dent | 35.3 | 2 | 165 | 1 | 1/39 | 1/39 | 165.00 | 4.64 | 213.0 | 0 | 0 |
| DM Housego | 6.0 | 0 | 25 | 0 | - | - | - | 4.16 | - | 0 | 0 |

**Catches/Stumpings:**

18 Herring (inc 1st), 15 Rouse (inc 2st), 14 Roderick, A Gidman, 11 Klinger, Tavaré, 9 Dent, 8 Howell, 7 Cockbain, 6 Jones, 5 W Gidman, Smith, 3 Payne, 2 Miles, Marshall, Taylor, 1 McCarter, Fuller, Norwell

# ROYAL LONDON ONE-DAY CUP AVERAGES 2014

Batting

| | Mat | Inns | NO | Runs | HS | Ave | SR | 100 | 50 | 4s | 6s |
|---|---|---|---|---|---|---|---|---|---|---|---|
| M Klinger | 7 | 7 | 3 | 228 | 98 | 57.00 | 70.58 | 0 | 2 | 22 | 0 |
| WRS Gidman | 8 | 7 | 2 | 236 | 71* | 47.20 | 87.73 | 0 | 1 | 28 | 1 |
| BAC Howell | 8 | 5 | 2 | 115 | 43* | 38.33 | 74.67 | 0 | 0 | 5 | 2 |
| WA Tavaré | 3 | 3 | 0 | 100 | 77 | 33.33 | 91.74 | 0 | 1 | 12 | 0 |
| CDJ Dent | 8 | 8 | 1 | 214 | 70 | 30.57 | 91.45 | 0 | 1 | 28 | 5 |
| APR Gidman | 4 | 4 | 1 | 91 | 47 | 30.33 | 70.00 | 0 | 0 | 11 | 0 |
| JMR Taylor | 7 | 4 | 0 | 117 | 53 | 29.25 | 112.50 | 0 | 1 | 7 | 7 |
| IA Cockbain | 8 | 6 | 1 | 136 | 98* | 27.20 | 72.72 | 0 | 1 | 15 | 0 |
| GH Roderick | 6 | 4 | 0 | 88 | 43 | 22.00 | 65.67 | 0 | 0 | 7 | 1 |
| CN Miles | 8 | 4 | 1 | 29 | 12 | 9.66 | 61.70 | 0 | 0 | 4 | 0 |
| HJH Marshall | 8 | 8 | 0 | 62 | 22 | 7.75 | 63.26 | 0 | 0 | 7 | 1 |
| DA Payne | 8 | 4 | 2 | 14 | 5* | 7.00 | 77.77 | 0 | 0 | 1 | 0 |
| TMJ Smith | 3 | 2 | 1 | 5 | 4* | 5.00 | 31.25 | 0 | 0 | 0 | 0 |
| AP Rouse | 2 | 2 | 0 | 8 | 4 | 4.00 | 88.88 | 0 | 0 | 1 | 0 |

Bowling

| | Overs | Mdns | Runs | Wkts | BBI | Ave | Econ | SR | 4w | 5w |
|---|---|---|---|---|---|---|---|---|---|---|
| BAC Howell | 61.0 | 2 | 243 | 5 | 1/15 | 48.60 | 3.98 | 73.2 | 0 | 0 |
| WRS Gidman | 56.0 | 3 | 252 | 12 | 4/41 | 21.00 | 4.50 | 28.0 | 1 | 0 |
| DA Payne | 57.3 | 4 | 279 | 17 | 5/44 | 16.41 | 4.85 | 20.2 | 1 | 1 |
| JMR Taylor | 44.0 | 1 | 220 | 9 | 4/38 | 24.44 | 5.00 | 29.3 | 1 | 0 |
| CDJ Dent | 19.0 | 0 | 103 | 1 | 1/25 | 103.00 | 5.42 | 114.0 | 0 | 0 |
| CN Miles | 56.5 | 1 | 316 | 8 | 3/48 | 39.50 | 5.56 | 42.6 | 0 | 0 |
| TMJ Smith | 9.1 | 0 | 61 | 2 | 2/55 | 30.50 | 6.65 | 27.5 | 0 | 0 |

**Catches/Stumpings:**

11 Roderick, 7 Cockbain, 4 Rouse (inc 1st), 2 Howell, A Gidman, Smith, 1 Taylor, Klinger, Marshall

# NATWEST T20 BLAST AVERAGES 2014

| | Mat | Inns | NO | Runs | HS | Ave | SR | 100 | 50 | 4s | 6s |
|---|---|---|---|---|---|---|---|---|---|---|---|
| WRS Gidman | 5 | 5 | 3 | 76 | 26* | 38.00 | 128.81 | 0 | 0 | 6 | 2 |
| CL Herring | 4 | 4 | 2 | 55 | 23* | 27.50 | 144.73 | 0 | 0 | 4 | 2 |
| IA Cockbain | 14 | 14 | 1 | 354 | 84 | 27.23 | 117.60 | 0 | 3 | 24 | 9 |
| M Klinger | 11 | 11 | 0 | 298 | 70 | 27.09 | 110.78 | 0 | 1 | 30 | 5 |
| TMJ Smith | 13 | 5 | 3 | 54 | 30* | 27.00 | 150.00 | 0 | 0 | 4 | 1 |
| HJH Marshall | 14 | 12 | 1 | 285 | 74 | 25.90 | 123.91 | 0 | 2 | 24 | 2 |
| GO Jones | 2 | 2 | 0 | 50 | 37 | 25.00 | 238.09 | 0 | 0 | 3 | 5 |
| BAC Howell | 14 | 14 | 2 | 254 | 50 | 21.16 | 114.41 | 0 | 1 | 13 | 9 |
| APR Gidman | 14 | 14 | 0 | 236 | 55 | 16.85 | 114.00 | 0 | 1 | 29 | 3 |
| JMR Taylor | 11 | 8 | 4 | 67 | 19* | 16.75 | 176.31 | 0 | 0 | 3 | 5 |
| JK Fuller | 3 | 2 | 0 | 30 | 21 | 15.00 | 125.00 | 0 | 0 | 1 | 1 |
| GJ McCarter | 13 | 4 | 2 | 28 | 16* | 14.00 | 155.55 | 0 | 0 | 3 | 1 |
| AP Rouse | 7 | 7 | 2 | 61 | 35* | 12.20 | 117.30 | 0 | 0 | 7 | 1 |
| CDJ Dent | 10 | 10 | 1 | 109 | 55* | 12.11 | 119.78 | 0 | 1 | 9 | 5 |
| DM Housego | 3 | 2 | 1 | 11 | 6* | 11.00 | 68.75 | 0 | 0 | 0 | 0 |
| GH Roderick | 1 | 1 | 0 | 3 | 3 | 3.00 | 60.00 | 0 | 0 | 0 | 0 |
| RJ Montgomery | 1 | 1 | 1 | 8 | 8* | - | 200.00 | 0 | 0 | 0 | 1 |
| LC Norwell | 5 | 2 | 2 | 2 | 1* | - | 66.66 | 0 | 0 | 0 | 0 |
| DA Payne | 9 | 1 | 1 | 1 | 1* | - | 100.00 | 0 | 0 | 0 | 0 |

Batting

| | Overs | Mdns | Runs | Wkts | BBI | Ave | Econ | SR | 4w | 5w |
|---|---|---|---|---|---|---|---|---|---|---|
| WRS Gidman | 14.0 | 0 | 97 | 5 | 2/23 | 19.40 | 6.92 | 16.8 | 0 | 0 |
| CDJ Dent | 6.0 | 0 | 42 | 2 | 1/4 | 21.00 | 7.00 | 18.0 | 0 | 0 |
| BAC Howell | 41.0 | 0 | 294 | 15 | 4/26 | 19.60 | 7.17 | 16.4 | 1 | 0 |
| JK Fuller | 12.0 | 0 | 88 | 7 | 4/32 | 12.57 | 7.33 | 10.2 | 1 | 0 |
| TMJ Smith | 40.0 | 0 | 297 | 12 | 2/24 | 24.75 | 7.42 | 20.0 | 0 | 0 |
| LC Norwell | 15.0 | 0 | 116 | 5 | 3/27 | 23.20 | 7.73 | 18.0 | 0 | 0 |
| JMR Taylor | 28.4 | 0 | 223 | 9 | 3/12 | 24.77 | 7.77 | 19.1 | 0 | 0 |
| DA Payne | 27.3 | 1 | 237 | 8 | 2/14 | 29.62 | 8.61 | 20.6 | 0 | 0 |
| GJ McCarter | 38.0 | 0 | 345 | 16 | 5/35 | 21.56 | 9.07 | 14.2 | 0 | 1 |
| RJ Montgomery | 3.0 | 0 | 50 | 0 | - | - | 16.66 | - | 0 | 0 |

Bowling

**Catches/Stumpings:**
8 Rouse (inc 4st), 7 McCarter, 5 Marshall, 4 Howell, Klinger, 3 Payne, Housego, 2 Dent, Smith, Taylor, Herring (inc 1st), 1 W Gidman, Fuller, Norwell, Roderick

# HAMPSHIRE

**FORMED:** 1863
**HOME GROUND:** The Ageas Bowl, Southampton
**CAPTAIN:** Jimmy Adams (Championship and RL50), James Vince (NWT20)
**2014 RESULTS:** CC2: Winners; RL50: 9/9 Group A; NWT20: Semi-finalists
**HONOURS:** Championship: (2) 1961, 1973; Gillette/NatWest/C&G/FP Trophy: (3) 1991, 2005, 2009; Benson & Hedges Cup: (2) 1988, 1992; Pro40/National League/CB40/YB40/RL50: 2012; Sunday League: (3) 1975, 1978, 1986; Twenty20 Cup: (2) 2010, 2012

## THE LOWDOWN

After an unusually quiet 2013 season, Hampshire bounced back last summer with promotion in the County Championship and a semi-final spot in the T20 Blast. Their greatest asset was undoubtedly James Vince, who added grit to his naturally stylish game and compiled 1,525 Championship runs. He also showed a canny captaincy ability in the T20 Blast. Jimmy Adams passed 1,000 runs for the fifth time in his career – there are few batsmen more underrated in county cricket – while Will Smith, who also reached four figures, proved to be an astute signing. The greatest mystery of the season was their atrocious form in the RL Cup, where they finished bottom of their group with just one win. The squad hasn't been strengthened massively over the winter, with Andre Adams – who will turn 40 during the summer – a surprising signing from Nottinghamshire, while Yasir Arafat makes Hampshire his sixth county. Australian fast bowler Jackson Bird will be available for the first three months of the season, and will hope to match the impact Kyle Abbott had with the ball last year.

## FIRST-TEAM COACH: DALE BENKENSTEIN

Topping Division Two in his first season as head coach was an emphatic way for Benkenstein to begin his post-playing career. Working under director of cricket Giles White, it was his first crack at heading up a team following work as batting coach with Sunfoil Dolphins in South Africa. Benkenstein helped Durham win three County Championship titles during his time as a player – becoming a Wisden Cricketer of the Year in 2009 – and also played 23 ODIs for South Africa.

# COUNTY CHAMPIONSHIP AVERAGES 2014

Batting

| | Mat | Inns | NO | Runs | HS | Ave | SR | 100 | 50 | 4s | 6s |
|---|---|---|---|---|---|---|---|---|---|---|---|
| NJ Rimmington | 1 | 2 | 1 | 65 | 65* | 65.00 | 48.87 | 0 | 1 | 9 | 0 |
| JM Vince | 16 | 28 | 3 | 1525 | 240 | 61.00 | 76.86 | 4 | 7 | 225 | 4 |
| GJ Maxwell | 1 | 2 | 0 | 109 | 85 | 54.50 | 100.00 | 0 | 1 | 13 | 3 |
| WR Smith | 16 | 27 | 4 | 1187 | 151* | 51.60 | 48.60 | 2 | 6 | 144 | 1 |
| DJ Balcombe | 4 | 4 | 2 | 91 | 65* | 45.50 | 63.19 | 0 | 1 | 12 | 0 |
| SM Ervine | 16 | 23 | 4 | 856 | 121 | 45.05 | 61.89 | 2 | 4 | 110 | 10 |
| JHK Adams | 16 | 29 | 1 | 1215 | 231 | 43.39 | 47.89 | 1 | 8 | 163 | 7 |
| MA Carberry | 12 | 21 | 1 | 847 | 125 | 42.35 | 51.52 | 3 | 3 | 119 | 12 |
| AJA Wheater | 12 | 20 | 1 | 610 | 107 | 32.10 | 76.05 | 1 | 3 | 81 | 3 |
| CP Wood | 4 | 6 | 1 | 132 | 61 | 26.40 | 79.04 | 0 | 1 | 19 | 1 |
| MD Bates | 7 | 10 | 3 | 181 | 50 | 25.85 | 46.29 | 0 | 1 | 20 | 0 |
| JA Tomlinson | 16 | 16 | 10 | 135 | 51 | 22.50 | 40.29 | 0 | 1 | 16 | 1 |
| Imran Tahir | 2 | 4 | 2 | 44 | 22* | 22.00 | 68.75 | 0 | 0 | 6 | 1 |
| LA Dawson | 10 | 18 | 1 | 354 | 64 | 20.82 | 42.90 | 0 | 1 | 36 | 1 |
| DR Briggs | 8 | 10 | 4 | 116 | 38* | 19.33 | 54.71 | 0 | 0 | 16 | 0 |
| JS Gatting | 8 | 12 | 1 | 191 | 67 | 17.36 | 43.40 | 0 | 1 | 21 | 2 |
| KJ Abbott | 9 | 10 | 1 | 127 | 40 | 14.11 | 43.64 | 0 | 0 | 13 | 1 |
| MT Coles | 15 | 18 | 0 | 251 | 83 | 13.94 | 75.37 | 0 | 1 | 37 | 5 |
| TP Alsop | 2 | 4 | 0 | 50 | 33 | 12.50 | 37.87 | 0 | 0 | 4 | 1 |
| BJ Taylor | 1 | 1 | 0 | 1 | 1 | 1.00 | 5.88 | 0 | 0 | 0 | 0 |

Bowling

| | Overs | Mdns | Runs | Wkts | BBI | BBM | Ave | Econ | SR | 5w | 10w |
|---|---|---|---|---|---|---|---|---|---|---|---|
| GJ Maxwell | 6.0 | 0 | 33 | 2 | 2/33 | 2/33 | 16.50 | 5.50 | 18.0 | 0 | 0 |
| CP Wood | 83.0 | 22 | 252 | 15 | 5/39 | 6/68 | 16.80 | 3.03 | 33.2 | 1 | 0 |
| KJ Abbott | 251.0 | 77 | 732 | 36 | 5/44 | 8/67 | 20.33 | 2.91 | 41.8 | 2 | 0 |
| WR Smith | 33.5 | 6 | 114 | 5 | 2/27 | 2/27 | 22.80 | 3.36 | 40.6 | 0 | 0 |
| NJ Rimmington | 16.0 | 4 | 51 | 2 | 2/51 | 2/51 | 25.50 | 3.18 | 48.0 | 0 | 0 |
| JA Tomlinson | 416.5 | 103 | 1215 | 47 | 6/48 | 7/86 | 25.85 | 2.91 | 53.2 | 1 | 0 |
| DR Briggs | 250.1 | 73 | 705 | 27 | 5/50 | 7/72 | 26.11 | 2.81 | 55.5 | 1 | 0 |
| MT Coles | 353.3 | 80 | 1165 | 41 | 4/84 | 7/175 | 28.41 | 3.29 | 51.7 | 0 | 0 |
| Imran Tahir | 49.4 | 8 | 180 | 6 | 3/140 | 3/40 | 30.00 | 3.62 | 49.6 | 0 | 0 |
| LA Dawson | 175.3 | 40 | 529 | 17 | 4/58 | 6/129 | 31.11 | 3.01 | 61.9 | 0 | 0 |
| SM Ervine | 217.0 | 43 | 686 | 19 | 3/22 | 4/60 | 36.10 | 3.16 | 68.5 | 0 | 0 |
| DJ Balcombe | 63.0 | 10 | 244 | 5 | 3/53 | 3/53 | 48.80 | 3.87 | 75.6 | 0 | 0 |
| BJ Taylor | 19.0 | 3 | 74 | 1 | 1/64 | 1/74 | 74.00 | 3.89 | 114.0 | 0 | 0 |
| JM Vince | 57.0 | 7 | 190 | 2 | 1/10 | 1/26 | 95.00 | 3.33 | 171.0 | 0 | 0 |
| JS Gatting | 3.0 | 0 | 22 | 0 | - | - | - | 7.33 | - | 0 | 0 |
| MA Carberry | 5.0 | 0 | 31 | 0 | - | - | - | 6.20 | - | 0 | 0 |

**Catches/Stumpings:**

22 Wheater (inc 2st), Vince, 18 Bates (inc 2st), 14 Dawson, 13 Ervine, 12 Smith, 7 Adams, 6 Coles, 5 Carberry, 3 Imran Tahir, 2 Tomlinson, Briggs, Gatting, Alsop, 1 Wood, Taylor

# ROYAL LONDON ONE-DAY CUP AVERAGES 2014

**Batting**

| | Mat | Inns | NO | Runs | HS | Ave | SR | 100 | 50 | 4s | 6s |
|---|---|---|---|---|---|---|---|---|---|---|---|
| GJ Maxwell | 2 | 2 | 0 | 181 | 146 | 90.50 | 154.70 | 1 | 0 | 26 | 4 |
| JHK Adams | 8 | 7 | 1 | 258 | 91* | 43.00 | 85.14 | 0 | 1 | 32 | 4 |
| SP Terry | 4 | 4 | 1 | 126 | 63 | 42.00 | 92.64 | 0 | 2 | 10 | 4 |
| WR Smith | 7 | 6 | 0 | 243 | 59 | 40.50 | 81.54 | 0 | 1 | 12 | 2 |
| AJA Wheater | 5 | 5 | 0 | 191 | 135 | 38.20 | 115.06 | 1 | 0 | 14 | 6 |
| JM Vince | 4 | 4 | 0 | 141 | 79 | 35.25 | 100.00 | 0 | 1 | 15 | 2 |
| MA Carberry | 6 | 6 | 1 | 175 | 61 | 35.00 | 103.55 | 0 | 2 | 25 | 5 |
| SM Ervine | 7 | 6 | 0 | 144 | 64 | 24.00 | 76.19 | 0 | 1 | 10 | 2 |
| DR Briggs | 8 | 7 | 4 | 56 | 18* | 18.66 | 101.81 | 0 | 0 | 5 | 0 |
| JA Tomlinson | 7 | 6 | 5 | 18 | 11* | 18.00 | 64.28 | 0 | 0 | 1 | 0 |
| LA Dawson | 8 | 7 | 0 | 98 | 30 | 14.00 | 73.13 | 0 | 0 | 6 | 0 |
| JS Gatting | 1 | 1 | 0 | 13 | 13 | 13.00 | 76.47 | 0 | 0 | 1 | 0 |
| CP Wood | 7 | 6 | 0 | 76 | 27 | 12.66 | 81.72 | 0 | 0 | 5 | 0 |
| MD Bates | 3 | 2 | 0 | 19 | 19 | 9.50 | 61.29 | 0 | 0 | 3 | 0 |
| MT Coles | 8 | 7 | 0 | 30 | 25 | 4.28 | 55.55 | 0 | 0 | 2 | 1 |
| BMR Akram | 1 | 1 | 0 | 1 | 1 | 1.00 | 11.11 | 0 | 0 | 0 | 0 |
| TP Alsop | 1 | 1 | 0 | 0 | 0 | 0.00 | 0.00 | 0 | 0 | 0 | 0 |
| TE Barber | 1 | 1 | 0 | 0 | 0 | 0.00 | 0.00 | 0 | 0 | 0 | 0 |

**Bowling**

| | Overs | Mdns | Runs | Wkts | BBI | Ave | Econ | SR | 4w | 5w |
|---|---|---|---|---|---|---|---|---|---|---|
| WR Smith | 23.0 | 0 | 125 | 3 | 1/17 | 41.66 | 5.43 | 46.0 | 0 | 0 |
| CP Wood | 38.5 | 4 | 213 | 7 | 2/27 | 30.42 | 5.48 | 33.2 | 0 | 0 |
| TE Barber | 4.0 | 0 | 22 | 2 | 2/22 | 11.00 | 5.50 | 12.0 | 0 | 0 |
| DR Briggs | 39.2 | 0 | 228 | 4 | 2/46 | 57.00 | 5.79 | 59.0 | 0 | 0 |
| LA Dawson | 34.0 | 0 | 201 | 3 | 2/56 | 67.00 | 5.91 | 68.0 | 0 | 0 |
| JA Tomlinson | 29.2 | 0 | 177 | 9 | 2/23 | 19.66 | 6.03 | 19.5 | 0 | 0 |
| MT Coles | 45.5 | 2 | 292 | 9 | 3/62 | 32.44 | 6.37 | 30.5 | 0 | 0 |
| JM Vince | 2.0 | 0 | 13 | 0 | - | - | 6.50 | - | 0 | 0 |
| SM Ervine | 19.0 | 0 | 124 | 1 | 1/34 | 124.00 | 6.52 | 114.0 | 0 | 0 |
| GJ Maxwell | 3.0 | 0 | 23 | 0 | - | - | 7.66 | - | 0 | 0 |
| BMR Akram | 2.0 | 0 | 24 | 0 | - | - | 12.00 | - | 0 | 0 |

**Catches/Stumpings:**
4 Vince, Maxwell, 2 Wood, Dawson, Adams, Bates, Wheater, 1 Smith, Briggs, Coles, Ervine, Carberry, Gatting

# NATWEST T20 BLAST AVERAGES 2014

| | Mat | Inns | NO | Runs | HS | Ave | SR | 100 | 50 | 4s | 6s |
|---|---|---|---|---|---|---|---|---|---|---|---|
| OA Shah | 6 | 6 | 3 | 156 | 50* | 52.00 | 122.83 | 0 | 1 | 8 | 7 |
| MA Carberry | 14 | 14 | 1 | 424 | 87* | 32.61 | 134.17 | 0 | 4 | 43 | 20 |
| JHK Adams | 16 | 16 | 1 | 447 | 69* | 29.80 | 144.66 | 0 | 4 | 46 | 14 |
| JM Vince | 16 | 16 | 2 | 399 | 93* | 28.50 | 148.88 | 0 | 4 | 52 | 12 |
| AJA Wheater | 11 | 7 | 2 | 114 | 34 | 22.80 | 105.55 | 0 | 0 | 7 | 2 |
| WR Smith | 16 | 13 | 5 | 179 | 37 | 22.37 | 136.64 | 0 | 0 | 16 | 4 |
| SM Ervine | 16 | 14 | 2 | 262 | 47 | 21.83 | 126.57 | 0 | 0 | 17 | 10 |
| MT Coles | 15 | 11 | 2 | 175 | 54 | 19.44 | 157.65 | 0 | 1 | 10 | 12 |
| LA Dawson | 4 | 2 | 1 | 17 | 10* | 17.00 | 100.00 | 0 | 0 | 1 | 0 |
| KJ Abbott | 12 | 3 | 1 | 27 | 16 | 13.50 | 180.00 | 0 | 0 | 1 | 1 |
| MD Bates | 5 | 5 | 2 | 38 | 15 | 12.66 | 115.15 | 0 | 0 | 4 | 0 |
| CP Wood | 15 | 7 | 2 | 63 | 27 | 12.60 | 105.00 | 0 | 0 | 4 | 2 |
| GJ Maxwell | 11 | 11 | 0 | 127 | 30 | 11.54 | 118.69 | 0 | 0 | 8 | 6 |
| NJ Rimmington | 1 | 1 | 0 | 0 | 0 | 0.00 | 0.00 | 0 | 0 | 0 | 0 |
| JS Gatting | 2 | 1 | 1 | 5 | 5* | - | 125.00 | 0 | 0 | 0 | 0 |
| DR Briggs | 15 | 5 | 5 | 3 | 1* | - | 50.00 | 0 | 0 | 0 | 0 |
| BJ Taylor | 1 | - | - | - | - | - | - | - | - | - | - |

Batting

| | Overs | Mdns | Runs | Wkts | BBI | Ave | Econ | SR | 4w | 5w |
|---|---|---|---|---|---|---|---|---|---|---|
| WR Smith | 57.0 | 0 | 395 | 20 | 3/15 | 19.75 | 6.92 | 17.1 | 0 | 0 |
| DR Briggs | 59.0 | 0 | 435 | 21 | 4/28 | 20.71 | 7.37 | 16.8 | 1 | 0 |
| NJ Rimmington | 4.0 | 0 | 30 | 0 | - | - | 7.50 | - | 0 | 0 |
| LA Dawson | 16.0 | 0 | 129 | 3 | 2/36 | 43.00 | 8.06 | 32.0 | 0 | 0 |
| KJ Abbott | 46.0 | 1 | 377 | 7 | 2/14 | 53.85 | 8.19 | 39.4 | 0 | 0 |
| MT Coles | 57.0 | 0 | 469 | 18 | 2/24 | 26.05 | 8.22 | 19.0 | 0 | 0 |
| CP Wood | 54.4 | 0 | 470 | 17 | 4/24 | 27.64 | 8.59 | 19.2 | 1 | 0 |
| JM Vince | 2.0 | 0 | 19 | 1 | 1/19 | 19.00 | 9.50 | 12.0 | 0 | 0 |
| GJ Maxwell | 3.0 | 0 | 34 | 0 | - | - | 11.33 | - | 0 | 0 |
| SM Ervine | 12.0 | 0 | 141 | 1 | 1/16 | 141.00 | 11.75 | 72.0 | 0 | 0 |
| BJ Taylor | 1.0 | 0 | 16 | 0 | - | - | 16.00 | - | 0 | 0 |

Bowling

**Catches/Stumpings:**
8 Adams, 6 Bates (inc 4st), Maxwell, 4 Briggs, Vince, Wheater, 3 Smith, Ervine, 2 Dawson, Abbott, Wood, Bates, Carberry, Shah, 1 Taylor

# KENT



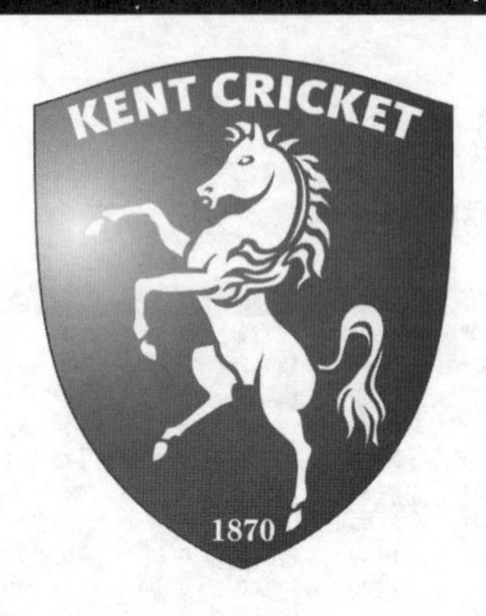


**FORMED:** 1870
**HOME GROUND:** The Spitfire Ground, St Lawrence
**ONE-DAY NAME:** Kent Spitfires
**CAPTAIN:** Rob Key
**2014 RESULTS:** CC2: 6/9; RL50: Semi-finalists; NWT20: 6/9 South Division
**HONOURS:** Championship: (7) 1906, 1909, 1910, 1913, 1970, 1977(s), 1978; Gillette/NatWest/C&G/FP Trophy: (2) 1967, 1974; Pro40/National League/CB40/RL50: 2001; Benson & Hedges Cup: (3) 1973, 1976, 1978; Sunday League: (4) 1972, 1973, 1976, 1995; Twenty20 Cup: 2007

---

## THE LOWDOWN

All of the talk in the first half of the season was about young offspinner Adam Riley, while it was another youngster, Sam Billings, who finished the season on everyone's lips. Riley, 23, is already being touted as a future England spinner after taking 48 Championship wickets while Billings, 23, highlighted his explosive potential with 458 runs at a strike-rate of 154.20 as Kent made the semi-finals of the RL Cup. While a sixth-place finish in Division Two of the Championship and a tepid T20 display ensured the season was an overall disappointment, Billings and Riley are the faces of a potentially bright future – if the county can keep hold of them. Opener Daniel Bell-Drummond, 22 this summer, finished just 45 runs shy of 1,000 and another encouraging sign was the renaissance of Sam Northeast. Now 25, he has long flattered to deceive and things reached a nadir last term when he was dropped to the 2nd XIs after a poor start to the season, but he responded magnificently on his return to the first team, hitting four centuries from his new position at No.5. With the experienced trio of Darren Stevens, Rob Key and Brendan Nash showing the young players the way, Kent fans have genuine cause for optimism for the season.

---

## HEAD COACH: JIMMY ADAMS

Now in his fourth season as Kent's head coach, Adams' work with the county's youth academy is beginning to pay off. As a player, Adams had a stunning start to his Test career when he averaged 87 after 12 matches. He went on to play 54 Tests and 127 ODIs, and captained West Indies for 15 Tests before stepping down following a 5-0 whitewash in Australia. After his playing career he moved into a coaching role with West Indies U19.

---

# COUNTY CHAMPIONSHIP AVERAGES 2014

**Batting**

| | Mat | Inns | NO | Runs | HS | Ave | SR | 100 | 50 | 4s | 6s |
|---|---|---|---|---|---|---|---|---|---|---|---|
| DJ Bell-Drummond | 16 | 28 | 3 | 955 | 153 | 38.20 | 40.27 | 2 | 6 | 124 | 0 |
| SA Northeast | 14 | 24 | 1 | 872 | 128 | 37.91 | 53.10 | 4 | 4 | 107 | 3 |
| BP Nash | 15 | 25 | 2 | 839 | 126 | 36.47 | 62.10 | 1 | 4 | 111 | 7 |
| DI Stevens | 16 | 26 | 2 | 859 | 105 | 35.79 | 71.34 | 1 | 4 | 118 | 17 |
| SW Billings | 16 | 24 | 2 | 755 | 92 | 34.31 | 56.46 | 0 | 7 | 103 | 3 |
| AJ Ball | 8 | 10 | 2 | 268 | 50 | 33.50 | 44.66 | 0 | 1 | 41 | 0 |
| BW Harmison | 15 | 24 | 0 | 642 | 125 | 26.75 | 42.97 | 1 | 1 | 90 | 1 |
| DE Bollinger | 8 | 9 | 5 | 91 | 33* | 22.75 | 81.98 | 0 | 0 | 11 | 3 |
| RWT Key | 15 | 26 | 1 | 561 | 126 | 22.44 | 48.23 | 1 | 2 | 67 | 1 |
| CJ Haggett | 4 | 7 | 0 | 119 | 44 | 17.00 | 44.07 | 0 | 0 | 18 | 0 |
| ME Claydon | 15 | 22 | 2 | 291 | 77 | 14.55 | 58.43 | 0 | 1 | 43 | 3 |
| RH Joseph | 6 | 7 | 2 | 70 | 29* | 14.00 | 41.66 | 0 | 0 | 10 | 1 |
| FK Cowdrey | 4 | 7 | 0 | 85 | 21 | 12.14 | 38.63 | 0 | 0 | 11 | 0 |
| AEN Riley | 15 | 20 | 9 | 132 | 23* | 12.00 | 30.13 | 0 | 0 | 16 | 0 |
| JC Tredwell | 4 | 7 | 0 | 81 | 29 | 11.57 | 48.79 | 0 | 0 | 11 | 0 |
| DA Griffiths | 1 | 2 | 0 | 18 | 12 | 9.00 | 35.29 | 0 | 0 | 1 | 0 |
| CF Hartley | 2 | 3 | 0 | 2 | 2 | 0.66 | 4.76 | 0 | 0 | 0 | 0 |
| MD Hunn | 2 | 3 | 2 | 0 | 0* | 0.00 | 0.00 | 0 | 0 | 0 | 0 |

**Bowling**

| | Overs | Mdns | Runs | Wkts | BBI | BBM | Ave | Econ | SR | 5w | 10w |
|---|---|---|---|---|---|---|---|---|---|---|---|
| DA Griffiths | 27.3 | 5 | 85 | 6 | 6/63 | 6/85 | 14.16 | 3.09 | 27.5 | 1 | 0 |
| FK Cowdrey | 12.4 | 1 | 59 | 3 | 3/59 | 3/59 | 19.66 | 4.65 | 25.3 | 0 | 0 |
| DE Bollinger | 241.4 | 54 | 713 | 27 | 5/29 | 7/81 | 26.40 | 2.95 | 53.7 | 2 | 0 |
| DI Stevens | 515.4 | 121 | 1517 | 56 | 6/64 | 9/89 | 27.08 | 2.94 | 55.2 | 6 | 0 |
| ME Claydon | 506.5 | 90 | 1711 | 55 | 5/61 | 9/151 | 31.10 | 3.37 | 55.2 | 3 | 0 |
| AEN Riley | 460.4 | 79 | 1564 | 48 | 5/78 | 9/155 | 32.58 | 3.39 | 57.5 | 2 | 0 |
| CF Hartley | 48.0 | 6 | 190 | 5 | 2/40 | 3/91 | 38.00 | 3.95 | 57.6 | 0 | 0 |
| RH Joseph | 142.0 | 30 | 464 | 12 | 3/43 | 5/92 | 38.66 | 3.26 | 71.0 | 0 | 0 |
| JC Tredwell | 139.0 | 23 | 426 | 11 | 4/102 | 8/212 | 38.72 | 3.06 | 75.8 | 0 | 0 |
| BW Harmison | 35.1 | 3 | 141 | 3 | 2/26 | 2/26 | 47.00 | 4.00 | 70.3 | 0 | 0 |
| MD Hunn | 36.0 | 6 | 155 | 3 | 1/7 | 2/82 | 51.66 | 4.30 | 72.0 | 0 | 0 |
| AJ Ball | 82.2 | 8 | 335 | 5 | 1/9 | 2/56 | 67.00 | 4.06 | 98.8 | 0 | 0 |
| CJ Haggett | 94.0 | 9 | 353 | 5 | 2/48 | 3/110 | 70.60 | 3.75 | 112.8 | 0 | 0 |
| BP Nash | 25.0 | 3 | 100 | 1 | 1/15 | 1/15 | 100.00 | 4.00 | 150.0 | 0 | 0 |
| SW Billings | 0.1 | 0 | 4 | 0 | - | - | - | 24.00 | - | 0 | 0 |
| SA Northeast | 1.0 | 0 | 4 | 0 | - | - | - | 4.00 | - | 0 | 0 |
| RWT Key | 2.0 | 0 | 12 | 0 | - | - | - | 6.00 | - | 0 | 0 |

**Catches/Stumpings:**

56 Billings (inc 6st), 14 Stevens, 12 Harmison, 10 Riley, 9 Tredwell, 8 Nash, 5 Ball, Northeast, Key, Bell-Drummond, 4 Bollinger, 2 Joseph, 1 Cowdrey, Claydon, Hunn

# ROYAL LONDON ONE-DAY CUP AVERAGES 2014

Batting

| | Mat | Inns | NO | Runs | HS | Ave | SR | 100 | 50 | 4s | 6s |
|---|---|---|---|---|---|---|---|---|---|---|---|
| SW Billings | 9 | 7 | 3 | 458 | 135* | 114.50 | 154.20 | 1 | 4 | 46 | 17 |
| SA Northeast | 9 | 9 | 0 | 406 | 132 | 45.11 | 72.89 | 1 | 2 | 40 | 1 |
| FK Cowdrey | 9 | 9 | 1 | 329 | 75 | 41.12 | 80.44 | 0 | 2 | 23 | 1 |
| DJ Bell-Drummond | 6 | 6 | 0 | 218 | 83 | 36.33 | 80.14 | 0 | 3 | 22 | 0 |
| JC Tredwell | 7 | 5 | 3 | 69 | 38* | 34.50 | 106.15 | 0 | 0 | 6 | 2 |
| BW Harmison | 6 | 6 | 1 | 124 | 43 | 24.80 | 77.98 | 0 | 0 | 13 | 1 |
| RWT Key | 3 | 3 | 0 | 72 | 47 | 24.00 | 68.57 | 0 | 0 | 6 | 2 |
| DI Stevens | 9 | 8 | 1 | 132 | 62* | 18.85 | 83.54 | 0 | 1 | 11 | 4 |
| DE Bollinger | 7 | 2 | 1 | 15 | 12* | 15.00 | 125.00 | 0 | 0 | 3 | 0 |
| AJ Blake | 8 | 7 | 1 | 81 | 21 | 13.50 | 65.32 | 0 | 0 | 5 | 0 |
| CJ Haggett | 7 | 5 | 0 | 55 | 36 | 11.00 | 96.49 | 0 | 0 | 5 | 2 |
| BP Nash | 4 | 4 | 0 | 39 | 21 | 9.75 | 58.20 | 0 | 0 | 3 | 0 |
| AJ Ball | 1 | 1 | 0 | 6 | 6 | 6.00 | 60.00 | 0 | 0 | 0 | 0 |
| ME Claydon | 9 | 6 | 1 | 24 | 8 | 4.80 | 70.58 | 0 | 0 | 2 | 0 |
| AEN Riley | 3 | 1 | 0 | 0 | 0 | 0.00 | 0.00 | 0 | 0 | 0 | 0 |
| DA Griffiths | 2 | 2 | 2 | 14 | 12* | - | 42.42 | 0 | 0 | 0 | 0 |

Bowling

| | Overs | Mdns | Runs | Wkts | BBI | Ave | Econ | SR | 4w | 5w |
|---|---|---|---|---|---|---|---|---|---|---|
| DA Griffiths | 16.3 | 0 | 65 | 4 | 2/29 | 16.25 | 3.93 | 24.7 | 0 | 0 |
| BW Harmison | 17.0 | 0 | 77 | 4 | 3/40 | 19.25 | 4.52 | 25.5 | 0 | 0 |
| JC Tredwell | 63.0 | 4 | 291 | 8 | 4/27 | 36.37 | 4.61 | 47.2 | 1 | 0 |
| DI Stevens | 68.0 | 3 | 336 | 7 | 2/36 | 48.00 | 4.94 | 58.2 | 0 | 0 |
| AEN Riley | 24.0 | 0 | 129 | 3 | 1/30 | 43.00 | 5.37 | 48.0 | 0 | 0 |
| FK Cowdrey | 42.0 | 1 | 226 | 5 | 2/28 | 45.20 | 5.38 | 50.4 | 0 | 0 |
| ME Claydon | 73.5 | 2 | 428 | 14 | 3/26 | 30.57 | 5.79 | 31.6 | 0 | 0 |
| CJ Haggett | 36.0 | 0 | 214 | 4 | 2/54 | 53.50 | 5.94 | 54.0 | 0 | 0 |
| DE Bollinger | 59.4 | 1 | 364 | 15 | 5/35 | 24.26 | 6.10 | 23.8 | 0 | 1 |
| DJ Bell-Drummond | 2.0 | 0 | 15 | 0 | - | - | 7.50 | - | 0 | 0 |

**Catches/Stumpings:**

7 Billings, 5 Stevens, 4 Cowdrey, 3 Tredwell, Haggett, Bollinger, 2 Harmison, Riley, Blake, Nash, 1 Claydon, Key, Northeast

# NATWEST T20 BLAST AVERAGES 2014

Batting

| | Mat | Inns | NO | Runs | HS | Ave | SR | 100 | 50 | 4s | 6s |
|---|---|---|---|---|---|---|---|---|---|---|---|
| RWT Key | 12 | 12 | 1 | 384 | 89* | 34.90 | 152.98 | 0 | 3 | 38 | 12 |
| AJ Blake | 14 | 14 | 4 | 311 | 58* | 31.10 | 140.72 | 0 | 2 | 24 | 16 |
| SA Northeast | 14 | 14 | 1 | 358 | 75 | 27.53 | 137.16 | 0 | 3 | 35 | 12 |
| DI Stevens | 14 | 14 | 1 | 351 | 71 | 27.00 | 158.82 | 0 | 3 | 21 | 21 |
| DJ Bell-Drummond | 14 | 14 | 0 | 264 | 59 | 18.85 | 114.28 | 0 | 1 | 25 | 5 |
| SW Billings | 14 | 14 | 2 | 210 | 33 | 17.50 | 137.25 | 0 | 0 | 17 | 7 |
| FK Cowdrey | 6 | 6 | 0 | 99 | 55 | 16.50 | 98.01 | 0 | 1 | 9 | 0 |
| AJ Ball | 11 | 7 | 2 | 67 | 18 | 13.40 | 91.78 | 0 | 0 | 3 | 1 |
| BW Harmison | 6 | 5 | 3 | 23 | 18* | 11.50 | 104.54 | 0 | 0 | 1 | 1 |
| JC Tredwell | 12 | 7 | 4 | 18 | 9 | 6.00 | 94.73 | 0 | 0 | 1 | 0 |
| AEN Riley | 9 | 2 | 0 | 9 | 5 | 4.50 | 81.81 | 0 | 0 | 1 | 0 |
| DE Bollinger | 9 | 2 | 0 | 4 | 3 | 2.00 | 40.00 | 0 | 0 | 0 | 0 |
| ME Claydon | 12 | 6 | 2 | 7 | 5* | 1.75 | 41.17 | 0 | 0 | 0 | 0 |
| DA Griffiths | 7 | 1 | 1 | 18 | 18* | - | 128.57 | 0 | 0 | 0 | 1 |

Bowling

| | Overs | Mdns | Runs | Wkts | BBI | Ave | Econ | SR | 4w | 5w |
|---|---|---|---|---|---|---|---|---|---|---|
| JC Tredwell | 41.3 | 0 | 313 | 11 | 2/12 | 28.45 | 7.54 | 22.6 | 0 | 0 |
| DI Stevens | 46.0 | 2 | 350 | 18 | 4/17 | 19.44 | 7.60 | 15.3 | 1 | 0 |
| FK Cowdrey | 14.5 | 0 | 116 | 3 | 2/28 | 38.66 | 7.82 | 29.6 | 0 | 0 |
| DE Bollinger | 30.0 | 0 | 236 | 15 | 3/19 | 15.73 | 7.86 | 12.0 | 0 | 0 |
| ME Claydon | 38.0 | 0 | 311 | 13 | 3/24 | 23.92 | 8.18 | 17.5 | 0 | 0 |
| AEN Riley | 26.0 | 0 | 213 | 9 | 4/22 | 23.66 | 8.19 | 17.3 | 1 | 0 |
| DA Griffiths | 19.1 | 0 | 170 | 8 | 4/22 | 21.25 | 8.86 | 14.3 | 1 | 0 |
| AJ Ball | 26.3 | 0 | 264 | 4 | 1/7 | 66.00 | 9.96 | 39.7 | 0 | 0 |
| BW Harmison | 15.0 | 1 | 168 | 7 | 3/35 | 24.00 | 11.20 | 12.8 | 0 | 0 |

**Catches/Stumpings:**
11 Billings (inc 1st), 9 Griffiths, 6 Stevens, 5 Cowdrey, Bell-Drummond, Blake, 4 Northeast, 3 Tredwell, Griffiths, 2 Claydon, Riley, Key, 1 Bollinger, Harmison

# LANCASHIRE

**Lancashire County Cricket Club**

FORMED: 1864
HOME GROUND: Emirates Old Trafford, Manchester
ONE-DAY NAME: Lancashire Lightning
CAPTAIN: Tom Smith
2014 RESULTS: CC1: 8/9; RL50: 8/9 Group A; NWT20: Finalists
HONOURS: Championship: (9) 1897, 1904, 1926, 1927, 1928, 1930, 1934, 1950(s), 2011; Gillette/NatWest/C&G/FP Trophy: (7) 1970, 1971, 1972, 1985, 1990, 1996, 1998; Benson & Hedges Cup: (4) 1984, 1990, 1995, 1996; Pro40/National League/CB40/YB40/RL50: 1999; Sunday League: (4) 1969, 1970, 1989, 1998

## THE LOWDOWN

New coach, new captain. A second relegation in three seasons for Lancashire means it is all change at the county. Ashley Giles comes in as head coach to replace director of cricket Mike Watkinson and will hope to have the same galvanising effect on Lancashire as he did when getting Warwickshire promoted in 2011 before leading them to the Championship title in 2012. Tom Smith replaces stalwart Glen Chapple as skipper, with Chapple staying on in a player/coach role. Smith was one of Lancashire's few bright spots last season as they won just five matches across the Championship and the RL Cup. South African Alviro Petersen has been signed on a two-year deal after retiring with 36 Tests to his name and will add class to a meek batting order, with only his fellow countryman Ashwell Prince passing 1,000 runs last season. Lancashire will be hoping for more from young opener Luis Reece after a poor 2014, while they have signed paceman Nathan Buck from Leicestershire and Australian star Peter Siddle until the end of July as they look to offset the blow of Kyle Hogg's early retirement.

## HEAD COACH: ASHLEY GILES

After being overlooked for England's head coach role, Giles will be keen to show that his success with Warwickshire wasn't a one-off. He won the County Championship with the Bears in 2012, as well as the C&G Cup in 2010. As a player he played 54 Tests for England, helping to win the 2005 Ashes, and spent 14 seasons with Warwickshire.

# COUNTY CHAMPIONSHIP AVERAGES 2014

Batting

| | Mat | Inns | NO | Runs | HS | Ave | SR | 100 | 50 | 4s | 6s |
|---|---|---|---|---|---|---|---|---|---|---|---|
| SJ Croft | 12 | 20 | 3 | 786 | 156 | 46.23 | 54.43 | 2 | 4 | 87 | 6 |
| AG Prince | 16 | 28 | 1 | 1160 | 257* | 42.96 | 54.05 | 3 | 3 | 121 | 5 |
| JC Buttler | 10 | 18 | 1 | 633 | 100* | 37.23 | 55.72 | 1 | 5 | 68 | 9 |
| TC Smith | 15 | 27 | 4 | 773 | 79 | 33.60 | 45.84 | 0 | 7 | 106 | 3 |
| PJ Horton | 16 | 30 | 2 | 891 | 140 | 31.82 | 43.29 | 2 | 3 | 107 | 0 |
| UT Khawaja | 7 | 13 | 0 | 413 | 117 | 31.76 | 46.56 | 1 | 3 | 51 | 1 |
| AL Davies | 10 | 17 | 0 | 469 | 62 | 27.58 | 46.90 | 0 | 3 | 73 | 1 |
| TE Bailey | 3 | 5 | 3 | 55 | 25* | 27.50 | 51.40 | 0 | 0 | 8 | 0 |
| LA Procter | 7 | 12 | 1 | 273 | 81* | 24.81 | 42.39 | 0 | 1 | 31 | 0 |
| G Chapple | 15 | 23 | 4 | 459 | 45* | 24.15 | 67.79 | 0 | 0 | 58 | 3 |
| SD Parry | 3 | 5 | 0 | 98 | 37 | 19.60 | 64.47 | 0 | 0 | 14 | 0 |
| JM Anderson | 4 | 8 | 3 | 93 | 28 | 18.60 | 110.71 | 0 | 0 | 18 | 0 |
| AP Agathangelou | 6 | 12 | 1 | 185 | 48 | 16.81 | 50.82 | 0 | 0 | 26 | 1 |
| Kabir Ali | 7 | 11 | 3 | 134 | 26 | 16.75 | 44.96 | 0 | 0 | 12 | 1 |
| LM Reece | 9 | 17 | 1 | 262 | 53 | 16.37 | 35.40 | 0 | 1 | 34 | 0 |
| KR Brown | 6 | 10 | 1 | 112 | 29 | 12.44 | 37.20 | 0 | 0 | 18 | 0 |
| KW Hogg | 8 | 10 | 1 | 98 | 47* | 10.88 | 43.36 | 0 | 0 | 12 | 0 |
| SC Kerrigan | 16 | 24 | 6 | 156 | 33 | 8.66 | 35.05 | 0 | 0 | 15 | 1 |
| WA White | 4 | 6 | 1 | 37 | 13 | 7.40 | 40.65 | 0 | 0 | 6 | 0 |
| KM Jarvis | 2 | 3 | 2 | 1 | 1* | 1.00 | 4.34 | 0 | 0 | 0 | 0 |
| Junaid Khan | 1 | - | - | - | - | - | - | - | - | - | - |

Bowling

| | Overs | Mdns | Runs | Wkts | BBI | BBM | Ave | Econ | SR | 5w | 10w |
|---|---|---|---|---|---|---|---|---|---|---|---|
| TC Smith | 365.3 | 83 | 1105 | 54 | 5/42 | 8/132 | 20.46 | 3.02 | 40.6 | 4 | 0 |
| JM Anderson | 166.4 | 43 | 432 | 21 | 5/41 | 10/89 | 20.57 | 2.59 | 47.6 | 3 | 1 |
| KW Hogg | 212.4 | 59 | 563 | 21 | 6/70 | 9/119 | 26.80 | 2.64 | 60.7 | 1 | 0 |
| Kabir Ali | 146.4 | 31 | 517 | 17 | 3/17 | 6/95 | 30.41 | 3.52 | 51.7 | 0 | 0 |
| SC Kerrigan | 530.0 | 99 | 1556 | 44 | 4/38 | 8/147 | 35.36 | 2.93 | 72.2 | 0 | 0 |
| G Chapple | 500.4 | 99 | 1415 | 39 | 5/51 | 7/132 | 36.28 | 2.82 | 77.0 | 1 | 0 |
| LA Procter | 59.3 | 10 | 205 | 5 | 4/50 | 4/58 | 41.00 | 3.44 | 71.4 | 0 | 0 |
| WA White | 87.0 | 12 | 331 | 8 | 2/41 | 2/71 | 41.37 | 3.80 | 65.2 | 0 | 0 |
| SJ Croft | 113.0 | 10 | 357 | 8 | 3/25 | 3/42 | 44.62 | 3.15 | 84.7 | 0 | 0 |
| TE Bailey | 85.0 | 19 | 272 | 6 | 2/36 | 3/82 | 45.33 | 3.20 | 85.0 | 0 | 0 |
| Junaid Khan | 47.0 | 11 | 147 | 3 | 3/84 | 3/147 | 49.00 | 3.12 | 94.0 | 0 | 0 |
| SD Parry | 60.0 | 5 | 197 | 4 | 3/109 | 3/109 | 49.25 | 3.28 | 90.0 | 0 | 0 |
| KM Jarvis | 49.0 | 7 | 201 | 2 | 2/88 | 2/101 | 100.50 | 4.10 | 147.0 | 0 | 0 |
| LM Reece | 14.0 | 2 | 59 | 0 | - | - | - | 4.21 | - | 0 | 0 |

**Catches/Stumpings:**

28 Buttler, 17 Davies (inc 1st), 16 Croft, Horton, 11 Prince, 10 Smith, 8 Khawaja, 7 Agathangelou, 5 Kerrigan, Brown, 4 Chapple, Reece, 3 Anderson, 2 Procter, White, 1 Parry

# ROYAL LONDON ONE-DAY CUP AVERAGES 2014

Batting

| | Mat | Inns | NO | Runs | HS | Ave | SR | 100 | 50 | 4s | 6s |
|---|---|---|---|---|---|---|---|---|---|---|---|
| KR Brown | 7 | 7 | 1 | 373 | 129 | 62.16 | 89.44 | 1 | 2 | 37 | 7 |
| TC Smith | 1 | 1 | 0 | 54 | 54 | 54.00 | 114.89 | 0 | 1 | 7 | 2 |
| PJ Horton | 7 | 7 | 1 | 224 | 57 | 37.33 | 93.33 | 0 | 1 | 20 | 0 |
| SJ Croft | 7 | 6 | 1 | 186 | 51 | 37.20 | 93.00 | 0 | 3 | 13 | 3 |
| AG Prince | 5 | 5 | 0 | 168 | 69 | 33.60 | 81.15 | 0 | 2 | 21 | 0 |
| LM Reece | 2 | 2 | 0 | 61 | 54 | 30.50 | 84.72 | 0 | 1 | 7 | 0 |
| AL Davies | 7 | 5 | 0 | 152 | 53 | 30.40 | 95.59 | 0 | 1 | 17 | 1 |
| J Clark | 7 | 5 | 2 | 90 | 22 | 30.00 | 102.27 | 0 | 0 | 6 | 2 |
| UT Khawaja | 6 | 6 | 1 | 116 | 31 | 23.20 | 89.92 | 0 | 0 | 20 | 0 |
| WA White | 6 | 5 | 1 | 53 | 26* | 13.25 | 101.92 | 0 | 0 | 3 | 3 |
| KM Jarvis | 5 | 2 | 1 | 10 | 6* | 10.00 | 76.92 | 0 | 0 | 2 | 0 |
| Kabir Ali | 3 | 2 | 0 | 11 | 7 | 5.50 | 57.89 | 0 | 0 | 0 | 0 |
| KW Hogg | 1 | 1 | 0 | 1 | 1 | 1.00 | 100.00 | 0 | 0 | 0 | 0 |
| SD Parry | 4 | 2 | 1 | 1 | 1 | 1.00 | 33.33 | 0 | 0 | 0 | 0 |
| TE Bailey | 4 | 1 | 1 | 4 | 4* | - | 133.33 | 0 | 0 | 1 | 0 |
| AM Lilley | 1 | 1 | 1 | 2 | 2* | - | 100.00 | 0 | 0 | 0 | 0 |
| GT Griffiths | 1 | - | - | - | - | - | - | - | - | - | - |
| SC Kerrigan | 2 | - | - | - | - | - | - | - | - | - | - |
| LA Procter | 1 | - | - | - | - | - | - | - | - | - | - |

Bowling

| | Overs | Mdns | Runs | Wkts | BBI | Ave | Econ | SR | 4w | 5w |
|---|---|---|---|---|---|---|---|---|---|---|
| SC Kerrigan | 17.0 | 2 | 76 | 0 | - | - | 4.47 | - | 0 | 0 |
| SD Parry | 37.0 | 0 | 185 | 9 | 3/23 | 20.55 | 5.00 | 24.6 | 0 | 0 |
| LA Procter | 4.0 | 0 | 20 | 1 | 1/20 | 20.00 | 5.00 | 24.0 | 0 | 0 |
| TC Smith | 4.1 | 0 | 21 | 2 | 2/21 | 10.50 | 5.04 | 12.5 | 0 | 0 |
| TE Bailey | 38.0 | 0 | 194 | 7 | 3/41 | 27.71 | 5.10 | 32.5 | 0 | 0 |
| GT Griffiths | 8.0 | 0 | 41 | 0 | - | - | 5.12 | - | 0 | 0 |
| KW Hogg | 8.0 | 0 | 41 | 0 | - | - | 5.12 | - | 0 | 0 |
| SJ Croft | 42.0 | 1 | 219 | 3 | 2/32 | 73.00 | 5.21 | 84.0 | 0 | 0 |
| Kabir Ali | 22.0 | 1 | 117 | 6 | 3/26 | 19.50 | 5.31 | 22.0 | 0 | 0 |
| AM Lilley | 6.0 | 0 | 36 | 2 | 2/36 | 18.00 | 6.00 | 18.0 | 0 | 0 |
| WA White | 49.3 | 0 | 318 | 10 | 4/33 | 31.80 | 6.42 | 29.7 | 1 | 0 |
| KM Jarvis | 32.0 | 1 | 214 | 3 | 2/68 | 71.33 | 6.68 | 64.0 | 0 | 0 |
| J Clark | 41.0 | 0 | 287 | 6 | 2/41 | 47.83 | 7.00 | 41.0 | 0 | 0 |
| KR Brown | 1.0 | 0 | 17 | 0 | - | - | 17.00 | - | 0 | 0 |

**Catches/Stumpings:**

11 Davies (inc 1st), 5 Croft, Brown, Horton, 2 Parry, Griffiths, Clark, Khawaja, 1 Smith, Jarvis, Prince, Reece

 

# NATWEST T20 BLAST AVERAGES 2014

| | Mat | Inns | NO | Runs | HS | Ave | SR | 100 | 50 | 4s | 6s |
|---|---|---|---|---|---|---|---|---|---|---|---|
| AG Prince | 9 | 9 | 1 | 372 | 72* | 46.50 | 146.45 | 0 | 3 | 42 | 9 |
| KR Brown | 15 | 15 | 1 | 467 | 67* | 33.35 | 131.92 | 0 | 4 | 41 | 17 |
| UT Khawaja | 4 | 4 | 0 | 128 | 67 | 32.00 | 126.73 | 0 | 1 | 15 | 1 |
| JC Buttler | 10 | 10 | 2 | 251 | 58* | 31.37 | 170.74 | 0 | 2 | 18 | 10 |
| SJ Croft | 15 | 15 | 5 | 268 | 76* | 26.80 | 127.01 | 0 | 1 | 23 | 7 |
| J Clark | 15 | 11 | 5 | 159 | 44 | 26.50 | 126.19 | 0 | 0 | 11 | 5 |
| PJ Horton | 15 | 13 | 2 | 275 | 71* | 25.00 | 123.31 | 0 | 2 | 23 | 6 |
| TC Smith | 14 | 14 | 0 | 339 | 74 | 24.21 | 139.50 | 0 | 3 | 40 | 9 |
| A Flintoff | 3 | 2 | 1 | 21 | 20* | 21.00 | 175.00 | 0 | 0 | 0 | 2 |
| AP Agathangelou | 3 | 2 | 0 | 21 | 21 | 10.50 | 110.52 | 0 | 0 | 0 | 1 |
| Kabir Ali | 11 | 5 | 2 | 28 | 19* | 9.33 | 121.73 | 0 | 0 | 2 | 1 |
| Junaid Khan | 10 | 1 | 0 | 9 | 9 | 9.00 | 100.00 | 0 | 0 | 1 | 0 |
| WA White | 4 | 4 | 1 | 25 | 11* | 8.33 | 125.00 | 0 | 0 | 3 | 0 |
| AM Lilley | 9 | 5 | 2 | 13 | 12* | 4.33 | 185.71 | 0 | 0 | 1 | 1 |
| AL Davies | 7 | 6 | 0 | 18 | 7 | 3.00 | 72.00 | 0 | 0 | 0 | 1 |
| JM Anderson | 4 | 1 | 0 | 0 | 0 | 0.00 | 0.00 | 0 | 0 | 0 | 0 |
| SD Parry | 15 | 5 | 5 | 16 | 10* | - | 100.00 | 0 | 0 | 1 | 0 |
| KM Jarvis | 2 | - | - | - | - | - | - | - | - | - | - |

Batting

| | Overs | Mdns | Runs | Wkts | BBI | Ave | Econ | SR | 4w | 5w |
|---|---|---|---|---|---|---|---|---|---|---|
| SJ Croft | 46.0 | 0 | 286 | 14 | 3/31 | 20.42 | 6.21 | 19.7 | 0 | 0 |
| Junaid Khan | 39.0 | 1 | 266 | 19 | 4/12 | 14.00 | 6.82 | 12.3 | 1 | 0 |
| KM Jarvis | 7.0 | 0 | 50 | 3 | 2/25 | 16.66 | 7.14 | 14.0 | 0 | 0 |
| SD Parry | 50.0 | 0 | 377 | 8 | 2/12 | 47.12 | 7.54 | 37.5 | 0 | 0 |
| Kabir Ali | 39.0 | 1 | 299 | 20 | 3/19 | 14.95 | 7.66 | 11.7 | 0 | 0 |
| AM Lilley | 24.0 | 0 | 193 | 5 | 2/28 | 38.60 | 8.04 | 28.8 | 0 | 0 |
| A Flintoff | 10.0 | 0 | 82 | 6 | 3/26 | 13.66 | 8.20 | 10.0 | 0 | 0 |
| J Clark | 29.1 | 1 | 255 | 9 | 4/22 | 28.33 | 8.74 | 19.4 | 1 | 0 |
| TC Smith | 20.0 | 0 | 176 | 7 | 2/28 | 25.14 | 8.80 | 17.1 | 0 | 0 |
| WA White | 14.0 | 0 | 124 | 4 | 2/31 | 31.00 | 8.85 | 21.0 | 0 | 0 |
| JM Anderson | 13.0 | 0 | 128 | 4 | 2/24 | 32.00 | 9.84 | 19.5 | 0 | 0 |

Bowling

**Catches/Stumpings:**
9 Brown, 8 Horton, 6 Croft, Parry, Smith, 5 Buttler (inc 2st), Davies (inc 1st), 4 White, Prince, 3 Clark,, 2 Lilley, Khawaja, 1 Junaid Khan, Jarvis, Agathangelou

# LEICESTERSHIRE

FORMED: 1879
HOME GROUND: County Ground, Grace Road, Leicester
ONE-DAY NAME: Leicestershire Foxes
CAPTAIN: Mark Cosgrove
2014 RESULTS: CC2: 9/9; RL50: 5/9 Group A; NWT20: 8/9 North Division
HONOURS: Championship: (3) 1975, 1996, 1998; Benson & Hedges Cup: (3) 1972, 1975, 1985; Sunday League: (2) 1974, 1977; Twenty20 Cup: (3) 2004, 2006, 2011

---

THE LOWDOWN

Leicestershire's place at the foot of the County Championship is beginning to become as much part of the English summer as Wimbledon, rain and sunburn. For the second successive season they failed to win a single Championship match, while last summer they also failed to take 20 wickets in any game and only reached maximum batting points on three occasions. Their limited-overs form was little better, as they failed to make it out of their group in either competition. Things got worse at the end of the season, with the departures of Nathan Buck, Josh Cobb, Greg Smith and Shiv Thakor; that two of them have left to join Derbyshire and Northamptonshire hints at where the club is at. There are positives, though. Turning around Leicestershire may be considered the toughest job in county cricket but Wasim Khan, who worked wonders with Chance to Shine, has been appointed as chief executive and is already beginning to breathe life into the county. They have also done well to keep hold of the talented Angus Robson and Niall O'Brien, while Australian seamer Clint McKay could prove to be a canny overseas signing.

---

HEAD COACH: ANDREW MCDONALD

McDonald had two stints with Leicestershire in 2010 and 2011 and returns as coach with a brief to reinvigorate the county. He arrives with a reputation for developing young talent and also comes with Test match experience, having played four times for Australia. He replaces director of cricket Phil Whitticase, who stepped down at the end of last season.

---

# COUNTY CHAMPIONSHIP AVERAGES 2014

Batting

| | Mat | Inns | NO | Runs | HS | Ave | SR | 100 | 50 | 4s | 6s |
|---|---|---|---|---|---|---|---|---|---|---|---|
| NJ O'Brien | 15 | 28 | 3 | 971 | 133 | 38.84 | 60.08 | 2 | 5 | 125 | 8 |
| AJ Robson | 16 | 30 | 0 | 1086 | 115 | 36.20 | 54.71 | 1 | 9 | 161 | 0 |
| JJ Cobb | 14 | 26 | 3 | 803 | 137 | 34.91 | 52.38 | 1 | 7 | 117 | 7 |
| GP Smith | 15 | 28 | 0 | 862 | 118 | 30.78 | 54.17 | 2 | 4 | 124 | 2 |
| DJ Redfern | 9 | 17 | 1 | 463 | 64 | 28.93 | 62.90 | 0 | 5 | 76 | 1 |
| EJH Eckersley | 16 | 30 | 0 | 818 | 119 | 27.26 | 47.22 | 2 | 1 | 101 | 3 |
| MAG Boyce | 5 | 9 | 0 | 209 | 68 | 23.22 | 48.60 | 0 | 1 | 35 | 0 |
| RML Taylor | 15 | 27 | 1 | 567 | 98 | 21.80 | 68.06 | 0 | 4 | 82 | 6 |
| NL Buck | 9 | 15 | 6 | 192 | 29* | 21.33 | 47.76 | 0 | 0 | 31 | 1 |
| JKH Naik | 13 | 22 | 6 | 338 | 59* | 21.12 | 44.06 | 0 | 1 | 41 | 1 |
| MA Thornely | 1 | 1 | 0 | 21 | 21 | 21.00 | 29.57 | 0 | 0 | 4 | 0 |
| BA Raine | 7 | 13 | 1 | 239 | 55 | 19.91 | 40.99 | 0 | 1 | 32 | 0 |
| CE Shreck | 15 | 23 | 6 | 332 | 56 | 19.52 | 75.11 | 0 | 1 | 53 | 1 |
| RR Sarwan | 5 | 10 | 0 | 184 | 60 | 18.40 | 46.23 | 0 | 1 | 24 | 1 |
| TJ Wells | 1 | 2 | 0 | 28 | 15 | 14.00 | 54.90 | 0 | 0 | 4 | 0 |
| AJ Ireland | 6 | 10 | 2 | 111 | 52 | 13.87 | 49.77 | 0 | 1 | 11 | 4 |
| ACF Wyatt | 3 | 5 | 0 | 59 | 32 | 11.80 | 70.23 | 0 | 0 | 9 | 0 |
| JS Sykes | 3 | 6 | 1 | 35 | 8* | 7.00 | 36.08 | 0 | 0 | 4 | 0 |
| A Sheikh | 4 | 7 | 2 | 24 | 12 | 4.80 | 57.14 | 0 | 0 | 4 | 0 |
| RA Jones | 1 | 2 | 0 | 9 | 6 | 4.50 | 40.90 | 0 | 0 | 1 | 0 |
| OH Freckingham | 3 | 4 | 1 | 12 | 6 | 4.00 | 25.00 | 0 | 0 | 1 | 0 |

Bowling

| | Overs | Mdns | Runs | Wkts | BBI | BBM | Ave | Econ | SR | 5w | 10w |
|---|---|---|---|---|---|---|---|---|---|---|---|
| NL Buck | 327.1 | 54 | 1290 | 42 | 5/76 | 7/140 | 30.71 | 3.94 | 46.7 | 3 | 0 |
| DJ Redfern | 62.0 | 10 | 251 | 8 | 2/20 | 3/64 | 31.37 | 4.04 | 46.5 | 0 | 0 |
| RML Taylor | 349.3 | 66 | 1231 | 35 | 5/55 | 6/120 | 35.17 | 3.52 | 59.9 | 2 | 0 |
| BA Raine | 196.0 | 45 | 656 | 18 | 3/47 | 4/145 | 36.44 | 3.34 | 65.3 | 0 | 0 |
| AJ Ireland | 176.1 | 24 | 600 | 15 | 3/81 | 5/135 | 40.00 | 3.40 | 70.4 | 0 | 0 |
| CE Shreck | 560.0 | 135 | 1759 | 42 | 3/44 | 4/102 | 41.88 | 3.14 | 80.0 | 0 | 0 |
| OH Freckingham | 81.5 | 12 | 362 | 8 | 4/138 | 6/203 | 45.25 | 4.42 | 61.3 | 0 | 0 |
| RA Jones | 28.0 | 6 | 93 | 2 | 2/36 | 2/93 | 46.50 | 3.32 | 84.0 | 0 | 0 |
| JS Sykes | 110.0 | 13 | 381 | 8 | 3/72 | 5/180 | 47.62 | 3.46 | 82.5 | 0 | 0 |
| A Sheikh | 98.5 | 16 | 444 | 9 | 4/97 | 4/153 | 49.33 | 4.49 | 65.8 | 0 | 0 |
| ACF Wyatt | 60.0 | 14 | 214 | 4 | 3/61 | 3/61 | 53.50 | 3.56 | 90.0 | 0 | 0 |
| JKH Naik | 445.2 | 81 | 1535 | 20 | 3/76 | 3/98 | 76.75 | 3.44 | 133.6 | 0 | 0 |
| MA Thornely | 2.0 | 0 | 6 | 0 | - | - | - | 3.00 | - | 0 | 0 |
| EJH Eckersley | 3.3 | 0 | 16 | 0 | - | - | - | 4.57 | - | 0 | 0 |
| TJ Wells | 5.0 | 1 | 34 | 0 | - | - | - | 6.80 | - | 0 | 0 |
| JJ Cobb | 22.0 | 1 | 84 | 0 | - | - | - | 3.81 | - | 0 | 0 |
| AJ Robson | 16.3 | 1 | 84 | 0 | - | - | - | 5.09 | - | 0 | 0 |

**Catches/Stumpings:**
47 O'Brien (inc 4st), 14 Smith, 12 Eckersley, Robson, 11 Naik, 8 Cobb, 7 Taylor, 4 Shreck, Boyce, 3 Sarwan, 2 Raine, Sykes, 1 Sheikh, Wells

# ROYAL LONDON ONE-DAY CUP AVERAGES 2014

**Batting**

| | Mat | Inns | NO | Runs | HS | Ave | SR | 100 | 50 | 4s | 6s |
|---|---|---|---|---|---|---|---|---|---|---|---|
| JJ Cobb | 2 | 2 | 1 | 78 | 58 | 78.00 | 73.58 | 0 | 1 | 10 | 1 |
| BA Raine | 1 | 1 | 0 | 43 | 43 | 43.00 | 122.85 | 0 | 0 | 5 | 2 |
| MAG Boyce | 6 | 6 | 2 | 160 | 74* | 40.00 | 73.05 | 0 | 2 | 15 | 0 |
| GP Smith | 7 | 7 | 2 | 196 | 55* | 39.20 | 76.56 | 0 | 1 | 19 | 1 |
| NJ O'Brien | 7 | 7 | 1 | 203 | 105* | 33.83 | 98.54 | 1 | 0 | 16 | 8 |
| SB Styris | 6 | 5 | 1 | 111 | 44* | 27.75 | 86.04 | 0 | 0 | 9 | 1 |
| EJH Eckersley | 1 | 1 | 0 | 24 | 24 | 24.00 | 80.00 | 0 | 0 | 1 | 0 |
| DJ Redfern | 6 | 5 | 0 | 97 | 43 | 19.40 | 64.23 | 0 | 0 | 5 | 0 |
| AJ Robson | 6 | 6 | 0 | 92 | 28 | 15.33 | 80.00 | 0 | 0 | 12 | 0 |
| TJ Wells | 6 | 5 | 1 | 60 | 24 | 15.00 | 55.04 | 0 | 0 | 5 | 0 |
| JKH Naik | 5 | 4 | 1 | 38 | 36* | 12.66 | 84.44 | 0 | 0 | 4 | 0 |
| JS Sykes | 2 | 1 | 0 | 11 | 11 | 11.00 | 73.33 | 0 | 0 | 2 | 0 |
| AJ Ireland | 7 | 5 | 2 | 13 | 8 | 4.33 | 68.42 | 0 | 0 | 1 | 1 |
| SJ Thakor | 6 | 4 | 0 | 14 | 11 | 3.50 | 32.55 | 0 | 0 | 0 | 0 |
| NL Buck | 2 | 1 | 0 | 2 | 2 | 2.00 | 50.00 | 0 | 0 | 0 | 0 |
| CE Shreck | 6 | 3 | 2 | 2 | 1* | 2.00 | 16.66 | 0 | 0 | 0 | 0 |
| OH Freckingham | 1 | - | - | - | - | - | - | - | - | - | - |

**Bowling**

| | Overs | Mdns | Runs | Wkts | BBI | Ave | Econ | SR | 4w | 5w |
|---|---|---|---|---|---|---|---|---|---|---|
| CE Shreck | 40.2 | 2 | 177 | 8 | 3/33 | 22.12 | 4.38 | 30.2 | 0 | 0 |
| SB Styris | 22.0 | 0 | 97 | 2 | 2/25 | 48.50 | 4.40 | 66.0 | 0 | 0 |
| JS Sykes | 16.0 | 0 | 76 | 4 | 3/34 | 19.00 | 4.75 | 24.0 | 0 | 0 |
| JKH Naik | 35.1 | 0 | 179 | 4 | 1/24 | 44.75 | 5.09 | 52.7 | 0 | 0 |
| DJ Redfern | 24.0 | 0 | 123 | 4 | 2/19 | 30.75 | 5.12 | 36.0 | 0 | 0 |
| AJ Ireland | 47.0 | 4 | 243 | 8 | 4/31 | 30.37 | 5.17 | 35.2 | 1 | 0 |
| SJ Thakor | 26.5 | 1 | 161 | 8 | 4/49 | 20.12 | 6.00 | 20.1 | 1 | 0 |
| OH Freckingham | 6.0 | 0 | 38 | 2 | 2/38 | 19.00 | 6.33 | 18.0 | 0 | 0 |
| TJ Wells | 6.0 | 0 | 39 | 0 | - | - | 6.50 | - | 0 | 0 |
| NL Buck | 16.4 | 0 | 124 | 1 | 1/60 | 124.00 | 7.44 | 100.0 | 0 | 0 |
| BA Raine | 6.0 | 0 | 57 | 1 | 1/57 | 57.00 | 9.50 | 36.0 | 0 | 0 |

**Catches/Stumpings:**

6 O'Brien (inc 1st), 4 Styris, Wells, 3 Boyce, 2 Shreck, Ireland, 1 Sykes, Naik, Redfern, Thakor, Freckingham, Robson, Smith

# NATWEST T20 BLAST AVERAGES 2014

**Batting**

| | Mat | Inns | NO | Runs | HS | Ave | SR | 100 | 50 | 4s | 6s |
|---|---|---|---|---|---|---|---|---|---|---|---|
| JKH Naik | 13 | 5 | 4 | 39 | 16* | 39.00 | 95.12 | 0 | 0 | 1 | 1 |
| RR Sarwan | 1 | 1 | 0 | 37 | 37 | 37.00 | 100.00 | 0 | 0 | 3 | 0 |
| GP Smith | 14 | 13 | 1 | 390 | 102 | 32.50 | 123.02 | 1 | 3 | 41 | 6 |
| MAG Boyce | 11 | 9 | 2 | 211 | 47 | 30.14 | 113.44 | 0 | 0 | 24 | 1 |
| JJ Cobb | 14 | 13 | 0 | 357 | 70 | 27.46 | 134.21 | 0 | 2 | 30 | 16 |
| TJ Wells | 14 | 13 | 5 | 203 | 51 | 25.37 | 127.67 | 0 | 1 | 10 | 12 |
| SB Styris | 10 | 9 | 1 | 168 | 63* | 21.00 | 129.23 | 0 | 1 | 15 | 6 |
| EJH Eckersley | 13 | 11 | 1 | 185 | 43 | 18.50 | 121.71 | 0 | 0 | 14 | 5 |
| BA Raine | 11 | 8 | 4 | 61 | 20* | 15.25 | 98.38 | 0 | 0 | 6 | 1 |
| NJ O'Brien | 12 | 11 | 0 | 122 | 24 | 11.09 | 128.42 | 0 | 0 | 18 | 2 |
| A Sheikh | 3 | 2 | 0 | 21 | 14 | 10.50 | 105.00 | 0 | 0 | 0 | 2 |
| DJ Redfern | 2 | 2 | 0 | 14 | 14 | 7.00 | 116.66 | 0 | 0 | 2 | 0 |
| RML Taylor | 8 | 6 | 1 | 27 | 20 | 5.40 | 112.50 | 0 | 0 | 0 | 1 |
| CE Shreck | 7 | 2 | 0 | 10 | 10 | 5.00 | 76.92 | 0 | 0 | 0 | 1 |
| AJ Ireland | 10 | 2 | 0 | 7 | 6 | 3.50 | 116.66 | 0 | 0 | 0 | 1 |
| MA Thornely | 2 | 1 | 1 | 13 | 13* | - | 130.00 | 0 | 0 | 1 | 0 |
| NL Buck | 6 | 1 | 1 | 3 | 3* | - | 75.00 | 0 | 0 | 0 | 0 |
| RA Jones | 1 | - | - | - | - | - | - | - | - | - | - |
| JS Sykes | 1 | - | - | - | - | - | - | - | - | - | - |
| ACF Wyatt | 1 | - | - | - | - | - | - | - | - | - | - |

**Bowling**

| | Overs | Mdns | Runs | Wkts | BBI | Ave | Econ | SR | 4w | 5w |
|---|---|---|---|---|---|---|---|---|---|---|
| A Sheikh | 8.0 | 0 | 43 | 2 | 2/11 | 21.50 | 5.37 | 24.0 | 0 | 0 |
| SB Styris | 22.0 | 0 | 119 | 6 | 1/10 | 19.83 | 5.40 | 22.0 | 0 | 0 |
| JKH Naik | 51.0 | 0 | 344 | 15 | 3/30 | 22.93 | 6.74 | 20.4 | 0 | 0 |
| BA Raine | 36.0 | 0 | 269 | 15 | 3/12 | 17.93 | 7.47 | 14.4 | 0 | 0 |
| DJ Redfern | 6.0 | 0 | 45 | 0 | - | - | 7.50 | - | 0 | 0 |
| JJ Cobb | 37.1 | 0 | 279 | 14 | 3/18 | 19.92 | 7.50 | 15.9 | 0 | 0 |
| ACF Wyatt | 3.0 | 0 | 23 | 0 | - | - | 7.66 | - | 0 | 0 |
| CE Shreck | 23.3 | 0 | 192 | 7 | 3/13 | 27.42 | 8.17 | 20.1 | 0 | 0 |
| RA Jones | 4.0 | 0 | 34 | 5 | 5/34 | 6.80 | 8.50 | 4.8 | 0 | 1 |
| AJ Ireland | 34.5 | 1 | 305 | 17 | 5/22 | 17.94 | 8.75 | 12.2 | 0 | 1 |
| JS Sykes | 4.0 | 0 | 38 | 0 | - | - | 9.50 | - | 0 | 0 |
| NL Buck | 22.1 | 0 | 218 | 9 | 3/26 | 24.22 | 9.83 | 14.7 | 0 | 0 |
| RML Taylor | 21.4 | 0 | 237 | 4 | 1/26 | 59.25 | 10.93 | 32.5 | 0 | 0 |

**Catches/Stumpings:**

11 O'Brien (inc 2st), 10 Eckersley (inc 1st), 9 Cobb, 7 Smith, 6 Boyce, 5 Naik, Taylor, 3 Raine, 2 Redfern, Shreck, Ireland, 1 Sheikh, Styris, Buck

# MIDDLESEX



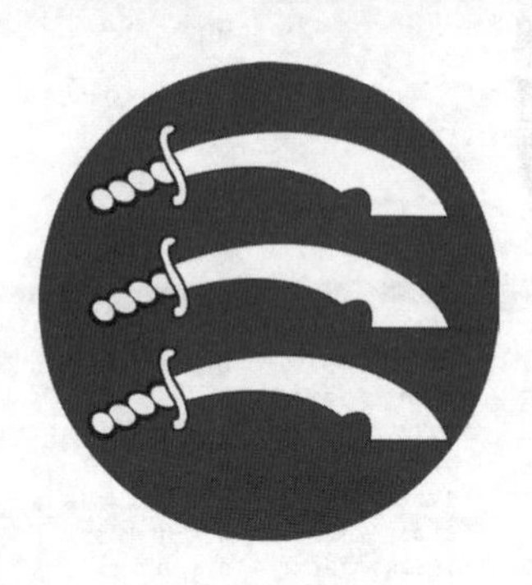

**FORMED:** 1864
**HOME GROUND:** Lord's Cricket Ground
**CAPTAIN:** Adam Voges (Championship), Eoin Morgan (RL50 and NWT20)
**2014 RESULTS:** CC1: 7/9; RL50: 7/9 Group B; NWT20: 9/9 South Division
**HONOURS:** Championship: (12) 1903, 1920, 1921, 1947, 1949(s), 1976, 1977(s), 1980, 1982, 1985, 1990, 1993; Gillette/NatWest/C&G/FP Trophy: (4) 1977, 1980, 1984, 1988; Benson & Hedges Cup: (2) 1983, 1986; Sunday League: 1992; Twenty20 Cup: 2008

## THE LOWDOWN

Top of the Championship in June after winning four of their first six matches, Middlesex then failed to win any of their remaining 10 games and avoided relegation only on the final day of the season. One of the pre-season favourites for the title, they once again relied too heavily on the runs of Chris Rogers. The bad news is Middlesex will be without Rogers this season, although they welcome the return of Nick Compton from Somerset. Australian Adam Voges has joined as Rogers' overseas replacement and will captain the Championship side. Gareth Berg's allround talents were sorely missed after he was sidelined through injury, and he has since signed for Hampshire. The county have recruited New Zealand allrounder James Franklin on a two-year deal – although he too has struggled with injuries over the last 18 months. Tim Murtagh led a decent bowling attack and was well backed up by the resurgent Steven Finn and Toby Roland-Jones, but they will hope for more from James Harris, who struggled and was sent on loan to Glamorgan. There is also great hope for 17-year-old Max Holden, called the Little Chef because of his similar batting style to Alastair Cook, but this season may come too soon.

## HEAD COACH: RICHARD SCOTT

Alongside director of cricket Angus Fraser, Scott has helped to turn the club into a Division One side since coming on board as head coach in 2009. He enjoyed a six-year county career with Hampshire and Gloucestershire – as well as turning out for Middlesex 2nd XI – before returning to Lord's in 2007 to take charge of the 2nd XI.



www.middlesexccc.com / tel: 0207 289 1300

# COUNTY CHAMPIONSHIP AVERAGES 2014

## Batting

| | Mat | Inns | NO | Runs | HS | Ave | SR | 100 | 50 | 4s | 6s |
|---|---|---|---|---|---|---|---|---|---|---|---|
| CJL Rogers | 15 | 28 | 4 | 1333 | 241* | 55.54 | 62.28 | 4 | 4 | 197 | 2 |
| EJG Morgan | 11 | 20 | 1 | 871 | 191 | 45.84 | 52.62 | 2 | 4 | 118 | 6 |
| DJ Malan | 15 | 26 | 1 | 1137 | 154* | 45.48 | 50.35 | 2 | 4 | 182 | 1 |
| PR Stirling | 6 | 10 | 2 | 351 | 66* | 43.87 | 61.04 | 0 | 4 | 47 | 2 |
| SD Robson | 11 | 20 | 3 | 674 | 163 | 39.64 | 55.24 | 1 | 4 | 95 | 0 |
| NRT Gubbins | 4 | 7 | 0 | 240 | 95 | 34.28 | 45.97 | 0 | 3 | 28 | 4 |
| JA Simpson | 15 | 23 | 3 | 669 | 110 | 33.45 | 52.22 | 2 | 4 | 86 | 5 |
| TS Roland-Jones | 13 | 19 | 3 | 500 | 77 | 31.25 | 70.72 | 0 | 3 | 71 | 7 |
| NJ Dexter | 13 | 22 | 3 | 535 | 163* | 28.15 | 43.39 | 1 | 3 | 69 | 8 |
| JL Denly | 9 | 14 | 0 | 327 | 70 | 23.35 | 46.91 | 0 | 3 | 45 | 1 |
| OP Rayner | 8 | 11 | 0 | 229 | 77 | 20.81 | 53.75 | 0 | 1 | 30 | 1 |
| JAR Harris | 7 | 9 | 3 | 105 | 41* | 17.50 | 34.53 | 0 | 0 | 14 | 0 |
| TJ Murtagh | 14 | 17 | 3 | 231 | 42 | 16.50 | 72.18 | 0 | 0 | 33 | 1 |
| RH Patel | 7 | 6 | 4 | 27 | 18 | 13.50 | 36.48 | 0 | 0 | 3 | 0 |
| ST Finn | 11 | 15 | 5 | 125 | 37* | 12.50 | 60.97 | 0 | 0 | 16 | 2 |
| TG Helm | 1 | 2 | 1 | 11 | 11* | 11.00 | 45.83 | 0 | 0 | 2 | 0 |
| AM Rossington | 3 | 5 | 0 | 25 | 8 | 5.00 | 39.68 | 0 | 0 | 3 | 1 |
| GS Sandhu | 1 | 1 | 1 | 6 | 6* | - | 30.00 | 0 | 0 | 1 | 0 |
| GK Berg | 1 | - | - | - | - | - | - | - | - | - | - |

## Bowling

| | Overs | Mdns | Runs | Wkts | BBI | BBM | Ave | Econ | SR | 5w | 10w |
|---|---|---|---|---|---|---|---|---|---|---|---|
| DJ Malan | 30.3 | 9 | 90 | 4 | 2/16 | 2/16 | 22.50 | 2.95 | 45.7 | 0 | 0 |
| TJ Murtagh | 527.4 | 116 | 1646 | 58 | 6/60 | 10/192 | 28.37 | 3.11 | 54.5 | 5 | 1 |
| ST Finn | 393.1 | 58 | 1475 | 48 | 6/80 | 9/173 | 30.72 | 3.75 | 49.1 | 2 | 0 |
| TS Roland-Jones | 406.1 | 87 | 1337 | 43 | 6/50 | 12/105 | 31.09 | 3.29 | 56.6 | 3 | 1 |
| TG Helm | 32.0 | 5 | 74 | 2 | 2/30 | 2/74 | 37.00 | 2.31 | 96.0 | 0 | 0 |
| JL Denly | 43.2 | 7 | 157 | 4 | 2/31 | 2/31 | 39.25 | 3.62 | 65.0 | 0 | 0 |
| NJ Dexter | 256.0 | 65 | 771 | 17 | 6/63 | 6/83 | 45.35 | 3.01 | 90.3 | 1 | 0 |
| PR Stirling | 14.0 | 2 | 49 | 1 | 1/45 | 1/45 | 49.00 | 3.50 | 84.0 | 0 | 0 |
| JAR Harris | 198.0 | 49 | 666 | 12 | 4/80 | 5/135 | 55.50 | 3.36 | 99.0 | 0 | 0 |
| RH Patel | 210.5 | 37 | 647 | 10 | 3/49 | 3/94 | 64.70 | 3.06 | 126.5 | 0 | 0 |
| GS Sandhu | 30.0 | 3 | 118 | 1 | 1/118 | 1/118 | 118.00 | 3.93 | 180.0 | 0 | 0 |
| OP Rayner | 219.0 | 36 | 596 | 5 | 2/101 | 2/101 | 119.20 | 2.72 | 262.8 | 0 | 0 |
| CJL Rogers | 1.0 | 0 | 2 | 0 | - | - | - | 2.00 | - | 0 | 0 |
| SD Robson | 1.0 | 0 | 6 | 0 | - | - | - | 6.00 | - | 0 | 0 |
| EJG Morgan | 0.5 | 0 | 7 | 0 | - | - | - | 8.40 | - | 0 | 0 |
| GK Berg | 20.0 | 7 | 50 | 0 | - | - | - | 2.50 | - | 0 | 0 |

**Catches/Stumpings:**

39 Simpson (inc 3st), 21 Malan, 12 Rayner, Robson, 10 Rogers, 7 Morgan, 6 Finn, 4 Harris, 3 Murtagh, Roland-Jones, Dexter, 2 Patel, 1 Helm, Denly, Stirling, Rossington

**Batting**

| | Mat | Inns | NO | Runs | HS | Ave | SR | 100 | 50 | 4s | 6s |
|---|---|---|---|---|---|---|---|---|---|---|---|
| EJG Morgan | 8 | 6 | 2 | 222 | 128* | 55.50 | 106.73 | 1 | 0 | 24 | 8 |
| CJL Rogers | 8 | 7 | 1 | 264 | 96 | 44.00 | 74.78 | 0 | 2 | 27 | 0 |
| NJ Dexter | 8 | 5 | 2 | 111 | 47* | 37.00 | 64.53 | 0 | 0 | 7 | 1 |
| DJ Malan | 8 | 7 | 1 | 218 | 82 | 36.33 | 66.26 | 0 | 2 | 21 | 0 |
| PR Stirling | 5 | 4 | 1 | 72 | 40 | 24.00 | 78.26 | 0 | 0 | 6 | 0 |
| NRT Gubbins | 3 | 3 | 0 | 63 | 38 | 21.00 | 63.63 | 0 | 0 | 6 | 1 |
| RF Higgins | 6 | 5 | 0 | 80 | 27 | 16.00 | 77.66 | 0 | 0 | 7 | 1 |
| JA Simpson | 8 | 4 | 0 | 56 | 23 | 14.00 | 76.71 | 0 | 0 | 3 | 2 |
| JL Denly | 1 | 1 | 0 | 14 | 14 | 14.00 | 40.00 | 0 | 0 | 1 | 1 |
| JAR Harris | 1 | 1 | 0 | 10 | 10 | 10.00 | 76.92 | 0 | 0 | 0 | 1 |
| TS Roland-Jones | 7 | 4 | 1 | 20 | 9 | 6.66 | 105.26 | 0 | 0 | 0 | 1 |
| TJ Murtagh | 6 | 2 | 1 | 6 | 6* | 6.00 | 100.00 | 0 | 0 | 1 | 0 |
| RH Patel | 5 | 1 | 0 | 0 | 0 | 0.00 | 0.00 | 0 | 0 | 0 | 0 |
| ST Finn | 3 | 2 | 2 | 48 | 42* | - | 54.54 | 0 | 0 | 5 | 0 |
| OP Rayner | 3 | 1 | 1 | 37 | 37* | - | 115.62 | 0 | 0 | 4 | 1 |
| HW Podmore | 6 | 1 | 1 | 1 | 1* | - | 50.00 | 0 | 0 | 0 | 0 |
| TG Helm | 1 | - | - | - | - | - | - | - | - | - | - |
| GS Sandhu | 1 | - | - | - | - | - | - | - | - | - | - |

**Bowling**

| | Overs | Mdns | Runs | Wkts | BBI | Ave | Econ | SR | 4w | 5w |
|---|---|---|---|---|---|---|---|---|---|---|
| GS Sandhu | 7.0 | 0 | 20 | 1 | 1/20 | 20.00 | 2.85 | 42.0 | 0 | 0 |
| ST Finn | 28.0 | 3 | 120 | 4 | 2/47 | 30.00 | 4.28 | 42.0 | 0 | 0 |
| TG Helm | 9.0 | 0 | 39 | 1 | 1/39 | 39.00 | 4.33 | 54.0 | 0 | 0 |
| DJ Malan | 37.1 | 1 | 180 | 6 | 2/25 | 30.00 | 4.84 | 37.1 | 0 | 0 |
| TJ Murtagh | 41.0 | 4 | 199 | 4 | 2/36 | 49.75 | 4.85 | 61.5 | 0 | 0 |
| TS Roland-Jones | 58.0 | 6 | 287 | 12 | 4/42 | 23.91 | 4.94 | 29.0 | 1 | 0 |
| OP Rayner | 18.0 | 0 | 91 | 1 | 1/42 | 91.00 | 5.05 | 108.0 | 0 | 0 |
| RH Patel | 48.0 | 0 | 244 | 4 | 2/35 | 61.00 | 5.08 | 72.0 | 0 | 0 |
| NJ Dexter | 37.2 | 0 | 212 | 1 | 1/39 | 212.00 | 5.67 | 224.0 | 0 | 0 |
| JL Denly | 5.0 | 0 | 31 | 2 | 2/31 | 15.50 | 6.20 | 15.0 | 0 | 0 |
| HW Podmore | 39.2 | 0 | 272 | 4 | 2/46 | 68.00 | 6.91 | 59.0 | 0 | 0 |
| JAR Harris | 9.0 | 0 | 87 | 0 | - | - | 9.66 | - | 0 | 0 |

**Catches/Stumpings:**
10 Simpson (inc 2st), 5 Malan, 3 Rayner, Rogers, 2 Dexter, 1 Helm, Murtagh, Roland-Jones, Patel, Denly, Morgan

# NATWEST T20 BLAST AVERAGES 2014

**Batting**

| | Mat | Inns | NO | Runs | HS | Ave | SR | 100 | 50 | 4s | 6s |
|---|---|---|---|---|---|---|---|---|---|---|---|
| DJ Malan | 14 | 13 | 3 | 393 | 86* | 39.30 | 124.36 | 0 | 2 | 44 | 5 |
| RF Higgins | 8 | 7 | 2 | 151 | 44* | 30.20 | 116.15 | 0 | 0 | 8 | 6 |
| EJG Morgan | 11 | 10 | 0 | 297 | 77 | 29.70 | 137.50 | 0 | 2 | 30 | 11 |
| JA Simpson | 14 | 11 | 6 | 131 | 47* | 26.20 | 103.96 | 0 | 0 | 9 | 1 |
| TS Roland-Jones | 5 | 3 | 1 | 45 | 30 | 22.50 | 136.36 | 0 | 0 | 3 | 3 |
| DT Christian | 14 | 12 | 0 | 268 | 129 | 22.33 | 138.86 | 1 | 0 | 20 | 16 |
| JL Denly | 13 | 12 | 1 | 209 | 98* | 19.00 | 123.66 | 0 | 1 | 23 | 6 |
| PR Stirling | 7 | 7 | 0 | 128 | 64 | 18.28 | 130.61 | 0 | 1 | 16 | 4 |
| NJ Dexter | 12 | 9 | 1 | 97 | 33 | 12.12 | 93.26 | 0 | 0 | 6 | 3 |
| OP Rayner | 12 | 8 | 2 | 63 | 18 | 10.50 | 84.00 | 0 | 0 | 5 | 1 |
| JAR Harris | 12 | 5 | 2 | 31 | 18 | 10.33 | 110.71 | 0 | 0 | 4 | 0 |
| HW Podmore | 7 | 2 | 1 | 10 | 7 | 10.00 | 66.66 | 0 | 0 | 0 | 0 |
| AM Rossington | 3 | 3 | 0 | 12 | 5 | 4.00 | 70.58 | 0 | 0 | 1 | 0 |
| RH Patel | 14 | 3 | 2 | 2 | 1* | 2.00 | 66.66 | 0 | 0 | 0 | 0 |
| A Balbirnie | 2 | 2 | 0 | 2 | 2 | 1.00 | 33.33 | 0 | 0 | 0 | 0 |
| ST Finn | 4 | 3 | 3 | 13 | 6* | - | 92.85 | 0 | 0 | 1 | 0 |
| GS Sandhu | 2 | - | - | - | - | - | - | - | - | - | - |

**Bowling**

| | Overs | Mdns | Runs | Wkts | BBI | Ave | Econ | SR | 4w | 5w |
|---|---|---|---|---|---|---|---|---|---|---|
| PR Stirling | 6.0 | 0 | 38 | 2 | 1/11 | 19.00 | 6.33 | 18.0 | 0 | 0 |
| RH Patel | 53.0 | 0 | 336 | 18 | 3/36 | 18.66 | 6.33 | 17.6 | 0 | 0 |
| NJ Dexter | 29.0 | 0 | 206 | 8 | 3/34 | 25.75 | 7.10 | 21.7 | 0 | 0 |
| HW Podmore | 22.1 | 0 | 165 | 9 | 3/13 | 18.33 | 7.44 | 14.7 | 0 | 0 |
| ST Finn | 14.0 | 0 | 109 | 4 | 2/23 | 27.25 | 7.78 | 21.0 | 0 | 0 |
| DT Christian | 39.3 | 0 | 313 | 10 | 2/6 | 31.30 | 7.92 | 23.7 | 0 | 0 |
| OP Rayner | 39.0 | 0 | 317 | 4 | 2/23 | 79.25 | 8.12 | 58.5 | 0 | 0 |
| TS Roland-Jones | 18.2 | 0 | 164 | 3 | 3/25 | 54.66 | 8.94 | 36.6 | 0 | 0 |
| JAR Harris | 38.0 | 0 | 342 | 11 | 2/10 | 31.09 | 9.00 | 20.7 | 0 | 0 |
| GS Sandhu | 7.4 | 0 | 75 | 2 | 1/34 | 37.50 | 9.78 | 23.0 | 0 | 0 |

**Catches/Stumpings:**

12 Simpson (inc 4st), 8 Malan, 7 Denly, 5 Morgan, 4 Dexter, 3 Patel, Podmore, Christian, Rossington, 2 Stirling, Rayner, Harris, Higgins, 1 Roland-Jones, Sandhu, Balbirnie

# NORTHAMPTONSHIRE

**FORMED:** 1878
**HOME GROUND:** County Ground, Northampton
**ONE-DAY NAME:** Northamptonshire Steelbacks
**CAPTAIN:** Alex Wakely
**2014 RESULTS:** CC1: 9/9; RL50: 6/9 Group A; NWT20: 7/9 North Division
**HONOURS:** Gillette/NatWest/C&G/FP Trophy: (2) 1976, 1992; Benson & Hedges Cup: 1980; Twenty20 Cup: 2013

## THE LOWDOWN

The 2014 season started badly for Northamptonshire, got worse and then finished without a whimper. They were relegated from Division One of the County Championship with a record-low points total of 79 and failed to make it out of their groups in the RL Cup and the T20 Blast. They were hindered by injury throughout 2014, with Alex Wakely missing the entire season and David Willey plagued with problems, while they struggled to land an overseas player and the normally reliable Stephen Peters laboured under the pressure of skippering a struggling side. A disastrous season was met with change, with Andrew Hall, David Sales, Matt Spriegel and James Middlebrook – who won the Player of the Year award – all released. David Smith also stepped down as chief executive. Peters was relieved of the captaincy and Wakely will now lead in all formats. They have signed aggressive batsman Josh Cobb from Leicestershire, as well as bringing in the two South Africans Richard Levi and Rory Kleinveldt for the entirety of the season across all formats. Kleinveldt in particular should be well suited to England's seamer-friendly wickets. Shahid Afridi's arrival for the first six matches of the T20 Blast will also ensure some much-needed excitement at the county, while young batsman Ben Duckett offers homegrown hope.

## HEAD COACH: DAVID RIPLEY

A Northamptonshire stalwart, Ripley scored over 10,000 runs for the county and took over 1,000 dismissals as wicketkeeper during a 17-year career. After retiring in 2001 he moved on to become 2nd XI coach before moving up to head coach in 2012.

# COUNTY CHAMPIONSHIP AVERAGES 2014

Batting

| | Mat | Inns | NO | Runs | HS | Ave | SR | 100 | 50 | 4s | 6s |
|---|---|---|---|---|---|---|---|---|---|---|---|
| AM Rossington | 6 | 10 | 0 | 440 | 103 | 44.00 | 75.60 | 1 | 2 | 61 | 8 |
| BM Duckett | 13 | 23 | 1 | 615 | 144* | 27.95 | 54.76 | 1 | 5 | 82 | 4 |
| JD Middlebrook | 16 | 30 | 0 | 825 | 87 | 27.50 | 46.29 | 0 | 5 | 119 | 0 |
| AJ Hall | 16 | 29 | 3 | 693 | 75 | 26.65 | 49.60 | 0 | 4 | 90 | 2 |
| SP Crook | 8 | 15 | 1 | 373 | 131 | 26.64 | 86.14 | 1 | 1 | 57 | 3 |
| JM Kettleborough | 8 | 15 | 0 | 398 | 73 | 26.53 | 45.74 | 0 | 3 | 59 | 1 |
| RI Keogh | 8 | 13 | 1 | 317 | 129 | 26.41 | 51.79 | 1 | 1 | 41 | 2 |
| IG Butler | 2 | 4 | 1 | 76 | 48* | 25.33 | 29.92 | 0 | 0 | 11 | 0 |
| SD Peters | 13 | 25 | 1 | 594 | 88 | 24.75 | 54.74 | 0 | 3 | 83 | 0 |
| MNW Spriegel | 12 | 24 | 2 | 494 | 97 | 22.45 | 34.98 | 0 | 2 | 72 | 0 |
| RI Newton | 12 | 24 | 2 | 473 | 114 | 21.50 | 43.55 | 1 | 0 | 67 | 1 |
| RE Levi | 3 | 6 | 0 | 120 | 59 | 20.00 | 53.09 | 0 | 1 | 20 | 0 |
| KJ Coetzer | 9 | 17 | 0 | 323 | 54 | 19.00 | 51.43 | 0 | 2 | 53 | 1 |
| DJG Sales | 3 | 6 | 0 | 103 | 43 | 17.16 | 55.97 | 0 | 0 | 15 | 1 |
| DJ Willey | 8 | 15 | 0 | 241 | 53 | 16.06 | 64.43 | 0 | 2 | 32 | 7 |
| Azharullah | 14 | 25 | 15 | 137 | 28 | 13.70 | 47.90 | 0 | 0 | 21 | 3 |
| D Murphy | 5 | 10 | 3 | 74 | 23* | 10.57 | 27.40 | 0 | 0 | 7 | 0 |
| MA Chambers | 8 | 15 | 3 | 107 | 20 | 8.91 | 28.60 | 0 | 0 | 15 | 0 |
| OP Stone | 5 | 9 | 2 | 46 | 15 | 6.57 | 21.90 | 0 | 0 | 6 | 0 |
| N Wagner | 5 | 8 | 0 | 52 | 18 | 6.50 | 38.80 | 0 | 0 | 7 | 1 |
| GG White | 2 | 3 | 0 | 12 | 6 | 4.00 | 37.50 | 0 | 0 | 1 | 0 |

Bowling

| | Overs | Mdns | Runs | Wkts | BBI | BBM | Ave | Econ | SR | 5w | 10w |
|---|---|---|---|---|---|---|---|---|---|---|---|
| OP Stone | 154.3 | 36 | 503 | 19 | 5/48 | 6/90 | 26.47 | 3.25 | 48.7 | 1 | 0 |
| DJ Willey | 163.1 | 36 | 515 | 19 | 4/46 | 7/111 | 27.10 | 3.15 | 51.5 | 0 | 0 |
| Azharullah | 462.1 | 92 | 1504 | 46 | 7/76 | 10/158 | 32.69 | 3.25 | 60.2 | 1 | 1 |
| AJ Hall | 451.1 | 83 | 1481 | 35 | 4/77 | 5/72 | 42.31 | 3.28 | 77.3 | 0 | 0 |
| IG Butler | 51.0 | 11 | 179 | 4 | 4/41 | 4/118 | 44.75 | 3.50 | 76.5 | 0 | 0 |
| JD Middlebrook | 414.3 | 93 | 1307 | 29 | 5/62 | 7/123 | 45.06 | 3.15 | 85.7 | 2 | 0 |
| MNW Spriegel | 99.0 | 11 | 378 | 8 | 3/26 | 3/26 | 47.25 | 3.81 | 74.2 | 0 | 0 |
| RI Keogh | 39.0 | 6 | 111 | 2 | 1/5 | 1/5 | 55.50 | 2.84 | 117.0 | 0 | 0 |
| MA Chambers | 222.3 | 37 | 814 | 13 | 2/23 | 4/130 | 62.61 | 3.65 | 102.6 | 0 | 0 |
| SP Crook | 210.0 | 22 | 833 | 13 | 3/26 | 4/122 | 64.07 | 3.96 | 96.9 | 0 | 0 |
| N Wagner | 182.0 | 26 | 728 | 10 | 5/104 | 5/104 | 72.80 | 4.00 | 109.2 | 1 | 0 |
| KJ Coetzer | 22.0 | 2 | 77 | 1 | 1/26 | 1/26 | 77.00 | 3.50 | 132.0 | 0 | 0 |
| GG White | 19.0 | 2 | 104 | 0 | - | - | - | 5.47 | - | 0 | 0 |

**Catches/Stumpings:**

16 Rossington (inc 3st), 15 Duckett (inc 1st), Hall, 14 Middlebrook, 7 Murphy, 6 Newton, 5 Spriegel, Crook, Kettleborough, 4 Chambers, Peters, 3 Coetzer, 2 Stone, Sales, 1 Willey, Wagner

# ROYAL LONDON ONE-DAY CUP AVERAGES 2014

Batting

| | Mat | Inns | NO | Runs | HS | Ave | SR | 100 | 50 | 4s | 6s |
|---|---|---|---|---|---|---|---|---|---|---|---|
| DJ Willey | 3 | 3 | 1 | 168 | 113 | 84.00 | 112.75 | 1 | 0 | 17 | 5 |
| RE Levi | 7 | 6 | 0 | 291 | 84 | 48.50 | 101.74 | 0 | 3 | 33 | 5 |
| AM Rossington | 7 | 6 | 0 | 214 | 82 | 35.66 | 84.92 | 0 | 2 | 27 | 1 |
| RI Keogh | 2 | 2 | 0 | 65 | 50 | 32.50 | 112.06 | 0 | 1 | 8 | 0 |
| SP Crook | 2 | 2 | 0 | 59 | 36 | 29.50 | 118.00 | 0 | 0 | 6 | 1 |
| AJ Hall | 4 | 3 | 1 | 58 | 43 | 29.00 | 131.81 | 0 | 0 | 7 | 0 |
| JM Kettleborough | 1 | 1 | 0 | 26 | 26 | 26.00 | 76.47 | 0 | 0 | 3 | 0 |
| JD Middlebrook | 5 | 4 | 2 | 51 | 24 | 25.50 | 71.83 | 0 | 0 | 2 | 1 |
| OP Stone | 2 | 1 | 0 | 21 | 21 | 21.00 | 48.83 | 0 | 0 | 1 | 0 |
| BM Duckett | 7 | 6 | 0 | 125 | 49 | 20.83 | 88.65 | 0 | 0 | 9 | 2 |
| MNW Spriegel | 7 | 6 | 0 | 87 | 32 | 14.50 | 58.78 | 0 | 0 | 4 | 0 |
| GG White | 7 | 5 | 1 | 53 | 21* | 13.25 | 86.88 | 0 | 0 | 7 | 0 |
| KJ Coetzer | 7 | 6 | 0 | 35 | 11 | 5.83 | 48.61 | 0 | 0 | 5 | 0 |
| SD Peters | 3 | 2 | 1 | 4 | 4* | 4.00 | 66.66 | 0 | 0 | 0 | 0 |
| MA Chambers | 5 | 3 | 1 | 3 | 1* | 1.50 | 33.33 | 0 | 0 | 0 | 0 |
| Azharullah | 7 | 2 | 1 | 0 | 0* | 0.00 | 0.00 | 0 | 0 | 0 | 0 |
| ML Turner | 1 | 1 | 1 | 4 | 4* | - | 66.66 | 0 | 0 | 0 | 0 |

Bowling

| | Overs | Mdns | Runs | Wkts | BBI | Ave | Econ | SR | 4w | 5w |
|---|---|---|---|---|---|---|---|---|---|---|
| MNW Spriegel | 28.0 | 2 | 118 | 2 | 1/31 | 59.00 | 4.21 | 84.0 | 0 | 0 |
| GG White | 43.0 | 2 | 216 | 5 | 2/48 | 43.20 | 5.02 | 51.6 | 0 | 0 |
| SP Crook | 19.0 | 0 | 96 | 5 | 3/42 | 19.20 | 5.05 | 22.8 | 0 | 0 |
| DJ Willey | 29.0 | 3 | 152 | 9 | 4/33 | 16.88 | 5.24 | 19.3 | 1 | 0 |
| OP Stone | 14.0 | 0 | 76 | 0 | - | - | 5.42 | - | 0 | 0 |
| JD Middlebrook | 29.0 | 0 | 160 | 4 | 2/36 | 40.00 | 5.51 | 43.5 | 0 | 0 |
| Azharullah | 50.1 | 1 | 296 | 8 | 5/38 | 37.00 | 5.90 | 37.6 | 0 | 1 |
| AJ Hall | 28.0 | 0 | 167 | 5 | 3/39 | 33.40 | 5.96 | 33.6 | 0 | 0 |
| MA Chambers | 31.1 | 0 | 208 | 7 | 3/29 | 29.71 | 6.67 | 26.7 | 0 | 0 |
| KJ Coetzer | 3.0 | 0 | 21 | 0 | - | - | 7.00 | - | 0 | 0 |

**Catches/Stumpings:**
7 White, 6 Spriegel, 4 Duckett (inc 1st), Rossington, 3 Coetzer, 2 Middlebrook, 1 Levi, Peters

# NATWEST T20 BLAST AVERAGES 2014

**Batting**

| | Mat | Inns | NO | Runs | HS | Ave | SR | 100 | 50 | 4s | 6s |
|---|---|---|---|---|---|---|---|---|---|---|---|
| AM Rossington | 6 | 6 | 1 | 157 | 52* | 31.40 | 155.44 | 0 | 1 | 15 | 7 |
| DJ Willey | 13 | 12 | 0 | 306 | 95 | 25.50 | 140.36 | 0 | 1 | 26 | 16 |
| RE Levi | 13 | 12 | 0 | 283 | 76 | 23.58 | 129.22 | 0 | 2 | 20 | 15 |
| SP Crook | 13 | 12 | 2 | 213 | 51* | 21.30 | 131.48 | 0 | 1 | 17 | 6 |
| KJ Coetzer | 11 | 11 | 0 | 222 | 67 | 20.18 | 112.12 | 0 | 1 | 21 | 2 |
| RI Keogh | 4 | 3 | 0 | 56 | 28 | 18.66 | 109.80 | 0 | 0 | 3 | 1 |
| DJG Sales | 5 | 4 | 0 | 70 | 25 | 17.50 | 81.39 | 0 | 0 | 4 | 2 |
| BM Duckett | 13 | 11 | 2 | 155 | 39* | 17.22 | 110.71 | 0 | 0 | 11 | 1 |
| GG White | 12 | 8 | 3 | 71 | 34 | 14.20 | 208.82 | 0 | 0 | 6 | 5 |
| IG Butler | 4 | 4 | 2 | 24 | 13* | 12.00 | 104.34 | 0 | 0 | 1 | 1 |
| MNW Spriegel | 13 | 11 | 2 | 97 | 32 | 10.77 | 127.63 | 0 | 0 | 9 | 2 |
| RI Newton | 4 | 3 | 0 | 21 | 12 | 7.00 | 70.00 | 0 | 0 | 2 | 0 |
| JD Middlebrook | 8 | 5 | 1 | 20 | 13 | 5.00 | 80.00 | 0 | 0 | 1 | 1 |
| OP Stone | 11 | 7 | 4 | 15 | 6* | 5.00 | 83.33 | 0 | 0 | 1 | 0 |
| Azharullah | 12 | 4 | 4 | 9 | 4* | - | 75.00 | 0 | 0 | 1 | 0 |
| MA Chambers | 1 | - | - | - | - | - | - | - | - | - | - |

**Bowling**

| | Overs | Mdns | Runs | Wkts | BBI | Ave | Econ | SR | 4w | 5w |
|---|---|---|---|---|---|---|---|---|---|---|
| JD Middlebrook | 18.0 | 0 | 126 | 6 | 2/26 | 21.00 | 7.00 | 18.0 | 0 | 0 |
| SP Crook | 39.0 | 1 | 278 | 13 | 3/19 | 21.38 | 7.12 | 18.0 | 0 | 0 |
| IG Butler | 11.0 | 0 | 94 | 6 | 4/25 | 15.66 | 8.54 | 11.0 | 1 | 0 |
| OP Stone | 32.1 | 2 | 275 | 6 | 2/18 | 45.83 | 8.54 | 32.1 | 0 | 0 |
| MNW Spriegel | 15.0 | 0 | 129 | 4 | 2/13 | 32.25 | 8.60 | 22.5 | 0 | 0 |
| GG White | 33.0 | 0 | 303 | 6 | 2/25 | 50.50 | 9.18 | 33.0 | 0 | 0 |
| DJ Willey | 27.0 | 0 | 248 | 5 | 1/8 | 49.60 | 9.18 | 32.4 | 0 | 0 |
| Azharullah | 35.1 | 0 | 330 | 13 | 3/31 | 25.38 | 9.38 | 16.2 | 0 | 0 |
| KJ Coetzer | 5.0 | 0 | 48 | 0 | - | - | 9.60 | - | 0 | 0 |
| MA Chambers | 2.0 | 0 | 26 | 0 | - | - | 13.00 | - | 0 | 0 |

**Catches/Stumpings:**
7 Duckett (inc 1st), Willey, 5 Crook, Coetzer, 4 Azharullah, 3 Keogh, 2 Middlebrook, Spriegel, White, 1 Butler, Stone, Levi, Rossington

# NOTTINGHAMSHIRE

**FORMED:** 1841
**HOME GROUND:** Trent Bridge, Nottingham
**ONE-DAY NAME:** Notts Outlaws
**CAPTAIN:** Chris Read (Championship), James Taylor (RL50 and NWT20)
**2014 RESULTS:** CC1: 4/9; RL50: Semi-finalists; NWT20: Quarter-finalists
**HONOURS:** County Championship: (6) 1907, 1929, 1981, 1987, 2005, 2010; Gillette/NatWest/C&G/FP Trophy: 1987; Pro40/National League/CB40/YB40/RL50: 2013; Benson & Hedges Cup: 1989; Sunday League: 1991

## THE LOWDOWN

A late-season collapse turned a very promising season into one of missed opportunities. Still challenging for the treble as the summer entered August, they were beaten in the T20 Blast quarter-finals, thrashed by a Ben Stokes-inspired Durham in the RL Cup semis and then let their Championship form deflate. There was still much to be positive about, with Alex Hales showing signs of fulfilling his natural talent and Riki Wessels scoring over 1,800 runs across all formats. James Taylor was explosive in the RL Cup, hitting three centuries at 88, but scored just a solitary hundred in the Championship. Samit Patel also had another wonderful all-round season after once again being overlooked by England. Nottinghamshire's bowlers struggled, with no one reaching 40 wickets. They have brought in seamers Vernon Philander and Ben Hilfenhaus to share the overseas duties, while they have also made the excellent signing of Will Gidman from Gloucestershire and once again raided Leicestershire, taking opener Greg Smith off their books. Ajmal Shahzad, who disappointed, has moved to Sussex in another attempt to resurrect his career while Notts stalwart Andre Adams, who struggled with injuries throughout the season, has headed to Hampshire.

## DIRECTOR OF CRICKET: MICK NEWELL

The longest-serving coach on the county circuit, Newell has been coach at Nottinghamshire since 2002. In that time he has led the county to two Championship titles and victory in the YB40. Last season he was also added to England's board of selectors, replacing Ashley Giles, after missing out on the role of national coach to Peter Moores. As a player, Newell spent eight seasons with Nottinghamshire, opening the batting between 1984 and 1992.

# COUNTY CHAMPIONSHIP AVERAGES 2014

Batting

| | Mat | Inns | NO | Runs | HS | Ave | SR | 100 | 50 | 4s | 6s |
|---|---|---|---|---|---|---|---|---|---|---|---|
| JD Libby | 1 | 2 | 0 | 120 | 108 | 60.00 | 40.95 | 1 | 0 | 18 | 0 |
| AD Hales | 11 | 20 | 1 | 954 | 183 | 50.21 | 72.38 | 3 | 4 | 136 | 11 |
| PA Jaques | 11 | 20 | 2 | 894 | 150* | 49.66 | 62.43 | 2 | 6 | 134 | 1 |
| MH Wessels | 16 | 29 | 4 | 1197 | 158 | 47.88 | 62.14 | 1 | 8 | 150 | 22 |
| CMW Read | 16 | 25 | 5 | 877 | 96 | 43.85 | 58.70 | 0 | 6 | 120 | 5 |
| JWA Taylor | 15 | 28 | 2 | 992 | 126 | 38.15 | 50.84 | 1 | 8 | 133 | 3 |
| SR Patel | 16 | 30 | 0 | 1098 | 156 | 36.60 | 67.81 | 2 | 6 | 165 | 3 |
| JEC Franklin | 1 | 2 | 0 | 63 | 39 | 31.50 | 35.59 | 0 | 0 | 6 | 0 |
| A Shahzad | 8 | 12 | 5 | 203 | 68* | 29.00 | 55.76 | 0 | 1 | 22 | 3 |
| MJ Lumb | 14 | 26 | 0 | 740 | 99 | 28.46 | 47.46 | 0 | 3 | 104 | 2 |
| PM Siddle | 11 | 16 | 5 | 250 | 48* | 22.72 | 83.05 | 0 | 0 | 27 | 4 |
| SJ Mullaney | 11 | 21 | 0 | 380 | 91 | 18.09 | 49.15 | 0 | 3 | 56 | 2 |
| L Wood | 1 | 2 | 1 | 17 | 12 | 17.00 | 43.58 | 0 | 0 | 3 | 0 |
| LJ Fletcher | 11 | 19 | 0 | 240 | 49 | 12.63 | 46.78 | 0 | 0 | 25 | 3 |
| JT Ball | 4 | 7 | 0 | 56 | 20 | 8.00 | 54.36 | 0 | 0 | 8 | 0 |
| G Keedy | 3 | 6 | 3 | 19 | 15* | 6.33 | 20.21 | 0 | 0 | 4 | 0 |
| HF Gurney | 10 | 17 | 8 | 51 | 15 | 5.66 | 39.84 | 0 | 0 | 5 | 0 |
| AR Adams | 9 | 11 | 0 | 61 | 19 | 5.54 | 81.33 | 0 | 0 | 4 | 3 |
| A Carter | 5 | 7 | 1 | 27 | 11* | 4.50 | 39.70 | 0 | 0 | 4 | 0 |
| SCJ Broad | 2 | 2 | 0 | 8 | 8 | 4.00 | 38.09 | 0 | 0 | 2 | 0 |

Bowling

| | Overs | Mdns | Runs | Wkts | BBI | BBM | Ave | Econ | SR | 5w | 10w |
|---|---|---|---|---|---|---|---|---|---|---|---|
| A Carter | 127.5 | 24 | 441 | 17 | 5/55 | 7/95 | 25.94 | 3.44 | 45.1 | 1 | 0 |
| LJ Fletcher | 338.5 | 79 | 1054 | 38 | 4/76 | 6/120 | 27.73 | 3.11 | 53.5 | 0 | 0 |
| AR Adams | 294.5 | 47 | 1013 | 36 | 5/65 | 6/113 | 28.13 | 3.43 | 49.1 | 1 | 0 |
| JT Ball | 83.0 | 14 | 264 | 9 | 3/60 | 5/108 | 29.33 | 3.18 | 55.3 | 0 | 0 |
| PM Siddle | 351.5 | 80 | 1165 | 37 | 4/61 | 8/136 | 31.48 | 3.31 | 57.0 | 0 | 0 |
| SJ Mullaney | 93.2 | 15 | 286 | 9 | 2/35 | 2/35 | 31.77 | 3.06 | 62.2 | 0 | 0 |
| HF Gurney | 335.3 | 58 | 1248 | 38 | 4/22 | 6/71 | 32.84 | 3.71 | 52.9 | 0 | 0 |
| SCJ Broad | 51.0 | 10 | 177 | 5 | 3/78 | 5/109 | 35.40 | 3.47 | 61.2 | 0 | 0 |
| G Keedy | 127.0 | 12 | 465 | 13 | 5/163 | 5/163 | 35.76 | 3.66 | 58.6 | 1 | 0 |
| JEC Franklin | 9.0 | 1 | 36 | 1 | 1/14 | 1/36 | 36.00 | 4.00 | 54.0 | 0 | 0 |
| A Shahzad | 192.2 | 32 | 730 | 18 | 4/46 | 7/90 | 40.55 | 3.79 | 64.1 | 0 | 0 |
| SR Patel | 278.0 | 49 | 979 | 22 | 3/13 | 4/23 | 44.50 | 3.52 | 75.8 | 0 | 0 |
| L Wood | 39.0 | 4 | 180 | 3 | 2/87 | 3/180 | 60.00 | 4.61 | 78.0 | 0 | 0 |
| AD Hales | 2.0 | 0 | 4 | 0 | - | - | - | 2.00 | - | 0 | 0 |
| MH Wessels | 5.0 | 0 | 19 | 0 | - | - | - | 3.80 | - | 0 | 0 |
| PA Jaques | - | - | - | - | - | - | - | - | - | - | - |
| JD Libby | - | - | - | - | - | - | - | - | - | - | - |
| MJ Lumb | - | - | - | - | - | - | - | - | - | - | - |
| CMW Read | - | - | - | - | - | - | - | - | - | - | - |
| JWA Taylor | - | - | - | - | - | - | - | - | - | - | - |

**Catches/Stumpings:**
55 Read (inc 1st), 22 Wessels, 18 Patel, 13 Hales, 9 Adams, 8 Mullaney, 7 Taylor, 5 Siddle, 4 Fletcher, Lumb, 3 Jaques, 2 Keedy, Shahzad, 1 Gurney, Libby

# ROYAL LONDON ONE-DAY CUP AVERAGES 2014

Batting

| | Mat | Inns | NO | Runs | HS | Ave | SR | 100 | 50 | 4s | 6s |
|---|---|---|---|---|---|---|---|---|---|---|---|
| JWA Taylor | 7 | 7 | 2 | 444 | 146* | 88.80 | 96.52 | 3 | 1 | 29 | 15 |
| AD Hales | 5 | 5 | 0 | 384 | 141 | 76.80 | 120.00 | 3 | 0 | 45 | 10 |
| MJ Lumb | 9 | 9 | 0 | 319 | 81 | 35.44 | 78.96 | 0 | 2 | 39 | 2 |
| CMW Read | 9 | 8 | 3 | 167 | 42 | 33.40 | 85.20 | 0 | 0 | 15 | 2 |
| SR Patel | 9 | 9 | 1 | 244 | 55 | 30.50 | 82.15 | 0 | 2 | 26 | 1 |
| SJ Mullaney | 9 | 8 | 1 | 213 | 63* | 30.42 | 113.90 | 0 | 2 | 20 | 6 |
| MH Wessels | 9 | 8 | 0 | 221 | 65 | 27.62 | 96.08 | 0 | 1 | 19 | 7 |
| JEC Franklin | 9 | 8 | 1 | 190 | 59* | 27.14 | 74.50 | 0 | 1 | 10 | 3 |
| JT Ball | 6 | 4 | 3 | 24 | 11* | 24.00 | 171.42 | 0 | 0 | 3 | 1 |
| LJ Fletcher | 8 | 4 | 2 | 43 | 19 | 21.50 | 122.85 | 0 | 0 | 5 | 0 |
| A Shahzad | 8 | 6 | 2 | 81 | 33* | 20.25 | 105.19 | 0 | 0 | 6 | 2 |
| S Kelsall | 2 | 2 | 0 | 35 | 30 | 17.50 | 56.45 | 0 | 0 | 4 | 0 |
| SKW Wood | 3 | 2 | 0 | 23 | 22 | 11.50 | 65.71 | 0 | 0 | 2 | 0 |
| HF Gurney | 6 | 2 | 2 | 1 | 1* | - | 50.00 | 0 | 0 | 0 | 0 |

Bowling

| | Overs | Mdns | Runs | Wkts | BBI | Ave | Econ | SR | 4w | 5w |
|---|---|---|---|---|---|---|---|---|---|---|
| SJ Mullaney | 63.0 | 4 | 261 | 7 | 4/33 | 37.28 | 4.14 | 54.0 | 1 | 0 |
| JEC Franklin | 23.0 | 0 | 115 | 7 | 3/32 | 16.42 | 5.00 | 19.7 | 0 | 0 |
| LJ Fletcher | 60.5 | 5 | 314 | 14 | 4/44 | 22.42 | 5.16 | 26.0 | 1 | 0 |
| SR Patel | 58.3 | 1 | 305 | 8 | 4/49 | 38.12 | 5.21 | 43.8 | 1 | 0 |
| SKW Wood | 6.0 | 0 | 35 | 0 | - | - | 5.83 | - | 0 | 0 |
| A Shahzad | 54.3 | 0 | 322 | 11 | 3/33 | 29.27 | 5.90 | 29.7 | 0 | 0 |
| HF Gurney | 52.0 | 2 | 325 | 9 | 4/16 | 36.11 | 6.25 | 34.6 | 1 | 0 |
| JT Ball | 44.0 | 0 | 297 | 7 | 3/57 | 42.42 | 6.75 | 37.7 | 0 | 0 |

**Catches/Stumpings:**
8 Read (inc 3st), Wessels, 4 Mullaney, Franklin, Taylor, 3 Shahzad, Lumb, 2 Patel, 1 Fletcher, Wood, Gurney, Ball, Hales

# NATWEST T20 BLAST AVERAGES 2014

| | Mat | Inns | NO | Runs | HS | Ave | SR | 100 | 50 | 4s | 6s |
|---|---|---|---|---|---|---|---|---|---|---|---|
| MH Wessels | 13 | 13 | 2 | 470 | 95* | 42.72 | 149.20 | 0 | 4 | 48 | 15 |
| JWA Taylor | 13 | 12 | 4 | 272 | 52* | 34.00 | 123.07 | 0 | 1 | 26 | 6 |
| SR Patel | 13 | 13 | 1 | 379 | 63 | 31.58 | 130.68 | 0 | 3 | 28 | 11 |
| AD Hales | 13 | 13 | 0 | 365 | 67 | 28.07 | 136.70 | 0 | 3 | 41 | 14 |
| SJ Mullaney | 13 | 11 | 5 | 164 | 36 | 27.33 | 154.71 | 0 | 0 | 19 | 8 |
| MJ Lumb | 7 | 7 | 0 | 128 | 39 | 18.28 | 124.27 | 0 | 0 | 14 | 5 |
| JEC Franklin | 6 | 5 | 1 | 68 | 27 | 17.00 | 109.67 | 0 | 0 | 2 | 4 |
| CMW Read | 13 | 11 | 3 | 92 | 23 | 11.50 | 117.94 | 0 | 0 | 5 | 3 |
| PA Jaques | 3 | 3 | 0 | 33 | 22 | 11.00 | 117.85 | 0 | 0 | 6 | 0 |
| A Shahzad | 13 | 5 | 2 | 32 | 11* | 10.66 | 78.04 | 0 | 0 | 0 | 1 |
| SKW Wood | 10 | 5 | 2 | 30 | 13* | 10.00 | 136.36 | 0 | 0 | 1 | 1 |
| LJ Fletcher | 10 | 4 | 1 | 12 | 6 | 4.00 | 109.09 | 0 | 0 | 0 | 1 |
| A Carter | 5 | 1 | 1 | 5 | 5* | - | 125.00 | 0 | 0 | 0 | 0 |
| HF Gurney | 10 | 2 | 2 | 1 | 1* | - | 100.00 | 0 | 0 | 0 | 0 |
| JT Ball | 1 | - | - | - | - | - | - | - | - | - | - |

Batting

| | Overs | Mdns | Runs | Wkts | BBI | Ave | Econ | SR | 4w | 5w |
|---|---|---|---|---|---|---|---|---|---|---|
| LJ Fletcher | 38.3 | 1 | 272 | 13 | 3/11 | 20.92 | 7.06 | 17.7 | 0 | 0 |
| A Carter | 18.0 | 0 | 129 | 9 | 3/31 | 14.33 | 7.16 | 12.0 | 0 | 0 |
| HF Gurney | 36.3 | 0 | 272 | 12 | 2/24 | 22.66 | 7.45 | 18.2 | 0 | 0 |
| SR Patel | 49.0 | 0 | 373 | 15 | 3/26 | 24.86 | 7.61 | 19.6 | 0 | 0 |
| A Shahzad | 49.0 | 1 | 376 | 13 | 2/29 | 28.92 | 7.67 | 22.6 | 0 | 0 |
| SJ Mullaney | 43.0 | 0 | 354 | 11 | 4/25 | 32.18 | 8.23 | 23.4 | 1 | 0 |
| JT Ball | 4.0 | 0 | 38 | 3 | 3/38 | 12.66 | 9.50 | 8.0 | 0 | 0 |
| SKW Wood | 12.0 | 0 | 117 | 3 | 2/21 | 39.00 | 9.75 | 24.0 | 0 | 0 |
| JEC Franklin | 6.0 | 0 | 60 | 3 | 2/26 | 20.00 | 10.00 | 12.0 | 0 | 0 |

Bowling

**Catches/Stumpings:**
11 Mullaney, 10 Read (inc 3st), 9 Wessels, 8 Hales, 5 Taylor, Lumb, 4 Franklin, 3 Gurney, 1 Carter, Patel, Shahzad, Wood, Jaques

# SOMERSET

**FORMED:** 1875
**HOME GROUND:** County Ground, Taunton
**CAPTAIN:** Marcus Trescothick (Championship), Alfonso Thomas (RL50 and NWT20)
**2014 RESULTS:** CC1: 6/9; RL50: 6/9 Group B; NWT20: 5/9, South Division
**HONOURS:** Gillette/NatWest/C&G/FP Trophy: (3) 1979, 1983, 2001; Benson & Hedges Cup: (2) 1981, 1982, Sunday League: 1979; Twenty20 Cup: 2005

## THE LOWDOWN

It all seems to have gone a little stale for Somerset. After a decade of being bridesmaids across all three competitions, 2014 was rather flat in all formats. Peter Trego and Alfonso Thomas had their usual solid seasons, while Marcus Trescothick passed 1,000 Championship runs for the sixth time in his career after struggling badly in 2013. Matthew Maynard has been brought in as director of cricket, replacing Dave Nosworthy after two seasons of underwhelming results. Maynard received an early blow by losing Nick Compton, who has returned to Middlesex, while there are doubts over Craig Kieswetter's career following eye surgery, but Maynard has freshened up the side with three key signings. Jim Allenby has joined after two seasons as Glamorgan's leading run-scorer (as well as taking 52 Championship wickets last season) while Abdur Rehman returns as a canny overseas signing after enjoying a profitable 2012 at Taunton – despite a 12-week ban for smoking cannabis – and he will also aid the development of Somerset's young slow left-armers George Dockrell and Jack Leach. Maynard has also given Australian-born batsman Tom Cooper his first chance in county cricket after he impressed in the Sheffield Shield and for Netherlands.

## DIRECTOR OF CRICKET: MATTHEW MAYNARD

A dashing batsman for Glamorgan during a 20-year career, Maynard played four Tests and 14 ODIs for England. This is his first return to coaching in England since he resigned his role as director of cricket with Glamorgan in 2010. Before that he had been England's assistant coach during the 2005 Ashes, and has recently coached Titans in South Africa and the St Lucia Zouks in the Caribbean.

# COUNTY CHAMPIONSHIP AVERAGES 2014

Batting

| | Mat | Inns | NO | Runs | HS | Ave | SR | 100 | 50 | 4s | 6s |
|---|---|---|---|---|---|---|---|---|---|---|---|
| NRD Compton | 16 | 25 | 3 | 961 | 156 | 43.68 | 44.28 | 2 | 5 | 117 | 4 |
| AWR Barrow | 4 | 7 | 2 | 218 | 88 | 43.60 | 51.53 | 0 | 1 | 37 | 0 |
| ME Trescothick | 16 | 25 | 0 | 1049 | 133 | 41.96 | 53.14 | 4 | 5 | 168 | 8 |
| TB Abell | 4 | 7 | 0 | 292 | 95 | 41.71 | 47.94 | 0 | 3 | 33 | 0 |
| AN Petersen | 11 | 16 | 1 | 605 | 155 | 40.33 | 54.35 | 1 | 4 | 66 | 7 |
| C Kieswetter | 13 | 17 | 3 | 508 | 78* | 36.28 | 57.20 | 0 | 5 | 67 | 8 |
| PD Trego | 15 | 20 | 1 | 644 | 107* | 33.89 | 77.03 | 1 | 3 | 79 | 8 |
| JC Hildreth | 15 | 24 | 1 | 763 | 182 | 33.17 | 53.35 | 1 | 4 | 100 | 3 |
| C Overton | 12 | 16 | 3 | 431 | 99 | 33.15 | 65.10 | 0 | 3 | 50 | 6 |
| JG Myburgh | 12 | 17 | 1 | 521 | 91 | 32.56 | 48.64 | 0 | 3 | 72 | 1 |
| L Gregory | 9 | 11 | 1 | 296 | 69 | 29.60 | 74.00 | 0 | 1 | 37 | 10 |
| MJ Leach | 3 | 3 | 1 | 59 | 43 | 29.50 | 60.20 | 0 | 0 | 11 | 0 |
| CAJ Meschede | 5 | 6 | 1 | 142 | 59* | 28.40 | 70.29 | 0 | 1 | 19 | 4 |
| CR Jones | 8 | 12 | 0 | 339 | 87 | 28.25 | 43.18 | 0 | 3 | 50 | 1 |
| GH Dockrell | 9 | 11 | 7 | 109 | 27 | 27.25 | 50.23 | 0 | 0 | 12 | 2 |
| J Overton | 7 | 8 | 3 | 133 | 56 | 26.60 | 104.72 | 0 | 2 | 20 | 4 |
| CA Ingram | 1 | 2 | 0 | 51 | 37 | 25.50 | 45.13 | 0 | 0 | 8 | 0 |
| AC Thomas | 14 | 17 | 5 | 193 | 54 | 16.08 | 36.14 | 0 | 1 | 19 | 0 |
| TD Groenewald | 2 | 3 | 0 | 3 | 1 | 1.00 | 9.37 | 0 | 0 | 0 | 0 |

Bowling

| | Overs | Mdns | Runs | Wkts | BBI | BBM | Ave | Econ | SR | 5w | 10w |
|---|---|---|---|---|---|---|---|---|---|---|---|
| AC Thomas | 469.3 | 124 | 1313 | 53 | 5/40 | 8/107 | 24.77 | 2.79 | 53.1 | 3 | 0 |
| L Gregory | 332.0 | 74 | 1121 | 43 | 6/47 | 11/122 | 26.06 | 3.37 | 46.3 | 3 | 1 |
| PD Trego | 442.4 | 92 | 1391 | 49 | 7/84 | 11/153 | 28.38 | 3.14 | 54.2 | 1 | 1 |
| C Overton | 339.1 | 65 | 1181 | 40 | 5/63 | 7/150 | 29.52 | 3.48 | 50.8 | 1 | 0 |
| MJ Leach | 121.0 | 34 | 286 | 8 | 3/40 | 4/116 | 35.75 | 2.36 | 90.7 | 0 | 0 |
| GH Dockrell | 279.1 | 50 | 751 | 21 | 3/44 | 5/108 | 35.76 | 2.69 | 79.7 | 0 | 0 |
| JC Hildreth | 14.0 | 1 | 48 | 1 | 1/21 | 1/21 | 48.00 | 3.42 | 84.0 | 0 | 0 |
| JG Myburgh | 212.1 | 39 | 581 | 11 | 2/13 | 3/124 | 52.81 | 2.73 | 115.7 | 0 | 0 |
| CAJ Meschede | 101.0 | 19 | 387 | 7 | 3/105 | 4/136 | 55.28 | 3.83 | 86.5 | 0 | 0 |
| J Overton | 165.0 | 14 | 708 | 10 | 2/35 | 4/85 | 70.80 | 4.29 | 99.0 | 0 | 0 |
| AN Petersen | 32.0 | 5 | 78 | 1 | 1/37 | 1/37 | 78.00 | 2.43 | 192.0 | 0 | 0 |
| TD Groenewald | 64.0 | 10 | 205 | 2 | 2/56 | 2/118 | 102.50 | 3.20 | 192.0 | 0 | 0 |
| NRD Compton | 1.0 | 0 | 8 | 0 | - | - | - | 8.00 | - | 0 | 0 |
| TB Abell | 2.0 | 0 | 11 | 0 | - | - | - | 5.50 | - | 0 | 0 |

**Catches/Stumpings:**
39 Kieswetter (inc 4st), 23 Trescothick, 19 Hildreth, 14 Barrow, 9 Compton, 8 Petersen, Jones, 5 Gregory, 4 Trego, Abell, 3 C Overton, Myburgh, 2 Dockrell, Meschede, Groenewald, 1 Ingram

# ROYAL LONDON ONE-DAY CUP AVERAGES 2014

SOMERSET
CRICKET CLUB

Batting

| | Mat | Inns | NO | Runs | HS | Ave | SR | 100 | 50 | 4s | 6s |
|---|---|---|---|---|---|---|---|---|---|---|---|
| AC Thomas | 8 | 4 | 3 | 87 | 49* | 87.00 | 114.47 | 0 | 0 | 12 | 0 |
| JC Hildreth | 8 | 8 | 4 | 304 | 146* | 76.00 | 99.34 | 1 | 1 | 25 | 3 |
| TD Groenewald | 8 | 6 | 3 | 159 | 57 | 53.00 | 159.00 | 0 | 2 | 17 | 6 |
| CA Ingram | 7 | 7 | 0 | 298 | 72 | 42.57 | 81.42 | 0 | 3 | 26 | 6 |
| L Gregory | 8 | 6 | 1 | 206 | 105* | 41.20 | 136.42 | 1 | 0 | 22 | 3 |
| PD Trego | 8 | 8 | 0 | 314 | 120 | 39.25 | 83.28 | 2 | 0 | 25 | 7 |
| ME Trescothick | 8 | 8 | 0 | 244 | 80 | 30.50 | 94.57 | 0 | 2 | 26 | 7 |
| NRD Compton | 8 | 8 | 0 | 214 | 68 | 26.75 | 69.25 | 0 | 2 | 25 | 0 |
| AWR Barrow | 8 | 8 | 2 | 132 | 54 | 22.00 | 98.50 | 0 | 1 | 18 | 0 |
| C Overton | 4 | 3 | 0 | 45 | 36 | 15.00 | 187.50 | 0 | 0 | 6 | 0 |
| JG Myburgh | 3 | 2 | 0 | 27 | 24 | 13.50 | 77.14 | 0 | 0 | 2 | 0 |
| MJ Leach | 6 | 2 | 0 | 18 | 18 | 9.00 | 51.42 | 0 | 0 | 2 | 0 |
| CAJ Meschede | 2 | 1 | 0 | 0 | 0 | 0.00 | 0.00 | 0 | 0 | 0 | 0 |
| GH Dockrell | 2 | - | - | - | - | - | - | - | - | - | - |

Bowling

| | Overs | Mdns | Runs | Wkts | BBI | Ave | Econ | SR | 4w | 5w |
|---|---|---|---|---|---|---|---|---|---|---|
| C Overton | 25.0 | 2 | 112 | 3 | 2/42 | 37.33 | 4.48 | 50.0 | 0 | 0 |
| PD Trego | 42.0 | 3 | 210 | 4 | 1/29 | 52.50 | 5.00 | 63.0 | 0 | 0 |
| JG Myburgh | 14.0 | 0 | 70 | 1 | 1/20 | 70.00 | 5.00 | 84.0 | 0 | 0 |
| MJ Leach | 52.0 | 1 | 262 | 8 | 3/53 | 32.75 | 5.03 | 39.0 | 0 | 0 |
| CAJ Meschede | 11.1 | 0 | 62 | 1 | 1/25 | 62.00 | 5.55 | 67.0 | 0 | 0 |
| TD Groenewald | 67.0 | 4 | 383 | 11 | 3/37 | 34.81 | 5.71 | 36.5 | 0 | 0 |
| L Gregory | 73.0 | 3 | 465 | 14 | 4/48 | 33.21 | 6.36 | 31.2 | 1 | 0 |
| AC Thomas | 72.0 | 2 | 469 | 10 | 3/30 | 46.90 | 6.51 | 43.2 | 0 | 0 |
| GH Dockrell | 10.0 | 0 | 82 | 0 | - | - | 8.20 | - | 0 | 0 |

**Catches/Stumpings:**
6 Barrow (inc 1st), Trescothick, 4 Leach, Gregory, Dockrell, Hildreth, 3 Compton, 2 Trego, Myburgh, Groenewald, Thomas, Ingram, 1 C Overton

# NATWEST T20 BLAST AVERAGES 2014

SOMERSET
CRICKET CLUB

**Batting**

| | Mat | Inns | NO | Runs | HS | Ave | SR | 100 | 50 | 4s | 6s |
|---|---|---|---|---|---|---|---|---|---|---|---|
| C Kieswetter | 11 | 10 | 0 | 497 | 74 | 49.70 | 125.50 | 0 | 6 | 45 | 10 |
| AN Petersen | 9 | 9 | 3 | 225 | 51 | 37.50 | 124.30 | 0 | 1 | 14 | 5 |
| AC Thomas | 13 | 4 | 3 | 35 | 19* | 35.00 | 140.00 | 0 | 0 | 5 | 0 |
| CA Ingram | 4 | 4 | 1 | 95 | 37* | 31.66 | 169.64 | 0 | 0 | 8 | 5 |
| PD Trego | 14 | 13 | 2 | 344 | 94* | 31.27 | 136.50 | 0 | 2 | 39 | 5 |
| JC Hildreth | 14 | 13 | 5 | 247 | 58* | 30.87 | 140.34 | 0 | 1 | 20 | 7 |
| NRD Compton | 6 | 6 | 1 | 136 | 58 | 27.20 | 149.45 | 0 | 1 | 17 | 4 |
| L Gregory | 6 | 4 | 2 | 39 | 20 | 19.50 | 125.80 | 0 | 0 | 3 | 1 |
| CR Jones | 4 | 4 | 0 | 56 | 28 | 14.00 | 98.24 | 0 | 0 | 7 | 0 |
| TD Groenewald | 6 | 2 | 0 | 22 | 17 | 11.00 | 137.50 | 0 | 0 | 4 | 0 |
| ME Trescothick | 10 | 9 | 0 | 89 | 46 | 9.88 | 105.95 | 0 | 0 | 14 | 0 |
| C Overton | 10 | 5 | 1 | 35 | 15 | 8.75 | 87.50 | 0 | 0 | 2 | 0 |
| CAJ Meschede | 9 | 6 | 2 | 30 | 13* | 7.50 | 96.77 | 0 | 0 | 3 | 1 |
| JE Burke | 3 | 1 | 0 | 4 | 4 | 4.00 | 66.66 | 0 | 0 | 0 | 0 |
| MTC Waller | 12 | 2 | 1 | 2 | 1* | 2.00 | 50.00 | 0 | 0 | 0 | 0 |
| DP Nannes | 14 | 1 | 1 | 4 | 4* | - | 133.33 | 0 | 0 | 0 | 0 |
| GH Dockrell | 5 | - | - | - | - | - | - | - | - | - | - |
| JG Myburgh | 4 | - | - | - | - | - | - | - | - | - | - |

**Bowling**

| | Overs | Mdns | Runs | Wkts | BBI | Ave | Econ | SR | 4w | 5w |
|---|---|---|---|---|---|---|---|---|---|---|
| JG Myburgh | 2.0 | 0 | 12 | 0 | - | - | 6.00 | - | 0 | 0 |
| MTC Waller | 39.0 | 0 | 280 | 10 | 3/22 | 28.00 | 7.17 | 23.4 | 0 | 0 |
| TD Groenewald | 19.0 | 0 | 142 | 4 | 1/28 | 35.50 | 7.47 | 28.5 | 0 | 0 |
| DP Nannes | 46.3 | 0 | 373 | 24 | 5/31 | 15.54 | 8.02 | 11.6 | 1 | 1 |
| L Gregory | 15.0 | 0 | 121 | 6 | 2/28 | 20.16 | 8.06 | 15.0 | 0 | 0 |
| PD Trego | 19.0 | 0 | 156 | 6 | 2/18 | 26.00 | 8.21 | 19.0 | 0 | 0 |
| CAJ Meschede | 22.0 | 0 | 185 | 5 | 2/26 | 37.00 | 8.40 | 26.4 | 0 | 0 |
| AC Thomas | 38.1 | 0 | 322 | 13 | 3/34 | 24.76 | 8.43 | 17.6 | 0 | 0 |
| GH Dockrell | 15.0 | 0 | 145 | 4 | 2/31 | 36.25 | 9.66 | 22.5 | 0 | 0 |
| C Overton | 24.0 | 0 | 243 | 4 | 1/23 | 60.75 | 10.12 | 36.0 | 0 | 0 |

**Catches/Stumpings:**
8 Waller, 7 Kieswetter (inc 2st), 5 C Overton, Hildreth, Trescothick, 4 Trego, Thomas, 3 Myburgh, Dockrell, Jones, 2 Groenewald, Nannes, Gregory, Ingram, Petersen, 1 Meschede, Compton

# SURREY

**FORMED:** 1845
**GROUND:** The Kia Oval, London
**CAPTAIN:** Gareth Batty
**2014 RESULTS:** CC2: 5/9; RL50: 9/9 Group B; NWT20: Semi-finalists
**HONOURS:** Championship: (19) 1890, 1891, 1892, 1894, 1895, 1899, 1914, 1950, 1952, 1953, 1954, 1955, 1956, 1957, 1958, 1971, 1999, 2000, 2002; Gillette/NatWest/C&G/FP Trophy: 1982; Benson & Hedges Cup: (3) 1974, 1997, 2001; Pro40/National League/CB40/YB40/RL50: (2) 2003, 2011; Sunday League: 1996; Twenty20 Cup: 2003

## THE LOWDOWN

Aside from a semi-final appearance in the T20 Blast, Surrey spent much of 2014 underperforming. They were hindered by the early forced retirement of captain Graeme Smith at the end of May and never seemed to recover. Jason Roy provided the biggest ray of light. Labelled as a one-day specialist – he hit nine fifties in the T20 Blast – he also proved his four-day worth by scoring 1,042 runs at over 50. Young openers Rory Burns and Zafar Ansari didn't set the world alight but produced solid seasons – both finishing just shy of 1,000 runs – that suggested they have enough potential bubbling away to provide Surrey with a bright future. Hotly-tipped Dom Sibley had a season to forget but, at 19, has the talent to come back stronger. Stuart Meaker, Chris Tremlett and Jade Dernbach struggled with injury but had their moments and, if they can remain fit, pose a serious pace threat. Young quick Matt Dunn picked up 39 wickets but proved costly too often and will be looking to tighten up. They have also added to their fast-bowling stocks with the signing of David Balcombe from Hampshire. The stellar signing of Kumar Sangakkara and the announcement that Gareth Batty will captain means a young side will also have plenty of experience.

## HEAD COACH: GRAHAM FORD

Ford played just seven first-class matches in his native South Africa, but that hasn't held him back as a coach of distinction. After impressing with Natal – winning both domestic titles in 1996/97 – he went on to become assistant to national coach Bob Woolmer in 1999 before eventually replacing him in the top job after that year's World Cup. He has previous experience in county cricket with Kent, and also coached Sri Lanka before joining Surrey for the 2014 season.

# COUNTY CHAMPIONSHIP AVERAGES 2014

Batting

| | Mat | Inns | NO | Runs | HS | Ave | SR | 100 | 50 | 4s | 6s |
|---|---|---|---|---|---|---|---|---|---|---|---|
| JJ Roy | 16 | 23 | 3 | 1042 | 121* | 52.10 | 84.78 | 3 | 5 | 130 | 19 |
| ZS Ansari | 16 | 26 | 7 | 913 | 112 | 48.05 | 35.88 | 2 | 5 | 104 | 0 |
| GC Wilson | 15 | 20 | 4 | 750 | 160* | 46.87 | 57.25 | 1 | 5 | 100 | 5 |
| SM Davies | 16 | 23 | 0 | 937 | 174 | 40.73 | 62.55 | 2 | 5 | 130 | 0 |
| RJ Burns | 16 | 28 | 4 | 950 | 199 | 39.58 | 46.70 | 2 | 4 | 126 | 1 |
| VS Solanki | 10 | 16 | 1 | 567 | 143 | 37.80 | 59.62 | 1 | 5 | 80 | 3 |
| TM Dilshan | 3 | 5 | 0 | 185 | 69 | 37.00 | 78.72 | 0 | 2 | 30 | 0 |
| GC Smith | 5 | 8 | 0 | 263 | 103 | 32.87 | 63.83 | 1 | 1 | 34 | 0 |
| A Harinath | 5 | 9 | 1 | 250 | 63 | 31.25 | 40.19 | 0 | 2 | 25 | 2 |
| CT Tremlett | 10 | 11 | 2 | 273 | 90 | 30.33 | 48.66 | 0 | 2 | 25 | 11 |
| HM Amla | 4 | 4 | 0 | 118 | 71 | 29.50 | 71.95 | 0 | 1 | 18 | 0 |
| SC Meaker | 8 | 12 | 2 | 228 | 58 | 22.80 | 39.17 | 0 | 2 | 31 | 0 |
| KJ O'Brien | 1 | 1 | 0 | 17 | 17 | 17.00 | 43.58 | 0 | 0 | 3 | 0 |
| GJ Batty | 11 | 14 | 3 | 175 | 29 | 15.90 | 52.71 | 0 | 0 | 20 | 3 |
| A Kapil | 2 | 4 | 0 | 60 | 38 | 15.00 | 53.57 | 0 | 0 | 9 | 0 |
| MP Dunn | 12 | 10 | 5 | 57 | 31* | 11.40 | 22.80 | 0 | 0 | 9 | 0 |
| JW Dernbach | 9 | 10 | 3 | 76 | 24 | 10.85 | 54.67 | 0 | 0 | 9 | 2 |
| DP Sibley | 5 | 8 | 0 | 79 | 34 | 9.87 | 27.62 | 0 | 0 | 9 | 0 |
| TE Linley | 6 | 9 | 3 | 41 | 21* | 6.83 | 29.92 | 0 | 0 | 6 | 0 |
| TK Curran | 6 | 6 | 3 | 16 | 9* | 5.33 | 28.07 | 0 | 0 | 1 | 0 |

Bowling

| | Overs | Mdns | Runs | Wkts | BBI | BBM | Ave | Econ | SR | 5w | 10w |
|---|---|---|---|---|---|---|---|---|---|---|---|
| A Harinath | 2.0 | 1 | 1 | 2 | 2/1 | 2/1 | 0.50 | 0.50 | 6.0 | 0 | 0 |
| VS Solanki | 7.1 | 1 | 20 | 2 | 2/20 | 2/20 | 10.00 | 2.79 | 21.5 | 0 | 0 |
| A Kapil | 12.2 | 3 | 52 | 4 | 2/23 | 4/52 | 13.00 | 4.21 | 18.5 | 0 | 0 |
| TM Dilshan | 15.0 | 3 | 29 | 2 | 2/29 | 2/29 | 14.50 | 1.93 | 45.0 | 0 | 0 |
| RJ Burns | 6.0 | 1 | 18 | 1 | 1/18 | 1/18 | 18.00 | 3.00 | 36.0 | 0 | 0 |
| GJ Batty | 400.3 | 113 | 915 | 39 | 8/68 | 8/68 | 23.46 | 2.28 | 61.6 | 1 | 0 |
| TK Curran | 143.4 | 25 | 477 | 16 | 5/51 | 5/89 | 29.81 | 3.32 | 53.8 | 1 | 0 |
| SC Meaker | 273.4 | 35 | 1028 | 32 | 7/90 | 11/196 | 32.12 | 3.75 | 51.3 | 1 | 1 |
| CT Tremlett | 260.1 | 48 | 811 | 25 | 6/59 | 7/95 | 32.44 | 3.11 | 62.4 | 2 | 0 |
| TE Linley | 177.4 | 36 | 558 | 16 | 4/79 | 4/129 | 34.87 | 3.14 | 66.6 | 0 | 0 |
| ZS Ansari | 294.5 | 51 | 884 | 24 | 5/93 | 6/115 | 36.83 | 2.99 | 73.7 | 1 | 0 |
| MP Dunn | 374.2 | 71 | 1444 | 39 | 5/48 | 6/105 | 37.02 | 3.85 | 57.5 | 2 | 0 |
| JW Dernbach | 256.3 | 49 | 900 | 23 | 4/72 | 6/126 | 39.13 | 3.50 | 66.9 | 0 | 0 |
| JJ Roy | 78.0 | 9 | 283 | 6 | 3/9 | 4/47 | 47.16 | 3.62 | 78.0 | 0 | 0 |
| DP Sibley | 16.4 | 2 | 60 | 1 | 1/41 | 1/42 | 60.00 | 3.60 | 100.0 | 0 | 0 |
| HM Amla | 1.0 | 0 | 2 | 0 | - | - | - | 2.00 | - | 0 | 0 |
| KJ O'Brien | 3.0 | 0 | 19 | 0 | - | - | - | 6.33 | - | 0 | 0 |

**Catches/Stumpings:**
37 Wilson (inc 2st), 22 Burns, 18 Roy, 10 Solanki, Smith, 9 Davies, 6 Ansari, 5 Batty, Sibley, Amla, 4 Dunn, 2 Harinath, Tremlett, Dernbach, 1 Kapil, Dilshan, Curran, Meaker, Linley

# ROYAL LONDON ONE-DAY CUP AVERAGES 2014

Batting

| | Mat | Inns | NO | Runs | HS | Ave | SR | 100 | 50 | 4s | 6s |
|---|---|---|---|---|---|---|---|---|---|---|---|
| A Kapil | 3 | 3 | 1 | 104 | 59 | 52.00 | 88.13 | 0 | 1 | 10 | 1 |
| TM Dilshan | 6 | 6 | 0 | 276 | 115 | 46.00 | 87.34 | 1 | 2 | 30 | 0 |
| ZS Ansari | 4 | 4 | 2 | 86 | 28 | 43.00 | 106.17 | 0 | 0 | 4 | 2 |
| SM Davies | 7 | 7 | 0 | 287 | 58 | 41.00 | 106.69 | 0 | 4 | 42 | 2 |
| Azhar Mahmood | 6 | 6 | 0 | 224 | 57 | 37.33 | 104.67 | 0 | 2 | 24 | 5 |
| RJ Burns | 7 | 7 | 0 | 216 | 87 | 30.85 | 83.39 | 0 | 1 | 19 | 2 |
| VS Solanki | 7 | 7 | 0 | 197 | 83 | 28.14 | 69.36 | 0 | 2 | 19 | 4 |
| JJ Roy | 2 | 2 | 0 | 44 | 34 | 22.00 | 97.77 | 0 | 0 | 8 | 0 |
| RJ Peterson | 1 | 1 | 0 | 17 | 17 | 17.00 | 100.00 | 0 | 0 | 2 | 0 |
| A Harinath | 3 | 3 | 1 | 31 | 12 | 15.50 | 67.39 | 0 | 0 | 2 | 0 |
| GC Wilson | 7 | 7 | 0 | 106 | 45 | 15.14 | 62.72 | 0 | 0 | 11 | 1 |
| TE Linley | 3 | 3 | 2 | 11 | 7* | 11.00 | 84.61 | 0 | 0 | 1 | 0 |
| GJ Batty | 4 | 3 | 0 | 27 | 13 | 9.00 | 79.41 | 0 | 0 | 1 | 0 |
| CT Tremlett | 2 | 2 | 0 | 13 | 12 | 6.50 | 108.33 | 0 | 0 | 1 | 1 |
| SC Meaker | 5 | 3 | 1 | 9 | 5* | 4.50 | 60.00 | 0 | 0 | 0 | 0 |
| FOE van den Bergh | 3 | 1 | 1 | 29 | 29* | - | 107.40 | 0 | 0 | 2 | 1 |
| GA Edwards | 4 | 2 | 2 | 9 | 8* | - | 128.57 | 0 | 0 | 1 | 0 |
| DP Sibley | 1 | 1 | 1 | 4 | 4* | - | 40.00 | 0 | 0 | 0 | 0 |
| JW Dernbach | 1 | - | - | - | - | - | - | - | - | - | - |
| JR Winslade | 1 | - | - | - | - | - | - | - | - | - | - |

Bowling

| | Overs | Mdns | Runs | Wkts | BBI | Ave | Econ | SR | 4w | 5w |
|---|---|---|---|---|---|---|---|---|---|---|
| JW Dernbach | 9.0 | 0 | 37 | 1 | 1/37 | 37.00 | 4.11 | 54.0 | 0 | 0 |
| GJ Batty | 36.0 | 2 | 150 | 2 | 1/33 | 75.00 | 4.16 | 108.0 | 0 | 0 |
| RJ Peterson | 10.0 | 0 | 45 | 2 | 2/45 | 22.50 | 4.50 | 30.0 | 0 | 0 |
| FOE van den Bergh | 26.0 | 0 | 122 | 0 | - | - | 4.69 | - | 0 | 0 |
| CT Tremlett | 17.0 | 0 | 83 | 5 | 4/38 | 16.60 | 4.88 | 20.4 | 1 | 0 |
| A Harinath | 3.0 | 0 | 16 | 0 | - | - | 5.33 | - | 0 | 0 |
| ZS Ansari | 30.5 | 1 | 176 | 5 | 3/38 | 35.20 | 5.70 | 37.0 | 0 | 0 |
| Azhar Mahmood | 43.0 | 5 | 247 | 7 | 2/30 | 35.28 | 5.74 | 36.8 | 0 | 0 |
| TM Dilshan | 33.0 | 0 | 213 | 2 | 1/34 | 106.50 | 6.45 | 99.0 | 0 | 0 |
| TE Linley | 23.1 | 0 | 169 | 6 | 3/68 | 28.16 | 7.29 | 23.1 | 0 | 0 |
| GA Edwards | 21.0 | 0 | 157 | 1 | 1/29 | 157.00 | 7.47 | 126.0 | 0 | 0 |
| SC Meaker | 43.3 | 1 | 353 | 8 | 4/78 | 44.12 | 8.11 | 32.6 | 1 | 0 |
| JR Winslade | 6.3 | 0 | 61 | 1 | 1/61 | 61.00 | 9.38 | 39.0 | 0 | 0 |

**Catches/Stumpings:**
8 Wilson (inc 1st), 5 Ansari, 4 Burns, Solanki, 3 Edwards, 2 Meaker, 1 Mahmood, Dilshan, Linley, Sibley

# NATWEST T20 BLAST AVERAGES 2014

## Batting

| | Mat | Inns | NO | Runs | HS | Ave | SR | 100 | 50 | 4s | 6s |
|---|---|---|---|---|---|---|---|---|---|---|---|
| HM Amla | 4 | 4 | 1 | 164 | 61* | 54.66 | 113.10 | 0 | 2 | 18 | 1 |
| JJ Roy | 15 | 15 | 1 | 677 | 81* | 48.35 | 157.07 | 0 | 9 | 77 | 27 |
| GC Wilson | 16 | 15 | 3 | 368 | 63* | 30.66 | 121.05 | 0 | 2 | 37 | 4 |
| TM Dilshan | 7 | 7 | 0 | 173 | 46 | 24.71 | 127.20 | 0 | 0 | 21 | 3 |
| Azhar Mahmood | 16 | 13 | 4 | 208 | 36* | 23.11 | 130.00 | 0 | 0 | 20 | 5 |
| KP Pietersen | 13 | 12 | 2 | 225 | 39 | 22.50 | 107.14 | 0 | 0 | 23 | 5 |
| ZS Ansari | 15 | 7 | 5 | 38 | 15* | 19.00 | 108.57 | 0 | 0 | 3 | 1 |
| KJ O'Brien | 10 | 7 | 2 | 91 | 40* | 18.20 | 126.38 | 0 | 0 | 6 | 4 |
| SM Davies | 11 | 10 | 0 | 173 | 39 | 17.30 | 119.31 | 0 | 0 | 19 | 1 |
| RJ Peterson | 16 | 10 | 4 | 99 | 24* | 16.50 | 130.26 | 0 | 0 | 10 | 3 |
| GC Smith | 2 | 2 | 0 | 27 | 20 | 13.50 | 100.00 | 0 | 0 | 3 | 1 |
| RJ Burns | 4 | 4 | 1 | 31 | 28 | 10.33 | 134.78 | 0 | 0 | 2 | 1 |
| GJ Batty | 14 | 5 | 3 | 17 | 7 | 8.50 | 80.95 | 0 | 0 | 1 | 0 |
| JW Dernbach | 9 | 1 | 1 | 24 | 24* | - | 171.42 | 0 | 0 | 3 | 0 |
| VS Solanki | 1 | 1 | 1 | 13 | 13* | - | 108.33 | 0 | 0 | 1 | 0 |
| CT Tremlett | 2 | 1 | 1 | 11 | 11* | - | 137.50 | 0 | 0 | 1 | 0 |
| A Kapil | 2 | 1 | 1 | 2 | 2* | - | 200.00 | 0 | 0 | 0 | 0 |
| SC Meaker | 2 | 1 | 1 | 1 | 1* | - | 100.00 | 0 | 0 | 0 | 0 |
| TK Curran | 9 | - | - | - | - | - | - | - | - | - | - |
| MP Dunn | 7 | - | - | - | - | - | - | - | - | - | - |
| GA Edwards | 1 | - | - | - | - | - | - | - | - | - | - |

## Bowling

| | Overs | Mdns | Runs | Wkts | BBI | Ave | Econ | SR | 4w | 5w |
|---|---|---|---|---|---|---|---|---|---|---|
| TM Dilshan | 20.0 | 0 | 119 | 5 | 2/21 | 23.80 | 5.95 | 24.0 | 0 | 0 |
| CT Tremlett | 3.0 | 0 | 18 | 2 | 1/5 | 9.00 | 6.00 | 9.0 | 0 | 0 |
| GA Edwards | 2.0 | 0 | 12 | 0 | - | - | 6.00 | - | 0 | 0 |
| GJ Batty | 51.0 | 0 | 361 | 12 | 2/26 | 30.08 | 7.07 | 25.5 | 0 | 0 |
| RJ Peterson | 47.0 | 0 | 352 | 10 | 2/12 | 35.20 | 7.48 | 28.2 | 0 | 0 |
| KJ O'Brien | 21.0 | 0 | 158 | 6 | 2/22 | 26.33 | 7.52 | 21.0 | 0 | 0 |
| Azhar Mahmood | 61.2 | 1 | 467 | 17 | 3/38 | 27.47 | 7.61 | 21.6 | 0 | 0 |
| TK Curran | 25.0 | 0 | 193 | 9 | 3/23 | 21.44 | 7.72 | 16.6 | 0 | 0 |
| ZS Ansari | 23.0 | 0 | 184 | 8 | 3/27 | 23.00 | 8.00 | 17.2 | 0 | 0 |
| SC Meaker | 7.0 | 0 | 60 | 4 | 4/30 | 15.00 | 8.57 | 10.5 | 1 | 0 |
| MP Dunn | 25.0 | 0 | 215 | 13 | 3/8 | 16.53 | 8.60 | 11.5 | 0 | 0 |
| JW Dernbach | 30.0 | 0 | 260 | 9 | 2/22 | 28.88 | 8.66 | 20.0 | 0 | 0 |
| A Kapil | 1.0 | 0 | 11 | 1 | 1/11 | 11.00 | 11.00 | 6.0 | 0 | 0 |
| JJ Roy | 1.0 | 0 | 16 | 0 | - | - | 16.00 | - | 0 | 0 |

**Catches/Stumpings:**
13 Wilson (inc 4st), 6 O'Brien, 5 Ansari, Roy, 4 Batty, Pietersen, 3 Peterson, Mahmood, Davies, 2 Dunn, Smith, 1 Burns (1st), Curran, Dernbach, Kapil

# SUSSEX

**FORMED:** 1839
**HOME GROUND:** The BrightonandHoveJobs.com County Ground, Hove
**ONE-DAY NAME:** Sussex Sharks
**CAPTAIN:** Ed Joyce (Championship and RL50), Luke Wright (NWT20)
**2014 RESULTS:** CC1: 3/9; RL50: 8/9 Group B; NWT20: 7/9 South Division
**HONOURS:** Championship: (3) 2003, 2006, 2007; Gillette/NatWest/C&G/FP Trophy: (5) 1963, 1964, 1978, 1986, 2006; Pro40/National League/CB40/YB40/RL50: (2) 2008, 2009; Sunday League: 1982; Twenty20 Cup: 2009

## THE LOWDOWN

Sussex's third-place Championship finish went some way to making up for a surprisingly poor showing in the two one-day tournaments. Captain Ed Joyce's seven Championship centuries was the most by anyone across both divisions while only Mark Footitt took more than Steve Magoffin's 72 wickets. Luke Wright recovered his four-day form with 933 runs at 51.83, as well as inflicting his customary T20 damage by scoring 601 runs. Coach Mark Robinson once again got the most out of a rather middle-of-the-road squad in the Championship. Sussex fans will hope young batsmen Luke Wells and Matt Machan will kick on after disappointing seasons while leg-spinner Will Beer, who impressed in the T20 Blast with 13 wickets, made just one Championship appearance. Matt Prior, depending on his recovery from injury, could be available for much of the season and, with England enjoying plenty of options among fast bowlers, Sussex may also see more of Chris Jordan. The pace attack is boosted by Ajmal Shahzad, who makes Sussex his fourth county after moving on from Nottinghamshire. Rory Hamilton-Brown has been forced to retire due to a wrist injury.

## HEAD COACH: MARK ROBINSON

A seam bowler who had spells with Northamptonshire, Yorkshire and Sussex, Robinson has established himself as one of English cricket's brightest coaches. He has coached Sussex since the start of the 2006 season, in which time he has led them to six trophies. His coaching credentials have been recognised by the England management, who asked him to coach England Lions on their winter tours in 2013/14 and 2014/15.



www.sussexcricket.co.uk / tel: 0844 264 0202

# COUNTY CHAMPIONSHIP AVERAGES 2014

Batting

| | Mat | Inns | NO | Runs | HS | Ave | SR | 100 | 50 | 4s | 6s |
|---|---|---|---|---|---|---|---|---|---|---|---|
| MJ Prior | 2 | 3 | 1 | 174 | 125 | 87.00 | 72.50 | 1 | 0 | 26 | 1 |
| EC Joyce | 14 | 23 | 2 | 1398 | 164* | 66.57 | 60.15 | 7 | 3 | 173 | 8 |
| LJ Wright | 12 | 21 | 3 | 933 | 189 | 51.83 | 65.84 | 3 | 3 | 128 | 7 |
| C Cachopa | 5 | 10 | 1 | 441 | 84 | 49.00 | 55.05 | 0 | 5 | 69 | 5 |
| CD Nash | 12 | 22 | 0 | 867 | 178 | 39.40 | 62.87 | 1 | 6 | 135 | 0 |
| LWP Wells | 15 | 27 | 1 | 942 | 162 | 36.23 | 43.93 | 1 | 7 | 127 | 4 |
| JC Tredwell | 5 | 8 | 1 | 218 | 50* | 31.14 | 54.63 | 0 | 1 | 35 | 0 |
| MH Yardy | 8 | 13 | 0 | 361 | 139 | 27.76 | 50.20 | 1 | 1 | 36 | 0 |
| BC Brown | 15 | 23 | 2 | 579 | 163 | 27.57 | 53.36 | 1 | 0 | 68 | 3 |
| MW Machan | 7 | 12 | 3 | 218 | 44* | 24.22 | 49.20 | 0 | 0 | 30 | 0 |
| Ashar Zaidi | 9 | 11 | 0 | 266 | 88 | 24.18 | 56.59 | 0 | 2 | 34 | 2 |
| SJ Magoffin | 15 | 21 | 10 | 245 | 51 | 22.27 | 45.11 | 0 | 1 | 28 | 0 |
| RJ Hamilton-Brown | 7 | 14 | 1 | 265 | 62 | 20.38 | 50.00 | 0 | 2 | 30 | 2 |
| J Lewis | 8 | 10 | 1 | 174 | 61 | 19.33 | 62.58 | 0 | 1 | 24 | 1 |
| WAT Beer | 1 | 2 | 0 | 37 | 29 | 18.50 | 35.57 | 0 | 0 | 6 | 0 |
| SA Piolet | 6 | 10 | 0 | 180 | 32 | 18.00 | 38.87 | 0 | 0 | 18 | 1 |
| JE Anyon | 7 | 9 | 0 | 155 | 50 | 17.22 | 39.14 | 0 | 1 | 21 | 0 |
| CJ Jordan | 5 | 8 | 1 | 109 | 41 | 15.57 | 41.92 | 0 | 0 | 14 | 0 |
| LJ Hatchett | 8 | 11 | 5 | 62 | 20* | 10.33 | 24.89 | 0 | 0 | 5 | 0 |
| ME Hobden | 3 | 4 | 1 | 4 | 4 | 1.33 | 14.28 | 0 | 0 | 1 | 0 |
| CJ Liddle | 1 | 2 | 1 | 0 | 0* | 0.00 | 0.00 | 0 | 0 | 0 | 0 |

Bowling

| | Overs | Mdns | Runs | Wkts | BBI | BBM | Ave | Econ | SR | 5w | 10w |
|---|---|---|---|---|---|---|---|---|---|---|---|
| RJ Hamilton-Brown | 6.5 | 0 | 30 | 2 | 2/5 | 2/5 | 15.00 | 4.39 | 20.5 | 0 | 0 |
| SJ Magoffin | 539.0 | 144 | 1405 | 72 | 6/60 | 8/40 | 19.51 | 2.60 | 44.9 | 4 | 0 |
| CJ Jordan | 196.0 | 32 | 668 | 25 | 5/76 | 6/136 | 26.72 | 3.40 | 47.0 | 1 | 0 |
| ME Hobden | 68.0 | 4 | 342 | 12 | 3/49 | 5/83 | 28.50 | 5.02 | 34.0 | 0 | 0 |
| Ashar Zaidi | 189.2 | 24 | 579 | 19 | 3/36 | 5/124 | 30.47 | 3.05 | 59.7 | 0 | 0 |
| J Lewis | 204.5 | 58 | 546 | 17 | 4/34 | 6/55 | 32.11 | 2.66 | 72.2 | 0 | 0 |
| LWP Wells | 60.4 | 6 | 227 | 6 | 3/38 | 3/40 | 37.83 | 3.74 | 60.6 | 0 | 0 |
| JC Tredwell | 170.0 | 35 | 518 | 12 | 4/7 | 5/88 | 43.16 | 3.04 | 85.0 | 0 | 0 |
| JE Anyon | 159.2 | 23 | 706 | 16 | 3/67 | 4/93 | 44.12 | 4.43 | 59.7 | 0 | 0 |
| LJ Hatchett | 246.5 | 32 | 974 | 22 | 5/113 | 6/188 | 44.27 | 3.94 | 67.3 | 1 | 0 |
| LJ Wright | 51.0 | 6 | 170 | 3 | 2/31 | 2/31 | 56.66 | 3.33 | 102.0 | 0 | 0 |
| SA Piolet | 78.1 | 9 | 289 | 5 | 2/61 | 3/82 | 57.80 | 3.69 | 93.8 | 0 | 0 |
| CD Nash | 85.3 | 12 | 309 | 4 | 2/91 | 2/114 | 77.25 | 3.61 | 128.2 | 0 | 0 |
| BC Brown | 4.0 | 1 | 14 | 0 | - | - | - | 3.50 | - | 0 | 0 |
| CJ Liddle | 23.0 | 3 | 70 | 0 | - | - | - | 3.04 | - | 0 | 0 |
| WAT Beer | 13.0 | 1 | 76 | 0 | - | - | - | 5.84 | - | 0 | 0 |

**Catches/Stumpings:**
53 Brown (inc 4st), 11 Wells, Joyce, Yardy, 10 Jordan, 7 Tredwell, 6 Hatchett, Nash, 5 Prior, 4 Hamilton-Brown, Lewis, Piolet, 3 Zaidi, Machan, 2 Wright, Cachopa, 1 Anyon

# ROYAL LONDON ONE-DAY CUP AVERAGES 2014

## Batting

| | Mat | Inns | NO | Runs | HS | Ave | SR | 100 | 50 | 4s | 6s |
|---|---|---|---|---|---|---|---|---|---|---|---|
| EC Joyce | 8 | 7 | 1 | 320 | 59 | 53.33 | 83.55 | 0 | 2 | 36 | 3 |
| LJ Wright | 6 | 6 | 0 | 292 | 127 | 48.66 | 110.60 | 1 | 1 | 40 | 6 |
| MW Machan | 8 | 8 | 2 | 232 | 47* | 38.66 | 86.24 | 0 | 0 | 21 | 3 |
| Yasir Arafat | 7 | 5 | 1 | 125 | 55* | 31.25 | 93.98 | 0 | 1 | 14 | 0 |
| SA Piolet | 7 | 6 | 2 | 118 | 63* | 29.50 | 88.05 | 0 | 1 | 14 | 1 |
| C Cachopa | 8 | 8 | 0 | 214 | 58 | 26.75 | 78.96 | 0 | 1 | 19 | 7 |
| WAT Beer | 8 | 6 | 2 | 99 | 45* | 24.75 | 105.31 | 0 | 0 | 11 | 2 |
| CD Nash | 8 | 8 | 0 | 183 | 65 | 22.87 | 79.22 | 0 | 1 | 21 | 5 |
| LWP Wells | 2 | 2 | 0 | 45 | 23 | 22.50 | 56.25 | 0 | 0 | 3 | 0 |
| BC Brown | 8 | 6 | 0 | 92 | 34 | 15.33 | 78.63 | 0 | 0 | 6 | 2 |
| Ashar Zaidi | 1 | 1 | 0 | 11 | 11 | 11.00 | 64.70 | 0 | 0 | 2 | 0 |
| LJ Hatchett | 8 | 3 | 2 | 8 | 5 | 8.00 | 44.44 | 0 | 0 | 0 | 0 |
| CJ Liddle | 6 | 4 | 2 | 15 | 8* | 7.50 | 88.23 | 0 | 0 | 2 | 0 |
| HZ Finch | 1 | 1 | 1 | 92 | 92* | - | 158.62 | 0 | 1 | 12 | 2 |
| SJ Magoffin | 1 | 1 | 1 | 2 | 2* | - | 100.00 | 0 | 0 | 0 | 0 |
| FJ Hudson-Prentice | 1 | - | - | - | - | - | - | - | - | - | - |

## Bowling

| | Overs | Mdns | Runs | Wkts | BBI | Ave | Econ | SR | 4w | 5w |
|---|---|---|---|---|---|---|---|---|---|---|
| SJ Magoffin | 7.0 | 0 | 31 | 0 | - | - | 4.42 | - | 0 | 0 |
| Ashar Zaidi | 7.0 | 0 | 33 | 0 | - | - | 4.71 | - | 0 | 0 |
| SA Piolet | 58.0 | 0 | 277 | 7 | 2/35 | 39.57 | 4.77 | 49.7 | 0 | 0 |
| Yasir Arafat | 60.5 | 3 | 309 | 17 | 5/36 | 18.17 | 5.07 | 21.4 | 1 | 1 |
| LJ Hatchett | 70.0 | 3 | 391 | 9 | 3/44 | 43.44 | 5.58 | 46.6 | 0 | 0 |
| WAT Beer | 58.0 | 0 | 343 | 7 | 3/60 | 49.00 | 5.91 | 49.7 | 0 | 0 |
| CJ Liddle | 46.0 | 0 | 306 | 6 | 3/39 | 51.00 | 6.65 | 46.0 | 0 | 0 |
| CD Nash | 27.0 | 0 | 186 | 0 | - | - | 6.88 | - | 0 | 0 |
| MW Machan | 7.4 | 0 | 60 | 0 | - | - | 7.82 | - | 0 | 0 |
| FJ Hudson-Prentice | 6.0 | 0 | 51 | 0 | - | - | 8.50 | - | 0 | 0 |

**Catches/Stumpings:**
9 Brown, 5 Machan, 4 Cachopa, Wright, 3 Hatchett, 2 Yasir Arafat, Beer, Nash, 1 Piolet

# NATWEST T20 BLAST AVERAGES 2014

Batting

| | Mat | Inns | NO | Runs | HS | Ave | SR | 100 | 50 | 4s | 6s |
|---|---|---|---|---|---|---|---|---|---|---|---|
| LJ Wright | 14 | 14 | 2 | 601 | 153* | 50.08 | 162.43 | 2 | 3 | 56 | 28 |
| MJ Prior | 1 | 1 | 0 | 39 | 39 | 39.00 | 162.50 | 0 | 0 | 5 | 1 |
| EC Joyce | 7 | 7 | 0 | 186 | 56 | 26.57 | 112.72 | 0 | 1 | 16 | 3 |
| CJ Jordan | 3 | 3 | 0 | 78 | 37 | 26.00 | 127.86 | 0 | 0 | 6 | 2 |
| RJ Hamilton-Brown | 9 | 9 | 0 | 195 | 49 | 21.66 | 122.64 | 0 | 0 | 13 | 10 |
| CD Nash | 12 | 12 | 1 | 209 | 74* | 19.00 | 134.83 | 0 | 1 | 19 | 7 |
| MW Machan | 13 | 13 | 2 | 206 | 41* | 18.72 | 104.04 | 0 | 0 | 16 | 3 |
| BC Brown | 14 | 13 | 3 | 177 | 33* | 17.70 | 133.08 | 0 | 0 | 12 | 7 |
| WAT Beer | 12 | 9 | 3 | 98 | 37 | 16.33 | 163.33 | 0 | 0 | 10 | 5 |
| HZ Finch | 4 | 4 | 0 | 61 | 22 | 15.25 | 105.17 | 0 | 0 | 7 | 0 |
| C Cachopa | 4 | 4 | 0 | 49 | 24 | 12.25 | 122.50 | 0 | 0 | 6 | 1 |
| Yasir Arafat | 12 | 9 | 3 | 71 | 36* | 11.83 | 136.53 | 0 | 0 | 8 | 1 |
| Ashar Zaidi | 5 | 4 | 1 | 35 | 19 | 11.66 | 94.59 | 0 | 0 | 1 | 0 |
| SA Piolet | 13 | 8 | 3 | 45 | 25 | 9.00 | 115.38 | 0 | 0 | 5 | 1 |
| MH Yardy | 4 | 3 | 1 | 18 | 12 | 9.00 | 90.00 | 0 | 0 | 2 | 0 |
| SJ Magoffin | 2 | 1 | 0 | 9 | 9 | 9.00 | 81.81 | 0 | 0 | 0 | 0 |
| CJ Liddle | 9 | 4 | 2 | 9 | 4* | 4.50 | 100.00 | 0 | 0 | 1 | 0 |
| LWP Wells | 3 | 3 | 0 | 4 | 3 | 1.33 | 40.00 | 0 | 0 | 0 | 0 |
| JE Anyon | 3 | 1 | 0 | 0 | 0 | 0.00 | 0.00 | 0 | 0 | 0 | 0 |
| LJ Hatchett | 8 | 3 | 2 | 0 | 0* | 0.00 | 0.00 | 0 | 0 | 0 | 0 |
| ME Hobden | 1 | - | - | - | - | - | - | - | - | - | - |
| J Lewis | 1 | - | - | - | - | - | - | - | - | - | - |

Bowling

| | Overs | Mdns | Runs | Wkts | BBI | Ave | Econ | SR | 4w | 5w |
|---|---|---|---|---|---|---|---|---|---|---|
| RJ Hamilton-Brown | 3.0 | 0 | 19 | 1 | 1/12 | 19.00 | 6.33 | 18.0 | 0 | 0 |
| JE Anyon | 10.0 | 0 | 67 | 4 | 2/23 | 16.75 | 6.70 | 15.0 | 0 | 0 |
| WAT Beer | 37.3 | 0 | 253 | 13 | 3/14 | 19.46 | 6.74 | 17.3 | 0 | 0 |
| CD Nash | 22.0 | 0 | 162 | 6 | 1/14 | 27.00 | 7.36 | 22.0 | 0 | 0 |
| MH Yardy | 13.2 | 0 | 100 | 3 | 1/19 | 33.33 | 7.50 | 26.6 | 0 | 0 |
| SA Piolet | 46.0 | 0 | 349 | 15 | 3/14 | 23.26 | 7.58 | 18.4 | 0 | 0 |
| SJ Magoffin | 8.0 | 0 | 62 | 1 | 1/26 | 62.00 | 7.75 | 48.0 | 0 | 0 |
| Yasir Arafat | 45.4 | 1 | 355 | 15 | 3/32 | 23.66 | 7.77 | 18.2 | 0 | 0 |
| CJ Jordan | 11.0 | 0 | 94 | 3 | 1/25 | 31.33 | 8.54 | 22.0 | 0 | 0 |
| LJ Hatchett | 27.5 | 0 | 249 | 11 | 3/23 | 22.63 | 8.94 | 15.1 | 0 | 0 |
| J Lewis | 4.0 | 0 | 36 | 0 | - | - | 9.00 | - | 0 | 0 |
| CJ Liddle | 32.4 | 0 | 305 | 5 | 1/31 | 61.00 | 9.33 | 39.2 | 0 | 0 |
| Ashar Zaidi | 6.0 | 0 | 60 | 3 | 3/32 | 20.00 | 10.00 | 12.0 | 0 | 0 |
| ME Hobden | 2.0 | 0 | 36 | 0 | - | - | 18.00 | - | 0 | 0 |

**Catches/Stumpings:**

9 Machan, 6 Hamilton-Brown, 5 Beer, Nash, Wright, 4 Piolet, Brown, Joyce, 3 Jordan, 2 Cachopa, Prior, 1 Magoffin, Yasir Arafat, Finch, Wells

# WARWICKSHIRE

**FORMED:** 1882
**HOME GROUND:** Edgbaston Stadium
**T20 BLAST NAME:** Birmingham Bears
**CAPTAIN:** Varun Chopra
**2014 RESULTS:** CC1: 2/9; RL50: Finalists; NWT20: Winners
**HONOURS:** Championship: (7) 1911, 1951, 1972, 1994, 1995, 2004, 2012; Gillette/NatWest/C&G/FP Trophy: (5) 1966, 1968, 1989, 1993, 1995; Benson & Hedges Cup: (2) 1994, 2002; Pro40/National League/CB40/YB40/RL50: 2010; Sunday League: (3) 1980, 1994, 1997; Twenty20 Cup: 2014

## THE LOWDOWN

Twenty years after securing a famous treble, Warwickshire almost repeated the trick. In the end they had to settle for one trophy – a first T20 title – and two runners-up slots. Varun Chopra looked like a natural leader after the enforced retirement of Jim Troughton and has been appointed captain permanently. Warwickshire boasted the top-rated player in the MVP rankings, with Jeetan Patel taking over 100 wickets across all formats and regularly excelling on flat wickets. He has also improved his batting, often offering vital lower-order runs. Rikki Clarke also developed into one of the county circuit's most consistent allrounders and remains one of the game's finest slip-catchers, while Keith Barker picked up another 50 wickets. Whether Warwickshire can go a step further in the Championship this season may depend on Jonathan Trott. If he remains in the England reckoning then Warwickshire could be short of runs, as they occasionally were in 2014 – none of their batsmen passed four figures. Their highest run-scorer was Sam Hain, who is starting to get tongues wagging. He turns 20 this summer and, after being brought up in Australia by British parents, has confirmed his allegiance to England. He hit four centuries – including a double against Northamptonshire – to establish himself as one of England's hottest prospects.

## DIRECTOR OF CRICKET: DOUGIE BROWN

An underrated allrounder, Brown played for both England and Scotland. His averages were the right way round – with 30 as a batsman and 28 as a bowler – and he was famous for his never-say-die attitude. After a stint as assistant coach at Warwickshire from 2008, Brown stepped up to director of cricket after Ashley Giles' departure in 2013.

# COUNTY CHAMPIONSHIP AVERAGES 2014

Batting

| | Mat | Inns | NO | Runs | HS | Ave | SR | 100 | 50 | 4s | 6s |
|---|---|---|---|---|---|---|---|---|---|---|---|
| IR Bell | 4 | 8 | 1 | 506 | 189* | 72.28 | 58.29 | 2 | 2 | 55 | 7 |
| SR Hain | 12 | 18 | 2 | 823 | 208 | 51.43 | 47.29 | 4 | 1 | 95 | 3 |
| IJL Trott | 8 | 13 | 0 | 620 | 164 | 47.69 | 55.65 | 3 | 1 | 92 | 1 |
| WTS Porterfield | 14 | 23 | 1 | 778 | 118 | 35.36 | 44.68 | 1 | 5 | 107 | 2 |
| R Clarke | 12 | 18 | 2 | 550 | 94 | 34.37 | 63.58 | 0 | 5 | 82 | 4 |
| V Chopra | 16 | 25 | 2 | 785 | 160 | 34.13 | 50.51 | 2 | 4 | 102 | 1 |
| JO Troughton | 2 | 3 | 0 | 101 | 69 | 33.66 | 61.21 | 0 | 1 | 14 | 1 |
| IJ Westwood | 8 | 11 | 0 | 370 | 129 | 33.63 | 46.19 | 1 | 1 | 53 | 0 |
| TR Ambrose | 15 | 24 | 2 | 712 | 167 | 32.36 | 53.37 | 1 | 4 | 100 | 1 |
| JS Patel | 16 | 20 | 3 | 510 | 105 | 30.00 | 80.31 | 1 | 2 | 57 | 11 |
| KHD Barker | 15 | 20 | 5 | 444 | 102* | 29.60 | 62.97 | 1 | 1 | 59 | 1 |
| PJ McKay | 1 | 1 | 0 | 28 | 28 | 28.00 | 35.44 | 0 | 0 | 3 | 0 |
| CR Woakes | 9 | 16 | 2 | 317 | 91 | 22.64 | 48.69 | 0 | 1 | 47 | 0 |
| CJC Wright | 11 | 15 | 3 | 221 | 65 | 18.41 | 60.71 | 0 | 2 | 37 | 0 |
| OJ Hannon-Dalby | 8 | 9 | 4 | 73 | 40 | 14.60 | 44.78 | 0 | 0 | 10 | 1 |
| A Javid | 6 | 10 | 2 | 108 | 28 | 13.50 | 29.75 | 0 | 0 | 8 | 0 |
| RA Jones | 3 | 5 | 0 | 57 | 35 | 11.40 | 38.77 | 0 | 0 | 4 | 2 |
| LJ Evans | 7 | 12 | 0 | 127 | 24 | 10.58 | 32.90 | 0 | 0 | 19 | 0 |
| WB Rankin | 7 | 8 | 3 | 35 | 12 | 7.00 | 41.17 | 0 | 0 | 5 | 0 |
| RO Gordon | 2 | 1 | 1 | 14 | 14* | - | 30.43 | 0 | 0 | 2 | 0 |

Bowling

| | Overs | Mdns | Runs | Wkts | BBI | BBM | Ave | Econ | SR | 5w | 10w |
|---|---|---|---|---|---|---|---|---|---|---|---|
| WB Rankin | 165.4 | 31 | 548 | 28 | 3/16 | 6/115 | 19.57 | 3.30 | 35.5 | 0 | 0 |
| RO Gordon | 38.2 | 2 | 125 | 6 | 4/53 | 4/80 | 20.83 | 3.26 | 38.3 | 0 | 0 |
| OJ Hannon-Dalby | 161.3 | 28 | 491 | 22 | 4/57 | 5/92 | 22.31 | 3.04 | 44.0 | 0 | 0 |
| CR Woakes | 283.1 | 68 | 912 | 40 | 5/35 | 8/140 | 22.80 | 3.22 | 42.4 | 2 | 0 |
| JS Patel | 536.2 | 136 | 1553 | 59 | 5/49 | 8/145 | 26.32 | 2.89 | 54.5 | 1 | 0 |
| KHD Barker | 442.5 | 93 | 1377 | 50 | 6/46 | 8/66 | 27.54 | 3.10 | 53.1 | 2 | 0 |
| RA Jones | 69.0 | 7 | 275 | 9 | 4/81 | 5/80 | 30.55 | 3.98 | 46.0 | 0 | 0 |
| A Javid | 12.0 | 0 | 33 | 1 | 1/1 | 1/1 | 33.00 | 2.75 | 72.0 | 0 | 0 |
| CJC Wright | 291.1 | 47 | 1076 | 31 | 4/56 | 7/104 | 34.70 | 3.69 | 56.3 | 0 | 0 |
| R Clarke | 249.0 | 46 | 743 | 19 | 3/54 | 4/73 | 39.10 | 2.98 | 78.6 | 0 | 0 |
| IJL Trott | 20.0 | 2 | 79 | 1 | 1/27 | 1/27 | 79.00 | 3.95 | 120.0 | 0 | 0 |
| LJ Evans | 1.0 | 0 | 15 | 0 | - | - | - | 15.00 | - | 0 | 0 |

**Catches/Stumpings:**
62 Ambrose (5st), 18 Clarke, Porterfield, 17 Chopra, 9 Patel, 8 Trott, Bell, 6 Evans, Hain, 5 Barker, 4 Woakes, 3 Westwood, 2 Hannon-Dalby, McKay, Troughton, 1 Rankin, Gordon, Javid, Wright

Batting

| | Mat | Inns | NO | Runs | HS | Ave | SR | 100 | 50 | 4s | 6s |
|---|---|---|---|---|---|---|---|---|---|---|---|
| V Chopra | 9 | 9 | 2 | 471 | 111 | 67.28 | 68.55 | 1 | 3 | 32 | 4 |
| TR Ambrose | 9 | 6 | 1 | 277 | 98 | 55.40 | 87.38 | 0 | 3 | 28 | 0 |
| IJL Trott | 10 | 9 | 0 | 488 | 108 | 54.22 | 85.16 | 2 | 3 | 53 | 0 |
| A Javid | 10 | 8 | 4 | 108 | 22* | 27.00 | 79.41 | 0 | 0 | 6 | 1 |
| LJ Evans | 10 | 10 | 1 | 227 | 50 | 25.22 | 104.12 | 0 | 1 | 22 | 5 |
| CR Woakes | 1 | 1 | 0 | 23 | 23 | 23.00 | 74.19 | 0 | 0 | 4 | 0 |
| WTS Porterfield | 10 | 10 | 0 | 212 | 83 | 21.20 | 73.35 | 0 | 1 | 18 | 3 |
| R Clarke | 10 | 9 | 1 | 148 | 68 | 18.50 | 94.26 | 0 | 1 | 13 | 2 |
| FRJ Coleman | 2 | 2 | 0 | 32 | 25 | 16.00 | 61.53 | 0 | 0 | 4 | 0 |
| JS Patel | 10 | 7 | 3 | 54 | 16* | 13.50 | 114.89 | 0 | 0 | 4 | 2 |
| OJ Hannon-Dalby | 10 | 3 | 1 | 17 | 11 | 8.50 | 85.00 | 0 | 0 | 1 | 1 |
| JE Poysden | 5 | 2 | 1 | 3 | 2* | 3.00 | 30.00 | 0 | 0 | 0 | 0 |
| WB Rankin | 5 | 2 | 0 | 4 | 3 | 2.00 | 40.00 | 0 | 0 | 0 | 0 |
| RO Gordon | 5 | 1 | 0 | 0 | 0 | 0.00 | 0.00 | 0 | 0 | 0 | 0 |
| PJ McKay | 1 | 1 | 1 | 22 | 22* | - | 244.44 | 0 | 0 | 1 | 2 |
| RA Jones | 2 | 1 | 1 | 0 | 0* | - | - | 0 | 0 | 0 | 0 |
| AD Thomason | 1 | 1 | 1 | 0 | 0* | - | - | 0 | 0 | 0 | 0 |

Bowling

| | Overs | Mdns | Runs | Wkts | BBI | Ave | Econ | SR | 4w | 5w |
|---|---|---|---|---|---|---|---|---|---|---|
| R Clarke | 77.0 | 8 | 305 | 12 | 3/40 | 25.41 | 3.96 | 38.5 | 0 | 0 |
| WB Rankin | 42.0 | 1 | 174 | 7 | 3/34 | 24.85 | 4.14 | 36.0 | 0 | 0 |
| JS Patel | 90.0 | 3 | 391 | 23 | 4/24 | 17.00 | 4.34 | 23.4 | 3 | 0 |
| IJL Trott | 16.0 | 0 | 72 | 0 | - | - | 4.50 | - | 0 | 0 |
| RO Gordon | 39.0 | 0 | 214 | 7 | 3/25 | 30.57 | 5.48 | 33.4 | 0 | 0 |
| OJ Hannon-Dalby | 77.1 | 5 | 431 | 14 | 4/44 | 30.78 | 5.58 | 33.0 | 1 | 0 |
| AD Thomason | 4.0 | 0 | 23 | 0 | - | - | 5.75 | - | 0 | 0 |
| JE Poysden | 28.3 | 0 | 166 | 5 | 2/49 | 33.20 | 5.82 | 34.2 | 0 | 0 |
| A Javid | 41.0 | 0 | 264 | 5 | 3/48 | 52.80 | 6.43 | 49.2 | 0 | 0 |
| CR Woakes | 7.2 | 0 | 50 | 0 | - | - | 6.81 | - | 0 | 0 |
| RA Jones | 12.0 | 0 | 89 | 1 | 1/59 | 89.00 | 7.41 | 72.0 | 0 | 0 |

**Catches/Stumpings:**
14 Ambrose, 8 Chopra, Porterfield, 5 Clarke, 4 Evans, 3 Rankin, 2 Poysden, Javid, 1 Patel, Trott, Hannon-Dalby, Jones, McKay

# NATWEST T20 BLAST AVERAGES 2014

Batting

| | Mat | Inns | NO | Runs | HS | Ave | SR | 100 | 50 | 4s | 6s |
|---|---|---|---|---|---|---|---|---|---|---|---|
| V Chopra | 15 | 15 | 2 | 525 | 86* | 40.38 | 122.37 | 0 | 5 | 46 | 13 |
| Shoaib Malik | 6 | 6 | 1 | 200 | 50 | 40.00 | 130.71 | 0 | 1 | 13 | 9 |
| WTS Porterfield | 15 | 15 | 1 | 504 | 81* | 36.00 | 142.37 | 0 | 4 | 53 | 15 |
| LJ Evans | 15 | 13 | 4 | 276 | 69* | 30.66 | 147.59 | 0 | 2 | 30 | 8 |
| CR Woakes | 6 | 5 | 3 | 58 | 22* | 29.00 | 141.46 | 0 | 0 | 6 | 0 |
| A Javid | 14 | 11 | 6 | 132 | 27 | 26.40 | 128.15 | 0 | 0 | 12 | 2 |
| R Clarke | 12 | 11 | 1 | 215 | 70* | 21.50 | 125.73 | 0 | 1 | 14 | 9 |
| IR Bell | 2 | 2 | 0 | 42 | 38 | 21.00 | 175.00 | 0 | 0 | 4 | 2 |
| IJL Trott | 2 | 2 | 0 | 40 | 39 | 20.00 | 88.88 | 0 | 0 | 0 | 1 |
| JS Patel | 15 | 6 | 3 | 44 | 21* | 14.66 | 162.96 | 0 | 0 | 1 | 4 |
| JP Webb | 11 | 11 | 0 | 154 | 50 | 14.00 | 110.00 | 0 | 1 | 17 | 3 |
| TR Ambrose | 13 | 7 | 2 | 58 | 22 | 11.60 | 85.29 | 0 | 0 | 4 | 0 |
| CJC Wright | 9 | 3 | 2 | 5 | 3* | 5.00 | 71.42 | 0 | 0 | 0 | 0 |
| KHD Barker | 3 | 2 | 0 | 4 | 4 | 2.00 | 133.33 | 0 | 0 | 1 | 0 |
| WB Rankin | 9 | 2 | 1 | 2 | 1* | 2.00 | 66.66 | 0 | 0 | 0 | 0 |
| FRJ Coleman | 1 | 1 | 1 | 20 | 20* | - | 142.85 | 0 | 0 | 3 | 0 |
| OJ Hannon-Dalby | 7 | 1 | 1 | 2 | 2* | - | 66.66 | 0 | 0 | 0 | 0 |
| PM Best | 1 | - | - | - | - | - | - | - | - | - | - |
| RO Gordon | 6 | - | - | - | - | - | - | - | - | - | - |
| PJ McKay | 2 | - | - | - | - | - | - | - | - | - | - |
| JE Poysden | 1 | - | - | - | - | - | - | - | - | - | - |

Bowling

| | Overs | Mdns | Runs | Wkts | BBI | Ave | Econ | SR | 4w | 5w |
|---|---|---|---|---|---|---|---|---|---|---|
| A Javid | 37.3 | 0 | 229 | 9 | 2/13 | 25.44 | 6.10 | 25.0 | 0 | 0 |
| JS Patel | 53.0 | 0 | 324 | 25 | 4/19 | 12.96 | 6.11 | 12.7 | 1 | 0 |
| R Clarke | 31.0 | 0 | 212 | 7 | 1/5 | 30.28 | 6.83 | 26.5 | 0 | 0 |
| PM Best | 4.0 | 0 | 29 | 0 | - | - | 7.25 | - | 0 | 0 |
| KHD Barker | 10.5 | 0 | 79 | 3 | 2/18 | 26.33 | 7.29 | 21.6 | 0 | 0 |
| WB Rankin | 34.0 | 0 | 280 | 14 | 3/34 | 20.00 | 8.23 | 14.5 | 0 | 0 |
| Shoaib Malik | 20.0 | 0 | 166 | 4 | 2/21 | 41.50 | 8.30 | 30.0 | 0 | 0 |
| CR Woakes | 23.0 | 0 | 198 | 8 | 2/33 | 24.75 | 8.60 | 17.2 | 0 | 0 |
| OJ Hannon-Dalby | 23.5 | 0 | 206 | 8 | 3/31 | 25.75 | 8.64 | 17.8 | 0 | 0 |
| RO Gordon | 17.0 | 0 | 147 | 9 | 3/18 | 16.33 | 8.64 | 11.3 | 0 | 0 |
| JE Poysden | 3.0 | 0 | 26 | 0 | - | - | 8.66 | - | 0 | 0 |
| CJC Wright | 34.0 | 0 | 322 | 10 | 3/37 | 32.20 | 9.47 | 20.4 | 0 | 0 |
| LJ Evans | 2.0 | 0 | 20 | 0 | - | - | 10.00 | - | 0 | 0 |

**Catches/Stumpings:**
11 Ambrose (inc 3st), 9 Chopra, 8 Porterfield, Evans, 5 Javid, Patel, 3 Clarke, Wright, Webb, 2 Barker, Shoaib Malik, McKay, 1 Best, Woakes, Hannon-Dalby, Bell

# WORCESTERSHIRE

**FORMED:** 1865
**HOME GROUND:** County Ground, New Road, Worcester
**ONE-DAY NAME:** Worcestershire Rapids
**CAPTAIN:** Daryl Mitchell
**2014 RESULTS:** CC2: 2/9; RL50: 7/9 Group A; NWT20: Quarter-finalists
**HONOURS:** Championship: (5) 1964, 1965, 1974, 1988, 1989; Gillette/NatWest/C&G/FP Trophy: 1994; Benson & Hedges Cup: 1991; Pro40/National League/CB40/YB40/RL50: 2007; Sunday League: (3) 1971, 1987, 1988

## THE LOWDOWN

While promotion was more nail-biting than it had looked like being for much of the season, Worcestershire defied early predictions that they might struggle. They were hugely grateful for Saeed Ajmal's 63 wickets, but that brought its own controversy after he was banned from bowling after the season because of an illegal action. Paul Grayson, Essex's head coach, even went as far as to bemoan the umpires' lack of intervention while Ajmal was bowling. It wasn't just the Ajmal show, however. Seam bowler Charlie Morris was a surprise success, taking 52 Championship wickets in his debut season with a nagging line while Jack Shantry had a fine campaign, also passing 50 wickets and chipping in with surprising runs. Daryl Mitchell struck five centuries as he revelled in the pressures of captaincy and at times held the batting together, especially after Moeen Ali missed much of the season following his England call-up. There is much expected of Tom Fell, 21 and, although he struggled at times last season he compiled two good centuries that hinted at his genuine promise. The signing of Alex Gidman will bring some experience to a young side and solidity to the middle order as Worcestershire aim to avoid following promotion with relegation for the fifth successive time.

## DIRECTOR OF CRICKET: STEVE RHODES

Rhodes moved to New Road in 1985 after beginning his career at his home county Yorkshire and has since become a Worcestershire institution. He played 11 Tests for England and earned a reputation as a skilful wicketkeeper and a nuggety batsman who made the most of his talents. He has been director of cricket at Worcestershire since 2006.



www.wccc.co.uk / tel: 01905 748474

# COUNTY CHAMPIONSHIP AVERAGES 2014

Batting

| | Mat | Inns | NO | Runs | HS | Ave | SR | 100 | 50 | 4s | 6s |
|---|---|---|---|---|---|---|---|---|---|---|---|
| MM Ali | 8 | 11 | 0 | 676 | 162 | 61.45 | 65.31 | 1 | 6 | 78 | 15 |
| DKH Mitchell | 16 | 27 | 4 | 1334 | 172* | 58.00 | 48.28 | 5 | 4 | 163 | 3 |
| RK Oliver | 7 | 14 | 0 | 558 | 179 | 39.85 | 83.15 | 1 | 4 | 90 | 1 |
| AD Hales | 1 | 2 | 0 | 78 | 63 | 39.00 | 57.35 | 0 | 1 | 10 | 1 |
| AN Kervezee | 16 | 26 | 1 | 829 | 110 | 33.16 | 57.97 | 2 | 5 | 109 | 4 |
| TC Fell | 12 | 20 | 1 | 563 | 133 | 29.63 | 42.65 | 2 | 1 | 68 | 1 |
| JD Shantry | 16 | 24 | 7 | 481 | 101* | 28.29 | 61.98 | 1 | 0 | 68 | 6 |
| OB Cox | 16 | 25 | 2 | 604 | 104 | 26.26 | 58.58 | 1 | 3 | 82 | 6 |
| BL D'Oliveira | 1 | 2 | 0 | 51 | 44 | 25.50 | 60.71 | 0 | 0 | 6 | 1 |
| MG Pardoe | 9 | 13 | 1 | 284 | 52 | 23.66 | 43.69 | 0 | 1 | 39 | 2 |
| J Leach | 12 | 19 | 0 | 447 | 74 | 23.52 | 58.12 | 0 | 4 | 61 | 5 |
| SH Choudhry | 6 | 10 | 1 | 209 | 44 | 23.22 | 44.75 | 0 | 0 | 32 | 0 |
| T Kohler-Cadmore | 13 | 23 | 0 | 516 | 99 | 22.43 | 52.92 | 0 | 4 | 71 | 4 |
| GM Andrew | 4 | 6 | 1 | 108 | 71* | 21.60 | 59.34 | 0 | 1 | 10 | 5 |
| Saeed Ajmal | 9 | 10 | 2 | 156 | 53* | 19.50 | 88.63 | 0 | 1 | 20 | 2 |
| RA Whiteley | 9 | 12 | 0 | 214 | 43 | 17.83 | 44.67 | 0 | 0 | 23 | 8 |
| MJ McClenaghan | 4 | 7 | 1 | 86 | 27 | 14.33 | 42.57 | 0 | 0 | 10 | 0 |
| CAJ Morris | 16 | 20 | 14 | 72 | 24 | 12.00 | 27.58 | 0 | 0 | 11 | 0 |
| CJ Russell | 1 | - | - | - | - | - | - | - | - | - | - |

Bowling

| | Overs | Mdns | Runs | Wkts | BBI | BBM | Ave | Econ | SR | 5w | 10w |
|---|---|---|---|---|---|---|---|---|---|---|---|
| GM Andrew | 106.0 | 25 | 319 | 20 | 5/40 | 8/85 | 15.95 | 3.00 | 31.8 | 1 | 0 |
| Saeed Ajmal | 417.3 | 116 | 1038 | 63 | 7/19 | 13/94 | 16.47 | 2.48 | 39.7 | 6 | 2 |
| JD Shantry | 497.0 | 124 | 1336 | 56 | 6/53 | 10/131 | 23.85 | 2.68 | 53.2 | 2 | 1 |
| CAJ Morris | 499.4 | 135 | 1371 | 52 | 5/54 | 6/96 | 26.36 | 2.74 | 57.6 | 1 | 0 |
| J Leach | 268.5 | 48 | 988 | 33 | 5/36 | 6/116 | 29.93 | 3.67 | 48.8 | 1 | 0 |
| MJ McClenaghan | 120.0 | 27 | 466 | 13 | 5/78 | 5/169 | 35.84 | 3.88 | 55.3 | 1 | 0 |
| CJ Russell | 14.0 | 1 | 73 | 2 | 2/73 | 2/73 | 36.50 | 5.21 | 42.0 | 0 | 0 |
| MM Ali | 190.5 | 36 | 552 | 15 | 3/43 | 4/162 | 36.80 | 2.89 | 76.3 | 0 | 0 |
| SH Choudhry | 108.1 | 13 | 384 | 8 | 3/79 | 3/106 | 48.00 | 3.55 | 81.1 | 0 | 0 |
| BL D'Oliveira | 14.0 | 1 | 73 | 1 | 1/73 | 1/73 | 73.00 | 5.21 | 84.0 | 0 | 0 |
| MG Pardoe | 10.0 | 2 | 24 | 0 | - | - | - | 2.40 | - | 0 | 0 |
| DKH Mitchell | 9.0 | 3 | 26 | 0 | - | - | - | 2.88 | - | 0 | 0 |
| AN Kervezee | 7.3 | 0 | 34 | 0 | - | - | - | 4.53 | - | 0 | 0 |
| RA Whiteley | 12.0 | 1 | 44 | 0 | - | - | - | 3.66 | - | 0 | 0 |

**Catches/Stumpings:**

35 Cox (inc 3st), 28 Mitchell, 15 Kohler-Cadmore, 13 Fell, 8 Kervezee, 7 Shantry, Morris, 6 Ali, Pardoe, 4 Saeed Ajmal, 3 Whiteley, 2 Leach, Choudhry, Oliver, 1 Hales

**Batting**

| | Mat | Inns | NO | Runs | HS | Ave | SR | 100 | 50 | 4s | 6s |
|---|---|---|---|---|---|---|---|---|---|---|---|
| J Leach | 8 | 6 | 4 | 157 | 45* | 78.50 | 103.97 | 0 | 0 | 19 | 0 |
| TC Fell | 7 | 7 | 0 | 341 | 89 | 48.71 | 80.42 | 0 | 4 | 41 | 1 |
| RA Whiteley | 8 | 7 | 1 | 219 | 53 | 36.50 | 86.22 | 0 | 2 | 20 | 9 |
| DKH Mitchell | 8 | 7 | 0 | 234 | 88 | 33.42 | 68.42 | 0 | 1 | 23 | 0 |
| AN Kervezee | 8 | 7 | 1 | 200 | 80 | 33.33 | 85.83 | 0 | 2 | 21 | 1 |
| SH Choudhry | 6 | 5 | 2 | 83 | 44* | 27.66 | 112.16 | 0 | 0 | 11 | 0 |
| T Kohler-Cadmore | 7 | 6 | 0 | 130 | 71 | 21.66 | 62.50 | 0 | 1 | 14 | 0 |
| OB Cox | 8 | 6 | 0 | 102 | 39 | 17.00 | 97.14 | 0 | 0 | 10 | 2 |
| CAJ Morris | 6 | 4 | 1 | 24 | 16* | 8.00 | 72.72 | 0 | 0 | 2 | 0 |
| JD Shantry | 6 | 3 | 1 | 14 | 7 | 7.00 | 42.42 | 0 | 0 | 2 | 0 |
| RK Oliver | 5 | 5 | 0 | 34 | 14 | 6.80 | 73.91 | 0 | 0 | 3 | 0 |
| MJ McClenaghan | 6 | 3 | 0 | 18 | 16 | 6.00 | 52.94 | 0 | 0 | 2 | 0 |
| GM Andrew | 4 | 2 | 0 | 8 | 7 | 4.00 | 72.72 | 0 | 0 | 1 | 0 |
| CJ Russell | 1 | 1 | 1 | 1 | 1* | - | 100.00 | 0 | 0 | 0 | 0 |

**Bowling**

| | Overs | Mdns | Runs | Wkts | BBI | Ave | Econ | SR | 4w | 5w |
|---|---|---|---|---|---|---|---|---|---|---|
| DKH Mitchell | 13.4 | 0 | 64 | 4 | 4/19 | 16.00 | 4.68 | 20.5 | 1 | 0 |
| SH Choudhry | 24.0 | 1 | 113 | 1 | 1/41 | 113.00 | 4.70 | 144.0 | 0 | 0 |
| JD Shantry | 39.0 | 3 | 186 | 3 | 2/32 | 62.00 | 4.76 | 78.0 | 0 | 0 |
| CAJ Morris | 35.4 | 1 | 182 | 4 | 2/54 | 45.50 | 5.10 | 53.5 | 0 | 0 |
| J Leach | 46.5 | 2 | 259 | 7 | 2/53 | 37.00 | 5.53 | 40.1 | 0 | 0 |
| MJ McClenaghan | 45.0 | 4 | 265 | 10 | 3/46 | 26.50 | 5.88 | 27.0 | 0 | 0 |
| RA Whiteley | 16.3 | 0 | 117 | 1 | 1/61 | 117.00 | 7.09 | 99.0 | 0 | 0 |
| AN Kervezee | 2.0 | 0 | 17 | 0 | - | - | 8.50 | - | 0 | 0 |
| CJ Russell | 4.0 | 0 | 35 | 0 | - | - | 8.75 | - | 0 | 0 |

**Catches/Stumpings:**

8 Cox (inc 1st), 4 Kervezee, 3 Fell, 2 Andrew, 1 Choudhry, Leach, Oliver

# NATWEST T20 BLAST AVERAGES 2014

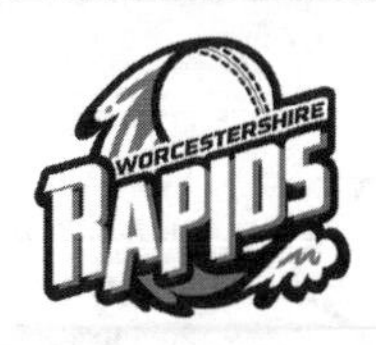


Batting

| | Mat | Inns | NO | Runs | HS | Ave | SR | 100 | 50 | 4s | 6s |
|---|---|---|---|---|---|---|---|---|---|---|---|
| BL D'Oliveira | 10 | 5 | 4 | 49 | 15 | 49.00 | 148.48 | 0 | 0 | 2 | 2 |
| OB Cox | 13 | 11 | 7 | 157 | 46 | 39.25 | 138.93 | 0 | 0 | 17 | 4 |
| DKH Mitchell | 13 | 13 | 3 | 372 | 68* | 37.20 | 134.29 | 0 | 3 | 40 | 4 |
| RA Whiteley | 13 | 12 | 4 | 237 | 84* | 29.62 | 151.92 | 0 | 1 | 12 | 16 |
| C Munro | 13 | 13 | 1 | 332 | 65 | 27.66 | 141.27 | 0 | 1 | 30 | 14 |
| MM Ali | 4 | 4 | 0 | 101 | 41 | 25.25 | 150.74 | 0 | 0 | 11 | 4 |
| RK Oliver | 13 | 13 | 0 | 279 | 77 | 21.46 | 136.09 | 0 | 1 | 32 | 7 |
| T Kohler-Cadmore | 11 | 11 | 0 | 227 | 51 | 20.63 | 133.52 | 0 | 1 | 29 | 7 |
| GM Andrew | 1 | 1 | 0 | 20 | 20 | 20.00 | 166.66 | 0 | 0 | 1 | 1 |
| AN Kervezee | 10 | 8 | 1 | 130 | 43 | 18.57 | 120.37 | 0 | 0 | 7 | 2 |
| Saeed Ajmal | 10 | 1 | 0 | 16 | 16 | 16.00 | 228.57 | 0 | 0 | 1 | 1 |
| J Leach | 3 | 2 | 0 | 25 | 20 | 12.50 | 104.16 | 0 | 0 | 1 | 1 |
| JD Shantry | 13 | 4 | 1 | 24 | 12* | 8.00 | 100.00 | 0 | 0 | 1 | 1 |
| SH Choudhry | 3 | 2 | 1 | 5 | 4 | 5.00 | 100.00 | 0 | 0 | 0 | 0 |
| MJ McClenaghan | 3 | 2 | 2 | 7 | 4* | - | 175.00 | 0 | 0 | 1 | 0 |
| CAJ Morris | 2 | 1 | 1 | 2 | 2* | - | 50.00 | 0 | 0 | 0 | 0 |
| CJ Russell | 8 | - | - | - | - | - | - | - | - | - | - |

Bowling

| | Overs | Mdns | Runs | Wkts | BBI | Ave | Econ | SR | 4w | 5w |
|---|---|---|---|---|---|---|---|---|---|---|
| J Leach | 9.0 | 0 | 54 | 5 | 2/22 | 10.80 | 6.00 | 10.8 | 0 | 0 |
| Saeed Ajmal | 39.0 | 1 | 237 | 12 | 3/17 | 19.75 | 6.07 | 19.5 | 0 | 0 |
| MM Ali | 16.0 | 0 | 112 | 4 | 2/23 | 28.00 | 7.00 | 24.0 | 0 | 0 |
| JD Shantry | 50.3 | 0 | 418 | 15 | 3/25 | 27.86 | 8.27 | 20.2 | 0 | 0 |
| BL D'Oliveira | 21.0 | 0 | 176 | 1 | 1/21 | 176.00 | 8.38 | 126.0 | 0 | 0 |
| DKH Mitchell | 27.0 | 0 | 234 | 8 | 5/28 | 29.25 | 8.66 | 20.2 | 0 | 1 |
| SH Choudhry | 10.3 | 0 | 91 | 3 | 2/21 | 30.33 | 8.66 | 21.0 | 0 | 0 |
| CJ Russell | 30.2 | 0 | 280 | 16 | 4/40 | 17.50 | 9.23 | 11.3 | 1 | 0 |
| C Munro | 22.0 | 0 | 204 | 7 | 2/37 | 29.14 | 9.27 | 18.8 | 0 | 0 |
| MJ McClenaghan | 11.0 | 0 | 112 | 3 | 1/26 | 37.33 | 10.18 | 22.0 | 0 | 0 |
| CAJ Morris | 8.0 | 0 | 82 | 2 | 2/44 | 41.00 | 10.25 | 24.0 | 0 | 0 |
| RA Whiteley | 3.0 | 0 | 41 | 0 | - | - | 13.66 | - | 0 | 0 |

**Catches/Stumpings:**
12 Mitchell, 10 Cox (inc 5st), 6 Russell, 5 Shantry, Kervezee, Kohler-Cadmore, 3 Munro, Whiteley, 2 Leach, D'Oliveria, Choudhry, Oliver, 1 Saeed Ajmal, McClenaghan, Andrew

# YORKSHIRE

**FORMED:** 1863
**HOME GROUND:** Headingley Carnegie
**ONE-DAY NAME:** Yorkshire Vikings
**CAPTAIN:** Andrew Gale
**2014 RESULTS:** CC1: Champions; RL50: Quarter-finalists; NWT20: 5/9 North Division
**HONOURS:** County Championship: (32) 1893, 1896, 1898, 1900, 1901, 1902, 1905, 1908, 1912, 1919, 1922, 1923, 1924, 1925, 1931, 1932, 1933, 1935, 1937, 1938, 1939, 1946, 1949, 1959, 1960, 1962, 1963, 1966, 1967, 1968, 2001, 2014; Gillette/NatWest/C&G/FP Trophy: (3) 1965, 1969, 2002; Benson & Hedges Cup: 1987; Sunday League: 1983

### THE LOWDOWN

A first County Championship title since 2001 was richly deserved for Yorkshire, who looked head and shoulders above their competition. Their depth is staggering, and they barely skipped a beat while losing the likes of Joe Root and Gary Ballance to England. Most counties would struggle in such a situation but Yorkshire appear to always have someone fully ready to step in and take their place. Openers Adam Lyth and Alex Lees scored 2,460 runs between them, while captain Andrew Gale, Ballance and Adil Rashid also added two centuries apiece. Rashid has been transformed under the guidance of head coach Jason Gillespie, offering a key spin threat to complement the pace attack of Ryan Sidebottom, Liam Plunkett, Jack Brooks, Tim Bresnan and Steve Patterson. Championship overseas duties will be shared by Younis Khan, Aaron Finch and Kane Williamson, while they have great hope for another batch of Academy products such as Matt Fisher, Will Rhodes and Karl Carver. Yorkshire showed decent form in the one-day tournaments, narrowly missing out on the quarter-finals of the T20 Blast and losing in the quarter-finals of the RL Cup, but will feel they have the squad to challenge for the treble this season.

### HEAD COACH: JASON GILLESPIE

Gillespie has had an almost perfect record since he took over at Yorkshire in 2012. Promotion in the first season, narrowly missing out on the title in his second and, in his third, leading them to their 32nd County Championship triumph. It is no surprise that he is being linked with national coaching roles. Gillespie had a stellar career in Australia's great sides of the late 1990s and early 2000s, finishing his career with 402 international wickets.

# COUNTY CHAMPIONSHIP AVERAGES 2014

## Batting

| | Mat | Inns | NO | Runs | HS | Ave | SR | 100 | 50 | 4s | 6s |
|---|---|---|---|---|---|---|---|---|---|---|---|
| A Lyth | 16 | 23 | 1 | 1489 | 251 | 67.68 | 52.41 | 6 | 6 | 189 | 6 |
| GS Ballance | 6 | 9 | 0 | 585 | 174 | 65.00 | 59.87 | 2 | 3 | 70 | 9 |
| KS Williamson | 9 | 13 | 2 | 629 | 189 | 57.18 | 48.38 | 1 | 4 | 81 | 1 |
| AJ Finch | 5 | 6 | 0 | 291 | 110 | 48.50 | 72.02 | 1 | 1 | 27 | 6 |
| JM Bairstow | 13 | 17 | 3 | 647 | 161* | 46.21 | 61.91 | 1 | 4 | 76 | 6 |
| JE Root | 4 | 6 | 0 | 275 | 97 | 45.83 | 71.61 | 0 | 3 | 37 | 2 |
| AZ Lees | 15 | 22 | 0 | 971 | 138 | 44.13 | 48.28 | 2 | 5 | 127 | 7 |
| AW Gale | 13 | 16 | 3 | 562 | 126* | 43.23 | 57.40 | 2 | 1 | 71 | 1 |
| RM Pyrah | 6 | 6 | 2 | 161 | 62 | 40.25 | 61.45 | 0 | 1 | 19 | 0 |
| JA Leaning | 10 | 14 | 2 | 465 | 99 | 38.75 | 46.08 | 0 | 4 | 47 | 4 |
| AU Rashid | 14 | 18 | 3 | 577 | 159* | 38.46 | 60.22 | 2 | 1 | 80 | 2 |
| LE Plunkett | 7 | 8 | 2 | 209 | 86 | 34.83 | 93.30 | 0 | 2 | 26 | 5 |
| TT Bresnan | 10 | 10 | 0 | 338 | 95 | 33.80 | 45.24 | 0 | 4 | 44 | 3 |
| AJ Hodd | 5 | 6 | 1 | 144 | 55 | 28.80 | 64.28 | 0 | 1 | 22 | 0 |
| JA Brooks | 16 | 14 | 8 | 142 | 37* | 23.66 | 60.16 | 0 | 0 | 18 | 2 |
| Azeem Rafiq | 1 | 1 | 0 | 14 | 14 | 14.00 | 51.85 | 0 | 0 | 1 | 0 |
| SA Patterson | 15 | 14 | 1 | 178 | 43 | 13.69 | 36.77 | 0 | 0 | 26 | 0 |
| RJ Sidebottom | 12 | 12 | 2 | 112 | 25 | 11.20 | 27.45 | 0 | 0 | 11 | 0 |
| K Carver | 1 | 1 | 1 | 2 | 2* | - | 10.00 | 0 | 0 | 0 | 0 |

## Bowling

| | Overs | Mdns | Runs | Wkts | BBI | BBM | Ave | Econ | SR | 5w | 10w |
|---|---|---|---|---|---|---|---|---|---|---|---|
| RJ Sidebottom | 351.1 | 84 | 881 | 48 | 7/44 | 9/65 | 18.35 | 2.50 | 43.8 | 2 | 0 |
| K Carver | 20.0 | 4 | 65 | 3 | 2/27 | 3/65 | 21.66 | 3.25 | 40.0 | 0 | 0 |
| LE Plunkett | 167.0 | 27 | 596 | 24 | 4/42 | 5/97 | 24.83 | 3.56 | 41.7 | 0 | 0 |
| AU Rashid | 369.4 | 71 | 1199 | 46 | 5/117 | 8/194 | 26.06 | 3.24 | 48.2 | 1 | 0 |
| SA Patterson | 403.4 | 133 | 1001 | 36 | 4/54 | 5/69 | 27.80 | 2.47 | 67.2 | 0 | 0 |
| JA Brooks | 523.2 | 105 | 1906 | 68 | 5/36 | 8/112 | 28.02 | 3.64 | 46.1 | 2 | 0 |
| TT Bresnan | 331.0 | 76 | 947 | 30 | 4/112 | 7/155 | 31.56 | 2.86 | 66.2 | 0 | 0 |
| A Lyth | 59.2 | 12 | 160 | 5 | 2/18 | 2/18 | 32.00 | 2.69 | 71.2 | 0 | 0 |
| KS Williamson | 61.4 | 21 | 160 | 5 | 2/45 | 2/45 | 32.00 | 2.59 | 74.0 | 0 | 0 |
| AJ Finch | 15.0 | 4 | 39 | 1 | 1/20 | 1/31 | 39.00 | 2.60 | 90.0 | 0 | 0 |
| JE Root | 13.0 | 1 | 40 | 1 | 1/26 | 1/26 | 40.00 | 3.07 | 78.0 | 0 | 0 |
| RM Pyrah | 99.0 | 26 | 309 | 6 | 3/37 | 3/67 | 51.50 | 3.12 | 99.0 | 0 | 0 |
| Azeem Rafiq | 38.0 | 6 | 110 | 1 | 1/79 | 1/110 | 110.00 | 2.89 | 228.0 | 0 | 0 |
| JM Bairstow | 1.0 | 0 | 1 | 0 | - | - | - | 1.00 | - | 0 | 0 |
| JA Leaning | 6.0 | 1 | 13 | 0 | - | - | - | 2.16 | - | 0 | 0 |

**Catches/Stumpings:**
42 Bairstow (inc 4st), 19 Hodd (inc 1st), 10 Williamson, Lees, 9 Rashid, 8 Finch, 7 Ballance, 5 Bresnan, 4 Plunkett, Brooks, Leaning, 2 Sidebottom, Pyrah, Gale, 1 Carver, Patterson, Root, Rafiq

# ROYAL LONDON ONE-DAY CUP AVERAGES 2014

| Batting | Mat | Inns | NO | Runs | HS | Ave | SR | 100 | 50 | 4s | 6s |
|---|---|---|---|---|---|---|---|---|---|---|---|
| AJ Hodd | 5 | 2 | 1 | 111 | 69* | 111.00 | 135.36 | 0 | 1 | 12 | 2 |
| GS Ballance | 1 | 1 | 0 | 61 | 61 | 61.00 | 68.53 | 0 | 1 | 3 | 0 |
| RM Pyrah | 9 | 4 | 3 | 57 | 29* | 57.00 | 103.63 | 0 | 0 | 4 | 2 |
| JA Leaning | 8 | 7 | 3 | 220 | 111* | 55.00 | 87.64 | 1 | 1 | 12 | 5 |
| AZ Lees | 9 | 9 | 1 | 368 | 102 | 46.00 | 78.80 | 1 | 3 | 46 | 1 |
| A Lyth | 9 | 9 | 1 | 317 | 84 | 39.62 | 85.67 | 0 | 2 | 40 | 2 |
| AU Rashid | 9 | 7 | 3 | 142 | 71 | 35.50 | 92.20 | 0 | 1 | 16 | 2 |
| KS Williamson | 9 | 8 | 0 | 184 | 70 | 23.00 | 73.89 | 0 | 1 | 21 | 2 |
| JM Bairstow | 4 | 4 | 1 | 63 | 45* | 21.00 | 84.00 | 0 | 0 | 5 | 2 |
| AW Gale | 9 | 8 | 1 | 142 | 45 | 20.28 | 69.60 | 0 | 0 | 15 | 1 |
| TT Bresnan | 9 | 5 | 1 | 77 | 32 | 19.25 | 132.75 | 0 | 0 | 10 | 1 |
| SA Patterson | 7 | 2 | 1 | 9 | 8 | 9.00 | 60.00 | 0 | 0 | 1 | 0 |
| JA Brooks | 8 | 2 | 0 | 0 | 0 | 0.00 | 0.00 | 0 | 0 | 0 | 0 |
| MD Fisher | 3 | - | - | - | - | - | - | - | - | - | - |

| Bowling | Overs | Mdns | Runs | Wkts | BBI | Ave | Econ | SR | 4w | 5w |
|---|---|---|---|---|---|---|---|---|---|---|
| MD Fisher | 24.0 | 1 | 101 | 2 | 1/29 | 50.50 | 4.20 | 72.0 | 0 | 0 |
| SA Patterson | 56.0 | 3 | 238 | 9 | 3/39 | 26.44 | 4.25 | 37.3 | 0 | 0 |
| JA Brooks | 72.0 | 5 | 323 | 11 | 3/30 | 29.36 | 4.48 | 39.2 | 0 | 0 |
| AU Rashid | 86.5 | 4 | 409 | 21 | 5/33 | 19.47 | 4.71 | 24.8 | 0 | 1 |
| TT Bresnan | 75.2 | 6 | 371 | 15 | 4/28 | 24.73 | 4.92 | 30.1 | 1 | 0 |
| RM Pyrah | 66.4 | 3 | 333 | 15 | 4/51 | 22.20 | 4.99 | 26.6 | 1 | 0 |
| JA Leaning | 6.0 | 0 | 38 | 0 | - | - | 6.33 | - | 0 | 0 |
| A Lyth | 11.0 | 1 | 72 | 1 | 1/24 | 72.00 | 6.54 | 66.0 | 0 | 0 |

**Catches/Stumpings:**
11 Hodd (inc 2st), 10 Lyth, 8 Bairstow, 6 Bresnan, 4 Leaning, Williamson, 2 Brooks, Ballance, Lees, 1 Rashid, Pyrah, Gale

# NATWEST T20 BLAST AVERAGES 2014

Batting

| | Mat | Inns | NO | Runs | HS | Ave | SR | 100 | 50 | 4s | 6s |
|---|---|---|---|---|---|---|---|---|---|---|---|
| JM Bairstow | 11 | 11 | 4 | 355 | 102* | 50.71 | 143.14 | 1 | 2 | 24 | 12 |
| TT Bresnan | 10 | 9 | 5 | 175 | 45* | 43.75 | 143.44 | 0 | 0 | 15 | 5 |
| AZ Lees | 10 | 10 | 2 | 315 | 67* | 39.37 | 128.57 | 0 | 2 | 34 | 4 |
| LE Plunkett | 2 | 1 | 0 | 36 | 36 | 36.00 | 163.63 | 0 | 0 | 6 | 0 |
| AJ Finch | 10 | 10 | 0 | 256 | 89 | 25.60 | 128.00 | 0 | 2 | 19 | 13 |
| AU Rashid | 11 | 5 | 1 | 98 | 29* | 24.50 | 113.95 | 0 | 0 | 10 | 2 |
| KS Williamson | 5 | 5 | 0 | 93 | 41 | 18.60 | 113.41 | 0 | 0 | 13 | 1 |
| RM Pyrah | 11 | 6 | 3 | 48 | 16* | 16.00 | 129.72 | 0 | 0 | 3 | 2 |
| AW Gale | 10 | 10 | 0 | 135 | 55 | 13.50 | 104.65 | 0 | 1 | 13 | 1 |
| JE Root | 1 | 1 | 0 | 13 | 13 | 13.00 | 108.33 | 0 | 0 | 2 | 0 |
| GS Ballance | 1 | 1 | 0 | 12 | 12 | 12.00 | 120.00 | 0 | 0 | 2 | 0 |
| A Lyth | 10 | 7 | 1 | 66 | 46* | 11.00 | 120.00 | 0 | 0 | 3 | 1 |
| RJ Sidebottom | 8 | 2 | 1 | 2 | 2 | 2.00 | 50.00 | 0 | 0 | 0 | 0 |
| OE Robinson | 7 | 3 | 0 | 5 | 3 | 1.66 | 35.71 | 0 | 0 | 0 | 0 |
| Azeem Rafiq | 9 | 3 | 3 | 13 | 7* | - | 118.18 | 0 | 0 | 1 | 0 |
| JA Brooks | 3 | - | - | - | - | - | - | - | - | - | - |
| JA Leaning | 1 | - | - | - | - | - | - | - | - | - | - |
| SA Patterson | 1 | - | - | - | - | - | - | - | - | - | - |

Bowling

| | Overs | Mdns | Runs | Wkts | BBI | Ave | Econ | SR | 4w | 5w |
|---|---|---|---|---|---|---|---|---|---|---|
| SA Patterson | 3.0 | 0 | 16 | 2 | 2/16 | 8.00 | 5.33 | 9.0 | 0 | 0 |
| JE Root | 1.0 | 0 | 6 | 0 | - | - | 6.00 | - | 0 | 0 |
| KS Williamson | 6.0 | 0 | 37 | 3 | 2/26 | 12.33 | 6.16 | 12.0 | 0 | 0 |
| Azeem Rafiq | 28.4 | 0 | 184 | 14 | 3/20 | 13.14 | 6.41 | 12.2 | 0 | 0 |
| LE Plunkett | 7.0 | 0 | 45 | 4 | 2/20 | 11.25 | 6.42 | 10.5 | 0 | 0 |
| AU Rashid | 39.0 | 1 | 272 | 14 | 3/14 | 19.42 | 6.97 | 16.7 | 0 | 0 |
| TT Bresnan | 36.0 | 0 | 262 | 9 | 2/22 | 29.11 | 7.27 | 24.0 | 0 | 0 |
| A Lyth | 3.3 | 0 | 26 | 2 | 2/5 | 13.00 | 7.42 | 10.5 | 0 | 0 |
| RM Pyrah | 36.0 | 0 | 274 | 13 | 3/19 | 21.07 | 7.61 | 16.6 | 0 | 0 |
| RJ Sidebottom | 28.5 | 1 | 247 | 11 | 3/24 | 22.45 | 8.56 | 15.7 | 0 | 0 |
| JA Brooks | 9.0 | 0 | 82 | 0 | - | - | 9.11 | - | 0 | 0 |
| OE Robinson | 17.0 | 0 | 162 | 6 | 2/25 | 27.00 | 9.52 | 17.0 | 0 | 0 |
| JA Leaning | 1.0 | 0 | 12 | 0 | - | - | 12.00 | - | 0 | 0 |

**Catches/Stumpings:**

14 Finch, 8 Bairstow (inc 4st), Rafiq, 6 Lyth, 5 Bresnan, 4 Pyrah, Lees, 3 Rashid, Robinson, 2 Gale, 1 Williamson, Sidebottom, Brooks, Ballance

# THE SHOW MUST GO ON

*A century of club cricket in the south*

From the game's struggle for survival through the ravages of two world wars to the multicultural leagues of today, *The Show Must Go On* is a celebration of a century of club cricket in the south of England.

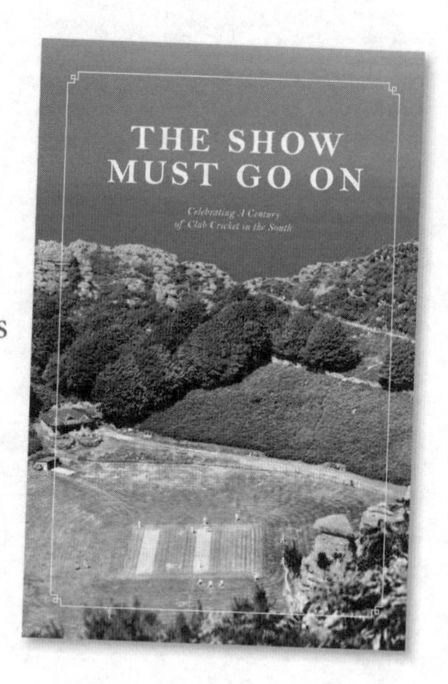


To order your copy for £19.99

contact Donna Black at the CCC

Email: **donna.black@club-cricket.co.uk**

Phone: **020 8973 1612**

# County Ins and Outs

# COUNTY INS AND OUTS 2014/15

**DERBYSHIRE**

▶IN: Tillakaratne Dilshan (SL), Martin Guptill (NZ), Nathan Rimmington (Aus), Shiv Thakor (Lei), Wayne White (Lan)

◀OUT: Paul Borrington (rel), Paul Burgoyne (rel), Gareth Cross (rel), Tim Groenewald (Som), Matt Higginbottom (rel), Richard Johnson (ret), Stephen Moore (ret), Mark Turner (rel)

**DURHAM**

▶IN: John Hastings (Aus)

◀OUT: Gareth Breese (rel)

**ESSEX**

▶IN: Shaun Tait (Aus)

◀OUT: Tom Craddock (rel), Ben Foakes (Sur), Tymal Mills (Sus), Tim Phillips (ret)

**GLAMORGAN**

▶IN: Colin Ingram (SA), James Kettleborough (Nor), Craig Meschede (Som, season-long loan)

◀OUT: Jim Allenby (Som), John Glover (ret), Murray Goodwin (ret), Tom Lancefield (rel), Mike Reed (rel), Gareth Rees (ret), Stewart Walters (rel)

**GLOUCESTERSHIRE**

▶IN: Kieran Noema-Barnett (NZ), Tom Hampton (Bucks), Peter Handscomb (Aus), Geraint Jones (Ken)

◀OUT: Alex Gidman (Wor), Will Gidman (Not), Dan Housego (rel), Graeme McCarter (rel)

**HAMPSHIRE**

▶IN: Andre Adams (Not), Yasir Arafat (Pak), Gareth Berg (Mid), Jackson Bird (Aus), Owais Shah (free agent)

◀OUT: David Balcombe (Sur), Michael Bates (rel), Ruel Brathwaite (rel), Matt Coles (Ken)

**KENT**

▶IN: Matt Coles (Han), Joe Denly (Mid)

◀OUT: Mark Davies (ret), Geraint Jones (Glo)

**LANCASHIRE**

▶IN: Nathan Buck (Lei), George Edwards (Sur), Alviro Petersen (SA), Peter Siddle (Aus)

◀OUT: Andrew Agathangelou (rel), Kyle Hogg (ret), Oliver Newby (rel), Wayne White (Der)

**LEICESTERSHIRE**

▶IN: Mark Cosgrove (Aus), Grant Elliott (NZ), Clint McKay (Aus)

◀OUT: Nathan Buck (Lan), Josh Cobb (Nor), Anthony Ireland (rel), Greg Smith (Not), Shiv Thakor (Der), Michael Thornely (rel)

# COUNTY INS AND OUTS 2014/15

**MIDDLESEX**

▶IN: Nick Compton (Som), James Franklin (NZ), Adam Voges (Aus)

◀OUT: Gareth Berg (Han), Joe Denly (Ken), Adam Rossington (Nor), Ollie Wilkin (rel)

**NORTHAMPTONSHIRE**

▶IN: Shahid Afridi (Pak), Josh Cobb (Lei), Rory Kleinveldt (SA), Richard Levi (Som), Adam Rossington (Mid)

◀OUT: Andrew Hall (rel), James Kettleborough (Gla), James Middlebrook (rel), David Sales (ret), Matthew Spriegel (rel)

**NOTTINGHAMSHIRE**

▶IN: Will Gidman (Glo), Ben Hilfenhaus (Aus), Vernon Philander (SA), Darren Sammy (WI), Greg Smith (Lei), Brendan Taylor (Zim)

◀OUT: Andre Adams (Hants), Ajmal Shahzad (Sus)

**SOMERSET**

▶IN: Jim Allenby (Gla), Corey Anderson (NZ), Tom Cooper (Aus), Tim Groenewald (Der), Sohail Tanvir (Pak)

◀OUT: James Burke (Sur), Nick Compton (Mid), Steve Kirby (ret), Craig Meschede (Gla, loan)

**SURREY**

▶IN: David Balcombe (Han), James Burke (Som), Ben Foakes (Ess), Azhar Mahmood (Pak), Kumar Sangakkara (SL)

◀OUT: George Edwards (Lan), Tom Jewell (rel), Jack Winslade (rel)

**SUSSEX**

▶IN: Mahela Jayawardene (SL), Tymal Mills (Ess), Ajmal Shahzad (Not)

◀OUT: Rory Hamilton-Brown (ret), Jon Lewis (ret)

**WARWICKSHIRE**

◀OUT: Jim Troughton (ret)

**WORCESTERSHIRE**

▶IN: Saeed Ajmal (Pak), Alex Gidman (Glo), Colin Munro (NZ)

◀OUT: Graeme Cressford (rel), Nick Harrison (rel), Matt Pardoe (rel)

**YORKSHIRE**

▶IN: Aaron Finch (Aus), Younis Khan (Pak), Glenn Maxwell (Aus), Kane Williamson (NZ)

◀OUT: Azeem Rafiq (rel), Oliver Robinson (rel)

# YOUR GAME

# WE'RE GAME

# SPORT.

# IT'S WHAT WE DO

PRINT / MAGAZINES / PROGRAMMES / PRINT MANAGEMENT / DIGITAL / WEBSITES
TABLETS / DIGIMAGS / E-MARKETING / EDITORIAL / COPYWRITING / DESIGN / AD SALE
SPONSORSHIP SOLUTIONS / CONSULTANCY / EVENTS / SURVEYS

www.trinorth.co.uk

TriNorth
Communications

# *The* Players

# TOM ABELL RHB RM R0 W0

FULL NAME: Thomas Benjamin Abell
BORN: March 5, 1994, Taunton
SQUAD NO: 28
TEAMS: Somerset
CAREER: First-class: 2014

BEST BATTING: 95 Somerset vs Warwickshire, Taunton, 2014

MOST MARKED CHARACTERISTIC? Probably my dodgy-looking hair
SUPERSTITIONS? I am quite superstitious when I bat. I have to make sure all my kit feels right, so I adjust everything after each ball – pads, gloves, etc
CRICKETING HEROES? Brian Lara, Andrew Flintoff, Marcus Trescothick
NON-CRICKETING HEROES? Sonny Bill Williams, David Haye, Jonny Wilkinson
IF YOU WEREN'T A CRICKETER? Doing something in the sport/sports science field
DESERT ISLAND DISC? The Kooks – Naive
FAVOURITE TV? Geordie Shore
ACCOMPLISHMENTS? Hockey success with school team (four national finals). Runner-up in Aviva/Telegraph School Sport Matters Awards
SURPRISING FACT? I was Somerset U8 tennis champion
FANTASY SLIP CORDON? Keeper: James Corden, 1st: Lee Mack, 2nd: Jimmy Carr, 3rd: Jonny Wilkinson, Gully: Yohan Blake
TWITTER FEED: @tomabell1

| Batting | Mat | Inns | NO | Runs | HS | Ave | SR | 100 | 50 | Ct | St |
|---|---|---|---|---|---|---|---|---|---|---|---|
| First-class | 4 | 7 | 0 | 292 | 95 | 41.71 | 47.94 | 0 | 3 | 4 | 0 |
| **Bowling** | **Mat** | **Balls** | **Runs** | **Wkts** | **BBI** | **BBM** | **Ave** | **Econ** | **SR** | **5w** | **10** |
| First-class | 4 | 12 | 11 | 0 | - | - | - | 5.50 | - | 0 | 0 |

## MARK ADAIR

## RHB RFM R0 W0

FULL NAME: Mark Richard Adair
BORN: March 27, 1996, Belfast
SQUAD NO: 27
HEIGHT: 6ft 4in
NICKNAME: Sparky, Beefy, Fabio
EDUCATION: Sullivan Upper School
TEAMS: Warwickshire 2nd XI, Ireland U19
CAREER: Yet to make first-team debut



---

FAMILY TIES? My dad played cricket for Ulster and my brother Ross played for Ireland U19
CAREER HIGHLIGHTS? Playing my first match at Edgbaston, playing for Ireland and getting a few four-fers for the seconds
TIP FOR THE TOP? Pete McKay
MOST MARKED CHARACTERISTIC? I have a terrible accent
SUPERSTITIONS? I only tie my laces once I'm across the rope
NON-CRICKETING HEROES? Harvey Specter – although he's not real, he's just an all-round boss
CRICKET RULE YOU'D CHANGE? How wide you could bowl it. I'd go for fewer runs
IF YOU COULD BE SOMEONE ELSE FOR A DAY? Barack Obama
DESERT ISLAND DISC? Jessie J – Sexy Lady
FAVOURITE TV? Friday Night Lights
PET HATE? Double standards
SURPRISING FACT? I'm one of the worst football tennis players of my generation
FANTASY SLIP CORDON? Keeper: Pete McKay, 1st: Muhammad Ali, 2nd: Mike Tyson, 3rd: My mum, Gully: Will Ferrell (all of them are very funny with a lot to say! And who doesn't want to spend a day with their mum?)
TWITTER FEED: @Markkadairr

# ANDRE ADAMS

RHB RFM R0 W3

FULL NAME: Andre Ryan Adams
BORN: July 17, 1975, Auckland , New Zealand
SQUAD NO: 41
HEIGHT: 5ft 11in
NICKNAME: Dre
EDUCATION: Westlake Boys' High School, Auckland
TEAMS: New Zealand, Hampshire, Auckland, Essex, Kolkata Tigers, Nottinghamshire
CAREER: Test: 2002; ODI: 2001; T20I: 2005; First-class: 1998; List A: 1997; T20: 2004

BEST BATTING: 124 Essex vs Leicestershire, Leicester, 2014
BEST BOWLING: 7-32 Nottinghamshire vs Lancashire, Manchester, 2012
COUNTY CAPS: 2004 (Essex); 2007 (Nottinghamshire)

FAMILY TIES? My parents are West Indian. I had no choice!
CAREER HIGHLIGHTS? Winning the Championship, playing in a World Cup, playing a Test
CRICKETING HEROES? Michael Holding, Viv Richards
IF YOU WEREN'T A CRICKETER? Running a hunting lodge
SURPRISING FACT? My grandfather is Corsican and my grandmother is Scottish
FANTASY SLIP CORDON? Keeper: Chris Read (the best I have seen), 1st: Stephen Fleming (he has hands like buckets and it may earn me an invite to his wine collection), 2nd: 'Super' Graeme Swann (no need to explain), 3rd: Beyoncé Knowles
TWITTER FEED: @AndreAdams

| Batting | Mat | Inns | NO | Runs | HS | Ave | SR | 100 | 50 | Ct | St |
|---|---|---|---|---|---|---|---|---|---|---|---|
| Tests | 1 | 2 | 0 | 18 | 11 | 9.00 | 90.00 | 0 | 0 | 1 | 0 |
| ODIs | 42 | 34 | 10 | 419 | 45 | 17.45 | 100.47 | 0 | 0 | 8 | 0 |
| T20Is | 4 | 2 | 1 | 13 | 7 | 13.00 | 108.33 | 0 | 0 | 1 | 0 |
| First-class | 170 | 232 | 23 | 4482 | 124 | 21.44 | | 3 | 20 | 111 | 0 |
| List A | 165 | 119 | 29 | 1504 | 90* | 16.71 | | 0 | 1 | 40 | 0 |
| Twenty20 | 71 | 42 | 14 | 417 | 54* | 14.89 | 131.96 | 0 | 1 | 21 | 0 |
| **Bowling** | **Mat** | **Balls** | **Runs** | **Wkts** | **BBI** | **BBM** | **Ave** | **Econ** | **SR** | **5w** | **10** |
| Tests | 1 | 190 | 105 | 6 | 3/44 | 6/105 | 17.50 | 3.31 | 31.6 | 0 | 0 |
| ODIs | 42 | 1885 | 1643 | 53 | 5/22 | 5/22 | 31.00 | 5.22 | 35.5 | 1 | 0 |
| T20Is | 4 | 77 | 105 | 3 | 2/20 | 2/20 | 35.00 | 8.18 | 25.6 | 0 | 0 |
| First-class | 170 | 32660 | 16218 | 683 | 7/32 | | 23.74 | 2.97 | 47.8 | 32 | 6 |
| List A | 165 | 7561 | 5957 | 209 | 5/7 | 5/7 | 28.50 | 4.72 | 36.1 | 4 | 0 |
| Twenty20 | 71 | 1498 | 1914 | 87 | 5/20 | 5/20 | 22.00 | 7.66 | 17.2 | 1 | 0 |

# JIMMY ADAMS LHB LM R5 W0 MVP36

FULL NAME: James Henry Kenneth Adams
BORN: September 23, 1980, Winchester, Hampshire
SQUAD NO: 4
HEIGHT: 6ft
NICKNAME: Bison
EDUCATION: Twyford School; Sherborne School; Loughborough University
TEAMS: Hampshire, Auckland, England Lions
CAREER: First-class: 2002; List A: 2002; T20: 2005



BEST BATTING: 262* Hampshire vs Nottinghamshire, Nottingham, 2006
BEST BOWLING: 2-16 Hampshire vs Durham, Chester-le-Street, 2004
COUNTY CAPS: 2006; BENEFIT YEAR: 2015

FAMILY TIES? My dad played a bit for Kent Schoolboys and my brothers played Hampshire age-group until they decided to pursue other things
CAREER HIGHLIGHTS? Batting on debut with Robin Smith who'd been my hero growing up. Being fortunate enough to play and win two finals at Lord's, and being part of the teams that won the T20 (2010 and 2012), especially 2010 at our home ground
MOST MARKED CHARACTERISTIC? Indecisiveness and an over-sized big toe
CRICKETING HEROES? Robin Smith, Jimmy Adams
NON-CRICKETING HEROES? Jimmy Page, Keith Moon
DESERT ISLAND DISC? The Who – Live At Leeds
FAVOURITE TV? Most detective series
FANTASY SLIP CORDON? Keeper: Me, 1st: Bill Bailey (funny bloke and a bit random), 2nd: The Dude from The Big Lebowski (ditto 1st slip reason), 3rd: Jimmy Page (he's bound to have some good tales), Gully: Eddie Vedder (imagine he's had a pretty interesting life too)
TWITTER FEED: @jhkadams

| Batting | Mat | Inns | NO | Runs | HS | Ave | SR | 100 | 50 | Ct | St |
|---|---|---|---|---|---|---|---|---|---|---|---|
| First-class | 175 | 308 | 27 | 11026 | 262* | 39.23 | | 20 | 57 | 141 | 0 |
| List A | 91 | 86 | 11 | 2978 | 131 | 39.70 | 86.06 | 2 | 22 | 37 | 0 |
| Twenty20 | 119 | 109 | 13 | 2444 | 101* | 25.45 | 122.93 | 2 | 8 | 33 | 0 |
| **Bowling** | **Mat** | **Balls** | **Runs** | **Wkts** | **BBI** | **BBM** | **Ave** | **Econ** | **SR** | **5w** | **10** |
| First-class | 175 | 1063 | 718 | 13 | 2/16 | | 55.23 | 4.05 | 81.7 | 0 | 0 |
| List A | 91 | 79 | 105 | 1 | 1/34 | 1/34 | 105.00 | 7.97 | 79.0 | 0 | 0 |
| Twenty20 | 119 | 36 | 60 | 0 | - | - | - | 10.00 | - | 0 | 0 |

# BASIL AKRAM

RHB RFM R0 W0

FULL NAME: Basil Mohammad R Akram
BORN: February 23, 1993, Enfield, London
SQUAD NO: 46
NICKNAME: Baz
TEAMS: Hampshire
CAREER: First-class: 2014, List A: 2014

BEST BATTING: 36 Loughborough MCCU vs Sussex, Hove, 2014
BEST BOWLING: 2-82 Loughborough MCCU vs Sussex, Hove, 2014

CRICKETING HEROES? Jacques Kallis
DESERT ISLAND DISC? Michael Jackson – Thriller
FAVOURITE TV? The Fresh Prince Of Bel-Air
NOTES: A fast-bowling allrounder, Akram had spells in Essex's and Northamptonshire's 2nd XIs. He joined Hampshire in 2014 after making his first-class debut for Loughborough MCCU against Sussex in April 2014. He played one match for Hampshire last season, making his one-day debut in the RL Cup against Yorkshire in August

| Batting | Mat | Inns | NO | Runs | HS | Ave | SR | 100 | 50 | Ct | St |
|---|---|---|---|---|---|---|---|---|---|---|---|
| First-class | 1 | 2 | 0 | 37 | 36 | 18.50 | 51.38 | 0 | 0 | 0 | 0 |
| List A | 1 | 1 | 0 | 1 | 1 | 1.00 | 11.11 | 0 | 0 | 0 | 0 |
| **Bowling** | **Mat** | **Balls** | **Runs** | **Wkts** | **BBI** | **BBM** | **Ave** | **Econ** | **SR** | **5w** | **10** |
| First-class | 1 | 102 | 88 | 2 | 2/82 | 2/88 | 44.00 | 5.17 | 51.0 | 0 | 0 |
| List A | 1 | 12 | 24 | 0 | - | - | - | 12.00 | - | 0 | 0 |

## AADIL ALI

## RHB OB R0 W0

FULL NAME: Aadil Ali
BORN: December 29, 1994, Leicester
SQUAD NO: 14
HEIGHT: 5ft 11in
EDUCATION: Lancaster Boys; Wyggeston and Queen Elizabeth I College
TEAMS: Leicestershire 2nd XI
CAREER: Yet to make first-team debut



---

CAREER HIGHLIGHTS? Getting my first professional contract
BEST PLAYER IN COUNTY CRICKET? Ravi Bopara
TIP FOR THE TOP? Atif Sheikh
MOST MARKED CHARACTERISTIC? My pads
CRICKETING HEROES? Tendulkar, obviously
CRICKET RULE YOU'D CHANGE? If the ball goes out of the ground, it should count as 12 runs
IF YOU WEREN'T A CRICKETER? Struggling at university
IF YOU COULD BE SOMEONE ELSE FOR A DAY? Floyd Mayweather
FAVOURITE TV? NCIS: Los Angeles
ACCOMPLISHMENTS? Passing Maths (GCSE level)
PET HATE? Poor table manners
FANTASY SLIP CORDON? Keeper: David Beckham, 1st: Me, 2nd: Beyoncé, 3rd: Kevin Hart, Gully: Russell Spiers aka Legend
TWITTER FEED: @aadil_ali94

# MOEEN ALI

LHB OB R2 W0

WORCESTERSHIRE

FULL NAME: Moeen Munir Ali
BORN: June 18, 1987, Birmingham
SQUAD NO: 8
HEIGHT: 6ft
NICKNAME: Brother Mo
EDUCATION: Moseley School
TEAMS: England, Worcestershire, Warwickshire
CAREER: Test: 2014; ODI: 2014; T20I: 2014; First-class: 2005; List A: 2006; T20: 2007

BEST BATTING: 250 Worcestershire vs Glamorgan, Worcester, 2013
BEST BOWLING: 6-29 Worcestershire vs Lancashire, Manchester, 2012
COUNTY CAPS: 2007

FAMILY TIES? My cousin Kabir played for England, brother Kadeer played for England A
TIP FOR THE TOP? Tom Fell, Sam Hain
CRICKETING HEROES? Saeed Anwar and Brian Lara
CRICKET RULE YOU'D CHANGE? I'd have more Powerplays
IF YOU WEREN'T A CRICKETER? Working in a chippy!
IF YOU COULD BE SOMEONE ELSE FOR A DAY? The Incredible Hulk
FAVOURITE TV? Match Of The Day
FANTASY SLIP CORDON? Keeper: Muhammad Ali, 1st: Me, 2nd: Chris Jordan, 3rd Ravi Bopara, Gully: Sachin Tendulkar

| Batting | Mat | Inns | NO | Runs | HS | Ave | SR | 100 | 50 | Ct | St |
|---|---|---|---|---|---|---|---|---|---|---|---|
| Tests | 7 | 10 | 1 | 286 | 108* | 31.77 | 37.93 | 1 | 0 | 4 | 0 |
| ODIs | 21 | 21 | 0 | 713 | 128 | 33.95 | 103.48 | 2 | 3 | 8 | 0 |
| T20Is | 7 | 7 | 0 | 57 | 36 | 8.14 | 103.63 | 0 | 0 | 1 | 0 |
| First-class | 124 | 211 | 18 | 7484 | 250 | 38.77 | 53.94 | 14 | 46 | 79 | 0 |
| List A | 122 | 117 | 2 | 3563 | 158 | 30.98 | 101.39 | 9 | 16 | 36 | 0 |
| Twenty20 | 85 | 82 | 3 | 1697 | 85 | 21.48 | 125.42 | 0 | 8 | 23 | 0 |
| **Bowling** | **Mat** | **Balls** | **Runs** | **Wkts** | **BBI** | **BBM** | **Ave** | **Econ** | **SR** | **5w** | **10** |
| Tests | 7 | 1054 | 618 | 22 | 6/67 | 8/129 | 28.09 | 3.51 | 47.9 | 1 | 0 |
| ODIs | 21 | 984 | 791 | 20 | 2/34 | 2/34 | 39.55 | 4.82 | 49.2 | 0 | 0 |
| T20Is | 7 | 48 | 72 | 1 | 1/31 | 1/31 | 72.00 | 9.00 | 48.0 | 0 | 0 |
| First-class | 124 | 11341 | 6586 | 169 | 6/29 | 12/96 | 38.97 | 3.48 | 67.1 | 5 | 1 |
| List A | 122 | 3213 | 2910 | 74 | 3/28 | 3/28 | 39.32 | 5.43 | 43.4 | 0 | 0 |
| Twenty20 | 85 | 1046 | 1279 | 48 | 5/34 | 5/34 | 26.64 | 7.33 | 21.7 | 1 | 0 |

# JIM ALLENBY

RHB RM R0 W1 MVP3

FULL NAME: James Allenby
BORN: September 12, 1982, Perth, Australia
SQUAD NO: 6
HEIGHT: 6ft
NICKNAME: Hank
EDUCATION: Christ Church Grammar School, Perth
TEAMS: Somerset, Glamorgan, Leicestershire, Western Australia
CAREER: First-class: 2006; List A: 2003; T20: 2005



BEST BATTING: 138* Leicestershire vs Bangladesh A, Leicester, 2008
BEST BOWLING: 6-54 Glamorgan vs Hampshire, Cardiff, 2014
COUNTY CAPS: 2010 (Glamorgan)

FAMILY TIES? My father was CEO of the WACA in the late '90s and my great-grandfather played for Yorkshire and Hampshire
CAREER HIGHLIGHTS? Winning the T20 Cup, scoring a hundred on Championship debut, scoring two T20 hundreds, taking a double hat-trick in the T20 Cup, getting my county cap at Glamorgan, taking 10 wickets in my last game for Glamorgan and signing for Somerset
CRICKETING HEROES? Steve Waugh – had an amazing ability to win games from tough situations. Dean Jones – extraordinary self-belief
CRICKET RULE YOU'D CHANGE? New ball after 60 overs
IF YOU WEREN'T A CRICKETER? Probably lawn-mowing
IF YOU COULD BE SOMEONE ELSE FOR A DAY? Any golfer (preferably a good one) playing during the Masters
SURPRISING FACT? I was a gardener and then a short-order chef in my first five years in England while I was trialling. Loved both of those jobs, and still back my egg-cooking ability!
TWITTER FEED: @jimallenby

| Batting | Mat | Inns | NO | Runs | HS | Ave | SR | 100 | 50 | Ct | St |
|---|---|---|---|---|---|---|---|---|---|---|---|
| First-class | 121 | 191 | 28 | 6656 | 138* | 40.83 | 59.41 | 10 | 46 | 121 | 0 |
| List A | 95 | 90 | 10 | 2096 | 91* | 26.20 | 87.47 | 0 | 10 | 33 | 0 |
| Twenty20 | 97 | 89 | 14 | 2407 | 110 | 32.09 | 124.58 | 2 | 16 | 26 | 0 |
| **Bowling** | **Mat** | **Balls** | **Runs** | **Wkts** | **BBI** | **BBM** | **Ave** | **Econ** | **SR** | **5w** | **10** |
| First-class | 121 | 14785 | 6551 | 254 | 6/54 | 10/128 | 25.79 | 2.65 | 58.2 | 5 | 1 |
| List A | 95 | 3096 | 2548 | 80 | 5/43 | 5/43 | 31.85 | 4.93 | 38.7 | 1 | 0 |
| Twenty20 | 97 | 1288 | 1685 | 52 | 5/21 | 5/21 | 32.40 | 7.84 | 24.7 | 2 | 0 |

## TIM AMBROSE

RHB WK R0 W0 MVP46

FULL NAME: Timothy Raymond Ambrose
BORN: December 1, 1982, Newcastle, Australia
SQUAD NO: 11
HEIGHT: 5ft 7in
NICKNAME: Freak
EDUCATION: Merewether Selective High, New South Wales
TEAMS: England, Warwickshire, Sussex
CAREER: Test: 2008; ODI: 2008; T20I: 2008; First-class: 2001; List A: 2001; T20: 2003

BEST BATTING: 251* Warwickshire vs Worcestershire, Worcester, 2007
COUNTY CAPS: 2003 (Sussex); 2007 (Warwickshire)

FAMILY TIES? Father played for Nelson Bay
CAREER HIGHLIGHTS? Winning the Championship with Sussex in 2003; any time I've played for England
SUPERSTITIONS? Left pad before right
CRICKETING HEROES? Steve Waugh, Adam Gilchrist, Mushtaq Ahmed
NON-CRICKETING HEROES? Peter Griffin, Eric Cantona
FAVOURITE TV? Dexter, Family Guy
SURPRISING FACT? Learning to play guitar

| Batting | Mat | Inns | NO | Runs | HS | Ave | SR | 100 | 50 | Ct | St |
|---|---|---|---|---|---|---|---|---|---|---|---|
| Tests | 11 | 16 | 1 | 447 | 102 | 29.80 | 46.41 | 1 | 3 | 31 | 0 |
| ODIs | 5 | 5 | 1 | 10 | 6 | 2.50 | 29.41 | 0 | 0 | 3 | 0 |
| T20Is | 1 | - | - | - | - | - | - | - | - | 1 | 1 |
| First-class | 181 | 274 | 26 | 8438 | 251* | 34.02 | 52.94 | 12 | 52 | 464 | 28 |
| List A | 145 | 119 | 18 | 3074 | 135 | 30.43 | 76.14 | 3 | 15 | 139 | 28 |
| Twenty20 | 68 | 50 | 15 | 858 | 77 | 24.51 | 112.15 | 0 | 2 | 40 | 20 |
| **Bowling** | **Mat** | **Balls** | **Runs** | **Wkts** | **BBI** | **BBM** | **Ave** | **Econ** | **SR** | **5w** | **10** |
| Tests | 11 | - | - | - | - | - | - | - | - | - | - |
| ODIs | 5 | - | - | - | - | - | - | - | - | - | - |
| T20Is | 1 | - | - | - | - | - | - | - | - | - | - |
| First-class | 181 | 6 | 1 | 0 | - | - | - | 1.00 | - | 0 | 0 |
| List A | 145 | - | - | - | - | - | - | - | - | - | - |
| Twenty20 | 68 | - | - | - | - | - | - | - | - | - | - |

## JAMES ANDERSON LHB RFM R0 W2

FULL NAME: James Michael Anderson
BORN: July 30, 1982, Burnley, Lancashire
SQUAD NO: 9
HEIGHT: 6ft 2in
NICKNAME: Jimmy, Jimbo, Jimbob
EDUCATION: St Theodore's RC High School; St Theodore's RC Sixth Form Centre, Burnley
TEAMS: England, Lancashire, Auckland
CAREER: Test: 2003; ODI: 2002; T20I: 2007; First-class: 2002; List A: 2000; T20: 2004



BEST BATTING: 81 England vs India, Nottingham, 2014
BEST BOWLING: 7-43 England vs New Zealand, Nottingham, 2008
COUNTY CAPS: 2003; BENEFIT YEAR: 2012

FAMILY TIES? My dad played for Burnley and uncle and cousin still play club cricket
CAREER HIGHLIGHTS? Three Ashes wins, County Championship winners' medal
CRICKETING HEROES? Allan Donald, Peter Martin, Glen Chapple
NON-CRICKETING HEROES? Ian Wright, Steve Davis (ex Burnley FC), Boris Becker
IF YOU WEREN'T A CRICKETER? Busking with my recorder
ACCOMPLISHMENTS? Marriage and kids, scaling Kilimanjaro
SURPRISING FACT? I can peel a potato in 2.4 seconds. I have a personality
FANTASY SLIP CORDON? Keeper: Inspector Gadget, Gully: Me
TWITTER FEED: @jimmy9

| Batting | Mat | Inns | NO | Runs | HS | Ave | SR | 100 | 50 | Ct | St |
|---|---|---|---|---|---|---|---|---|---|---|---|
| Tests | 99 | 135 | 48 | 949 | 81 | 10.90 | 39.94 | 0 | 1 | 57 | 0 |
| ODIs | 193 | 79 | 43 | 273 | 28 | 7.58 | 48.66 | 0 | 0 | 53 | 0 |
| T20Is | 19 | 4 | 3 | 1 | 1* | 1.00 | 50.00 | 0 | 0 | 3 | 0 |
| First-class | 174 | 217 | 79 | 1452 | 81 | 10.52 | | 0 | 1 | 95 | 0 |
| List A | 246 | 100 | 60 | 366 | 28 | 9.15 | | 0 | 0 | 62 | 0 |
| Twenty20 | 44 | 10 | 6 | 23 | 16 | 5.75 | 88.46 | 0 | 0 | 8 | 0 |
| **Bowling** | **Mat** | **Balls** | **Runs** | **Wkts** | **BBI** | **BBM** | **Ave** | **Econ** | **SR** | **5w** | **10** |
| Tests | 99 | 22114 | 11295 | 380 | 7/43 | 11/71 | 29.72 | 3.06 | 58.1 | 16 | 2 |
| ODIs | 193 | 9542 | 7843 | 268 | 5/23 | 5/23 | 29.26 | 4.93 | 35.6 | 2 | 0 |
| T20Is | 19 | 422 | 552 | 18 | 3/23 | 3/23 | 30.66 | 7.84 | 23.4 | 0 | 0 |
| First-class | 174 | 35184 | 18027 | 664 | 7/43 | | 27.14 | 3.07 | 52.9 | 32 | 5 |
| List A | 246 | 11952 | 9639 | 342 | 5/23 | 5/23 | 28.18 | 4.83 | 34.9 | 2 | 0 |
| Twenty20 | 44 | 933 | 1318 | 41 | 3/23 | 3/23 | 32.14 | 8.47 | 22.7 | 0 | 0 |

# GARETH ANDREW

LHB RMF R0 W1

FULL NAME: Gareth Mark Andrew
BORN: December 27, 1983, Yeovil, Somerset
SQUAD NO: 14
HEIGHT: 6ft
NICKNAME: Gaz, Brad, Golden Gary
EDUCATION: Ansford Community School; Richard Huish College
TEAMS: Worcestershire, Canterbury, Somerset
CAREER: First-class: 2003; List A: 2000; T20: 2003

BEST BATTING: 180* Canterbury vs Auckland, Auckland, 2012
BEST BOWLING: 5-40 Worcestershire vs Glamorgan, Cardiff, 2014

CAREER HIGHLIGHTS? Winning the 2005 T20 Cup with Somerset, getting promotion to Division One with Worcestershire in 2008 and 2010 and helping Worcestershire avoid relegation in 2011
MOST MARKED CHARACTERISTIC? I love a list
CRICKETING HEROES? Ian Botham, Keith Parsons, Ivan Short
NON-CRICKETING HEROES? Keith Lemon
IF YOU WEREN'T A CRICKETER? I'd be an archaeologist, like Indiana Jones
DESERT ISLAND DISC? Kings Of Leon – Only By The Night
FAVOURITE TV? Strike Back
ACCOMPLISHMENTS? I've got a few qualifications and I like to do my bit for charities
SURPRISING FACT? I'm seriously colourblind
FANTASY SLIP CORDON? Keeper: Angelina Jolie, 1st: John Bishop, 2nd: Myself, 3rd: Keith Lemon, Gully: Dynamo
TWITTER FEED: @GAndrew14

| Batting | Mat | Inns | NO | Runs | HS | Ave | SR | 100 | 50 | Ct | St |
|---|---|---|---|---|---|---|---|---|---|---|---|
| First-class | 87 | 132 | 17 | 2757 | 180* | 23.97 | 55.40 | 1 | 16 | 30 | 0 |
| List A | 114 | 80 | 15 | 1175 | 104 | 18.07 | | 1 | 2 | 39 | 0 |
| Twenty20 | 103 | 72 | 22 | 807 | 65* | 16.14 | 136.31 | 0 | 4 | 28 | 0 |
| **Bowling** | **Mat** | **Balls** | **Runs** | **Wkts** | **BBI** | **BBM** | **Ave** | **Econ** | **SR** | **5w** | **10** |
| First-class | 87 | 11787 | 7482 | 221 | 5/40 | | 33.85 | 3.80 | 53.3 | 5 | 0 |
| List A | 114 | 3524 | 3667 | 104 | 5/31 | 5/31 | 35.25 | 6.24 | 33.8 | 1 | 0 |
| Twenty20 | 103 | 1751 | 2492 | 87 | 4/22 | 4/22 | 28.64 | 8.53 | 20.1 | 0 | 0 |

# ZAFAR ANSARI

## LHB SLA R1 W0 MVP64

FULL NAME: Zafar Shahaan Ansari
BORN: December 10, 1991, Ascot, Berkshire
SQUAD NO: 22
HEIGHT: 6ft
NICKNAME: PM, Zaf
EDUCATION: Hampton School; University of Cambridge
TEAMS: Surrey
CAREER: First-class: 2011; List A: 2010; T20: 2011



BEST BATTING: 112 Surrey vs Glamorgan, Colwyn Bay, 2014
BEST BOWLING: 5-33 CMCCU vs Surrey, Fenner's, 2011

FAMILY TIES? My father played a couple of first-class matches in Pakistan, my brother Akbar captained Cambridge Blues, played first-class cricket for Cambridge MCCU, and 2nd XI cricket for various counties
CAREER HIGHLIGHTS? Winning the CB40 in 2011 and the T20 Finals Days in 2013 and 2014
MOST MARKED CHARACTERISTIC? Bookishness
CRICKETING HEROES? Wasim Akram – because he is Pakistani and a left-armer
NON-CRICKETING HEROES? Angela Davis and Frantz Fanon, for their anti-colonial activism
CRICKET RULE YOU'D CHANGE? Not really a rule, but I'd get rid of individual statistics. It would make it into a genuine team sport
COACHING TIP? Do not change your technique if things aren't going well, if it is a technique that has worked for you in the past
ACCOMPLISHMENTS? Gaining a double first in my Cambridge degree
PET HATE? Lateness, because it's selfish
FANTASY SLIP CORDON? Keeper: Malcolm X, 1st: Rosa Luxemburg, 2nd: Chimamanda Adichie, 3rd: Angela Davis, Gully: Myself

| Batting | Mat | Inns | NO | Runs | HS | Ave | SR | 100 | 50 | Ct | St |
|---|---|---|---|---|---|---|---|---|---|---|---|
| First-class | 41 | 67 | 12 | 1659 | 112 | 30.16 | 35.70 | 2 | 9 | 17 | 0 |
| List A | 27 | 23 | 8 | 474 | 62 | 31.60 | 93.86 | 0 | 2 | 17 | 0 |
| Twenty20 | 48 | 34 | 16 | 463 | 38* | 25.72 | 107.17 | 0 | 0 | 9 | 0 |
| **Bowling** | **Mat** | **Balls** | **Runs** | **Wkts** | **BBI** | **BBM** | **Ave** | **Econ** | **SR** | **5w** | **10** |
| First-class | 41 | 4059 | 2068 | 54 | 5/33 | 6/115 | 38.29 | 3.05 | 75.1 | 2 | 0 |
| List A | 27 | 797 | 767 | 25 | 4/42 | 4/42 | 30.68 | 5.77 | 31.8 | 0 | 0 |
| Twenty20 | 48 | 618 | 784 | 23 | 3/27 | 3/27 | 34.08 | 7.61 | 26.8 | 0 | 0 |

# JAMES ANYON

LHB RFM R0 W2

FULL NAME: James Edward Anyon
BORN: May 5, 1983, Lancaster
SQUAD NO: 30
HEIGHT: 6ft 2in
NICKNAME: Jimmy
EDUCATION: Garstang High School; Preston College; Loughborough University
TEAMS: Sussex, Surrey, Warwickshire
CAREER: First-class: 2003; List A: 2004; T20: 2005

BEST BATTING: 64* Sussex vs Surrey, Horsham, 2012
BEST BOWLING: 6-82 Warwickshire vs Glamorgan, Cardiff, 2008
COUNTY CAPS: 2011

FAMILY TIES? My dad played for Calder CC. Great hands!
CAREER HIGHLIGHTS? My T20 hat-trick vs Somerset in 2005. My Man of the Match performance against Nottinghamshire in 2011
MOST MARKED CHARACTERISTIC? Grumpiness
CRICKETING HEROES? Curtly Ambrose, Glenn McGrath, Darren Gough, Mike Atherton
NON-CRICKETING HEROES? Fred Dibnah
CRICKET RULE YOU'D CHANGE? Back-foot no-balls
IF YOU WEREN'T A CRICKETER? A fitness instructor
FAVOURITE TV? Anything on the History or Discovery channels
ACCOMPLISHMENTS? Getting married
SURPRISING FACT? I represented the North-West in a cow-judging competition
FANTASY SLIP CORDON? I wouldn't have any. Spread the field and let's have some quiet, no?
TWITTER FEED: @Landskilljames

| Batting | Mat | Inns | NO | Runs | HS | Ave | SR | 100 | 50 | Ct | St |
|---|---|---|---|---|---|---|---|---|---|---|---|
| First-class | 110 | 143 | 43 | 1450 | 64* | 14.50 | 37.40 | 0 | 5 | 32 | 0 |
| List A | 43 | 14 | 6 | 43 | 12 | 5.37 | 72.88 | 0 | 0 | 9 | 0 |
| Twenty20 | 26 | 6 | 3 | 18 | 8* | 6.00 | 66.66 | 0 | 0 | 3 | 0 |
| **Bowling** | **Mat** | **Balls** | **Runs** | **Wkts** | **BBI** | **BBM** | **Ave** | **Econ** | **SR** | **5w** | **10** |
| First-class | 110 | 17494 | 10954 | 311 | 6/82 | | 35.22 | 3.75 | 56.2 | 7 | 0 |
| List A | 43 | 1557 | 1436 | 47 | 3/6 | 3/6 | 30.55 | 5.53 | 33.1 | 0 | 0 |
| Twenty20 | 26 | 423 | 587 | 30 | 3/6 | 3/6 | 19.56 | 8.32 | 14.1 | 0 | 0 |

## YASIR ARAFAT RHB RFM R0 W0

**FULL NAME:** Yasir Arafat Satti
**BORN:** March 12, 1982, Rawalpindi, Pakistan
**SQUAD NO:** 99
**NICKNAME:** Yas
**TEAMS:** Pakistan, Scotland, Hampshire, Barisal Burners, Canterbury, Dolphins, Kent, Khan Research Labs, Lancashire, Otago, Rawalpindi, Reco Pakistan Ltd, Somerset, Surrey, Sussex
**CAREER:** Test: 2007; ODI: 2000; T20I: 2007; First-class: 1997; List A: 1997; T20: 2006



**BEST BATTING:** 170 Khan Research Laboratories vs Multan, Multan, 2011
**BEST BOWLING:** 9-35 Khan Research Laboratories vs Sui Southern Gas Company, Rawalpindi, 2008
**COUNTY CAPS:** 2006 (Sussex); 2007 (Kent)

**NOTES:** Arafat has a wealth of experience in county cricket having represented Sussex, Surrey, Kent, Somerset and Lancashire. He joins Hampshire for the RL Cup and the T20 Blast. He is third on the all-time list of T20 wicket-takers with 255 scalps, behind Dirk Nannes and Lasith Malinga. He took 33 one-day wickets for Sussex last season. He represented Pakistan as recently as 2012 but has only ever featured sporadically for his country. He took five wickets in the space of six balls in a Pakistani domestic game in 2004, a feat matched only by three other bowlers in the history of the game

| Batting | Mat | Inns | NO | Runs | HS | Ave | SR | 100 | 50 | Ct | St |
|---|---|---|---|---|---|---|---|---|---|---|---|
| Tests | 3 | 3 | 1 | 94 | 50* | 47.00 | 46.76 | 0 | 1 | 0 | 0 |
| ODIs | 11 | 8 | 3 | 74 | 27 | 14.80 | 67.27 | 0 | 0 | 2 | 0 |
| T20Is | 13 | 11 | 4 | 92 | 17 | 13.14 | 116.45 | 0 | 0 | 1 | 0 |
| First-class | 200 | 291 | 41 | 6784 | 170 | 27.13 | | 5 | 35 | 54 | 0 |
| List A | 244 | 176 | 49 | 2721 | 110* | 21.42 | | 1 | 9 | 52 | 0 |
| Twenty20 | 197 | 125 | 45 | 1156 | 49 | 14.45 | 119.42 | 0 | 0 | 29 | 0 |
| **Bowling** | **Mat** | **Balls** | **Runs** | **Wkts** | **BBI** | **BBM** | **Ave** | **Econ** | **SR** | **5w** | **10** |
| Tests | 3 | 627 | 438 | 9 | 5/161 | 7/210 | 48.66 | 4.19 | 69.6 | 1 | 0 |
| ODIs | 11 | 414 | 373 | 4 | 1/28 | 1/28 | 93.25 | 5.40 | 103.5 | 0 | 0 |
| T20Is | 13 | 236 | 316 | 16 | 3/18 | 3/18 | 19.75 | 8.03 | 14.7 | 0 | 0 |
| First-class | 200 | 32657 | 18663 | 773 | 9/35 | | 24.14 | 3.42 | 42.2 | 43 | 5 |
| List A | 244 | 11577 | 9599 | 393 | 6/24 | 6/24 | 24.42 | 4.97 | 29.4 | 8 | 0 |
| Twenty20 | 197 | 4086 | 5401 | 255 | 4/5 | 4/5 | 21.18 | 7.93 | 16.0 | 0 | 0 |

## USMAN ARSHAD RHB RFM R0 W0



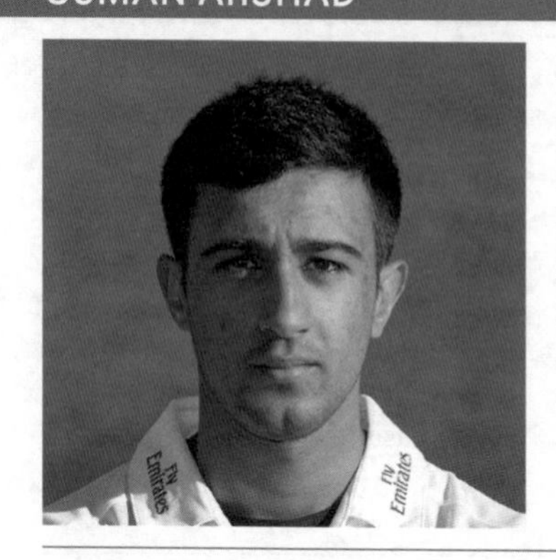


FULL NAME: Usman Arshad
BORN: January 9, 1993, Bradford, Yorkshire
SQUAD NO: 78
HEIGHT: 5ft 11in
NICKNAME: Benny
EDUCATION: Beckfoot Grammar School
TEAMS: Durham
CAREER: First-class: 2013; List A: 2013; T20: 2014

BEST BATTING: 83 Durham vs Sussex, Hove, 2013
BEST BOWLING: 4-78 Durham vs Northamptonshire, Northampton, 2014
COUNTY CAPS: 2014

CAREER HIGHLIGHTS? Making my first-class debut
SUPERSTITIONS? I always put my right pad on first
CRICKETING HEROES? Wasim Akram
IF YOU WEREN'T A CRICKETER? Doctor
DESERT ISLAND DISC? J. Cole – Born Sinner
FAVOURITE TV? EastEnders, Family Guy
ACCOMPLISHMENTS? I raised £1,455 for charity
SURPRISING FACT? I played for Yorkshire when I was 14
FANTASY SLIP CORDON? Keeper: Chris Martin, 1st: Ryan Buckley, 2nd: Keaton Jennings, 3rd: Waj from Four Lions, Gully: Faisal from Four Lions
TWITTER FEED: @usman_arshad65

| Batting | Mat | Inns | NO | Runs | HS | Ave | SR | 100 | 50 | Ct | St |
|---|---|---|---|---|---|---|---|---|---|---|---|
| First-class | 11 | 14 | 1 | 318 | 83 | 24.46 | 51.53 | 0 | 1 | 2 | 0 |
| List A | 1 | - | - | - | - | - | - | - | - | 0 | 0 |
| Twenty20 | 10 | 3 | 0 | 17 | 10 | 5.66 | 80.95 | 0 | 0 | 4 | 0 |
| **Bowling** | **Mat** | **Balls** | **Runs** | **Wkts** | **BBI** | **BBM** | **Ave** | **Econ** | **SR** | **5w** | **10** |
| First-class | 11 | 1100 | 628 | 31 | 4/78 | 6/34 | 20.25 | 3.42 | 35.4 | 0 | 0 |
| List A | 1 | 18 | 13 | 0 | - | - | - | 4.33 | - | 0 | 0 |
| Twenty20 | 10 | 163 | 222 | 8 | 2/21 | 2/21 | 27.75 | 8.17 | 20.3 | 0 | 0 |

# MOIN ASHRAF

## RHB RFM R0 W0

FULL NAME: Moin Aqeeb Ashraf
BORN: January 5, 1992, Bradford, Yorkshire
SQUAD NO: 23
NICKNAME: MoJo, Mo, The Official
EDUCATION: Dixons City Academy; Leeds Metropolitan University
TEAMS: Yorkshire
CAREER: First-class: 2010; List A: 2011; T20: 2012



BEST BATTING: 10 Yorkshire vs Kent, Leeds, 2010
BEST BOWLING: 5-32 Yorkshire vs Kent, Leeds, 2010

FAMILY TIES? My brothers and two of my uncles played club cricket in the Bradford League. They were the ones who got me playing. Dad has always been a keen cricketer but he's never been any good!
CAREER HIGHLIGHTS? Taking 5-32 vs Kent at Headingley on my home debut, 4-16 against Derbyshire in the T20 and playing in the Champions League in South Africa
MOST MARKED CHARACTERISTIC? My hair
SUPERSTITIONS? Not a superstition but I pray to God for the health and well-being of everyone in attendance at the game I am taking part in
CRICKETING HEROES? Imran Khan
NON-CRICKETING HEROES? Muhammad Ali, Cristiano Ronaldo
CRICKET RULE YOU'D CHANGE? The rule. If it's going on to hit the wickets it's out, regardless of where it pitches
IF YOU WEREN'T A CRICKETER? Actor
SURPRISING FACT? It takes me an hour to do my hair each morning
TWITTER FEED: @MoinA23

| Batting | Mat | Inns | NO | Runs | HS | Ave | SR | 100 | 50 | Ct | St |
|---|---|---|---|---|---|---|---|---|---|---|---|
| First-class | 21 | 19 | 5 | 56 | 10 | 4.00 | 18.66 | 0 | 0 | 2 | 0 |
| List A | 23 | 6 | 4 | 3 | 3* | 1.50 | 50.00 | 0 | 0 | 4 | 0 |
| Twenty20 | 17 | 1 | 0 | 4 | 4 | 4.00 | 66.66 | 0 | 0 | 1 | 0 |
| **Bowling** | **Mat** | **Balls** | **Runs** | **Wkts** | **BBI** | **BBM** | **Ave** | **Econ** | **SR** | **5w** | **10** |
| First-class | 21 | 2336 | 1268 | 43 | 5/32 | 6/45 | 29.48 | 3.25 | 54.3 | 1 | 0 |
| List A | 23 | 930 | 920 | 25 | 3/38 | 3/38 | 36.80 | 5.93 | 37.2 | 0 | 0 |
| Twenty20 | 17 | 345 | 462 | 17 | 4/18 | 4/18 | 27.17 | 8.03 | 20.2 | 0 | 0 |

# MOHAMMAD AZHARULLAH RHB RFM R0 W0 MVP63

FULL NAME: Mohammad Azharullah
BORN: December 25, 1983, Burewala, Pakistan
SQUAD NO: 92
TEAMS: Northamptonshire, Multan Region, Multan Tigers, Quetta Bears, Water and Power Development Authority
CAREER: First-class: 2004; List A: 2005; T20: 2005

BEST BATTING: 41 Water and Power Development Authority vs Kerachi Whites, Kerachi, 2007
BEST BOWLING: 7-74 Quetta vs Lahore Ravi, Quetta, 2005

TWITTER FEED: @Azhar_ullah
NOTES: The Pakistan-born seamer signed for Northamptonshire ahead of the 2013 season and finished the campaign as the leading wicket-taker in the Friends Life t20 with a haul of 27, helping his side to the trophy. He also took 25 first-class wickets at 28.68 as Northants won promotion to Division One of the County Championship, earning himself a new two-year deal. He was Northants' leading bowler last season, taking 46 wickets in the Championship. Azharullah played first-class cricket in Pakistan before moving to England in 2010 and had to wait three years to gain UK citizenship and in turn qualification for a county side. Married to Emma Taylor, the scorer at his Bradford League club Pudsey Congs

| Batting | Mat | Inns | NO | Runs | HS | Ave | SR | 100 | 50 | Ct | St |
|---|---|---|---|---|---|---|---|---|---|---|---|
| First-class | 76 | 105 | 59 | 634 | 41 | 13.78 | | 0 | 0 | 17 | 0 |
| List A | 41 | 16 | 9 | 57 | 9 | 8.14 | 57.57 | 0 | 0 | 9 | 0 |
| Twenty20 | 32 | 10 | 9 | 16 | 5* | 16.00 | 69.56 | 0 | 0 | 6 | 0 |

| Bowling | Mat | Balls | Runs | Wkts | BBI | BBM | Ave | Econ | SR | 5w | 10 |
|---|---|---|---|---|---|---|---|---|---|---|---|
| First-class | 76 | 12619 | 7258 | 261 | 7/74 | | 27.80 | 3.45 | 48.3 | 12 | 2 |
| List A | 41 | 1841 | 1665 | 63 | 5/38 | 5/38 | 26.42 | 5.42 | 29.2 | 2 | 0 |
| Twenty20 | 32 | 638 | 864 | 41 | 4/14 | 4/14 | 21.07 | 8.12 | 15.5 | 0 | 0 |

# TOM BAILEY

RHB RFM R0 W0

FULL NAME: Tom Ernest Bailey
BORN: April 21, 1991, Preston, Lancashire
SQUAD NO: 8
HEIGHT: 6ft 4in
NICKNAME: Jebby
EDUCATION: Myerscough College
TEAMS: Lancashire
CAREER: First-class: 2012; List A: 2014



BEST BATTING: 25* Lancashire vs Yorkshire, Manchester, 2014
BEST BOWLING: 2-36 Lancashire vs Middlesex, Manchester, 2014

FAMILY TIES? My dad played for a local side and I used to watch him every weekend as a kid
CAREER HIGHLIGHTS? Making my first-class debut for my home county
BEST PLAYER IN COUNTY CRICKET? Paul Horton
TIP FOR THE TOP? Haseeb Hameed
MOST MARKED CHARACTERISTIC? Daydreaming
CRICKETING HEROES? Steve Harmison – I just wanted to bowl fast!
CRICKET RULE YOU'D CHANGE? No DRS. Umpires are there for a reason
COACHING TIP? See ball, hit ball
IF YOU WEREN'T A CRICKETER? Making millions
IF YOU COULD BE SOMEONE ELSE FOR A DAY? Prince Harry
DESERT ISLAND DISC? Fugees – Greatest Hits
FAVOURITE TV? Cricket
LEAST FAVOURITE TV? Big Brother
ACCOMPLISHMENTS? I managed to read a book
SURPRISING FACT? I'm actually really smart
TWITTER FEED: @tombaildog

| Batting | Mat | Inns | NO | Runs | HS | Ave | SR | 100 | 50 | Ct | St |
|---|---|---|---|---|---|---|---|---|---|---|---|
| First-class | 4 | 5 | 3 | 55 | 25* | 27.50 | 51.40 | 0 | 0 | 0 | 0 |
| List A | 4 | 1 | 1 | 4 | 4* | - | 133.33 | 0 | 0 | 0 | 0 |
| **Bowling** | **Mat** | **Balls** | **Runs** | **Wkts** | **BBI** | **BBM** | **Ave** | **Econ** | **SR** | **5w** | **10** |
| First-class | 4 | 612 | 339 | 7 | 2/36 | 3/82 | 48.42 | 3.32 | 87.4 | 0 | 0 |
| List A | 4 | 228 | 194 | 7 | 3/41 | 3/41 | 27.71 | 5.10 | 32.5 | 0 | 0 |

# JONNY BAIRSTOW RHB WK R1 W0 MVP57



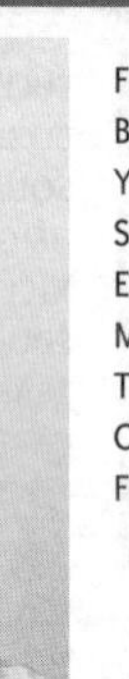

FULL NAME: Jonathan Marc Bairstow
BORN: September 26, 1989, Bradford, Yorkshire
SQUAD NO: 21
EDUCATION: St. Peter's School, York; Leeds Metropolitan University
TEAMS: England, Yorkshire
CAREER: Test: 2012; ODI: 2011; T20I: 2011; First-class: 2009; List A: 2009; T20: 2010

BEST BATTING: 205 Yorkshire vs Nottinghamshire, Nottingham, 2011
COUNTY CAPS: 2011

FAMILY TIES? My father David played for Yorkshire and England
CAREER HIGHLIGHTS? Making my Test debut and being named MotM on my ODI debut
CRICKETING HEROES? Sachin Tendulkar
NON-CRICKETING HEROES? Jonny Wilkinson and Steve Irwin
IF YOU WEREN'T A CRICKETER? I'd be a rugby player
DESERT ISLAND DISC? Vengaboys or David Guetta
SURPRISING FACT? I played football for the Leeds United Academy for seven years
FANTASY SLIP CORDON? Keeper: David Bairstow, 1st: Me, 2nd: David Beckham, 3rd: Mila Kunis, 4th: Ray Mears, Gully: Elisha Cuthbert
TWITTER FEED: @jbairstow21

| Batting | Mat | Inns | NO | Runs | HS | Ave | SR | 100 | 50 | Ct | St |
|---|---|---|---|---|---|---|---|---|---|---|---|
| Tests | 14 | 24 | 2 | 593 | 95 | 26.95 | 48.36 | 0 | 4 | 16 | 0 |
| ODIs | 7 | 6 | 1 | 119 | 41* | 23.80 | 76.77 | 0 | 0 | 3 | 0 |
| T20Is | 18 | 14 | 4 | 194 | 60* | 19.40 | 108.37 | 0 | 1 | 21 | 0 |
| First-class | 103 | 166 | 23 | 6136 | 205 | 42.90 | | 11 | 36 | 239 | 10 |
| List A | 63 | 56 | 7 | 1551 | 123 | 31.65 | 98.41 | 2 | 8 | 44 | 4 |
| Twenty20 | 72 | 61 | 13 | 1088 | 102* | 22.66 | 122.52 | 1 | 4 | 39 | 8 |
| **Bowling** | **Mat** | **Balls** | **Runs** | **Wkts** | **BBI** | **BBM** | **Ave** | **Econ** | **SR** | **5w** | **10** |
| Tests | 14 | - | - | - | - | - | - | - | - | - | - |
| ODIs | 7 | - | - | - | - | - | - | - | - | - | - |
| T20Is | 18 | - | - | - | - | - | - | - | - | - | - |
| First-class | 103 | 6 | 1 | 0 | - | - | - | 1.00 | - | 0 | 0 |
| List A | 63 | - | - | - | - | - | - | - | - | - | - |
| Twenty20 | 72 | - | - | - | - | - | - | - | - | - | - |

# ANDY BALBIRNIE

RHB OB WK R0 W0

FULL NAME: Andrew Balbirnie
BORN: December 28, 1990, Dublin, Ireland
SQUAD NO: 15
HEIGHT: 6ft 1in
NICKNAME: Balbo, Big Head, Planet Head
EDUCATION: St. Andrew's College Dublin; Cardiff Metropolitan University
TEAMS: Ireland, Middlesex
CAREER: ODI: 2010; First-class: 2012; List A: 2010



BEST BATTING: 38 Ireland vs Scotland, Dublin, 2013
BEST BOWLING: 1-5 Ireland vs Netherlands, Deventer, 2013

FAMILY TIES? My grandfather played for Leinster and my youngest brother Jack plays for Ireland U19
CAREER HIGHLIGHTS? My Middlesex and Ireland debuts
BEST PLAYER IN COUNTY CRICKET? Ed Joyce
MOST MARKED CHARACTERISTIC? Some say I have a big head. But I don't believe them
CRICKETING HEROES? Michael Vaughan – because I thought he was very elegant to watch. Sachin Tendulker as well due to what he has done for the game
CRICKET RULE YOU'D CHANGE? Tea should be longer than 20 minutes
COACHING TIP? Keep your head still while batting as it is the heaviest part of your body
IF YOU WEREN'T A CRICKETER? Something in sport, maybe photography. I would like to go into journalism potentially
PET HATE? An obnoxious laugh
TWITTER FEED: @balbo90

| Batting | Mat | Inns | NO | Runs | HS | Ave | SR | 100 | 50 | Ct | St |
|---|---|---|---|---|---|---|---|---|---|---|---|
| ODIs | 15 | 14 | 1 | 351 | 97 | 27.00 | 67.37 | 0 | 2 | 1 | 0 |
| First-class | 9 | 13 | 1 | 181 | 38 | 15.08 | 52.76 | 0 | 0 | 6 | 0 |
| List A | 20 | 18 | 1 | 520 | 129 | 30.58 | 76.35 | 1 | 2 | 4 | 0 |
| Twenty20 | 2 | 2 | 0 | 2 | 2 | 1.00 | 33.33 | 0 | 0 | 1 | 0 |
| **Bowling** | **Mat** | **Balls** | **Runs** | **Wkts** | **BBI** | **BBM** | **Ave** | **Econ** | **SR** | **5w** | **10** |
| ODIs | 15 | 60 | 68 | 2 | 1/26 | 1/26 | 34.00 | 6.80 | 30.0 | 0 | 0 |
| First-class | 9 | 168 | 95 | 2 | 1/5 | 2/25 | 47.50 | 3.39 | 84.0 | 0 | 0 |
| List A | 20 | 84 | 95 | 2 | 1/26 | 1/26 | 47.50 | 6.78 | 42.0 | 0 | 0 |
| Twenty20 | 2 | - | - | - | - | - | - | - | - | - | - |

## DAVID BALCOMBE

RHB RMF R0 W1

FULL NAME: David John Balcombe
BORN: December 24, 1984, City of London
SQUAD NO: 84
HEIGHT: 6ft 3in
NICKNAME: Balcs
EDUCATION: St John's School, Leatherhead; Durham University
TEAMS: Surrey, Hampshire, Kent
CAREER: First-class: 2005; List A: 2007; T20: 2006

BEST BATTING: 73 vs Hampshire vs Leicestershire, Leicester, 2012
BEST BOWLING: 8-71 Hampshire vs Gloucestershire, Southampton, 2012
COUNTY CAPS: 2013 (Hampshire)

CAREER HIGHLIGHTS? Taking 8 for 71, my best-ever Championship figures at the Ageas Bowl and my maiden first-class five-fer at The Oval (a wonderful memory at a wonderful ground)
BEST PLAYER IN COUNTY CRICKET? Kumar Sangakkara
TIP FOR THE TOP? Tom Curran
MOST MARKED CHARACTERISTIC? I look like Boris Johnson
CRICKETING HEROES? Craig McDermott, Paul Reiffel
CRICKET RULE YOU'D CHANGE? Double-Plays
IF YOU WEREN'T A CRICKETER? A property magnate
IF YOU COULD BE SOMEONE ELSE FOR A DAY? Prince Harry
DESERT ISLAND DISC? Taking just one record would make me very bored
PET HATE? Ignorance on public transport
FANTASY SLIP CORDON? Keeper: Boris Johnson, 1st: Mark Wahlberg, 2nd: Alex Tysoe (Surrey's head physio), 3rd: Me, Gully: James Corden
TWITTER FEED: @DavidBalcombe1

| Batting | Mat | Inns | NO | Runs | HS | Ave | SR | 100 | 50 | Ct | St |
|---|---|---|---|---|---|---|---|---|---|---|---|
| First-class | 67 | 83 | 20 | 958 | 73 | 15.20 | 53.40 | 0 | 3 | 14 | 0 |
| List A | 14 | 5 | 0 | 10 | 6 | 2.00 | 32.25 | 0 | 0 | 5 | 0 |
| Twenty20 | 3 | 2 | 1 | 3 | 3 | 3.00 | 60.00 | 0 | 0 | 0 | 0 |
| **Bowling** | **Mat** | **Balls** | **Runs** | **Wkts** | **BBI** | **BBM** | **Ave** | **Econ** | **SR** | **5w** | **10** |
| First-class | 67 | 11278 | 6436 | 196 | 8/71 | | 32.83 | 3.42 | 57.5 | 9 | 2 |
| List A | 14 | 519 | 492 | 18 | 4/38 | 4/38 | 27.33 | 5.68 | 28.8 | 0 | 0 |
| Twenty20 | 3 | 49 | 61 | 1 | 1/23 | 1/23 | 61.00 | 7.46 | 49.0 | 0 | 0 |

# ADAM BALL

RHB LFM R0 W0

FULL NAME: Adam James Ball
BORN: March 1, 1993, Greenwich, London
SQUAD NO: 24
HEIGHT: 6ft 2in
NICKNAME: Bally
EDUCATION: Beths Grammar School, Bexley
TEAMS: Kent
CAREER: First-class: 2011; List A: 2010; T20: 2011



BEST BATTING: 69 Kent vs Lancashire, Canterbury, 2013
BEST BOWLING: 3-36 Kent vs Leicestershire, Leicester, 2011

CAREER HIGHLIGHTS? Signing my first professional contract with Kent and being named as England U19 captain
CRICKETING HEROES? Andrew Flintoff
DESERT ISLAND DISC? Taio Cruz
TWITTER FEED: @AdamBall2
NOTES: Left-arm seamer Ball was handed his Kent List A debut in 2010 and was called up to the England U19 team in the same year. He made nine Championship appearances in 2011, taking 15 wickets including career-best figures of 3-36 vs Leicestershire at Leicester. In 2012 he captained the England U19 side and was Kent's leading T20 wicket-taker with 12 at an average of 18. He was plagued by injury in 2013 and made only two County Championship appearances. He made his highest first-class score in one of these, hitting 69 in the final game of the season against Lancashire at Canterbury. He struggled for form in 2014, picking up just 18 wickets across all formats

| Batting | Mat | Inns | NO | Runs | HS | Ave | SR | 100 | 50 | Ct | St |
|---|---|---|---|---|---|---|---|---|---|---|---|
| First-class | 20 | 28 | 3 | 560 | 69 | 22.40 | 41.57 | 0 | 2 | 10 | 0 |
| List A | 26 | 18 | 6 | 164 | 28 | 13.66 | 91.11 | 0 | 0 | 4 | 0 |
| Twenty20 | 33 | 16 | 4 | 128 | 18 | 10.66 | 101.58 | 0 | 0 | 21 | 0 |
| **Bowling** | **Mat** | **Balls** | **Runs** | **Wkts** | **BBI** | **BBM** | **Ave** | **Econ** | **SR** | **5w** | **10** |
| First-class | 20 | 1652 | 1094 | 25 | 3/36 | 3/45 | 43.76 | 3.97 | 66.0 | 0 | 0 |
| List A | 26 | 825 | 781 | 22 | 3/36 | 3/36 | 35.50 | 5.68 | 37.5 | 0 | 0 |
| Twenty20 | 33 | 558 | 761 | 26 | 2/18 | 2/18 | 29.26 | 8.18 | 21.4 | 0 | 0 |

# JAKE BALL

## RHB RFM R0 W0

FULL NAME: Jacob Timothy Ball
BORN: March 14, 1991, Mansfield, Nottinghamshire
SQUAD NO: 28
HEIGHT: 6ft 3in
NICKNAME: Yak
EDUCATION: Meden School
TEAMS: Nottinghamshire
CAREER: First-class: 2011; List A: 2009; T20: 2011

BEST BATTING: 31 Nottinghamshire vs Oxford MCCU, Oxford, 2014
BEST BOWLING: 3-18 Nottinghamshire vs Durham MCCU, Oxford, 2013

FAMILY TIES? My uncle is Bruce French, who kept wicket for England and Notts
CAREER HIGHLIGHTS? Getting Man of the Match in a Pro40 semi-final
BEST PLAYER IN COUNTY CRICKET? Ben Stokes
TIP FOR THE TOP? Luke Wood
MOST MARKED CHARACTERISTIC? Being lanky
SUPERSTITIONS? I always wear Calvin Klein boxers to bowl in
CRICKETING HEROES? Dale Steyn – he's the best in the world
CRICKET RULE YOU'D CHANGE? Have five fielders outside of the circle in one-day cricket
IF YOU WEREN'T A CRICKETER? Working in property
IF YOU COULD BE SOMEONE ELSE FOR A DAY? David Beckham
DESERT ISLAND DISC? The Beatles – 1
FAVOURITE TV? I love watching Suits – I like to think I could be a lawyer!
PET HATE? People stopping in front of you in a shopping centre
TWITTER FEED: @Jakeball30

| Batting | Mat | Inns | NO | Runs | HS | Ave | SR | 100 | 50 | Ct | St |
|---|---|---|---|---|---|---|---|---|---|---|---|
| First-class | 7 | 11 | 1 | 106 | 31 | 10.60 | 61.62 | 0 | 0 | 0 | 0 |
| List A | 33 | 14 | 6 | 86 | 19* | 10.75 | 110.25 | 0 | 0 | 2 | 0 |
| Twenty20 | 11 | 1 | 1 | 1 | 1* | - | 100.00 | 0 | 0 | 3 | 0 |
| **Bowling** | **Mat** | **Balls** | **Runs** | **Wkts** | **BBI** | **BBM** | **Ave** | **Econ** | **SR** | **5w** | **10** |
| First-class | 7 | 768 | 420 | 17 | 3/18 | 5/108 | 24.70 | 3.28 | 45.1 | 0 | 0 |
| List A | 33 | 1159 | 1137 | 37 | 4/25 | 4/25 | 30.72 | 5.88 | 31.3 | 0 | 0 |
| Twenty20 | 11 | 210 | 306 | 11 | 3/38 | 3/38 | 27.81 | 8.74 | 19.0 | 0 | 0 |

# GARY BALLANCE LHB LB R2 W0 MVP25

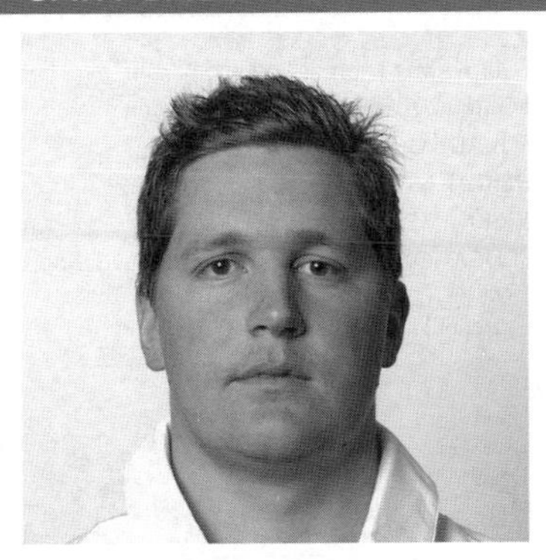

FULL NAME: Gary Simon Ballance
BORN: November 22, 1989, Harare, Zimbabwe
SQUAD NO: 19
NICKNAME: Gazza
EDUCATION: Peterhouse, Zimbabwe; Harrow School
TEAMS: England, Yorkshire, Mid West Rhinos, Zimbabwe U19
CAREER: Test: 2014; ODI: 2013; First-class: 2008; List A: 2006; T20: 2010



BEST BATTING: 210 Midwest Rhinos vs Southern Rocks, Masvingo, 2011
COUNTY CAPS: 2012

NOTES: A close family friend of former Zimbabwe skipper David Houghton, Ballance signed for Derbyshire at 16 before joining the Yorkshire Academy in 2008. He played for Zimbabwe U19 at the World Cup in 2006 before qualifying to play for England. Toured Australia with the England Lions squad in February 2013 and made his ODI debut against Ireland Iin 2013 before being selected in England's Ashes tour party, making his Test bow at Sydney in January. He had an exceptional summer in Test cricket in 2014, hitting three centuries to cement his place at No.3

| Batting | Mat | Inns | NO | Runs | HS | Ave | SR | 100 | 50 | Ct | St |
|---|---|---|---|---|---|---|---|---|---|---|---|
| Tests | 8 | 13 | 1 | 729 | 156 | 60.75 | 50.87 | 3 | 3 | 7 | 0 |
| ODIs | 16 | 15 | 1 | 297 | 79 | 21.21 | 67.04 | 0 | 2 | 8 | 0 |
| First-class | 82 | 126 | 15 | 6162 | 210 | 55.51 | 52.97 | 24 | 28 | 78 | 0 |
| List A | 73 | 69 | 11 | 2827 | 139 | 48.74 | 88.31 | 6 | 17 | 34 | 0 |
| Twenty20 | 57 | 52 | 8 | 1170 | 68 | 26.59 | 120.49 | 0 | 5 | 30 | 0 |
| **Bowling** | **Mat** | **Balls** | **Runs** | **Wkts** | **BBI** | **BBM** | **Ave** | **Econ** | **SR** | **5w** | **10** |
| Tests | 8 | 12 | 5 | 0 | - | - | - | 2.50 | - | 0 | 0 |
| ODIs | 16 | - | - | - | - | - | - | - | - | - | - |
| First-class | 82 | 156 | 143 | 0 | - | - | - | 5.50 | - | 0 | 0 |
| List A | 73 | - | - | - | - | - | - | - | - | - | - |
| Twenty20 | 57 | - | - | - | - | - | - | - | - | - | - |

## TOM BARBER

## RBH LFM R0 W0

HAMPSHIRE

FULL NAME: Thomas Edward Barber
BORN: August 8, 1995, Poole, Dorset
SQUAD NO: 20
HEIGHT: 6ft 3in
NICKNAME: Barbs
EDUCATION: Bournemouth Grammar School
TEAMS: Hampshire
CAREER: List A: 2014

FAMILY TIES? My two brothers played cricket through the Dorset age groups and my dad is an umpire in the Dorset and Hampshire leagues
CAREER HIGHLIGHTS? Making my debut for Hampshire in 2014 in a RL Cup match against Yorkshire, in which I took two wickets in two balls, and representing England U19
BEST PLAYER IN COUNTY CRICKET? James Vince
TIP FOR THE TOP? Tom Alsop, Lewis McManus and Ryan Higgins
SUPERSTITIONS? I have a few. One is tucking my shirt in at the end of every over I bowl and another is scratching my run-up mark at the start of every over
CRICKETING HEROES? Andrew flintoff and Brett Lee – watching them during the 2005 Ashes really inspired me to be a fast bowler. Dale Steyn – he never stops running in and bowling fast. Shane Warne – for the way he made the game look so simple
NON-CRICKETING HEROES? My family – for everything they have done for me. Brian Cox – for inspiring me to have an interest in science
COACHING TIP? If you're a fast bowler, do what you've been put in the team to do and bowl fast!
IF YOU COULD BE SOMEONE ELSE FOR A DAY? Cristiano Ronaldo
FAVOURITE TV? Top Gear, The Big Bang Theory, An Idiot Abroad
FANTASY SLIP CORDON? Keeper: Ricky Gervais, 1st: Karl Pilkington, 2nd: Myself, 3rd: Frankie Boyle, Gully: Jonty Rhodes
TWITTER FEED: @Tom_Barber20

| Batting | Mat | Inns | NO | Runs | HS | Ave | SR | 100 | 50 | Ct | St |
|---|---|---|---|---|---|---|---|---|---|---|---|
| List A | 2 | 1 | 0 | 0 | 0 | 0.00 | 0.00 | 0 | 0 | 0 | 0 |
| **Bowling** | **Mat** | **Balls** | **Runs** | **Wkts** | **BBI** | **BBM** | **Ave** | **Econ** | **SR** | **5w** | **10** |
| List A | 2 | 48 | 50 | 2 | 2/22 | 2/22 | 25.00 | 6.25 | 24.0 | 0 | 0 |

# KEITH BARKER

LHB LFM RO W2 MVP59

FULL NAME: Keith Hubert Douglas Barker
BORN: October 21, 1986, Manchester
SQUAD NO: 13
HEIGHT: 6ft 2in
NICKNAME: Barks, Barksy
EDUCATION: Moorhead High School; Preston College
TEAMS: Warwickshire
CAREER: First-class: 2009; List A: 2009; T20: 2009



BEST BATTING: 125 Warwickshire vs Surrey, Guildford, 2013
BEST BOWLING: 6-40 Warwickshire vs Somerset, Taunton, 2012

FAMILY TIES? My father Keith played for British Guiana
CAREER HIGHLIGHTS? Winning the County Championship, CB40 and T20
CRICKETING HEROES? Brian Lara was great to watch and I liked how he was always scoring runs quickly and I enjoyed his technique
NON-CRICKETING HEROES? Lewis Hamilton – very confident and pushes the boundaries
CRICKET RULE YOU'D CHANGE? Anything that helps the bowlers rather than the batsman
COACHING TIP? In anything you do, remember it takes time and won't happen overnight
IF YOU WEREN'T A CRICKETER? Still trying to be a footballer
IF YOU COULD BE SOMEONE ELSE FOR A DAY? Jay Z
FAVOURITE TV? House Of Cards, Homeland, Breaking Bad
ACCOMPLISHMENTS? Represented England U18-20 at football
FANTASY SLIP CORDON? Keeper: Neo from The Matrix, 1st: Keith Barker Jnr, 2nd: Keith Barker Snr, 3rd: Kevin Hart, Gully: Usman Awan (Neo would slow everything down so it would be easy to catch and the rest of us could just joke around and have a laugh)
TWITTER FEED: KBarks13

| Batting | Mat | Inns | NO | Runs | HS | Ave | SR | 100 | 50 | Ct | St |
|---|---|---|---|---|---|---|---|---|---|---|---|
| First-class | 59 | 71 | 12 | 1660 | 125 | 28.13 | 57.63 | 4 | 3 | 21 | 0 |
| List A | 43 | 30 | 7 | 397 | 56 | 17.26 | 89.01 | 0 | 1 | 8 | 0 |
| Twenty20 | 54 | 28 | 5 | 310 | 46 | 13.47 | 106.16 | 0 | 0 | 15 | 0 |
| **Bowling** | **Mat** | **Balls** | **Runs** | **Wkts** | **BBI** | **BBM** | **Ave** | **Econ** | **SR** | **5w** | **10** |
| First-class | 59 | 9199 | 4746 | 181 | 6/40 | 10/70 | 26.22 | 3.09 | 50.8 | 9 | 1 |
| List A | 43 | 1498 | 1468 | 48 | 4/33 | 4/33 | 30.58 | 5.87 | 31.2 | 0 | 0 |
| Twenty20 | 54 | 984 | 1257 | 58 | 4/19 | 4/19 | 21.67 | 7.66 | 16.9 | 0 | 0 |

# ED BARNARD

RHB RFM R0 W0

FULL NAME: Edward George Barnard
BORN: November 20, 1995, Shrewsbury, Shropshire
SQUAD NO: 30
HEIGHT: 6ft
NICKNAME: Barn
EDUCATION: Shrewsbury School
TEAMS: Worcestershire 2nd XI; England U19
CAREER: Yet to make first-team debut

---

FAMILY TIES? My dad Andy played for Shropshire and my brother Mike played a first-class match for Oxford MCCU
CAREER HIGHLIGHTS? Scoring a hundred on debut for England U19 and winning the National Club Championship with Shrewsbury
BEST PLAYER IN COUNTY CRICKET? Moeen Ali
TIP FOR THE TOP? Joe Clarke, Matthew Fisher, Haseeb Hameed
CRICKETING HEROES? Andrew Flintoff – because of the way he played the game and the way he could change games
NON-CRICKETING HEROES? Nelson Mandela – for standing up for what he believed in. Alan Shearer – because I'm a big Newcastle United fan
CRICKET RULE YOU'D CHANGE? Eight runs for hitting it out of the ground
IF YOU COULD BE SOMEONE ELSE FOR A DAY? David Beckham – coolest man on earth
FAVOURITE TV? Match Of The Day
LEAST FAVOURITE TV? Antiques Roadshow
PET HATE? People who are overly arrogant. If you're good then let whatever you're good at do the talking
SURPRISING FACT? My dad played rugby for London Wasps
FANTASY SLIP CORDON? Keeper: Nelson Mandela, 1st: Graeme Swann, 2nd: Mila Kunis, 3rd: Myself, Gully: Kevin Hart
TWITTER FEED: @EdBarn95

# ALEX BARROW

## RHB OB R0 W0

FULL NAME: Alexander William Rodgerson Barrow
BORN: May 6, 1992, Bath, Somerset
SQUAD NO: 18
HEIGHT: 5ft 8in
NICKNAME: Baz, Bazrick
EDUCATION: King's College, Taunton
TEAMS: Somerset
CAREER: First-class: 2011; List A: 2012



BEST BATTING: 88 Somerset vs Northamptonshire, Taunton, 2014
BEST BOWLING: 1-4 Somerset vs Hampshire, Southampton, 2011

CAREER HIGHLIGHTS? Pulling my Somerset cap on
MOST MARKED CHARACTERISTIC? The eight scars from the four operations I've had
CRICKETING HEROES? Jonty Rhodes – amazing fielder. Michael Clarke – love watching him bat. Ian Bell – I enjoy watching him and I would love to play against him. Darren Gough – he inspired me when I was really young
NON-CRICKETING HEROES? Carl Fogarty – as a boy I used to have his video of winning all the championships and watched it regularly!
IF YOU WEREN'T A CRICKETER? Maybe working in the bat-making industry
IF YOU COULD BE SOMEONE ELSE FOR A DAY? Someone close to me, then I'd probably realise how annoying I am!
FAVOURITE TV? I love TV series and always have one on the go, but Prison Break hasn't been beaten yet! Homeland, Suits, Scandal, Luther and Breaking Bad would be my recommendations if someone asked!
ACCOMPLISHMENTS? Playing rugby for Bath as a boy
PET HATE? Loud eaters!
TWITTER FEED: @bazrick18

| Batting | Mat | Inns | NO | Runs | HS | Ave | SR | 100 | 50 | Ct | St |
|---|---|---|---|---|---|---|---|---|---|---|---|
| First-class | 30 | 50 | 3 | 1000 | 88 | 21.27 | 46.18 | 0 | 4 | 44 | 0 |
| List A | 17 | 14 | 4 | 276 | 72 | 27.60 | 87.89 | 0 | 2 | 14 | 1 |
| **Bowling** | **Mat** | **Balls** | **Runs** | **Wkts** | **BBI** | **BBM** | **Ave** | **Econ** | **SR** | **5w** | **10** |
| First-class | 30 | 42 | 36 | 1 | 1/4 | 1/4 | 36.00 | 5.14 | 42.0 | 0 | 0 |
| List A | 17 | - | - | - | - | - | - | - | - | - | - |

# GARETH BATTY

RHB OB R0 W2 MVP92

FULL NAME: Gareth Jon Batty
BORN: October 13, 1977, Bradford, Yorkshire
SQUAD NO: 13
HEIGHT: 5ft 11in
NICKNAME: Bats, Stuta, Boom Boom
EDUCATION: Bingley Grammar School
TEAMS: England, Surrey, Worcestershire, Yorkshire
CAREER: Test: 2003; ODI: 2002; T20I: 2009; First-class: 1997; List A: 1998; T20: 2003

BEST BATTING: 133 Worcestershire vs Surrey, The Oval, 2004
BEST BOWLING: 8-68 Surrey vs Essex, Chelmsford, 2014
COUNTY CAPS: 2011 (Surrey)

FAMILY TIES? My dad played for and coached at Yorkshire Academy. My brother Jeremy played for Yorkshire and Somerset
CAREER HIGHLIGHTS? Playing for England
NON-CRICKETING HEROES? Margaret Thatcher, Winston Churchill, James Bond
FAVOURITE TV? Only Fools And Horses
PET HATE? Laziness and a blame culture
FANTASY SLIP CORDON? Keeper: Harry Redknapp (old-school sportsman, must have great stories), 1st: Me, 2nd: James Bond (never fails to deliver), 3rd: Rick Astley (to sing us a song when we get bored), Gully: Radha Mitchell

| Batting | Mat | Inns | NO | Runs | HS | Ave | SR | 100 | 50 | Ct | St |
|---|---|---|---|---|---|---|---|---|---|---|---|
| Tests | 7 | 8 | 1 | 144 | 38 | 20.57 | 27.01 | 0 | 0 | 3 | 0 |
| ODIs | 10 | 8 | 2 | 30 | 17 | 5.00 | 41.09 | 0 | 0 | 4 | 0 |
| T20Is | 1 | 1 | 0 | 4 | 4 | 4.00 | 57.14 | 0 | 0 | 0 | 0 |
| First-class | 206 | 311 | 49 | 6202 | 133 | 23.67 | | 2 | 28 | 152 | 0 |
| List A | 227 | 174 | 35 | 2230 | 83* | 16.04 | | 0 | 5 | 76 | 0 |
| Twenty20 | 107 | 68 | 20 | 550 | 87 | 11.45 | 105.36 | 0 | 1 | 35 | 0 |
| **Bowling** | **Mat** | **Balls** | **Runs** | **Wkts** | **BBI** | **BBM** | **Ave** | **Econ** | **SR** | **5w** | **10** |
| Tests | 7 | 1394 | 733 | 11 | 3/55 | 5/153 | 66.63 | 3.15 | 126.7 | 0 | 0 |
| ODIs | 10 | 440 | 366 | 5 | 2/40 | 2/40 | 73.20 | 4.99 | 88.0 | 0 | 0 |
| T20Is | 1 | 18 | 17 | 0 | - | - | - | 5.66 | - | 0 | 0 |
| First-class | 206 | 37518 | 18186 | 544 | 8/68 | | 33.43 | 2.90 | 68.9 | 22 | 2 |
| List A | 227 | 8729 | 6639 | 207 | 5/35 | 5/35 | 32.07 | 4.56 | 42.1 | 1 | 0 |
| Twenty20 | 107 | 1932 | 2320 | 88 | 4/13 | 4/13 | 26.36 | 7.20 | 21.9 | 0 | 0 |

# AARON BEARD RHB RFM R0 W0

FULL NAME: Aaron Paul Beard
BORN: October 15, 1997, Chelmsford
SQUAD NO: 14
HEIGHT: 5ft 10in
NICKNAME: Beardy
EDUCATION: Great Baddow Sixth Form
TEAMS: Essex U15
CAREER: Yet to make first-team debut



FAMILY TIES? My dad and uncle both used to play for the same club and I used to go and watch them every time they were playing
CAREER HIGHLIGHTS? Captaining county age groups for three years. Attaining a place at Bunbury Festival. Being a member of the England Development Programme for a year. Fielding for England and Essex in the Ashes warm-up game when I was 15. Given a first-class contract to enable me to be able to play to a professional standard
BEST PLAYER IN COUNTY CRICKET? Joe Root – class batsman with a very good technique. Also a very good fielder in most positions and is a very handy bowler to have as well
TIP FOR THE TOP? Matt Salisbury, Kishen Velani, Jamie Porter, Haseeb Hameed
CRICKETING HEROES? Andrew Flintoff – grew up loving the way he played his cricket in an aggressive, exciting manner and always giving his all. Didn't let things happening off the field affect his performance on the field
NON-CRICKETING HEROES? David Beckham
COACHING TIP? Bowling – try and aim your bowling arm at the point of release at 2 o'clock, which enables your arm to be vertical, where it should be
IF YOU WEREN'T A CRICKETER? Cristiano Ronaldo – love the way he plays his football, skilful and is the best football player in the world in my eyes
FAVOURITE TV? Only Fools And Horses
LEAST FAVOURITE TV? Gardening programmes
PET HATE? Disrespectful people
SURPRISING FACT? I enjoy fishing as a hobby and a form of relaxation
TWITTER FEED: @aaronbeard_14

# WILL BEER

RHB LB R0 W0

FULL NAME: William Andrew Thomas Beer
BORN: October 8, 1988, Crawley, Sussex
SQUAD NO: 18
TEAMS: Sussex
CAREER: First-class: 2008; List A: 2009; T20: 2008

BEST BATTING: 39 Sussex vs Middlesex, Lord's, 2013
BEST BOWLING: 3-31 Sussex vs Worcestershire, Worcester, 2010

FAMILY TIES? My dad played for Sussex 2nd XI
CAREER HIGHLIGHTS? Winning the T20 domestic tournament in 2009 and going to the Champions League
CRICKETING HEROES? Shane Warne, Michael Yardy
NON-CRICKETING HEROES? David Beckham, Joey Essex
IF YOU WEREN'T A CRICKETER? Professional golfer
FAVOURITE TV? The Only Way Is Essex
ACCOMPLISHMENTS? My 25m swimming badge. Orange belt in judo
TWITTER FEED: @willbeer18

| Batting | Mat | Inns | NO | Runs | HS | Ave | SR | 100 | 50 | Ct | St |
|---|---|---|---|---|---|---|---|---|---|---|---|
| First-class | 9 | 12 | 2 | 219 | 39 | 21.90 | 30.88 | 0 | 0 | 3 | 0 |
| List A | 37 | 20 | 8 | 236 | 45* | 19.66 | 91.11 | 0 | 0 | 10 | 0 |
| Twenty20 | 64 | 35 | 12 | 220 | 37 | 9.56 | 133.33 | 0 | 0 | 12 | 0 |
| **Bowling** | **Mat** | **Balls** | **Runs** | **Wkts** | **BBI** | **BBM** | **Ave** | **Econ** | **SR** | **5w** | **10** |
| First-class | 9 | 898 | 519 | 13 | 3/31 | 3/36 | 39.92 | 3.46 | 69.0 | 0 | 0 |
| List A | 37 | 1518 | 1322 | 35 | 3/27 | 3/27 | 37.77 | 5.22 | 43.3 | 0 | 0 |
| Twenty20 | 64 | 1167 | 1389 | 50 | 3/14 | 3/14 | 27.78 | 7.14 | 23.3 | 0 | 0 |

# IAN BELL

RHB RM R4 W0

FULL NAME: Ian Ronald Bell
BORN: April 11, 1982, Walsgrave, Coventry, Warwickshire
SQUAD NO: 4
HEIGHT: 5ft 10in
NICKNAME: Belly
EDUCATION: Princethorpe College, Rugby
TEAMS: England, Warwickshire
CAREER: Test: 2004; ODI: 2004; T20I: 2006; First-class: 1999; List A: 1999; T20: 2003



BEST BATTING: 262* Warwickshire vs Sussex, Horsham, 2004
BEST BOWLING: 4-4 Warwickshire vs Middlesex, Lord's, 2004
COUNTY CAPS: 2001; BENEFIT YEAR: 2011

CAREER HIGHLIGHTS? Winning the County Championship with Warwickshire and Ashes victories
BEST PLAYER IN COUNTY CRICKET? Marcus Trescothick
CRICKETING HEROES? Ricky Ponting, Dominic Ostler, Jeetan Patel
NON-CRICKETING HEROES? Gary Shaw, Gordon Cowans
IF YOU WEREN'T A CRICKETER? I'd be sitting at the Holte End watching the Villa
ACCOMPLISHMENTS? Honorary doctorate at Coventry University
TWITTER FEED: @Ian_Bell

| Batting | Mat | Inns | NO | Runs | HS | Ave | SR | 100 | 50 | Ct | St |
|---|---|---|---|---|---|---|---|---|---|---|---|
| Tests | 105 | 181 | 22 | 7156 | 235 | 45.00 | 49.97 | 21 | 42 | 88 | 0 |
| ODIs | 159 | 155 | 13 | 5301 | 141 | 37.33 | 77.03 | 4 | 33 | 54 | 0 |
| T20Is | 8 | 8 | 1 | 188 | 60* | 26.85 | 115.33 | 0 | 1 | 4 | 0 |
| First-class | 246 | 415 | 46 | 16938 | 262* | 45.90 | | 48 | 87 | 188 | 0 |
| List A | 289 | 278 | 27 | 10017 | 158 | 39.90 | | 11 | 70 | 102 | 0 |
| Twenty20 | 47 | 46 | 6 | 981 | 85 | 24.52 | 115.68 | 0 | 4 | 17 | 0 |
| **Bowling** | **Mat** | **Balls** | **Runs** | **Wkts** | **BBI** | **BBM** | **Ave** | **Econ** | **SR** | **5w** | **10** |
| Tests | 105 | 108 | 76 | 1 | 1/33 | 1/33 | 76.00 | 4.22 | 108.0 | 0 | 0 |
| ODIs | 159 | 88 | 88 | 6 | 3/9 | 3/9 | 14.66 | 6.00 | 14.6 | 0 | 0 |
| T20Is | 8 | - | - | - | - | - | - | - | - | - | - |
| First-class | 246 | 2827 | 1598 | 47 | 4/4 | | 34.00 | 3.39 | 60.1 | 0 | 0 |
| List A | 289 | 1290 | 1138 | 33 | 5/41 | 5/41 | 34.48 | 5.29 | 39.0 | 1 | 0 |
| Twenty20 | 47 | 132 | 186 | 3 | 1/12 | 1/12 | 62.00 | 8.45 | 44.0 | 0 | 0 |

# DANIEL BELL-DRUMMOND RHB RM R1 W0

FULL NAME: Daniel James Bell-Drummond
BORN: August 4, 1993, Lewisham, London
SQUAD NO: 23
HEIGHT: 5ft 11in
NICKNAME: DBD, Deebs
EDUCATION: Millfield School
TEAMS: Kent
CAREER: First-class: 2011; List A: 2011; T20: 2011

BEST BATTING: 153 Kent vs Hampshire, Southampton, 2014

FAMILY TIES? My father got me into cricket. I've always really enjoyed spending time at my local club Catford Wanderers CC
CAREER HIGHLIGHTS? Making my first-class debut
CRICKETING HEROES? Brian Lara, Kevin Pietersen, Chris Gayle
NON-CRICKETING HEROES? Nelson Mandela, Muhammad Ali
IF YOU WEREN'T A CRICKETER? I'd be a musician
FAVOURITE TV? EastEnders
FANTASY SLIP CORDON? Keeper: Floyd Mayweather Jr, 1st: Me, 2nd: Robin van Persie, 3rd: Lee Evans, Gully: Brian Lara
TWITTER FEED: @deebzz23

| Batting | Mat | Inns | NO | Runs | HS | Ave | SR | 100 | 50 | Ct | St |
|---|---|---|---|---|---|---|---|---|---|---|---|
| First-class | 38 | 63 | 5 | 1977 | 153 | 34.08 | 44.51 | 4 | 12 | 17 | 0 |
| List A | 13 | 13 | 0 | 352 | 83 | 27.07 | 82.24 | 0 | 3 | 1 | 0 |
| Twenty20 | 20 | 20 | 0 | 356 | 59 | 17.80 | 112.65 | 0 | 1 | 6 | 0 |
| **Bowling** | **Mat** | **Balls** | **Runs** | **Wkts** | **BBI** | **BBM** | **Ave** | **Econ** | **SR** | **5w** | **10** |
| First-class | 38 | 41 | 54 | 0 | - | - | - | 7.90 | - | 0 | 0 |
| List A | 13 | 12 | 15 | 0 | - | - | - | 7.50 | - | 0 | 0 |
| Twenty20 | 20 | - | - | - | - | - | - | - | - | - | - |

# PAUL BEST

## LHB SLA R0 W0

FULL NAME: Paul Merwood Best
BORN: March 8, 1991, Nuneaton, Warwickshire
SQUAD NO: 15
EDUCATION: Bablake School, Coventry; Cambridge University
TEAMS: Warwickshire, Northamptonshire
CAREER: First-class: 2011; List A: 2011; T20: 2012



BEST BATTING: 150 CMCCU vs Warwickshire, Fenner's, 2011
BEST BOWLING: 6-86 Cambridge University vs Oxford University, Fenner's, 2011

FAMILY TIES? My dad played club cricket and my younger brother Mark is in the Warwickshire Academy
CAREER HIGHLIGHTS? Captaining England U19 in 2009 and 2010. Scoring 150* for Cambridge MCCU vs Surrey in 2011 and winning the game. Getting a six-fer vs Middlesex for Cambridge MCCU in 2011. Making my Warwickshire Championship debut. Being in the Cambridge team that won the treble vs Oxford in 2011
CRICKETING HEROES? Daniel Vettori
NON-CRICKETING HEROES? Hugh Laurie
IF YOU WEREN'T A CRICKETER? Either in the City or owning my own set of delicatessens
FAVOURITE TV? The Wire
ACCOMPLISHMENTS? Getting to Cambridge University
SURPRISING FACT? The subjects I studied at university are Anglo Saxon, Norse and Celtic
FANTASY SLIP CORDON? Keeper: Frankie Boyle, 1st: Shakespeare, 2nd: King Aethelred the Unready, 3rd: Me, Gully: Jamie Oliver
TWITTER FEED: @MerwoodBest

| Batting | Mat | Inns | NO | Runs | HS | Ave | SR | 100 | 50 | Ct | St |
|---|---|---|---|---|---|---|---|---|---|---|---|
| First-class | 11 | 13 | 3 | 428 | 150 | 42.80 | 48.69 | 1 | 2 | 5 | 0 |
| List A | 13 | 9 | 4 | 57 | 16* | 11.40 | 75.00 | 0 | 0 | 3 | 0 |
| Twenty20 | 4 | - | - | - | - | - | - | - | - | 2 | 0 |
| **Bowling** | **Mat** | **Balls** | **Runs** | **Wkts** | **BBI** | **BBM** | **Ave** | **Econ** | **SR** | **5w** | **10** |
| First-class | 11 | 2449 | 1445 | 32 | 6/86 | 9/131 | 45.15 | 3.54 | 76.5 | 2 | 0 |
| List A | 13 | 443 | 463 | 11 | 3/43 | 3/43 | 42.09 | 6.27 | 40.2 | 0 | 0 |
| Twenty20 | 4 | 84 | 90 | 4 | 3/19 | 3/19 | 22.50 | 6.42 | 21.0 | 0 | 0 |

## SAM BILLINGS RHB WK R0 W0 MVP56

FULL NAME: Samuel William Billings
BORN: June 15, 1991, Pembury, Kent
SQUAD NO: 20
HEIGHT: 6ft
NICKNAME: Bilbo, Skittles
EDUCATION: Haileybury College; Loughborough University
TEAMS: Kent
CAREER: First-class: 2011; List A: 2011; T20: 2011

BEST BATTING: 131 Loughborough MCCU vs Northamptonshire, Loughborough, 2011

CAREER HIGHLIGHTS? EPP tour to Sri Lanka, England Lions tour to South Africa, 135 off 58 balls vs Somerset, scoring 131 on first-class debut and Kent's Player of the Year 2014
BEST PLAYER IN COUNTY CRICKET? Gary Ballance
TIP FOR THE TOP? Matthew Dunn, Daniel Bell-Drummond, Shiv Thakor
CRICKETING HEROES? Adam Gilchrist and Sachin Tendulkar – both phenomenal players. One is the best ever in my opinion and the other single-handedly changed the role of a wicketkeeper in any team
NON-CRICKETING HEROES? Lewis Hamilton, David Beckham and Cristiano Ronaldo
CRICKET RULE YOU'D CHANGE? Have Supersubs in T20 … could be fun
COACHING TIP? Focus on the 90% you're good at; too many people are quick to pick up on what you can't do!
IF YOU COULD BE SOMEONE ELSE FOR A DAY? Cristiano Ronaldo
FAVOURITE TV? Made In Chelsea
LEAST FAVOURITE TV? I don't watch enough TV to have one
PET HATE? People getting in my personal space!
TWITTER FEED: @sambillings

| Batting | Mat | Inns | NO | Runs | HS | Ave | SR | 100 | 50 | Ct | St |
|---|---|---|---|---|---|---|---|---|---|---|---|
| First-class | 25 | 37 | 3 | 1153 | 131 | 33.91 | 54.51 | 1 | 8 | 63 | 7 |
| List A | 34 | 31 | 7 | 1019 | 143 | 42.45 | 114.75 | 2 | 7 | 25 | 5 |
| Twenty20 | 38 | 36 | 3 | 627 | 59 | 19.00 | 113.17 | 0 | 1 | 25 | 1 |
| **Bowling** | **Mat** | **Balls** | **Runs** | **Wkts** | **BBI** | **BBM** | **Ave** | **Econ** | **SR** | **5w** | **10** |
| First-class | 25 | 1 | 4 | 0 | - | - | - | 24.00 | - | 0 | 0 |
| List A | 34 | - | - | - | - | - | - | - | - | - | - |
| Twenty20 | 38 | - | - | - | - | - | - | - | - | - | - |

# JACKSON BIRD

RHB RFM R0 W0

FULL NAME: Jackson Munro Bird
BORN: December 11, 1986, Sydney, Australia
SQUAD NO: 22
HEIGHT: 6ft 4in
NICKNAME: Squid
EDUCATION: St Puis X College, Sydney; St Ignatius College, Riverview
TEAMS: Australia, Hampshire, Melbourne Stars, Tasmania
CAREER: Test: 2012; First-class: 2011; List A: 2011; T20: 2012



BEST BATTING: 26 Tasmania vs Western Australia, Hobart, 2012
BEST BOWLING: 6-25 Tasmania vs Western Australia, Hobart, 2012

NOTES: The Australian fast bowler signed a deal with Hampshire to play in all three formats for the first three months of the county season ahead of any potential involvement in the Ashes. Having made his Test debut in the 2012 Boxing Day Test against Sri Lanka, Bird played in the Chester-le-Street Test during the 2013 Ashes before he was forced to leave the tour early following the recurrence of a back injury. He took 53 first-class wickets at 16 in his first season of professional cricket in 2011/12, finishing the campaign as Sheffield Shield Player of the Year, and took 38 at 19.28 in 2012/13. He was due to play for Northamptonshire last season but was ruled out by injury

| Batting | Mat | Inns | NO | Runs | HS | Ave | SR | 100 | 50 | Ct | St |
|---|---|---|---|---|---|---|---|---|---|---|---|
| Tests | 3 | 4 | 3 | 7 | 6* | 7.00 | 13.20 | 0 | 0 | 1 | 0 |
| First-class | 30 | 33 | 16 | 148 | 26 | 8.70 | 33.48 | 0 | 0 | 14 | 0 |
| List A | 7 | 2 | 1 | 7 | 5* | 7.00 | 175.00 | 0 | 0 | 3 | 0 |
| Twenty20 | 24 | 3 | 1 | 3 | 3 | 1.50 | 60.00 | 0 | 0 | 10 | 0 |
| **Bowling** | **Mat** | **Balls** | **Runs** | **Wkts** | **BBI** | **BBM** | **Ave** | **Econ** | **SR** | **5w** | **10** |
| Tests | 3 | 633 | 303 | 13 | 4/41 | 7/117 | 23.30 | 2.87 | 48.6 | 0 | 0 |
| First-class | 30 | 5705 | 2831 | 132 | 6/25 | 11/95 | 21.44 | 2.97 | 43.2 | 7 | 2 |
| List A | 7 | 382 | 277 | 8 | 3/39 | 3/39 | 34.62 | 4.35 | 47.7 | 0 | 0 |
| Twenty20 | 24 | 525 | 626 | 28 | 4/31 | 4/31 | 22.35 | 7.15 | 18.7 | 0 | 0 |

# ALEX BLAKE

LHB RM R0 W0

FULL NAME: Alexander James Blake
BORN: January 25, 1989, Farnborough, Kent
SQUAD NO: 18
HEIGHT: 6ft 2in
NICKNAME: Blakey, Butler, TS
EDUCATION: Hayes Secondary School; Leeds Metropolitan University
TEAMS: Kent
CAREER: First-class: 2008; List A: 2007; T20: 2010

---

BEST BATTING: 105* Kent vs Yorkshire, Leeds, 2010
BEST BOWLING: 2-9 Kent vs Pakistanis, Canterbury, 2010

---

CAREER HIGHLIGHTS? Maiden first-class century at Headingley and representing England U19
CRICKETING HEROES? Graham Thorpe, Freddie Flintoff
NON-CRICKETING HEROES? David Beckham
IF YOU WEREN'T A CRICKETER? Busker
ACCOMPLISHMENTS? A second-class Honours degree
SURPRISING FACT? I lived with Jonny Bairstow at university, I can name all the countries of the world and I have a pet budgie
FANTASY SLIP CORDON? Keeper: Calvin Harris (to bust out some beats), 1st: Karl Pilkington (to entertain us all day by not having a clue), 2nd: Me, 3rd: Joey Barton (chief sledger), Gully: Joey Essex
TWITTER FEED: @aj_blake10

| Batting | Mat | Inns | NO | Runs | HS | Ave | SR | 100 | 50 | Ct | St |
|---|---|---|---|---|---|---|---|---|---|---|---|
| First-class | 28 | 47 | 2 | 993 | 105* | 22.06 | 56.80 | 1 | 4 | 17 | 0 |
| List A | 45 | 36 | 7 | 632 | 81* | 21.79 | 90.02 | 0 | 3 | 21 | 0 |
| Twenty20 | 50 | 43 | 8 | 618 | 58* | 17.65 | 126.63 | 0 | 2 | 25 | 0 |
| **Bowling** | **Mat** | **Balls** | **Runs** | **Wkts** | **BBI** | **BBM** | **Ave** | **Econ** | **SR** | **5w** | **10** |
| First-class | 28 | 204 | 129 | 3 | 2/9 | 2/9 | 43.00 | 3.79 | 68.0 | 0 | 0 |
| List A | 45 | 84 | 74 | 3 | 2/13 | 2/13 | 24.66 | 5.28 | 28.0 | 0 | 0 |
| Twenty20 | 50 | - | - | - | - | - | - | - | - | - | - |

# RAVI BOPARA RHB RM R1 W0 MVP65

FULL NAME: Ravinder Singh Bopara
BORN: May 4, 1985, Forest Gate, London
SQUAD NO: 25
HEIGHT: 5 ft 10 in
NICKNAME: Puppy
EDUCATION: Brampton Manor School
TEAMS: England, Essex, Chittagong Kings, Dolphins, Gloucestershire, Kings XI Punjab, Prime Bank Cricket Club, Sydney Sixers
CAREER: Test: 2007; ODI: 2007; T20I: 2008; First-class: 2002; List A: 2002; T20: 2003



BEST BATTING: 229 Essex vs Northamptonshire, Chelmsford, 2007
BEST BOWLING: 5-75 Essex vs Surrey, Colchester, 2006
COUNTY CAPS: 2005; BENEFIT YEAR: 2015

FAMILY TIES? Brother played Essex age-group
CAREER HIGHLIGHTS? Playing for England, playing for Essex, scoring 201* vs Leics in a one-day match, playing in the IPL and BPL, and scoring three centuries in a row for England
CRICKETING HEROES? Sachin Tendulkar
DESERT ISLAND DISC? A Drake or Jay Z album
SURPRISING FACT? I have a fast-food business
FANTASY SLIP CORDON? Keeper: Robert De Niro, 1st: Ronnie Kray, 2nd: Reggie Kray, Gully: Sachin Tendulkar. They all achieved great things in their respective fields
TWITTER FEED: @ravibopara

| Batting | Mat | Inns | NO | Runs | HS | Ave | SR | 100 | 50 | Ct | St |
|---|---|---|---|---|---|---|---|---|---|---|---|
| Tests | 13 | 19 | 1 | 575 | 143 | 31.94 | 52.89 | 3 | 0 | 6 | 0 |
| ODIs | 119 | 109 | 21 | 2695 | 101* | 30.62 | 77.84 | 1 | 14 | 34 | 0 |
| T20Is | 38 | 35 | 10 | 711 | 65* | 28.44 | 118.69 | 0 | 3 | 7 | 0 |
| First-class | 151 | 249 | 29 | 9201 | 229 | 41.82 | 52.61 | 25 | 34 | 82 | 0 |
| List A | 280 | 262 | 49 | 8416 | 201* | 39.51 | | 13 | 50 | 85 | 0 |
| Twenty20 | 179 | 166 | 31 | 3605 | 105* | 26.70 | 118.66 | 1 | 17 | 56 | 0 |
| **Bowling** | **Mat** | **Balls** | **Runs** | **Wkts** | **BBI** | **BBM** | **Ave** | **Econ** | **SR** | **5w** | **10** |
| Tests | 13 | 434 | 290 | 1 | 1/39 | 1/39 | 290.00 | 4.00 | 434.0 | 0 | 0 |
| ODIs | 119 | 1812 | 1492 | 38 | 4/38 | 4/38 | 39.26 | 4.94 | 47.6 | 0 | 0 |
| T20Is | 38 | 322 | 387 | 16 | 4/10 | 4/10 | 24.18 | 7.21 | 20.1 | 0 | 0 |
| First-class | 151 | 10546 | 6583 | 160 | 5/75 | | 41.14 | 3.74 | 65.9 | 1 | 0 |
| List A | 280 | 6313 | 5501 | 198 | 5/63 | 5/63 | 27.78 | 5.22 | 31.8 | 1 | 0 |
| Twenty20 | 179 | 2283 | 2873 | 108 | 4/10 | 4/10 | 26.60 | 7.55 | 21.1 | 0 | 0 |

# SCOTT BORTHWICK LHB LB R2 W0 MVP37

FULL NAME: Scott George Borthwick
BORN: April 19, 1990, Sunderland, Co Durham
SQUAD NO: 16
HEIGHT: 5ft 10in
NICKNAME: Badger
EDUCATION: Farringdon Community Sports College, Sunderland
TEAMS: England, Durham
CAREER: Test: 2014; ODI: 2011; T20I: 2011; First-class 2009; List A: 2009; T20: 2008

BEST BATTING: 216 Durham vs Middlesex, Chester-le-Street, 2014
BEST BOWLING: 6-70 Durham vs Surrey, The Oval, 2013

FAMILY TIES? Dad. Club-cricket slogger
CAREER HIGHLIGHTS? Playing for England
TWITTER FEED: @Borthwick16

| Batting | Mat | Inns | NO | Runs | HS | Ave | SR | 100 | 50 | Ct | St |
|---|---|---|---|---|---|---|---|---|---|---|---|
| Tests | 1 | 2 | 0 | 5 | 4 | 2.50 | 26.31 | 0 | 0 | 2 | 0 |
| ODIs | 2 | 2 | 0 | 18 | 15 | 9.00 | 112.50 | 0 | 0 | 0 | 0 |
| T20Is | 1 | 1 | 0 | 14 | 14 | 14.00 | 87.50 | 0 | 0 | 1 | 0 |
| First-class | 87 | 141 | 17 | 4173 | 216 | 33.65 | 54.92 | 8 | 21 | 115 | 0 |
| List A | 63 | 42 | 9 | 520 | 80 | 15.75 | 74.71 | 0 | 2 | 18 | 0 |
| Twenty20 | 49 | 31 | 7 | 401 | 62 | 16.70 | 97.80 | 0 | 1 | 18 | 0 |
| **Bowling** | **Mat** | **Balls** | **Runs** | **Wkts** | **BBI** | **BBM** | **Ave** | **Econ** | **SR** | **5w** | **10** |
| Tests | 1 | 78 | 82 | 4 | 3/33 | 4/82 | 20.50 | 6.30 | 19.5 | 0 | 0 |
| ODIs | 2 | 54 | 72 | 0 | - | - | - | 8.00 | - | 0 | 0 |
| T20Is | 1 | 24 | 15 | 1 | 1/15 | 1/15 | 15.00 | 3.75 | 24.0 | 0 | 0 |
| First-class | 87 | 7579 | 4948 | 143 | 6/70 | 8/84 | 34.60 | 3.91 | 53.0 | 2 | 0 |
| List A | 63 | 1782 | 1731 | 46 | 4/51 | 4/51 | 37.63 | 5.82 | 38.7 | 0 | 0 |
| Twenty20 | 49 | 559 | 761 | 34 | 3/19 | 3/19 | 22.38 | 8.16 | 16.4 | 0 | 0 |

# MATT BOYCE

## LHB RM R0 W0

FULL NAME: Matthew Andrew Golding Boyce
BORN: August 13, 1985, Cheltenham
SQUAD NO: 11
HEIGHT: 5ft 10in
NICKNAME: Boycey, Weasel
EDUCATION: Oakham School; University of Nottingham
TEAMS: Leicestershire
CAREER: First-class: 2006; List A: 2007; T20: 2008



BEST BATTING: 135 Leicestershire vs Kent, Leicester, 2013

CAREER HIGHLIGHTS? My maiden first-class ton and winning the T20 in 2011
BEST PLAYER IN COUNTY CRICKET? Jim Allenby
TIP FOR THE TOP? Tom Wells, Shiv Thakor
CRICKETING HEROES? Brian Lara, Graham Thorpe
NON-CRICKETING HEROES? Jonny Wilkinson
CRICKET RULE YOU'D CHANGE? Longer tea break
IF YOU WEREN'T A CRICKETER? Something in finance
IF YOU COULD BE SOMEONE ELSE FOR A DAY? Ollie Freckingham...
FAVOURITE TV? Game Of Thrones
ACCOMPLISHMENTS? Walking the length of the country off road to raise £18,000 for charity
PET HATE? People who over-complicate things
SURPRISING FACT? I'm planning on setting up my own wealth-management business
FANTASY SLIP CORDON? Keeper: Winston Churchill, 1st: Jonny Wilkinson, 2nd: Ed Stafford
TWITTER FEED: @boycey85

| Batting | Mat | Inns | NO | Runs | HS | Ave | SR | 100 | 50 | Ct | St |
|---|---|---|---|---|---|---|---|---|---|---|---|
| First-class | 98 | 172 | 9 | 4622 | 135 | 28.35 | 41.13 | 6 | 22 | 60 | 0 |
| List A | 67 | 62 | 5 | 1499 | 80 | 26.29 | 82.09 | 0 | 10 | 19 | 0 |
| Twenty20 | 51 | 38 | 8 | 675 | 63* | 22.50 | 112.12 | 0 | 1 | 13 | 0 |
| **Bowling** | **Mat** | **Balls** | **Runs** | **Wkts** | **BBI** | **BBM** | **Ave** | **Econ** | **SR** | **5w** | **10** |
| First-class | 98 | 54 | 72 | 0 | - | - | - | 8.00 | - | 0 | 0 |
| List A | 67 | - | - | - | - | - | - | - | - | - | - |
| Twenty20 | 51 | - | - | - | - | - | - | - | - | - | - |

# WILL BRAGG

## LHB WK R2 W0

FULL NAME: Will David Bragg
BORN: October 24, 1986, Newport
SQUAD NO: 22
HEIGHT: 5ft 10in
NICKNAME: BPOT, Shelf
EDUCATION: Rougemont School, Newport; University of Wales Institute
TEAMS: Glamorgan
CAREER: First-class 2007; List A: 2005; T20: 2010

BEST BATTING: 110 Glamorgan vs Leicestershire, Colwyn Bay, 2011
BEST BOWLING: 2-10 Glamorgan vs Worcestershire, Cardiff, 2013

FAMILY TIES? Dad played club cricket in the South Wales League
CAREER HIGHLIGHTS? Scoring 1,000 runs in my first full season in 2011
SUPERSTITIONS? Always go to the toilet before batting!
CRICKETING HEROES? Herschelle Gibbs, Brian Lara, Daryl Cullinan
NON-CRICKETING HEROES? Kenny Powers, Ricky Gervais
IF YOU WEREN'T A CRICKETER? Working abroad in some kind of financial environment
FAVOURITE TV? The Office
ACCOMPLISHMENTS? Getting a BSc degree in Civil Engineering
SURPRISING FACT? I play acoustic guitar
FANTASY SLIP CORDON? Keeper: Ricky Gervais, 1st: Karl Pilkington, 2nd: Piers Morgan, 3rd: Britney Spears, Gully: Peggy Mitchell
TWITTER FEED: @WDBragg22

| Batting | Mat | Inns | NO | Runs | HS | Ave | SR | 100 | 50 | Ct | St |
|---|---|---|---|---|---|---|---|---|---|---|---|
| First-class | 77 | 134 | 5 | 3823 | 110 | 29.63 | 49.22 | 2 | 25 | 31 | 1 |
| List A | 25 | 24 | 1 | 638 | 88 | 27.73 | 75.68 | 0 | 4 | 2 | 0 |
| Twenty20 | 1 | 1 | 0 | 15 | 15 | 15.00 | 68.18 | 0 | 0 | 0 | 0 |
| **Bowling** | **Mat** | **Balls** | **Runs** | **Wkts** | **BBI** | **BBM** | **Ave** | **Econ** | **SR** | **5w** | **10** |
| First-class | 77 | 496 | 344 | 4 | 2/10 | 2/10 | 86.00 | 4.16 | 124.0 | 0 | 0 |
| List A | 25 | 44 | 54 | 1 | 1/11 | 1/11 | 54.00 | 7.36 | 44.0 | 0 | 0 |
| Twenty20 | 1 | - | - | - | - | - | - | - | - | - | - |

# TIM BRESNAN

RHB RFM R0 W0 MVP26

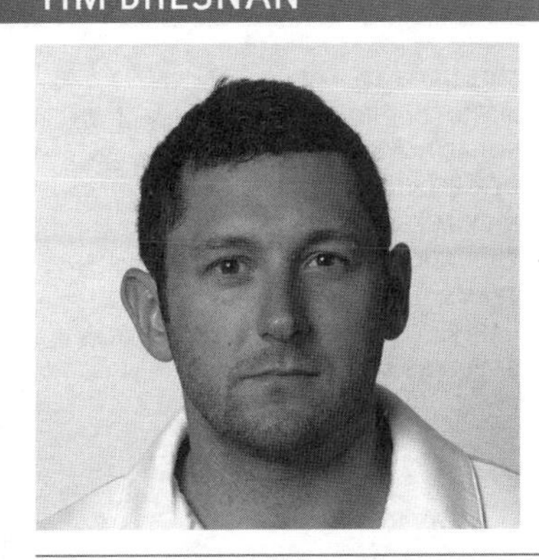

FULL NAME: Timothy Thomas Bresnan
BORN: February 28, 1985, Pontefract, Yorkshire
SQUAD NO: 16
HEIGHT: 6ft
NICKNAME: Brezy Lad, Brez
EDUCATION: Castleford High School, Pontefract New College
TEAMS: England, Yorkshire
CAREER: Test: 2009; ODI: 2006; T20I: 2006; First-class: 2003; List A: 2001; T20: 2003



BEST BATTING: 126* England Lions vs Indians, Chelmsford, 2007
BEST BOWLING: 5-42 Yorkshire vs Worcestershire, Worcester, 2005
COUNTY CAPS: 2006

CAREER HIGHLIGHTS? The Ashes in 2010/11
CRICKETING HEROES? Jacques Kallis
NON-CRICKETING HEROES? Sir Steve Redgrave
IF YOU WEREN'T A CRICKETER? Secret agent
FAVOURITE TV? Homeland
SURPRISING FACT? I'm very handy around the house, shelves, flooring etc
FANTASY SLIP CORDON? Keeper: Roy Chubby Brown, 1st: Myself, 2nd: Michael McIntyre, 3rd: Sean Lock, 4th: Keith Lemon. Should be a good laugh
TWITTER FEED: @timbresnan

| Batting | Mat | Inns | NO | Runs | HS | Ave | SR | 100 | 50 | Ct | St |
|---|---|---|---|---|---|---|---|---|---|---|---|
| Tests | 23 | 26 | 4 | 575 | 91 | 26.13 | 39.43 | 0 | 3 | 8 | 0 |
| ODIs | 84 | 64 | 20 | 871 | 80 | 19.79 | 90.25 | 0 | 1 | 20 | 0 |
| T20Is | 34 | 22 | 9 | 216 | 47* | 16.61 | 127.05 | 0 | 0 | 10 | 0 |
| First-class | 140 | 180 | 29 | 4103 | 126* | 27.17 | 46.87 | 3 | 21 | 56 | 0 |
| List A | 236 | 167 | 49 | 2184 | 80 | 18.50 | 91.18 | 0 | 4 | 62 | 0 |
| Twenty20 | 100 | 72 | 28 | 841 | 47* | 19.11 | 123.13 | 0 | 0 | 31 | 0 |
| **Bowling** | **Mat** | **Balls** | **Runs** | **Wkts** | **BBI** | **BBM** | **Ave** | **Econ** | **SR** | **5w** | **10** |
| Tests | 23 | 4674 | 2357 | 72 | 5/48 | 8/141 | 32.73 | 3.02 | 64.9 | 1 | 0 |
| ODIs | 84 | 4185 | 3802 | 108 | 5/48 | 5/48 | 35.20 | 5.45 | 38.7 | 1 | 0 |
| T20Is | 34 | 663 | 887 | 24 | 3/10 | 3/10 | 36.95 | 8.02 | 27.6 | 0 | 0 |
| First-class | 140 | 24449 | 12448 | 398 | 5/42 | | 31.27 | 3.05 | 61.4 | 6 | 0 |
| List A | 236 | 10527 | 9115 | 271 | 5/48 | 5/48 | 33.63 | 5.19 | 38.8 | 1 | 0 |
| Twenty20 | 100 | 2006 | 2541 | 88 | 3/10 | 3/10 | 28.87 | 7.60 | 22.7 | 0 | 0 |

## DANNY BRIGGS RHB SLA R0 W0

FULL NAME: Danny Richard Briggs
BORN: April 30, 1991, Newport, Isle of Wight
SQUAD NO: 19
HEIGHT: 6ft 2in
NICKNAME: Briggsy
EDUCATION: Carisbrooke High School
TEAMS: England, Hampshire
CAREER: ODI: 2012; T20I: 2012; First-class: 2009; List A: 2009; T20: 2010

BEST BATTING: 54 Hampshire vs Gloucestershire, Bristol, 2011
BEST BOWLING: 6-45 England Lions vs Windward Islands, Roseau, 2011
COUNTY CAPS: 2012

CAREER HIGHLIGHTS? Winning the T20 Cup in 2010
CRICKETING HEROES? Daniel Vettori
IF YOU WEREN'T A CRICKETER? Anything to do with sport
DESERT ISLAND DISC? Any 80s music
FAVOURITE TV? Any comedy
FANTASY SLIP CORDON? Keeper: Happy Gilmore, 1st: Viv Richards, 2nd: James Tomlinson, 3rd: Pelé
TWITTER FEED: @DannyBriggs19

| Batting | Mat | Inns | NO | Runs | HS | Ave | SR | 100 | 50 | Ct | St |
|---|---|---|---|---|---|---|---|---|---|---|---|
| ODIs | 1 | - | - | - | - | - | - | - | - | 0 | 0 |
| T20Is | 7 | 1 | 1 | 0 | 0* | - | - | 0 | 0 | 1 | 0 |
| First-class | 58 | 68 | 16 | 731 | 54 | 14.05 | | 0 | 1 | 19 | 0 |
| List A | 65 | 29 | 11 | 201 | 25 | 11.16 | 89.73 | 0 | 0 | 18 | 0 |
| Twenty20 | 87 | 17 | 12 | 35 | 10 | 7.00 | 100.00 | 0 | 0 | 18 | 0 |
| **Bowling** | **Mat** | **Balls** | **Runs** | **Wkts** | **BBI** | **BBM** | **Ave** | **Econ** | **SR** | **5w** | **10** |
| ODIs | 1 | 60 | 39 | 2 | 2/39 | 2/39 | 19.50 | 3.90 | 30.0 | 0 | 0 |
| T20Is | 7 | 108 | 199 | 5 | 2/25 | 2/25 | 39.80 | 11.05 | 21.6 | 0 | 0 |
| First-class | 58 | 10633 | 5416 | 170 | 6/45 | 9/96 | 31.85 | 3.05 | 62.5 | 6 | 0 |
| List A | 65 | 2846 | 2391 | 69 | 4/32 | 4/32 | 34.65 | 5.04 | 41.2 | 0 | 0 |
| Twenty20 | 87 | 1819 | 2143 | 108 | 5/19 | 5/19 | 19.84 | 7.06 | 16.8 | 1 | 0 |

## STUART BROAD LHB RFM R0 W0

FULL NAME: Stuart Christopher John Broad
BORN: June 24, 1986, Nottingham
SQUAD NO: 16
HEIGHT: 6ft 5in
NICKNAME: Broady
EDUCATION: Oakham School
TEAMS: England, Nottinghamshire, Kings XI Punjab, Leicestershire,
CAREER: Test: 2007; ODI: 2006; T20I: 2006; First-class: 2005; List A: 2005; T20: 2006



BEST BATTING: 169 England vs Pakistan, Lord's, 2010
BEST BOWLING: 8-52 Nottinghamshire vs Warwickshire, Birmingham, 2010
COUNTY CAPS: 2007 (Leicestershire)

FAMILY TIES? My father Chris played for England, Nottinghamshire and Gloucestershire and is now an ICC match official
CRICKETING HEROES? Glenn McGrath, Shaun Pollock
NON-CRICKETING HEROES? Brian Clough, Lewis Hamilton
IF YOU WEREN'T A CRICKETER? Traffic warden
SURPRISING FACT? I often dream in French
FANTASY SLIP CORDON? Keeper: Mark Crossley, 1st: Des Lyttle, 2nd: Steve Chettle, 3rd: Des Walker, 4th: Stuart Pearce
TWITTER FEED: @StuartBroad8

| Batting | Mat | Inns | NO | Runs | HS | Ave | SR | 100 | 50 | Ct | St |
|---|---|---|---|---|---|---|---|---|---|---|---|
| Tests | 74 | 104 | 13 | 2193 | 169 | 24.09 | 66.61 | 1 | 10 | 21 | 0 |
| ODIs | 118 | 66 | 25 | 510 | 45* | 12.43 | 74.88 | 0 | 0 | 27 | 0 |
| T20Is | 56 | 26 | 10 | 118 | 18* | 7.37 | 100.00 | 0 | 0 | 21 | 0 |
| First-class | 131 | 176 | 28 | 3403 | 169 | 22.99 | 61.47 | 1 | 17 | 41 | 0 |
| List A | 136 | 73 | 26 | 556 | 45* | 11.82 | 73.54 | 0 | 0 | 29 | 0 |
| Twenty20 | 74 | 28 | 11 | 127 | 18* | 7.47 | 96.94 | 0 | 0 | 24 | 0 |
| **Bowling** | **Mat** | **Balls** | **Runs** | **Wkts** | **BBI** | **BBM** | **Ave** | **Econ** | **SR** | **5w** | **10** |
| Tests | 74 | 15515 | 7894 | 264 | 7/44 | 11/121 | 29.90 | 3.05 | 58.7 | 12 | 2 |
| ODIs | 118 | 5965 | 5257 | 176 | 5/23 | 5/23 | 29.86 | 5.28 | 33.8 | 1 | 0 |
| T20Is | 56 | 1173 | 1491 | 65 | 4/24 | 4/24 | 22.93 | 7.62 | 18.0 | 0 | 0 |
| First-class | 131 | 25256 | 13467 | 478 | 8/52 | | 28.17 | 3.19 | 52.8 | 22 | 3 |
| List A | 136 | 6789 | 5974 | 204 | 5/23 | 5/23 | 29.28 | 5.27 | 33.2 | 1 | 0 |
| Twenty20 | 74 | 1575 | 1863 | 91 | 4/24 | 4/24 | 20.47 | 7.09 | 17.3 | 0 | 0 |

# JACK BROOKS

## RHB RFM R0 W1 MVP29

FULL NAME: Jack Alexander Brooks
BORN: June 4, 1984, Oxford
SQUAD NO: 70
HEIGHT: 6ft 2in
NICKNAME: Brooksy, Animal, Ferret, SuBo, Headband Warrior, King of Oxford, Therapist
EDUCATION: Wheatley Park School
TEAMS: Yorkshire, England Lions, Northamptonshire
CAREER: First-class: 2009; List A: 2009; T20: 2010

---

BEST BATTING: 53* England Lions vs South Africa A, Paarl, 2015
BEST BOWLING: 5-23 Northamptonshire vs Leicestershire, Leicester, 2011
COUNTY CAPS: 2012 (Northamptonshire)

---

CAREER HIGHLIGHTS? First-class debut vs Australia in 2009, winning the County Championship with Yorkshire in 2014
CRICKETING HEROES? Curtly Ambrose, Allan Donald, Darren Gough, Dennis Lillee – all characters I admired for ability, personality and aggression
CRICKET RULE YOU'D CHANGE? Allow two bouncers in T20
IF YOU WEREN'T A CRICKETER? Farmer? Maybe travelling the world feeding my soul
DESERT ISLAND DISC? Oasis – any of the early stuff. Whatever is a massive tune
ACCOMPLISHMENTS? Oxfordshire U13 badminton champion. Only turned up because two of my mates who played county badminton were there and I won it. Hilarious
SURPRISING FACT? I chose my middle name. Official SuBo lookalike
FANTASY SLIP CORDON? Keeper: David Beckham (legend), 1st: James Hunt (great stories and personality), 2nd: Lee Evans (my fave comedian and makes great silly noises), 3rd: Myself, Gully: Ben Howgego (one of my best mates in cricket and makes me laugh constantly)
TWITTER FEED: @brooksyferret

| Batting | Mat | Inns | NO | Runs | HS | Ave | SR | 100 | 50 | Ct | St |
|---|---|---|---|---|---|---|---|---|---|---|---|
| First-class | 67 | 72 | 30 | 628 | 53* | 14.95 | 53.90 | 0 | 2 | 18 | 0 |
| List A | 32 | 13 | 4 | 42 | 10 | 4.66 | 64.61 | 0 | 0 | 3 | 0 |
| Twenty20 | 44 | 10 | 6 | 59 | 33* | 14.75 | 134.09 | 0 | 0 | 9 | 0 |
| **Bowling** | **Mat** | **Balls** | **Runs** | **Wkts** | **BBI** | **BBM** | **Ave** | **Econ** | **SR** | **5w** | **10** |
| First-class | 67 | 11219 | 6377 | 226 | 5/23 | 8/112 | 28.21 | 3.41 | 49.6 | 7 | 0 |
| List A | 32 | 1410 | 1138 | 33 | 3/30 | 3/30 | 34.48 | 4.84 | 42.7 | 0 | 0 |
| Twenty20 | 44 | 798 | 971 | 38 | 5/21 | 5/21 | 25.55 | 7.30 | 21.0 | 1 | 0 |

# BEN BROWN

## RHB WK R0 W0

FULL NAME: Ben Christopher Brown
BORN: November 23, 1988, Crawley, Sussex
SQUAD NO: 26
HEIGHT: 5ft 8in
NICKNAME: Brownie, Goblin
EDUCATION: Ardingly College
TEAMS: Sussex
CAREER: First-class: 2007; List A: 2007; T20: 2008



BEST BATTING: 163 Sussex vs Durham, Hove, 2014
COUNTY CAPS: 2014

CAREER HIGHLIGHTS? Being capped at Sussex
BEST PLAYER IN COUNTY CRICKET? Luke Wright
TIP FOR THE TOP? Matt Hobden
CRICKETING HEROES? Adam Gilchrist – he changed the modern game
NON-CRICKETING HEROES? All my family for supporting me through my career, and José Mourinho!
CRICKET RULE YOU'D CHANGE? Let's cancel LBW
IF YOU WEREN'T A CRICKETER? Possibly trying my hand in journalism or media
IF YOU COULD BE SOMEONE ELSE FOR A DAY? Didier Drogba in the Champions League final vs Bayern Munich, 2012
DESERT ISLAND DISC? Rod Stewart!
LEAST FAVOURITE TV? Anything with a vampire in it
FANTASY SLIP CORDON? Keeper: Me, 1st: Frank Lampard, 2nd: Jack Bauer, 3rd: Rocket Rod Stewart, Gully: Henry VIII
TWITTER FEED: @Ben_brown26

| Batting | Mat | Inns | NO | Runs | HS | Ave | SR | 100 | 50 | Ct | St |
|---|---|---|---|---|---|---|---|---|---|---|---|
| First-class | 67 | 104 | 15 | 2970 | 163 | 33.37 | 57.77 | 5 | 16 | 177 | 14 |
| List A | 46 | 34 | 9 | 513 | 60 | 20.52 | 93.61 | 0 | 3 | 43 | 9 |
| Twenty20 | 49 | 42 | 7 | 505 | 68 | 14.42 | 108.83 | 0 | 1 | 19 | 5 |
| **Bowling** | **Mat** | **Balls** | **Runs** | **Wkts** | **BBI** | **BBM** | **Ave** | **Econ** | **SR** | **5w** | **10** |
| First-class | 67 | 24 | 14 | 0 | - | - | - | 3.50 | - | 0 | 0 |
| List A | 46 | - | - | - | - | - | - | - | - | - | - |
| Twenty20 | 49 | - | - | - | - | - | - | - | - | - | - |

## KARL BROWN

## RHB RM R0 W0

FULL NAME: Karl Robert Brown
BORN: May 17, 1988, Bolton, Lancashire
SQUAD NO: 14
HEIGHT: 5ft 10in
NICKNAME: Browny, Charlie
EDUCATION: Hesketh Fletcher CofE High School
TEAMS: Lancashire
CAREER: First-class: 2006; List A: 2007; T20: 2011

BEST BATTING: 114 Lancashire vs Sussex, Liverpool, 2011
BEST BOWLING: 2-30 Lancashire vs Nottinghamshire, Nottingham, 2009

FAMILY TIES? My dad played league cricket for Atherton CC and was the professional for Clifton CC
CAREER HIGHLIGHTS? Scoring my maiden first-class and one-day hundreds and playing for England U19
CRICKETING HEROES? Andrew Flintoff, Stuart Law
NON-CRICKETING HEROES? Kevin Davies, Lionel Messi, Ronnie O'Sullivan, Phil Taylor, Sergio Garcia
FAVOURITE TV? Celebrity Juice
ACCOMPLISHMENTS? Playing football for Wigan Athletic
TWITTER FEED: @karlos173

| Batting | Mat | Inns | NO | Runs | HS | Ave | SR | 100 | 50 | Ct | St |
|---|---|---|---|---|---|---|---|---|---|---|---|
| First-class | 61 | 102 | 6 | 2402 | 114 | 25.02 | 46.64 | 1 | 13 | 33 | 0 |
| List A | 53 | 50 | 9 | 1656 | 129 | 40.39 | 85.58 | 2 | 9 | 13 | 0 |
| Twenty20 | 45 | 43 | 7 | 1112 | 67* | 30.88 | 129.15 | 0 | 8 | 17 | 0 |
| **Bowling** | **Mat** | **Balls** | **Runs** | **Wkts** | **BBI** | **BBM** | **Ave** | **Econ** | **SR** | **5w** | **10** |
| First-class | 61 | 84 | 49 | 2 | 2/30 | 2/37 | 24.50 | 3.50 | 42.0 | 0 | 0 |
| List A | 53 | 6 | 17 | 0 | - | - | - | 17.00 | - | 0 | 0 |
| Twenty20 | 45 | - | - | - | - | - | - | - | - | - | - |

# NICK BROWNE LHB LB R0 W0

FULL NAME: Nicholas Laurence Joseph Browne
BORN: March 24, 1991, Leytonstone, Essex
SQUAD NO: 10
EDUCATION: Trinity College, Essex
TEAMS: Essex
CAREER: First-class: 2013



BEST BATTING: 132* Essex vs Derbyshire, Chesterfield, 2014

NOTES: Made his first-class debut for Essex in 2013. Last season he made history when he became the first Essex player to score two unbeaten centuries in a match, against Derbyshire at Chesterfield. He added a further Championship hundred and earned himself a two-year contract

| Batting | Mat | Inns | NO | Runs | HS | Ave | SR | 100 | 50 | Ct | St |
|---|---|---|---|---|---|---|---|---|---|---|---|
| First-class | 12 | 20 | 4 | 676 | 132* | 42.25 | 44.41 | 3 | 2 | 10 | 0 |
| **Bowling** | **Mat** | **Balls** | **Runs** | **Wkts** | **BBI** | **BBM** | **Ave** | **Econ** | **SR** | **5w** | **10** |
| First-class | 12 | 233 | 153 | 0 | - | - | - | 3.93 | - | 0 | 0 |

# NATHAN BUCK

RHB RFM R0 W0

FULL NAME: Nathan Liam Buck
BORN: April 26, 1991, Leicester
SQUAD NO: 11
HEIGHT: 6ft 3in
EDUCATION: Ashby Grammar School
TEAMS: Lancashire, Leicestershire
CAREER: First-class: 2009; List A: 2009; T20: 2010

---

BEST BATTING: 29* Leicestershire vs Worcestershire, Worcester, 2014
BEST BOWLING: 5-76 Leicestershire vs Essex, Chelmsford, 2014
COUNTY CAPS: 2011 (Leicestershire)

---

CAREER HIGHLIGHTS? England Lions tours in 2010 and 2011, receiving my Leicestershire cap and signing for Lancashire
BEST PLAYER IN COUNTY CRICKET? Darren Stevens
TIP FOR THE TOP? Liam Livingstone, Liam Kinch, Angus Robson
MOST MARKED CHARACTERISTIC? My 'shlid'
NON-CRICKETING HEROES? Peter Griffin
COACHING TIP? Never over-complicate things
IF YOU WEREN'T A CRICKETER? Struggling
IF YOU COULD BE SOMEONE ELSE FOR A DAY? Kyle Jarvis
FAVOURITE TV? Victoria's Secret Fashion Show
ACCOMPLISHMENTS? I once cooked one-minute noodles in 58 seconds
PET HATE? Slow walkers
TWITTER FEED: @nathanbuck17

| Batting | Mat | Inns | NO | Runs | HS | Ave | SR | 100 | 50 | Ct | St |
|---|---|---|---|---|---|---|---|---|---|---|---|
| First-class | 60 | 82 | 24 | 613 | 29* | 10.56 | | 0 | 0 | 8 | 0 |
| List A | 36 | 15 | 6 | 80 | 21 | 8.88 | 66.11 | 0 | 0 | 7 | 0 |
| Twenty20 | 24 | 5 | 4 | 19 | 8* | 19.00 | 95.00 | 0 | 0 | 5 | 0 |
| **Bowling** | **Mat** | **Balls** | **Runs** | **Wkts** | **BBI** | **BBM** | **Ave** | **Econ** | **SR** | **5w** | **10** |
| First-class | 60 | 9659 | 5667 | 150 | 5/76 | 7/79 | 37.78 | 3.52 | 64.3 | 4 | 0 |
| List A | 36 | 1525 | 1572 | 43 | 4/39 | 4/39 | 36.55 | 6.18 | 35.4 | 0 | 0 |
| Twenty20 | 24 | 495 | 723 | 29 | 3/16 | 3/16 | 24.93 | 8.76 | 17.0 | 0 | 0 |

# KIERAN BULL

RHB OB R0 W0

FULL NAME: Kieran Andrew Bull
BORN: April 5, 1995, Haverfordwest, Pembrokeshire
SQUAD NO: 11
HEIGHT: 6ft 2in
NICKNAME: Bully
EDUCATION: Queen Elizabeth High School; Cardiff Metropolitan University
TEAMS: Glamorgan
CAREER: First-class: 2014



BEST BATTING: 12 Glamorgan vs Kent, Canterbury, 2014
BEST BOWLING: 4-62 Glamorgan vs Kent, Canterbury, 2014

FAMILY TIES? My father played club cricket
CAREER HIGHLIGHTS? Successful season with Wales Minor Counties, making my Glamorgan debut and receiving the Glamorgan Academy Most Promising Player Award
MOST MARKED CHARACTERISTIC? Bucket hands
CRICKETING HEROES? Darren Gough and Andrew Flintoff
NON-CRICKETING HEROES? Steven Gerrard and Muhammad Ali
IF YOU WEREN'T A CRICKETER? Studying at university
DESERT ISLAND DISC? Arctic Monkeys – AM
FAVOURITE TV? Two And A Half Men
ACCOMPLISHMENTS? Being a Cardiff City Junior Academy football player and passing my driving test (third attempt)
SURPRISING FACT? I moved to Spain aged 10 to take up a place in a tennis academy and lived there for two years, representing Spain at age-group level vs Qatar. I was also ball boy for Rafael Nadal
FANTASY SLIP CORDON? Keeper: James Corden, 1st: Myself, 2nd: John Bishop, 3rd: Dynamo, Gully: Bruce Grobbelaar
TWITTER FEED: @Kieran_Bull89

| Batting | Mat | Inns | NO | Runs | HS | Ave | SR | 100 | 50 | Ct | St |
|---|---|---|---|---|---|---|---|---|---|---|---|
| First-class | 3 | 6 | 2 | 31 | 12 | 7.75 | 24.21 | 0 | 0 | 0 | 0 |
| **Bowling** | **Mat** | **Balls** | **Runs** | **Wkts** | **BBI** | **BBM** | **Ave** | **Econ** | **SR** | **5w** | **10** |
| First-class | 3 | 267 | 168 | 7 | 4/62 | 4/62 | 24.00 | 3.77 | 38.1 | 0 | 0 |

# JAMES BURKE RHB RMF R0 W0

FULL NAME: James Edward Burke
BORN: January 25, 1991, Plymouth, Devon
SQUAD NO: 8
HEIGHT: 6ft 3in
NICKNAME: Burkey
EDUCATION: Plymouth College School; Open University
TEAMS: Surrey, Somerset
CAREER: First-class: 2012; T20: 2014

BEST BOWLING: 2-51 Somerset vs Cardiff MCCU, Taunton, 2012

CAREER HIGHLIGHTS? Playing for England U19 and first-class cricket
BEST PLAYER IN COUNTY CRICKET? James Vince
TIP FOR THE TOP? Tom Abell
MOST MARKED CHARACTERISTIC? Tanned
CRICKETING HEROES? Brett Lee – loved his aggression and pace
NON-CRICKETING HEROES? Tube and Berger – they make sick music. Lawrence Krauss and Richard Dawkins – leading the struggle for spreading logic and reason
CRICKET RULE YOU'D CHANGE? Overthrows for hitting the stumps because it's punishing the fielder for executing their skill
COACHING TIP? When bowling, imagine that you are pulling down an invisible rope with your front arm
IF YOU WEREN'T A CRICKETER? Scientist
IF YOU COULD BE SOMEONE ELSE FOR A DAY? Benedict Cumberbatch
PET HATE? Conforming to the social paradigm without questioning it first
SURPRISING FACT? I love Classical music
FANTASY SLIP CORDON? Keeper: Leonardo da Vinci, 1st: Benedict Cumberbatch, 2nd: Myself, 3rd: Lawrence Krauss, Gully: Chris Jones

| Batting | Mat | Inns | NO | Runs | HS | Ave | SR | 100 | 50 | Ct | St |
|---|---|---|---|---|---|---|---|---|---|---|---|
| First-class | 1 | - | - | - | - | - | - | - | - | 0 | 0 |
| Twenty20 | 3 | 1 | 0 | 4 | 4 | 4.00 | 66.66 | 0 | 0 | 0 | 0 |
| **Bowling** | **Mat** | **Balls** | **Runs** | **Wkts** | **BBI** | **BBM** | **Ave** | **Econ** | **SR** | **5w** | **10** |
| First-class | 1 | 108 | 68 | 2 | 2/51 | 2/68 | 34.00 | 3.77 | 54.0 | 0 | 0 |
| Twenty20 | 3 | - | - | - | - | - | - | - | - | - | - |

# RORY BURNS — LHB RM WK R1 W0

FULL NAME: Rory Joseph Burns
BORN: August 26, 1990, Epsom, Surrey
SQUAD NO: 17
HEIGHT: 5ft 10in
NICKNAME: Fong, Burnsy
EDUCATION: Whitgift School; City of London Freemen's; Cardiff Metropolitan University
TEAMS: Surrey
CAREER: First-class: 2011; List A: 2012; T20: 2012



BEST BATTING: 199 Surrey vs Gloucestershire, Gloucester, 2014
BEST BOWLING: 1-18 Surrey vs Middlesex, Lord's, 2013

CAREER HIGHLIGHTS? First-class debut, county cap and first Championship hundred
BEST PLAYER IN COUNTY CRICKET? Darren Stevens
TIP FOR THE TOP? Dom Sibley, Jason Roy, Matthew Dunn, Daniel Bell-Drummond
MOST MARKED CHARACTERISTIC? Mischievous
CRICKETING HEROES? Brian Lara – legend
NON-CRICKETING HEROES? Jonny Wilkinson – loved his work ethic
CRICKET RULE YOU'D CHANGE? Double-Plays like you have in baseball for T20 and one-dayers
IF YOU WEREN'T A CRICKETER? Student, teacher or amateur rugby playmaker
DESERT ISLAND DISC? Ed Sheeran – X
FAVOURITE TV? Game Of Thrones
ACCOMPLISHMENTS? Proud owner of a VW polo called Shaniqua
PET HATE? Loud noises
SURPRISING FACT? I play the saxophone
TWITTER FEED: @roryburns17

| Batting | Mat | Inns | NO | Runs | HS | Ave | SR | 100 | 50 | Ct | St |
|---|---|---|---|---|---|---|---|---|---|---|---|
| First-class | 45 | 78 | 7 | 2748 | 199 | 38.70 | 45.66 | 6 | 13 | 46 | 0 |
| List A | 15 | 15 | 1 | 387 | 87 | 27.64 | 89.17 | 0 | 1 | 7 | 0 |
| Twenty20 | 9 | 9 | 1 | 100 | 28 | 12.50 | 102.04 | 0 | 0 | 2 | 1 |
| **Bowling** | **Mat** | **Balls** | **Runs** | **Wkts** | **BBI** | **BBM** | **Ave** | **Econ** | **SR** | **5w** | **10** |
| First-class | 45 | 126 | 108 | 2 | 1/18 | 1/18 | 54.00 | 5.14 | 63.0 | 0 | 0 |
| List A | 15 | - | - | - | - | - | - | - | - | - | - |
| Twenty20 | 9 | - | - | - | - | - | - | - | - | - | - |

# JOS BUTTLER RHB WK R0 W0



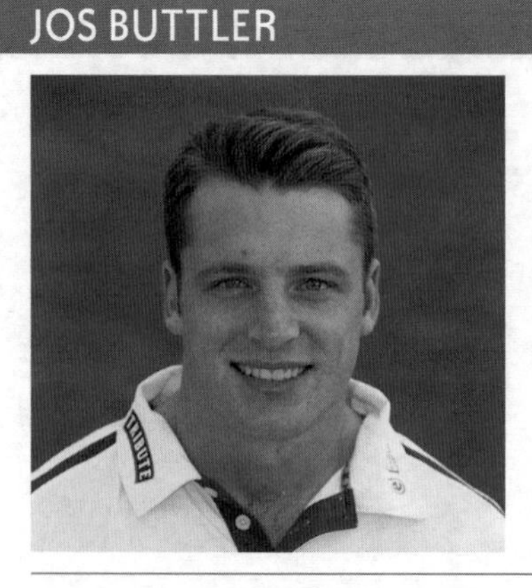

FULL NAME: Joseph Charles Buttler
BORN: September 8, 1990, Taunton
SQUAD NO: 6
HEIGHT: 5ft 11in
EDUCATION: King's College, Taunton
TEAMS: England, Lancashire, Somerset
CAREER: Test: 2014; ODI: 2012; T20I: 2011; First-class: 2009; List A: 2009; T20: 2009

BEST BATTING: 144 Somerset vs Hampshire, Southampton, 2013

NOTES: Signed for Lancashire in September 2013 to pursue more opportunities as a keeper after sharing duties with Craig Kieswetter at Somerset. Came to prominence after scoring 55 from 25 balls in the 2010 FPt20 semi-final between Somerset and Notts. Scored 440 runs at 55 in the 2010 CB40 and 411 runs at 137 in 2011, including 86 from 72 balls in the final. A successful tour with England Lions to Sri Lanka in early 2012 (262 runs at 87.33) led to a call-up for England's limited-overs squads for the series against Pakistan in UAE. Moved to Lancashire from Somerset ahead of the 2014 season and usurped Matt Prior as England's No.1 Test wicketkeeper, scoring 85 on Test debut against India at Southampton. Scored England's fastest one-day hundred in May last year, off 61 balls against Sri Lanka at Lord's

| Batting | Mat | Inns | NO | Runs | HS | Ave | SR | 100 | 50 | Ct | St |
|---|---|---|---|---|---|---|---|---|---|---|---|
| Tests | 3 | 3 | 0 | 200 | 85 | 66.66 | 69.93 | 0 | 2 | 11 | 0 |
| ODIs | 54 | 47 | 7 | 1280 | 121 | 32.00 | 111.30 | 1 | 7 | 72 | 8 |
| T20Is | 37 | 31 | 7 | 516 | 67 | 21.50 | 131.96 | 0 | 2 | 10 | 1 |
| First-class | 61 | 91 | 7 | 2864 | 144 | 34.09 | 59.86 | 4 | 16 | 121 | 2 |
| List A | 116 | 100 | 27 | 3278 | 121 | 44.90 | 118.04 | 3 | 22 | 118 | 13 |
| Twenty20 | 122 | 104 | 24 | 2043 | 72* | 25.53 | 142.66 | 0 | 10 | 64 | 13 |
| **Bowling** | **Mat** | **Balls** | **Runs** | **Wkts** | **BBI** | **BBM** | **Ave** | **Econ** | **SR** | **5w** | **10** |
| Tests | 3 | - | - | - | - | - | - | - | - | - | - |
| ODIs | 54 | - | - | - | - | - | - | - | - | - | - |
| T20Is | 37 | - | - | - | - | - | - | - | - | - | - |
| First-class | 61 | 12 | 11 | 0 | - | - | - | 5.50 | - | 0 | 0 |
| List A | 116 | - | - | - | - | - | - | - | - | - | - |
| Twenty20 | 122 | - | - | - | - | - | - | - | - | - | - |

# CRAIG CACHOPA

RHB WK R0 W0

FULL NAME: Craig Cachopa
BORN: January 17, 1992, Welkom, South Africa
SQUAD NO: 12
HEIGHT: 5ft 7in
NICKNAME: Chops, Booney
EDUCATION: Westlake Boys High School; Massey University
TEAMS: Sussex, Auckland, Wellington
CAREER: First-class: 2012; List A: 2011; T20: 2011



BEST BATTING: 203 Auckland vs Wellington, Auckland, 2014

FAMILY TIES? I have two brothers – Carl and Bradley – playing first-class cricket in New Zealand
CAREER HIGHLIGHTS? First-class debut, my maiden double-ton and signing for Sussex
BEST PLAYER IN COUNTY CRICKET? Ed Joyce
CRICKETING HEROES? Jonty Rhodes – amazing fielder! AB de Villiers – brilliant in all three forms of the game
NON-CRICKETING HEROES? My grandfather and my father – well grounded and always guiding me! Iron Man – self-explanatory
COACHING TIP? Don't be afraid to get out in the nets. It's the best place to learn things and see what you can do
IF YOU COULD BE SOMEONE ELSE FOR A DAY? Richard Branson
ACCOMPLISHMENTS? Competitive hockey player
PET HATE? Inconsiderate drivers. They just frustrate me
FANTASY SLIP CORDON? Keeper: Me, 1st: Kevin Hart, 2nd: Chris Nash, 3rd: Hugh Hefner, Gully: Dan Bilzerian
TWITTER FEED: @craigcachopa

| Batting | Mat | Inns | NO | Runs | HS | Ave | SR | 100 | 50 | Ct | St |
|---|---|---|---|---|---|---|---|---|---|---|---|
| First-class | 27 | 46 | 2 | 2179 | 203 | 49.52 | 60.27 | 5 | 13 | 18 | 0 |
| List A | 41 | 41 | 1 | 1102 | 121 | 27.55 | 94.26 | 2 | 6 | 22 | 0 |
| Twenty20 | 40 | 37 | 8 | 848 | 79* | 29.24 | 131.47 | 0 | 1 | 18 | 1 |
| **Bowling** | **Mat** | **Balls** | **Runs** | **Wkts** | **BBI** | **BBM** | **Ave** | **Econ** | **SR** | **5w** | **10** |
| First-class | 27 | 42 | 73 | 0 | - | - | - | 10.42 | - | 0 | 0 |
| List A | 41 | - | - | - | - | - | - | - | - | - | - |
| Twenty20 | 40 | - | - | - | - | - | - | - | - | - | - |

## MICHAEL CARBERRY — LHB OB R3 W0 MVP83

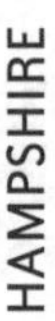


FULL NAME: Michael Alexander Carberry
BORN: September 29, 1980, Croydon, Surrey
SQUAD NO: 15
HEIGHT: 5ft 11in
NICKNAME: Carbs
EDUCATION: St John Rigby College
TEAMS: England, Hampshire, Kent, Surrey
CAREER: Test: 2010; ODIs: 2013; T20I: 2014; First-class: 2001; List A: 1999; T20: 2003

---

BEST BATTING: 300* Hampshire vs Yorkshire, Southampton, 2011
BEST BOWLING: 2-85 Hampshire vs Durham, Chester-le-Street, 2006
COUNTY CAPS: 2006 (Hampshire)

---

CAREER HIGHLIGHTS? Every day is a highlight
CRICKETING HEROES? Ricky Ponting, Brian Lara
TWITTER FEED: @carbs646
NOTES: Carberry made his Test debut against Bangladesh in 2010, scoring 30 and 34. It was three years until his next chance, when he was drafted in for the doomed tour of Australia in 2013/14. He was England's second-highest run-scorer overall in the series with 281 but hasn't played a Test since. Scored 300* against Yorkshire in Southampton 2011. Helped Hampshire to two titles, the FL t20 and CB40, in 2012. He hit three Championship centuries in 12 appearances in 2014 and also scored four half-centures in the T20 Blast

| Batting | Mat | Inns | NO | Runs | HS | Ave | SR | 100 | 50 | Ct | St |
|---|---|---|---|---|---|---|---|---|---|---|---|
| Tests | 6 | 12 | 0 | 345 | 60 | 28.75 | 41.31 | 0 | 1 | 7 | 0 |
| ODIs | 6 | 6 | 0 | 114 | 63 | 19.00 | 63.33 | 0 | 1 | 2 | 0 |
| T20Is | 1 | 1 | 0 | 7 | 7 | 7.00 | 100.00 | 0 | 0 | 1 | 0 |
| First-class | 166 | 289 | 23 | 11499 | 300* | 43.22 | 51.64 | 32 | 53 | 82 | 0 |
| List A | 160 | 150 | 15 | 4470 | 150* | 33.11 | | 6 | 32 | 59 | 0 |
| Twenty20 | 110 | 103 | 15 | 2799 | 100* | 31.80 | 121.22 | 1 | 22 | 40 | 0 |
| **Bowling** | **Mat** | **Balls** | **Runs** | **Wkts** | **BBI** | **BBM** | **Ave** | **Econ** | **SR** | **5w** | **10** |
| Tests | 6 | - | - | - | - | - | - | - | - | - | - |
| ODIs | 6 | 6 | 12 | 0 | - | - | - | 12.00 | - | 0 | 0 |
| T20Is | 1 | - | - | - | - | - | - | - | - | - | - |
| First-class | 166 | 1459 | 1041 | 16 | 2/85 | | 65.06 | 4.28 | 91.1 | 0 | 0 |
| List A | 160 | 322 | 297 | 11 | 3/37 | 3/37 | 27.00 | 5.53 | 29.2 | 0 | 0 |
| Twenty20 | 110 | 18 | 19 | 1 | 1/16 | 1/16 | 19.00 | 6.33 | 18.0 | 0 | 0 |

# ANDY CARTER

RHB RF R0 W0

FULL NAME: Andrew Carter
BORN: August 27, 1988, Lincoln
SQUAD NO: 37
HEIGHT: 6ft 5in
NICKNAME: Carts
EDUCATION: Lincoln College
TEAMS: Nottinghamshire, Essex
CAREER: First-class: 2009; List A: 2009; T20: 2010



BEST BATTING: 17* Nottinghamshire vs Sussex, Hove, 2012
BEST BOWLING: 5-40 Essex vs Kent, Canterbury, 2010

CAREER HIGHLIGHTS? Staying fit
MOST MARKED CHARACTERISTIC? I'm ginger
SUPERSTITIONS? I always carry a rabbit's foot
CRICKETING HEROES? Mike Hendrick, Luke Fletcher, Matthew Hoggard
NON-CRICKETING HEROES? Ted Nugent, butchers
IF YOU WEREN'T A CRICKETER? Plumber
DESERT ISLAND DISC? Iron Maiden – The Number Of The Beast
FAVOURITE TV? Jimmy's Farm
ACCOMPLISHMENTS? My charity work
SURPRISING FACT? I was Lincolnshire trampoline junior champion
FANTASY SLIP CORDON? Keeper: My dog, 1st: Luke Fletcher, 2nd and 3rd: The Hairy Bikers, 4th: Lisa Riley, Gully: Nigel Dennis
TWITTER FEED: @andy_carter2011

| Batting | Mat | Inns | NO | Runs | HS | Ave | SR | 100 | 50 | Ct | St |
|---|---|---|---|---|---|---|---|---|---|---|---|
| First-class | 24 | 27 | 8 | 137 | 17* | 7.21 | | 0 | 0 | 4 | 0 |
| List A | 20 | 8 | 2 | 35 | 12 | 5.83 | 52.23 | 0 | 0 | 7 | 0 |
| Twenty20 | 23 | 1 | 1 | 5 | 5* | - | 125.00 | 0 | 0 | 5 | 0 |
| **Bowling** | **Mat** | **Balls** | **Runs** | **Wkts** | **BBI** | **BBM** | **Ave** | **Econ** | **SR** | **5w** | **10** |
| First-class | 24 | 3768 | 2080 | 70 | 5/40 | 7/95 | 29.71 | 3.31 | 53.8 | 2 | 0 |
| List A | 20 | 657 | 702 | 26 | 4/45 | 4/45 | 27.00 | 6.41 | 25.2 | 0 | 0 |
| Twenty20 | 23 | 449 | 600 | 27 | 4/20 | 4/20 | 22.22 | 8.01 | 16.6 | 0 | 0 |

# KARL CARVER

LHB SLA R0 W0



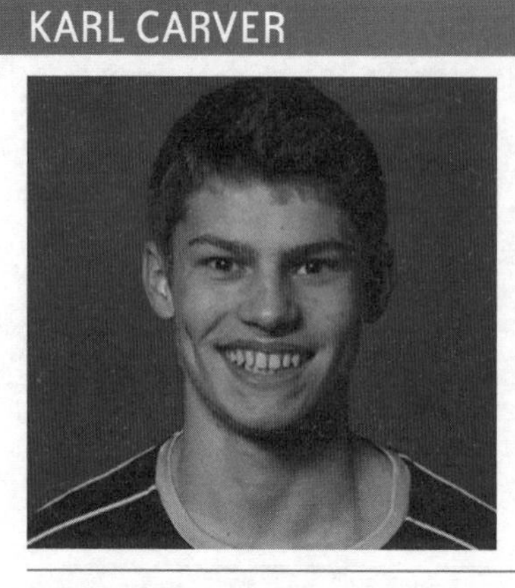

FULL NAME: Karl Carver
BORN: March 26, 1996, Northallerton, Yorkshire
SQUAD NO: 29
HEIGHT: 5ft 10in
NICKNAME: Curley, Keith Curle, Carves
EDUCATION: Thirsk School and Sixth Form College
TEAMS: Yorkshire
CAREER: First-class: 2014

BEST BATTING: 2* Yorkshire vs Warwickshire, Birmingham, 2014
BEST BOWLING: 2- 27 Yorkshire vs Warwickshire, Birmingham, 2014

CAREER HIGHLIGHTS? Making my first-class debut for Yorkshire and taking my first first-class wicket, being in a Championship-winning side and representing England U19
BEST PLAYER IN COUNTY CRICKET? Adam Lyth
TIP FOR THE TOP? Matthew Fisher, Ryan Higgins, Haseeb Hameed, Will Rhodes
SUPERSTITIONS? Often bowling in my sunglasses
CRICKETING HEROES? Brian Lara – because of what he achieved and how he achieved it. Shane Warne – because of the way he played the game. Joe Root – because of his passion for the game and his character
CRICKET RULE YOU'D CHANGE? Have free hits in Test matches
COACHING TIP? As a bowler and fielder, have good match-awareness to work the batter out and watch where he plays
IF YOU COULD BE SOMEONE ELSE FOR A DAY? Leonardo DiCaprio
DESERT ISLAND DISC? A Clean Bandit album or a Bee Gees album
ACCOMPLISHMENTS? Catching golden trout and winning a fishing competition
PET HATE? Over-complicating simple situations or being spoken down to
FANTASY SLIP CORDON? Keeper: James Corden, 1st: Me, 2nd: Jack Whitehall, 3rd: Matt LeBlanc, Gully: Peter Kay
TWITTER FEED: @Carver_Karl

| Batting | Mat | Inns | NO | Runs | HS | Ave | SR | 100 | 50 | Ct | St |
|---|---|---|---|---|---|---|---|---|---|---|---|
| First-class | 1 | 1 | 1 | 2 | 2* | - | 10.00 | 0 | 0 | 1 | 0 |
| **Bowling** | **Mat** | **Balls** | **Runs** | **Wkts** | **BBI** | **BBM** | **Ave** | **Econ** | **SR** | **5w** | **10** |
| First-class | 1 | 120 | 65 | 3 | 2/27 | 3/65 | 21.66 | 3.25 | 40.0 | 0 | 0 |

# MAURICE CHAMBERS RHB RFM R0 W0

FULL NAME: Maurice Anthony Chambers
BORN: September 14, 1987, Port Antonio, Jamaica
SQUAD NO: 29
HEIGHT: 6ft 3in
NICKNAME: Moza
EDUCATION: Homerton College of Technology; George Monoux College
TEAMS: Northamptonshire, Essex, England Lions, Warwickshire
CAREER: First-class: 2005; List A: 2008; T20: 2010



BEST BATTING: 58 Warwickshire vs Derbyshire, Derby, 2013
BEST BOWLING: 6-68 Essex vs Nottinghamshire, Chelmsford, 2010

CAREER HIGHLIGHTS? Getting selected for the England Lions tour to Australia in 2010 and the tour to the West Indies in 2011
MOST MARKED CHARACTERISTIC? Calm and steadfast in the face of adversity
SUPERSTITIONS? No sexy time before cricket
CRICKETING HEROES? Courtney Walsh and Curtly Ambrose
NON-CRICKETING HEROES? Usain Bolt
DESERT ISLAND DISC? Ne-Yo – Year Of The Gentleman
FAVOURITE TV? The Big Bang Theory
ACCOMPLISHMENTS? Getting through college and passing my driving test
FANTASY SLIP CORDON? Keeper: James Foster (fantastic man and the best keeper in the country), 1st: Usain Bolt, 2nd: Will Smith, 3rd: Chris Gayle (Will and him will make me laugh until my belly hurts), Gully: Me
TWITTER FEED: @Maurice29chamb

| Batting | Mat | Inns | NO | Runs | HS | Ave | SR | 100 | 50 | Ct | St |
|---|---|---|---|---|---|---|---|---|---|---|---|
| First-class | 58 | 77 | 24 | 388 | 58 | 7.32 | | 0 | 1 | 18 | 0 |
| List A | 12 | 5 | 2 | 6 | 2 | 2.00 | 37.50 | 0 | 0 | 2 | 0 |
| Twenty20 | 19 | 8 | 5 | 28 | 10* | 9.33 | 96.55 | 0 | 0 | 6 | 0 |
| **Bowling** | **Mat** | **Balls** | **Runs** | **Wkts** | **BBI** | **BBM** | **Ave** | **Econ** | **SR** | **5w** | **10** |
| First-class | 58 | 8246 | 4968 | 141 | 6/68 | | 35.23 | 3.61 | 58.4 | 3 | 1 |
| List A | 12 | 415 | 465 | 14 | 3/29 | 3/29 | 33.21 | 6.72 | 29.6 | 0 | 0 |
| Twenty20 | 19 | 324 | 487 | 17 | 3/31 | 3/31 | 28.64 | 9.01 | 19.0 | 0 | 0 |

## ZAK CHAPPELL

RHB RFM R0 W0

FULL NAME: Zachariah Chappell
BORN: August 21, 1996, Grantham, Lincolnshire
SQUAD NO: 32
HEIGHT: 6ft 4in
NICKNAME: Chappo
EDUCATION: Stamford Boys School
TEAMS: Leicestershire Academy
CAREER: Yet to make first-team debut

---

BEST PLAYER IN COUNTY CRICKET? James Anderson
TIP FOR THE TOP? Atif Sheikh is very quick. Proved himself by picking up a hat-trick last season
MOST MARKED CHARACTERISTIC? Raw pace
SUPERSTITIONS? No
CRICKETING HEROES? Brett Lee and Andrew Flintoff. Both quick and hostile fast bowlers
NON-CRICKETING HEROES? Muhammad Ali for his charisma and showmanship
CRICKET RULE YOU'D CHANGE? No bent arm at all when bowling
COACHING TIP? Try and make everything as smooth as possible in your action to reduce injury
IF YOU COULD BE SOMEONE ELSE FOR A DAY? Dan Bilzerian
DESERT ISLAND DISC? Scouting For Girls
FAVOURITE TV? Any ball sports or The Office
LEAST FAVOURITE TV? Soaps
ACCOMPLISHMENTS? Playing squash for Huntingdonshire
PET HATE? Fat people complaining they're fat. People talking through TV programmes
SURPRISING FACT? Got some quality shapes and play county squash
FANTASY SLIP CORDON? 1st: Michael Holding, 2nd: Michael McIntyre, 3rd: Cheryl Cole, Gully: Dan Bilzerian
TWITTER FEED: @ZakkChappell

# GLEN CHAPPLE RHB RMF R0 W7 MVP100

FULL NAME: Glen Chapple
BORN: January 23, 1974, Skipton, Yorkshire
SQUAD NO: 3
HEIGHT: 6ft 2in
NICKNAME: Chappie, Boris
EDUCATION: West Craven High School; Nelson and Colne College
TEAMS: England, Lancashire
CAREER: ODI: 2006; First-class: 1992; List A: 1993; T20: 2003



BEST BATTING: 155 Lancashire vs Somerset, Manchester, 2001
BEST BOWLING: 7-53 Lancashire vs Durham, Blackpool, 2007
COUNTY CAPS: 1994; BENEFIT YEAR: 2004

FAMILY TIES? Father played in Lancashire League for Nelson CC and was a professional for Darwen and Earby
CRICKETING HEROES? Dennis Lillee, Robin Smith
DESERT ISLAND DISC? U2, Oasis, Stone Roses
TWITTER FEED: @chappie03
NOTES: After making his Lancashire debut in 1992, club legend Chapple takes on a new player/coach role for 2015. He has played once for England, an ODI against Ireland in 2006. He has 975 first-class wickets going into the 2015 season. He has won seven trophies at Lancashire, including winning the County Championship in 2011 as captain. He is one of only three Lancashire allrounders to have passed 7,000 runs and 800 wickets

| Batting | Mat | Inns | NO | Runs | HS | Ave | SR | 100 | 50 | Ct | St |
|---|---|---|---|---|---|---|---|---|---|---|---|
| ODIs | 1 | 1 | 0 | 14 | 14 | 14.00 | 200.00 | 0 | 0 | 0 | 0 |
| First-class | 310 | 431 | 74 | 8674 | 155 | 24.29 | | 6 | 37 | 102 | 0 |
| List A | 283 | 160 | 44 | 2062 | 81* | 17.77 | | 0 | 9 | 66 | 0 |
| Twenty20 | 66 | 36 | 13 | 301 | 55* | 13.08 | 110.25 | 0 | 1 | 16 | 0 |
| **Bowling** | **Mat** | **Balls** | **Runs** | **Wkts** | **BBI** | **BBM** | **Ave** | **Econ** | **SR** | **5w** | **10** |
| ODIs | 1 | 24 | 14 | 0 | - | - | - | 3.50 | - | 0 | 0 |
| First-class | 310 | 53453 | 25825 | 975 | 7/53 | | 26.48 | 2.89 | 54.8 | 39 | 3 |
| List A | 283 | 12165 | 9138 | 320 | 6/18 | 6/18 | 28.55 | 4.50 | 38.0 | 5 | 0 |
| Twenty20 | 66 | 1300 | 1586 | 68 | 3/36 | 3/36 | 23.32 | 7.32 | 19.1 | 0 | 0 |

# VARUN CHOPRA

## RHB OB R3 W0 MVP10

FULL NAME: Varun Chopra
BORN: June 21, 1987, Barking, Essex
SQUAD NO: 3
HEIGHT: 6ft 1in
NICKNAME: Chops, Tidz
EDUCATION: Ilford County High School
TEAMS: Warwickshire, England Lions, Essex
CAREER: First-class: 2006; List A: 2006; T20: 2006

BEST BATTING: 233* Tamil Union vs Sinhalese Sports Club, Colombo, 2012
COUNTY CAPS: 2012 (Warwickshire)

CAREER HIGHLIGHTS? Winning the Championship in 2012 and scoring back-to-back double-hundreds
CRICKETING HEROES? Sachin Tendulkar and Shane Warne. Pure admiration for their talents and they're both the best at what they do
NON-CRICKETING HEROES? Roger Federer – makes the game look simple and effortless
CRICKET RULE YOU'D CHANGE? No heavy roller in one-day cricket. Also, the ball to have to go over the rope for a boundary to avoid the time wasted on checking if the fielder was in contact with the rope and ball at the same time
COACHING TIP? Never be afraid to try new things
LEAST FAVOURITE TV? Anything vampire related
PET HATE? People eating loudly! Cannot stand it!
SURPRISING FACT? I'm allergic to cats!
FANTASY SLIP CORDON? Keeper: Mark Zuckerburg, 1st: Me, 2nd: Dan Bilzerian, 3rd: Barack Obama, Gully: Scarlett Johansson
TWITTER FEED: @vchops3

| Batting | Mat | Inns | NO | Runs | HS | Ave | SR | 100 | 50 | Ct | St |
|---|---|---|---|---|---|---|---|---|---|---|---|
| First-class | 136 | 224 | 16 | 7815 | 233* | 37.57 | 51.06 | 16 | 39 | 152 | 0 |
| List A | 85 | 83 | 5 | 3289 | 115 | 42.16 | 74.83 | 7 | 22 | 30 | 0 |
| Twenty20 | 63 | 61 | 9 | 1399 | 86* | 26.90 | 109.04 | 0 | 10 | 16 | 0 |
| **Bowling** | **Mat** | **Balls** | **Runs** | **Wkts** | **BBI** | **BBM** | **Ave** | **Econ** | **SR** | **5w** | **10** |
| First-class | 136 | 192 | 116 | 0 | - | - | - | 3.62 | - | 0 | 0 |
| List A | 85 | 18 | 18 | 0 | - | - | - | 6.00 | - | 0 | 0 |
| Twenty20 | 63 | - | - | - | - | - | - | - | - | - | - |

# SHAAIQ CHOUDHRY RHB SLA R0 W0

FULL NAME: Shaaiq Hussain Choudhry
BORN: November 3, 1985, Rotherham, Yorkshire
SQUAD NO: 28
HEIGHT: 5ft 11in
NICKNAME: Shaqs, Chouds
EDUCATION: Fir Vale School; Rotherham College of Arts and Technology; University of Bradford
TEAMS: Worcestershire, Warwickshire
CAREER: First-class: 2007; List A: 2010; T20: 2010



BEST BATTING: 75 Warwickshire vs Durham UCCE, Durham University, 2009
BEST BOWLING: 4-38 Worcestershire vs Lancashire, Manchester, 2012

CAREER HIGHLIGHTS? Promotion last season, 4-54 vs Surrey in List A, 4-38 vs Lancashire in the Championship
TIP FOR THE TOP? Tom Fell, Tom Kohler-Cadmore
CRICKETING HEROES? Sachin Tendulkar – for maintaining such high standards throughout a career spanning over two decades. Shane Warne – for his sheer brilliance and game-changing ability. Saeed Ajmal – for his variations and ability to control them so well
NON-CRICKETING HEROES? Muhammad Ali – he achieved so much and had so many setbacks to overcome through his career
CRICKET RULE YOU'D CHANGE? Teams have to have specialist fielders which means batters and bowlers don't always have to field
IF YOU WEREN'T A CRICKETER? I would probably be a graphic designer
IF YOU COULD BE SOMEONE ELSE FOR A DAY? David Beckham
FAVOURITE TV? I love Top Gear, Two And A Half Men, The Fresh Prince Of Bel-Air, Friends
LEAST FAVOURITE TV? EastEnders, Coronation Street, Hollyoaks
TWITTER FEED: @ShaaiqChoudhry

| Batting | Mat | Inns | NO | Runs | HS | Ave | SR | 100 | 50 | Ct | St |
|---|---|---|---|---|---|---|---|---|---|---|---|
| First-class | 22 | 35 | 7 | 629 | 75 | 22.46 | 38.75 | 0 | 4 | 8 | 0 |
| List A | 29 | 21 | 9 | 246 | 44* | 20.50 | 94.25 | 0 | 0 | 8 | 0 |
| Twenty20 | 24 | 14 | 9 | 84 | 26* | 16.80 | 105.00 | 0 | 0 | 5 | 0 |
| **Bowling** | **Mat** | **Balls** | **Runs** | **Wkts** | **BBI** | **BBM** | **Ave** | **Econ** | **SR** | **5w** | **10** |
| First-class | 22 | 2319 | 1189 | 33 | 4/38 | 6/54 | 36.03 | 3.07 | 70.2 | 0 | 0 |
| List A | 29 | 822 | 794 | 18 | 4/54 | 4/54 | 44.11 | 5.79 | 45.6 | 0 | 0 |
| Twenty20 | 24 | 381 | 458 | 13 | 2/21 | 2/21 | 35.23 | 7.21 | 29.3 | 0 | 0 |

# JONATHAN CLARE

## RHB RMF R0 W0

FULL NAME: Jonathan Luke Clare
BORN: June 14, 1986, Burnley, Lancashire
SQUAD NO: 13
HEIGHT: 6ft 3in
NICKNAME: JC
EDUCATION: St Theodore's RC High School and Sixth Form
TEAMS: Derbyshire, Lancashire
CAREER: First-class: 2007; List A: 2007; T20: 2008

---

BEST BATTING: 130 Derbyshire vs Glamorgan, Derby, 2011
BEST BOWLING: 7-74 Derbyshire vs Northamptonshire, Northampton, 2008
COUNTY CAPS: 2012

---

CAREER HIGHLIGHTS? Taking 5-90 on debut vs Notts, scoring 129* and taking 7-79 in the same innings vs Northants, winning Division Two
BEST PLAYER IN COUNTY CRICKET? Chris Woakes
TIP FOR THE TOP? Harvey Hosein, Ben Cotton, Greg Cork
CRICKETING HEROES? Carl Hooper, Brian Lara, Allan Donald, Andrew Flintoff
NON-CRICKETING HEROES? Sean Dyche – Burnley manager, Dean Marney – Burnley player (best in the world), Derrick Rose – Chicago Bulls, Ray Lewis – Baltimore Ravens
IF YOU COULD BE SOMEONE ELSE FOR A DAY? Batman
DESERT ISLAND DISC? Any Arctic Monkeys record
PET HATE? People who watch The X Factor
SURPRISING FACT? Golf handicap of 8
FANTASY SLIP CORDON? Keeper: Alex Turner, 1st: Sean Dyche, 2nd: Me, 3rd: My British bulldogs Humpty and Hilda, Gully: David Beckham
TWITTER FEED: @jcfalcons13

| Batting | Mat | Inns | NO | Runs | HS | Ave | SR | 100 | 50 | Ct | St |
|---|---|---|---|---|---|---|---|---|---|---|---|
| First-class | 56 | 81 | 9 | 1721 | 130 | 23.90 | 66.39 | 2 | 8 | 28 | 0 |
| List A | 41 | 31 | 3 | 321 | 57 | 11.46 | 96.39 | 0 | 1 | 11 | 0 |
| Twenty20 | 37 | 25 | 10 | 215 | 35* | 14.33 | 110.25 | 0 | 0 | 14 | 0 |
| **Bowling** | **Mat** | **Balls** | **Runs** | **Wkts** | **BBI** | **BBM** | **Ave** | **Econ** | **SR** | **5w** | **10** |
| First-class | 56 | 6947 | 4190 | 154 | 7/74 | 11/57 | 27.20 | 3.61 | 45.1 | 6 | 1 |
| List A | 41 | 1292 | 1204 | 30 | 3/39 | 3/39 | 40.13 | 5.59 | 43.0 | 0 | 0 |
| Twenty20 | 37 | 346 | 500 | 9 | 2/20 | 2/20 | 55.55 | 8.67 | 38.4 | 0 | 0 |

# JORDAN CLARK

RHB RM WK R0 W0

FULL NAME: Jordan Clark
BORN: October 14, 1990, Whitehaven, Cumbria
SQUAD NO: 16
HEIGHT: 6ft 4in
NICKNAME: Clarky
EDUCATION: Sedbergh School
TEAMS: Lancashire
CAREER: List A: 2010; T20: 2011



FAMILY TIES? My dad plays cricket so me and my two brothers followed. My younger brother Graham has a scholarship at Durham CCC
CAREER HIGHLIGHTS? Hitting six sixes in an over and being involved in the one-day format at Lancashire
SUPERSTITIONS? Batting in a jumper
CRICKETING HEROES? Adam Gilchrist, Andrew Flintoff
NON-CRICKETING HEROES? Jeremy Piven
CRICKET RULE YOU'D CHANGE? Can't be out slogging
IF YOU WEREN'T A CRICKETER? Writing books, poetry, newsreader
DESERT ISLAND DISC? Anything by Drake
FAVOURITE TV? Breaking Bad, Entourage, Geordie Shore
SURPRISING FACT? I have an arm of tattoos
TWITTER FEED: @Clarksy16

| Batting | Mat | Inns | NO | Runs | HS | Ave | SR | 100 | 50 | Ct | St |
|---|---|---|---|---|---|---|---|---|---|---|---|
| List A | 20 | 12 | 3 | 275 | 72 | 30.55 | 96.49 | 0 | 1 | 3 | 0 |
| Twenty20 | 25 | 19 | 7 | 286 | 44 | 23.83 | 131.19 | 0 | 0 | 7 | 0 |
| **Bowling** | **Mat** | **Balls** | **Runs** | **Wkts** | **BBI** | **BBM** | **Ave** | **Econ** | **SR** | **5w** | **10** |
| List A | 20 | 414 | 480 | 9 | 2/41 | 2/41 | 53.33 | 6.95 | 46.0 | 0 | 0 |
| Twenty20 | 25 | 187 | 270 | 9 | 4/22 | 4/22 | 30.00 | 8.66 | 20.7 | 0 | 0 |

## JOE CLARKE RHB WK R0 W0

FULL NAME: Joe Michael Clarke
BORN: May 26, 1996, Shrewsbury, Shropshire
SQUAD NO: 33
HEIGHT: 5ft 11in
EDUCATION: Llanfyllin High School
TEAMS: Worcestershire 2nd XI, England U19
CAREER: Yet to make first-team debut

---

CAREER HIGHLIGHTS? Representing England at the 2014 U19 World Cup and signing my first professional contract with Worcestershire
BEST PLAYER IN COUNTY CRICKET? Moeen Ali
TIP FOR THE TOP? Will Rhodes, Ryan Higgins, Rob Sayer, Tom Kohler-Cadmore
MOST MARKED CHARACTERISTIC? Cheekiness
SUPERSTITIONS? I always put my right pad on first
CRICKETING HEROES? Adam Gilchrist – he inspired me to play cricket
IF YOU COULD BE SOMEONE ELSE FOR A DAY? David Beckham
DESERT ISLAND DISC? Drake – Nothing Was The Same
FAVOURITE TV? Geordie Shore
LEAST FAVOURITE TV? Emmerdale
ACCOMPLISHMENTS? Played regional football and tennis
PET HATE? Poor chat when 'sledging'
FANTASY SLIP CORDON? Keeper: Myself, 1st: George Best, 2nd: David Beckham, 3rd: Margot Robbie, Gully: Lee Nelson
TWITTER FEED: @joeclarke10

# RIKKI CLARKE

## RHB RFM R1 W0 MVP27

FULL NAME: Rikki Clarke
BORN: September 29, 1981, Orsett, Essex
SQUAD NO: 81
HEIGHT: 6ft 4in
NICKNAME: Clarkey, Crouchy
EDUCATION: Broadwater Secondary; Godalming College
TEAMS: England, Warwickshire, Derbyshire, Surrey
CAREER: Test: 2003; ODI: 2003; First-class: 2002; List A: 2001; T20: 2003



BEST BATTING: 214 Surrey vs Somerset, Guildford, 2006
BEST BOWLING: 6-63 Warwickshire vs Kent, Canterbury, 2010
COUNTY CAPS: 2005 (Surrey); 2011 (Warwickshire)

CAREER HIGHLIGHTS? England Test and ODI debuts, winning the County Championship with Surrey and Warwickshire, winning the first-ever T20 Cup with Surrey, taking a wicket with my first ball in international cricket, becoming joint world-record holder for catches taken by an outfielder in a first-class innings, and CB40 winner with Warwickshire in 2010
BEST PLAYER IN COUNTY CRICKET? Samit Patel
DESERT ISLAND DISC? Being on a desert island I'd need something upbeat to keep my spirits high… so let's go for the Kiss Does Funky House Compilation
FAVOURITE TV? Celebrity Juice, TOWIE, Geordie Shore – I would like to say the wife makes me watch them but secretly it's me that records them!
SURPRISING FACT? I was named after Ricky Villa, Spurs 1981 FA Cup winner
TWITTER FEED: @rikkiclarke81

| Batting | Mat | Inns | NO | Runs | HS | Ave | SR | 100 | 50 | Ct | St |
|---|---|---|---|---|---|---|---|---|---|---|---|
| Tests | 2 | 3 | 0 | 96 | 55 | 32.00 | 37.94 | 0 | 1 | 1 | 0 |
| ODIs | 20 | 13 | 0 | 144 | 39 | 11.07 | 62.06 | 0 | 0 | 11 | 0 |
| First-class | 177 | 270 | 31 | 8454 | 214 | 35.37 | | 16 | 42 | 269 | 0 |
| List A | 196 | 164 | 22 | 3653 | 98* | 25.72 | | 0 | 19 | 92 | 0 |
| Twenty20 | 109 | 101 | 26 | 1600 | 79* | 21.33 | 121.76 | 0 | 4 | 48 | 0 |
| **Bowling** | **Mat** | **Balls** | **Runs** | **Wkts** | **BBI** | **BBM** | **Ave** | **Econ** | **SR** | **5w** | **10** |
| Tests | 2 | 174 | 60 | 4 | 2/7 | 3/11 | 15.00 | 2.06 | 43.5 | 0 | 0 |
| ODIs | 20 | 469 | 415 | 11 | 2/28 | 2/28 | 37.72 | 5.30 | 42.6 | 0 | 0 |
| First-class | 177 | 16634 | 9861 | 284 | 6/63 | | 34.72 | 3.55 | 58.5 | 2 | 0 |
| List A | 196 | 4772 | 4344 | 115 | 4/28 | 4/28 | 37.77 | 5.46 | 41.4 | 0 | 0 |
| Twenty20 | 109 | 1158 | 1513 | 56 | 3/11 | 3/11 | 27.01 | 7.83 | 20.6 | 0 | 0 |

# MITCHELL CLAYDON

## LHB RMF R0 W1 MVP40

FULL NAME: Mitchell Eric Claydon
BORN: November 25, 1982, Fairfield, Australia
SQUAD NO: 8
HEIGHT: 6ft 3in
NICKNAME: Ellen, Precious, Lips
EDUCATION: Westfield Sports High School
TEAMS: Kent, Durham, Yorkshire
CAREER: First-class: 2005; List A: 2006; T20: 2006

BEST BATTING: 77 Kent vs Leicestershire, Leicester, 2014
BEST BOWLING: 6-104 Durham vs Somerset, Taunton, 2011
COUNTY CAPS: 2012 (Durham)

CAREER HIGHLIGHTS? Winning trophies with Durham and players' player at Kent in 2014
BEST PLAYER IN COUNTY CRICKET? Darren Stevens
TIP FOR THE TOP? Sam Billings, Adam Riley
MOST MARKED CHARACTERISTIC? Joking around
CRICKETING HEROES? Ricky Ponting
CRICKET RULE YOU'D CHANGE? Lunch and tea should be 30 minutes each instead of 40 and 20 minutes
IF YOU WEREN'T A CRICKETER? A policeman
IF YOU COULD BE SOMEONE ELSE FOR A DAY? David Beckham
DESERT ISLAND DISC? Foo Fighters
PET HATE? Being late – so being friends with Darren Stevens is very tough
SURPRISING FACT? I'm a magician, a keen surfer and I love to play a prank or two
TWITTER FEED: @mitchellclaydon

| Batting | Mat | Inns | NO | Runs | HS | Ave | SR | 100 | 50 | Ct | St |
|---|---|---|---|---|---|---|---|---|---|---|---|
| First-class | 69 | 89 | 16 | 1107 | 77 | 15.16 | 58.41 | 0 | 2 | 9 | 0 |
| List A | 76 | 38 | 10 | 211 | 19 | 7.53 | 82.42 | 0 | 0 | 4 | 0 |
| Twenty20 | 89 | 29 | 15 | 107 | 19 | 7.64 | 91.45 | 0 | 0 | 21 | 0 |
| **Bowling** | **Mat** | **Balls** | **Runs** | **Wkts** | **BBI** | **BBM** | **Ave** | **Econ** | **SR** | **5w** | **10** |
| First-class | 69 | 10039 | 5910 | 189 | 6/104 |  | 31.26 | 3.53 | 53.1 | 5 | 0 |
| List A | 76 | 3237 | 2948 | 97 | 4/39 | 4/39 | 30.39 | 5.46 | 33.3 | 0 | 0 |
| Twenty20 | 89 | 1752 | 2346 | 98 | 5/26 | 5/26 | 23.93 | 8.03 | 17.8 | 2 | 0 |

## BEN COAD

## RHB RFM R0 W0

FULL NAME: Benjamin Oliver Coad
BORN: January 10, 1994, Harrogate, Yorkshire
SQUAD NO: 10
HEIGHT: 6ft 3in
NICKNAME: Coady
EDUCATION: Thirsk School and Sixth Form College
TEAMS: Yorkshire
CAREER: List A: 2013



FAMILY TIES? All my family are involved with Studley Royal CC. My brothers have played junior representative cricket and my dad has played Minor County cricket for Suffolk
CAREER HIGHLIGHTS? Making my first-team debut against Gloucestershire in 2013 and being awarded my second-team cap for Yorkshire
TIP FOR THE TOP? Matthew Fisher
CRICKET RULE YOU'D CHANGE? LBW – in that you're not allowed to be out if the ball hits you outside the line of off stump when playing a shot
IF YOU COULD BE SOMEONE ELSE FOR A DAY? David Beckham
DESERT ISLAND DISC? Arctic Monkeys – Whatever People Say I Am, That's What I Am Not
FAVOURITE TV? Friends
FANTASY SLIP CORDON? Keeper: Kevin Hart, 1st: Me, 2nd: Will Smith, 3rd: Alan Shearer, Gully: Usain Bolt
TWITTER FEED: @BenCoad10

| Batting | Mat | Inns | NO | Runs | HS | Ave | SR | 100 | 50 | Ct | St |
|---|---|---|---|---|---|---|---|---|---|---|---|
| List A | 7 | 3 | 3 | 3 | 2* | - | 27.27 | 0 | 0 | 3 | 0 |
| **Bowling** | **Mat** | **Balls** | **Runs** | **Wkts** | **BBI** | **BBM** | **Ave** | **Econ** | **SR** | **5w** | **10** |
| List A | 7 | 260 | 282 | 3 | 1/34 | 1/34 | 94.00 | 6.50 | 86.6 | 0 | 0 |

## JOSH COBB RHB LB R0 W0 MVP84

FULL NAME: Joshua James Cobb
BORN: August 17, 1990, Leicester
SQUAD NO: 4
HEIGHT: 6ft
NICKNAME: Cobby, Tuck Shop
EDUCATION: Bosworth College; Oakham School
TEAMS: Northamptonshire, Leicestershire, Dhaka Gladiators
CAREER: First-class: 2007; List A: 2008; T20: 2008

BEST BATTING: 148* Leicestershire vs Middlesex, Lord's, 2008
BEST BOWLING: 2-11 Leicestershire vs Gloucestershire, Leicester, 2011

FAMILY TIES? My dad Russell played for Leics and is head coach at Loughborough MCCU
IF YOU WEREN'T A CRICKETER? At Oakham I was a member of the debating society and took an active interest in historical and modern British politics. Had my cricket career not taken off, I would most likely be involved in local politics and government. I still take a number of books and papers with me to away games which keeps me busy during rain delays, much to the dismay of most of my teammates who could only look at books with pictures in
IF YOU COULD BE SOMEONE ELSE FOR A DAY? I would love to spend a day in the life of Leicestershire's James Sykes. It would be fascinating to get under the skin of one of the most influential fashion icons of his time and to see how he felt the first time he wore the now infamous leather T-shirt
ACCOMPLISHMENTS? I released a book of rural landscape sketches from some of my favourite winter walks in and around the East Midlands countryside
PET HATE? Itchy polo-neck jumpers
SURPRISING FACT? I was once a childhood model for Next … where did it all go wrong?
TWITTER FEED: @cobby24

| Batting | Mat | Inns | NO | Runs | HS | Ave | SR | 100 | 50 | Ct | St |
|---|---|---|---|---|---|---|---|---|---|---|---|
| First-class | 77 | 135 | 11 | 3133 | 148* | 25.26 | 47.81 | 3 | 19 | 38 | 0 |
| List A | 60 | 57 | 5 | 1921 | 137 | 36.94 | 99.68 | 5 | 9 | 17 | 0 |
| Twenty20 | 80 | 74 | 8 | 1398 | 70 | 21.18 | 136.39 | 0 | 6 | 41 | 0 |
| **Bowling** | **Mat** | **Balls** | **Runs** | **Wkts** | **BBI** | **BBM** | **Ave** | **Econ** | **SR** | **5w** | **10** |
| First-class | 77 | 1297 | 816 | 9 | 2/11 | 2/11 | 90.66 | 3.77 | 144.1 | 0 | 0 |
| List A | 60 | 1122 | 1093 | 22 | 3/34 | 3/34 | 49.68 | 5.84 | 51.0 | 0 | 0 |
| Twenty20 | 80 | 740 | 996 | 40 | 4/22 | 4/22 | 24.90 | 8.07 | 18.5 | 0 | 0 |

# IAN COCKBAIN

RHB RM R0 W0

FULL NAME: Ian Andrew Cockbain
BORN: February 17, 1987, Liverpool
SQUAD NO: 28
HEIGHT: 6ft
NICKNAME: Coey, Gramps
EDUCATION: Maghull High School; Liverpool John Moores University
TEAMS: Gloucestershire
CAREER: First-class: 2011; List A: 2011; T20: 2011

BEST BATTING: 151* Gloucestershire vs Surrey, Bristol, 2014
COUNTY CAPS: 2011

FAMILY TIES? My dad Ian played for Lancs back in the day
CAREER HIGHLIGHTS? Scoring 151* and batting for almost nine hours vs Surrey last season
CRICKETING HEROES? AB de Villiers currently is awesome and I love watching him bat and go about his business
NON-CRICKETING HEROES? Roger Federer – love the way he carries himself and he's just so chilled
CRICKET RULE YOU'D CHANGE? Double-Plays in T20 and runs based on how big sixes are
COACHING TIP? Play in the 'V' until 23
IF YOU COULD BE SOMEONE ELSE FOR A DAY? David Beckham!
LEAST FAVOURITE TV? Hate watching any reality TV
SURPRISING FACT? Back home in Liverpool we have four tortoises and four chickens in our back garden along with two ducks. My mother is going a bit off her head!
FANTASY SLIP CORDON? Keeper: Blake Lively, 1st: Myself, 2nd: Kelly Brook, 3rd: Shane Warne, Gully: John Legend
TWITTER FEED: @iancoey

| Batting | Mat | Inns | NO | Runs | HS | Ave | SR | 100 | 50 | Ct | St |
|---|---|---|---|---|---|---|---|---|---|---|---|
| First-class | 37 | 63 | 4 | 1751 | 151* | 29.67 | 41.22 | 3 | 10 | 30 | 0 |
| List A | 44 | 38 | 8 | 917 | 98* | 30.56 | 91.24 | 0 | 7 | 32 | 0 |
| Twenty20 | 43 | 40 | 4 | 883 | 84 | 24.52 | 114.52 | 0 | 6 | 20 | 0 |
| **Bowling** | **Mat** | **Balls** | **Runs** | **Wkts** | **BBI** | **BBM** | **Ave** | **Econ** | **SR** | **5w** | **10** |
| First-class | 37 | - | - | - | - | - | - | - | - | - | - |
| List A | 44 | - | - | - | - | - | - | - | - | - | - |
| Twenty20 | 43 | - | - | - | - | - | - | - | - | - | - |

## KYLE COETZER RHB RM R0 W0

FULL NAME: Kyle James Coetzer
BORN: April 14, 1984, Aberdeen
SQUAD NO: 30
HEIGHT: 5ft 11in
NICKNAME: Costa, Meerkat, Shortbread
EDUCATION: Aberdeen Grammar School
TEAMS: Scotland, Northamptonshire, Durham, Western Province
CAREER: ODI: 2008; T20I: 2008; First-class: 2004; List A: 2003; T20: 2007

BEST BATTING: 219 Northamptonshire vs Leicestershire, Leicester, 2013
BEST BOWLING: 2-16 Scotland vs Kenya, Gymkhana Club Ground, 2009

FAMILY TIES? My elder brothers Shaun and Stuart both played some level of cricket for Scotland. Grandfather Sid Dugmore played for Eastern Province and so did my uncle Grant Dugmore, who has coached and played for Argentina. He is now the development officer for the Americas
SUPERSTITIONS? I touch my bat in the crease after each ball
CRICKETING HEROES? Brian McMillan, Allan Donald, Jacques Kallis, Robin Smith, Jack Brooks
DESERT ISLAND DISC? Kenny Rogers – The Gambler
SURPRISING FACT? I was given a Meerkat toy by my ex-teammate Paul Wiseman who claimed I looked like it. It has never left my kitbag since, hence the nickname
TWITTER FEED: @MeerGoose11

| Batting | Mat | Inns | NO | Runs | HS | Ave | SR | 100 | 50 | Ct | St |
|---|---|---|---|---|---|---|---|---|---|---|---|
| ODIs | 24 | 23 | 1 | 971 | 156 | 44.13 | 82.84 | 2 | 6 | 9 | 0 |
| T20Is | 20 | 20 | 1 | 442 | 62 | 23.26 | 101.14 | 0 | 1 | 10 | 0 |
| First-class | 84 | 142 | 11 | 4183 | 219 | 31.93 | 48.58 | 8 | 18 | 41 | 0 |
| List A | 121 | 117 | 12 | 3565 | 156 | 33.95 | 79.82 | 6 | 21 | 45 | 0 |
| Twenty20 | 77 | 74 | 7 | 1617 | 71* | 24.13 | 105.34 | 0 | 4 | 27 | 0 |
| **Bowling** | **Mat** | **Balls** | **Runs** | **Wkts** | **BBI** | **BBM** | **Ave** | **Econ** | **SR** | **5w** | **10** |
| ODIs | 24 | 150 | 164 | 1 | 1/35 | 1/35 | 164.00 | 6.56 | 150.0 | 0 | 0 |
| T20Is | 20 | 66 | 71 | 5 | 3/25 | 3/25 | 14.20 | 6.45 | 13.2 | 0 | 0 |
| First-class | 84 | 660 | 402 | 6 | 2/16 | 2/16 | 67.00 | 3.65 | 110.0 | 0 | 0 |
| List A | 121 | 390 | 412 | 4 | 1/2 | 1/2 | 103.00 | 6.33 | 97.5 | 0 | 0 |
| Twenty20 | 77 | 150 | 183 | 7 | 3/25 | 3/25 | 26.14 | 7.32 | 21.4 | 0 | 0 |

# FREDDIE COLEMAN RHB OB R0 W0

FULL NAME: Freddie Robert John Coleman
BORN: December 15, 1991, Edinburgh
SQUAD NO: 21
TEAMS: Scotland, Warwickshire
CAREER: ODI: 2013; T20I: 2013; First-class: 2012; List A: 2010; T20: 2013

BEST BATTING: 110 Oxford MCCU vs Worcestershire, Oxford, 2012

CAREER HIGHLIGHTS? My maiden first-class century and qualifying for the 2015 World Cup with Scotland
TIP FOR THE TOP? Jonny Webb and Sam Hain
MOST MARKED CHARACTERISTIC? Scot without an accent
SUPERSTITIONS? Lucky socks
CRICKETING HEROES? AB de Villiers
NON-CRICKETING HEROES? Ray Lewis
IF YOU WEREN'T A CRICKETER? Business
DESERT ISLAND DISC? Red Hot Chili Peppers – By the Way
FAVOURITE TV? The Mentalist
SURPRISING FACT? I played the bagpipes when I was 12
TWITTER FEED: @FRJcoleman

| Batting | Mat | Inns | NO | Runs | HS | Ave | SR | 100 | 50 | Ct | St |
|---|---|---|---|---|---|---|---|---|---|---|---|
| ODIs | 14 | 12 | 0 | 141 | 40 | 11.75 | 53.61 | 0 | 0 | 4 | 0 |
| T20Is | 1 | 1 | 0 | 9 | 9 | 9.00 | 69.23 | 0 | 0 | 0 | 0 |
| First-class | 7 | 12 | 0 | 219 | 110 | 18.25 | 49.32 | 1 | 0 | 4 | 0 |
| List A | 38 | 33 | 1 | 675 | 64* | 21.09 | 70.16 | 0 | 4 | 8 | 0 |
| Twenty20 | 5 | 2 | 1 | 29 | 20* | 29.00 | 107.40 | 0 | 0 | 1 | 0 |
| **Bowling** | **Mat** | **Balls** | **Runs** | **Wkts** | **BBI** | **BBM** | **Ave** | **Econ** | **SR** | **5w** | **10** |
| ODIs | 14 | - | - | - | - | - | - | - | - | - | - |
| T20Is | 1 | - | - | - | - | - | - | - | - | - | - |
| First-class | 7 | - | - | - | - | - | - | - | - | - | - |
| List A | 38 | - | - | - | - | - | - | - | - | - | - |
| Twenty20 | 5 | - | - | - | - | - | - | - | - | - | - |

# MATT COLES

LHB RFM R0 W1 MVP44

FULL NAME: Matthew Thomas Coles
BORN: May 26, 1990, Maidstone, Kent
SQUAD NO: 26
HEIGHT: 6ft 3in
NICKNAME: Colesy
EDUCATION: Maplesden Noakes Secondary School
TEAMS: Kent, England Lions, Hampshire
CAREER: First-class: 2009; List A: 2009; T20: 2010

BEST BATTING: 103* Kent vs Yorkshire, Leeds, 2012
BEST BOWLING: 6-51 Kent vs Northamptonshire, Northampton, 2012
COUNTY CAPS: 2012

CRICKETING HEROES? Andrew Flintoff
DESERT ISLAND DISC? Red Hot Chili Peppers
TWITTER FEED: @MattColes_90
NOTES: A powerful allrounder, Coles caught the eye with a maiden Championship century against Yorkshire at Headingley in 2012, a season in which he also took 59 first-class wickets at 22.72. In 2012-13 he was picked for the England Lions tour of Australia but was sent home with Ben Stokes after twice breaching discipline rules. In 2013 he moved to Hampshire on loan towards the end of the season and picked up 24 wickets in five matches. He signed permanently in 2014 and although he managed only one half-century he took 41 wickets at 28.41 to help Hampshire get promoted. He left Hampshire and returned to Kent in March 2015

| Batting | Mat | Inns | NO | Runs | HS | Ave | SR | 100 | 50 | Ct | St |
|---|---|---|---|---|---|---|---|---|---|---|---|
| First-class | 70 | 92 | 13 | 1547 | 103* | 19.58 | 66.16 | 1 | 7 | 24 | 0 |
| List A | 44 | 24 | 4 | 187 | 47 | 9.35 | 93.03 | 0 | 0 | 13 | 0 |
| Twenty20 | 49 | 34 | 6 | 349 | 54 | 12.46 | 142.44 | 0 | 1 | 16 | 0 |
| **Bowling** | **Mat** | **Balls** | **Runs** | **Wkts** | **BBI** | **BBM** | **Ave** | **Econ** | **SR** | **5w** | **10** |
| First-class | 70 | 9749 | 5749 | 195 | 6/51 | 10/154 | 29.48 | 3.53 | 49.9 | 7 | 1 |
| List A | 44 | 1500 | 1532 | 64 | 6/32 | 6/32 | 23.93 | 6.12 | 23.4 | 1 | 0 |
| Twenty20 | 49 | 924 | 1352 | 46 | 3/14 | 3/14 | 29.39 | 8.77 | 20.0 | 0 | 0 |

# PAUL COLLINGWOOD RHB RM R2 W0 MVP9

FULL NAME: Paul David Collingwood
BORN: May 26, 1976, Shotley Bridge, County Durham
SQUAD NO: 5
HEIGHT: 5ft 11in
NICKNAME: Colly, Weed, Wobbles
EDUCATION: Blackfyne Comprehensive School; Derwentside College
TEAMS: England, Durham, Delhi Daredevils, Impi, Perth Scorchers, Rajasthan Royals
CAREER: Test: 2003; ODI: 2001; T20I: 2005; First-class: 1996; List A: 1995; T20:2005



BEST BATTING: 206 England vs Australia, Adelaide, 2006
BEST BOWLING: 5-52 Durham vs Somerset, Grangefield Road, 2005
BENEFIT YEAR: 2007

FAMILY TIES? My dad and brother played for Shotley Bridge
CAREER HIGHLIGHTS? Playing for England, winning the World T20 and the three Ashes wins
SUPERSTITIONS? Left pad on first and a little jig as I walk out to bat, but it's getting harder as it involves squatting three times!
SURPRISING FACT? I'm an artist
FANTASY SLIP CORDON? Keeper: Phil Mustard (to provide the one-liners), 1st: Me, 2nd: Candice Swanepoel, 3rd: Graeme Swann (so I can wind him up about his beloved Newcastle Utd), Gully: Keith Lemon
TWITTER FEED: @Colly622

| Batting | Mat | Inns | NO | Runs | HS | Ave | SR | 100 | 50 | Ct | St |
|---|---|---|---|---|---|---|---|---|---|---|---|
| Tests | 68 | 115 | 10 | 4259 | 206 | 40.56 | 46.44 | 10 | 20 | 96 | 0 |
| ODIs | 197 | 181 | 37 | 5092 | 120* | 35.36 | 76.98 | 5 | 26 | 108 | 0 |
| T20Is | 35 | 33 | 2 | 583 | 79 | 18.80 | 127.01 | 0 | 3 | 14 | 0 |
| First-class | 250 | 429 | 39 | 14105 | 206 | 36.16 | | 29 | 74 | 280 | 0 |
| List A | 405 | 379 | 68 | 10616 | 120* | 34.13 | | 9 | 60 | 199 | 0 |
| Twenty20 | 103 | 89 | 8 | 1494 | 79 | 18.44 | 119.90 | 0 | 7 | 31 | 0 |
| **Bowling** | **Mat** | **Balls** | **Runs** | **Wkts** | **BBI** | **BBM** | **Ave** | **Econ** | **SR** | **5w** | **10** |
| Tests | 68 | 1905 | 1018 | 17 | 3/23 | 3/35 | 59.88 | 3.20 | 112.0 | 0 | 0 |
| ODIs | 197 | 5186 | 4294 | 111 | 6/31 | 6/31 | 38.68 | 4.96 | 46.7 | 1 | 0 |
| T20Is | 35 | 222 | 329 | 16 | 4/22 | 4/22 | 20.56 | 8.89 | 13.8 | 0 | 0 |
| First-class | 250 | 11084 | 5623 | 143 | 5/52 | | 39.32 | 3.04 | 77.5 | 1 | 0 |
| List A | 405 | 10678 | 8576 | 256 | 6/31 | 6/31 | 33.50 | 4.81 | 41.7 | 1 | 0 |
| Twenty20 | 103 | 1057 | 1249 | 74 | 5/6 | 5/6 | 16.87 | 7.08 | 14.2 | 2 | 0 |

# NICK COMPTON

## RHB OB R5 W0

FULL NAME: Nicholas Richard Denis Compton
BORN: June 26, 1983, Durban, South Africa
SQUAD NO: 3
HEIGHT: 6ft 2in
NICKNAME: Compdog, Compo
EDUCATION: Harrow School; Durham University
TEAMS: England, Middlesex, Somerset, Marshonaland Eagles
CAREER: Test: 2012; First-class: 2004; List A: 2001; T20: 2004

BEST BATTING: 254* Somerset vs Durham, Chester-le-Street, 2011
BEST BOWLING: 1-1 Somerset vs Hampshire, Southampton, 2010
COUNTY CAPS: 2006 (Middlesex); 2011 (Somerset)

FAMILY TIES? My grandfather Denis played for England, my great-uncle Leslie played for Middlesex, my father Richard played first-class cricket in South Africa and my uncle Patrick played a few games too
CAREER HIGHLIGHTS? England's series win in India, back-to-back Test centuries, Wisden Player of the Year and back-to-back Player of the Year awards at Somerset
SUPERSTITIONS? I wear a pair of adidas speedos to bat in
SURPRISING FACT? I was voted national science expo champion aged 12
FANTASY SLIP CORDON? Keeper: David Nash (funniest bloke on a cricket field I know), 1st: Myself, 2nd: My mother (the only person that would laugh at my jokes), 3rd: Phil Hughes (because I miss him and that cheeky grin), 4th: Matthew McConaughey (just for being cool), 5th: My grandfather (to shine the ball with a lather of Brylcreem)
TWITTER FEED: @thecompdog

| Batting | Mat | Inns | NO | Runs | HS | Ave | SR | 100 | 50 | Ct | St |
|---|---|---|---|---|---|---|---|---|---|---|---|
| Tests | 9 | 17 | 2 | 479 | 117 | 31.93 | 34.68 | 2 | 1 | 4 | 0 |
| First-class | 139 | 240 | 31 | 9163 | 254* | 43.84 | 47.00 | 22 | 44 | 71 | 0 |
| List A | 109 | 100 | 20 | 3016 | 131 | 37.70 | 79.32 | 6 | 19 | 45 | 0 |
| Twenty20 | 78 | 66 | 7 | 1191 | 74 | 20.18 | 113.32 | 0 | 6 | 29 | 0 |
| **Bowling** | **Mat** | **Balls** | **Runs** | **Wkts** | **BBI** | **BBM** | **Ave** | **Econ** | **SR** | **5w** | **10** |
| Tests | 9 | - | - | - | - | - | - | - | - | - | - |
| First-class | 139 | 170 | 223 | 3 | 1/1 | 1/1 | 74.33 | 7.87 | 56.6 | 0 | 0 |
| List A | 109 | 61 | 53 | 1 | 1/0 | 1/0 | 53.00 | 5.21 | 61.0 | 0 | 0 |
| Twenty20 | 78 | - | - | - | - | - | - | - | - | - | - |

# ALASTAIR COOK LHB OB R5 W0

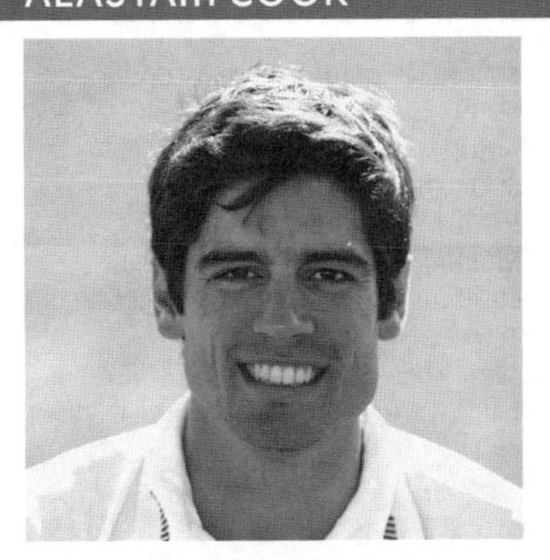

FULL NAME: Alastair Nathan Cook
BORN: December 25, 1984, Gloucester
SQUAD NO: 26
HEIGHT: 6ft 2in
NICKNAME: Cookie, Chef
EDUCATION: Bedford School
TEAMS: England, Essex
CAREER: Test: 2006; ODI: 2006; T20I: 2007; First-class: 2003; List A: 2003; T20: 2005



BEST BATTING: 294 England vs India, Birmingham, 2011
BEST BOWLING: 3-13 Essex vs Northamptonshire, Chelmsford, 2005
COUNTY CAPS: 2005

FAMILY TIES? Dad played for the local club side and was a very good opening bat, while my mum made the teas. Brothers played for Maldon Cricket Club
CAREER HIGHLIGHTS? Ashes wins home and away, becoming world No.1 Test team, Essex winning the 50-over comp, making England debut
NON-CRICKETING HEROES? Graham Gooch – I watched him playing for Essex at the County Ground
IF YOU WEREN'T A CRICKETER? Farmer
FANTASY SLIP CORDON? Keeper: Mark Pettini, 1st: Me, 2nd: Charlize Theron, 3rd: James Corden

| Batting | Mat | Inns | NO | Runs | HS | Ave | SR | 100 | 50 | Ct | St |
|---|---|---|---|---|---|---|---|---|---|---|---|
| Tests | 109 | 194 | 11 | 8423 | 294 | 46.02 | 46.82 | 25 | 38 | 108 | 0 |
| ODIs | 92 | 92 | 4 | 3204 | 137 | 36.40 | 77.13 | 5 | 19 | 36 | 0 |
| T20Is | 4 | 4 | 0 | 61 | 26 | 15.25 | 112.96 | 0 | 0 | 1 | 0 |
| First-class | 209 | 371 | 27 | 16262 | 294 | 47.27 | 51.39 | 47 | 79 | 205 | 0 |
| List A | 150 | 148 | 10 | 5204 | 137 | 37.71 | 78.95 | 9 | 31 | 63 | 0 |
| Twenty20 | 31 | 29 | 2 | 884 | 100* | 32.74 | 128.11 | 1 | 5 | 12 | 0 |
| **Bowling** | **Mat** | **Balls** | **Runs** | **Wkts** | **BBI** | **BBM** | **Ave** | **Econ** | **SR** | **5w** | **10** |
| Tests | 109 | 18 | 7 | 1 | 1/6 | 1/6 | 7.00 | 2.33 | 18.0 | 0 | 0 |
| ODIs | 92 | - | - | - | - | - | - | - | - | - | - |
| T20Is | 4 | - | - | - | - | - | - | - | - | - | - |
| First-class | 209 | 282 | 211 | 7 | 3/13 |  | 30.14 | 4.48 | 40.2 | 0 | 0 |
| List A | 150 | 18 | 10 | 0 | - | - | - | 3.33 | - | 0 | 0 |
| Twenty20 | 31 | - | - | - | - | - | - | - | - | - | - |

## CHRIS COOKE RHB WK R0 W0

FULL NAME: Christopher Barry Cooke
BORN: May 30, 1986, Johannesburg, South Africa
SQUAD NO: 46
HEIGHT: 5ft 11in
NICKNAME: Minty, Shapeless, Cookie
EDUCATION: Bishops; University of Cape Town
TEAMS: Glamorgan, Western Province
CAREER: First-class: 2009; List A: 2009; T20: 2011

BEST BATTING: 171 Glamorgan vs Kent, Canterbury, 2014

CAREER HIGHLIGHTS? Scoring my maiden List A hundred at Newlands, hitting my second, third and fourth balls for six on my Glamorgan T20 debut and scoring my first hundred for the county in a 40-over match at Taunton and it becoming the fourth highest one-day score for Glamorgan
MOST MARKED CHARACTERISTIC? My back-lift probably!
SUPERSTITIONS? Batting: left pad on first. Keeping: right pad on first
CRICKETING HEROES? Kevin Pietersen, Hylton Ackerman
NON-CRICKETING HEROES? Nelson Mandela
IF YOU WEREN'T A CRICKETER? International DJ
DESERT ISLAND DISC? Surely an iPod would be easier to take!?
FAVOURITE TV? 24
SURPRISING FACT? I'm allergic to shellfish, I'm a massive Chelsea fan and I have to have the volume on an even number!
FANTASY SLIP CORDON? Keeper: Shane Warne, 1st: José Mourinho, 2nd: Georgie Thompson, 3rd: Myself, Gully: Jimmy Carr
TWITTER FEED: @Cooky_24

| Batting | Mat | Inns | NO | Runs | HS | Ave | SR | 100 | 50 | Ct | St |
|---|---|---|---|---|---|---|---|---|---|---|---|
| First-class | 26 | 43 | 3 | 1450 | 171 | 36.25 | 50.84 | 1 | 11 | 18 | 1 |
| List A | 53 | 50 | 7 | 1535 | 137* | 35.69 | 97.83 | 2 | 9 | 21 | 2 |
| Twenty20 | 46 | 39 | 6 | 729 | 65* | 22.09 | 144.07 | 0 | 3 | 21 | 0 |
| **Bowling** | **Mat** | **Balls** | **Runs** | **Wkts** | **BBI** | **BBM** | **Ave** | **Econ** | **SR** | **5w** | **10** |
| First-class | 26 | - | - | - | - | - | - | - | - | - | - |
| List A | 53 | - | - | - | - | - | - | - | - | - | - |
| Twenty20 | 46 | - | - | - | - | - | - | - | - | - | - |

# GREG CORK RHB LMF R0 W0

FULL NAME: Gregory Teodor Gerald Cork
BORN: September 29, 1994, Derby
SQUAD NO: 14
HEIGHT: 6ft 1in
NICKNAME: Corky
EDUCATION: Denstone College; Leeds Metropolitan University
TEAMS: Derbyshire
CAREER: T20: 2014



FAMILY TIES? My dad is [former England bowler] Dominic Cork
CAREER HIGHLIGHTS? Signing my first professional contract this summer; hitting my first 2nd XI 100 vs Warwickshire; playing against India in a tourist game and getting a wicket; playing in six T20 matches for Derbyshire; being awarded 2nd XI player of the year in 2014
BEST PLAYER IN COUNTY CRICKET? Mark Footitt
TIP FOR THE TOP? Harvey Hosein
CRICKETING HEROES? Andrew Flintoff – massive character in the game and is a game-changer. Ian Botham – one of the greatest English allrounders to ever play the game
CRICKET RULE YOU'D CHANGE? Play the different formats of county cricket in the same block of the summer
COACHING TIP? Batting – before and while playing a shot, keep as still as possible to give you the best chance of hitting the ball in the middle of the bat and to where you want it to go
IF YOU COULD BE SOMEONE ELSE FOR A DAY? Lord Alan Sugar
DESERT ISLAND DISC? Take That – Greatest Hits
FAVOURITE TV? Made In Chelsea, Gogglebox
LEAST FAVOURITE TV? Location, Location, Location
SURPRISING FACT? I'm a quarter Italian
FANTASY SLIP CORDON? Keeper: Spencer Matthews, 1st: David Beckham, 2nd: Lee Evans, 3rd: Brian Badonde, Gully: Ricky Pointing
TWITTER FEED: @greg_cork

| Batting | Mat | Inns | NO | Runs | HS | Ave | SR | 100 | 50 | Ct | St |
|---|---|---|---|---|---|---|---|---|---|---|---|
| Twenty20 | 6 | 5 | 2 | 35 | 13* | 11.66 | 97.22 | 0 | 0 | 3 | 0 |
| **Bowling** | **Mat** | **Balls** | **Runs** | **Wkts** | **BBI** | **BBM** | **Ave** | **Econ** | **SR** | **5w** | **10** |
| Twenty20 | 6 | 90 | 168 | 5 | 2/36 | 2/36 | 33.60 | 11.20 | 18.0 | 0 | 0 |

# DEAN COSKER

RHB SLA R0 W1 MVP62

FULL NAME: Dean Andrew Cosker
BORN: January 7, 1978, Weymouth, Dorset
SQUAD NO: 23
HEIGHT: 5ft 11in
NICKNAME: Lurks, The Lurker
EDUCATION: Millfield School
TEAMS: Glamorgan
CAREER: First-class: 1996; List A: 1996; T20: 2003



BEST BATTING: 52 Glamorgan vs Gloucestershire, Bristol, 2005
BEST BOWLING: 6-91 Glamorgan vs Essex, Cardiff, 2009
COUNTY CAPS: 2000; BENEFIT YEAR: 2010

CAREER HIGHLIGHTS? My debut at Glamorgan in 1997, Championship medal in 1997, England A caps and trophies with Glamorgan
CRICKETING HEROES? Mike Kasprowicz, Matt Elliott, Matt Maynard, Robert Croft, Steve Watkin, Graham Thorpe
DESERT ISLAND DISC? Bananarama
TWITTER FEED: @DCosker23
NOTES: Leading wicket-taker on England A tour of Zimbabwe and South Africa in 1998/99. Third youngest Glamorgan player to receive his county cap

| Batting | Mat | Inns | NO | Runs | HS | Ave | SR | 100 | 50 | Ct | St |
|---|---|---|---|---|---|---|---|---|---|---|---|
| First-class | 242 | 322 | 92 | 3296 | 52 | 14.33 | | 0 | 1 | 144 | 0 |
| List A | 243 | 129 | 56 | 819 | 50* | 11.21 | | 0 | 1 | 89 | 0 |
| Twenty20 | 105 | 31 | 22 | 152 | 21* | 16.88 | 91.56 | 0 | 0 | 32 | 0 |
| **Bowling** | **Mat** | **Balls** | **Runs** | **Wkts** | **BBI** | **BBM** | **Ave** | **Econ** | **SR** | **5w** | **10** |
| First-class | 242 | 44293 | 21032 | 589 | 6/91 | | 35.70 | 2.84 | 75.2 | 12 | 1 |
| List A | 243 | 10255 | 8213 | 254 | 5/54 | 5/54 | 32.33 | 4.80 | 40.3 | 1 | 0 |
| Twenty20 | 105 | 1907 | 2492 | 75 | 3/11 | 3/11 | 33.22 | 7.84 | 25.4 | 0 | 0 |

## BEN COTTON RHB RMF R0 W0

FULL NAME: Benjamin David Cotton
BORN: September 13, 1993, Stoke-on-Trent, Staffordshire
SQUAD NO: 36
HEIGHT: 6ft 5in
NICKNAME: Cotts, BC, Fearne, Dot
EDUCATION: Clayton Hall Business and Language College; Staffordshire University
TEAMS: Derbyshire
CAREER: First-class: 2014; List A 2014; T20: 2014



BEST BATTING: 21 Derbyshire vs Leicestershire, Derby, 2014
BEST BOWLING: 4-20 Derbyshire vs Leicestershire, Derby, 2014

CAREER HIGHLIGHTS? Playing in a tour match against India, making my first-class debut, reaching the Royal London Cup quarter-final
BEST PLAYER IN COUNTY CRICKET? Mark Footitt
TIP FOR THE TOP? Harvey Hosein, Ben Slater
SUPERSTITIONS? Put gloves, boots, pads etc on the left side first
CRICKETING HEROES? Glenn McGrath, Andrew Flintoff
NON-CRICKETING HEROES? Ian Poulter
CRICKET RULE YOU'D CHANGE? Tea should be longer
IF YOU WEREN'T A CRICKETER? Removing asbestos roofs or finishing uni
IF YOU COULD BE SOMEONE ELSE FOR A DAY? Any pro-golfer!
DESERT ISLAND DISC? Arctic Monkeys – Whatever People Say I Am, That's What I'm Not
PET HATE? People who don't bring toiletries and always borrow them and then never bring them back
SURPRISING FACT? I'm learning to DJ
TWITTER FEED: @cotts1993

| Batting | Mat | Inns | NO | Runs | HS | Ave | SR | 100 | 50 | Ct | St |
|---|---|---|---|---|---|---|---|---|---|---|---|
| First-class | 2 | 2 | 0 | 36 | 21 | 18.00 | 62.06 | 0 | 0 | 0 | 0 |
| List A | 4 | 2 | 1 | 28 | 18* | 28.00 | 84.84 | 0 | 0 | 0 | 0 |
| Twenty20 | 2 | - | - | - | - | - | - | - | - | 0 | 0 |
| **Bowling** | **Mat** | **Balls** | **Runs** | **Wkts** | **BBI** | **BBM** | **Ave** | **Econ** | **SR** | **5w** | **10** |
| First-class | 2 | 235 | 111 | 8 | 4/20 | 5/33 | 13.87 | 2.83 | 29.3 | 0 | 0 |
| List A | 4 | 183 | 186 | 4 | 2/42 | 2/42 | 46.50 | 6.09 | 45.7 | 0 | 0 |
| Twenty20 | 2 | 48 | 105 | 2 | 1/49 | 1/49 | 52.50 | 13.12 | 24.0 | 0 | 0 |

## FABIAN COWDREY RHB SLA R0 W0

FULL NAME: Fabian Kruuse Cowdrey
BORN: January 30, 1993, Canterbury
SQUAD NO: 30
HEIGHT: 6ft
NICKNAME: Cow, Fabs, Fabes
EDUCATION: Tonbridge School; Cardiff Metropolitan University
TEAMS: Kent
CAREER: First-class: 2013; List A: 2013; T20: 2013

BEST BATTING: 62 Kent vs CMCCU, Cardiff, 2013
BEST BOWLING: 3-59 Kent vs Hampshire, Canterbury, 2014

FAMILY TIES? My father Chris, uncle Graham and grandfather Colin played for Kent. My father and grandfather also played for and captained England
CRICKETING HEROES? AB de Villiers and Viv Richards – both impossible to tie down and devastating to the greatest of bowling attacks
NON-CRICKETING HEROES? Phil Taylor, for his mental strength. José Mourinho – I'm a Chelsea man!
CRICKET RULE YOU'D CHANGE? I wouldn't change a rule, I'd just add first-ball grace!
IF YOU WEREN'T A CRICKETER? Singer? Lyricist! Writer
IF YOU COULD BE SOMEONE ELSE FOR A DAY? Hugh Hefner
DESERT ISLAND DISC? Imagine Dragons
FAVOURITE TV? Jeremy Kyle
LEAST FAVOURITE TV? Family Guy
SURPRISING FACT? I always missed out on choir solos at ages 6-13 due to my brother's vocal abilities!
TWITTER FEED: @fkcowdrey

| Batting | Mat | Inns | NO | Runs | HS | Ave | SR | 100 | 50 | Ct | St |
|---|---|---|---|---|---|---|---|---|---|---|---|
| First-class | 6 | 10 | 1 | 185 | 62 | 20.55 | 47.92 | 0 | 1 | 1 | 0 |
| List A | 14 | 14 | 3 | 439 | 75 | 39.90 | 84.26 | 0 | 3 | 4 | 0 |
| Twenty20 | 12 | 12 | 2 | 272 | 55 | 27.20 | 110.12 | 0 | 2 | 5 | 0 |
| **Bowling** | **Mat** | **Balls** | **Runs** | **Wkts** | **BBI** | **BBM** | **Ave** | **Econ** | **SR** | **5w** | **10** |
| First-class | 6 | 172 | 129 | 3 | 3/59 | 3/59 | 43.00 | 4.50 | 57.3 | 0 | 0 |
| List A | 14 | 282 | 250 | 5 | 2/28 | 2/28 | 50.00 | 5.31 | 56.4 | 0 | 0 |
| Twenty20 | 12 | 137 | 183 | 4 | 2/28 | 2/28 | 45.75 | 8.01 | 34.2 | 0 | 0 |

# BEN COX

RHB WK R0 W0

FULL NAME: Oliver Benjamin Cox
BORN: February 2, 1992, Wordsley, Stourbridge, Worcestershire
SQUAD NO: 10
HEIGHT: 5ft 10in
NICKNAME: Cocko, Cockballs
EDUCATION: Bromsgrove School
TEAMS: Worcestershire
CAREER: First-class: 2009; List A: 2010; T20: 2010



BEST BATTING: 104 Worcestershire vs Hampshire, Worcester, 2014

CAREER HIGHLIGHTS? My debut, promotion in 2010 and promotion last season
BEST PLAYER IN COUNTY CRICKET? Moeen Ali
TIP FOR THE TOP? Tom Kohler-Cadmore, Charlie Morris
MOST MARKED CHARACTERISTIC? Not being quiet behind the stumps ... EVER
CRICKETING HEROES? Phil Hughes – he always found a way around a problem. His attitude towards his game, how he loved being on the field and at the crease. He always wanted to improve and did so in his own way
CRICKET RULE YOU'D CHANGE? Double-Play – if a batsmen nicks it and also gets stumped off the same ball, then the batting side lose two wickets. So the next batter is out for 0 off 0
COACHING TIP? Keeping – the secret to being a successful keeper is posture. A good strong and powerful squat will get you out of tricky situations
FAVOURITE TV? Breaking Bad
LEAST FAVOURITE TV? The Valleys
ACCOMPLISHMENTS? England U18 rugby trial – unfortunately I couldn't train due to shoulder injuries
TWITTER FEED: @bencox10

| Batting | Mat | Inns | NO | Runs | HS | Ave | SR | 100 | 50 | Ct | St |
|---|---|---|---|---|---|---|---|---|---|---|---|
| First-class | 41 | 69 | 13 | 1323 | 104 | 23.62 | 55.98 | 1 | 7 | 99 | 6 |
| List A | 34 | 23 | 5 | 266 | 39 | 14.77 | 94.66 | 0 | 0 | 25 | 4 |
| Twenty20 | 31 | 25 | 12 | 309 | 46 | 23.76 | 130.37 | 0 | 0 | 12 | 8 |
| **Bowling** | **Mat** | **Balls** | **Runs** | **Wkts** | **BBI** | **BBM** | **Ave** | **Econ** | **SR** | **5w** | **10** |
| First-class | 41 | - | - | - | - | - | - | - | - | - | - |
| List A | 34 | - | - | - | - | - | - | - | - | - | - |
| Twenty20 | 31 | - | - | - | - | - | - | - | - | - | - |

## STEVEN CROFT RHB RMF/OB R0 W0 MVP34

FULL NAME: Steven John Croft
BORN: October 11, 1984, Blackpool, Lancashire
SQUAD NO: 15
HEIGHT: 5ft 11in
NICKNAME: Crofty
EDUCATION: Highfield High School, Blackpool; Myerscough College
TEAMS: Lancashire, Auckland, Northern Districts
CAREER: First-class: 2005; List A: 2003; T20: 2006

BEST BATTING: 156 Lancashire vs Northamptonshire, Manchester, 2014
BEST BOWLING: 6-41 Lancashire vs Worcestershire, Manchester, 2012
COUNTY CAPS: 2010

FAMILY TIES? My family moved out to Sri Lanka was I was seven years old for three years and I played nothing but cricket out there. My father was a bad leg-spinner
CAREER HIGHLIGHTS? Winning the County Championship with Lancashire in 2011 and hitting the winning runs. Being included in the 2012 provisional World T20 squad
CRICKETING HEROES? Andrew Flintoff, Jacques Kallis, Stuart Law
NON-CRICKETING HEROES? Denzel Washington
CRICKET RULE YOU'D CHANGE? The Duckworth Lewis method
DESERT ISLAND DISC? Anything by Kings Of Leon
SURPRISING FACT? I run a personal training business with ex-Lancashire player Steven Cheetham – www.ProSportPT.co.uk
FANTASY SLIP CORDON? Keeper: Will Ferrell (funniest man alive), 1st: Denzel Washington (favourite actor), 2nd: Me, 3rd: David Beckham (one cool dude), Gully: Brad Pitt and Angelina Jolie (we know why!)
TWITTER FEED: @Stevenjcroft

| Batting | Mat | Inns | NO | Runs | HS | Ave | SR | 100 | 50 | Ct | St |
|---|---|---|---|---|---|---|---|---|---|---|---|
| First-class | 114 | 179 | 18 | 5293 | 156 | 32.87 | 52.35 | 8 | 31 | 104 | 0 |
| List A | 121 | 109 | 21 | 3074 | 107 | 34.93 | | 1 | 24 | 60 | 0 |
| Twenty20 | 119 | 111 | 22 | 2699 | 88 | 30.32 | 123.35 | 0 | 15 | 67 | 0 |
| **Bowling** | **Mat** | **Balls** | **Runs** | **Wkts** | **BBI** | **BBM** | **Ave** | **Econ** | **SR** | **5w** | **10** |
| First-class | 114 | 4169 | 2404 | 59 | 6/41 | 9/105 | 40.74 | 3.45 | 70.6 | 1 | 0 |
| List A | 121 | 2212 | 2002 | 54 | 4/24 | 4/24 | 37.07 | 5.43 | 40.9 | 0 | 0 |
| Twenty20 | 119 | 951 | 1214 | 43 | 3/6 | 3/6 | 28.23 | 7.65 | 22.1 | 0 | 0 |

# STEVEN CROOK RHB RFM R0 W0 MVP78

FULL NAME: Steven Paul Crook
BORN: May 28, 1983, Adelaide, Australia
SQUAD NO: 25
HEIGHT: 5ft 11in
NICKNAME: Crooky
EDUCATION: Rostrevor College
TEAMS: Northamptonshire, Lancashire, Middlesex
CAREER: First-class: 2003; List A: 2003; T20: 2004



BEST BATTING: 131 Northamptonshire vs Middlesex, Lord's, 2014
BEST BOWLING: 5-48 Middlesex vs Lancashire, Lord's, 2012

FAMILY TIES? My brother Andrew has played for South Australia, Lancashire and Northants
CAREER HIGHLIGHTS? Winning the FPt20 in 2013 with Northants
BEST PLAYER IN COUNTY CRICKET? Graham Napier
TIP FOR THE TOP? Olly Stone
CRICKETING HEROES? Anyone who bowls fast and hits lots of sixes and fours
NON-CRICKETING HEROES? Richard Branson – he's done pretty well for himself
CRICKET RULE YOU'D CHANGE? One hand, one bounce in Powerplays
IF YOU COULD BE SOMEONE ELSE FOR A DAY? Jim Morrison in the early '70s
DESERT ISLAND DISC? The Very Best of The Doors
FAVOURITE TV? Bad drivers
SURPRISING FACT? My father was a professional footballer and played for Australia
FANTASY SLIP CORDON? Keeper: Spider-Man, 1st: Jim Morrison, 2nd: Mila Kunis, 3rd: God
TWITTER FEED: @stevecrook25

| Batting | Mat | Inns | NO | Runs | HS | Ave | SR | 100 | 50 | Ct | St |
|---|---|---|---|---|---|---|---|---|---|---|---|
| First-class | 75 | 97 | 12 | 2470 | 131 | 29.05 | 75.23 | 1 | 17 | 26 | 0 |
| List A | 64 | 46 | 4 | 814 | 100 | 19.38 | 100.74 | 1 | 4 | 15 | 0 |
| Twenty20 | 79 | 56 | 11 | 778 | 63 | 17.28 | 135.06 | 0 | 2 | 17 | 0 |
| **Bowling** | **Mat** | **Balls** | **Runs** | **Wkts** | **BBI** | **BBM** | **Ave** | **Econ** | **SR** | **5w** | **10** |
| First-class | 75 | 9711 | 6290 | 162 | 5/48 | | 38.82 | 3.88 | 59.9 | 3 | 0 |
| List A | 64 | 2374 | 2254 | 71 | 5/36 | 5/36 | 31.74 | 5.69 | 33.4 | 1 | 0 |
| Twenty20 | 79 | 1045 | 1401 | 55 | 3/19 | 3/19 | 25.47 | 8.04 | 19.0 | 0 | 0 |

# TOM CURRAN

RHB RFM R0 W0



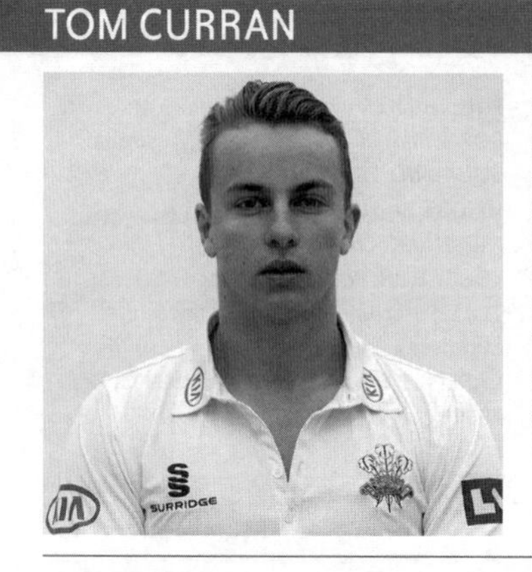

FULL NAME: Thomas Kevin Curran
BORN: March 12, 1995, Cape Town, South Africa
SQUAD NO: 59
HEIGHT: 6ft
NICKNAME: TC
EDUCATION: Wellington College, Berkshire
TEAMS: Surrey
CAREER: First-class: 2014; List A: 2013; T20: 2014

BEST BATTING: 9* Surrey vs Derbyshire, Derby, 2014
BEST BOWLING: 5-51 Surrey vs Derbyshire, Derby, 2014

FAMILY TIES? My father Kevin played for Northants and Zimbabwe
CAREER HIGHLIGHTS? My first five-fer against Scotland in one-day cricket
BEST PLAYER IN COUNTY CRICKET? Jason Roy
TIP FOR THE TOP? Saif Zaib, Dominic Sibley
CRICKETING HEROES? Hamilton Masakadza – he smashes it
NON-CRICKETING HEROES? Dan Bilzerian – lives the dream
CRICKET RULE YOU'D CHANGE? Four-ball overs
IF YOU WEREN'T A CRICKETER? I would still be fishing like last year
FAVOURITE TV? The Vampire Diaries
LEAST FAVOURITE TV? Game Of Thrones
PET HATE? Jason Roy getting in my locker area and my grill
SURPRISING FACT? I play guitar and sing to an extremely high standard
FANTASY SLIP CORDON? Keeper: Michelangelo the Mutant Ninja Turtle, 1st: Me, 2nd: Margot Robbie, 3rd: Rey Mysterio
TWITTER FEED: @TommyCurran159

| Batting | Mat | Inns | NO | Runs | HS | Ave | SR | 100 | 50 | Ct | St |
|---|---|---|---|---|---|---|---|---|---|---|---|
| First-class | 7 | 7 | 3 | 16 | 9* | 4.00 | 27.11 | 0 | 0 | 2 | 0 |
| List A | 5 | 4 | 1 | 3 | 1* | 1.00 | 18.75 | 0 | 0 | 2 | 0 |
| Twenty20 | 9 | - | - | - | - | - | - | - | - | 1 | 0 |
| **Bowling** | **Mat** | **Balls** | **Runs** | **Wkts** | **BBI** | **BBM** | **Ave** | **Econ** | **SR** | **5w** | **10** |
| First-class | 7 | 926 | 526 | 19 | 5/51 | 5/89 | 27.68 | 3.40 | 48.7 | 1 | 0 |
| List A | 5 | 193 | 202 | 9 | 5/34 | 5/34 | 22.44 | 6.27 | 21.4 | 1 | 0 |
| Twenty20 | 9 | 150 | 193 | 9 | 3/23 | 3/23 | 21.44 | 7.72 | 16.6 | 0 | 0 |

# BRETT D'OLIVEIRA

## RHB LB R0 W0

FULL NAME: Brett Louis D'Oliveira
BORN: February 28, 1992, Worcester
SQUAD NO: 15
NICKNAME: Dolly, Bdol
EDUCATION: Blessed Edward Oldcorne; Worcester Sixth Form College
TEAMS: Worcestershire
CAREER: First-class: 2012; List A: 2011; T20: 2012



BEST BATTING: 44 Worcestershire vs Essex, Chelmsford, 2014
BEST BOWLING: 1-73 Worcestershire vs Essex, Chelmsford, 2014

FAMILY TIES? My grandad Basil played for England and Worcestershire and also went on to coach Worcestershire. My Dad Damian played for Worcestershire and went on to be assistant coach and academy director
BEST PLAYER IN COUNTY CRICKET? Moeen Ali
TIP FOR THE TOP? Tom Kohler-Cadmore
MOST MARKED CHARACTERISTIC? I'm tiny and round
SUPERSTITIONS? I always touch the white line and say a couple of personal thoughts to myself before going on the field
CRICKETING HEROES? Shane Warne – outstanding performer and could win games just by himself. Moeen Ali – class batter, top spinner, serious fielder and an even better bloke around the changing rooms
NON-CRICKETING HEROES? Nelson Mandela – achieved a lot during Apartheid but I feel there is a link between what my grandad also achieved and that's why it's special
FAVOURITE TV? The Fresh Prince Of Bel-Air
SURPRISING FACT? Have a coaching level in basketball

| Batting | Mat | Inns | NO | Runs | HS | Ave | SR | 100 | 50 | Ct | St |
|---|---|---|---|---|---|---|---|---|---|---|---|
| First-class | 4 | 8 | 0 | 113 | 44 | 14.12 | 49.13 | 0 | 0 | 0 | 0 |
| List A | 20 | 14 | 7 | 149 | 28 | 21.28 | 103.47 | 0 | 0 | 6 | 0 |
| Twenty20 | 26 | 11 | 10 | 81 | 15 | 81.00 | 152.83 | 0 | 0 | 3 | 0 |
| **Bowling** | **Mat** | **Balls** | **Runs** | **Wkts** | **BBI** | **BBM** | **Ave** | **Econ** | **SR** | **5w** | **10** |
| First-class | 4 | 342 | 271 | 1 | 1/73 | 1/73 | 271.00 | 4.75 | 342.0 | 0 | 0 |
| List A | 20 | 582 | 537 | 15 | 3/35 | 3/35 | 35.80 | 5.53 | 38.8 | 0 | 0 |
| Twenty20 | 26 | 270 | 371 | 6 | 3/20 | 3/20 | 61.83 | 8.24 | 45.0 | 0 | 0 |

# JOSH DAVEY

RHB RMF R0 W0

FULL NAME: Joshua Henry Davey
BORN: August 3, 1990, Aberdeen
SQUAD NO: 38
EDUCATION: Culford School
TEAMS: Scotland, Somerset, Middlesex
CAREER: ODI: 2010; T20I: 2012; First-class: 2010; List A: 2010; T20I: 2010

BEST BATTING: 72 Middlesex vs Oxford MCCU, Oxford, 2010
BEST BOWLING: 4-53 Scotland vs Afghanistan, Abu Dhabi, 2013

TWITTER FEED: @JoshDavey38
NOTES: After four years at Middlesex, he was released at the end of 2013 and excelled for Somerset 2nd XI in 2014, which led to a full contract at the county. Made his highest first-class score of 72 on his debut for Middlesex against Oxford University in 2010. Hit an unbeaten 48 and took 3-41 for Scotland against Ireland at Edinburgh in the 2011 Tri-Nation Tournament to help his country to a five-wicket win. Attended the Darren Lehmann Cricket Academy in Adelaide in 2009. Tookf 5-9 for Scotland against Afghanistan at Ayr in 2010. In January 2015, against the same opponents, he took 6-28 and scored 53*. He played for Scotland in the 2015 World Cup, finishing as his team's highest wicket-taker

| Batting | Mat | Inns | NO | Runs | HS | Ave | SR | 100 | 50 | Ct | St |
|---|---|---|---|---|---|---|---|---|---|---|---|
| ODIs | 22 | 20 | 5 | 398 | 64 | 26.53 | 65.24 | 0 | 2 | 8 | 0 |
| T20Is | 1 | 1 | 0 | 7 | 7 | 7.00 | 116.66 | 0 | 0 | 1 | 0 |
| First-class | 7 | 13 | 1 | 307 | 72 | 25.58 | 42.52 | 0 | 3 | 3 | 0 |
| List A | 54 | 51 | 10 | 1035 | 91 | 25.24 | 65.46 | 0 | 5 | 18 | 0 |
| Twenty20 | 13 | 9 | 4 | 72 | 18* | 14.40 | 114.28 | 0 | 0 | 10 | 0 |
| **Bowling** | **Mat** | **Balls** | **Runs** | **Wkts** | **BBI** | **BBM** | **Ave** | **Econ** | **SR** | **5w** | **10** |
| ODIs | 22 | 887 | 741 | 39 | 6/28 | 6/28 | 19.00 | 5.01 | 22.7 | 2 | 0 |
| T20Is | 1 | 24 | 23 | 3 | 3/23 | 3/23 | 7.66 | 5.75 | 8.0 | 0 | 0 |
| First-class | 7 | 333 | 186 | 7 | 4/53 | 4/53 | 26.57 | 3.35 | 47.5 | 0 | 0 |
| List A | 54 | 1733 | 1625 | 63 | 6/28 | 6/28 | 25.79 | 5.62 | 27.5 | 2 | 0 |
| Twenty20 | 13 | 72 | 104 | 4 | 3/23 | 3/23 | 26.00 | 8.66 | 18.0 | 0 | 0 |

# ALEX DAVIES

## RHB WK R0 W0

FULL NAME: Alexander Luke Davies
BORN: August 23, 1994, Darwen, Lancashire
SQUAD NO: 17
HEIGHT: 5ft 8in
NICKNAME: Davo, AD, Chikwambo
EDUCATION: Queen Elizabeth's Grammar School, Blackburn
TEAMS: Lancashire
CAREER: First-class: 2012; List A: 2011; T20: 2014



BEST BATTING: 62 Lancashire vs Somerset, Manchester, 2014

CAREER HIGHLIGHTS? Representing England at the U19 World Cup and making my first-class debut for Lancashire at T20 Finals Day
BEST PLAYER IN COUNTY CRICKET? Simon Kerrigan, Tom Smith
TIP FOR THE TOP? Tom Bailey, Arron Lilley
MOST MARKED CHARACTERISTIC? Height … lack of
CRICKETING HEROES? Ricky Ponting – small and a fighter. Sachin Tendulkar – I tried to be like him from a young age
COACHING TIP? If you're going to swing, swing hard
IF YOU WEREN'T A CRICKETER? Studying at university and travelling
IF YOU COULD BE SOMEONE ELSE FOR A DAY? Dan Bilzerian – need I say why?
FAVOURITE TV? Eggheads
LEAST FAVOURITE TV? Hollyoaks
ACCOMPLISHMENTS? Playing football for Blackburn Rovers
PET HATE? Listening to other people brush their teeth
SURPRISING FACT? I can bowl with both arms
TWITTER FEED: @aldavies23

| Batting | Mat | Inns | NO | Runs | HS | Ave | SR | 100 | 50 | Ct | St |
|---|---|---|---|---|---|---|---|---|---|---|---|
| First-class | 14 | 20 | 1 | 527 | 62 | 27.73 | 47.52 | 0 | 3 | 21 | 1 |
| List A | 9 | 7 | 1 | 171 | 53 | 28.50 | 91.93 | 0 | 1 | 12 | 1 |
| Twenty20 | 7 | 6 | 0 | 18 | 7 | 3.00 | 72.00 | 0 | 0 | 4 | 1 |
| **Bowling** | **Mat** | **Balls** | **Runs** | **Wkts** | **BBI** | **BBM** | **Ave** | **Econ** | **SR** | **5w** | **10** |
| First-class | 14 | - | - | - | - | - | - | - | - | - | - |
| List A | 9 | - | - | - | - | - | - | - | - | - | - |
| Twenty20 | 7 | - | - | - | - | - | - | - | - | - | - |

## RYAN DAVIES RHB WK R0 W0

FULL NAME: Ryan Christopher Davies
BORN: November 5, 1996, Thanet, Kent
SQUAD NO: 7
HEIGHT: 5ft 9in
NICKNAME: Rizzlar, Riz, Davi
EDUCATION: Sandwich Technology School; Canterbury Academy
TEAMS: Kent 2nd XI
CAREER: Yet to make first-team debut

FAMILY TIES? Dad used to play for Kent when he was younger
CAREER HIGHLIGHTS? Making the EDP U19 squad and gaining a professional contract
BEST PLAYER IN COUNTY CRICKET? Jason Roy
TIP FOR THE TOP? Sam Billings, Haseeb Hameed, Callum Taylor
CRICKETING HEROES? Kevin Pietersen – for the flair he bats with and crowds mainly only went to watch him
NON-CRICKETING HEROES? Who doesn't love Ronaldo? Always challenging himself to break records and be the best in the world
CRICKET RULE YOU'D CHANGE? Being caught – only because that's how I mainly get out
COACHING TIP? For takes down the legside: hands always going first with feet and head following
IF YOU COULD BE SOMEONE ELSE FOR A DAY? Probably Richard Branson – see what that kind of lifestyle is like
DESERT ISLAND DISC? OneRepublic
FAVOURITE TV? Two And A Half Men
LEAST FAVOURITE TV? EastEnders
PET HATE? People who spit while walking down the street
SURPRISING FACT? I have dropped five iPhones in the bath
FANTASY SLIP CORDON? Keeper: Karl Pilkington, 1st: Jack Whitehall, 2nd: Ronaldo, 3rd: Daniel Radcliffe, Gully: José Mourinho
TWITTER FEED: @Frikinrizzlar

# STEVEN DAVIES LHB WK R5 W0

FULL NAME: Steven Michael Davies
BORN: June 17, 1986, Bromsgrove, Worcestershire
SQUAD NO: 9
HEIGHT: 5ft 11in
NICKNAME: Davo
EDUCATION: King Charles High School
TEAMS: England, Surrey, Worcestershire
CAREER: ODI: 2009; T20I: 2009; First-class: 2005; List A: 2003; T20: 2006



BEST BATTING: 192 Worcestershire vs Gloucestershire, Bristol, 2006
COUNTY CAPS: 2011 (Surrey)

CAREER HIGHLIGHTS? Playing for England
BEST PLAYER IN COUNTY CRICKET? Kumar Sangakkara
CRICKETING HEROES? Adam Gilchrist – because he changed the way the game was played
NON-CRICKETING HEROES? Roger Federer
CRICKET RULE YOU'D CHANGE? I would like to see a longer pitch
IF YOU WEREN'T A CRICKETER? I would be a tennis player
IF YOU COULD BE SOMEONE ELSE FOR A DAY? Gareth Batty – and what a day that would be
ACCOMPLISHMENTS? Being an international-graded pianist
SURPRISING FACT? I have played at Wimbledon
FANTASY SLIP CORDON? Keeper: Ricky Gervais, 1st: Alex Tysoe (Surrey's head physio), 2nd: Kevin Hart, 3rd: Me, Gully: Roger Federer
TWITTER FEED: @SteveDavies43

| Batting | Mat | Inns | NO | Runs | HS | Ave | SR | 100 | 50 | Ct | St |
|---|---|---|---|---|---|---|---|---|---|---|---|
| ODIs | 8 | 8 | 0 | 244 | 87 | 30.50 | 105.62 | 0 | 1 | 8 | 0 |
| T20Is | 5 | 5 | 0 | 102 | 33 | 20.40 | 124.39 | 0 | 0 | 2 | 1 |
| First-class | 154 | 252 | 25 | 8912 | 192 | 39.25 | 62.23 | 16 | 43 | 393 | 20 |
| List A | 150 | 139 | 13 | 4554 | 127* | 36.14 |  | 6 | 30 | 126 | 41 |
| Twenty20 | 103 | 95 | 8 | 2024 | 99* | 23.26 | 140.55 | 0 | 10 | 53 | 18 |
| **Bowling** | **Mat** | **Balls** | **Runs** | **Wkts** | **BBI** | **BBM** | **Ave** | **Econ** | **SR** | **5w** | **10** |
| ODIs | 8 | - | - | - | - | - | - | - | - | - | - |
| T20Is | 5 | - | - | - | - | - | - | - | - | - | - |
| First-class | 154 | - | - | - | - | - | - | - | - | - | - |
| List A | 150 | - | - | - | - | - | - | - | - | - | - |
| Twenty20 | 103 | - | - | - | - | - | - | - | - | - | - |

## LIAM DAWSON

RHB SLA R1 W0

FULL NAME: Liam Andrew Dawson
BORN: March 1, 1990, Swindon
SQUAD NO: 8
HEIGHT: 5ft 8in
NICKNAME: Daws, Chav, Leemo
EDUCATION: John Bentley School
TEAMS: Hampshire, England Lions
CAREER: First-class: 2007; List A: 2007; T20: 2008

BEST BATTING: 169 Hampshire vs Somerset, Southampton, 2011
BEST BOWLING: 7-51 Mountaineers vs Mashonaland Eagles, Mutare Sports Club, 2011

FAMILY TIES? My dad and brother both played for Goatacre CC in Wiltshire
CAREER HIGHLIGHTS? Winning five trophies in the space of seven years with a group of lads I've grown up with from the academy
BEST PLAYER IN COUNTY CRICKET? Michael Carberry
TIP FOR THE TOP? Craig Miles
MOST MARKED CHARACTERISTIC? Being stubborn
CRICKETING HEROES? Shane Warne – genius how he played cricket
CRICKET RULE YOU'D CHANGE? If a game is a boring draw, both teams should agree to shake hands at any time on the fourth day
IF YOU WEREN'T A CRICKETER? Radio pundit
DESERT ISLAND DISC? Lorde – Royals
PET HATE? Umpires deciding to look at conditions again in 40 minutes' time but there's no chance it's going to be any different to when they looked before
TWITTER FEED: @Daws128

| Batting | Mat | Inns | NO | Runs | HS | Ave | SR | 100 | 50 | Ct | St |
|---|---|---|---|---|---|---|---|---|---|---|---|
| First-class | 89 | 143 | 15 | 4243 | 169 | 33.14 | 48.03 | 6 | 23 | 110 | 0 |
| List A | 100 | 82 | 15 | 1856 | 113* | 27.70 | 92.43 | 1 | 7 | 51 | 0 |
| Twenty20 | 63 | 41 | 13 | 347 | 30 | 12.39 | 103.89 | 0 | 0 | 32 | 0 |
| **Bowling** | **Mat** | **Balls** | **Runs** | **Wkts** | **BBI** | **BBM** | **Ave** | **Econ** | **SR** | **5w** | **10** |
| First-class | 89 | 5590 | 3069 | 81 | 7/51 | 7/84 | 37.88 | 3.29 | 69.0 | 2 | 0 |
| List A | 100 | 3114 | 2542 | 66 | 4/45 | 4/45 | 38.51 | 4.89 | 47.1 | 0 | 0 |
| Twenty20 | 63 | 790 | 1007 | 34 | 4/19 | 4/19 | 29.61 | 7.64 | 23.2 | 0 | 0 |

# JOE DENLY RHB LB R2 W0

FULL NAME: Joseph Liam Denly
BORN: March 16, 1986, Canterbury
SQUAD NO: 6
HEIGHT: 6ft
NICKNAME: JD, Denners
EDUCATION: Chaucer Technology School
TEAMS: England, Kent, Middlesex
CAREER: ODI: 2009; T20I: 2009; First-class: 2004; List A: 2004; T20: 2004



BEST BATTING: 199 Kent vs Derbyshire, Derby, 2011
BEST BOWLING: 3-43 Kent vs Surrey, The Oval, 2011
COUNTY CAPS: 2008 (Kent); 2012 (Middlesex)

CAREER HIGHLIGHTS? Winning the T20. Playing for England
SUPERSTITIONS? Left pad on first
IF YOU WEREN'T A CRICKETER? Football
IF YOU COULD BE SOMEONE ELSE FOR A DAY? David Beckham
FAVOURITE TV? Gogglebox
LEAST FAVOURITE TV? The Only Way Is Essex
ACCOMPLISHMENTS? The wife
PET HATE? Loud eaters
TWITTER FEED: @joed1986

| Batting | Mat | Inns | NO | Runs | HS | Ave | SR | 100 | 50 | Ct | St |
|---|---|---|---|---|---|---|---|---|---|---|---|
| ODIs | 9 | 9 | 0 | 268 | 67 | 29.77 | 65.52 | 0 | 2 | 5 | 0 |
| T20Is | 5 | 5 | 0 | 20 | 14 | 4.00 | 68.96 | 0 | 0 | 1 | 0 |
| First-class | 127 | 223 | 13 | 6952 | 199 | 33.10 | 57.09 | 15 | 35 | 51 | 0 |
| List A | 111 | 107 | 10 | 3282 | 115 | 33.83 | 73.70 | 4 | 18 | 37 | 0 |
| Twenty20 | 116 | 112 | 10 | 2553 | 100 | 25.02 | 113.26 | 1 | 16 | 44 | 0 |
| **Bowling** | **Mat** | **Balls** | **Runs** | **Wkts** | **BBI** | **BBM** | **Ave** | **Econ** | **SR** | **5w** | **10** |
| ODIs | 9 | - | - | - | - | - | - | - | - | - | - |
| T20Is | 5 | 6 | 9 | 1 | 1/9 | 1/9 | 9.00 | 9.00 | 6.0 | 0 | 0 |
| First-class | 127 | 2341 | 1324 | 27 | 3/43 | 6/114 | 49.03 | 3.39 | 86.7 | 0 | 0 |
| List A | 111 | 398 | 315 | 17 | 3/19 | 3/19 | 18.52 | 4.74 | 23.4 | 0 | 0 |
| Twenty20 | 116 | 48 | 76 | 1 | 1/9 | 1/9 | 76.00 | 9.50 | 48.0 | 0 | 0 |

# CHRIS DENT

## LHB SLA WK R1 W0

FULL NAME: Christopher David James Dent
BORN: January 11, 1991, Bristol
SQUAD NO: 15
HEIGHT: 5ft 10in
NICKNAME: Denty
EDUCATION: Backwell School; Filton College
TEAMS: Gloucestershire
CAREER: First-class: 2010; List A: 2009; T20: 2010

---

BEST BATTING: 203* Gloucestershire vs Cardiff MCCU, Bristol, 2014
BEST BOWLING: 1-12 Gloucestershire vs Hampshire, Bristol, 2013
COUNTY CAPS: 2010

---

CAREER HIGHLIGHTS? My first first-class hundred at Cheltenham
BEST PLAYER IN COUNTY CRICKET? Will Gidman
TIP FOR THE TOP? Craig Miles
CRICKETING HEROES? Kane Williamson – amazing cricketer and great guy
NON-CRICKETING HEROES? Family, but especially my uncle!
CRICKET RULE YOU'D CHANGE? Batsmen don't field
IF YOU COULD BE SOMEONE ELSE FOR A DAY? Usain Bolt
DESERT ISLAND DISC? Bohemian Rhapsody – Queen
FAVOURITE TV? Breaking Bad
LEAST FAVOURITE TV? Made In Chelsea
ACCOMPLISHMENTS? Renovating a house
SURPRISING FACT? I can handstand until boredom sets in
FANTASY SLIP CORDON? Keeper: Ricky Gervais, 1st: Karl Pilkington, 2nd: Me, 3rd: Sean Lock, Gully: Joe Wilkinson

| Batting | Mat | Inns | NO | Runs | HS | Ave | SR | 100 | 50 | Ct | St |
|---|---|---|---|---|---|---|---|---|---|---|---|
| First-class | 66 | 117 | 9 | 3565 | 203* | 33.00 | 53.96 | 5 | 20 | 82 | 0 |
| List A | 32 | 27 | 3 | 723 | 151* | 30.12 | 99.44 | 1 | 2 | 7 | 0 |
| Twenty20 | 28 | 27 | 2 | 460 | 63* | 18.40 | 117.64 | 0 | 3 | 6 | 0 |
| **Bowling** | **Mat** | **Balls** | **Runs** | **Wkts** | **BBI** | **BBM** | **Ave** | **Econ** | **SR** | **5w** | **10** |
| First-class | 66 | 472 | 308 | 2 | 1/12 | 1/12 | 154.00 | 3.91 | 236.0 | 0 | 0 |
| List A | 32 | 390 | 348 | 10 | 4/43 | 4/43 | 34.80 | 5.35 | 39.0 | 0 | 0 |
| Twenty20 | 28 | 108 | 140 | 4 | 1/4 | 1/4 | 35.00 | 7.77 | 27.0 | 0 | 0 |

# JADE DERNBACH

## RHB RFM R0 W1

FULL NAME: Jade Winston Dernbach
BORN: March 3, 1986, Johannesburg, South Africa
SQUAD NO: 16
HEIGHT: 6ft 2in
NICKNAME: Dirtbag
EDUCATION: St John the Baptist School, Woking
TEAMS: England, Surrey
CAREER: ODI: 2011; T20I: 2011; First-class: 2003; List A: 2005; T20: 2005



BEST BATTING: 56* Surrey vs Northamptonshire, Northampton, 2011
BEST BOWLING: 6-47 Surrey vs Leicestershire, Leicester, 2010
COUNTY CAPS: 2011 (Surrey)

CAREER HIGHLIGHTS? Playing for England, winning the CB40 and guiding Ricky Ponting to a hundred in his final first-class innings
BEST PLAYER IN COUNTY CRICKET? Jason Roy
TIP FOR THE TOP? Tom Curran
CRICKETING HEROES? Allan Donald
IF YOU WEREN'T A CRICKETER? A lawyer
ACCOMPLISHMENTS? Completing my mind-reading course to an international standard
SURPRISING FACT? I have fought in a kick-boxing ring
FANTASY SLIP CORDON? Keeper: Candice Swanepoel, 1st: Me, 2nd: Michelle Keegan, 3rd: George Bush, Gully: Micky Flanagan
TWITTER FEED: @Jwd_16

| Batting | Mat | Inns | NO | Runs | HS | Ave | SR | 100 | 50 | Ct | St |
|---|---|---|---|---|---|---|---|---|---|---|---|
| ODIs | 24 | 8 | 1 | 19 | 5 | 2.71 | 48.71 | 0 | 0 | 5 | 0 |
| T20Is | 34 | 7 | 2 | 24 | 12 | 4.80 | 114.28 | 0 | 0 | 8 | 0 |
| First-class | 93 | 119 | 43 | 724 | 56* | 9.52 | | 0 | 1 | 12 | 0 |
| List A | 115 | 42 | 15 | 197 | 31 | 7.29 | 79.43 | 0 | 0 | 22 | 0 |
| Twenty20 | 102 | 23 | 10 | 90 | 24* | 6.92 | 103.44 | 0 | 0 | 21 | 0 |
| **Bowling** | **Mat** | **Balls** | **Runs** | **Wkts** | **BBI** | **BBM** | **Ave** | **Econ** | **SR** | **5w** | **10** |
| ODIs | 24 | 1234 | 1308 | 31 | 4/45 | 4/45 | 42.19 | 6.35 | 39.8 | 0 | 0 |
| T20Is | 34 | 702 | 1020 | 39 | 4/22 | 4/22 | 26.15 | 8.71 | 18.0 | 0 | 0 |
| First-class | 93 | 15080 | 8530 | 265 | 6/47 | | 32.18 | 3.39 | 56.9 | 10 | 0 |
| List A | 115 | 4877 | 4954 | 173 | 5/31 | 5/31 | 28.63 | 6.09 | 28.1 | 2 | 0 |
| Twenty20 | 102 | 2008 | 2816 | 108 | 4/22 | 4/22 | 26.07 | 8.41 | 18.5 | 0 | 0 |

## NEIL DEXTER RHB RM R0 W0

FULL NAME: Neil John Dexter
BORN: August 21, 1984, Johannesburg, South Africa
SQUAD NO: 4
HEIGHT: 5ft 11in
NICKNAME: Dexy, Dex, Sexy Dexy
EDUCATION: Northwood High School
TEAMS: Middlesex, Essex, Kent
CAREER: First-class: 2005; List A: 2005; T20: 2006

BEST BATTING: 163* Middlesex vs Northamptonshire, Northampton, 2014
BEST BOWLING: 6-63 Middlesex vs Lancashire, Lord's, 2014
COUNTY CAPS: 2010 (Middlesex)

CAREER HIGHLIGHTS? Taking six wickets against Lancashire and reaching my PB with the bat against Northants in the 2014 season
BEST PLAYER IN COUNTY CRICKET? Adam Lyth
CRICKETING HEROES? Brett Lee – fast and aggressive but played game in the right spirit. AB de Villiers – the best player in the world in all formats and very humble
IF YOU WEREN'T A CRICKETER? Probably a scientist
IF YOU COULD BE SOMEONE ELSE FOR A DAY? My wife, so I can see how lucky she really is
DESERT ISLAND DISC? The Lonely Island – Motherlover
FAVOURITE TV? Dexter
LEAST FAVOURITE TV? Anything sci-fi
ACCOMPLISHMENTS? My daughter, and I've got two hole in ones in golf
PET HATE? People who eat loudly next to me and bad body odour
FANTASY SLIP CORDON? Keeper: Borat, 1st: Barney, 2nd: Cheryl Cole, 3rd: Einstein
TWITTER FEED: @dexy214

| Batting | Mat | Inns | NO | Runs | HS | Ave | SR | 100 | 50 | Ct | St |
|---|---|---|---|---|---|---|---|---|---|---|---|
| First-class | 107 | 176 | 22 | 5559 | 163* | 36.09 | 52.17 | 12 | 29 | 80 | 0 |
| List A | 92 | 76 | 17 | 1896 | 135* | 32.13 | 81.44 | 2 | 8 | 25 | 0 |
| Twenty20 | 99 | 83 | 10 | 1466 | 73 | 20.08 | 110.22 | 0 | 2 | 40 | 0 |
| **Bowling** | **Mat** | **Balls** | **Runs** | **Wkts** | **BBI** | **BBM** | **Ave** | **Econ** | **SR** | **5w** | **10** |
| First-class | 107 | 6057 | 3126 | 84 | 6/63 | | 37.21 | 3.09 | 72.1 | 2 | 0 |
| List A | 92 | 1975 | 1839 | 31 | 3/17 | 3/17 | 59.32 | 5.58 | 63.7 | 0 | 0 |
| Twenty20 | 99 | 1115 | 1424 | 51 | 4/21 | 4/21 | 27.92 | 7.66 | 21.8 | 0 | 0 |

# ADAM DIBBLE

RHB RFM R0 W0

FULL NAME: Adam John Dibble
BORN: March 9, 1991, Exeter, Devon
SQUAD NO: 23
HEIGHT: 6ft 4in
NICKNAME: Dibbs, Officer
EDUCATION: St John's School, Sidmouth; Taunton School
TEAMS: Somerset
CAREER: First-class: 2011; List A: 2011; T20: 2011



BEST BATTING: 43 Somerset vs Warwickshire, Birmingham, 2012
BEST BOWLING: 3-42 Somerset vs Warwickshire, Birmingham, 2012

FAMILY TIES? My dad played cricket for Sidmouth CC. My sister [Jodie] is in the England Women's Academy
CAREER HIGHLIGHTS? My Somerset debut and a Champions League T20 semi-final in 2011
TIP FOR THE TOP? Tom Abell
CRICKETING HEROES? Chris Gayle and Kumar Sangakkara
NON-CRICKETING HEROES? David Beckham, Jonny Wilkinson, Ricky Gervais
DESERT ISLAND DISC? Coldplay – Viva La Vida
FAVOURITE TV? Sherlock and Top Gear
FANTASY SLIP CORDON? Keeper: David Beckham, 1st: Ricky Gervais, 2nd: Jonny Wilkinson, 3rd: Jeremy Clarkson
TWITTER FEED: @adam_dibble

| Batting | Mat | Inns | NO | Runs | HS | Ave | SR | 100 | 50 | Ct | St |
|---|---|---|---|---|---|---|---|---|---|---|---|
| First-class | 3 | 6 | 2 | 84 | 43 | 21.00 | 72.41 | 0 | 0 | 0 | 0 |
| List A | 7 | 2 | 1 | 15 | 15 | 15.00 | 136.36 | 0 | 0 | 1 | 0 |
| Twenty20 | 2 | - | - | - | - | - | - | - | - | 0 | 0 |
| **Bowling** | **Mat** | **Balls** | **Runs** | **Wkts** | **BBI** | **BBM** | **Ave** | **Econ** | **SR** | **5w** | **10** |
| First-class | 3 | 294 | 184 | 5 | 3/42 | 3/42 | 36.80 | 3.75 | 58.8 | 0 | 0 |
| List A | 7 | 288 | 295 | 11 | 4/52 | 4/52 | 26.81 | 6.14 | 26.1 | 0 | 0 |
| Twenty20 | 2 | 48 | 44 | 2 | 1/20 | 1/20 | 22.00 | 5.50 | 24.0 | 0 | 0 |

# GEORGE DOCKRELL RHB SLA R0 W0

FULL NAME: George Henry Dockrell
BORN: July 22, 1992, Dublin
SQUAD NO: 20
HEIGHT: 6ft 4in
NICKNAME: Doc, Dockers
EDUCATION: Gonzaga College; Trinity College Dublin
TEAMS: Ireland, Somerset
CAREER: ODI: 2010; T20I: 2010; First-class: 2010; List A: 2010; T20: 2010

---

BEST BATTING: 53 Ireland vs Namibia, Belfast, 2011
BEST BOWLING: 6-27 Somerset vs Middlesex, Taunton, 2012

---

CAREER HIGHLIGHTS? Beating England at the 2011 World Cup and winning the ICC Associate Player of the Year award in 2012
MOST MARKED CHARACTERISTIC? I'm a thinker. Probably too much at times...
CRICKETING HEROES? Daniel Vettori – he has consistently performed at international level for a long period of time
NON-CRICKETING HEROES? Johnny Sexton and Brian O'Driscoll
IF YOU COULD BE SOMEONE ELSE FOR A DAY? Skateboarder Rob Dyrdek
ACCOMPLISHMENTS? Making the Irish U16 hockey squad
PET HATE? I travel a lot so people who take too long checking in or going through security at airports gets to me
SURPRISING FACT? I've never had a cup of tea or coffee before
TWITTER FEED: @georgedockrell

| Batting | Mat | Inns | NO | Runs | HS | Ave | SR | 100 | 50 | Ct | St |
|---|---|---|---|---|---|---|---|---|---|---|---|
| ODIs | 46 | 25 | 15 | 146 | 25 | 14.60 | 63.75 | 0 | 0 | 20 | 0 |
| T20Is | 26 | 3 | 2 | 2 | 2* | 2.00 | 25.00 | 0 | 0 | 7 | 0 |
| First-class | 39 | 47 | 18 | 422 | 53 | 14.55 | 31.65 | 0 | 1 | 14 | 0 |
| List A | 71 | 35 | 21 | 220 | 25 | 15.71 | 67.07 | 0 | 0 | 35 | 0 |
| Twenty20 | 65 | 8 | 6 | 4 | 2* | 2.00 | 21.05 | 0 | 0 | 37 | 0 |
| **Bowling** | **Mat** | **Balls** | **Runs** | **Wkts** | **BBI** | **BBM** | **Ave** | **Econ** | **SR** | **5w** | **10** |
| ODIs | 46 | 2229 | 1618 | 56 | 4/24 | 4/24 | 28.89 | 4.35 | 39.8 | 0 | 0 |
| T20Is | 26 | 520 | 539 | 33 | 4/20 | 4/20 | 16.33 | 6.21 | 15.7 | 0 | 0 |
| First-class | 39 | 7198 | 3422 | 119 | 6/27 | 9/71 | 28.75 | 2.85 | 60.4 | 6 | 0 |
| List A | 71 | 3165 | 2391 | 73 | 4/24 | 4/24 | 32.75 | 4.53 | 43.3 | 0 | 0 |
| Twenty20 | 65 | 1235 | 1396 | 72 | 4/20 | 4/20 | 19.38 | 6.78 | 17.1 | 0 | 0 |

# ANEURIN DONALD

## RHB OB R0 W0

FULL NAME: Aneurin Henry Thomas Donald
BORN: December 20, 1996, Swansea
SQUAD NO: 12
HEIGHT: 6ft 3in
NICKNAME: Sir Don, The Don
EDUCATION: Pontarddulais Comprehensive School
TEAMS: Glamorgan
CAREER: First-class: 2014

BEST BATTING: 59 Glamorgan vs Hampshire, Cardiff, 2014

FAMILY TIES? My recently late grand-uncle, Bernard Hedges, scored the first one-day century for Glamorgan. Also my brother Gafyn who played for the Wales age-groups and plays in the Welsh Premier League for Pontarddulais CC
CAREER HIGHLIGHTS? Captaining England Development Programme U17 vs Sri Lanka U17, Bangladesh U19 and Pakistan U19, and making my debut for Glamorgan
MOST MARKED CHARACTERISTIC? My remarkable resemblance to Jackson Bird, the Australian fast bowler
NON-CRICKETING HEROES? Kevin Pietersen, Jos Buttler
DESERT ISLAND DISC? Bastille – Bad Blood
FAVOURITE TV? Suits
ACCOMPLISHMENTS? Playing regional age-grade rugby and not failing my GCSEs!
SURPRISING FACT? When I used to go and net with my brother and father on a Saturday morning, Leigh Halfpenny would be there every week practising his goal-kicking. I could never get the courage to ask him to feed the bowling machine...
FANTASY SLIP CORDON? Keeper: Matt Taylor (Northamptonshire Academy – for general amusement and to make me feel better about myself), 1st: Me, 2nd: Leigh Halfpenny (to run after the ball as it goes through the rest of the cordon), 3rd: Piers Morgan (to add some controversy and to listen to his opinions on just about everything)
TWITTER FEED: @aneurindonald12

| Batting | Mat | Inns | NO | Runs | HS | Ave | SR | 100 | 50 | Ct | St |
|---|---|---|---|---|---|---|---|---|---|---|---|
| First-class | 1 | 2 | 0 | 63 | 59 | 31.50 | 82.89 | 0 | 1 | 1 | 0 |
| **Bowling** | **Mat** | **Balls** | **Runs** | **Wkts** | **BBI** | **BBM** | **Ave** | **Econ** | **SR** | **5w** | **10** |
| First-class | 1 | - | - | - | - | - | - | - | - | - | - |

# BEN DUCKETT

# LHB OB WK R0 W0

FULL NAME: Ben Matthew Duckett
BORN: October 17, 1994, Farnborough, Kent
SQUAD NO: 24
HEIGHT: 5ft 9in
NICKNAME: Ducky, Toilet
EDUCATION: Millfield School; Winchester House School; Stowe School
TEAMS: Northamptonshire
CAREER: First-class: 2013; List A: 2013; T20: 2012

BEST BATTING: 144* Northamptonshire vs Somerset, Taunton, 2014

FAMILY TIES? My dad played for Surrey 2nd XI and my grandad played a bit and was an umpire
CAREER HIGHLIGHTS? Scoring 144* against Somerset, winning the T20 Cup and getting promoted to Division One in my first season
TIP FOR THE TOP? Saif Zaib, Rob Keogh, James Kettleborough, Dom Sibley
CRICKETING HEROES? Brian Lara and Graham Thorpe – both left-handed batsmen like myself
NON-CRICKETING HEROES? Dan Bilzerian – he's got to be the best bloke out there! Can't really explain why but he's a legend!
IF YOU WEREN'T A CRICKETER? I'd be struggling – probably working at a bar or something
IF YOU COULD BE SOMEONE ELSE FOR A DAY? Beyoncé
DESERT ISLAND DISC? OMI – Cheerleader
FAVOURITE TV? Made In Chelsea
PET HATE? When people bite their fork while eating – does my head in
SURPRISING FACT? I have a tattoo of a duck on the side of my bottom
TWITTER FEED: @benduckett1

| Batting | Mat | Inns | NO | Runs | HS | Ave | SR | 100 | 50 | Ct | St |
|---|---|---|---|---|---|---|---|---|---|---|---|
| First-class | 18 | 30 | 2 | 763 | 144* | 27.25 | 56.22 | 1 | 6 | 18 | 2 |
| List A | 13 | 11 | 2 | 227 | 49 | 25.22 | 83.45 | 0 | 0 | 7 | 1 |
| Twenty20 | 17 | 14 | 5 | 175 | 39* | 19.44 | 110.75 | 0 | 0 | 7 | 1 |
| **Bowling** | **Mat** | **Balls** | **Runs** | **Wkts** | **BBI** | **BBM** | **Ave** | **Econ** | **SR** | **5w** | **10** |
| First-class | 18 | - | - | - | - | - | - | - | - | - | - |
| List A | 13 | - | - | - | - | - | - | - | - | - | - |
| Twenty20 | 17 | - | - | - | - | - | - | - | - | - | - |

# MATT DUNN

## LHB RFM R0 W0

FULL NAME: Matthew Peter Dunn
BORN: May 5, 1992, Egham, Surrey
SQUAD NO: 4
HEIGHT: 6ft 1in
NICKNAME: The Viking
EDUCATION: Bishopsgate School; Bearwood College
TEAMS: Surrey
CAREER: First-class: 2010; List A: 2011; T20: 2013



BEST BATTING: 31* Surrey vs Kent, Guildford, 2014
BEST BOWLING: 5-48 Surrey vs Gloucestershire, The Oval, 2014

CAREER HIGHLIGHTS? Taking my first five-fer at The Oval, Man-of-the-Match performance in front of a 20,000+ crowd in last year's T20 Blast and being selected for England Lions
BEST PLAYER IN COUNTY CRICKET? Darren Stevens
TIP FOR THE TOP? Tom Curran
MOST MARKED CHARACTERISTIC? My big cheesy smile!
CRICKETING HEROES? Dale Steyn, Jimmy Anderson, Dougie Bollinger
IF YOU WEREN'T A CRICKETER? I was never meant to do anything but cricket
IF YOU COULD BE SOMEONE ELSE FOR A DAY? Thor
DESERT ISLAND DISC? Mumford and Sons
FAVOURITE TV? Derek
LEAST FAVOURITE TV? The Only Way Is Essex
SURPRISING FACT? I lived in Norway for two years when I was younger
FANTASY SLIP CORDON? Keeper: Rory Burns, 1st: Thor, 2nd: Myself, 3rd: Ricky Gervais, Gully: Kyle Pilkington
TWITTER FEED: @MatthewDunn05

| Batting | Mat | Inns | NO | Runs | HS | Ave | SR | 100 | 50 | Ct | St |
|---|---|---|---|---|---|---|---|---|---|---|---|
| First-class | 21 | 19 | 12 | 69 | 31* | 9.85 | 22.47 | 0 | 0 | 4 | 0 |
| List A | 1 | - | - | - | - | - | - | - | - | 1 | 0 |
| Twenty20 | 8 | - | - | - | - | - | - | - | - | 3 | 0 |
| **Bowling** | **Mat** | **Balls** | **Runs** | **Wkts** | **BBI** | **BBM** | **Ave** | **Econ** | **SR** | **5w** | **10** |
| First-class | 21 | 3077 | 2057 | 64 | 5/48 | 6/84 | 32.14 | 4.01 | 48.0 | 3 | 0 |
| List A | 1 | 36 | 32 | 2 | 2/32 | 2/32 | 16.00 | 5.33 | 18.0 | 0 | 0 |
| Twenty20 | 8 | 162 | 236 | 13 | 3/8 | 3/8 | 18.15 | 8.74 | 12.4 | 0 | 0 |

# WES DURSTON

## RHB OB R1 W0 MVP45

FULL NAME: Wesley John Durston
BORN: October 6, 1980, Taunton
SQUAD NO: 3
HEIGHT: 5ft 9in
NICKNAME: The Durst, Bestie
EDUCATION: Millfield School; University College Worcester
TEAMS: Derbyshire, Somerset
CAREER: First-class: 2002; List A: 2000; T20: 2003

---

BEST BATTING: 151 Derbyshire vs Gloucestershire, Derby, 2011
BEST BOWLING: 5-19 Derbyshire vs Worcestershire, Derby, 2014
COUNTY CAPS: 2012 (Derbyshire)

---

CAREER HIGHLIGHTS? T20 success in 2005 and Division Two winners with Somerset in 2007. Also winning Division Two with Derbyshire in 2012. Proud to be the only player in Derbyshire history to have scored a hundred in all three forms of the game
SUPERSTITIONS? Yes I have some silly ones, but the main one is that I don't let anybody touch my bats on game day!
CRICKETING HEROES? Ian Botham, Shane Warne, Brian Lara, Steve Waugh
NON-CRICKETING HEROES? Eric Cantona was my absolute hero – he made the game look very easy and even though he had a chequered history that for me only added to his genius
CRICKET RULE YOU'D CHANGE? I'd like to see an experiment season where there was no toss at the start of the game which meant the visiting team could choose to bat or bowl first
COACHING TIP? Play to your strengths but train to your weaknesses
IF YOU COULD BE SOMEONE ELSE FOR A DAY? The England football manager on a big game day
TWITTER FEED: @Wjdurston3

| Batting | Mat | Inns | NO | Runs | HS | Ave | SR | 100 | 50 | Ct | St |
|---|---|---|---|---|---|---|---|---|---|---|---|
| First-class | 94 | 163 | 23 | 4832 | 151 | 34.51 | 59.98 | 6 | 30 | 98 | 0 |
| List A | 109 | 95 | 19 | 2583 | 134 | 33.98 | | 4 | 13 | 38 | 0 |
| Twenty20 | 97 | 88 | 13 | 1846 | 111 | 24.61 | 125.49 | 1 | 11 | 37 | 0 |
| **Bowling** | **Mat** | **Balls** | **Runs** | **Wkts** | **BBI** | **BBM** | **Ave** | **Econ** | **SR** | **5w** | **10** |
| First-class | 94 | 6067 | 3601 | 86 | 5/19 | | 41.87 | 3.56 | 70.5 | 2 | 0 |
| List A | 109 | 1959 | 1849 | 48 | 3/7 | 3/7 | 38.52 | 5.66 | 40.8 | 0 | 0 |
| Twenty20 | 97 | 894 | 1147 | 47 | 3/25 | 3/25 | 24.40 | 7.69 | 19.0 | 0 | 0 |

# NED ECKERSLEY RHB WK R1 W0

FULL NAME: Edmund James Holden Eckersley
BORN: August 9, 1989, Oxford
SQUAD NO: 33
HEIGHT: 5ft 11in
NICKNAME: Eckers
EDUCATION: St Benedict's School
TEAMS: Leicestershire
CAREER: First-class: 2011; List A: 2008; T20: 2011



BEST BATTING: 147 Leicestershire vs Essex, Chelmsford, 2013
BEST BOWLING: 2-29 Leicestershire vs Lancashire, Manchester, 2013
COUNTY CAPS: 2013

CAREER HIGHLIGHTS? Back-to-back centuries against Worcestershire in 2013 and being given my county cap during that game
BEST PLAYER IN COUNTY CRICKET? James Vince
TIP FOR THE TOP? Sam Hain
SUPERSTITIONS? Must always do a quick crouch down when I enter the pitch to bat
CRICKETING HEROES? Alec Stewart – I always wanted to be a batsman/wicketkeeper and he was England's keeper when I first started to watch
CRICKET RULE YOU'D CHANGE? No-ball rule – if a bowler bowls a no-ball the batsman should be allowed to decide if he wants the extra ball or not. A batsman can't get out off a no-ball (apart from run out) but can of the legitimate seventh ball
IF YOU WEREN'T A CRICKETER? Sports reporting
FAVOURITE TV? Any David Attenborough documentary
PET HATE? Suck-ups
TWITTER FEED: @nedeckersley

| Batting | Mat | Inns | NO | Runs | HS | Ave | SR | 100 | 50 | Ct | St |
|---|---|---|---|---|---|---|---|---|---|---|---|
| First-class | 57 | 101 | 7 | 3313 | 147 | 35.24 | 48.82 | 8 | 11 | 92 | 3 |
| List A | 22 | 21 | 3 | 517 | 108 | 28.72 | 100.38 | 1 | 2 | 17 | 1 |
| Twenty20 | 36 | 30 | 9 | 356 | 43 | 16.95 | 109.87 | 0 | 0 | 13 | 3 |
| **Bowling** | **Mat** | **Balls** | **Runs** | **Wkts** | **BBI** | **BBM** | **Ave** | **Econ** | **SR** | **5w** | **10** |
| First-class | 57 | 70 | 58 | 2 | 2/29 | 2/29 | 29.00 | 4.97 | 35.0 | 0 | 0 |
| List A | 22 | - | - | - | - | - | - | - | - | - | - |
| Twenty20 | 36 | - | - | - | - | - | - | - | - | - | - |

## GEORGE EDWARDS RHB RFM R0 W0

FULL NAME: George Alexander Edwards
BORN: July 29, 1992, King's College Hospital, Lambeth, London
SQUAD NO: 22
HEIGHT: 6ft 4in
NICKNAME: Chicken
EDUCATION: St Joseph's College, Upper Norwood
TEAMS: Lancashire, Surrey
CAREER: First-class: 2011; List A: 2013; T20: 2014

BEST BATTING: 19 Surrey vs Cambridge MCCU, Cambridge, 2011
BEST BOWLING: 4-44 Surrey vs Worcestershire, Worcester, 2012

CAREER HIGHLIGHTS? My Championship debut against Worcestershire
MOST MARKED CHARACTERISTIC? My height
CRICKETING HEROES? The West Indies team
IF YOU WEREN'T A CRICKETER? Working on Dave Chappelle's Show
DESERT ISLAND DISC? Kid Cudi – Man On The Moon Part II
FAVOURITE TV? Breaking Bad
FANTASY SLIP CORDON? Keeper: Kevin Garnett, 1st: Myself, 2nd: Alicia Keys, 3rd: Carmelo Anthony, Gully: Eva Mendes
TWITTER FEED: @GEdwards29

| Batting | Mat | Inns | NO | Runs | HS | Ave | SR | 100 | 50 | Ct | St |
|---|---|---|---|---|---|---|---|---|---|---|---|
| First-class | 4 | 5 | 1 | 56 | 19 | 14.00 | 38.35 | 0 | 0 | 1 | 0 |
| List A | 5 | 3 | 3 | 9 | 8* | - | 128.57 | 0 | 0 | 3 | 0 |
| Twenty20 | 1 | - | - | - | - | - | - | - | - | 0 | 0 |
| **Bowling** | **Mat** | **Balls** | **Runs** | **Wkts** | **BBI** | **BBM** | **Ave** | **Econ** | **SR** | **5w** | **10** |
| First-class | 4 | 602 | 346 | 8 | 4/44 | 5/92 | 43.25 | 3.44 | 75.2 | 0 | 0 |
| List A | 5 | 162 | 201 | 2 | 1/29 | 1/29 | 100.50 | 7.44 | 81.0 | 0 | 0 |
| Twenty20 | 1 | 12 | 12 | 0 | - | - | - | 6.00 | - | 0 | 0 |

# SCOTT ELSTONE

## RHB OB R0 W0

FULL NAME: Scott Liam Elstone
BORN: June 10, 1990, Burton-on-Trent, Staffordshire
SQUAD NO: 10
HEIGHT: 5ft 8in
EDUCATION: Friary School, Lichfield; Cathedral School
TEAMS: Derbyshire, Nottinghamshire
CAREER: First-class: 2014; List A: 2010; T20: 2010



BEST BATTING: 63 Derbyshire vs Gloucestershire, Derby, 2014
BEST BOWLING: 2-8 Derbyshire vs Leicestershire, Leicester, 2014

CRICKETING HEROES? AB de Villiers and Chris Read
NON-CRICKETING HEROES? Steven Gerrard
IF YOU WEREN'T A CRICKETER? I'd be at university
IF YOU COULD BE SOMEONE ELSE FOR A DAY?
DESERT ISLAND DISC? Jay Z – Watch The Throne
FAVOURITE TV? Entourage, Prison Break, The Walking Dead
FANTASY SLIP CORDON? Keeper: Tiger Woods, 1st: Jay Z, 2nd: Steven Gerrard, 3rd: Mark Francis, Gully: Kevin Bridges
TWITTER FEED: @scottelstone

| Batting | Mat | Inns | NO | Runs | HS | Ave | SR | 100 | 50 | Ct | St |
|---|---|---|---|---|---|---|---|---|---|---|---|
| First-class | 6 | 9 | 0 | 199 | 63 | 22.11 | 35.40 | 0 | 1 | 2 | 0 |
| List A | 33 | 32 | 5 | 562 | 75* | 20.81 | 87.81 | 0 | 1 | 11 | 0 |
| Twenty20 | 27 | 21 | 10 | 177 | 24* | 16.09 | 133.08 | 0 | 0 | 11 | 0 |
| **Bowling** | **Mat** | **Balls** | **Runs** | **Wkts** | **BBI** | **BBM** | **Ave** | **Econ** | **SR** | **5w** | **10** |
| First-class | 6 | 181 | 124 | 6 | 2/8 | 2/30 | 20.66 | 4.11 | 30.1 | 0 | 0 |
| List A | 33 | 58 | 58 | 1 | 1/22 | 1/22 | 58.00 | 6.00 | 58.0 | 0 | 0 |
| Twenty20 | 27 | 24 | 43 | 0 | - | - | - | 10.75 | - | 0 | 0 |

# SEAN ERVINE LHB RM R0 W0 MVP85

FULL NAME: Sean Michael Ervine
BORN: December 6, 1982, Harare, Zimbabwe
SQUAD NO: 7
HEIGHT: 6ft 2in
NICKNAME: Slug, Lion
EDUCATION: Lomagundi College
TEAMS: Zimbabwe, Hampshire, Southern Rocks, Western Australia
CAREER: Test: 2003; ODI: 2001; First-class: 2001; List A: 2001; T20: 2005

BEST BATTING: 237* Hampshire vs Somerset, Southampton, 2010
BEST BOWLING: 6-82 Midlands vs Mashonaland, Kwekwe Sports Club, 2003
COUNTY CAPS: 2005

FAMILY TIES? My father Rory played first-class cricket in Zimbabwe. Brother Craig plays for the current Zimbabwe team. Brother Ryan plays for Southern Rocks in Zimbabwe. Uncle Neil played first-class cricket in Zimbabwe
IF YOU WEREN'T A CRICKETER? I'd be a golfer, fisherman or African wildlife conservationist
FAVOURITE TV? Sky Sports News, Discovery and National Geographic
FANTASY SLIP CORDON? Keeper: Donald 'Bomber' Campbell (funniest guy I know), 1st: Myself, 2nd: David Livingston (he'd have some great stories to tell), 3rd: Bon Jovi (he can sing us a tune if we ever got bored), Gully: Spider-Man (he wouldn't drop a thing and would catch the rest of ours too)
TWITTER FEED: @Slug_7

| Batting | Mat | Inns | NO | Runs | HS | Ave | SR | 100 | 50 | Ct | St |
|---|---|---|---|---|---|---|---|---|---|---|---|
| Tests | 5 | 8 | 0 | 261 | 86 | 32.62 | 55.41 | 0 | 3 | 7 | 0 |
| ODIs | 42 | 34 | 7 | 698 | 100 | 25.85 | 85.53 | 1 | 2 | 5 | 0 |
| First-class | 184 | 285 | 33 | 8995 | 237* | 35.69 | | 16 | 47 | 154 | 0 |
| List A | 227 | 200 | 29 | 5251 | 167* | 30.70 | | 7 | 24 | 62 | 0 |
| Twenty20 | 151 | 137 | 31 | 2666 | 82 | 25.15 | 127.98 | 0 | 9 | 50 | 0 |
| **Bowling** | **Mat** | **Balls** | **Runs** | **Wkts** | **BBI** | **BBM** | **Ave** | **Econ** | **SR** | **5w** | **10** |
| Tests | 5 | 570 | 388 | 9 | 4/146 | 4/146 | 43.11 | 4.08 | 63.3 | 0 | 0 |
| ODIs | 42 | 1649 | 1561 | 41 | 3/29 | 3/29 | 38.07 | 5.67 | 40.2 | 0 | 0 |
| First-class | 184 | 18376 | 10807 | 262 | 6/82 | | 41.24 | 3.52 | 70.1 | 5 | 0 |
| List A | 227 | 7387 | 6904 | 203 | 5/50 | 5/50 | 34.00 | 5.60 | 36.3 | 2 | 0 |
| Twenty20 | 151 | 1374 | 2025 | 66 | 4/12 | 4/12 | 30.68 | 8.84 | 20.8 | 0 | 0 |

## STEVIE ESKINAZI RHB WK R0 W0

FULL NAME: Stephen Sean Eskinazi
BORN: March 28, 1994, Johannesburg, Transvaal, South Africa
SQUAD NO: 28
HEIGHT: 6ft 2in
NICKNAME: Eski, Esk, Roo
EDUCATION: Christ Church Grammar School, Western Australia; University of Western Australia
TEAMS: Middlesex 2nd XI, Western Australia U19
CAREER: Yet to make first-team debut



---

FAMILY TIES? My father thinks he is the best batting coach in the Southern Hemisphere!
CAREER HIGHLIGHTS? Signing my first contract for Middlesex, scoring my first hundred for the club
SUPERSTITIONS? Same routine every time I cross the line with my bat in hand
CRICKETING HEROES? Graeme Smith and Ricky Ponting – both legends at the top of the order. Both had technical issues at points in their career yet still managed to dominate all bowling almost all the time
NON-CRICKETING HEROES? My family – for their unwavering support even though we live on opposite ends of the world for most of the year!
CRICKET RULE YOU'D CHANGE? Batsmen should start their innings on 10!
IF YOU COULD BE SOMEONE ELSE FOR A DAY? Ryan Gosling
DESERT ISLAND DISC? Ben Howard – Every Kingdom
ACCOMPLISHMENTS? Selection as a reserve in the Australian U16 hockey team. Graduating from school in the top four per cent of the state
SURPRISING FACT? I have three passports! Two months before I played my first game for Middlesex I was selected in an Australian U19 squad
FANTASY SLIP CORDON? Keeper: Me, 1st: Jamie Laing, 2nd: Ariana Grande, 3rd: The big lad that took that beauty in the World Cup for Bermuda (Dwayne Leverock)! Gully: Katniss Everdeen!
TWITTER FEED: @seskinazi

# LAURIE EVANS

## RHB RM R0 W0

WARWICKSHIRE

FULL NAME: Laurie John Evans
BORN: October 12, 1987, Lambeth, London
SQUAD NO: 32
HEIGHT: 6ft
NICKNAME: Birmingham Beckham
EDUCATION: Whitgift School; The John Fisher School; Durham University
TEAMS: Warwickshire, Surrey
CAREER: First-class: 2007; List A: 2009; T20: 2009

---

BEST BATTING: 178 Warwickshire vs Nottinghamshire, Birmingham, 2013
BEST BOWLING: 1-30 Surrey vs Bangladeshis, The Oval, 2010

---

CAREER HIGHLIGHTS? Winning the Championship and winning the T20 Cup
BEST PLAYER IN COUNTY CRICKET? Jeetan Patel
CRICKETING HEROES? Brian Lara – pure class
IF YOU WEREN'T A CRICKETER? Rugby
DESERT ISLAND DISC? Ed Sheeran – X
FAVOURITE TV? Top Gear
PET HATE? Bad manners
TWITTER FEED: @LaurieEvans32

| Batting | Mat | Inns | NO | Runs | HS | Ave | SR | 100 | 50 | Ct | St |
|---|---|---|---|---|---|---|---|---|---|---|---|
| First-class | 36 | 59 | 3 | 1927 | 178 | 34.41 | 46.04 | 4 | 10 | 23 | 0 |
| List A | 20 | 20 | 4 | 391 | 50 | 24.43 | 92.87 | 0 | 1 | 9 | 0 |
| Twenty20 | 34 | 28 | 10 | 509 | 69* | 28.27 | 138.69 | 0 | 4 | 13 | 0 |
| **Bowling** | **Mat** | **Balls** | **Runs** | **Wkts** | **BBI** | **BBM** | **Ave** | **Econ** | **SR** | **5w** | **10** |
| First-class | 36 | 324 | 228 | 1 | 1/30 | 1/30 | 228.00 | 4.22 | 324.0 | 0 | 0 |
| List A | 20 | 30 | 41 | 0 | - | - | - | 8.20 | - | 0 | 0 |
| Twenty20 | 34 | 22 | 35 | 1 | 1/5 | 1/5 | 35.00 | 9.54 | 22.0 | 0 | 0 |

# TOM FELL

## RHB WK R0 W0

FULL NAME: Thomas Charles Fell
BORN: October 17, 1993, Hillingdon, Middlesex
SQUAD NO: 29
HEIGHT: 6ft
NICKNAME: Lord
EDUCATION: Oakham School
TEAMS: Worcestershire
CAREER: First-class: 2013; List A: 2013



BEST BATTING: 133 Worcestershire vs Glamorgan, Worcester, 2014

FAMILY TIES? Dad played a few first-class games for Cambridge University
CAREER HIGHLIGHTS? Promotion to Division One in 2014
MOST MARKED CHARACTERISTIC? Laid-back/posh
SUPERSTITIONS? I tread on the rope when walking out to bat
CRICKETING HEROES? George Rhodes
NON-CRICKETING HEROES? Alan Partridge – he's a comedy genius
CRICKET RULE YOU'D CHANGE? Cricket couldn't possibly be improved
IF YOU COULD BE SOMEONE ELSE FOR A DAY? Dan Bilzerian
DESERT ISLAND DISC? Ed Sheeran
FAVOURITE TV? Made In Chelsea or Family Guy
LEAST FAVOURITE TV? I don't watch my least favourite programmes
ACCOMPLISHMENTS? I've got a hole in one
PET HATE? The gym, because it's hard
SURPRISING FACT? I enjoy a glass of red wine from time to time
FANTASY SLIP CORDON? Keeper: Alan Partridge, 1st slip: Ricky Gervais, 2nd slip: Karl Pilkington, 3rd slip: Me

| Batting | Mat | Inns | NO | Runs | HS | Ave | SR | 100 | 50 | Ct | St |
|---|---|---|---|---|---|---|---|---|---|---|---|
| First-class | 22 | 36 | 3 | 1040 | 133 | 31.51 | 45.27 | 2 | 4 | 16 | 0 |
| List A | 14 | 14 | 1 | 483 | 89 | 37.15 | 78.92 | 0 | 5 | 4 | 0 |
| **Bowling** | **Mat** | **Balls** | **Runs** | **Wkts** | **BBI** | **BBM** | **Ave** | **Econ** | **SR** | **5w** | **10** |
| First-class | 22 | - | - | - | - | - | - | - | - | - | - |
| List A | 14 | - | - | - | - | - | - | - | - | - | - |

# AARON FINCH — RHB SLA R0 W0

FULL NAME: Aaron James Finch
BORN: November 17, 1986, Colac, Australia
SQUAD NO: 20
HEIGHT: 5ft 8in
NICKNAME: Finchy
TEAMS: Australia, Yorkshire, Auckland, Delhi Daredevils, Melbourne Renegades, Pune Warriors, Rajasthan Royals, Victoria
CAREER: ODI: 2013; T20I: 2013; First-class: 2007; List A: 2007; T20: 2009

BEST BATTING: 122 Australia A vs Zimbabwe XI, Harare, 2011
BEST BOWLING: 1-0 Victoria vs Western Australia, Perth, 2013

TWITTER FEED: @AaronFinch5
NOTES: Australian batsman Finch returns for a second season at Yorkshire and will be available after he finishes his IPL stint. Finch scored a Championship century against Warwickshire last season and also made two T20 half-centuries. He holds the record for the highest score in a T20 international, hitting 156 from from 63 balls against England at Southampton in 2013, with 16 sixes. He was Man of the Series in Australia's T20 series win over England in January 2014. He captains Melbourne Renegades in the Big Bash League and has previously played for Pune Warriors and Delhi Daredevils in the IPL

| Batting | Mat | Inns | NO | Runs | HS | Ave | SR | 100 | 50 | Ct | St |
|---|---|---|---|---|---|---|---|---|---|---|---|
| ODIs | 45 | 43 | 0 | 1624 | 148 | 37.76 | 87.97 | 6 | 6 | 23 | 0 |
| T20Is | 22 | 22 | 3 | 756 | 156 | 39.78 | 152.41 | 1 | 5 | 5 | 0 |
| First-class | 46 | 77 | 1 | 2240 | 122 | 29.47 | 54.87 | 3 | 15 | 46 | 0 |
| List A | 107 | 105 | 4 | 4004 | 154 | 39.64 | 86.31 | 10 | 20 | 45 | 0 |
| Twenty20 | 123 | 120 | 12 | 3730 | 156 | 34.53 | 133.78 | 2 | 25 | 51 | 0 |
| **Bowling** | **Mat** | **Balls** | **Runs** | **Wkts** | **BBI** | **BBM** | **Ave** | **Econ** | **SR** | **5w** | **10** |
| ODIs | 45 | 55 | 48 | 2 | 1/2 | 1/2 | 24.00 | 5.23 | 27.5 | 0 | 0 |
| T20Is | 22 | 12 | 27 | 0 | - | - | - | 13.50 | - | 0 | 0 |
| First-class | 46 | 320 | 246 | 4 | 1/0 | 1/0 | 61.50 | 4.61 | 80.0 | 0 | 0 |
| List A | 107 | 244 | 213 | 7 | 2/44 | 2/44 | 30.42 | 5.23 | 34.8 | 0 | 0 |
| Twenty20 | 123 | 181 | 281 | 5 | 1/11 | 1/11 | 56.20 | 9.31 | 36.2 | 0 | 0 |

# HARRY FINCH

RHB RM R0 W0

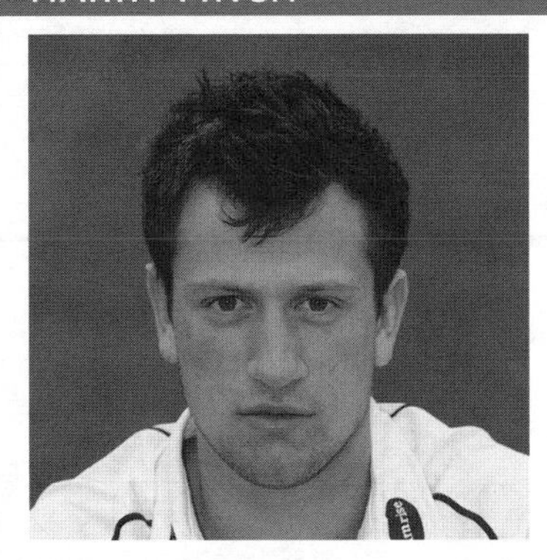

FULL NAME: Harry Zacariah Finch
BORN: February 10, 1995, Hastings, Sussex
SQUAD NO: 6
HEIGHT: 5ft 9in
NICKNAME: Chozza, Finchy
EDUCATION: Eastbourne College
TEAMS: Sussex
CAREER: First-class: 2013; List A:2013; T20I 2014



BEST BATTING: 11 Sussex vs Durham, Chester-le-Street, 2013
BEST BOWLING: 0-15 Sussex vs Durham, Chester-le-Street, 2013

FAMILY TIES? Played with my father [Jason], who is a Sussex junior coach
CAREER HIGHLIGHTS? Playing for England at the U19 World Cup, debuts in all forms for Sussex
BEST PLAYER IN COUNTY CRICKET? Ed Joyce
TIP FOR THE TOP? Craig Cachopa
CRICKETING HEROES? Ricky Ponting – aggressive style of cricket, Luke Wright – his attitude towards the game
NON-CRICKETING HEROES? Dad – for bringing me up and we both share the same passion
COACHING TIP? Concentrate on the ball not the player
IF YOU WEREN'T A CRICKETER? Struggling at uni
IF YOU COULD BE SOMEONE ELSE FOR A DAY? Gareth Bale
DESERT ISLAND DISC? Bastille
PET HATE? Moody people – they just bring people down
SURPRISING FACT? I've never been to a music festival or concert
TWITTER FEED: @hfinch72

| Batting | Mat | Inns | NO | Runs | HS | Ave | SR | 100 | 50 | Ct | St |
|---|---|---|---|---|---|---|---|---|---|---|---|
| First-class | 1 | 2 | 0 | 14 | 11 | 7.00 | 21.53 | 0 | 0 | 1 | 0 |
| List A | 2 | 1 | 1 | 92 | 92* | - | 158.62 | 0 | 1 | 0 | 0 |
| Twenty20 | 5 | 5 | 1 | 61 | 22 | 15.25 | 105.17 | 0 | 0 | 1 | 0 |
| **Bowling** | **Mat** | **Balls** | **Runs** | **Wkts** | **BBI** | **BBM** | **Ave** | **Econ** | **SR** | **5w** | **10** |
| First-class | 1 | 24 | 15 | 0 | - | - | - | 3.75 | - | 0 | 0 |
| List A | 2 | 6 | 2 | 0 | - | - | - | 2.00 | - | 0 | 0 |
| Twenty20 | 5 | - | - | - | - | - | - | - | - | - | - |

## STEVEN FINN RHB RF R0 W2 MVP74

FULL NAME: Steven Thomas Finn
BORN: April 4, 1989, Watford, Hertfordshire
SQUAD NO: 9
HEIGHT: 6ft 7in
NICKNAME: Finny, Cyril, Finndog
EDUCATION: Parmiter's School
TEAMS: England, Middlesex
CAREER: Test: 2010; ODI: 2011; T20I: 2011; First-class: 2005; List A: 2007; T20: 2008

BEST BATTING: 56 England vs New Zealand, Dunedin, 2013
BEST BOWLING: 9-37 Middlesex vs Worcestershire, Worcester, 2010
COUNTY CAPS: 2009

FAMILY TIES? My father, Terry, played Minor Counties cricket
CAREER HIGHLIGHTS? My Test debut, my first Test five-fer and winning the Ashes in Australia in 2010/11
CRICKETING HEROES? Glenn McGrath
NON-CRICKETING HEROES? Tony Soprano
FAVOURITE TV? Sopranos, Don't Tell The Bride, Come Dine With Me
LEAST FAVOURITE TV? Anything to do with hospitals
PET HATE? Loud eating. Can't stand it
TWITTER FEED: @finnysteve

| Batting | Mat | Inns | NO | Runs | HS | Ave | SR | 100 | 50 | Ct | St |
|---|---|---|---|---|---|---|---|---|---|---|---|
| Tests | 23 | 29 | 14 | 169 | 56 | 11.26 | 28.98 | 0 | 1 | 6 | 0 |
| ODIs | 56 | 23 | 9 | 114 | 35 | 8.14 | 60.31 | 0 | 0 | 11 | 0 |
| T20Is | 19 | 3 | 3 | 14 | 8* | - | 73.68 | 0 | 0 | 4 | 0 |
| First-class | 104 | 127 | 39 | 692 | 56 | 7.86 | 33.78 | 0 | 1 | 35 | 0 |
| List A | 110 | 41 | 15 | 247 | 42* | 9.50 | 58.11 | 0 | 0 | 18 | 0 |
| Twenty20 | 50 | 11 | 9 | 45 | 8* | 22.50 | 84.90 | 0 | 0 | 8 | 0 |
| **Bowling** | **Mat** | **Balls** | **Runs** | **Wkts** | **BBI** | **BBM** | **Ave** | **Econ** | **SR** | **5w** | **10** |
| Tests | 23 | 4348 | 2646 | 90 | 6/125 | 9/187 | 29.40 | 3.65 | 48.3 | 4 | 0 |
| ODIs | 56 | 2902 | 2416 | 86 | 5/33 | 5/33 | 28.09 | 4.99 | 33.7 | 2 | 0 |
| T20Is | 19 | 432 | 515 | 26 | 3/16 | 3/16 | 19.80 | 7.15 | 16.6 | 0 | 0 |
| First-class | 104 | 18889 | 11010 | 385 | 9/37 |  | 28.59 | 3.49 | 49.0 | 11 | 1 |
| List A | 110 | 5188 | 4362 | 157 | 5/33 | 5/33 | 27.78 | 5.04 | 33.0 | 3 | 0 |
| Twenty20 | 50 | 1058 | 1311 | 53 | 3/16 | 3/16 | 24.73 | 7.43 | 19.9 | 0 | 0 |

# MATTHEW FISHER

RHB RFM R0 W0

FULL NAME: Matthew David Fisher
BORN: November 9, 1997, York
SQUAD NO: 7
HEIGHT: 6ft 2in
EDUCATION: Easingwold School
TEAMS: Yorkshire
CAREER: List A: 2013



TWITTER FEED: @mfisher97

NOTES: Fisher became the youngest cricketer to play in a competitive county game when he made his debut for Yorkshire aged 15 years and 212 days in a YB40 match in 2013 against Leicestershire. He returned figures of 1-40, taking the wicket of Shiv Thakor. He has played 15 ODIs for England U19 and featured in the 2014 U19 World Cup in UAE, taking 10 wickets at 19.70 and earning the Man of the Match award against New Zealand for his spell of 3-18. He took three more wickets, for 55 runs, in the quarter-final win over India. Made a senior league century in 2011, aged only 13. Took 2-21 off 10 overs in the semi-final of the 2014 U19 World Cup

| Batting | Mat | Inns | NO | Runs | HS | Ave | SR | 100 | 50 | Ct | St |
|---|---|---|---|---|---|---|---|---|---|---|---|
| List A | 5 | 1 | 0 | 10 | 10 | 10.00 | 250.00 | 0 | 0 | 0 | 0 |
| **Bowling** | **Mat** | **Balls** | **Runs** | **Wkts** | **BBI** | **BBM** | **Ave** | **Econ** | **SR** | **5w** | **10** |
| List A | 5 | 228 | 186 | 3 | 1/29 | 1/29 | 62.00 | 4.89 | 76.0 | 0 | 0 |

# LUKE FLETCHER

RHB RFM R0 W0 MVP58

FULL NAME: Luke Jack Fletcher
BORN: September 18, 1988, Nottingham
SQUAD NO: 19
HEIGHT: 6ft 6in
NICKNAME: Fletch
EDUCATION: Henry Mellish Comprehensive School
TEAMS: Nottinghamshire, Wellington
CAREER: First-class: 2008; List A: 2008; T20: 2009

BEST BATTING: 92 Nottinghamshire vs Hampshire, Southampton, 2009
BEST BOWLING: 5-52 Nottinghamshire vs Warwickshire, Nottingham, 2013

CAREER HIGHLIGHTS? Winning a County Championship
SUPERSTITIONS? I always tap my bat down twice in the crease when the umpire calls over
CRICKETING HEROES? Freddie Flintoff
IF YOU WEREN'T A CRICKETER? Maybe a policeman
DESERT ISLAND DISC? Anything by Deadmau5
FAVOURITE TV? Match Of The Day
ACCOMPLISHMENTS? Played football at Wembley and Old Trafford as a youngster
TWITTER FEED: @fletcherluke

| Batting | Mat | Inns | NO | Runs | HS | Ave | SR | 100 | 50 | Ct | St |
|---|---|---|---|---|---|---|---|---|---|---|---|
| First-class | 65 | 97 | 19 | 1176 | 92 | 15.07 | 52.94 | 0 | 3 | 16 | 0 |
| List A | 40 | 20 | 7 | 142 | 40* | 10.92 | 94.66 | 0 | 0 | 4 | 0 |
| Twenty20 | 41 | 11 | 4 | 28 | 8 | 4.00 | 84.84 | 0 | 0 | 7 | 0 |
| Bowling | Mat | Balls | Runs | Wkts | BBI | BBM | Ave | Econ | SR | 5w | 10 |
| First-class | 65 | 11856 | 5910 | 202 | 5/52 | 9/108 | 29.25 | 2.99 | 58.6 | 3 | 0 |
| List A | 40 | 1633 | 1471 | 43 | 4/44 | 4/44 | 34.20 | 5.40 | 37.9 | 0 | 0 |
| Twenty20 | 41 | 885 | 1102 | 48 | 4/30 | 4/30 | 22.95 | 7.47 | 18.4 | 0 | 0 |

# ANDREW FLINTOFF RHB RFM R0 W0

FULL NAME: Andrew Flintoff
BORN: December 6, 1977, Preston, Lancashire
SQUAD NO: 26
HEIGHT: 6ft 4in
NICKNAME: Freddie
EDUCATION: Ribbleton Hall High School
TEAMS: England, Lancashire, Brisbane Heat, Chennai Super Kings, ICC World XI
CAREER: Test: 1998; ODI: 1999; T20I: 2005; First-class: 1995; List A: 1995; T20: 2004



BEST BATTING: 167 England vs West Indies, Birmingham, 2004
BEST BOWLING: 5-24 Lancashire vs Hampshire, Southampton, 1999

NOTES: Four years after apparently retiring from cricket, Flintoff made a comeback for Lancashire in the T20 Blast. Although it wasn't a dream return – Lancashire lost in the final – he showed enough to sign on for another season in 2015. He also turned out for Brisbane Heat in the 2014/15 Big Bash, although his stint will probably be remembered for singing Elvis songs while on the mic rather than any feats with bat or ball. He will be forever associated with England's stunning 2005 Ashes triumph, when he took 24 wickets and hit a century and three fifties to briefly emerge as the best player in the world. While he never quite reached those heights again, and suffered a 5-0 whitewash as England captain down under in 2006/07, he had one last international hurrah when he ran Ricky Ponting out at The Oval in 2009 to almost seal the Ashes

| Batting | Mat | Inns | NO | Runs | HS | Ave | SR | 100 | 50 | Ct | St |
|---|---|---|---|---|---|---|---|---|---|---|---|
| Tests | 79 | 130 | 9 | 3845 | 167 | 31.77 | 62.04 | 5 | 26 | 52 | 0 |
| ODIs | 141 | 122 | 16 | 3394 | 123 | 32.01 | 88.82 | 3 | 18 | 47 | 0 |
| T20Is | 7 | 7 | 1 | 76 | 31 | 12.66 | 126.66 | 0 | 0 | 5 | 0 |
| First-class | 183 | 290 | 23 | 9027 | 167 | 33.80 | | 15 | 53 | 185 | 0 |
| List A | 282 | 251 | 28 | 6641 | 143 | 29.78 | | 6 | 34 | 106 | 0 |
| Twenty20 | 39 | 36 | 6 | 683 | 93 | 22.76 | 142.88 | 0 | 3 | 19 | 0 |
| **Bowling** | **Mat** | **Balls** | **Runs** | **Wkts** | **BBI** | **BBM** | **Ave** | **Econ** | **SR** | **5w** | **10** |
| Tests | 79 | 14951 | 7410 | 226 | 5/58 | 8/156 | 32.78 | 2.97 | 66.1 | 3 | 0 |
| ODIs | 141 | 5624 | 4121 | 169 | 5/19 | 5/19 | 24.38 | 4.39 | 33.2 | 2 | 0 |
| T20Is | 7 | 150 | 161 | 5 | 2/23 | 2/23 | 32.20 | 6.44 | 30.0 | 0 | 0 |
| First-class | 183 | 22799 | 11059 | 350 | 5/24 | | 31.59 | 2.91 | 65.1 | 4 | 0 |
| List A | 282 | 9416 | 6536 | 289 | 5/19 | 5/19 | 22.61 | 4.16 | 32.5 | 2 | 0 |
| Twenty20 | 39 | 657 | 827 | 39 | 4/12 | 4/12 | 21.20 | 7.55 | 16.8 | 0 | 0 |

## BEN FOAKES

## RHB WK R0 W0

FULL NAME: Benjamin Thomas Foakes
BORN: February 15, 1993, Colchester, Essex
SQUAD NO: 4
HEIGHT: 6ft 2in
NICKNAME: Foakesy, The Rod
EDUCATION: Tendring Technology College
TEAMS: Surrey, England Lions, Essex
CAREER: First-class: 2011; List A: 2013; T20I: 2014

BEST BATTING: 132* Essex vs Gloucestershire, Bristol, 2014

FAMILY TIES? My old man bashed a few around in a local league but was a Premier League referee
CAREER HIGHLIGHTS? Getting my first ton in the Championship in 2013 and making my Lions debut against Australia A last year
BEST PLAYER IN COUNTY CRICKET? Darren Stevens
TIP FOR THE TOP? Jamie Porter and Nick Browne
MOST MARKED CHARACTERISTIC? Looking like Vincent Chase
SUPERSTITIONS? Itching my belly button and both lips between deliveries
CRICKETING HEROES? James Foster – I grew up watching him at Essex and he's the reason I took an interest in keeping
CRICKET RULE YOU'D CHANGE? First-ball grace!
IF YOU COULD BE SOMEONE ELSE FOR A DAY? Jean-Bernard Fernandez-Versini
DESERT ISLAND DISC? Akon – Lonely
PET HATE? When people are rude to service workers
SURPRISING FACT? I'm a better footballer than cricketer
TWITTER FEED: @Foakesey04

| Batting | Mat | Inns | NO | Runs | HS | Ave | SR | 100 | 50 | Ct | St |
|---|---|---|---|---|---|---|---|---|---|---|---|
| First-class | 32 | 45 | 6 | 1223 | 132* | 31.35 | 57.33 | 3 | 6 | 23 | 0 |
| List A | 11 | 10 | 1 | 161 | 56 | 17.88 | 95.26 | 0 | 2 | 6 | 1 |
| Twenty20 | 13 | 9 | 2 | 149 | 46 | 21.28 | 115.50 | 0 | 0 | 5 | 0 |
| **Bowling** | **Mat** | **Balls** | **Runs** | **Wkts** | **BBI** | **BBM** | **Ave** | **Econ** | **SR** | **5w** | **10** |
| First-class | 32 | 6 | 6 | 0 | - | - | - | 6.00 | - | 0 | 0 |
| List A | 11 | - | - | - | - | - | - | - | - | - | - |
| Twenty20 | 13 | - | - | - | - | - | - | - | - | - | - |

# MARK FOOTITT

## RHB LFM R0 W1 MVP21

FULL NAME: Mark Harold Alan Footitt
BORN: November 25, 1985, Nottingham
SQUAD NO: 4
HEIGHT: 6ft 2in
NICKNAME: Footy
EDUCATION: Carlton Le Willows School
TEAMS: Derbyshire, Nottinghamshire
CAREER: First-class: 2005; List A: 2002; T20: 2005



BEST BATTING: 30 Derbyshire vs Surrey, The Oval, 2010
BEST BOWLING: 6-48 Derbyshire vs Glamorgan, Derby, 2014

CAREER HIGHLIGHTS? Winning the 2012 Division Two Championship with Derbyshire
CRICKETING HEROES? Brett Lee
NON-CRICKETING HEROES? Adam Sandler and Sir Alex Ferguson
IF YOU WEREN'T A CRICKETER? Not too sure. A plumber?
DESERT ISLAND DISC? Anything from the 1980s
FAVOURITE TV? Boardwalk Empire
ACCOMPLISHMENTS? Becoming a dad to Heidi Footitt
SURPRISING FACT? I started off bowling right-arm then changed to left-arm
FANTASY SLIP CORDON? Keeper: Adam Sandler, 1st: Kevin James, 2nd: David Beckham 3rd: 'Stone Cold' Steve Austin, Gully: Hulk Hogan

| Batting | Mat | Inns | NO | Runs | HS | Ave | SR | 100 | 50 | Ct | St |
|---|---|---|---|---|---|---|---|---|---|---|---|
| First-class | 57 | 77 | 25 | 474 | 30 | 9.11 | 61.96 | 0 | 0 | 16 | 0 |
| List A | 28 | 7 | 3 | 24 | 11* | 6.00 | 75.00 | 0 | 0 | 4 | 0 |
| Twenty20 | 12 | 2 | 1 | 2 | 2* | 2.00 | 100.00 | 0 | 0 | 1 | 0 |
| **Bowling** | **Mat** | **Balls** | **Runs** | **Wkts** | **BBI** | **BBM** | **Ave** | **Econ** | **SR** | **5w** | **10** |
| First-class | 57 | 8813 | 5223 | 198 | 6/48 | | 26.37 | 3.55 | 44.5 | 11 | 0 |
| List A | 28 | 953 | 1026 | 36 | 5/28 | 5/28 | 28.50 | 6.45 | 26.4 | 2 | 0 |
| Twenty20 | 12 | 192 | 349 | 11 | 3/22 | 3/22 | 31.72 | 10.90 | 17.4 | 0 | 0 |

# JAMES FOSTER RHB WK R1 W0 MVP70

FULL NAME: James Savin Foster
BORN: April 15, 1980, Whipps Cross, Leytonstone, Essex
SQUAD NO: 7
HEIGHT: 6ft
NICKNAME: Fozzy, Chief
EDUCATION: Forest School; Durham University
TEAMS: England, Essex, Northern Districts
CAREER: Test: 2001; ODI: 2001; T20I: 2009; First-class: 2000; List A: 2000; T20: 2003

BEST BATTING: 212 Essex vs Leicestershire, Chelmsford, 2004
BEST BOWLING: 1-122 Essex vs Northamptonshire, Northampton, 2008
COUNTY CAPS: 2001; BENEFIT YEAR: 2011

FAMILY TIES? My dad played for Essex Amateurs
CAREER HIGHLIGHTS? Playing for my country
CRICKETING HEROES? Nasser Hussain, Stuart Law, Robert Rollins, Ian Healy, Jack Russell, Alec Stewart, Adam Gilchrist
NOTES: Current Essex captain in four-day cricket. Achieved the 'double' of 1,037 runs and 51 dismissals in 2004. In a Pro40 match against Durham in September 2009, he hit five sixes in consecutive balls from Scott Borthwick. Was the first wicketkeeper to stump Sachin Tendulkar in a Test, at Bangalore in 2001

| Batting | Mat | Inns | NO | Runs | HS | Ave | SR | 100 | 50 | Ct | St |
|---|---|---|---|---|---|---|---|---|---|---|---|
| Tests | 7 | 12 | 3 | 226 | 48 | 25.11 | 34.55 | 0 | 0 | 17 | 1 |
| ODIs | 11 | 6 | 3 | 41 | 13 | 13.66 | 57.74 | 0 | 0 | 13 | 7 |
| T20Is | 5 | 5 | 2 | 37 | 14* | 12.33 | 115.62 | 0 | 0 | 3 | 3 |
| First-class | 240 | 361 | 47 | 11805 | 212 | 37.59 | | 21 | 60 | 681 | 55 |
| List A | 202 | 151 | 40 | 3124 | 83* | 28.14 | | 0 | 15 | 223 | 59 |
| Twenty20 | 135 | 110 | 32 | 1828 | 65* | 23.43 | 139.86 | 0 | 6 | 59 | 42 |
| **Bowling** | **Mat** | **Balls** | **Runs** | **Wkts** | **BBI** | **BBM** | **Ave** | **Econ** | **SR** | **5w** | **10** |
| Tests | 7 | - | - | - | - | - | - | - | - | - | - |
| ODIs | 11 | - | - | - | - | - | - | - | - | - | - |
| T20Is | 5 | - | - | - | - | - | - | - | - | - | - |
| First-class | 240 | 84 | 128 | 1 | 1/122 | 1/122 | 128.00 | 9.14 | 84.0 | 0 | 0 |
| List A | 202 | - | - | - | - | - | - | - | - | - | - |
| Twenty20 | 135 | - | - | - | - | - | - | - | - | - | - |

# JAMES FRANKLIN

LHB LMF R0 W0

FULL NAME: James Edward Charles Franklin
BORN: November 7, 1980, Wellington
SQUAD NO: tbc
HEIGHT: 6ft 4in
NICKNAME: Franky, Tank
EDUCATION: Wellington College; Victoria University
TEAMS: New Zealand, Middlesex, Essex, Glamorgan, Gloucestershire, Mumbai Indians, Nottinghamshire, Wellington
CAREER: Test: 2001; ODI: 2001; T20I: 2006; First-class: 1998; List A: 1999; T20: 2004



BEST BATTING: 219 Wellington vs Auckland, Auckland, 2008
BEST BOWLING: 7-14 Gloucestershire vs Derbyshire, Bristol, 2010

FAMILY TIES? An aunt, Jean Coulston, represented NZ in the 1950s
CAREER HIGHLIGHTS? Nothing beats being involved in a team that wins trophies
CRICKETING HEROES? Wasim Akram – genius!
NON-CRICKETING HEROES? Mike Horn – an explorer who is an absolute legend!
COACHING TIP? Don't fear the air – there are plenty of gaps above the fielders
IF YOU WEREN'T A CRICKETER? Working for NASA on their next space programme
IF YOU COULD BE SOMEONE ELSE FOR A DAY? George Best
FAVOURITE TV? Breaking Bad
SURPRISING FACT? I can wiggle my ears
TWITTER FEED: @jecfranklin

| Batting | Mat | Inns | NO | Runs | HS | Ave | SR | 100 | 50 | Ct | St |
|---|---|---|---|---|---|---|---|---|---|---|---|
| Tests | 31 | 46 | 7 | 808 | 122* | 20.71 | 37.35 | 1 | 2 | 12 | 0 |
| ODIs | 110 | 80 | 27 | 1270 | 98* | 23.96 | 76.92 | 0 | 4 | 26 | 0 |
| T20Is | 38 | 31 | 8 | 463 | 60 | 20.13 | 118.41 | 0 | 2 | 13 | 0 |
| First-class | 163 | 253 | 36 | 8001 | 219 | 36.87 | | 19 | 34 | 68 | 0 |
| List A | 261 | 217 | 63 | 5114 | 133* | 33.20 | | 4 | 28 | 82 | 0 |
| Twenty20 | 171 | 152 | 35 | 3466 | 90 | 29.62 | 125.30 | 0 | 14 | 59 | 0 |
| **Bowling** | **Mat** | **Balls** | **Runs** | **Wkts** | **BBI** | **BBM** | **Ave** | **Econ** | **SR** | **5w** | **10** |
| Tests | 31 | 4767 | 2786 | 82 | 6/119 | 7/117 | 33.97 | 3.50 | 58.1 | 3 | 0 |
| ODIs | 110 | 3848 | 3354 | 81 | 5/42 | 5/42 | 41.40 | 5.22 | 47.5 | 1 | 0 |
| T20Is | 38 | 327 | 417 | 20 | 4/15 | 4/15 | 20.85 | 7.65 | 16.3 | 0 | 0 |
| First-class | 163 | 22941 | 12110 | 449 | 7/14 | | 26.97 | 3.16 | 51.0 | 14 | 1 |
| List A | 261 | 8756 | 7216 | 209 | 5/42 | 5/42 | 34.52 | 4.94 | 41.8 | 2 | 0 |
| Twenty20 | 171 | 1797 | 2488 | 78 | 4/15 | 4/15 | 31.89 | 8.30 | 23.0 | 0 | 0 |

# PAUL FRANKS LHB RMF R0 W2

FULL NAME: Paul John Franks
BORN: February 3, 1979, Mansfield, Nottinghamshire
SQUAD NO: 8
HEIGHT: 6ft 2in
NICKNAME: Franksie, Pike, The General
EDUCATION: Minster School, Southwell
TEAMS: England, Nottinghamshire, Mid West Rhinos
CAREER: ODI: 2000; First-class: 1996; List A: 1997; T20: 2003

BEST BATTING: 123* Nottinghamshire vs Leicestershire, Leicester, 2003
BEST BOWLING: 7-56 Nottinghamshire vs Middlesex, Lord's, 2000
COUNTY CAPS: 1999; BENEFIT YEAR: 2007

CAREER HIGHLIGHTS? My England debut, County Championship wins in 2005 and 2010, T20 Finals Day
CRICKETING HEROES? Ian Botham, Andrew Flintoff, Graeme Swann
NON-CRICKETING HEROES? Eric Cantona, Seve Ballesteros
FANTASY SLIP CORDON? Keeper: Paul Gascoigne, 1st: Me, 2nd: Elle Macpherson, 3rd: David Beckham, Gully: Luke Fletcher
TWITTER FEED: @thegeneral_8

| Batting | Mat | Inns | NO | Runs | HS | Ave | SR | 100 | 50 | Ct | St |
|---|---|---|---|---|---|---|---|---|---|---|---|
| ODIs | 1 | 1 | 0 | 4 | 4 | 4.00 | 23.52 | 0 | 0 | 1 | 0 |
| First-class | 215 | 313 | 56 | 7185 | 123* | 27.95 | | 4 | 41 | 69 | 0 |
| List A | 184 | 135 | 41 | 2039 | 84* | 21.69 | | 0 | 7 | 28 | 0 |
| Twenty20 | 50 | 30 | 13 | 287 | 29* | 16.88 | 117.62 | 0 | 0 | 8 | 0 |
| **Bowling** | **Mat** | **Balls** | **Runs** | **Wkts** | **BBI** | **BBM** | **Ave** | **Econ** | **SR** | **5w** | **10** |
| ODIs | 1 | 54 | 48 | 0 | - | - | - | 5.33 | - | 0 | 0 |
| First-class | 215 | 31587 | 17322 | 524 | 7/56 | | 33.05 | 3.29 | 60.2 | 11 | 0 |
| List A | 184 | 6757 | 5701 | 198 | 6/27 | 6/27 | 28.79 | 5.06 | 34.1 | 3 | 0 |
| Twenty20 | 50 | 479 | 687 | 20 | 2/12 | 2/12 | 34.35 | 8.60 | 23.9 | 0 | 0 |

## OLLIE FRECKINGHAM RHB RFM R0 W0

FULL NAME: Oliver Henry Freckingham
BORN: November 12, 1988, Oakham, Rutland
SQUAD NO: 24
HEIGHT: 6ft 1in
NICKNAME: Frecko
EDUCATION: King Edward VII School, Melton Mowbray
TEAMS: Leicestershire
CAREER: First-class: 2013; List A: 2014



BEST BATTING: 30 Leicestershire vs Gloucestershire, Bristol, 2013
BEST BOWLING: 6-125 Leicestershire vs Northamptonshire, Northampton, 2013

CAREER HIGHLIGHTS? My first-class debut
BEST PLAYER IN COUNTY CRICKET? Kumar Sangakkara
TIP FOR THE TOP? Angus Robson, Shiv Thakor
MOST MARKED CHARACTERISTIC? Rapidly thinning hair
CRICKETING HEROES? Andrew Flintoff – legend
NON-CRICKETING HEROES? Tiger Woods – single-handedly changed golf to what it is today. Best sportsman ever
IF YOU WEREN'T A CRICKETER? Cutting greens at Rutland County Golf Club
IF YOU COULD BE SOMEONE ELSE FOR A DAY? Rory McIlroy
DESERT ISLAND DISC? Westlife – Coast To Coast
FAVOURITE TV? EastEnders
ACCOMPLISHMENTS? Being a scratch golfer – however I don't know how I managed it the way I hit it these days
PET HATE? Abbreviation in text messages, e.g. wbu, tbh, tbf
FANTASY SLIP CORDON? Keeper: David Beckham, 1st: James Corden, 2nd: Myself, 3rd: Kelly Brook, Gully: Michelle Keegan
TWITTER FEED: @olliefreck

| Batting | Mat | Inns | NO | Runs | HS | Ave | SR | 100 | 50 | Ct | St |
|---|---|---|---|---|---|---|---|---|---|---|---|
| First-class | 18 | 25 | 3 | 216 | 30 | 9.81 | 37.82 | 0 | 0 | 4 | 0 |
| List A | 1 | - | - | - | - | - | - | - | - | 1 | 0 |
| **Bowling** | **Mat** | **Balls** | **Runs** | **Wkts** | **BBI** | **BBM** | **Ave** | **Econ** | **SR** | **5w** | **10** |
| First-class | 18 | 2885 | 1946 | 44 | 6/125 | 9/188 | 44.22 | 4.04 | 65.5 | 1 | 0 |
| List A | 1 | 36 | 38 | 2 | 2/38 | 2/38 | 19.00 | 6.33 | 18.0 | 0 | 0 |

## JAMES FULLER RHB RF R0 W0

FULL NAME: James Kerr Fuller
BORN: January 24, 1990, Cape Town, South Africa
SQUAD NO: 26
HEIGHT: 6ft 3in
NICKNAME: Fuller, Foz, Fozzy
EDUCATION: Westlake Boys High School; University of Otago
TEAMS: Gloucestershire, Otago
CAREER: First-class: 2010; List A: 2011; T20: 2011

BEST BATTING: 57 Gloucestershire vs Leicestershire, Cheltenham, 2012
BEST BOWLING: 6-24 Otago vs Wellington, Dunedin, 2013
COUNTY CAPS: 2011

BEST PLAYER IN COUNTY CRICKET? Will Gidman
TIP FOR THE TOP? Tom Hampton
MOST MARKED CHARACTERISTIC? A great big bowlers' ass
CRICKETING HEROES? Brett Lee and Shaun Tait – because they bowl rockets. Glenn McGrath – because he's the best fast bowler ever. Chris Cairns and Lance Klusener – because they were big impact players and could do everything
IF YOU COULD BE SOMEONE ELSE FOR A DAY? I would be Usain Bolt at the Olympics
DESERT ISLAND DISC? Fall Out Boy – Centuries
ACCOMPLISHMENTS? Shooting par through 18 holes of golf, eighth generation on Titan Fall and doing a personal training course
PET HATE? Leaving the sponge in the sink. It stays wet which really grinds my gears
SURPRISING FACT? I can swim 50m under water and hold my breath for three minutes and 10 seconds (so far!)
TWITTER FEED: @James_Fuller246

| Batting | Mat | Inns | NO | Runs | HS | Ave | SR | 100 | 50 | Ct | St |
|---|---|---|---|---|---|---|---|---|---|---|---|
| First-class | 27 | 32 | 3 | 387 | 57 | 13.34 | 60.00 | 0 | 1 | 8 | 0 |
| List A | 26 | 21 | 7 | 295 | 43 | 21.07 | 104.98 | 0 | 0 | 7 | 0 |
| Twenty20 | 33 | 19 | 7 | 238 | 36 | 19.83 | 150.63 | 0 | 0 | 13 | 0 |
| **Bowling** | **Mat** | **Balls** | **Runs** | **Wkts** | **BBI** | **BBM** | **Ave** | **Econ** | **SR** | **5w** | **10** |
| First-class | 27 | 4137 | 2452 | 74 | 6/24 | 10/79 | 33.13 | 3.55 | 55.9 | 4 | 1 |
| List A | 26 | 1048 | 1012 | 43 | 6/35 | 6/35 | 23.53 | 5.79 | 24.3 | 1 | 0 |
| Twenty20 | 33 | 708 | 983 | 49 | 4/24 | 4/24 | 20.06 | 8.33 | 14.4 | 0 | 0 |

# ANDREW GALE LHB LB R1 W0

FULL NAME: Andrew William Gale
BORN: November 28, 1983, Dewsbury, Yorkshire
SQUAD NO: 26
HEIGHT: 6ft 1in
NICKNAME: Galey, Bobby, G
EDUCATION: Whitcliffe Mount School
TEAMS: Yorkshire, England Lions
CAREER: First-class: 2004; List A: 2002; T20: 2004

BEST BATTING: 272* Yorkshire vs Nottinghamshire, Scarborough, 2013
BEST BOWLING: 1-33 Yorkshire vs Loughborough UCCE, Leeds, 2007
COUNTY CAPS: 2008

CAREER HIGHLIGHTS? Captaining Yorkshire to winning the County Championship in 2014 and scoring 272 vs Notts
BEST PLAYER IN COUNTY CRICKET? Adam Lyth
TIP FOR THE TOP? Matt Fisher
SUPERSTITIONS? I hate odd numbers
CRICKETING HEROES? Ricky Ponting
NON-CRICKETING HEROES? Andy Booth – Huddersfield Town legend
IF YOU WEREN'T A CRICKETER? Cleaning toilets
IF YOU COULD BE SOMEONE ELSE FOR A DAY? Dan Bilzerian
DESERT ISLAND DISC? Only Fools And Horses theme tune
FAVOURITE TV? Game Of Thrones
LEAST FAVOURITE TV? Antiques Roadshow
SURPRISING FACT? Grade Two in piano
TWITTER FEED: @galeylad

| Batting | Mat | Inns | NO | Runs | HS | Ave | SR | 100 | 50 | Ct | St |
|---|---|---|---|---|---|---|---|---|---|---|---|
| First-class | 124 | 191 | 17 | 6601 | 272 | 37.93 | | 17 | 26 | 44 | 0 |
| List A | 132 | 123 | 12 | 3412 | 125* | 30.73 | | 2 | 18 | 26 | 0 |
| Twenty20 | 96 | 88 | 9 | 2014 | 91 | 25.49 | 121.76 | 0 | 15 | 30 | 0 |
| **Bowling** | **Mat** | **Balls** | **Runs** | **Wkts** | **BBI** | **BBM** | **Ave** | **Econ** | **SR** | **5w** | **10** |
| First-class | 124 | 115 | 238 | 1 | 1/33 | 1/33 | 238.00 | 12.41 | 115.0 | 0 | 0 |
| List A | 132 | - | - | - | - | - | - | - | - | - | - |
| Twenty20 | 96 | - | - | - | - | - | - | - | - | - | - |

# JOE GATTING RHB OB R0 W0

FULL NAME: Joe Stephen Gatting
BORN: November 25, 1987, Brighton
SQUAD NO: 6
HEIGHT: 5ft 11in
EDUCATION: Brighton College
TEAMS: Hampshire, Sussex
CAREER: First-class: 2009; List A: 2009; T20: 2009

BEST BATTING: 152 Sussex vs Cambridge UCCE, Fenner's, 2009
BEST BOWLING: 1-8 Sussex vs Nottinghamshire, Nottingham, 2011

FAMILY TIES? My uncle [Mike of England and Middlesex] and dad [Steve of Middlesex 2nd XI] both played
CAREER HIGHLIGHTS? Champions League in India. First centuries in first-class and List A cricket
SUPERSTITIONS? Left pad first
CRICKETING HEROES? My uncle, Brian Lara and Andrew Symonds
NON-CRICKETING HEROES? Tiger Woods
IF YOU WEREN'T A CRICKETER? Footballer
FAVOURITE TV? Celebrity Juice
ACCOMPLISHMENTS? Playing Championship football for Brighton and Hove Albion
SURPRISING FACT? I'm colour-blind (green and red)
FANTASY SLIP CORDON? Keeper: John Bishop (good for sledging), 1st: James Corden (funny banter and would have a supply of sweets), 2nd: Me, 3rd: Eric Cantona (arrogant and skilful), Gully: Mike Tyson (to scare the batsmen)
TWITTER FEED: @joegatting25

| Batting | Mat | Inns | NO | Runs | HS | Ave | SR | 100 | 50 | Ct | St |
|---|---|---|---|---|---|---|---|---|---|---|---|
| First-class | 43 | 62 | 5 | 1567 | 152 | 27.49 | 57.75 | 3 | 7 | 19 | 0 |
| List A | 45 | 41 | 5 | 988 | 122 | 27.44 | 86.06 | 1 | 4 | 16 | 0 |
| Twenty20 | 54 | 42 | 9 | 491 | 45* | 14.87 | 111.84 | 0 | 0 | 22 | 0 |
| **Bowling** | **Mat** | **Balls** | **Runs** | **Wkts** | **BBI** | **BBM** | **Ave** | **Econ** | **SR** | **5w** | **10** |
| First-class | 43 | 228 | 152 | 2 | 1/8 | 1/8 | 76.00 | 4.00 | 114.0 | 0 | 0 |
| List A | 45 | 20 | 22 | 0 | - | - | - | 6.60 | - | 0 | 0 |
| Twenty20 | 54 | 10 | 14 | 1 | 1/12 | 1/12 | 14.00 | 8.40 | 10.0 | 0 | 0 |

# ALEX GIDMAN

## RHB RM R6 W0 MVP80

FULL NAME: Alexander Peter Richard Gidman
BORN: June 22, 1981, High Wycombe, Buckinghamshire
SQUAD NO: 3
HEIGHT: 6ft 2in
NICKNAME: Gido
EDUCATION: Wycliffe College
TEAMS: Worcestershire, England Lions, Gloucestershire, Otago
CAREER: First-class: 2002; List A: 2001; T20: 2003



BEST BATTING: 264 Gloucestershire vs Leicestershire, Bristol, 2014
BEST BOWLING: 4-47 Gloucestershire vs Glamorgan, Cardiff, 2009
COUNTY CAPS: BENEFIT YEAR: 2012 (Gloucestershire)

FAMILY TIES? My brother Will plays for Notts
CAREER HIGHLIGHTS? Two Lord's final victories, captaining England A
MOST MARKED CHARACTERISTIC? Being grumpy, drinking espresso
CRICKETING HEROES? Steve Waugh – because of the way he played his cricket and the way he captained. Mark Ramprakash – for pure batsmanship
CRICKET RULE YOU'D CHANGE? I would change the structure of four-day cricket. Top secret, I'm afraid.
IF YOU WEREN'T A CRICKETER? A wannabe rock star
IF YOU COULD BE SOMEONE ELSE FOR A DAY? Caleb Followill
DESERT ISLAND DISC? Only By The Night – Kings of Leon
PET HATE? Burnt coffee, because it tastes disgusting!
SURPRISING FACT? I love cooking and taught myself the guitar five years ago
FANTASY SLIP CORDON? Keeper: Jack Russell, 1st: Me, 2nd: Caleb Followill, 3rd: Noel Gallagher, Gully: Steve Waugh (Music and cricket – perfect)

| Batting | Mat | Inns | NO | Runs | HS | Ave | SR | 100 | 50 | Ct | St |
|---|---|---|---|---|---|---|---|---|---|---|---|
| First-class | 191 | 328 | 26 | 11182 | 264 | 37.02 | 58.54 | 24 | 57 | 128 | 0 |
| List A | 194 | 182 | 20 | 4458 | 116 | 27.51 | | 5 | 21 | 67 | 0 |
| Twenty20 | 95 | 84 | 11 | 1448 | 64 | 19.83 | 119.37 | 0 | 4 | 22 | 0 |
| **Bowling** | **Mat** | **Balls** | **Runs** | **Wkts** | **BBI** | **BBM** | **Ave** | **Econ** | **SR** | **5w** | **10** |
| First-class | 191 | 7304 | 4521 | 102 | 4/47 | | 44.32 | 3.71 | 71.6 | 0 | 0 |
| List A | 194 | 3256 | 2786 | 71 | 5/42 | 5/42 | 39.23 | 5.13 | 45.8 | 1 | 0 |
| Twenty20 | 95 | 292 | 410 | 9 | 2/24 | 2/24 | 45.55 | 8.42 | 32.4 | 0 | 0 |

## WILL GIDMAN

## LHB RMF R1 W2 MVP16

FULL NAME: William Robert Simon Gidman
BORN: February 14, 1985, High Wycombe, Buckinghamshire
SQUAD NO: tbc
HEIGHT: 6ft 2in
NICKNAME: Giddo, Gidders, Wilbur
EDUCATION: Wycliffe College
TEAMS: Nottinghamshire, Durham, Gloucestershire
CAREER: First-class: 2007; List A: 2003; T20: 2011

BEST BATTING: 143 Gloucestershire vs Leicestershire, Bristol, 2013
BEST BOWLING: 6-15 Gloucestershire vs Leicestershire, Bristol, 2013
COUNTY CAPS: 2011 (Gloucestershire)

FAMILY TIES? My brother Alex plays for Worcestershire
CAREER HIGHLIGHTS? The 2011 season, any five-wicket hauls and any hundreds
TIP FOR THE TOP? Gareth Roderick, Jake Ball
MOST MARKED CHARACTERISTIC? My big nose
CRICKETING HEROES? Any allrounder – I love guys who give different things a go
NON-CRICKETING HEROES? Jonny Wilkinson – due to his sheer professionalism and work ethic. Muhammad Ali – because of his personality and love for sport and life
COACHING TIP? Bowling – practise yorkers sooner rather than later
IF YOU WEREN'T A CRICKETER? I'd own a coffee shop
IF YOU COULD BE SOMEONE ELSE FOR A DAY? David Beckham
DESERT ISLAND DISC? Meatloaf – Greatest Hits
PET HATE? Pessimism
SURPRISING FACT? Not really – I'm fairly plain
TWITTER FEED: @wgiddo

| Batting | Mat | Inns | NO | Runs | HS | Ave | SR | 100 | 50 | Ct | St |
|---|---|---|---|---|---|---|---|---|---|---|---|
| First-class | 56 | 85 | 16 | 2752 | 143 | 39.88 | 51.34 | 5 | 14 | 14 | 0 |
| List A | 46 | 30 | 6 | 615 | 76 | 25.62 | | 0 | 2 | 12 | 0 |
| Twenty20 | 13 | 12 | 4 | 154 | 40* | 19.25 | 103.35 | 0 | 0 | 3 | 0 |
| **Bowling** | **Mat** | **Balls** | **Runs** | **Wkts** | **BBI** | **BBM** | **Ave** | **Econ** | **SR** | **5w** | **10** |
| First-class | 56 | 8989 | 4294 | 194 | 6/15 | 10/43 | 22.13 | 2.86 | 46.3 | 9 | 1 |
| List A | 46 | 1602 | 1296 | 42 | 4/36 | 4/36 | 30.85 | 4.85 | 38.1 | 0 | 0 |
| Twenty20 | 13 | 132 | 173 | 6 | 2/23 | 2/23 | 28.83 | 7.86 | 22.0 | 0 | 0 |

# BILLY GODLEMAN LHB LB R0 W0

FULL NAME: Billy Ashley Godleman
BORN: February 11, 1989, Camden, London
SQUAD NO: 1
HEIGHT: 6ft 3in
EDUCATION: Islington Green School
TEAMS: Derbyshire, Essex, Middlesex
CAREER: First-class: 2005; List A: 2007; T20: 2006



BEST BATTING: 130 Essex vs Leicestershire, Leicester, 2011

NOTES: At 17, left-hander Godleman became the second-youngest debutant ever for Middlesex when he turned out for them against Cambridge at Fenner's in 2005. The first-youngest was Steven Finn, playing in the same game. He was called up for England U19 in 2007 for whom he made 149* against Pakistan at Grace Road and big things were expected of him. Joined Essex in 2009 where he hit his highest first-class score of 130 vs Leicestershire at Leicester two years later. After mixed success, he was released and joined Derbyshire in 2012. Did not feature heavily in the 2013 season but returned to the first team for the last two YB40 games, scoring 60 against Essex at Colchester. In 2014 he hit his first century for Derbyshire, scoring 104* against Surrey at The Oval

| Batting | Mat | Inns | NO | Runs | HS | Ave | SR | 100 | 50 | Ct | St |
|---|---|---|---|---|---|---|---|---|---|---|---|
| First-class | 88 | 152 | 5 | 4207 | 130 | 28.61 | 41.50 | 6 | 22 | 62 | 0 |
| List A | 30 | 29 | 4 | 698 | 96 | 27.92 | 69.10 | 0 | 3 | 14 | 0 |
| Twenty20 | 31 | 28 | 0 | 505 | 69 | 18.03 | 110.98 | 0 | 3 | 18 | 0 |
| **Bowling** | **Mat** | **Balls** | **Runs** | **Wkts** | **BBI** | **BBM** | **Ave** | **Econ** | **SR** | **5w** | **10** |
| First-class | 88 | 30 | 35 | 0 | - | - | - | 7.00 | - | 0 | 0 |
| List A | 30 | - | - | - | - | - | - | - | - | - | - |
| Twenty20 | 31 | - | - | - | - | - | - | - | - | - | - |

## RECORDO GORDON

## RHB RFM R0 W0

FULL NAME: Recordo Olton Gordon
BORN: October 12, 1991, St Elizabeth's, Jamaica
SQUAD NO: 44
EDUCATION: Aston Manor Academy; Hamstead Hall Sixth Form
TEAMS: Warwickshire
CAREER: First-class: 2013; List A: 2013; T20: 2014

BEST BATTING: 14 Warwickshire vs Somerset, Taunton, 2014
BEST BOWLING: 4-53 Warwickshire vs Somerset, Taunton, 2014

CRICKETING HEROES? Courtney Walsh and Curtly Ambrose
NON-CRICKETING HEROES? My father
IF YOU WEREN'T A CRICKETER? I'd be at universiy
FAVOURITE TV? The Big Bang Theory
ACCOMPLISHMENTS? Being head boy of my school
SURPRISING FACT? I'm a good cook and baker
TWITTER FEED: @recordogordon

| Batting | Mat | Inns | NO | Runs | HS | Ave | SR | 100 | 50 | Ct | St |
|---|---|---|---|---|---|---|---|---|---|---|---|
| First-class | 6 | 5 | 2 | 52 | 14* | 17.33 | 26.94 | 0 | 0 | 3 | 0 |
| List A | 7 | 2 | 0 | 1 | 1 | 0.50 | 20.00 | 0 | 0 | 0 | 0 |
| Twenty20 | 6 | - | - | - | - | - | - | - | - | 0 | 0 |
| **Bowling** | **Mat** | **Balls** | **Runs** | **Wkts** | **BBI** | **BBM** | **Ave** | **Econ** | **SR** | **5w** | **10** |
| First-class | 6 | 800 | 413 | 13 | 4/53 | 4/80 | 31.76 | 3.09 | 61.5 | 0 | 0 |
| List A | 7 | 318 | 336 | 9 | 3/25 | 3/25 | 37.33 | 6.33 | 35.3 | 0 | 0 |
| Twenty20 | 6 | 102 | 147 | 9 | 3/18 | 3/18 | 16.33 | 8.64 | 11.3 | 0 | 0 |

# LEWIS GREGORY RHB RFM R0 W0 MVP33

FULL NAME: Lewis Gregory
BORN: May 24, 1992, Plymouth
SQUAD NO: 24
EDUCATION: Hele's School, Plymouth
TEAMS: Somerset
CAREER: First-class: 2011; List A: 2010; T20: 2011



BEST BATTING: 69 Somerset vs Yorkshire, Taunton, 2014
BEST BOWLING: 6-47 Somerset vs Northamptonshire, Northampton, 2014

TWITTER FEED: @lewisgregory23
NOTES: Former England U19 skipper. Took a hat-trick for Somerset's 2nd XI against Essex in 2010. Claimed 4-49 on his List A debut in 2010 against the touring Pakistanis. The leading wicket-taker in the 2011 FL t20, claiming 18 wickets at 17. Returned figures of 4-39 in Somerset's 2012 FL t20 quarter-final win against Essex. In 2013 he played six first-class matches, taking 14 wickets at 25.57, including a career-best 5-38 against Middlesex at Lord's, and scored a maiden half-century against Derbyshire at Taunton. He had another good season in 2014, taking 43 wickets at 26.06 in the Championship, and hitting a maiden one-day century in the RL Cup

| Batting | Mat | Inns | NO | Runs | HS | Ave | SR | 100 | 50 | Ct | St |
|---|---|---|---|---|---|---|---|---|---|---|---|
| First-class | 26 | 34 | 4 | 593 | 69 | 19.76 | 57.91 | 0 | 2 | 8 | 0 |
| List A | 31 | 18 | 2 | 334 | 105* | 20.87 | 98.81 | 1 | 0 | 13 | 0 |
| Twenty20 | 28 | 14 | 5 | 149 | 22 | 16.55 | 110.37 | 0 | 0 | 9 | 0 |
| **Bowling** | **Mat** | **Balls** | **Runs** | **Wkts** | **BBI** | **BBM** | **Ave** | **Econ** | **SR** | **5w** | **10** |
| First-class | 26 | 3297 | 1930 | 70 | 6/47 | 11/122 | 27.57 | 3.51 | 47.1 | 4 | 1 |
| List A | 31 | 977 | 1031 | 39 | 4/27 | 4/27 | 26.43 | 6.33 | 25.0 | 0 | 0 |
| Twenty20 | 28 | 435 | 565 | 32 | 4/15 | 4/15 | 17.65 | 7.79 | 13.5 | 0 | 0 |

# DAVID GRIFFITHS LHB RF R0 W0

FULL NAME: David Andrew Griffiths
BORN: September 10, 1985, Newport, Isle of Wight
SQUAD NO: 18
HEIGHT: 5ft 11in
NICKNAME: Griffindor, SOG, Griffta
EDUCATION: Sandown High School
TEAMS: Kent, Hampshire
CAREER: First-class: 2006; List A: 2008; T20: 2007

BEST BATTING: 31* Hampshire vs Surrey, Southampton, 2007
BEST BOWLING: 6-63 Kent vs Gloucestershire, Canterbury, 2014

FAMILY TIES? My dad captained Wales and my step-dad and uncles have all played for Isle of Wight
CAREER HIGHLIGHTS? Winning a Pro40 final at Lord's off the last ball
SUPERSTITIONS? I always turn right at the end of my run-up and always put my left boot on first
CRICKETING HEROES? Darren Gough, Brett Lee, Graham Thorpe
NON-CRICKETING HEROES? David Beckham
IF YOU WEREN'T A CRICKETER? Anything outside, maybe a farmer
DESERT ISLAND DISC? Jack Johnson
FAVOURITE TV? Game Of Thrones
FANTASY SLIP CORDON? Keeper: Brian Lara, 1st: James Corden, 2nd: Charlize Theron, 3rd: Scarlett Johansson, Gully: Sir Alex Ferguson
TWITTER FEED: @griffta18

| Batting | Mat | Inns | NO | Runs | HS | Ave | SR | 100 | 50 | Ct | St |
|---|---|---|---|---|---|---|---|---|---|---|---|
| First-class | 38 | 52 | 19 | 220 | 31* | 6.66 | 26.34 | 0 | 0 | 4 | 0 |
| List A | 26 | 10 | 8 | 30 | 12* | 15.00 | 41.66 | 0 | 0 | 5 | 0 |
| Twenty20 | 16 | 2 | 2 | 22 | 18* | - | 88.00 | 0 | 0 | 4 | 0 |
| **Bowling** | **Mat** | **Balls** | **Runs** | **Wkts** | **BBI** | **BBM** | **Ave** | **Econ** | **SR** | **5w** | **10** |
| First-class | 38 | 6007 | 3828 | 113 | 6/63 | 7/102 | 33.87 | 3.82 | 53.1 | 4 | 0 |
| List A | 26 | 981 | 982 | 34 | 4/29 | 4/29 | 28.88 | 6.00 | 28.8 | 0 | 0 |
| Twenty20 | 16 | 301 | 407 | 17 | 4/22 | 4/22 | 23.94 | 8.11 | 17.7 | 0 | 0 |

# GAVIN GRIFFITHS

## RHB RFM R0 W0

FULL NAME: Gavin Timothy Griffiths
BORN: November 19, 1993, Ormskirk, Lancashire
SQUAD NO: 18
HEIGHT: 6ft 2in
NICKNAME: Gavlar
EDUCATION: St Mary's College, Crosby
TEAMS: Lancashire
CAREER: List A: 2014



CAREER HIGHLIGHTS? Making my first-team debut for Lancashire last season
BEST PLAYER IN COUNTY CRICKET? Ben Stokes
TIP FOR THE TOP? Haseeb Hameed, Liam Livingstone, Tom Bailey
MOST MARKED CHARACTERISTIC? My brick-head
CRICKETING HEROES? Allan Donald, Dale Steyn, Freddie Flintoff
CRICKET RULE YOU'D CHANGE? Red-ball cricket – new ball at both ends
IF YOU COULD BE SOMEONE ELSE FOR A DAY? Dan Bilzerian
DESERT ISLAND DISC? Coldplay
FAVOURITE TV? The Inbetweeners
ACCOMPLISHMENTS? Playing chess for England and being a goalkeeper at Everton's academy
PET HATE? Selfishness
TWITTER FEED: @Gavvlar

| Batting | Mat | Inns | NO | Runs | HS | Ave | SR | 100 | 50 | Ct | St |
|---|---|---|---|---|---|---|---|---|---|---|---|
| List A | 1 | - | - | - | - | - | - | - | - | 2 | 0 |
| **Bowling** | **Mat** | **Balls** | **Runs** | **Wkts** | **BBI** | **BBM** | **Ave** | **Econ** | **SR** | **5w** | **10** |
| List A | 1 | 48 | 41 | 0 | - | - | - | 5.12 | - | 0 | 0 |

# TIM GROENEWALD RHB RFM R0 W0

FULL NAME: Timothy Duncan Groenewald
BORN: January 10, 1984, Pietermaritzburg, South Africa
SQUAD NO: 5
HEIGHT: 6ft
NICKNAME: TG, Groeners
EDUCATION: Maritzburg College; University of South Africa
TEAMS: Somerset, Derbyshire, Warwickshire
CAREER: First-class: 2006; List A: 2006; T20: 2006

---

BEST BATTING: 78 Warwickshire vs Bangladesh A, Birmingham, 2008
BEST BOWLING: 6-50 Derbyshire vs Surrey, Whitgift School, 2009
COUNTY CAPS: 2011 (Derbyshire)

---

CAREER HIGHLIGHTS? My hat-trick vs Essex in the 2013 Championship
BEST PLAYER IN COUNTY CRICKET? Ed Joyce
CRICKETING HEROES? Hansie Cronje, Jonty Rhodes, Allan Donald
NON-CRICKETING HEROES? My little boy Jamie – he means the world to me!
CRICKET RULE YOU'D CHANGE? Edges through the slips for four don't count – it should be dead ball! And people who clap edged boundaries to be removed from the ground!
COACHING TIP? Decide what you're going to bowl at the top of your mark and focus on executing that ball. Don't change as you're about to bowl
IF YOU WEREN'T A CRICKETER? Coffee-shop owner
IF YOU COULD BE SOMEONE ELSE FOR A DAY? Mark Footitt – I'd love to know what goes through his head!
PET HATE? Bad drivers, slow golfers that don't let you through, bad manners, loud eaters!
SURPRISING FACT? I love cricket statistics
TWITTER FEED: @timmyg12

| Batting | Mat | Inns | NO | Runs | HS | Ave | SR | 100 | 50 | Ct | St |
|---|---|---|---|---|---|---|---|---|---|---|---|
| First-class | 91 | 126 | 34 | 1704 | 78 | 18.52 | 50.01 | 0 | 6 | 33 | 0 |
| List A | 77 | 46 | 15 | 550 | 57 | 17.74 | 110.00 | 0 | 2 | 19 | 0 |
| Twenty20 | 82 | 33 | 14 | 346 | 41 | 18.21 | 130.07 | 0 | 0 | 25 | 0 |
| **Bowling** | **Mat** | **Balls** | **Runs** | **Wkts** | **BBI** | **BBM** | **Ave** | **Econ** | **SR** | **5w** | **10** |
| First-class | 91 | 15439 | 7975 | 257 | 6/50 | 8/97 | 31.03 | 3.09 | 60.0 | 11 | 0 |
| List A | 77 | 2882 | 2642 | 82 | 4/22 | 4/22 | 32.21 | 5.50 | 35.1 | 0 | 0 |
| Twenty20 | 82 | 1475 | 1972 | 71 | 4/21 | 4/21 | 27.77 | 8.02 | 20.7 | 0 | 0 |

## NICK GUBBINS

## LHB LB R0 W0

FULL NAME: Nicholas Richard Trail Gubbins
BORN: December 31, 1993, Richmond, Surrey
SQUAD NO: 18
HEIGHT: 6ft
NICKNAME: Gubbs
EDUCATION: Radley College; University of Leeds
TEAMS: Middlesex
CAREER: First-class: 2013; List A: 2014



BEST BATTING: 95 Middlesex vs Somerset, Uxbridge, 2014

FAMILY TIES? My dad played a high standard of club cricket and ended up playing an ODI for Singapore Cricket Club against Malaysia when I was five
CAREER HIGHLIGHTS? Making my Middlesex first-team debut in 2014 and having a string of successful performances to help establish myself. Playing a one-day game against India at Lord's was also an incredible experience
BEST PLAYER IN COUNTY CRICKET? James Taylor
TIP FOR THE TOP? Ryan Higgins, Harry Podmore, Tom Helm
CRICKETING HEROES? Andrew Strauss – he is similarly an Old-Radleian and ex-Middlesex player. Have been fortunate enough to work with him since I was 17 and will continue to pick his brains
NON-CRICKETING HEROES? Didier Drogba – my childhood hero and just a bit of a Chelsea legend and good bloke!
CRICKET RULE YOU'D CHANGE? I think batsmen should get a free hit when there is a wide instead of one run extra
IF YOU COULD BE SOMEONE ELSE FOR A DAY? Gerard Piqué – some of you will understand!
PET HATE? Cats. Hate cats. Why would you not get a dog?
SURPRISING FACT? I grew up in Singapore
TWITTER FEED: @ngubbins18

| Batting | Mat | Inns | NO | Runs | HS | Ave | SR | 100 | 50 | Ct | St |
|---|---|---|---|---|---|---|---|---|---|---|---|
| First-class | 8 | 15 | 1 | 330 | 95 | 23.57 | 43.08 | 0 | 3 | 2 | 0 |
| List A | 3 | 3 | 0 | 63 | 38 | 21.00 | 63.63 | 0 | 0 | 0 | 0 |
| **Bowling** | **Mat** | **Balls** | **Runs** | **Wkts** | **BBI** | **BBM** | **Ave** | **Econ** | **SR** | **5w** | **10** |
| First-class | 8 | - | - | - | - | - | - | - | - | - | - |
| List A | 3 | - | - | - | - | - | - | - | - | - | - |

## MARTIN GUPTILL

## RHB OB R0 W0

FULL NAME: Martin James Guptill
BORN: September 30, 1986, Auckland, New Zealand
SQUAD NO: 31
TEAMS: New Zealand, Derbyshire, Guyana Amazon Warriors
CAREER: Test: 2009; ODI: 2009; T20I: 2009; First-class: 2006; List A: 2016; T20: 2006

BEST BATTING: 195* Auckland vs Canterbury, Rangiora, 2011
BEST BOWLING: 3-37 New Zealand vs Pakistan, Napier, 2009

NOTES: He was the leading run-scorer in New Zealand's State Shied in 2007-08, scoring 596 runs at 59.60. Scored 122 not out on his ODI debut against West Indies at Auckland in 2009. In 2011 he signed for Derbyshire and scored 537 runs in the Championship from eight matches, as well as scoring two centuries in the CB40. In 2012 he struck 101 not out in a T20 match against South Africa at East London, which means he has an international century in all three formats. Holds New Zealand two highest ODI score, hitting 189* off 155 balls against England at Southampton in 2013 and then smashing 237* against West Indies at Wellington in March, the highest score at a World Cup

| Batting | Mat | Inns | NO | Runs | HS | Ave | SR | 100 | 50 | Ct | St |
|---|---|---|---|---|---|---|---|---|---|---|---|
| Tests | 31 | 59 | 1 | 1718 | 189 | 29.62 | 43.40 | 2 | 12 | 33 | 0 |
| ODIs | 104 | 101 | 10 | 3348 | 189* | 36.79 | 80.13 | 5 | 22 | 46 | 0 |
| T20Is | 48 | 46 | 6 | 1273 | 101* | 31.82 | 121.58 | 1 | 5 | 24 | 0 |
| First-class | 81 | 147 | 9 | 4972 | 195* | 36.02 | 49.70 | 9 | 28 | 78 | 0 |
| List A | 155 | 150 | 13 | 5430 | 189* | 39.63 | 82.04 | 14 | 30 | 71 | 0 |
| Twenty20 | 131 | 126 | 17 | 3823 | 120* | 35.07 | 125.42 | 2 | 23 | 82 | 0 |
| **Bowling** | **Mat** | **Balls** | **Runs** | **Wkts** | **BBI** | **BBM** | **Ave** | **Econ** | **SR** | **5w** | **10** |
| Tests | 31 | 332 | 258 | 5 | 3/37 | 3/37 | 51.60 | 4.66 | 66.4 | 0 | 0 |
| ODIs | 104 | 91 | 78 | 2 | 2/7 | 2/7 | 39.00 | 5.14 | 45.5 | 0 | 0 |
| T20Is | 48 | 6 | 11 | 0 | - | - | - | 11.00 | - | 0 | 0 |
| First-class | 81 | 650 | 542 | 7 | 3/37 | 3/37 | 77.42 | 5.00 | 92.8 | 0 | 0 |
| List A | 155 | 91 | 78 | 2 | 2/7 | 2/7 | 39.00 | 5.14 | 45.5 | 0 | 0 |
| Twenty20 | 131 | 12 | 19 | 0 | - | - | - | 9.50 | - | 0 | 0 |

# HARRY GURNEY RHB LFM R0 W0 MVP96

FULL NAME: Harry Frederick Gurney
BORN: October 25, 1986, Nottingham
SQUAD NO: 11
HEIGHT: 6ft 2in
NICKNAME: Gramps
EDUCATION: University of Leeds
TEAMS: England, Nottinghamshire, Leicestershire
CAREER: ODI: 2014; T20I: 2014; First-class: 2007; ODI: 2009; T20: 2009



BEST BATTING: 24* Leicestershire vs Middlesex, Leicester, 2009
BEST BOWLING: 5-81 Nottinghamshire vs Somerset, Nottingham, 2013

CAREER HIGHLIGHTS? Playing for England, winning the Pro40 with Nottinghamshire, winning T20 with Leicestershire and taking a Championship hat-trick
CRICKET RULE YOU'D CHANGE? I would introduce two divisions of umpires based on performance
COACHING TIP? Forget technique, focus on outcomes!
IF YOU COULD BE SOMEONE ELSE FOR A DAY? Rory McIlroy
PET HATE? Bowlers wildly celebrating the wicket of a guy who has just pumped them all around the park. Head down, son
SURPRISING FACT? I play the piano to a decent standard
FANTASY SLIP CORDON? Keeper: Ricky Gervais, 1st: Me, 2nd: Tony Blair, Gully: Richard Branson
TWITTER FEED: @gurneyhf

| Batting | Mat | Inns | NO | Runs | HS | Ave | SR | 100 | 50 | Ct | St |
|---|---|---|---|---|---|---|---|---|---|---|---|
| ODIs | 10 | 6 | 4 | 15 | 6* | 7.50 | 45.45 | 0 | 0 | 1 | 0 |
| T20Is | 2 | - | - | - | - | - | - | - | - | 0 | 0 |
| First-class | 54 | 65 | 30 | 191 | 24* | 5.45 | 32.15 | 0 | 0 | 7 | 0 |
| List A | 59 | 19 | 10 | 41 | 13* | 4.55 | 48.80 | 0 | 0 | 5 | 0 |
| Twenty20 | 59 | 5 | 4 | 6 | 5* | 6.00 | 85.71 | 0 | 0 | 8 | 0 |
| **Bowling** | **Mat** | **Balls** | **Runs** | **Wkts** | **BBI** | **BBM** | **Ave** | **Econ** | **SR** | **5w** | **10** |
| ODIs | 10 | 455 | 432 | 11 | 4/55 | 4/55 | 39.27 | 5.69 | 41.3 | 0 | 0 |
| T20Is | 2 | 48 | 55 | 3 | 2/26 | 2/26 | 18.33 | 6.87 | 16.0 | 0 | 0 |
| First-class | 54 | 8591 | 4914 | 145 | 5/81 | 7/148 | 33.88 | 3.43 | 59.2 | 2 | 0 |
| List A | 59 | 2442 | 2275 | 68 | 5/24 | 5/24 | 33.45 | 5.58 | 35.9 | 2 | 0 |
| Twenty20 | 59 | 1208 | 1458 | 67 | 3/21 | 3/21 | 21.76 | 7.24 | 18.0 | 0 | 0 |

# CALUM HAGGETT

## LHB RM R0 W0

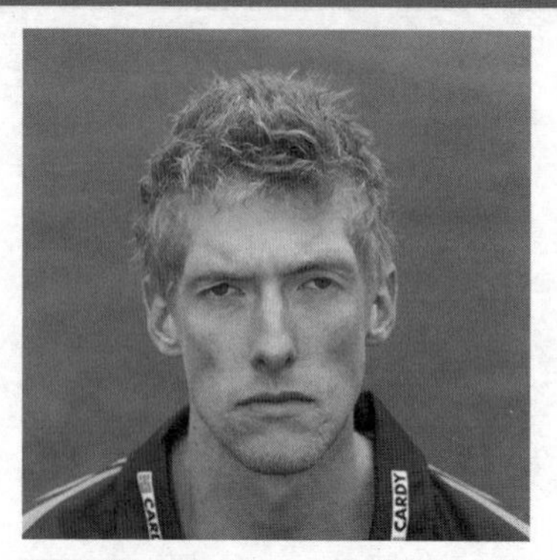


FULL NAME: Calum John Haggett
BORN: October 30, 1990, Taunton
SQUAD NO: 25
HEIGHT: 6ft 3in
NICKNAME: Haggs
EDUCATION: Millfield School
TEAMS: Kent, Somerset
CAREER: First-class: 2013; List A: 2013; T20: 2013

BEST BATTING: 44* Kent vs Gloucestershire, Canterbury, 2013
BEST BOWLING: 4-94 Kent vs Glamorgan, Canterbury, 2013

CAREER HIGHLIGHTS? Making my first-class debut
BEST PLAYER IN COUNTY CRICKET? Darren Stevens
TIP FOR THE TOP? Imran Qayyum
CRICKETING HEROES? Jacques Kallis – because he could make an impact in the game with both bat and ball
NON-CRICKETING HEROES? Johnny Wilkinson – he is the model professional
IF YOU WEREN'T A CRICKETER? Philosopher
IF YOU COULD BE SOMEONE ELSE FOR A DAY? Prince Harry
DESERT ISLAND DISC? Queen – Bohemian Rhapsody
FAVOURITE TV? Peep Show
LEAST FAVOURITE TV? Hollyoaks
PET HATE? Having bad manners
FANTASY SLIP CORDON? Keeper: Peter Kay, 1st: Winston Churchill, 2nd: Jimi Hendrix, Gully: Chris March

| Batting | Mat | Inns | NO | Runs | HS | Ave | SR | 100 | 50 | Ct | St |
|---|---|---|---|---|---|---|---|---|---|---|---|
| First-class | 16 | 21 | 7 | 368 | 44* | 26.28 | 42.74 | 0 | 0 | 3 | 0 |
| List A | 10 | 7 | 0 | 57 | 36 | 8.14 | 90.47 | 0 | 0 | 4 | 0 |
| Twenty20 | 5 | 3 | 1 | 4 | 2 | 2.00 | 80.00 | 0 | 0 | 1 | 0 |
| **Bowling** | **Mat** | **Balls** | **Runs** | **Wkts** | **BBI** | **BBM** | **Ave** | **Econ** | **SR** | **5w** | **10** |
| First-class | 16 | 2352 | 1260 | 31 | 4/94 | 4/94 | 40.64 | 3.21 | 75.8 | 0 | 0 |
| List A | 10 | 336 | 375 | 8 | 2/54 | 2/54 | 46.87 | 6.69 | 42.0 | 0 | 0 |
| Twenty20 | 5 | 48 | 71 | 1 | 1/15 | 1/15 | 71.00 | 8.87 | 48.0 | 0 | 0 |

# SAM HAIN RHB RM R0 W0

FULL NAME: Samuel Robert Hain
BORN: July 16, 1995, Hong Kong
SQUAD NO: 16
TEAMS: Warwickshire, Australia U19
CAREER: First-class: 2014; List A: 2013



BEST BATTING: 208 Warwickshire vs Northamptonshire, Birmingham, 2014

CAREER HIGHLIGHTS? Making my debut last year against Worcester
BEST PLAYER IN COUNTY CRICKET? Moeen Ali
MOST MARKED CHARACTERISTIC? Going round picking up all the lads' bats
CRICKETING HEROES? Michael Clarke and Freddie Flintoff back in the day were the ones I loved to watch
NON-CRICKETING HEROES? Kelly Slater
CRICKET RULE YOU'D CHANGE? Starting up day/night Test matches somewhere down the line would be exciting I think
FAVOURITE TV? Prison Break
FANTASY SLIP CORDON? Keeper: Jimmy Carr (absolutely hilarious), 1st: Sam Hain, 2nd: Mila Kunis (I don't think any explanation is needed), 3rd: Kelly Slater (would love to know what it's like surfing the big breaks around the world), Gully: Will Smith (just because he's the Fresh Prince Of Bel-Air)
TWITTER FEED: @SammieHain

| Batting | Mat | Inns | NO | Runs | HS | Ave | SR | 100 | 50 | Ct | St |
|---|---|---|---|---|---|---|---|---|---|---|---|
| First-class | 12 | 18 | 2 | 823 | 208 | 51.43 | 47.29 | 4 | 1 | 6 | 0 |
| List A | 1 | 1 | 0 | 1 | 1 | 1.00 | 33.33 | 0 | 0 | 0 | 0 |
| **Bowling** | **Mat** | **Balls** | **Runs** | **Wkts** | **BBI** | **BBM** | **Ave** | **Econ** | **SR** | **5w** | **10** |
| First-class | 12 | - | - | - | - | - | - | - | - | - | - |
| List A | 1 | - | - | - | - | - | - | - | - | - | - |

## ALEX HALES RHB RM R2 W0 MVP25

FULL NAME: Alexander Daniel Hales
BORN: January 3, 1989, Hillingdon, Middlesex
SQUAD NO: 10
HEIGHT: 6ft 5in
NICKNAME: Baz, Halesy, Trigg
TEAMS: England, Nottinghamshire, Duronto Rajshahi, Melbourne Renegades, Worcestershire
CAREER: ODI: 2014; T20I: 2011; First-class: 2008; List A: 2008; T20: 2009

BEST BATTING: 184 Nottinghamshire vs Somerset, Nottingham, 2011
BEST BOWLING: 2-63 Nottinghamshire vs Yorkshire, Nottingham, 2009
COUNTY CAPS: 2011

CAREER HIGHLIGHTS? My England debut
MOST MARKED CHARACTERISTIC? Patience
CRICKETING HEROES? Ian Bell
NON-CRICKETING HEROES? Steve Jobs, Paul Merson
IF YOU WEREN'T A CRICKETER? Groundsman
DESERT ISLAND DISC? Nicki Minaj – Pound The Alarm
FAVOURITE TV? Keeping Up With The Kardashians
ACCOMPLISHMENTS? I rowed across the English Channel in an old tin bath
FANTASY SLIP CORDON? Keeper: Bilal Shafayat, 1st: Maria Sharapova, 2nd: Arséne Wenger, 3rd: Kirstie Edwards, Gully: Jimmy Carr
TWITTER FEED: @AlexHales1

| Batting | Mat | Inns | NO | Runs | HS | Ave | SR | 100 | 50 | Ct | St |
|---|---|---|---|---|---|---|---|---|---|---|---|
| ODIs | 8 | 8 | 0 | 153 | 42 | 19.12 | 71.83 | 0 | 0 | 1 | 0 |
| T20Is | 33 | 33 | 5 | 1062 | 116* | 37.92 | 138.46 | 1 | 7 | 19 | 0 |
| First-class | 73 | 126 | 6 | 4399 | 184 | 36.65 | 59.23 | 9 | 27 | 71 | 0 |
| List A | 89 | 87 | 2 | 2968 | 150* | 34.91 | 98.27 | 8 | 13 | 28 | 0 |
| Twenty20 | 122 | 121 | 7 | 3351 | 116* | 29.39 | 139.50 | 1 | 23 | 49 | 0 |
| **Bowling** | **Mat** | **Balls** | **Runs** | **Wkts** | **BBI** | **BBM** | **Ave** | **Econ** | **SR** | **5w** | **10** |
| ODIs | 8 | - | - | - | - | - | - | - | - | - | - |
| T20Is | 33 | - | - | - | - | - | - | - | - | - | - |
| First-class | 73 | 293 | 171 | 3 | 2/63 | 2/63 | 57.00 | 3.50 | 97.6 | 0 | 0 |
| List A | 89 | 4 | 10 | 0 | - | - | - | 15.00 | - | 0 | 0 |
| Twenty20 | 122 | 3 | 7 | 0 | - | - | - | 14.00 | - | 0 | 0 |

# HASEEB HAMEED

RHB LB R0 W0

FULL NAME: Haseeb Hameed
BORN: January 17, 1997, Bolton, Lancashire
SQUAD NO: 23
EDUCATION: Bolton School
TEAMS: Lancashire 2nd XI, England U19
CAREER: Yet to make first-team debut



TWITTER FEED:@HaseebHameed97
NOTES: At just 18 Haseeb Hameed has been awarded a full contract with Lancashire and has been tipped as one of the hottest batting prospects in England. In August last year he hit 389 runs in five matches for England U19 against South Africa U19, an international record for a batsman in a youth bilateral one-day series, with consecutive scores of 97, 97 and 125

# MILES HAMMOND

LHB OB R0 W0

FULL NAME: Miles Arthur Halhead Hammond
BORN: January 11, 1996, Cheltenham, Gloucestershire
SQUAD NO: 88
HEIGHT: 6ft
NICKNAME: Hammo, Cryles
EDUCATION: St Edward's School
TEAMS: Gloucestershire
CAREER: First-class: 2013; List A: 2013; T20: 2013

BEST BATTING: 4 Gloucestershire vs Worcestershire, Cheltenham, 2013
BEST BOWLING: 1-96 Gloucestershire vs Glamorgan, Bristol, 2013

BEST PLAYER IN COUNTY CRICKET? Moeen Ali
TIP FOR THE TOP? Chris Dent, Will Tavaré
MOST MARKED CHARACTERISTIC? Chilled out (bit dopey)
SUPERSTITIONS? Left sock inside out and I wear my house key around my neck
CRICKETING HEROES? Moeen Ali – because he plays the game in the right way and is ridiculously skilful
CRICKET RULE YOU'D CHANGE? The LBW rule – scrap the impact-outside-the-line rule
IF YOU COULD BE SOMEONE ELSE FOR A DAY? Dan Bilzerian
DESERT ISLAND DISC? Matisyahu – Sunshine
FAVOURITE TV? Friends
LEAST FAVOURITE TV? I'm A Celebrity ... Get Me Out Of Here!
PET HATE? Getting up early, because sleeping is the best thing ever. People eating my food – it's insensitive
FANTASY SLIP CORDON? Keeper: Lee Evans, 1st: Dumbledore, 2nd: Mila Kunis, 3rd: Matisyahu, Gully: Kevin Pietersen

| Batting | Mat | Inns | NO | Runs | HS | Ave | SR | 100 | 50 | Ct | St |
|---|---|---|---|---|---|---|---|---|---|---|---|
| First-class | 2 | 2 | 0 | 4 | 4 | 2.00 | 28.57 | 0 | 0 | 1 | 0 |
| List A | 2 | - | - | - | - | - | - | - | - | 0 | 0 |
| Twenty20 | 1 | - | - | - | - | - | - | - | - | 0 | 0 |
| **Bowling** | **Mat** | **Balls** | **Runs** | **Wkts** | **BBI** | **BBM** | **Ave** | **Econ** | **SR** | **5w** | **10** |
| First-class | 2 | 294 | 196 | 1 | 1/96 | 1/155 | 196.00 | 4.00 | 294.0 | 0 | 0 |
| List A | 2 | 78 | 79 | 3 | 2/29 | 2/29 | 26.33 | 6.07 | 26.0 | 0 | 0 |
| Twenty20 | 1 | 12 | 17 | 0 | - | - | - | 8.50 | - | 0 | 0 |

# TOM HAMPTON

RHB RMF R0 W0

FULL NAME: Thomas Robert Gareth Hampton
BORN: October 5, 1990, Kingston, Surrey
SQUAD NO: 16
HEIGHT: 6ft
NICKNAME: Hampo, Snr
EDUCATION: John Hampden Grammar School
TEAMS: Gloucestershire
CAREER: First-class: 2010



FAMILY TIES? My brother Dan is an allrounder who has spent the last three years with the MCC Young Cricketers
CAREER HIGHLIGHTS? Signing my first professional contract with Gloucestershire
BEST PLAYER IN COUNTY CRICKET? Adam Lyth
TIP FOR THE TOP? Will Tavaré, Jamie Porter
CRICKETING HEROES? Glenn McGrath and Dale Steyn – great bowlers who play the game hard and give it their all
NON-CRICKETING HEROES? Grandad – a brilliant role model and truly great man. Mum and grandma have always been there for me and the rest of the family
IF YOU WEREN'T A CRICKETER? PE teacher or personal trainer
IF YOU COULD BE SOMEONE ELSE FOR A DAY? Sam Warburton on a match day in Cardiff
DESERT ISLAND DISC? Justin Timberlake – The 20/20 Experience
FAVOURITE TV? Game Of Thrones
LEAST FAVOURITE TV? Made In Chelsea
ACCOMPLISHMENTS? World rugby tour with school
PET HATE? Phone calls – texts are much easier!
SURPRISING FACT? I'm a castle-lover
FANTASY SLIP CORDON? Keeper: Muhammad Ali, 1st: Gareth Thomas, 2nd: Jonny Wilkinson, 3rd: David Beckham, Gully: Eminem
TWITTER FEED: @TrgHampton

| Batting | Mat | Inns | NO | Runs | HS | Ave | SR | 100 | 50 | Ct | St |
|---|---|---|---|---|---|---|---|---|---|---|---|
| First-class | 1 | 1 | 1 | 1 | 1* | - | 25.00 | 0 | 0 | 0 | 0 |
| **Bowling** | **Mat** | **Balls** | **Runs** | **Wkts** | **BBI** | **BBM** | **Ave** | **Econ** | **SR** | **5w** | **10** |
| First-class | 1 | 84 | 42 | 1 | 1/15 | 1/42 | 42.00 | 3.00 | 84.0 | 0 | 0 |

## OLIVER HANNON-DALBY LHB RFM R0 W0

FULL NAME: Oliver James Hannon-Dalby
BORN: June 20, 1989, Halifax, Yorkshire
SQUAD NO: 20
HEIGHT: 6ft 8in
NICKNAME: OHD, Dave, Schürrle
EDUCATION: Brooksbank School; Leeds Metropolitan University
TEAMS: Warwickshire, Yorkshire
CAREER: First-class: 2008; List A: 2011; T20: 2012

BEST BATTING: 40 Warwickshire vs Somerset, Taunton, 2014
BEST BOWLING: 5-68 Yorkshire vs Somerset, Leeds, 2010

CAREER HIGHLIGHTS? Winning the Natwest T20 Blast in 2014, Lord's final in the Royal London Cup in 2014, my first first-class five-fer
CRICKETING HEROES? Glenn McGrath, Brett Lee and Freddie Flintoff. Loved watching them all bowl, particularly in the 2005 Ashes
NON-CRICKETING HEROES? Arthur Guinness – makes a lovely pint
COACHING TIP? Keep your eyes fixed on your target throughout your run-up, delivery and follow-through
IF YOU COULD BE SOMEONE ELSE FOR A DAY? Hugh Hefner
DESERT ISLAND DISC? Oasis – The Masterplan
ACCOMPLISHMENTS? Captain of the Brooksbank School championship-winning quiz team
PET HATE? Littering – it's disgusting
SURPRISING FACT? Warwickshire CCC Karaoke Champion
FANTASY SLIP CORDON? Keeper: James Finch, 1st: Me, 2nd: Peter Griffin, 3rd: Stephen Fry, Gully: Chazz Michael Michaels
TWITTER FEED: @OHD20

| Batting | Mat | Inns | NO | Runs | HS | Ave | SR | 100 | 50 | Ct | St |
|---|---|---|---|---|---|---|---|---|---|---|---|
| First-class | 37 | 38 | 16 | 155 | 40 | 7.04 | 22.14 | 0 | 0 | 5 | 0 |
| List A | 16 | 4 | 2 | 38 | 21* | 19.00 | 126.66 | 0 | 0 | 4 | 0 |
| Twenty20 | 9 | 1 | 1 | 2 | 2* | - | 66.66 | 0 | 0 | 1 | 0 |
| **Bowling** | **Mat** | **Balls** | **Runs** | **Wkts** | **BBI** | **BBM** | **Ave** | **Econ** | **SR** | **5w** | **10** |
| First-class | 37 | 5040 | 2851 | 78 | 5/68 | 7/122 | 36.55 | 3.39 | 64.6 | 2 | 0 |
| List A | 16 | 660 | 678 | 20 | 4/44 | 4/44 | 33.90 | 6.16 | 33.0 | 0 | 0 |
| Twenty20 | 9 | 191 | 264 | 11 | 3/31 | 3/31 | 24.00 | 8.29 | 17.3 | 0 | 0 |

## ARUN HARINATH

LHB OB R0 W0

FULL NAME: Arun Harinath
BORN: April 3, 1987, Sutton, Surrey
SQUAD NO: 10
HEIGHT: 5ft 10in
NICKNAME: Baron
EDUCATION: Tiffin School; Loughborough University
TEAMS: Surrey
CAREER: First-class: 2007; List A: 2009



BEST BATTING: 154 Surrey vs Derbyshire, Derby, 2013
BEST BOWLING: 2-1 Surrey vs Middlesex, Lord's, 2013

FAMILY TIES? My dad played league cricket and my brother Muhunthan has also played for Surrey
CAREER HIGHLIGHTS? My maiden first-class hundred
TIP FOR THE TOP? Mathew Dunn
CRICKETING HEROES? Ricky Ponting – having met him and played with him he is not only one of the greatest cricketers of this generation, but a great person to have in the dressing room too
NON-CRICKETING HEROES? Jonny Wilkinson – a great professional and role model
CRICKET RULE YOU'D CHANGE? You're not allowed to have any slip fielders!
COACHING TIP? Always practise your strengths as well as working on your weaknesses
IF YOU COULD BE SOMEONE ELSE FOR A DAY? Sergio Garcia
DESERT ISLAND DISC? Coldplay – Parachutes
FAVOURITE TV? House Of Cards
ACCOMPLISHMENTS? Completing my degree
SURPRISING FACT? I can play the guitar – not brilliantly but not too bad
FANTASY SLIP CORDON? Keeper: Frank Sinatra, 1st: Me, 2nd: Bill Clinton, 3rd: Kevin Hart, 4th: Dalai Lama

| Batting | Mat | Inns | NO | Runs | HS | Ave | SR | 100 | 50 | Ct | St |
|---|---|---|---|---|---|---|---|---|---|---|---|
| First-class | 50 | 87 | 5 | 2384 | 154 | 29.07 | 40.99 | 3 | 14 | 13 | 0 |
| List A | 6 | 6 | 2 | 105 | 52 | 26.25 | 79.54 | 0 | 1 | 1 | 0 |
| **Bowling** | **Mat** | **Balls** | **Runs** | **Wkts** | **BBI** | **BBM** | **Ave** | **Econ** | **SR** | **5w** | **10** |
| First-class | 50 | 84 | 46 | 4 | 2/1 | 2/1 | 11.50 | 3.28 | 21.0 | 0 | 0 |
| List A | 6 | 18 | 16 | 0 | - | - | - | 5.33 | - | 0 | 0 |

# BEN HARMISON

LHB RMF R0 W0



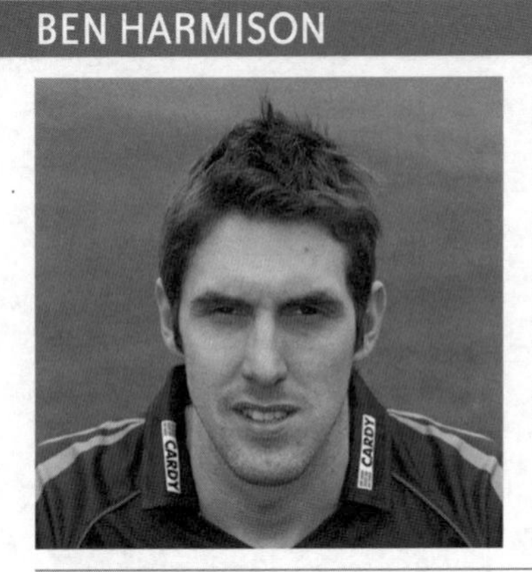

FULL NAME: Ben William Harmison
BORN: January 9, 1986, Ashington, Northumberland
SQUAD NO: 21
HEIGHT: 6ft 5in
NICKNAME: Harmy
EDUCATION: Ashington High School
TEAMS: Kent, Durham
CAREER: First-class: 2006; List A: 2005; T20: 2006

BEST BATTING: 125 Kent vs Gloucestershire, Bristol, 2014
BEST BOWLING: 4-27 Durham vs Surrey, Guildford, 2008

FAMILY TIES? My brother Steve played for Durham and England. Father Jim and brother James play league cricket for Ashington CC
CAREER HIGHLIGHTS? Signing my first professional contract at the age of 18. Consecutive hundreds in my first two first-class games for Durham
CRICKETING HEROES? Andrew Flintoff
DESERT ISLAND DISC? Take That
TWITTER FEED: @harmy14

| Batting | Mat | Inns | NO | Runs | HS | Ave | SR | 100 | 50 | Ct | St |
|---|---|---|---|---|---|---|---|---|---|---|---|
| First-class | 78 | 123 | 10 | 3218 | 125 | 28.47 | 44.57 | 6 | 14 | 46 | 0 |
| List A | 69 | 58 | 8 | 1177 | 67 | 23.54 | 72.29 | 0 | 3 | 24 | 0 |
| Twenty20 | 44 | 28 | 12 | 200 | 24 | 12.50 | 103.62 | 0 | 0 | 15 | 0 |
| **Bowling** | **Mat** | **Balls** | **Runs** | **Wkts** | **BBI** | **BBM** | **Ave** | **Econ** | **SR** | **5w** | **10** |
| First-class | 78 | 2104 | 1512 | 37 | 4/27 | 6/98 | 40.86 | 4.31 | 56.8 | 0 | 0 |
| List A | 69 | 1017 | 963 | 30 | 3/40 | 3/40 | 32.10 | 5.68 | 33.9 | 0 | 0 |
| Twenty20 | 44 | 438 | 639 | 30 | 3/20 | 3/20 | 21.30 | 8.75 | 14.6 | 0 | 0 |

# JAMES HARRIS

RHB RMF R0 W1

FULL NAME: James Alexander Russell Harris
BORN: May 16, 1990, Morriston, Swansea, Glamorgan
SQUAD NO: 5
HEIGHT: 6ft 1in
NICKNAME: Harry, Bones, Lloyd Christmas
EDUCATION: Pontarddulais Comprehensive School; Gorseinon College
TEAMS: Middlesex, Glamorgan, England Lions
CAREER: First-class: 2007; List A: 2007; T20: 2008



BEST BATTING: 87* Glamorgan vs Nottinghamshire, Swansea, 2007
BEST BOWLING: 7-66 Glamorgan vs Gloucestershire, Bristol, 2007
COUNTY CAPS: 2010 (Glamorgan)

CAREER HIGHLIGHTS? Being selected to tour with England to New Zealand in 2013 and two England Lions tours to Sri Lanka and the West Indies. Breaking records at the start of my career with Glamorgan, including being the youngest player to take 10 wickets in a match
CRICKETING HEROES? Glenn McGrath and Sachin Tendulkar
NON-CRICKETING HEROES? Jack Nicklaus, Seve Ballesteros – possibly the two greatest golfers ever. Cyclist Eddy Merckx – possibly one of the greatest winners in sporting history
CRICKET RULE YOU'D CHANGE? If batsmen can now use the bats that they do then the bowlers should be allowed to scratch the ball to make the game more of a 50/50 contest
PET HATE? Boys who throw kit everywhere in the dressing room. I must have a bit of OCD I guess as my kit is generally always kept tidy and neat with boots lined up etc
SURPRISING FACT? I won the Welsh Junior Sports Personality in 2007 and finished second in the national BBC Junior Sports Personality of the Year where I was pipped by Tom Daley. Third place was filled by one Mr Rory McIlroy
TWITTER FEED: @James_Harris9

| Batting | Mat | Inns | NO | Runs | HS | Ave | SR | 100 | 50 | Ct | St |
|---|---|---|---|---|---|---|---|---|---|---|---|
| First-class | 85 | 115 | 24 | 1877 | 87* | 20.62 | | 0 | 7 | 24 | 0 |
| List A | 47 | 29 | 7 | 227 | 29 | 10.31 | 68.99 | 0 | 0 | 10 | 0 |
| Twenty20 | 40 | 21 | 10 | 131 | 18 | 11.90 | 113.91 | 0 | 0 | 5 | 0 |
| **Bowling** | **Mat** | **Balls** | **Runs** | **Wkts** | **BBI** | **BBM** | **Ave** | **Econ** | **SR** | **5w** | **10** |
| First-class | 85 | 14911 | 8003 | 272 | 7/66 | 12/118 | 29.42 | 3.22 | 54.8 | 9 | 1 |
| List A | 47 | 1901 | 1836 | 62 | 4/48 | 4/48 | 29.61 | 5.79 | 30.6 | 0 | 0 |
| Twenty20 | 40 | 722 | 1065 | 35 | 4/23 | 4/23 | 30.42 | 8.85 | 20.6 | 0 | 0 |

# JAMIE HARRISON

RHB LFM R0 W0



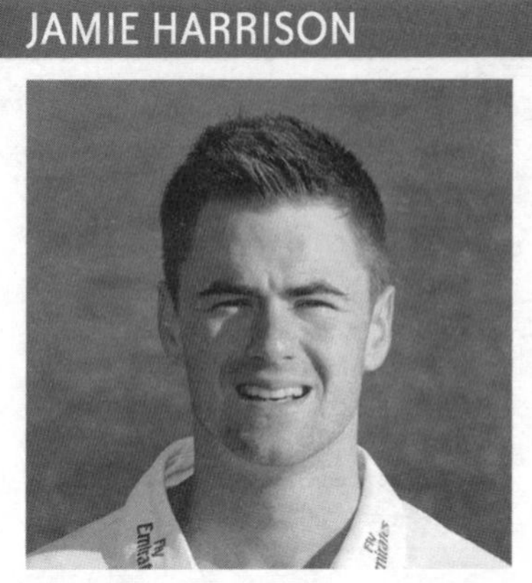

FULL NAME: Jamie Harrison
BORN: November 19, 1990, Whiston, Knowsley, Lancashire
SQUAD NO: 13
HEIGHT: 6ft 1in
NICKNAME: Bieber, Jay
EDUCATION: Sedbergh School
TEAMS: Durham
CAREER: First-class: 2012; List A: 2012

BEST BATTING: 65 Durham vs Northamptonshire, Northampton, 2014
BEST BOWLING: 5-31 Durham vs Surrey, Chester-le-Street, 2013

FAMILY TIES? My step-dad Simon played in the local Cumbria leagues
CAREER HIGHLIGHTS? Being part of a Championship-winning side
MOST MARKED CHARACTERISTIC? Unnecessary aggression, stuttering start to my run-up, my taste in music (good or bad)
SUPERSTITIONS? I pack my bag the night before, packing my training/warm-up gear in the left of the bag and playing whites to the right. The morning before the game I swim and stretch
CRICKETING HEROES? Wasim Akram, Glenn McGrath
NON-CRICKETING HEROES? Sean Long, Keiron Cunningham, my dad
IF YOU WEREN'T A CRICKETER? Who knows! Probably travelling the world blagging a living
DESERT ISLAND DISC? Dirty Vegas – Greatest Hits
FAVOURITE TV? Shameless
ACCOMPLISHMENTS? I became a part-time Justin Bieber lookalike
SURPRISING FACT? I own two budgies – Boris and Beryl!
TWITTER FEED: @jayharrison13

| Batting | Mat | Inns | NO | Runs | HS | Ave | SR | 100 | 50 | Ct | St |
|---|---|---|---|---|---|---|---|---|---|---|---|
| First-class | 13 | 20 | 5 | 337 | 65 | 22.46 | 51.76 | 0 | 1 | 0 | 0 |
| List A | 2 | 1 | 1 | 7 | 7* | - | 140.00 | 0 | 0 | 0 | 0 |
| **Bowling** | **Mat** | **Balls** | **Runs** | **Wkts** | **BBI** | **BBM** | **Ave** | **Econ** | **SR** | **5w** | **10** |
| First-class | 13 | 1824 | 1137 | 42 | 5/31 | 7/74 | 27.07 | 3.74 | 43.4 | 2 | 0 |
| List A | 2 | 72 | 83 | 2 | 2/51 | 2/51 | 41.50 | 6.91 | 36.0 | 0 | 0 |

# CHARLIE HARTLEY RHB RMF R0 W0

FULL NAME: Charles Frederick Hartley
BORN: 1994, Bromsgrove, Worcestershire
SQUAD NO: 22
HEIGHT: 6ft 2in
NICKNAME: Chappers, Chaps
EDUCATION: Millfield School
TEAMS: Kent
CAREER: First-class: 2014; List A: 2014



BEST BATTING: 2 Kent vs Leicestershire, Leicester, 2014
BEST BOWLING: 2-40 Kent vs Leicestershire, Leicester, 2014

CAREER HIGHLIGHTS? Signing a contract with Kent, closely followed by winning the National Club T20 with Millfield
TIP FOR THE TOP? Daniel Bell-Drummond
MOST MARKED CHARACTERISTIC? Over-thinking... actually, maybe not
CRICKETING HEROES? Andrew Flintoff
NON-CRICKETING HEROES? Jonny Wilkinson and Maximus Decimus Meridius from Gladiator
IF YOU WEREN'T A CRICKETER? Events hospitality/working hard to get into property
DESERT ISLAND DISC? Beach Boys – Pet Sounds
FAVOURITE TV? NCIS, Top Gear and 8 Out Of 10 Cats
SURPRISING FACT? I spent a lot of my time during school cricket being dropped from first teams and having my character tested. Keep pursuing and you will make it
FANTASY SLIP CORDON? Keeper: James Corden, 1st: Chris Stark, 2nd: Mila Kunis, 3rd: Will Smith, Gully: Jack Whitehall. I'd be listening over the stump mic
TWITTER FEED: @hartcf

| Batting | Mat | Inns | NO | Runs | HS | Ave | SR | 100 | 50 | Ct | St |
|---|---|---|---|---|---|---|---|---|---|---|---|
| First-class | 2 | 3 | 0 | 2 | 2 | 0.66 | 4.76 | 0 | 0 | 0 | 0 |
| List A | 2 | 2 | 0 | 9 | 5 | 4.50 | 50.00 | 0 | 0 | 0 | 0 |
| **Bowling** | **Mat** | **Balls** | **Runs** | **Wkts** | **BBI** | **BBM** | **Ave** | **Econ** | **SR** | **5w** | **10** |
| First-class | 2 | 288 | 190 | 5 | 2/40 | 3/91 | 38.00 | 3.95 | 57.6 | 0 | 0 |
| List A | 2 | 108 | 104 | 2 | 1/51 | 1/51 | 52.00 | 5.77 | 54.0 | 0 | 0 |

# JOHN HASTINGS RHB RFM R0 W0 MVP22

FULL NAME: John Wayne Hastings
BORN: November 4, 1985, Penrith, Australia
SQUAD NO: 2
HEIGHT: 6ft 4in
NICKNAME: The Duke
TEAMS: Australia, Durham, Kochi Tuskers Kerala, Victoria
CAREER: Test: 2012; ODI: 2010; T20I: 2010; First-class: 2007; List A: 2007; T20: 2007

BEST BATTING: 93 Victoria vs Tasmania, Hobart, 2010
BEST BOWLING: 5-30 Victoria vs Western Australia, Perth, 2014

NOTES: Hastings returns as Durham's overseas player for the 2015 season after impressing in 2014. He took 37 Championship wickets in just eight games and smashed two fifities in the T20 Blast. He signed as a T20 player for Sussex in the 2013 season but an ankle injury prevented him playing a game. The muscular allrounder built his reputation in Australian domestic cricket when in 2009/2010 he was Victoria's highest wicket-taker across all three formats, including 446 runs at 37.16 and 36 wickets at 26.13 in the Sheffield Shield. He was subsequently named Bradman Young Cricketer of the Year. Featured in Australia's limited-overs sides from 2010/2011 and was included in their 2011 T20 World Cup squad but has not played since. He played a solitary Test in 2012 against South Africa at Perth

| Batting | Mat | Inns | NO | Runs | HS | Ave | SR | 100 | 50 | Ct | St |
|---|---|---|---|---|---|---|---|---|---|---|---|
| Tests | 1 | 2 | 0 | 52 | 32 | 26.00 | 59.09 | 0 | 0 | 1 | 0 |
| ODIs | 11 | 9 | 4 | 82 | 21* | 16.40 | 105.12 | 0 | 0 | 2 | 0 |
| T20Is | 3 | 3 | 2 | 32 | 15 | 32.00 | 177.77 | 0 | 0 | 0 | 0 |
| First-class | 50 | 71 | 6 | 1505 | 93 | 23.15 | 49.76 | 0 | 7 | 22 | 0 |
| List A | 71 | 53 | 14 | 703 | 69* | 18.02 | 100.28 | 0 | 1 | 23 | 0 |
| Twenty20 | 58 | 40 | 10 | 427 | 80* | 14.23 | 151.95 | 0 | 2 | 15 | 0 |
| **Bowling** | **Mat** | **Balls** | **Runs** | **Wkts** | **BBI** | **BBM** | **Ave** | **Econ** | **SR** | **5w** | **10** |
| Tests | 1 | 234 | 153 | 1 | 1/51 | 1/153 | 153.00 | 3.92 | 234.0 | 0 | 0 |
| ODIs | 11 | 546 | 410 | 8 | 2/35 | 2/35 | 51.25 | 4.50 | 68.2 | 0 | 0 |
| T20Is | 3 | 60 | 66 | 3 | 3/14 | 3/14 | 22.00 | 6.60 | 20.0 | 0 | 0 |
| First-class | 50 | 9013 | 4214 | 163 | 5/30 | 8/118 | 25.85 | 2.80 | 55.2 | 5 | 0 |
| List A | 71 | 3681 | 3015 | 102 | 5/46 | 5/46 | 29.55 | 4.91 | 36.0 | 1 | 0 |
| Twenty20 | 58 | 1153 | 1455 | 69 | 4/26 | 4/26 | 21.08 | 7.57 | 16.7 | 0 | 0 |

# LEWIS HATCHETT

## LHB LMF R0 W0

FULL NAME: Lewis James Hatchett
BORN: January 21, 1990, Shoreham-by-Sea, Sussex
SQUAD NO: 5
TEAMS: Sussex
CAREER: First-class: 2010; List A: 2013; T20: 2013



BEST BATTING: 21 Sussex vs Yorkshire, Hove, 2013
BEST BOWLING: 5-47 Sussex vs Leicestershire, Leicester, 2010

CAREER HIGHLIGHTS? First-class debut. Maiden first-class five-fer. Signing a contract with my home county Sussex. All of these happening in the same year!
SUPERSTITIONS? I try not to move places when the team are doing well and I sometimes shave my head before games! I always turn left at the top of my run-up
CRICKETING HEROES? Grew up watching the old West Indian bowlers such as Courtney Walsh and Curtly Ambrose. Watched a lot of Jason Lewry at Sussex, which is probably where I learnt my action from
NON-CRICKETING HEROES? My family. Our country's servicemen, past and present
IF YOU WEREN'T A CRICKETER? I would love to have been a Marine
FAVOURITE TV? Scrubs
SURPRISING FACT? I suffer from Poland syndrome. I have my Sussex cap number tattooed under my left arm
FANTASY SLIP CORDON? Keeper: Will Ferrell, 1st: Jim Carrey, 2nd: Me, 3rd: Jonny Wilkinson, 4th: Tiger Woods, 5th: Nicki Minaj, Gully: Rihanna
TWITTER FEED: @lewis_hatchett

| Batting | Mat | Inns | NO | Runs | HS | Ave | SR | 100 | 50 | Ct | St |
|---|---|---|---|---|---|---|---|---|---|---|---|
| First-class | 22 | 29 | 9 | 169 | 21 | 8.45 | 28.11 | 0 | 0 | 8 | 0 |
| List A | 15 | 4 | 2 | 9 | 5 | 4.50 | 40.90 | 0 | 0 | 5 | 0 |
| Twenty20 | 10 | 3 | 2 | 0 | 0* | 0.00 | 0.00 | 0 | 0 | 0 | 0 |
| **Bowling** | **Mat** | **Balls** | **Runs** | **Wkts** | **BBI** | **BBM** | **Ave** | **Econ** | **SR** | **5w** | **10** |
| First-class | 22 | 3366 | 2108 | 62 | 5/47 | 8/64 | 34.00 | 3.75 | 54.2 | 2 | 0 |
| List A | 15 | 670 | 630 | 19 | 3/44 | 3/44 | 33.15 | 5.64 | 35.2 | 0 | 0 |
| Twenty20 | 10 | 185 | 304 | 11 | 3/23 | 3/23 | 27.63 | 9.85 | 16.8 | 0 | 0 |

# TOM HELM

RHB RMF R0 W0

FULL NAME: Thomas George Helm
BORN: May 7, 1994, Stoke Mandeville Hospital, Buckinghamshire
SQUAD NO: 14
HEIGHT: 6ft 4in
NICKNAME: Ched
EDUCATION: The Misbourne School
TEAMS: Middlesex, Glamorgan
CAREER: First-class: 2013; List A: 2013

BEST BATTING: 18 Middlesex vs Yorkshire, Leeds, 2013
BEST BOWLING: 3-46 Middlesex vs Yorkshire, Leeds, 2013

FAMILY TIES? My brother plays Minor Counties
CAREER HIGHLIGHTS? Making my Championship and List A debut vs Yorkshire at Headingley
BEST PLAYER IN COUNTY CRICKET? Moeen Ali
TIP FOR THE TOP? Ryan Higgins, Harry Podmore
MOST MARKED CHARACTERISTIC? My beanpole-like figure
SUPERSTITIONS? I slide and tap my bat at the end of each over I survive!
CRICKETING HEROES? James Anderson – the best swing bowler in the world
IF YOU COULD BE SOMEONE ELSE FOR A DAY? David Beckham
DESERT ISLAND DISC? Olly Murs
FAVOURITE TV? Game Of Thrones
LEAST FAVOURITE TV? Big Brother
ACCOMPLISHMENTS? Completing my A-Levels
PET HATE? Three-putting
FANTASY SLIP CORDON? Keeper: Micky Flanagan, 1st: Jennifer Aniston, 2nd: Myself, 3rd: Batman, Gully: Robert Downey Jnr
TWITTER FEED: @tomhelm7

| Batting | Mat | Inns | NO | Runs | HS | Ave | SR | 100 | 50 | Ct | St |
|---|---|---|---|---|---|---|---|---|---|---|---|
| First-class | 6 | 9 | 3 | 58 | 18 | 9.66 | 32.04 | 0 | 0 | 2 | 0 |
| List A | 3 | - | - | - | - | - | - | - | - | 1 | 0 |
| **Bowling** | **Mat** | **Balls** | **Runs** | **Wkts** | **BBI** | **BBM** | **Ave** | **Econ** | **SR** | **5w** | **10** |
| First-class | 6 | 804 | 428 | 14 | 3/46 | 5/78 | 30.57 | 3.19 | 57.4 | 0 | 0 |
| List A | 3 | 102 | 66 | 4 | 3/27 | 3/27 | 16.50 | 3.88 | 25.5 | 0 | 0 |

## ALEX HEPBURN

RHB RM R0 W0

FULL NAME: Alex Hepburn
BORN: December 21, 1995 , Subiaco, Australia
SQUAD NO: 26
HEIGHT: 5ft 10in
NICKNAME: Audrey, Heppers
EDUCATION: Aquinas College, Perth
TEAMS: Worcestershire 2nd XI
CAREER: Yet to make first-team debut



---

CAREER HIGHLIGHTS? Signing my first professional contract for Worcestershire in 2013
BEST PLAYER IN COUNTY CRICKET? Batsman – Daryl Mitchell. Bowler – Mark Footitt
TIP FOR THE TOP? Joe Clarke and Ed Barnard
MOST MARKED CHARACTERISTIC? My big blue eyes
SUPERSTITIONS? Must put all of my kit on in the same order
CRICKETING HEROES? Tom Hansell – former Surrey cricketer who has coached and been a part of my cricketing career from a young age. Michael Hussey – the player I wanted to become and strive towards
NON-CRICKETING HEROES? My aunt Elaine, who passed away in 2012 losing her battle to cancer at only 50 years of age. My dad, who has been a part of my cricketing ambitions from the day I started
IF YOU WEREN'T A CRICKETER? In Perth studying to become a teacher
IF YOU COULD BE SOMEONE ELSE FOR A DAY? Bruce Willis – the lifestyle of a big-time Hollywood actor
FAVOURITE TV? Prison Break
LEAST FAVOURITE TV? Big Brother
PET HATE? Arrogance and people who forget where they came from
SURPRISING FACT? I'm a Harry Potter nerd!
FANTASY SLIP CORDON? Keeper: Adam Gilchrist (legend of the game), 1st: Rodney Rude (have the cordon in stitches), 2nd: Myself, 3rd: Margot Robbie (self explanatory), Gully: Jonah Hill (pure entertainment)
TWITTER FEED: @AlexHepburn95

## CAMERON HERRING RHB WK R0 W0

FULL NAME: Cameron Lee Herring
BORN: July 15, 1994, Abergavenny, Monmouthshire
SQUAD NO: 29
HEIGHT: 5ft 6in
NICKNAME: Cam, Ellen
EDUCATION: Tredegar Comprehensive
TEAMS: Gloucestershire
CAREER: First-class: 2013; T20: 2014

BEST BATTING: 114* Gloucestershire vs Cardiff MCCU, Bristol, 2014

FAMILY TIES? My dad is an ECB elite coach and works with the Wales Cricket Board and my sister is an ex-Wales Women international
CAREER HIGHLIGHTS? My Championship debut against Essex at Chelmsford in April 2013 and my T20 debut against Middlesex last season in which I helped see the team home
BEST PLAYER IN COUNTY CRICKET? Moeen Ali
TIP FOR THE TOP? Miles Hammond
CRICKETING HEROES? AB de Villiers – as he is a keeper/batsmen like myself and watching him made me want to become as successful as he has been over the last few years
NON-CRICKETING HEROES? Steven Gerrard as his leadership skills are immense and he has single-handedly carried Liverpool for many years
COACHING TIP? I know it sounds simple but just to watch the ball as long as possible when both batting and keeping to help block out external pressures
FAVOURITE TV? Match Of The Day
LEAST FAVOURITE TV? Made In Chelsea or The Only Way Is Essex
ACCOMPLISHMENTS? Playing for Newport County academy in football at U16 and probably passing all my A-Levels
PET HATE? Drivers not indicating as it often makes you slow down for no reason!
TWITTER FEED: @camlee_196

| Batting | Mat | Inns | NO | Runs | HS | Ave | SR | 100 | 50 | Ct | St |
|---|---|---|---|---|---|---|---|---|---|---|---|
| First-class | 11 | 14 | 1 | 282 | 114* | 21.69 | 46.84 | 1 | 0 | 32 | 1 |
| Twenty20 | 4 | 4 | 2 | 55 | 23* | 27.50 | 144.73 | 0 | 0 | 1 | 1 |
| **Bowling** | **Mat** | **Balls** | **Runs** | **Wkts** | **BBI** | **BBM** | **Ave** | **Econ** | **SR** | **5w** | **10** |
| First-class | 11 | - | - | - | - | - | - | - | - | - | - |
| Twenty20 | 4 | - | - | - | - | - | - | - | - | - | - |

# RYAN HIGGINS

RHB OB R0 W0

FULL NAME: Ryan Francis Higgins
BORN: January 6, 1995, Harare, Zimbabwe
SQUAD NO: 11
HEIGHT: 6ft 5in
NICKNAME: Higgo, Zim, Pope, Vicor
EDUCATION: Bradfield College; Peterhouse
TEAMS: Middlesex
CAREER: List A: 2014; T20: 2014



CAREER HIGHLIGHTS? Playing in the U19 World Cup semi-final
TIP FOR THE TOP? Matt Fisher, Nick Gubbins
MOST MARKED CHARACTERISTIC? Fiery
CRICKETING HEROES? Michael Hussey – for the intensity in which he played the game. Also that he achieved success in all three forms
NON-CRICKETING HEROES? Mum and dad – they've always been there for me and have always inspired me
CRICKET RULE YOU'D CHANGE? No 50-over cricket because 40-overs is a better, more entertaining game
IF YOU WEREN'T A CRICKETER? I would probably be finding a way to go to uni
IF YOU COULD BE SOMEONE ELSE FOR A DAY? Lil Wayne
FAVOURITE TV? Vampire Diaries
LEAST FAVOURITE TV? Family Guy
FANTASY SLIP CORDON? Keeper: Jon Bon Jovi, 1st: Bruce Springsteen, 2nd: Myself, 3rd: Johnny Cash, Gully: Bryan Adams (to get all the stories from their life of partying and their rock 'n' roll lifestyle)
TWITTER FEED: @ryanhiggins21

| Batting | Mat | Inns | NO | Runs | HS | Ave | SR | 100 | 50 | Ct | St |
|---|---|---|---|---|---|---|---|---|---|---|---|
| List A | 6 | 5 | 0 | 80 | 27 | 16.00 | 77.66 | 0 | 0 | 0 | 0 |
| Twenty20 | 8 | 7 | 2 | 151 | 44* | 30.20 | 116.15 | 0 | 0 | 2 | 0 |
| **Bowling** | **Mat** | **Balls** | **Runs** | **Wkts** | **BBI** | **BBM** | **Ave** | **Econ** | **SR** | **5w** | **10** |
| List A | 6 | - | - | - | - | - | - | - | - | - | - |
| Twenty20 | 8 | - | - | - | - | - | - | - | - | - | - |

## JAMES HILDRETH

RHB RM R4 W0 MVP91

FULL NAME: James Charles Hildreth
BORN: September 9, 1984, Milton Keynes, Buckinghamshire
SQUAD NO: 25
HEIGHT: 5ft 10in
NICKNAME: Hildy, Hildz
EDUCATION: Millfield School
TEAMS: Somerset, England Lions
CAREER: First-class: 2003; List A: 2003; T20: 2004

BEST BATTING: 303* Somerset vs Warwickshire, Taunton, 2009
BEST BOWLING: 2-39 Somerset vs Hampshire, Taunton, 2009
COUNTY CAPS: 2007

CAREER HIGHLIGHTS? Winning the T20 in 2005, captaining England Lions and captaining Somerset
CRICKETING HEROES? Ricky Ponting
IF YOU WEREN'T A CRICKETER? Travelling or on a beach somewhere
FAVOURITE TV? The Big Bang Theory
SURPRISING FACT? I'm a big MK Dons fan
TWITTER FEED: @dreth25

| Batting | Mat | Inns | NO | Runs | HS | Ave | SR | 100 | 50 | Ct | St |
|---|---|---|---|---|---|---|---|---|---|---|---|
| First-class | 184 | 299 | 23 | 11717 | 303* | 42.45 | | 30 | 55 | 164 | 0 |
| List A | 168 | 157 | 30 | 4300 | 151 | 33.85 | | 6 | 17 | 63 | 0 |
| Twenty20 | 133 | 124 | 23 | 2378 | 107* | 23.54 | 120.52 | 1 | 10 | 56 | 0 |
| **Bowling** | **Mat** | **Balls** | **Runs** | **Wkts** | **BBI** | **BBM** | **Ave** | **Econ** | **SR** | **5w** | **10** |
| First-class | 184 | 576 | 492 | 6 | 2/39 | | 82.00 | 5.12 | 96.0 | 0 | 0 |
| List A | 168 | 150 | 185 | 6 | 2/26 | 2/26 | 30.83 | 7.40 | 25.0 | 0 | 0 |
| Twenty20 | 133 | 169 | 247 | 10 | 3/24 | 3/24 | 24.70 | 8.76 | 16.9 | 0 | 0 |

# BEN HILFENHAUS RHB RFM R0 W0

FULL NAME: Benjamin William Hilfenhaus
BORN: March 15, 1983, Ulverstone, Australia
SQUAD NO: tbc
HEIGHT: 6ft 1in
NICKNAME: Hilfy
TEAMS: Australia, Nottinghamshire, Chennai Super Kings, Hobart Hurricanes, Tasmania
CAREER: Test: 2009; ODI: 2007; T20I: 2007; First-class: 2005; List A: 2005; T20: 2006



BEST BATTING: 56* Australia vs Pakistan, Lord's, 2010
BEST BOWLING: 7-58 Tasmania vs New South Wales, Hobart, 2006

NOTES: Australian seamer Hilfenhaus will make his county cricket debut this season and will replace Vernon Philander from June 5. He has played 27 Tests, 25 ODIs and seven T20Is, although he hasn't played for Australia since 2012. He took 22 wickets in the 2009 Ashes. He became only the second fast bowler from Tasmania to play for Australia. In 2005 he was working on a building site but in 2007 he earned a national contract after taking 60 wickets in the Pura Cup

| Batting | Mat | Inns | NO | Runs | HS | Ave | SR | 100 | 50 | Ct | St |
|---|---|---|---|---|---|---|---|---|---|---|---|
| Tests | 27 | 38 | 12 | 355 | 56* | 13.65 | 54.19 | 0 | 1 | 7 | 0 |
| ODIs | 25 | 11 | 8 | 29 | 16 | 9.66 | 42.02 | 0 | 0 | 10 | 0 |
| T20Is | 7 | 3 | 1 | 2 | 2 | 1.00 | 20.00 | 0 | 0 | 0 | 0 |
| First-class | 100 | 141 | 36 | 1316 | 56* | 12.53 | | 0 | 3 | 29 | 0 |
| List A | 78 | 34 | 21 | 119 | 18* | 9.15 | 57.76 | 0 | 0 | 20 | 0 |
| Twenty20 | 65 | 27 | 16 | 121 | 38* | 11.00 | 96.03 | 0 | 0 | 11 | 0 |
| **Bowling** | **Mat** | **Balls** | **Runs** | **Wkts** | **BBI** | **BBM** | **Ave** | **Econ** | **SR** | **5w** | **10** |
| Tests | 27 | 6078 | 2822 | 99 | 5/75 | 8/97 | 28.50 | 2.78 | 61.3 | 2 | 0 |
| ODIs | 25 | 1216 | 1075 | 29 | 5/33 | 5/33 | 37.06 | 5.30 | 41.9 | 1 | 0 |
| T20Is | 7 | 156 | 161 | 9 | 2/15 | 2/15 | 17.88 | 6.19 | 17.3 | 0 | 0 |
| First-class | 100 | 22288 | 10974 | 379 | 7/58 | 10/87 | 28.95 | 2.95 | 58.8 | 13 | 1 |
| List A | 78 | 4169 | 3200 | 89 | 5/33 | 5/33 | 35.95 | 4.60 | 46.8 | 1 | 0 |
| Twenty20 | 65 | 1426 | 1754 | 78 | 4/27 | 4/27 | 22.48 | 7.38 | 18.2 | 0 | 0 |

# LEWIS HILL

RHB WK R0 W0

FULL NAME: Lewis John Hill
BORN: October 5, 1990, Leicester
SQUAD NO: 23
HEIGHT: 5ft 8in
NICKNAME: Lew Show, Lew
EDUCATION: Hastings High School; John Cleveland College
TEAMS: Leicestershire 2nd XI, Unicorns
CAREER: List A: 2012

CAREER HIGHLIGHTS? Signing my first professional contract. Playing at Lord's for the Unicorns in 2013
BEST PLAYER IN COUNTY CRICKET? Jos Buttler
TIP FOR THE TOP? Shiv Thakor
MOST MARKED CHARACTERISTIC? Eyebrows!
CRICKETING HEROES? Craig Wilson and Karl Smith – played 1st XI club cricket with them since I was young. Marcus Trescothick – watching him when I was younger
CRICKET RULE YOU'D CHANGE? Being a wicketkeeper, no byes would be ideal!
IF YOU WEREN'T A CRICKETER? Unfortunately maybe working for my dad!
FAVOURITE TV? The Inbetweeners, The Walking Dead, Game Of Thrones
PET HATE? Rude people
SURPRISING FACT? I've been a wicketkeeper for only two years. I was 'held up' twice in a newsagents before becoming a cricketer
FANTASY SLIP CORDON? Keeper: Myself, 1st: Ricky Ponting, 2nd: Mila Kunis, 3rd: Keith Lemon
TWITTER FEED: @lew_show_

| Batting | Mat | Inns | NO | Runs | HS | Ave | SR | 100 | 50 | Ct | St |
|---|---|---|---|---|---|---|---|---|---|---|---|
| List A | 11 | 11 | 1 | 169 | 35 | 16.90 | 81.25 | 0 | 0 | 4 | 1 |
| Bowling | Mat | Balls | Runs | Wkts | BBI | BBM | Ave | Econ | SR | 5w | 10 |
| List A | 11 | - | - | - | - | - | - | - | - | - | - |

# MATTHEW HOBDEN RHB RFM R0 W0

FULL NAME: Matthew Edward Hobden
BORN: March 27, 1993, Eastbourne, Sussex
SQUAD NO: 19
HEIGHT: 6ft 4in
NICKNAME: Hobbo, Shooter
EDUCATION: Eastbourne College; Cardiff Metropolitan University
TEAMS: Sussex
CAREER: First-class: 2012; List A: 2013; T20L 2014



BEST BATTING: 18 Cardiff MCCU vs Glamorgan, Cardiff, 2013
BEST BOWLING: 5-62 Cardiff MCCU vs Warwickshire, Birmingham, 2012

CAREER HIGHLIGHTS? My Championship debut against Notts
BEST PLAYER IN COUNTY CRICKET? Ed Joyce
TIP FOR THE TOP? Harry Finch
CRICKETING HEROES? Andrew Flintoff – watched him a lot when I was younger
IF YOU WEREN'T A CRICKETER? Travelling all over the place
IF YOU COULD BE SOMEONE ELSE FOR A DAY? A Formula One driver
DESERT ISLAND DISC? Bob Dylan – The Freewheelin'
TWITTER FEED: @hobs19

| Batting | Mat | Inns | NO | Runs | HS | Ave | SR | 100 | 50 | Ct | St |
|---|---|---|---|---|---|---|---|---|---|---|---|
| First-class | 7 | 6 | 2 | 37 | 18 | 9.25 | 28.46 | 0 | 0 | 0 | 0 |
| List A | 1 | 1 | 0 | 2 | 2 | 2.00 | 28.57 | 0 | 0 | 0 | 0 |
| Twenty20 | 1 | - | - | - | - | - | - | - | - | 0 | 0 |
| **Bowling** | **Mat** | **Balls** | **Runs** | **Wkts** | **BBI** | **BBM** | **Ave** | **Econ** | **SR** | **5w** | **10** |
| First-class | 7 | 1041 | 775 | 25 | 5/62 | 5/62 | 31.00 | 4.46 | 41.6 | 2 | 0 |
| List A | 1 | 48 | 39 | 1 | 1/39 | 1/39 | 39.00 | 4.87 | 48.0 | 0 | 0 |
| Twenty20 | 1 | 12 | 36 | 0 | - | - | - | 18.00 | - | 0 | 0 |

# ANDY HODD RHB WK R0 W0

FULL NAME: Andrew John Hodd
BORN: January 12, 1984, Chichester, West Sussex
SQUAD NO: 4
HEIGHT: 5ft 9in
NICKNAME: Hoddy
EDUCATION: Bexhill High School; Bexhill College; Loughborough University
TEAMS: Yorkshire, Surrey, Sussex
CAREER: First-class: 2003; List A: 2002: T20: 2005

BEST BATTING: 123 Sussex vs Yorkshire, Hove, 2007

TWITTER FEED: @Hoddfather
NOTES: Hodd began his career at Sussex before moving on to Surrey, but he returned to the south coast in 2006 to act as Matt Prior's deputy. He performed well for Sussex, including a career-best 123 against Yorkshire at Hove, but the emergence of Ben Brown meant Hodd's chances became fewer and he joined Yorkshire in August 2012 on a temporary contract after Jonny Bairstow's call-up for England. His performances earned him a two-year deal, which he signed at the end of 2012. He made nine first-class appearances for the White Rose in 2013, scoring 217 runs at 31. He was restricted to five Championship appearances in 2014. Toured Australia with England at U17 and U19 level

| Batting | Mat | Inns | NO | Runs | HS | Ave | SR | 100 | 50 | Ct | St |
|---|---|---|---|---|---|---|---|---|---|---|---|
| First-class | 75 | 104 | 18 | 2458 | 123 | 28.58 | 44.36 | 4 | 12 | 166 | 14 |
| List A | 55 | 42 | 11 | 752 | 91 | 24.25 | | 0 | 2 | 52 | 11 |
| Twenty20 | 53 | 30 | 6 | 282 | 26 | 11.75 | 101.80 | 0 | 0 | 24 | 11 |
| **Bowling** | **Mat** | **Balls** | **Runs** | **Wkts** | **BBI** | **BBM** | **Ave** | **Econ** | **SR** | **5w** | **10** |
| First-class | 75 | 10 | 7 | 0 | - | - | - | 4.20 | - | 0 | 0 |
| List A | 55 | - | - | - | - | - | - | - | - | - | - |
| Twenty20 | 53 | - | - | - | - | - | - | - | - | - | - |

# DAN HODGSON

RHB WK R0 W0

FULL NAME: Daniel Mark Hodgson
BORN: February 26, 1990, Northallerton, Yorkshire
SQUAD NO: 18
EDUCATION: Richmond School; Leeds University
TEAMS: Yorkshire, Mountaineers
CAREER: First-class: 2012; List A: 2012; T20: 2012



BEST BATTING: 94* Mountaineers vs Southern Rocks, Mutare, 2013

CAREER HIGHLIGHTS? Signing for Yorkshire
CRICKETING HEROES? Shane Warne, Kumar Sangakkara
NON-CRICKETING HEROES? My parents, Alan Shearer, The Rock, Jay Z
FAVOURITE TV? Match Of The Day, One Tree Hill, House
SURPRISING FACT? I can juggle fire
FANTASY SLIP CORDON? Keeper: Me, 1st: Sonny Bill Williams, 2nd: P. Diddy, 3rd: Peter Griffin, Gully: David Attenborough
TWITTER FEED: @dhodgson26

| Batting | Mat | Inns | NO | Runs | HS | Ave | SR | 100 | 50 | Ct | St |
|---|---|---|---|---|---|---|---|---|---|---|---|
| First-class | 12 | 22 | 2 | 450 | 94* | 22.50 | 46.39 | 0 | 4 | 33 | 2 |
| List A | 14 | 11 | 1 | 296 | 90 | 29.60 | 93.67 | 0 | 3 | 14 | 3 |
| Twenty20 | 17 | 15 | 2 | 225 | 52* | 17.30 | 96.15 | 0 | 1 | 10 | 1 |
| **Bowling** | **Mat** | **Balls** | **Runs** | **Wkts** | **BBI** | **BBM** | **Ave** | **Econ** | **SR** | **5w** | **10** |
| First-class | 12 | - | - | - | - | - | - | - | - | - | - |
| List A | 14 | - | - | - | - | - | - | - | - | - | - |
| Twenty20 | 17 | - | - | - | - | - | - | - | - | - | - |

## MICHAEL HOGAN RHB RFM R0 W2 MVP15

FULL NAME: Michael Garry Hogan
BORN: May 31, 1981, Newcastle, Australia
SQUAD NO: 31
HEIGHT: 6ft 5in
NICKNAME: Hulk, Hoges
TEAMS: Glamorgan, Western Australia
CAREER: First-class: 2009; List A: 2009; T20: 2010

BEST BATTING: 51 Glamorgan vs Gloucestershire, Bristol, 2013
BEST BOWLING: 7-92 Glamorgan vs Gloucestershire, Bristol, 2013

CAREER HIGHLIGHTS? Breaking the 100-wicket mark last season for Glamorgan was a nice personal achievement
CRICKETING HEROES? Glenn McGrath
IF YOU WEREN'T A CRICKETER? Probably a career in horticulture
DESERT ISLAND DISC? Jack Johnson – Sitting, Waiting, Wishing
FAVOURITE TV? The Simpsons
ACCOMPLISHMENTS? My two children
FANTASY SLIP CORDON? Keeper: Billy Connolly, 1st: Myself (you don't have to move at 1st), 2nd: James Taylor (the musician not the cricketer), 3rd: Ricky Ponting, Gully: Usain Bolt (someone fast to chase anything that goes behind the wicket)
TWITTER FEED: @Hoges31

| Batting | Mat | Inns | NO | Runs | HS | Ave | SR | 100 | 50 | Ct | St |
|---|---|---|---|---|---|---|---|---|---|---|---|
| First-class | 79 | 115 | 39 | 1191 | 51 | 15.67 | 82.08 | 0 | 1 | 39 | 0 |
| List A | 44 | 15 | 7 | 99 | 27 | 12.37 | 77.34 | 0 | 0 | 16 | 0 |
| Twenty20 | 38 | 7 | 4 | 17 | 5* | 5.66 | 77.27 | 0 | 0 | 16 | 0 |
| **Bowling** | **Mat** | **Balls** | **Runs** | **Wkts** | **BBI** | **BBM** | **Ave** | **Econ** | **SR** | **5w** | **10** |
| First-class | 79 | 17136 | 7758 | 317 | 7/92 | 10/125 | 24.47 | 2.71 | 54.0 | 13 | 1 |
| List A | 44 | 2310 | 1884 | 77 | 5/44 | 5/44 | 24.46 | 4.89 | 30.0 | 1 | 0 |
| Twenty20 | 38 | 816 | 1001 | 40 | 4/26 | 4/26 | 25.02 | 7.36 | 20.4 | 0 | 0 |

## MAX HOLDEN LHB OB R0 W0

FULL NAME: Max David Edward Holden
BORN: December 18, 1997, Cambridge
SQUAD NO: 24
HEIGHT: 5ft 11in
NICKNAME: Pepsi, Little Chef
EDUCATION: Sawston Village College; Hills Road Sixth Form College
TEAMS: Middlesex 2nd XI
CAREER: Yet to make first-team debut



CAREER HIGHLIGHTS? Playing for the England Development Programme, winning Middlesex Youth Player of the Year and receiving my first professional contract at Middlesex
BEST PLAYER IN COUNTY CRICKET? James Taylor
TIP FOR THE TOP? Haseeb Hameed
MOST MARKED CHARACTERISTIC? My smile
SUPERSTITIONS? I don't like odd numbers so I have to tap my bat two or four times before taking strike
CRICKETING HEROES? Alastair Cook – left-handed opening batsman like myself and has always been able to bat for long periods
CRICKET RULE YOU'D CHANGE? You can't be out caught down the leg-side as that is the most frustrating way of getting out
IF YOU COULD BE SOMEONE ELSE FOR A DAY? Arséne Wenger – so I could sign some good players for Arsenal
DESERT ISLAND DISC? Nico and Vinz – When The Day Comes
FAVOURITE TV? I'm A Celebrity ... Get Me Out Of Here!
LEAST FAVOURITE TV? Big Brother
ACCOMPLISHMENTS? Playing for the Cambridge United Youth Academy
PET HATE? Horror films
SURPRISING FACT? I am of Singaporean descent
FANTASY SLIP CORDON? Keeper: Morgan Freeman, 1st: Ollie Perry (my best mate), 2nd: Myself, 3rd: Alexis Sånchez, Gully: Sachin Tendulkar
TWITTER FEED: @maxholden24

# PAUL HORTON

RHB RM R3 W0 MVP60

FULL NAME: Paul James Horton
BORN: September 20, 1982, Sydney, Australia
SQUAD NO: 20
HEIGHT: 5ft 10in
NICKNAME: Horts, Lefty, Aussie
EDUCATION: Colo High School, Sydney; Broadgreen Camp Liverpool; St Margaret's High School
TEAMS: Lancashire, Matabeleland Tuskers
CAREER: First-class: 2003; List A: 2003; T20: 2005

BEST BATTING: 209 Matabeleland Tuskers vs Southern Rocks, Masvingo, 2011
COUNTY CAPS: 2007

CAREER HIGHLIGHTS? Nothing can top winning the County Championship in 2011 with Lancashire but every time I score a first-class hundred is pretty special. Back-to-back Logan Cup trophies with Matebeleland Tuskers in 2010/11 and 2011/12
CRICKETING HEROES? Mark Waugh, Dean Jones, Brian Lara
NON-CRICKETING HEROES? Roger Federer, Robbie Fowler
IF YOU WEREN'T A CRICKETER? Something in a suit!
FAVOURITE TV? Location, Location, Location
ACCOMPLISHMENTS? Finished school in one piece!
SURPRISING FACT? I was once held as an illegal immigrant!
FANTASY SLIP CORDON? Keeper: Tiger Woods, 1st: Myself, 2nd: Robbie Fowler, 3rd: Nelson Mandela, Gully: Wonder Woman
TWITTER FEED: @PJHorton20

| Batting | Mat | Inns | NO | Runs | HS | Ave | SR | 100 | 50 | Ct | St |
|---|---|---|---|---|---|---|---|---|---|---|---|
| First-class | 152 | 257 | 21 | 8911 | 209 | 37.75 | 47.86 | 20 | 46 | 152 | 1 |
| List A | 99 | 90 | 12 | 2463 | 111* | 31.57 | | 2 | 13 | 37 | 0 |
| Twenty20 | 75 | 69 | 13 | 1312 | 71* | 23.42 | 108.42 | 0 | 4 | 30 | 0 |
| **Bowling** | **Mat** | **Balls** | **Runs** | **Wkts** | **BBI** | **BBM** | **Ave** | **Econ** | **SR** | **5w** | **10** |
| First-class | 152 | 18 | 16 | 0 | - | - | - | 5.33 | - | 0 | 0 |
| List A | 99 | - | - | - | - | - | - | - | - | - | - |
| Twenty20 | 75 | - | - | - | - | - | - | - | - | - | - |

# HARVEY HOSEIN RHB WK R0 W0

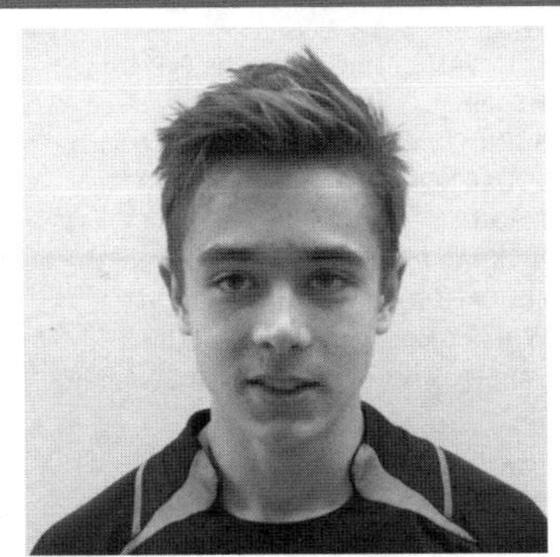

FULL NAME: Harvey Richard Hosein
BORN: August 12, 1996, Chesterfield, Derbyshire
SQUAD NO: 16
HEIGHT: 5ft 11in
EDUCATION: Denstone College
TEAMS: Derbyshire
CAREER: First-class: 2014



BEST BATTING: 13 Derbyshire vs Leicestershire, Derby, 2014

CAREER HIGHLIGHTS? Scoring 53* on Derbyshire debut against India and taking 11 catches on my first-class debut against Surrey at The Oval
BEST PLAYER IN COUNTY CRICKET? Jonathan Trott and Wayne Madsen
TIP FOR THE TOP? Shiv Thakor, Ben Cotton, Greg Cork
MOST MARKED CHARACTERISTIC? Worrying
CRICKETING HEROES? Adam Gilchrist – aggressive top-order batsman and wicketkeeper. Brian Lara – exciting player to watch
NON-CRICKETING HEROES? Roger Federer
CRICKET RULE YOU'D CHANGE? The wicketkeeper should be able to choose whether a batsman is caught or stumped if it happens in the same ball
DESERT ISLAND DISC? Take That – Greatest Hits
FAVOURITE TV? Law And Order
LEAST FAVOURITE TV? Most soaps
PET HATE? Bad smelling kit in the dressing room, especially if you're sat next to it
SURPRISING FACT? I used to play tennis at county level
TWITTER FEED: @HarveyHosein16

| Batting | Mat | Inns | NO | Runs | HS | Ave | SR | 100 | 50 | Ct | St |
|---|---|---|---|---|---|---|---|---|---|---|---|
| First-class | 2 | 2 | 0 | 17 | 13 | 8.50 | 26.56 | 0 | 0 | 15 | 0 |
| **Bowling** | **Mat** | **Balls** | **Runs** | **Wkts** | **BBI** | **BBM** | **Ave** | **Econ** | **SR** | **5w** | **10** |
| First-class | 2 | - | - | - | - | - | - | - | - | - | - |

GLOUCESTERSHIRE

## BENNY HOWELL RHB RMF R0 W0 MVP53

FULL NAME: Benny Alexander Cameron Howell
BORN: October 5, 1988, Bordeaux, France
SQUAD NO: 13
HEIGHT: 6ft
NICKNAME: Novak
EDUCATION: The Oratory School
TEAMS: Gloucestershire, Hampshire
CAREER: First-class: 2011; List A: 2010; T20: 2011

BEST BATTING: 83* Gloucestershire vs Yorkshire, Scarborough, 2012
BEST BOWLING: 5-57 Gloucestershire vs Leicestershire, Leicester, 2013
COUNTY CAPS: 2012

CAREER HIGHLIGHTS? Scoring 122 in the Pro40 vs Surrey and taking 8-97 in the Championship vs Leicestershire
CRICKETING HEROES? Steve Waugh – for his mental toughness. Brett Lee – because he was the ultimate athlete
IF YOU WEREN'T A CRICKETER? Professional gambler
IF YOU COULD BE SOMEONE ELSE FOR A DAY? Harry Styles
DESERT ISLAND DISC? Ed Sheeran
ACCOMPLISHMENTS? Youth champion at real tennis and winning a club baseball championship as a closing pitcher
PET HATE? When you think you're going to make the traffic lights and then they suddenly turn amber then red. Argh!
SURPRISING FACT? I often write in my spare time
FANTASY SLIP CORDON? Keeper: Ricky Gervais, 1st: Myself, 2nd: Whitney Houston, 3rd: Jessica Alba, Gully: Kevin Pietersen

| Batting | Mat | Inns | NO | Runs | HS | Ave | SR | 100 | 50 | Ct | St |
|---|---|---|---|---|---|---|---|---|---|---|---|
| First-class | 42 | 67 | 10 | 1524 | 83* | 26.73 | 52.67 | 0 | 10 | 21 | 0 |
| List A | 44 | 34 | 7 | 1004 | 122 | 37.18 | 91.43 | 1 | 5 | 14 | 0 |
| Twenty20 | 43 | 38 | 14 | 548 | 55* | 22.83 | 115.36 | 0 | 2 | 10 | 0 |
| **Bowling** | **Mat** | **Balls** | **Runs** | **Wkts** | **BBI** | **BBM** | **Ave** | **Econ** | **SR** | **5w** | **10** |
| First-class | 42 | 4194 | 2009 | 59 | 5/57 | 8/96 | 34.05 | 2.87 | 71.0 | 1 | 0 |
| List A | 44 | 1098 | 921 | 21 | 2/26 | 2/26 | 43.85 | 5.03 | 52.2 | 0 | 0 |
| Twenty20 | 43 | 492 | 607 | 28 | 4/26 | 4/26 | 21.67 | 7.40 | 17.5 | 0 | 0 |

## FYNN HUDSON-PRENTICE RHB RMF R0 W0

FULL NAME: Fynn Jake Hudson-Prentice
BORN: January 12, 1996, Haywards Heath, Sussex
SQUAD NO: 14
HEIGHT: 6ft
NICKNAME: Fynny, HP, Swampy
EDUCATION: Warden Park School; Bede's Senior School
TEAMS: Sussex
CAREER: List A: 2014



---

CAREER HIGHLIGHTS? Being selected for Sussex, scoring my first county century, then scoring three in a row and signing my first professional contract with Sussex
BEST PLAYER IN COUNTY CRICKET? Steve Magoffin
TIP FOR THE TOP? Sam Hain, Lewis Gregory, Matt Hobden, Rob Keogh
MOST MARKED CHARACTERISTIC? I'm always looking for a laugh
CRICKETING HEROES? Andrew Flintoff – he played the game the way it should be played, was a great team man and turned games around! He also knew how to have fun on and off the field!
CRICKET RULE YOU'D CHANGE? You should be able to have one substitution! You should be allowed to select a squad of 15 (including a 12th man) and be able to make one substitution at any point in the game, whether it be a fielder, batsmen or bowler!
COACHING TIP? 'Last six inches' is the best thing I have been taught. Watch the ball right onto the bat, watch the ball right into your hands (or gloves if you are a keeper), because the ball can move in the last six inches so don't take your eye off it!
IF YOU COULD BE SOMEONE ELSE FOR A DAY? Phil 'The Power' Taylor
DESERT ISLAND DISC? Ed Sheeran – X
FAVOURITE TV? How I Met Your Mother
LEAST FAVOURITE TV? Made In Chelsea, by a long stretch
PET HATE? People taking food off my plate without asking, because if I didn't want it or wanted to give it away, then it wouldn't be on my plate!
SURPRISING FACT? I am addicted to milk. I drink about three or four pints a day!
TWITTER FEED: @FJHPrentice

# ALEX HUGHES

RHB RM R0 W0

FULL NAME: Alex Lloyd Hughes
BORN: September 29, 1991, Wordsley, Staffordshire
SQUAD NO: 18
HEIGHT: 5ft 10in
NICKNAME: Yozza, Barry Horse
EDUCATION: Ounsdale High School; University of Worcester
TEAMS: Derbyshire, Staffordshire
CAREER: First-class: 2013; List A: 2012; T20: 2011

BEST BATTING: 82 Derbyshire vs Kent, Canterbury, 2014
BEST BOWLING: 4-46 Derbyshire vs Glamorgan, Derby, 2014

FAMILY TIES? My brother Liam is also contracted to Derbyshire
BEST PLAYER IN COUNTY CRICKET? Mark Footitt
TIP FOR THE TOP? Tommy Taylor and Ben Cotton
MOST MARKED CHARACTERISTIC? Full head of hair
SUPERSTITIONS? Kissing my lucky egg
CRICKETING HEROES? Dimi Mascarenhas and Mark Ealham
CRICKET RULE YOU'D CHANGE? Four inside the circle in one-day cricket. Too easy for batsmen
IF YOU WEREN'T A CRICKETER? Stuntman
IF YOU COULD BE SOMEONE ELSE FOR A DAY? Rory McIlroy
DESERT ISLAND DISC? Ed Sheeran – any album
FAVOURITE TV? Gogglebox
PET HATE? Cats
SURPRISING FACT? I got to The X Factor bootcamp in 2012
TWITTER FEED: @Yozza18

| Batting | Mat | Inns | NO | Runs | HS | Ave | SR | 100 | 50 | Ct | St |
|---|---|---|---|---|---|---|---|---|---|---|---|
| First-class | 19 | 32 | 4 | 584 | 82 | 20.85 | 41.68 | 0 | 3 | 8 | 0 |
| List A | 24 | 16 | 5 | 273 | 59* | 24.81 | 81.25 | 0 | 1 | 6 | 0 |
| Twenty20 | 19 | 15 | 4 | 128 | 43* | 11.63 | 114.28 | 0 | 0 | 7 | 0 |
| **Bowling** | **Mat** | **Balls** | **Runs** | **Wkts** | **BBI** | **BBM** | **Ave** | **Econ** | **SR** | **5w** | **10** |
| First-class | 19 | 1294 | 670 | 16 | 4/46 | 4/75 | 41.87 | 3.10 | 80.8 | 0 | 0 |
| List A | 24 | 761 | 710 | 16 | 3/56 | 3/56 | 44.37 | 5.59 | 47.5 | 0 | 0 |
| Twenty20 | 19 | 234 | 346 | 7 | 3/32 | 3/32 | 49.42 | 8.87 | 33.4 | 0 | 0 |

## CHESNEY HUGHES LHB SLA R0 W0

FULL NAME: Chesney Francis Hughes
BORN: January 20, 1991, Anguilla
SQUAD NO: 22
TEAMS: Derbyshire, Anguilla, Leeward Islands
CAREER: First-class: 2010; List A: 2007; T20: 2006



BEST BATTING: 270* Derbyshire vs Yorkshire, Leeds, 2013
BEST BOWLING: 2-9 Derbyshire vs Middlesex, Derby, 2011

TWITTER FEED: @ChesneyH22
NOTES: The Anguillan batsman made an immediate impact in his debut County Championship season in 2010, amassing 784 runs and averaging 41.26. His highest score came against Northamptonshire, when he hit 156 at Chesterfield. He was left out of Derbyshire's four-day side for the whole of 2012, playing just one game. Recorded career-best bowling figures in the YB40 vs Unicorns in the same season. Returned to the side for 2013 and scored 270* against Yorkshire at Headingley, with 40 fours and three sixes. Derbyshire's top-scorer in the YB40 in 2013 with 271 runs. He struggled for runs in 2014 and made only five Championship appearances

| Batting | Mat | Inns | NO | Runs | HS | Ave | SR | 100 | 50 | Ct | St |
|---|---|---|---|---|---|---|---|---|---|---|---|
| First-class | 44 | 79 | 3 | 2312 | 270* | 30.42 | 53.96 | 5 | 9 | 35 | 0 |
| List A | 64 | 60 | 2 | 1435 | 81 | 24.74 | | 0 | 12 | 12 | 0 |
| Twenty20 | 67 | 64 | 2 | 1141 | 65 | 18.40 | 109.50 | 0 | 3 | 19 | 0 |
| **Bowling** | **Mat** | **Balls** | **Runs** | **Wkts** | **BBI** | **BBM** | **Ave** | **Econ** | **SR** | **5w** | **10** |
| First-class | 44 | 940 | 581 | 15 | 2/9 | 2/17 | 38.73 | 3.70 | 62.6 | 0 | 0 |
| List A | 64 | 877 | 754 | 22 | 5/29 | 5/29 | 34.27 | 5.15 | 39.8 | 1 | 0 |
| Twenty20 | 67 | 630 | 793 | 26 | 4/23 | 4/23 | 30.50 | 7.55 | 24.2 | 0 | 0 |

# MATT HUNN

RHB RFM R0 W0

FULL NAME: Matthew David Hunn
BORN: March 22, 1994, Colchester
SQUAD NO: 14
HEIGHT: 6ft 5in
NICKNAME: Hunny
EDUCATION: St Joseph's College, Ipswich
TEAMS: Kent
CAREER: First-class: 2013

BEST BATTING: 0* Kent vs Essex, Chelmsford, 2014
BEST BOWLING: 2-51 Kent vs Lancashire, Canterbury, 2013

CAREER HIGHLIGHTS? Signing my first contract and making my debut
BEST PLAYER IN COUNTY CRICKET? Darren Stevens
MOST MARKED CHARACTERISTIC? My height
CRICKETING HEROES? Andrew Flintoff, Morne Morkel
NON-CRICKETING HEROES? Nelson Mandela
CRICKET RULE YOU'D CHANGE? Make the game more bowler-friendly
IF YOU WEREN'T A CRICKETER? Probably at university studying something
DESERT ISLAND DISC? Bastille
FAVOURITE TV? The Big Bang Theory or Top Gear
ACCOMPLISHMENTS? Holding a 24-hour, indoor rowing Guinness world record with my school
TWITTER FEED: @MattHunn10

| Batting | Mat | Inns | NO | Runs | HS | Ave | SR | 100 | 50 | Ct | St |
|---|---|---|---|---|---|---|---|---|---|---|---|
| First-class | 3 | 4 | 2 | 0 | 0* | 0.00 | 0.00 | 0 | 0 | 2 | 0 |
| **Bowling** | **Mat** | **Balls** | **Runs** | **Wkts** | **BBI** | **BBM** | **Ave** | **Econ** | **SR** | **5w** | **10** |
| First-class | 3 | 406 | 273 | 6 | 2/51 | 3/118 | 45.50 | 4.03 | 67.6 | 0 | 0 |

# BRETT HUTTON RHB RM R0 W0

FULL NAME: Brett Alan Hutton
BORN: February 6, 1993, Doncaster, Yorkshire
SQUAD NO: 26
HEIGHT: 6ft
NICKNAME: Hutts
EDUCATION: Worksop College
TEAMS: Nottinghamshire
CAREER: First-class: 2011; List A: 2011



BEST BATTING: 42 Nottinghamshire vs Somerset, Nottingham, 2013
BEST BOWLING: 1-31 Nottinghamshire vs Somerset. Nottingham, 2013

CAREER HIGHLIGHTS? Playing for England U19, Notts debut vs MCC in Abu Dhabi
MOST MARKED CHARACTERISTIC? Stubble
CRICKETING HEROES? Chris Tolley, Harold Larwood
NON-CRICKETING HEROES? Lee Westwood
IF YOU WEREN'T A CRICKETER? Window cleaner
DESERT ISLAND DISC? Nicki Minaj – Pink Friday
FAVOURITE TV? Emmerdale
SURPRISING FACT? I've got my own window cleaning round
FANTASY SLIP CORDON? Keeper: George Formby, 1st: Scarlett Johansson, 2nd: Tommy Johnson, 3rd: Stevie Wonder, 4th: Holly Willoughby

| Batting | Mat | Inns | NO | Runs | HS | Ave | SR | 100 | 50 | Ct | St |
|---|---|---|---|---|---|---|---|---|---|---|---|
| First-class | 2 | 4 | 1 | 71 | 42 | 23.66 | 75.53 | 0 | 0 | 1 | 0 |
| List A | 3 | 3 | 2 | 24 | 17* | 24.00 | 126.31 | 0 | 0 | 2 | 0 |
| **Bowling** | **Mat** | **Balls** | **Runs** | **Wkts** | **BBI** | **BBM** | **Ave** | **Econ** | **SR** | **5w** | **10** |
| First-class | 2 | 240 | 178 | 1 | 1/31 | 1/109 | 178.00 | 4.45 | 240.0 | 0 | 0 |
| List A | 3 | 144 | 169 | 2 | 1/60 | 1/60 | 84.50 | 7.04 | 72.0 | 0 | 0 |

# SAF IMTIAZ

## RHB WK R0 W0

ESSEX

FULL NAME: Saf Imtiaz
BORN: March 14, 1996, London
SQUAD NO: 15
HEIGHT: 5ft 11in
NICKNAME: Saffa
EDUCATION: Chigwell School
TEAMS: Essex 2nd XI
CAREER: Yet to make first-team debut

---

CAREER HIGHLIGHTS? Scoring 100 not out on Essex 2nd XI debut against Derbyshire and experiencing my first year on the Essex staff
BEST PLAYER IN COUNTY CRICKET? James Taylor
TIP FOR THE TOP? Jamie Porter
MOST MARKED CHARACTERISTIC? Hard worker
CRICKETING HEROES? Viv Richards – wasn't afraid to play his shots, had a lot of flare with his batting and took the game to the opposition.
NON-CRICKETING HEROES? Muhammad Ali – worked extremely hard to become the best in his field
CRICKET RULE YOU'D CHANGE? Batsmen to be given an extra chance once they are out because for a batsman it's a one-ball game
IF YOU WEREN'T A CRICKETER? Studying economics at university and eventually becoming a banker
IF YOU COULD BE SOMEONE ELSE FOR A DAY? Barack Obama
DESERT ISLAND DISC? Drake – Take Care
FAVOURITE TV? Friends
LEAST FAVOURITE TV? News
PET HATE? When you ask someone what do you want to do and they reply 'It's up to you' or 'I don't mind'. I wouldn't ask you if I didn't want your opinion
FANTASY SLIP CORDON? Keeper: Myself, 1st: Dwayne Johnson, 2nd: Andrew Flintoff, 3rd: Floyd Mayweather, Gully: Will Smith
TWITTER FEED: @safimtiaz_14

# COLIN INGRAM

LHB WK R0 W0

FULL NAME: Colin Alexander Ingram
BORN: July 3, 1985, Port Elizabeth, South Africa
SQUAD NO: 41
TEAMS: South Africa, Glamorgan, Delhi Daredevils, Eastern Province, Free State, Somerset, Warriors
CAREER: ODI: 2010; T20I: 2010; First-class: 2004; List A: 2005; T20: 2007



BEST BATTING: 190 Eastern Province vs KwaZulu-Natal, Port Elizabeth, 2009
BEST BOWLING: 4-16 Eastern Province vs Boland, Port Elizabeth, 2006

NOTES: An aggressive opening batsman, Colin Ingram joined Glamorgan as a Kolpak on a three-year deal, starting in 2015. He scored 124 on ODI debut for South Africa against Zimbabwe in 2010, putting on 136 with Hashim Amla. He took over as Warriors captain in 2014. In 2014 he signed for Somerset, playing 12 games across all three formats as a replacement for Alviro Petersen and scoring three fifties

| Batting | Mat | Inns | NO | Runs | HS | Ave | SR | 100 | 50 | Ct | St |
|---|---|---|---|---|---|---|---|---|---|---|---|
| ODIs | 31 | 29 | 3 | 843 | 124 | 32.42 | 82.32 | 3 | 3 | 12 | 0 |
| T20Is | 9 | 9 | 1 | 210 | 78 | 26.25 | 129.62 | 0 | 1 | 2 | 0 |
| First-class | 73 | 129 | 11 | 4584 | 190 | 38.84 | | 10 | 23 | 56 | 0 |
| List A | 132 | 129 | 13 | 5072 | 127 | 43.72 | 86.71 | 9 | 34 | 48 | 0 |
| Twenty20 | 81 | 79 | 8 | 1750 | 84 | 24.64 | 123.41 | 0 | 9 | 26 | 0 |
| **Bowling** | **Mat** | **Balls** | **Runs** | **Wkts** | **BBI** | **BBM** | **Ave** | **Econ** | **SR** | **5w** | **10** |
| ODIs | 31 | 6 | 17 | 0 | - | - | - | 17.00 | - | 0 | 0 |
| T20Is | 9 | - | - | - | - | - | - | - | - | - | - |
| First-class | 73 | 2234 | 1342 | 34 | 4/16 | 5/50 | 39.47 | 3.60 | 65.7 | 0 | 0 |
| List A | 132 | 396 | 340 | 11 | 2/13 | 2/13 | 30.90 | 5.15 | 36.0 | 0 | 0 |
| Twenty20 | 81 | 36 | 48 | 2 | 1/16 | 1/16 | 24.00 | 8.00 | 18.0 | 0 | 0 |

## CALLUM JACKSON

## RHB WK R0 W0

FULL NAME: Callum Frederick Jackson
BORN: September 7, 1994, Eastbourne, Sussex
SQUAD NO: 16
HEIGHT: 5ft 11in
NICKNAME: Jacko, CJ
EDUCATION: St Bede's School
TEAMS: Sussex
CAREER: First-class: 2013; List A: 2013; T20: 2013

BEST BATTING: 26 Sussex vs Australians, Hove, 2013

CAREER HIGHLIGHTS? Making my first-class debut against Australia at Hove, making my Sussex debut in all three formats and topping the one-day averages on the England U19 tour of South Africa
BEST PLAYER IN COUNTY CRICKET? Luke Wright
TIP FOR THE TOP? Matt Hobden, Tymal Mills
MOST MARKED CHARACTERISTIC? Probably my nose
SUPERSTITIONS? I always wear a sweatband when batting
CRICKETING HEROES? Ian Bell – because he looks stylish when he bats
CRICKET RULE YOU'D CHANGE? Stricter wides in the longer formats. As a keeper some of the byes given are unreachable
COACHING TIP? Relax from your shoulders down when keeping
DESERT ISLAND DISC? Alt J – This Is All Yours
PET HATE? People chewing with their mouth open and loud eaters! Argh
FANTASY SLIP CORDON? Keeper: Micky Flanagan, 1st: Will Smith, 2nd: Me, 3rd: Cheryl Cole, Gully: 50 Cent
TWITTER FEED: @callumjackson99

| Batting | Mat | Inns | NO | Runs | HS | Ave | SR | 100 | 50 | Ct | St |
|---|---|---|---|---|---|---|---|---|---|---|---|
| First-class | 1 | 1 | 0 | 26 | 26 | 26.00 | 52.00 | 0 | 0 | 1 | 0 |
| List A | 3 | - | - | - | - | - | - | - | - | 1 | 2 |
| Twenty20 | 3 | 1 | 0 | 3 | 3 | 3.00 | 75.00 | 0 | 0 | 0 | 3 |
| **Bowling** | **Mat** | **Balls** | **Runs** | **Wkts** | **BBI** | **BBM** | **Ave** | **Econ** | **SR** | **5w** | **10** |
| First-class | 1 | - | - | - | - | - | - | - | - | - | - |
| List A | 3 | - | - | - | - | - | - | - | - | - | - |
| Twenty20 | 3 | - | - | - | - | - | - | - | - | - | - |

# KYLE JARVIS

RHB RFM R0 W0

FULL NAME: Kyle Malcolm Jarvis
BORN: February 16, 1989, Harare, Zimbabwe
SQUAD NO: 27
HEIGHT: 6ft 2in
NICKNAME: Jarv
EDUCATION: St John's College, Harare; University of Pretoria
TEAMS: Zimbabwe, Lancashire, Central Districts, Mashonaland Eagles
CAREER: Test: 2011; ODI: 2009; T20I: 2011; First-class: 2009; List A: 2009; T20: 2011

BEST BATTING: 48 Mashonaland Eagles vs Mid West Rhinos, Harare, 2012
BEST BOWLING: 7-35 Mashonaland Eagles vs Matabeleland Tuskers, Bulawayo, 2012

FAMILY TIES? My father Malcolm played Test cricket for Zimbabwe
CAREER HIGHLIGHTS? Two Test five-wicket hauls against New Zealand and West Indies
TIP FOR THE TOP? Haseeb Hameed
CRICKET RULE YOU'D CHANGE? Stop making every rule in favour of the batsman
IF YOU WEREN'T A CRICKETER? Playing rugby
DESERT ISLAND DISC? Bob Marley
SURPRISING FACT? Spearfisherman extraordinaire, shockingly bad footballer
FANTASY SLIP CORDON? Keeper: Eminem, 1st: Wolf Of Wall Street (Jordan Belfort), 2nd: Myself, 3rd: Floyd Mayweather, Gully: Megan Fox
TWITTER FEED: @kylejarv89

| Batting | Mat | Inns | NO | Runs | HS | Ave | SR | 100 | 50 | Ct | St |
|---|---|---|---|---|---|---|---|---|---|---|---|
| Tests | 8 | 14 | 6 | 58 | 25* | 7.25 | 29.74 | 0 | 0 | 3 | 0 |
| ODIs | 24 | 15 | 5 | 52 | 13 | 5.20 | 40.62 | 0 | 0 | 6 | 0 |
| T20Is | 9 | 5 | 2 | 9 | 9* | 3.00 | 52.94 | 0 | 0 | 0 | 0 |
| First-class | 34 | 49 | 17 | 394 | 48 | 12.31 | 44.62 | 0 | 0 | 11 | 0 |
| List A | 41 | 25 | 11 | 102 | 33* | 7.28 | 41.63 | 0 | 0 | 12 | 0 |
| Twenty20 | 36 | 10 | 4 | 28 | 10 | 4.66 | 68.29 | 0 | 0 | 11 | 0 |
| **Bowling** | **Mat** | **Balls** | **Runs** | **Wkts** | **BBI** | **BBM** | **Ave** | **Econ** | **SR** | **5w** | **10** |
| Tests | 8 | 1569 | 952 | 30 | 5/54 | 7/115 | 31.73 | 3.64 | 52.3 | 2 | 0 |
| ODIs | 24 | 1217 | 1221 | 27 | 3/36 | 3/36 | 45.22 | 6.01 | 45.0 | 0 | 0 |
| T20Is | 9 | 193 | 270 | 10 | 3/15 | 3/15 | 27.00 | 8.39 | 19.3 | 0 | 0 |
| First-class | 34 | 5863 | 3448 | 135 | 7/35 | 10/53 | 25.54 | 3.52 | 43.4 | 8 | 1 |
| List A | 41 | 1865 | 1793 | 46 | 4/35 | 4/35 | 38.97 | 5.76 | 40.5 | 0 | 0 |
| Twenty20 | 36 | 751 | 1049 | 33 | 3/15 | 3/15 | 31.78 | 8.38 | 22.7 | 0 | 0 |

# ATEEQ JAVID

RHB RM/OB R0 W0

FULL NAME: Ateeq Javid
BORN: October 15, 1991, Birmingham
SQUAD NO: 17
TEAMS: Warwickshire
CAREER: First-class: 2009; List A: 2011; T20:2013

BEST BATTING: 133 Warwickshire vs Somerset, Birmingham, 2013
BEST BOWLING: 1-1 Warwickshire vs Lancashire, Manchester, 2014

CAREER HIGHLIGHTS? Playing against England for Warwickshire ahead of the 2009 Ashes
CRICKETING HEROES? Sachin Tendulkar
TWITTER FEED: @ateeqjavid2000
NOTES: Javid scored his maiden first-class century in 2013, against Somerset at Edgbaston in the County Championship, and followed it up with another against Surrey in September to finish the season with 619 runs at an average of 44.21. Last season he scored only one first-class half-century. A former England U19 player, he featured in four U19 Tests and 23 U19 ODIs between 2009 and 2011, scoring five half-centuries

| Batting | Mat | Inns | NO | Runs | HS | Ave | SR | 100 | 50 | Ct | St |
|---|---|---|---|---|---|---|---|---|---|---|---|
| First-class | 27 | 43 | 6 | 1004 | 133 | 27.13 | 36.16 | 2 | 3 | 12 | 0 |
| List A | 22 | 20 | 8 | 364 | 43 | 30.33 | 85.24 | 0 | 0 | 5 | 0 |
| Twenty20 | 24 | 16 | 6 | 196 | 41 | 19.60 | 116.66 | 0 | 0 | 5 | 0 |
| **Bowling** | **Mat** | **Balls** | **Runs** | **Wkts** | **BBI** | **BBM** | **Ave** | **Econ** | **SR** | **5w** | **10** |
| First-class | 27 | 450 | 266 | 3 | 1/1 | 1/1 | 88.66 | 3.54 | 150.0 | 0 | 0 |
| List A | 22 | 540 | 583 | 10 | 3/48 | 3/48 | 58.30 | 6.47 | 54.0 | 0 | 0 |
| Twenty20 | 24 | 393 | 444 | 20 | 4/17 | 4/17 | 22.20 | 6.77 | 19.6 | 0 | 0 |

## KEATON JENNINGS LHB RFM R0 W0

FULL NAME: Keaton Kent Jennings
BORN: June 19, 1992, Johannesburg, South Africa
SQUAD NO: 1
HEIGHT: 6ft 4in
NICKNAME: Jet, Keats
EDUCATION: King Edward VII School; University of South Africa
TEAMS: Durham, Gauteng
CAREER: First-class: 2011; List A: 2012; T20: 2014



BEST BATTING: 127 Durham vs Sussex, Hove, 2013
BEST BOWLING: 2-8 Gauteng vs Western Province, Cape Town, 2012

FAMILY TIES? My father Ray, brother Dylan and uncle Kenneth have all played first-class cricket
CAREER HIGHLIGHTS? Winning the County Championship and RL One-Day Cup
BEST PLAYER IN COUNTY CRICKET? Jeetan Patel
MOST MARKED CHARACTERISTIC? Discipline
CRICKETING HEROES? Michael Hussey – I really enjoyed the way he went about his cricket
NON-CRICKETING HEROES? Batman – he's done a lot of good work for Gotham City
COACHING TIP? Watch the ball – it's a tough game when you don't
IF YOU WEREN'T A CRICKETER? Finishing my degree
DESERT ISLAND DISC? U2 – Joshua Tree
FAVOURITE TV? Suits
PET HATE? Ironing
TWITTER FEED: @jetjennings

| Batting | Mat | Inns | NO | Runs | HS | Ave | SR | 100 | 50 | Ct | St |
|---|---|---|---|---|---|---|---|---|---|---|---|
| First-class | 44 | 77 | 3 | 2020 | 127 | 27.29 | 40.47 | 4 | 10 | 15 | 0 |
| List A | 16 | 16 | 4 | 526 | 71* | 43.83 | 73.25 | 0 | 6 | 2 | 0 |
| Twenty20 | 4 | 1 | 1 | 0 | 0* | - | - | 0 | 0 | 2 | 0 |
| **Bowling** | **Mat** | **Balls** | **Runs** | **Wkts** | **BBI** | **BBM** | **Ave** | **Econ** | **SR** | **5w** | **10** |
| First-class | 44 | 410 | 240 | 7 | 2/8 | 2/8 | 34.28 | 3.51 | 58.5 | 0 | 0 |
| List A | 16 | 108 | 109 | 1 | 1/9 | 1/9 | 109.00 | 6.05 | 108.0 | 0 | 0 |
| Twenty20 | 4 | 78 | 103 | 4 | 2/23 | 2/23 | 25.75 | 7.92 | 19.5 | 0 | 0 |

# DEWI JONES

RHB RF R0 W0

FULL NAME: Dewi Penrhyn Jones
BORN: September 9, 1994, Wrexham, Denbighshire
SQUAD NO: 30
HEIGHT: 6ft 1in
NICKNAME: Jonesy, Fiery Red
EDUCATION: Ellesmere College
TEAMS: Glamorgan
CAREER: List A: 2014

---

FAMILY TIES? My father played for Brymbo CC in the North Wales Cricket Premier League, which was my first club as a junior
CAREER HIGHLIGHTS? Representing my country Wales in the Minor Counties Championship, playing my first game for Glamorgan and getting my first wicket vs Middlesex
BEST PLAYER IN COUNTY CRICKET? James Taylor
TIP FOR THE TOP? Haseeb Hameed, Fynn Hudson-Prentice
MOST MARKED CHARACTERISTIC? My red hair
CRICKETING HEROES? Brett Lee – I love his action and that he continued to bowl so fast throughout his career
NON-CRICKETING HEROES? Welsh rugby player Leigh Halfpenny because he is at the top of his game and a fearless tackler
IF YOU WEREN'T A CRICKETER? A police officer
IF YOU COULD BE SOMEONE ELSE FOR A DAY? Spider-Man
PET HATE? Slow or no internet connection – it shouldn't happen in the 21st century
SURPRISING FACT? I have a dual kidney and therefore have three of them!
FANTASY SLIP CORDON? Keeper: Ricky Gervais, 1st: Freddie Flintoff, 2nd: Myself, 3rd: Adam Sandler, Gully: Lee Evans (this would be the funniest slip cordon that has ever played the game)
TWITTER FEED: @DewiPJones

| Batting | Mat | Inns | NO | Runs | HS | Ave | SR | 100 | 50 | Ct | St |
|---|---|---|---|---|---|---|---|---|---|---|---|
| List A | 1 | - | - | - | - | - | - | - | - | 0 | 0 |
| **Bowling** | **Mat** | **Balls** | **Runs** | **Wkts** | **BBI** | **BBM** | **Ave** | **Econ** | **SR** | **5w** | **10** |
| List A | 1 | 18 | 22 | 1 | 1/22 | 1/22 | 22.00 | 7.33 | 18.0 | 0 | 0 |

# GERAINT JONES

RHB WK R2 W0

FULL NAME: Geraint Owen Jones
BORN: July 14, 1976, Kundiawa, Papua New Guinea
SQUAD NO: 8
HEIGHT: 5ft 10in
NICKNAME: Joner, G
EDUCATION: Harristown State, Queensland
TEAMS: England, Papua New Guinea, Gloucestershire, Kent
CAREER: Test: 2004; ODI: 2004; T20I: 2005; First-class: 2001; List A: 2001; T20: 2003



BEST BATTING: 178 Kent vs Somerset, Canterbury, 2010
COUNTY CAPS: 2003 (Kent); BENEFIT YEAR: 2012 (Kent)

FAMILY TIES? My brother-in-law is James Tredwell
CRICKETING HEROES? Ian Healy
NON-CRICKETING HEROES? Rory McIlroy – simply the best golfer on the planet
COACHING TIP? Play the swinging ball late and the seaming ball early
IF YOU COULD BE SOMEONE ELSE FOR A DAY? Marty McFly
SURPRISING FACT? I make an outstanding focaccia bread
FANTASY SLIP CORDON? Keeper: Me, 1st : My mother (she died when I was 12 so I missed out on really getting to know her), 2nd: Micky Flanagan (makes me cry with laughter), 3rd: John Daly (would have plenty of stories to fill in the day)
TWITTER FEED: @Gojones623

| Batting | Mat | Inns | NO | Runs | HS | Ave | SR | 100 | 50 | Ct | St |
|---|---|---|---|---|---|---|---|---|---|---|---|
| Tests | 34 | 53 | 4 | 1172 | 100 | 23.91 | 54.13 | 1 | 6 | 128 | 5 |
| ODIs | 51 | 43 | 8 | 862 | 80 | 24.62 | 77.17 | 0 | 4 | 68 | 4 |
| T20Is | 2 | 2 | 1 | 33 | 19 | 33.00 | 132.00 | 0 | 0 | 2 | 0 |
| First-class | 193 | 293 | 28 | 8615 | 178 | 32.50 | | 15 | 46 | 586 | 36 |
| List A | 202 | 167 | 32 | 3335 | 86 | 24.70 | 80.90 | 0 | 13 | 207 | 42 |
| Twenty20 | 113 | 89 | 16 | 1312 | 56 | 17.97 | 111.75 | 0 | 3 | 50 | 20 |
| **Bowling** | **Mat** | **Balls** | **Runs** | **Wkts** | **BBI** | **BBM** | **Ave** | **Econ** | **SR** | **5w** | **10** |
| Tests | 34 | - | - | - | - | - | - | - | - | - | - |
| ODIs | 51 | - | - | - | - | - | - | - | - | - | - |
| T20Is | 2 | - | - | - | - | - | - | - | - | - | - |
| First-class | 193 | 24 | 26 | 0 | - | - | - | 6.50 | - | 0 | 0 |
| List A | 202 | - | - | - | - | - | - | - | - | - | - |
| Twenty20 | 113 | - | - | - | - | - | - | - | - | - | - |

## RICHARD JONES

## RHB RFM R0 W0

FULL NAME: Richard Alan Jones
BORN: November 6, 1986, Stourbridge, Worcestershire
SQUAD NO: 25
HEIGHT: 6ft 2in
NICKNAME: Dick, Jonah
EDUCATION: King Edward IV College; Manchester Metropolitan University
TEAMS: Warwickshire, Leicestershire, Worcestershire
CAREER: First-class: 2007; List A: 2008; T20: 2010

BEST BATTING: 62 Matabeleland Tuskers vs Southern Rocks, Bulawayo, 2012
BEST BOWLING: 7-115 Worcestershire vs Sussex, Hove, 2010
COUNTY CAPS: 2007 (Worcestershire)

CAREER HIGHLIGHTS? Being part of the Warwickshire squad last season that won the T20, and came runners-up in both the County Championship and RL50 competitions
BEST PLAYER IN COUNTY CRICKET? The correct answer is Jeetan Patel
MOST MARKED CHARACTERISTIC? My kneecaps are the size of dinner plates
SUPERSTITIONS? I always turn up to the first day of a Championship game in my whites
CRICKETING HEROES? Graeme Hick. To play with him on my debut was special
DESERT ISLAND DISC? Russ Abbot – Atmosphere
FAVOURITE TV? The Sopranos and Breaking Bad
LEAST FAVOURITE TV? The X Factor (only because I hate that I love it)
PET HATE? Mess – I can't stop thinking about it until it's tidied or cleaned
SURPRISING FACT? I was an (outstanding) usher at Daryl Mitchell's wedding. So much so that the vicar singled me out for the highest of praise in her speech to the congregation at the end of the ceremony
TWITTER FEED: @richardjones441

| Batting | Mat | Inns | NO | Runs | HS | Ave | SR | 100 | 50 | Ct | St |
|---|---|---|---|---|---|---|---|---|---|---|---|
| First-class | 49 | 75 | 13 | 720 | 62 | 11.61 | 40.72 | 0 | 2 | 18 | 0 |
| List A | 12 | 6 | 3 | 23 | 11* | 7.66 | 69.69 | 0 | 0 | 2 | 0 |
| Twenty20 | 7 | 2 | 1 | 14 | 9 | 14.00 | 77.77 | 0 | 0 | 7 | 0 |
| **Bowling** | **Mat** | **Balls** | **Runs** | **Wkts** | **BBI** | **BBM** | **Ave** | **Econ** | **SR** | **5w** | **10** |
| First-class | 49 | 6626 | 4534 | 146 | 7/115 | 8/105 | 31.05 | 4.10 | 45.3 | 5 | 0 |
| List A | 12 | 405 | 469 | 4 | 1/25 | 1/25 | 117.25 | 6.94 | 101.2 | 0 | 0 |
| Twenty20 | 7 | 90 | 153 | 7 | 5/34 | 5/34 | 21.85 | 10.20 | 12.8 | 1 | 0 |

# CHRIS JORDAN

RHB RFM R0 W1

FULL NAME: Christopher James Jordan
BORN: October 4, 1988, Barbados
SQUAD NO: 8
HEIGHT: 6ft 2in
NICKNAME: CJ
EDUCATION: Dulwich College
TEAMS: England, Sussex, Barbados, Surrey
CAREER: Test: 2014; ODI: 2013; T20I: 2014; First-class: 2007; List A: 2007; T20: 2008



BEST BATTING: 92 Sussex vs Derbyshire, Derby , 2013
BEST BOWLING: 7-43 Barbados vs Combined Campuses and Colleges, Bridgetown, 2013

TWITTER FEED: @ChrisJordan94
NOTES: Born in Barbados, Jordan is eligible to represent England through his grandmother and made his ODI debut in September 2013 against Australia at Southampton, when he took 3-51 in the match. His T20I debut came in February 2014 against Australia at Sydney. Took four wickets on first-class debut against Kent. Claimed career-best figures of 7-43 for Barbados in the 2013 close season and took 61 first-class wickets in the 2013 season. He made his Test debut against Sri Lanka in 2014 and took 5-29 in an ODI against the same team a month earlier

| Batting | Mat | Inns | NO | Runs | HS | Ave | SR | 100 | 50 | Ct | St |
|---|---|---|---|---|---|---|---|---|---|---|---|
| Tests | 5 | 6 | 0 | 125 | 35 | 20.83 | 57.87 | 0 | 0 | 8 | 0 |
| ODIs | 20 | 15 | 5 | 132 | 38* | 13.20 | 89.18 | 0 | 0 | 11 | 0 |
| T20Is | 7 | 6 | 2 | 80 | 27* | 20.00 | 135.59 | 0 | 0 | 5 | 0 |
| First-class | 69 | 92 | 13 | 1707 | 92 | 21.60 | | 0 | 6 | 71 | 0 |
| List A | 52 | 35 | 9 | 335 | 38* | 12.88 | | 0 | 0 | 26 | 0 |
| Twenty20 | 29 | 24 | 8 | 292 | 37 | 18.25 | 119.18 | 0 | 0 | 17 | 0 |
| **Bowling** | **Mat** | **Balls** | **Runs** | **Wkts** | **BBI** | **BBM** | **Ave** | **Econ** | **SR** | **5w** | **10** |
| Tests | 5 | 906 | 496 | 15 | 4/18 | 7/50 | 33.06 | 3.28 | 60.4 | 0 | 0 |
| ODIs | 20 | 1044 | 993 | 33 | 5/29 | 5/29 | 30.09 | 5.70 | 31.6 | 1 | 0 |
| T20Is | 7 | 134 | 181 | 9 | 3/39 | 3/39 | 20.11 | 8.10 | 14.8 | 0 | 0 |
| First-class | 69 | 10834 | 6358 | 201 | 7/43 | 9/58 | 31.63 | 3.52 | 53.9 | 7 | 0 |
| List A | 52 | 2362 | 2221 | 80 | 5/29 | 5/29 | 27.76 | 5.64 | 29.5 | 1 | 0 |
| Twenty20 | 29 | 523 | 749 | 25 | 3/39 | 3/39 | 29.96 | 8.59 | 20.9 | 0 | 0 |

# ED JOYCE

## LHB RM R8 W0 MVP14

FULL NAME: Edmund Christopher Joyce
BORN: September 22, 1978, Dublin
SQUAD NO: 24
HEIGHT: 5ft 10in
NICKNAME: Joycey, Spud, Piece
EDUCATION: Presentation College (Bray), Trinity College, Dublin
TEAMS: England, Ireland, Sussex, Middlesex
CAREER: ODI: 2006; T20I: 2006; First-class: 1997; List A: 1998; T20: 2003

BEST BATTING: 211 Middlesex vs Warwickshire, Birmingham, 2006
BEST BOWLING: 2-34 Middlesex vs Cambridge UCCE, Fenner's, 2004
COUNTY CAPS: 2002 (Middlesex)

TWITTER FEED: @edjoyce24
NOTES: Passed 1,000 first-class runs five English summers in a row between 2002 and 2006, also achieving the feat in 2011 and 2013. Has represented both Ireland and England in ODI cricket. Scored his one ODI century for England against Australia in the 2007 Commonwealth Bank Series. Appointed Sussex club captain ahead of the 2013 season. His brother, Dom, and sisters, Cecelia and Isobel, have all played international cricket for Ireland. Across 14 games at the ICC Trophies of 2001 and 2005 he averaged 84. Averaged 64 in first-class cricket in 2013, including a season-best 204* against Nottinghamshire at Trent Bridge. In 2014 he was named as the No.1 cricketer from non-Test playing nations by All Out Cricket and was the third-leading run-scorer in the County Championship with 1,398 runs, including seven hundreds

| Batting | Mat | Inns | NO | Runs | HS | Ave | SR | 100 | 50 | Ct | St |
|---|---|---|---|---|---|---|---|---|---|---|---|
| ODIs | 49 | 48 | 3 | 1587 | 116* | 35.26 | 71.51 | 3 | 10 | 16 | 0 |
| T20Is | 18 | 15 | 3 | 405 | 78* | 33.75 | 93.96 | 0 | 1 | 5 | 0 |
| First-class | 215 | 356 | 32 | 15419 | 211 | 47.58 | | 39 | 81 | 187 | 0 |
| List A | 266 | 252 | 27 | 8702 | 146 | 38.67 | | 14 | 52 | 88 | 0 |
| Twenty20 | 91 | 85 | 13 | 1453 | 78* | 20.18 | 96.35 | 0 | 2 | 29 | 0 |
| **Bowling** | **Mat** | **Balls** | **Runs** | **Wkts** | **BBI** | **BBM** | **Ave** | **Econ** | **SR** | **5w** | **10** |
| ODIs | 49 | - | - | - | - | - | - | - | - | - | - |
| T20Is | 18 | - | - | - | - | - | - | - | - | - | - |
| First-class | 215 | 1287 | 1025 | 11 | 2/34 | | 93.18 | 4.77 | 117.0 | 0 | 0 |
| List A | 266 | 264 | 309 | 6 | 2/10 | 2/10 | 51.50 | 7.02 | 44.0 | 0 | 0 |
| Twenty20 | 91 | 6 | 12 | 0 | - | - | - | 12.00 | - | 0 | 0 |

# ANEESH KAPIL

RHB RFM R0 W0

FULL NAME: Aneesh Kapil
BORN: August 3, 1993, Wolverhampton
SQUAD NO: 47
HEIGHT: 5ft 8in
NICKNAME: AK
EDUCATION: Denstone College
TEAMS: Surrey, Worcestershire
CAREER: First-class: 2011; List A: 2011; T20: 2011



BEST BATTING: 104* Surrey vs New Zealand A, The Oval, 2014
BEST BOWLING: 3-17 Worcestershire vs Nottinghamshire, Worcester, 2012

CAREER HIGHLIGHTS? My maiden first-class hundred against New Zealand A
BEST PLAYER IN COUNTY CRICKET? Gary Ballance
TIP FOR THE TOP? Dominic Sibley, Tom Curran and Sam Hain
CRICKETING HEROES? Vikram Solanki, Kevin Pietersen, Sachin Tendulkar
NON-CRICKETING HEROES? Muhammad Ali, Roger Federer, Floyd Mayweather, Manny Pacquiao
CRICKET RULE YOU'D CHANGE? If you have 10 play and misses in your innings you are out
IF YOU WEREN'T A CRICKETER? I would go to America and play baseball
IF YOU COULD BE SOMEONE ELSE FOR A DAY? Barack Obama
DESERT ISLAND DISC? Michael Jackson – Greatest Hits
FAVOURITE TV? Suits
LEAST FAVOURITE TV? The Only Way Is Essex
PET HATE? Ignorance
SURPRISING FACT? I can beatbox to a competent level
TWITTER FEED: @AneeshKapil22

| Batting | Mat | Inns | NO | Runs | HS | Ave | SR | 100 | 50 | Ct | St |
|---|---|---|---|---|---|---|---|---|---|---|---|
| First-class | 13 | 22 | 2 | 445 | 104* | 22.25 | 55.69 | 1 | 1 | 4 | 0 |
| List A | 18 | 15 | 4 | 282 | 59 | 25.63 | 77.47 | 0 | 1 | 3 | 0 |
| Twenty20 | 11 | 8 | 3 | 35 | 13 | 7.00 | 97.22 | 0 | 0 | 4 | 0 |
| **Bowling** | **Mat** | **Balls** | **Runs** | **Wkts** | **BBI** | **BBM** | **Ave** | **Econ** | **SR** | **5w** | **10** |
| First-class | 13 | 478 | 340 | 12 | 3/17 | 4/52 | 28.33 | 4.26 | 39.8 | 0 | 0 |
| List A | 18 | 209 | 263 | 4 | 1/18 | 1/18 | 65.75 | 7.55 | 52.2 | 0 | 0 |
| Twenty20 | 11 | 66 | 82 | 5 | 3/9 | 3/9 | 16.40 | 7.45 | 13.2 | 0 | 0 |

## GARY KEEDY

## LHB SLA R0 W4



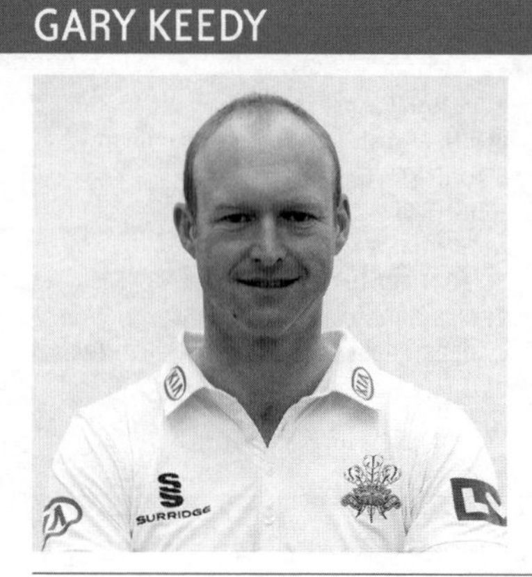


FULL NAME: Gary Keedy
BORN: November 27, 1974, Sandal, Wakefield, Yorkshire
SQUAD NO: 3
HEIGHT: 5ft 11in
NICKNAME: Keeds
EDUCATION: Garforth Comprehensive; University of Salford
TEAMS: Nottinghamshire, England Lions, Lancashire, Nottinghamshire, Surrey
CAREER: First-class: 1994; List A: 1995; T20: 2004

---

BEST BATTING: 64 Lancashire vs Sussex, Hove, 2008
BEST BOWLING: 7-68 Lancashire vs Durham, Manchester, 2010
COUNTY CAPS: 2000 (Lancashire); BENEFIT YEAR: 2009 (Lancashire)

---

CAREER HIGHLIGHTS? Winning the Championship in 2011 with Lancashire, getting capped by Lancashire, playing for England Lions against Australia and T20 Finals Days
MOST MARKED CHARACTERISTIC? Baldness
CRICKETING HEROES? Shane Warne and Graham Gooch
NON-CRICKETING HEROES? Jimmy Page
DESERT ISLAND DISC? The Beatles – Help!
FAVOURITE TV? MasterChef
ACCOMPLISHMENTS? My degree
SURPRISING FACT? I'm exceptionally good at playing the triangle
FANTASY SLIP CORDON? Keeper: Slash from Guns N' Roses, 1st: Gordon Ramsay, 2nd: Myself, 3rd: Karl Pilkington, Gully: Robert De Niro
TWITTER FEED: @keeds23

| Batting | Mat | Inns | NO | Runs | HS | Ave | SR | 100 | 50 | Ct | St |
|---|---|---|---|---|---|---|---|---|---|---|---|
| First-class | 226 | 262 | 128 | 1448 | 64 | 10.80 | | 0 | 2 | 56 | 0 |
| List A | 97 | 35 | 17 | 161 | 33 | 8.94 | | 0 | 0 | 14 | 0 |
| Twenty20 | 71 | 11 | 6 | 27 | 9* | 5.40 | 79.41 | 0 | 0 | 10 | 0 |
| **Bowling** | **Mat** | **Balls** | **Runs** | **Wkts** | **BBI** | **BBM** | **Ave** | **Econ** | **SR** | **5w** | **10** |
| First-class | 226 | 46231 | 21744 | 691 | 7/68 | | 31.46 | 2.82 | 66.9 | 35 | 7 |
| List A | 97 | 3936 | 3150 | 119 | 5/30 | 5/30 | 26.47 | 4.80 | 33.0 | 2 | 0 |
| Twenty20 | 71 | 1414 | 1541 | 72 | 4/15 | 4/15 | 21.40 | 6.53 | 19.6 | 0 | 0 |

# ROB KEOGH

## RHB OB R0 W0

FULL NAME: Robert Ian Keogh
BORN: October 21, 1991, Dunstable, Bedfordshire
SQUAD NO: 14
HEIGHT: 6ft 2in
NICKNAME: Keezy, Key Dog, Chav
EDUCATION: Queensbury Upper School
TEAMS: Northamptonshire
CAREER: First-class: 2012; List A: 2010; T20: 2011



BEST BATTING: 221 Northamptonshire vs Hampshire, Southampton, 2013
BEST BOWLING: 2-46 Northamptonshire vs Sri Lankans, Northampton, 2014

CAREER HIGHLIGHTS? Promotion and T20-winning year in 2013 with Northants, scoring a double-hundred against Hampshire and scoring a hundred against Sri Lanka in a tour match
TIP FOR THE TOP? Ben Duckett, Saif Zaib, James Kettleborough
SUPERSTITIONS? I put my kit on the same way and tap in the crease three times
NON-CRICKETING HEROES? David Beckham and Dan Bilzerian
IF YOU WEREN'T A CRICKETER? A terrible used-car salesman or selling dodgy goods
IF YOU COULD BE SOMEONE ELSE FOR A DAY? Dan Bilzerian
DESERT ISLAND DISC? Kanye West – The College Dropout
FAVOURITE TV? Entourage
ACCOMPLISHMENTS? I played football for Luton Town
FANTASY SLIP CORDON? Keeper: Mario Balotelli, 1st: Ariana Grande, 2nd: Myself, 3rd: Cheryl Cole, Gully: Jimmy Carr
TWITTER FEED: @RobKeogh91

| Batting | Mat | Inns | NO | Runs | HS | Ave | SR | 100 | 50 | Ct | St |
|---|---|---|---|---|---|---|---|---|---|---|---|
| First-class | 18 | 27 | 3 | 901 | 221 | 37.54 | 49.55 | 3 | 2 | 1 | 0 |
| List A | 11 | 10 | 1 | 233 | 61 | 25.88 | 83.21 | 0 | 2 | 2 | 0 |
| Twenty20 | 12 | 5 | 0 | 58 | 28 | 11.60 | 96.66 | 0 | 0 | 8 | 0 |
| **Bowling** | **Mat** | **Balls** | **Runs** | **Wkts** | **BBI** | **BBM** | **Ave** | **Econ** | **SR** | **5w** | **10** |
| First-class | 18 | 432 | 235 | 5 | 2/46 | 2/46 | 47.00 | 3.26 | 86.4 | 0 | 0 |
| List A | 11 | 114 | 115 | 0 | - | - | - | 6.05 | - | 0 | 0 |
| Twenty20 | 12 | 36 | 45 | 0 | - | - | - | 7.50 | - | 0 | 0 |

# SIMON KERRIGAN

## RHB SLA R0 W2

FULL NAME: Simon Christopher Kerrigan
BORN: May 10, 1989, Preston, Lancashire
SQUAD NO: 10
HEIGHT: 5ft 9in
NICKNAME: Kegs, Kegsy, Kegger, Bish
EDUCATION: Corpus Christi High School; Preston College; Edge Hill University
TEAMS: England, Lancashire
CAREER: Test: 2013; First-class: 2010; List A: 2011; T20: 2010

BEST BATTING: 62* Lancashire vs Hampshire, Southport, 2013
BEST BOWLING: 9-51 Lancashire vs Hampshire, Liverpool, 2011
COUNTY CAPS: 2013

CAREER HIGHLIGHTS? Winning the Championship in 2011
SUPERSTITIONS? Not really, they come and go
CRICKETING HEROES? Andrew Flintoff, Darren Gough
NON-CRICKETING HEROES? Phil Ivey
IF YOU WEREN'T A CRICKETER? Jobless
FAVOURITE TV? Modern Family
TWITTER FEED: @Kegs10

| Batting | Mat | Inns | NO | Runs | HS | Ave | SR | 100 | 50 | Ct | St |
|---|---|---|---|---|---|---|---|---|---|---|---|
| Tests | 1 | 1 | 1 | 1 | 1* | - | 8.33 | 0 | 0 | 0 | 0 |
| First-class | 71 | 82 | 28 | 546 | 62* | 10.11 | 32.40 | 0 | 1 | 21 | 0 |
| List A | 32 | 14 | 5 | 28 | 10 | 3.11 | 49.12 | 0 | 0 | 9 | 0 |
| Twenty20 | 24 | 4 | 4 | 9 | 4* | - | 180.00 | 0 | 0 | 11 | 0 |
| **Bowling** | **Mat** | **Balls** | **Runs** | **Wkts** | **BBI** | **BBM** | **Ave** | **Econ** | **SR** | **5w** | **10** |
| Tests | 1 | 48 | 53 | 0 | - | - | - | 6.62 | - | 0 | 0 |
| First-class | 71 | 13668 | 6521 | 229 | 9/51 | 12/192 | 28.47 | 2.86 | 59.6 | 11 | 2 |
| List A | 32 | 1328 | 1158 | 21 | 3/21 | 3/21 | 55.14 | 5.23 | 63.2 | 0 | 0 |
| Twenty20 | 24 | 516 | 595 | 20 | 3/17 | 3/17 | 29.75 | 6.91 | 25.8 | 0 | 0 |

# ALEXEI KERVEZEE

## RHB RM R1 W0

FULL NAME: Alexei Nicolaas Kervezee
BORN: September 11, 1989, Walvis Bay, Republic of South Africa (now Namibia)
SQUAD NO: 5
HEIGHT: 5ft 8in
NICKNAME: Cub, Dexter, Crazy Dutch B*stard
EDUCATION: Duneside High, Namibia; Segbroek College, Netherlands
TEAMS: Netherlands, Worcestershire
CAREER: ODI: 2006; T20I: 2009; First-class: 2005; List A: 2006; T20: 2009

---

BEST BATTING: 155 Worcestershire vs Derbyshire, Derby, 2010
BEST BOWLING: 1-14 Netherlands vs Namibia, Windhoek, 2008

---

FAMILY TIES? My uncle played cricket for Holland
CAREER HIGHLIGHTS? Two 50-over World Cups and a World T20 for Holland. First professional contract. Two promotions with Worcestershire
BEST PLAYER IN COUNTY CRICKET? Marcus Trescothick
CRICKETING HEROES? AB de Villiers – he can win you a game in any state
COACHING TIP? If it's in the V it's in the tree, if it's in the arch it's out of the park
IF YOU COULD BE SOMEONE ELSE FOR A DAY? Denzel Washington
FAVOURITE TV? Two And A Half Men (with Charlie Sheen)
LEAST FAVOURITE TV? The Only Way Is Essex, Made In Chelsea; anything like that
FANTASY SLIP CORDON? Keeper: John Bishop, 1st: Charlie Sheen, 2nd: Denzel Washington, 3rd: Myself, 4th: Nelson Mandela, Gully: Russell Howard
TWITTER FEED: @cubbo455

| Batting | Mat | Inns | NO | Runs | HS | Ave | SR | 100 | 50 | Ct | St |
|---|---|---|---|---|---|---|---|---|---|---|---|
| ODIs | 39 | 36 | 3 | 924 | 92 | 28.00 | 73.15 | 0 | 4 | 18 | 0 |
| T20Is | 10 | 10 | 1 | 289 | 58* | 32.11 | 110.30 | 0 | 2 | 4 | 0 |
| First-class | 87 | 147 | 8 | 4242 | 155 | 30.51 | | 6 | 25 | 45 | 0 |
| List A | 99 | 92 | 7 | 2494 | 121* | 29.34 | 78.67 | 2 | 12 | 38 | 0 |
| Twenty20 | 78 | 72 | 10 | 1234 | 58* | 19.90 | 112.28 | 0 | 4 | 32 | 0 |
| **Bowling** | **Mat** | **Balls** | **Runs** | **Wkts** | **BBI** | **BBM** | **Ave** | **Econ** | **SR** | **5w** | **10** |
| ODIs | 39 | 24 | 34 | 0 | - | - | - | 8.50 | - | 0 | 0 |
| T20Is | 10 | - | - | - | - | - | - | - | - | - | - |
| First-class | 87 | 228 | 179 | 2 | 1/14 | 1/14 | 89.50 | 4.71 | 114.0 | 0 | 0 |
| List A | 99 | 60 | 90 | 0 | - | - | - | 9.00 | - | 0 | 0 |
| Twenty20 | 78 | 12 | 13 | 0 | - | - | - | 6.50 | - | 0 | 0 |

## JAMES KETTLEBOROUGH RHB OB R0 W0

FULL NAME: James Michael Kettleborough
BORN: October 22, 1992, Huntingdon
SQUAD NO: 3
HEIGHT: 6ft
NICKNAME: Ketts
EDUCATION: Bedford School
TEAMS: Kent, Northamptonshire
CAREER: First-class: 2014; List A: 2014

BEST BATTING: 73 Northamptonshire vs Middlesex, Lord's, 2014

CAREER HIGHLIGHTS? My Championship debut at Lord's
BEST PLAYER IN COUNTY CRICKET? Adam Lyth
TIP FOR THE TOP? Saif Zaib
MOST MARKED CHARACTERISTIC? Grafting and hard working
SUPERSTITIONS? I lay my bat, gloves and helmet out in a certain way before waiting to bat and putting them on. Bit odd really and no idea why
CRICKETING HEROES? Stephen Peters – someone I look up to from a cricketing point of view and has been around for years. James Middlebrook – because he's an old-school, get-stuck-in-and-find-a-way character
NON-CRICKETING HEROES? My dad because he taught me a lot about what I know and do in cricket
CRICKET RULE YOU'D CHANGE? You can only get off the mark with a boundary – it would be good fun but I'd be pretty awful at it, mind
IF YOU COULD BE SOMEONE ELSE FOR A DAY? Probably my missus, so I could see what it was like to spend the day with me
PET HATE? People – and when I say people I mean my missus – fidgeting all of the time when I'm watching TV or at the cinema
TWITTER FEED: @jketts1305

| Batting | Mat | Inns | NO | Runs | HS | Ave | SR | 100 | 50 | Ct | St |
|---|---|---|---|---|---|---|---|---|---|---|---|
| First-class | 9 | 16 | 0 | 398 | 73 | 24.87 | 45.69 | 0 | 3 | 6 | 0 |
| List A | 1 | 1 | 0 | 26 | 26 | 26.00 | 76.47 | 0 | 0 | 0 | 0 |
| **Bowling** | **Mat** | **Balls** | **Runs** | **Wkts** | **BBI** | **BBM** | **Ave** | **Econ** | **SR** | **5w** | **10** |
| First-class | 9 | - | - | - | - | - | - | - | - | - | - |
| List A | 1 | - | - | - | - | - | - | - | - | - | - |

# ROB KEY RHB OB R7 W0

FULL NAME: Robert William Trevor Key
BORN: May 12, 1979, East Dulwich, London
SQUAD NO: 4
HEIGHT: 6ft 1in
NICKNAME: Keysy
EDUCATION: Colfe's School
TEAMS: England, Kent
CAREER: Test: 2002; ODI: 2003; T20I: 2009; First-class: 1998; List A: 1998; T20: 2004



BEST BATTING: 270* Kent vs Glamorgan, Cardiff, 2009
BEST BOWLING: 2-31 Kent vs Somerset, Canterbury, 2010
COUNTY CAPS: 2001; BENEFIT YEAR: 2011

CAREER HIGHLIGHTS? Scoring 221 vs West Indies for England at Lord's
CRICKETING HEROES? Philip Fussell
NON-CRICKETING HEROES? Will Ashby, George Digweed
DESERT ISLAND DISC? John Mayer – Free Fallin'
FAVOURITE TV? The Newsroom
ACCOMPLISHMENTS? Putting together a kids' trampoline
FANTASY SLIP CORDON? Keeper: George Digweed, 1st: Will Ashby, 2nd: James Fielding, 3rd: Glucka Wijesuriya, Gully: Andy Fussell
TWITTER FEED: @robkey612

| Batting | Mat | Inns | NO | Runs | HS | Ave | SR | 100 | 50 | Ct | St |
|---|---|---|---|---|---|---|---|---|---|---|---|
| Tests | 15 | 26 | 1 | 775 | 221 | 31.00 | 47.28 | 1 | 3 | 11 | 0 |
| ODIs | 5 | 5 | 0 | 54 | 19 | 10.80 | 40.00 | 0 | 0 | 0 | 0 |
| T20Is | 1 | 1 | 1 | 10 | 10* | - | 125.00 | 0 | 0 | 1 | 0 |
| First-class | 286 | 493 | 37 | 18461 | 270* | 40.48 | | 52 | 71 | 154 | 0 |
| List A | 225 | 218 | 17 | 6469 | 144* | 32.18 | | 8 | 37 | 46 | 0 |
| Twenty20 | 98 | 98 | 11 | 2239 | 98* | 25.73 | 124.59 | 0 | 13 | 25 | 0 |
| **Bowling** | **Mat** | **Balls** | **Runs** | **Wkts** | **BBI** | **BBM** | **Ave** | **Econ** | **SR** | **5w** | **10** |
| Tests | 15 | - | - | - | - | - | - | - | - | - | - |
| ODIs | 5 | - | - | - | - | - | - | - | - | - | - |
| T20Is | 1 | - | - | - | - | - | - | - | - | - | - |
| First-class | 286 | 484 | 331 | 3 | 2/31 | 2/31 | 110.33 | 4.10 | 161.3 | 0 | 0 |
| List A | 225 | - | - | - | - | - | - | - | - | - | - |
| Twenty20 | 98 | - | - | - | - | - | - | - | - | - | - |

## CRAIG KIESWETTER RHB OB WK R1 W0 MVP86

FULL NAME: Craig Kieswetter
BORN: November 28, 1987, Johannesburg, South Africa
SQUAD NO: 22
HEIGHT: 6ft
NICKNAME: Hobnob
EDUCATION: Bishop's Diocesan College; Millfield School
TEAMS: England, Somerset
CAREER: ODI: 2010; T20I: 2010; First-class: 2007; List A: 2007; T20: 2007

BEST BATTING: 164 Somerset vs Nottinghamshire, Nottingham, 2011
BEST BOWLING: 2-3 Somerset vs Worcestershire, Worcester, 2012
COUNTY CAPS: 2009

CAREER HIGHLIGHTS? Being awarded my cap for Somerset in 2009, being a World T20 winner in 2010 and being named Man of the Match in the final, becoming the second-youngest ODI centurion for England in 2010
TIP FOR THE TOP? Tom Abell
CRICKETING HEROES? Jonty Rhodes, Adam Gilchrist, Justin Langer
NON-CRICKETING HEROES? Ayrton Senna, Jose Mourinho
IF YOU WEREN'T A CRICKETER? I'd be studying Law
FAVOURITE TV? Game Of Thrones
ACCOMPLISHMENTS? Helping charities with donations of cricket equipment
TWITTER FEED: @kiesy_22

| Batting | Mat | Inns | NO | Runs | HS | Ave | SR | 100 | 50 | Ct | St |
|---|---|---|---|---|---|---|---|---|---|---|---|
| ODIs | 46 | 40 | 5 | 1054 | 107 | 30.11 | 89.93 | 1 | 5 | 53 | 12 |
| T20Is | 25 | 25 | 1 | 526 | 63 | 21.91 | 111.91 | 0 | 3 | 17 | 3 |
| First-class | 115 | 171 | 25 | 5728 | 164 | 39.23 | | 11 | 31 | 331 | 12 |
| List A | 134 | 124 | 16 | 4254 | 143 | 39.38 | 95.18 | 11 | 17 | 136 | 26 |
| Twenty20 | 124 | 121 | 15 | 3367 | 89* | 31.76 | 122.30 | 0 | 29 | 76 | 21 |
| **Bowling** | **Mat** | **Balls** | **Runs** | **Wkts** | **BBI** | **BBM** | **Ave** | **Econ** | **SR** | **5w** | **10** |
| ODIs | 46 | - | - | - | - | - | - | - | - | - | - |
| T20Is | 25 | - | - | - | - | - | - | - | - | - | - |
| First-class | 115 | 54 | 29 | 2 | 2/3 | 2/3 | 14.50 | 3.22 | 27.0 | 0 | 0 |
| List A | 134 | 12 | 19 | 1 | 1/19 | 1/19 | 19.00 | 9.50 | 12.0 | 0 | 0 |
| Twenty20 | 124 | - | - | - | - | - | - | - | - | - | - |

# RORY KLEINVELDT RHB RFM R0 W0

FULL NAME: Rory Keith Kleinveldt
BORN: March 15, 1983, Cape Town, South Africa
SQUAD NO: 6
TEAMS: South Africa, Northamptonshire, Cape Cobras, Hampshire, Western Province
CAREER: Test: 2012; ODI: 2013; T20I: 2008; First-class: 2002; List A: 2002; T20: 2004



BEST BATTING: 115 Western Province vs KwaZulu-Natal, Chatsworth, 2005
BEST BOWLING: 8-47 Cape Cobras vs Warriors, Stellenbosch, 2006

TWITTER FEED:@RoryK_9
NOTES: Kleinveldt was due to join Northamptonshire at the start of last season but had to withdraw through injury. He will be available for the entire season in all formats as the county's overseas player. A powerful, fast-bowling allrounder, Kleinveldt had played four Tests, 10 ODIs and six T20Is for South Africa but hasn't represented his country since 2013. He took nine wickets for South Africa A in the two unofficial Tests against England Lions in January 2015

| Batting | Mat | Inns | NO | Runs | HS | Ave | SR | 100 | 50 | Ct | St |
|---|---|---|---|---|---|---|---|---|---|---|---|
| Tests | 4 | 5 | 2 | 27 | 17* | 9.00 | 44.26 | 0 | 0 | 2 | 0 |
| ODIs | 10 | 7 | 0 | 105 | 43 | 15.00 | 84.67 | 0 | 0 | 4 | 0 |
| T20Is | 6 | 3 | 2 | 25 | 22 | 25.00 | 250.00 | 0 | 0 | 1 | 0 |
| First-class | 96 | 129 | 14 | 2201 | 115* | 19.13 | 68.84 | 1 | 10 | 39 | 0 |
| List A | 126 | 79 | 15 | 1114 | 55 | 17.40 | 109.00 | 0 | 2 | 23 | 0 |
| Twenty20 | 76 | 52 | 18 | 466 | 46 | 13.70 | 140.78 | 0 | 0 | 16 | 0 |
| **Bowling** | **Mat** | **Balls** | **Runs** | **Wkts** | **BBI** | **BBM** | **Ave** | **Econ** | **SR** | **5w** | **10** |
| Tests | 4 | 667 | 422 | 10 | 3/65 | 4/97 | 42.20 | 3.79 | 66.7 | 0 | 0 |
| ODIs | 10 | 513 | 448 | 12 | 4/22 | 4/22 | 37.33 | 5.23 | 42.7 | 0 | 0 |
| T20Is | 6 | 122 | 173 | 9 | 3/18 | 3/18 | 19.22 | 8.50 | 13.5 | 0 | 0 |
| First-class | 96 | 16319 | 7846 | 276 | 8/47 | | 28.42 | 2.88 | 59.1 | 10 | 1 |
| List A | 126 | 5654 | 4444 | 148 | 4/22 | 4/22 | 30.02 | 4.71 | 38.2 | 0 | 0 |
| Twenty20 | 76 | 1532 | 1981 | 63 | 3/18 | 3/18 | 31.44 | 7.75 | 24.3 | 0 | 0 |

# MICHAEL KLINGER

RHB R1 W0

FULL NAME: Michael Klinger
BORN: July 4, 1980, Kew, Melbourne, Australia
SQUAD NO: 2
HEIGHT: 5ft 11in
NICKNAME: Maxy
EDUCATION: Mount Scopus Memorial College; Deakin University
TEAMS: Gloucestershire, South Australia, Victoria, Western Australia, Worcestershire
CAREER: First-class: 1999; List A: 1999; T20: 2006

BEST BATTING: 255 South Australia vs Western Australia, Adelaide, 2008
COUNTY CAPS: 2012 (Worcestershire)

CAREER HIGHLIGHTS? Winning titles with South Australia and Western Australia
CRICKETING HEROES? Dean Jones – I grew up in Victoria where he was from and he was the best one-day cricketer in Australia at the time
NON-CRICKETING HEROES? My late mother – she was a fantastic role model and mother to myself, brother and sister
CRICKET RULE YOU'D CHANGE? Free hit off any no-ball in all forms
COACHING TIP? As a batter, there is always more time than you think
DESERT ISLAND DISC? Frozen soundtrack – it's constantly played at home
FAVOURITE TV? Modern Family
PET HATE? People standing too close at luggage carousel so others can't see if their bags are coming out
SURPRISING FACT? I once was declared on 99 not out in a first-class game
FANTASY SLIP CORDON? Keeper: Adam Gilchrist, 1st: Adam Scott, 2nd: Viv Richards, Two gullies: My two kids so I don't leave them every time I go off to play
TWITTER FEED: @maxyklinger

| Batting | Mat | Inns | NO | Runs | HS | Ave | SR | 100 | 50 | Ct | St |
|---|---|---|---|---|---|---|---|---|---|---|---|
| First-class | 146 | 259 | 25 | 8957 | 255 | 38.27 | 45.36 | 22 | 38 | 137 | 0 |
| List A | 136 | 135 | 19 | 5425 | 140* | 46.76 | | 11 | 36 | 50 | 0 |
| Twenty20 | 87 | 85 | 11 | 2404 | 108* | 32.48 | 122.46 | 2 | 13 | 30 | 0 |
| **Bowling** | **Mat** | **Balls** | **Runs** | **Wkts** | **BBI** | **BBM** | **Ave** | **Econ** | **SR** | **5w** | **10** |
| First-class | 146 | 6 | 3 | 0 | - | - | - | 3.00 | - | 0 | 0 |
| List A | 136 | - | - | - | - | - | - | - | - | - | - |
| Twenty20 | 87 | - | - | - | - | - | - | - | - | - | - |

# TOM KNIGHT

RHB SLA R0 W0

FULL NAME: Thomas Craig Knight
BORN: June 28, 1993, Sheffield, Yorkshire
SQUAD NO: 27
HEIGHT: 6ft 2in
NICKNAME: Knighty, Kizzle
EDUCATION: Eckington School
TEAMS: Derbyshire
CAREER: First-class: 2011; List A: 2011; T20: 2011



BEST BATTING: 14 Derbyshire vs Surrey, The Oval, 2011
BEST BOWLING: 2-32 Derbyshire vs Glamorgan, Cardiff, 2011

CAREER HIGHLIGHTS? Making my debut for Derbyshire and playing for England U19 at a World Cup
BEST PLAYER IN COUNTY CRICKET? Mark Footitt
TIP FOR THE TOP? Alex Hughes, Tom Taylor, Harvey Hosein
MOST MARKED CHARACTERISTIC? My mystery hole
CRICKETING HEROES? Shane Warne – the best spinner to play the game
NON-CRICKETING HEROES? David Beckham – boss man
CRICKET RULE YOU'D CHANGE? Go back to the old fielding restrictions in one-day cricket
IF YOU WEREN'T A CRICKETER? A fisherman
IF YOU COULD BE SOMEONE ELSE FOR A DAY? Dan Bilzerian
PET HATE? Boxer shorts
SURPRISING FACT? I used to have webbed fingers
FANTASY SLIP CORDON? Keeper: David Beckham, 1st: Anne Robinson, 2nd: Justin Timberlake, 3rd: Kaley Cuoco, 4th: Myself, Gully: Will Smith
TWITTER FEED: @tomknight28

| Batting | Mat | Inns | NO | Runs | HS | Ave | SR | 100 | 50 | Ct | St |
|---|---|---|---|---|---|---|---|---|---|---|---|
| First-class | 2 | 3 | 1 | 15 | 14 | 7.50 | 39.47 | 0 | 0 | 1 | 0 |
| List A | 9 | 7 | 4 | 16 | 10 | 5.33 | 38.09 | 0 | 0 | 1 | 0 |
| Twenty20 | 21 | 8 | 4 | 99 | 44* | 24.75 | 147.76 | 0 | 0 | 6 | 0 |
| **Bowling** | **Mat** | **Balls** | **Runs** | **Wkts** | **BBI** | **BBM** | **Ave** | **Econ** | **SR** | **5w** | **10** |
| First-class | 2 | 288 | 143 | 2 | 2/32 | 2/59 | 71.50 | 2.97 | 144.0 | 0 | 0 |
| List A | 9 | 360 | 321 | 9 | 3/36 | 3/36 | 35.66 | 5.35 | 40.0 | 0 | 0 |
| Twenty20 | 21 | 276 | 340 | 13 | 3/16 | 3/16 | 26.15 | 7.39 | 21.2 | 0 | 0 |

# TOM KOHLER-CADMORE RHB OB R0 W0

FULL NAME: Tom Kohler-Cadmore
BORN: August 19, 1994, Chatham, Kent
SQUAD NO: 32
HEIGHT: 6ft 3in
NICKNAME: Pepsi
EDUCATION: Malvern College
TEAMS: Worcestershire
CAREER: First-class: 2014; List A: 2013; T20: 2014

BEST BATTING: 99 Worcestershire v Leicestershire, Worcester, 2014

CAREER HIGHLIGHTS? Playing Surrey in the T20 quarter-finals and getting promoted
MOST MARKED CHARACTERISTIC? My nose
CRICKET RULE YOU'D CHANGE? Batsmen get a second chance
COACHING TIP? Watch the ball
IF YOU WEREN'T A CRICKETER? In the navy
IF YOU COULD BE SOMEONE ELSE FOR A DAY? George Rhodes
DESERT ISLAND DISC? Drake – Take Care
FAVOURITE TV? Family Guy
LEAST FAVOURITE TV? Made In Chelsea
ACCOMPLISHMENTS? I always win
PET HATE? Made In Chelsea and The Only Way Is Essex – it's just rubbish
FANTASY SLIP CORDON? Keeper: Peter Griffin, 1st: David Lucas, 2nd: Myself, 3rd: Will Ferrell, Gully: Winston Churchill
TWITTER FEED: @tomkohlercadmor

| Batting | Mat | Inns | NO | Runs | HS | Ave | SR | 100 | 50 | Ct | St |
|---|---|---|---|---|---|---|---|---|---|---|---|
| First-class | 13 | 23 | 0 | 516 | 99 | 22.43 | 52.92 | 0 | 4 | 15 | 0 |
| List A | 8 | 7 | 0 | 177 | 71 | 25.28 | 68.07 | 0 | 1 | 0 | 0 |
| Twenty20 | 11 | 11 | 0 | 227 | 51 | 20.63 | 133.52 | 0 | 1 | 5 | 0 |
| **Bowling** | **Mat** | **Balls** | **Runs** | **Wkts** | **BBI** | **BBM** | **Ave** | **Econ** | **SR** | **5w** | **10** |
| First-class | 13 | - | - | - | - | - | - | - | - | - | - |
| List A | 8 | - | - | - | - | - | - | - | - | - | - |
| Twenty20 | 11 | - | - | - | - | - | - | - | - | - | - |

# JEREMY LAWLOR RHB OB R0 W0

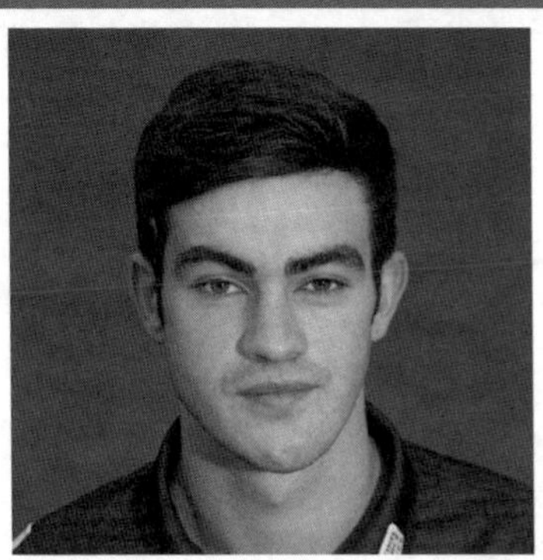

FULL NAME: Jeremy Lloyd Lawlor
BORN: November 4, 1995, Cardiff
SQUAD NO: 6
HEIGHT: 5ft 11in
NICKNAME: Jez
EDUCATION: Monmouth School; Cardiff Metropolitan University
TEAMS: Glamorgan 2nd XI
CAREER: Yet to make first-team debut



FAMILY TIES? My dad Peter played for Glamorgan
CAREER HIGHLIGHTS? Scoring a hundred at Lord's against England U17 and holding the record for the highest individual score of 203* at Monmouth School
BEST PLAYER IN COUNTY CRICKET? Michael Hogan
TIP FOR THE TOP? Jack Murphy
MOST MARKED CHARACTERISTIC? Relaxed
CRICKETING HEROES? Sachin Tendulkar – absolute genius
IF YOU WEREN'T A CRICKETER? Businessman
IF YOU COULD BE SOMEONE ELSE FOR A DAY? Cristiano Ronaldo
DESERT ISLAND DISC? Danza Kuduro
FAVOURITE TV? Match Of The Day
LEAST FAVOURITE TV? Emmerdale
PET HATE? People leaving rubbish in my car

## DANIEL LAWRENCE RHB LB R0 W0

FULL NAME: Daniel William Lawrence
BORN: July 12, 1997, Whipps Cross, Essex
SQUAD NO: 28
EDUCATION: Trinity Catholic High School
TEAMS: Essex 2nd XI
CAREER: Yet to make first-team debut

---

FAMILY TIES? My dad is the groundsman at Chingford Cricket Club. My great uncle played for England
CAREER HIGHLIGHTS? Playing a season for Essex 2nd XI and scoring a hundred for them
BEST PLAYER IN COUNTY CRICKET? Moeen Ali
MOST MARKED CHARACTERISTIC? Self belief and being sure of what I want to do when I get older
CRICKETING HEROES? Ricky Ponting, Graeme Smith, AB de Villiers
NON-CRICKETING HEROES? Martin Luther King, David Beckham
CRICKET RULE YOU'D CHANGE? You should be allowed to bowl as many overs as you want when you are young – no restrictions
DESERT ISLAND DISC? Red Hot Chili Peppers – Dani California
FAVOURITE TV? Hustle
SURPRISING FACT? I've got Grade Three on the saxophone but had to stop because of cricket
FANTASY SLIP CORDON? Keeper: Sheldon Cooper, 1st: The Rock, 2nd: Rafael Nadal, 3rd: Myself, Gully: Viv Richards

# JACK LEACH

## LHB SLA R0 W0

FULL NAME: Matthew Jack Leach
BORN: June 22, 1991, Taunton
SQUAD NO: 17
HEIGHT: 6ft
NICKNAME: Nut, Nutter
EDUCATION: Bishop Fox's Community School; Richard Huish College; Cardiff Metropolitan University
TEAMS: Somerset
CAREER: First-class: 2012; List A: 2012



BEST BATTING: 43 Somerset vs Yorkshire, Leeds, 2014
BEST BOWLING: 5-63 Somerset vs Warwickshire, Taunton, 2013

CAREER HIGHLIGHTS? Taking Hashim Amla's wicket, my first-class debut for Somerset and my maiden five-wicket haul against Warwickshire
BEST PLAYER IN COUNTY CRICKET? Marcus Trescothick
TIP FOR THE TOP? Tom Abell
MOST MARKED CHARACTERISTIC? The nut
CRICKETING HEROES? It pains me to say it but it used to be Marcus Trescothick! Now it's Jos Buttler – I like how he keeps his nut down and gets on with it
NON-CRICKETING HEROES? Terry Tibbs from Fonejacker
CRICKET RULE YOU'D CHANGE? All wickets have to be scarified!
IF YOU COULD BE SOMEONE ELSE FOR A DAY? James Yeabsley
FAVOURITE TV? The Big Bang Theory
ACCOMPLISHMENTS? Climbing Kilimanjaro
TWITTER FEED: @jackleach1991

| Batting | Mat | Inns | NO | Runs | HS | Ave | SR | 100 | 50 | Ct | St |
|---|---|---|---|---|---|---|---|---|---|---|---|
| First-class | 11 | 13 | 4 | 125 | 43 | 13.88 | 38.22 | 0 | 0 | 0 | 0 |
| List A | 9 | 3 | 0 | 20 | 18 | 6.66 | 44.44 | 0 | 0 | 4 | 0 |
| **Bowling** | **Mat** | **Balls** | **Runs** | **Wkts** | **BBI** | **BBM** | **Ave** | **Econ** | **SR** | **5w** | **10** |
| First-class | 11 | 1990 | 804 | 23 | 5/63 | 7/106 | 34.95 | 2.42 | 86.5 | 1 | 0 |
| List A | 9 | 426 | 352 | 9 | 3/53 | 3/53 | 39.11 | 4.95 | 47.3 | 0 | 0 |

# JOE LEACH

## RHB RFM R0 W0 MVP90

FULL NAME: Joseph Leach
BORN: October 30, 1990, Stafford, Staffordshire
SQUAD NO: 23
HEIGHT: 6ft 1in
NICKNAME: Leachy, SSSB
EDUCATION: Shrewsbury School; University of Leeds
TEAMS: Worcestershire
CAREER: First-class: 2012; List A: 2012; T20: 2013

---

BEST BATTING: 114 Worcestershire vs Gloucestershire, Cheltenham, 2013
BEST BOWLING: 5-36 Worcestershire vs Kent, Tunbridge Wells, 2014
COUNTY CAPS: 2012

---

FAMILY TIES? My brother Steve plays for Oxford MCCU
CAREER HIGHLIGHTS? Getting promoted into Division One last season and reaching the T20 quarter-finals
BEST PLAYER IN COUNTY CRICKET? Moeen Ali, James Taylor
TIP FOR THE TOP? Tom Fell, Charlie Morris, Tom Kohler-Cadmore
MOST MARKED CHARACTERISTIC? My massive head
CRICKETING HEROES? Jacques Kallis –a legend of the game and a genuine allrounder
CRICKET RULE YOU'D CHANGE? Make the tea break longer!
IF YOU COULD BE SOMEONE ELSE FOR A DAY? David Beckham
DESERT ISLAND DISC? The 1975
PET HATE? Lateness. I hate being late
FANTASY SLIP CORDON? Keeper: Ricky Gervais, 1st: Stephen Merchant, 2nd: Myself, 3rd: Shane Warne, Gully: Jacques Kallis
TWITTER FEED: @joeleach230

| Batting | Mat | Inns | NO | Runs | HS | Ave | SR | 100 | 50 | Ct | St |
|---|---|---|---|---|---|---|---|---|---|---|---|
| First-class | 26 | 42 | 3 | 921 | 114 | 23.61 | 53.23 | 1 | 7 | 5 | 0 |
| List A | 10 | 7 | 5 | 178 | 45* | 89.00 | 99.44 | 0 | 0 | 1 | 0 |
| Twenty20 | 11 | 8 | 3 | 75 | 20 | 15.00 | 117.18 | 0 | 0 | 2 | 0 |
| **Bowling** | **Mat** | **Balls** | **Runs** | **Wkts** | **BBI** | **BBM** | **Ave** | **Econ** | **SR** | **5w** | **10** |
| First-class | 26 | 2439 | 1520 | 51 | 5/36 | 6/116 | 29.80 | 3.73 | 47.8 | 1 | 0 |
| List A | 10 | 347 | 351 | 8 | 2/53 | 2/53 | 43.87 | 6.06 | 43.3 | 0 | 0 |
| Twenty20 | 11 | 127 | 177 | 9 | 3/20 | 3/20 | 19.66 | 8.36 | 14.1 | 0 | 0 |

# JACK LEANING

RHB RMF R0 W0

FULL NAME: Jack Andrew Leaning
BORN: October 18, 1993, Bristol
SQUAD NO: 34
HEIGHT: 6ft
EDUCATION: Archbishop Holgate's School, York; York College
TEAMS: Yorkshire
CAREER: First-class: 2013; List A: 2012; T20: 2013



BEST BATTING: 99 Yorkshire vs Sussex, Arundel, 2014

TWITTER FEED: @JackLeaning1
NOTES: Son of former York City goalkeeper Andy, Leaning wrote himself into the Yorkshire record-books as a 14-year-old, when he hit an unbeaten 164 during the U14 squad's clash with Cheshire. He won Yorkshire's Academy Player of the Year award in 2012 and made his List A debut in the same season, scoring 11 against Warwickshire. He made his first-class debut in 2013 against Surrey at Headingley and played 10 Championship matches last season, hitting four half-centuries and top-scoring with 99

| Batting | Mat | Inns | NO | Runs | HS | Ave | SR | 100 | 50 | Ct | St |
|---|---|---|---|---|---|---|---|---|---|---|---|
| First-class | 12 | 16 | 2 | 478 | 99 | 34.14 | 45.65 | 0 | 4 | 4 | 0 |
| List A | 14 | 13 | 4 | 342 | 111* | 38.00 | 88.83 | 1 | 2 | 7 | 0 |
| Twenty20 | 4 | 3 | 0 | 14 | 8 | 4.66 | 56.00 | 0 | 0 | 0 | 0 |
| **Bowling** | **Mat** | **Balls** | **Runs** | **Wkts** | **BBI** | **BBM** | **Ave** | **Econ** | **SR** | **5w** | **10** |
| First-class | 12 | 60 | 35 | 0 | - | - | - | 3.50 | - | 0 | 0 |
| List A | 14 | 156 | 141 | 7 | 5/22 | 5/22 | 20.14 | 5.42 | 22.2 | 1 | 0 |
| Twenty20 | 4 | 12 | 30 | 0 | - | - | - | 15.00 | - | 0 | 0 |

# ALEX LEES

LHB LB R1 W0 MVP50

FULL NAME: Alexander Zak Lees
BORN: April 14, 1993, Halifax, Yorkshire
SQUAD NO: 14
HEIGHT: 6ft 3in
NICKNAME: Leesy
EDUCATION: Holy Trinity Senior School
TEAMS: Yorkshire, England Lions
CAREER: First-class: 2010; List A: 2011; T20: 2013

BEST BATTING: 275* Yorkshire vs Derbyshire, Chesterfield, 2013

CAREER HIGHLIGHTS? My 275 not out against Derbyshire in 2013
BEST PLAYER IN COUNTY CRICKET? Gary Ballance
TIP FOR THE TOP? Sam Billings
CRICKETING HEROES? Brian Lara and Matthew Hayden
IF YOU WEREN'T A CRICKETER? I'd be a policeman
DESERT ISLAND DISC? Something by Drake
FAVOURITE TV? Band Of Brothers
SURPRISING FACT? I do a bit of magic on the side
FANTASY SLIP CORDON? Keeper: Steve Carell, 1st: Will Ferrell, 2nd: Sean Lock, 3rd: Jessica Alba, Gully: Disclosure
TWITTER FEED: @aleesy14

| Batting | Mat | Inns | NO | Runs | HS | Ave | SR | 100 | 50 | Ct | St |
|---|---|---|---|---|---|---|---|---|---|---|---|
| First-class | 33 | 51 | 4 | 1934 | 275* | 41.14 | 47.56 | 6 | 6 | 15 | 0 |
| List A | 21 | 20 | 2 | 714 | 102 | 39.66 | 78.63 | 1 | 6 | 5 | 0 |
| Twenty20 | 12 | 12 | 2 | 348 | 67* | 34.80 | 124.73 | 0 | 2 | 4 | 0 |
| **Bowling** | **Mat** | **Balls** | **Runs** | **Wkts** | **BBI** | **BBM** | **Ave** | **Econ** | **SR** | **5w** | **10** |
| First-class | 33 | 6 | 14 | 0 | - | - | - | 14.00 | - | 0 | 0 |
| List A | 21 | - | - | - | - | - | - | - | - | - | - |
| Twenty20 | 12 | - | - | - | - | - | - | - | - | - | - |

## RICHARD LEVI

RHB RM R0 W0

FULL NAME: Richard Ernst Levi
BORN: January 14, 1988, Johannesburg, South Africa
SQUAD NO: 88
HEIGHT: 6ft
NICKNAME: Beat
EDUCATION: Wynberg Boys' High School; University of South Africa
TEAMS: South Africa, Northamptonshire, Cape Cobras, Mumbai Indians, Somerset, Western Province
CAREER: T20I: 2012; First-class: 2006; List A: 2005; T20: 2008



BEST BATTING: 150* Western Province vs Eastern Province, Cape Town, 2007

CAREER HIGHLIGHTS? Making my debut for my province, South Africa and Northants
BEST PLAYER IN COUNTY CRICKET? Jesse Ryder
TIP FOR THE TOP? Olly Stone
MOST MARKED CHARACTERISTIC? I'm square
CRICKETING HEROES? Gary Kirsten – worked hard to get what he got and still does to this day
NON-CRICKETING HEROES? My old man – did everything for me, no questions asked
CRICKET RULE YOU'D CHANGE? One free life for batters!
IF YOU WEREN'T A CRICKETER? A lumberjack
IF YOU COULD BE SOMEONE ELSE FOR A DAY? Richard Branson
ACCOMPLISHMENTS? I have managed to stay alive
PET HATE? Liars and idiots – quite self-explanatory
SURPRISING FACT? I'm not that good at answering questionnaires
TWITTER FEED: @RichardLevi88

| Batting | Mat | Inns | NO | Runs | HS | Ave | SR | 100 | 50 | Ct | St |
|---|---|---|---|---|---|---|---|---|---|---|---|
| T20Is | 13 | 13 | 2 | 236 | 117* | 21.45 | 141.31 | 1 | 1 | 4 | 0 |
| First-class | 52 | 86 | 9 | 2897 | 150* | 37.62 | 65.99 | 5 | 19 | 38 | 0 |
| List A | 90 | 84 | 5 | 2995 | 166 | 37.91 | 104.72 | 6 | 15 | 28 | 0 |
| Twenty20 | 127 | 122 | 9 | 3071 | 117* | 27.17 | 140.03 | 3 | 19 | 32 | 0 |
| **Bowling** | **Mat** | **Balls** | **Runs** | **Wkts** | **BBI** | **BBM** | **Ave** | **Econ** | **SR** | **5w** | **10** |
| T20Is | 13 | - | - | - | - | - | - | - | - | - | - |
| First-class | 52 | - | - | - | - | - | - | - | - | - | - |
| List A | 90 | - | - | - | - | - | - | - | - | - | - |
| Twenty20 | 127 | - | - | - | - | - | - | - | - | - | - |

## TOM LEWIS

## LHB RM R0 W0

FULL NAME: Thomas Peter Lewis
BORN: March 7, 1991, Coventry, Warwickshire
SQUAD NO: 7
TEAMS: Warwickshire 2nd XI
CAREER: Yet to make first-team debut

---

FAMILY TIES? Mark Lewis (Oxford UCCE, Warwickshire)
CAREER HIGHLIGHTS? Being a MCC Young Cricketer and signing my first contract
MOST MARKED CHARACTERISTIC? My off-drive
SUPERSTITIONS? I put my pads on before my thigh guard
CRICKETING HEROES? Andrew Flintoff, Graham Thorpe, Marcus Trescothick
NON-CRICKETING HEROES? Paul Scholes
IF YOU WEREN'T A CRICKETER? Studying at university
DESERT ISLAND DISC? Drake – Take Care
FAVOURITE TV? Breaking Bad, Prison Break, Entourage
TWITTER FEED: @tom_lewis

# JAKE LIBBY RHB OB R0 W0

FULL NAME: Jacob Daniel Libby
BORN: January 3, 1993, Plymouth
SQUAD NO: tbc
HEIGHT: 5ft 9in
NICKNAME: Libs
EDUCATION: Plymouth College; Truro College; Cardiff Metropolitan University
TEAMS: Nottinghamshire
CAREER: First-class: 2014



BEST BATTING: 108 Nottinghamshire vs Sussex, Nottingham, 2014
BEST BOWLING: 1-18 Cardiff MCCU vs Glamorgan, Cardiff, 2014

FAMILY TIES? My dad played to a reasonably high level of club cricket and my brother plays in the Cornish Premier League
CAREER HIGHLIGHTS? Scoring 108 on my first-class debut vs Sussex at Trent Bridge and scoring a double-hundred vs Warwickshire 2nd XI at Edgbaston
BEST PLAYER IN COUNTY CRICKET? James Taylor
SUPERSTITIONS? I always put my pads on the same way, and I like to cross the rope after my batting partner when walking out
CRICKETING HEROES? Sachin Tendulkar – I just loved watching him bat
CRICKET RULE YOU'D CHANGE? Being run out while backing up – I have been on the receiving end of this and it just feels like you've been cheated!
IF YOU WEREN'T A CRICKETER? I'd like to say a pilot – flying amazes me
FAVOURITE TV? Family Guy
LEAST FAVOURITE TV? Friends
PET HATE? Losing on FIFA – there's nothing more frustrating!
SURPRISING FACT? I used to be a massive fan of The Powerpuff Girls on Cartoon Network!
FANTASY SLIP CORDON? Keeper: Dave Waters, 1st: The Rock, 2nd: Myself, 3rd: Mila Kunis, 4th: Peter Griffin (no catches would be taken but it would be entertaining!)
TWITTER FEED: @JakeLibby1

| Batting | Mat | Inns | NO | Runs | HS | Ave | SR | 100 | 50 | Ct | St |
|---|---|---|---|---|---|---|---|---|---|---|---|
| First-class | 3 | 5 | 1 | 201 | 108 | 50.25 | 41.44 | 1 | 1 | 1 | 0 |
| **Bowling** | **Mat** | **Balls** | **Runs** | **Wkts** | **BBI** | **BBM** | **Ave** | **Econ** | **SR** | **5w** | **10** |
| First-class | 3 | 155 | 104 | 1 | 1/18 | 1/41 | 104.00 | 4.02 | 155.0 | 0 | 0 |

## CHRIS LIDDLE

## RHB LMF R0 W0

FULL NAME: Christopher John Liddle
BORN: February 1, 1984, Middlesbrough, Yorkshire
SQUAD NO: 11
HEIGHT: 6ft 4in
NICKNAME: Lids
EDUCATION: Nunthorpe Comprehensive, Middlesborough; Teeside Tertiary College
TEAMS: Sussex, Dhaka Gladiators, Leicestershire
CAREER: First-class: 2005; List A: 2006; T20: 2008

BEST BATTING: 53 Sussex vs Worcestershire, Hove, 2007
BEST BOWLING: 3-42 Leicestershire vs Somerset, Leicester, 2006

FAMILY TIES? My brother Andrew plays in the NYSD cricket league
CAREER HIGHLIGHTS? My T20 debut. The 2011 season having previously missed the 2009 and 2010 seasons with injury
CRICKETING HEROES? Darren Gough, AB de Villiers, Marc Rosenberg
NON-CRICKETING HEROES? Jamie Redknapp
IF YOU WEREN'T A CRICKETER? I'd be an electrician
FAVOURITE TV? An Idiot Abroad, Emmerdale
SURPRISING FACT? Occasional DJ for friends
FANTASY SLIP CORDON? Keeper: Karl Pilkington, 1st: Cheryl Cole, 2nd: Jamie Redknapp, 3rd: Mila Kunis, 4th: Me, Gully: Jessica Biel
TWITTER FEED: @chrisliddle11

| Batting | Mat | Inns | NO | Runs | HS | Ave | SR | 100 | 50 | Ct | St |
|---|---|---|---|---|---|---|---|---|---|---|---|
| First-class | 21 | 21 | 11 | 125 | 53 | 12.50 | 51.44 | 0 | 1 | 6 | 0 |
| List A | 56 | 20 | 5 | 89 | 15 | 5.93 | 72.35 | 0 | 0 | 15 | 0 |
| Twenty20 | 64 | 16 | 9 | 54 | 16 | 7.71 | 71.05 | 0 | 0 | 15 | 0 |
| Bowling | Mat | Balls | Runs | Wkts | BBI | BBM | Ave | Econ | SR | 5w | 10 |
| First-class | 21 | 2457 | 1345 | 24 | 3/42 | 4/82 | 56.04 | 3.28 | 102.3 | 0 | 0 |
| List A | 56 | 2083 | 2064 | 75 | 5/18 | 5/18 | 27.52 | 5.94 | 27.7 | 1 | 0 |
| Twenty20 | 64 | 1233 | 1639 | 73 | 5/17 | 5/17 | 22.45 | 7.97 | 16.8 | 1 | 0 |

# ARRON LILLEY

RHB OB R0 W0

FULL NAME: Arron Mark Lilley
BORN: April 1, 1991, Tameside, Lancashire
SQUAD NO: 19
HEIGHT: 6ft 1in
NICKNAME: The Bigshow
EDUCATION: Mossley Hollins High School; Ashton Sixth Form
TEAMS: Lancashire
CAREER: First-class: 2013; List A: 2012; T20: 2013



BEST BATTING: 35* Lancashire vs Glamorgan, Manchester, 2013
BEST BOWLING: 1-41 Lancashire vs Worcestershire, Worcester, 2013

CAREER HIGHLIGHTS? T20 debut against Yorkshire at Headingley; Fred's comeback on T20 Finals Day; making my first-class debut against Glamorgan
BEST PLAYER IN COUNTY CRICKET? Jeetan Patel
TIP FOR THE TOP? Haseeb Hameed
CRICKETING HEROES? Shane Warne – greatest spinner to have graced the game. Graeme Swann – great to watch. Andrew Flintoff – charismatic
NON-CRICKETING HEROES? Jim Carrey – funniest guy in the world
IF YOU WEREN'T A CRICKETER? Physiotherapy
IF YOU COULD BE SOMEONE ELSE FOR A DAY? David Beckham
DESERT ISLAND DISC? The Courteeners – You're Not 19 Forever
FAVOURITE TV? Prison Break
LEAST FAVOURITE TV? Friends
PET HATE? People clapping on a plane when the plane has landed at its destination!
TWITTER FEED: @Arronlilley20

| Batting | Mat | Inns | NO | Runs | HS | Ave | SR | 100 | 50 | Ct | St |
|---|---|---|---|---|---|---|---|---|---|---|---|
| First-class | 2 | 2 | 2 | 39 | 35* | - | 108.33 | 0 | 0 | 0 | 0 |
| List A | 7 | 3 | 1 | 12 | 10 | 6.00 | 120.00 | 0 | 0 | 3 | 0 |
| Twenty20 | 17 | 8 | 3 | 37 | 18 | 7.40 | 160.86 | 0 | 0 | 5 | 0 |
| **Bowling** | **Mat** | **Balls** | **Runs** | **Wkts** | **BBI** | **BBM** | **Ave** | **Econ** | **SR** | **5w** | **10** |
| First-class | 2 | 414 | 212 | 2 | 1/41 | 2/83 | 106.00 | 3.07 | 207.0 | 0 | 0 |
| List A | 7 | 264 | 208 | 12 | 4/30 | 4/30 | 17.33 | 4.72 | 22.0 | 0 | 0 |
| Twenty20 | 17 | 306 | 380 | 10 | 2/28 | 2/28 | 38.00 | 7.45 | 30.6 | 0 | 0 |

# TIM LINLEY

RHB RFM R0 W1

FULL NAME: Timothy Edward Linley
BORN: March 23, 1982, Horsforth, Leeds
SQUAD NO: 12
HEIGHT: 6ft 3in
NICKNAME: Linners, The Viscount, Ned
EDUCATION: Oxford Brookes University
TEAMS: Surrey, Sussex
CAREER: First-class: 2003; List A: 2009; T20: 2009

BEST BATTING: 42 Oxford UCCE vs Derbyshire, The Parks, 2005
BEST BOWLING: 6-57 Surrey vs Leicestershire, Leicester, 2011

CAREER HIGHLIGHTS? My Surrey debut vs Middlesex. It was a T20 in front of 16,000, the biggest crowd I had played in front of by about 15,950
BEST PLAYER IN COUNTY CRICKET? Darren Stevens
TIP FOR THE TOP? Matthew Dunn
MOST MARKED CHARACTERISTIC? My laugh and my voice. Both too loud. You tend to hear me before you see me
CRICKETING HEROES? Curtly Ambrose – for his pace and bounce and his aura on the cricket field. Shaun Pollock, Glenn McGrath, Angus Fraser for their unerring accuracy and keep-it-simple game plan
CRICKET RULE YOU'D CHANGE? I want more wickets. How about three misses and you're out!
DESERT ISLAND DISC? Radiohead – The Bends
FAVOURITE TV? I love watching the darts
FANTASY SLIP CORDON? As long as you can catch I don't care!
TWITTER FEED: @ViscountLinley

| Batting | Mat | Inns | NO | Runs | HS | Ave | SR | 100 | 50 | Ct | St |
|---|---|---|---|---|---|---|---|---|---|---|---|
| First-class | 62 | 85 | 18 | 536 | 42 | 8.00 | 34.09 | 0 | 0 | 21 | 0 |
| List A | 25 | 13 | 9 | 84 | 20* | 21.00 | 86.59 | 0 | 0 | 3 | 0 |
| Twenty20 | 7 | 2 | 0 | 9 | 8 | 4.50 | 112.50 | 0 | 0 | 2 | 0 |
| **Bowling** | **Mat** | **Balls** | **Runs** | **Wkts** | **BBI** | **BBM** | **Ave** | **Econ** | **SR** | **5w** | **10** |
| First-class | 62 | 10621 | 5296 | 191 | 6/57 | | 27.72 | 2.99 | 55.6 | 5 | 1 |
| List A | 25 | 898 | 910 | 23 | 3/50 | 3/50 | 39.56 | 6.08 | 39.0 | 0 | 0 |
| Twenty20 | 7 | 122 | 148 | 6 | 2/28 | 2/28 | 24.66 | 7.27 | 20.3 | 0 | 0 |

# LIAM LIVINGSTONE RHB LB R0 W0

FULL NAME: Liam Stephen Livingstone
BORN: August 4, 1993, Barrow-in-Furness, Cumbria
SQUAD NO: 7
HEIGHT: 6ft 1in
NICKNAME: Livi
EDUCATION: Chetwynde School
TEAMS: Lancashire 2nd XI
CAREER: Yet to make first-team debut



BEST PLAYER IN COUNTY CRICKET? Jason Roy
TIP FOR THE TOP? Haseeb Hameed
MOST MARKED CHARACTERISTIC? I'm laid-back
SUPERSTITIONS? I put my left pad on first and I always step onto a pitch left-foot first
CRICKETING HEROES? Shane Warne – I was a legspinner when I was younger. Andrew Flintoff – great to watch as a kid
NON-CRICKETING HEROES? Cristiano Ronaldo – ridiculous athlete and great to watch
CRICKET RULE YOU'D CHANGE? You can't be caught down the leg side!
IF YOU WEREN'T A CRICKETER? Not a clue...
IF YOU COULD BE SOMEONE ELSE FOR A DAY? Sheikh Mohammed
DESERT ISLAND DISC? One Direction's greatest hits
FAVOURITE TV? Prison Break
LEAST FAVOURITE TV? Any soaps
SURPRISING FACT? My record for head keepy-ups is 257
TWITTER FEED: @Liaml4893

# DAVID LLOYD

RHB OB R0 W0

GLAMORGAN

FULL NAME: David Liam Lloyd
BORN: June 15, 1992, St Asaph, Flintshire
SQUAD NO: 14
HEIGHT: 5ft 9in
NICKNAME: Ram
EDUCATION: Darland School; Shrewsbury School
TEAMS: Glamorgan
CAREER: First-class: 2012; List A: 2014; T20: 2014

BEST BATTING: 41 Glamorgan vs Kent, Canterbury, 2014
BEST BOWLING: 2-22 Glamorgan vs Derbyshire, Cardiff, 2014

FAMILY TIES? My father and both of my uncles played local cricket and represented Wales Minor Counties
CRICKETING HEROES? Jacques Kallis and Brendon McCullum – both like to play attacking cricket and they are really enjoyable to watch
NON-CRICKETING HEROES? Usain Bolt – trains hard but still has a smile on his face
IF YOU WEREN'T A CRICKETER? I would like to become a brewer
IF YOU COULD BE SOMEONE ELSE FOR A DAY? David Beckham – just to live his lifestyle for a day would be amazing
DESERT ISLAND DISC? Beach Boys – Greatest Hits
FAVOURITE TV? Breaking Bad
ACCOMPLISHMENTS? Winning the English Schools Football Cup
SURPRISING FACT? I'm a prolific goalscorer for Wrexham Lager FC
FANTASY SLIP CORDON? Keeper: Joey Barton, 1st: Bryan Cranston, 2nd: Jose Mourinho, 3rd: Myself, Gully: David Moyes
TWITTER FEED: @lloyddl2010

| Batting | Mat | Inns | NO | Runs | HS | Ave | SR | 100 | 50 | Ct | St |
|---|---|---|---|---|---|---|---|---|---|---|---|
| First-class | 7 | 11 | 1 | 109 | 41 | 10.90 | 41.76 | 0 | 0 | 2 | 0 |
| List A | 7 | 5 | 0 | 53 | 32 | 10.60 | 73.61 | 0 | 0 | 1 | 0 |
| Twenty20 | 3 | 2 | 0 | 3 | 3 | 1.50 | 42.85 | 0 | 0 | 0 | 0 |
| **Bowling** | **Mat** | **Balls** | **Runs** | **Wkts** | **BBI** | **BBM** | **Ave** | **Econ** | **SR** | **5w** | **10** |
| First-class | 7 | 210 | 126 | 4 | 2/22 | 2/22 | 31.50 | 3.60 | 52.5 | 0 | 0 |
| List A | 7 | 186 | 149 | 8 | 4/10 | 4/10 | 18.62 | 4.80 | 23.2 | 0 | 0 |
| Twenty20 | 3 | - | - | - | - | - | - | - | - | - | - |

# MICHAEL LUMB

LHB RM R3 W0

FULL NAME: Michael John Lumb
BORN: February 12, 1980, Johannesburg, South Africa
SQUAD NO: 45
HEIGHT: 6ft
NICKNAME: Joe, Lumby, China, Slumdog
EDUCATION: St Stithians College
TEAMS: England, Nottinghamshire, Deccan Chargers, Hampshire, Queensland, Rajasthan Royals, Sydney Sixers, Yorkshire
CAREER: ODI: 2014; T20I: 2010; First-class: 2000; List A: 2001; T20: 2003



BEST BATTING: 221* Nottinghamshire vs Derbyshire, Nottingham, 2013
BEST BOWLING: 2-10 Yorkshire vs Kent, Canterbury, 2001
COUNTY CAPS: 2003 (Yorkshire); 2008 (Hampshire); 2012

FAMILY TIES? My father Richard played for Yorkshire and my uncle Tich played for Natal and South Africa
CAREER HIGHLIGHTS? It would have to be playing for England and winning the World T20, beating the Aussies in the final!
SUPERSTITIONS? Too many to mention, they call me Rain Man!
CRICKETING HEROES? Graham Thorpe, Darren Lehmann, Stephen Fleming, Craig White, Shane Warne, Jacques Kallis
NON-CRICKETING HEROES? Nelson Mandela
IF YOU WEREN'T A CRICKETER? Game ranger
FAVOURITE TV? Entourage, 24, CSI

| Batting | Mat | Inns | NO | Runs | HS | Ave | SR | 100 | 50 | Ct | St |
|---|---|---|---|---|---|---|---|---|---|---|---|
| ODIs | 3 | 3 | 0 | 165 | 106 | 55.00 | 81.28 | 1 | 0 | 1 | 0 |
| T20Is | 27 | 27 | 1 | 552 | 63 | 21.23 | 133.65 | 0 | 3 | 8 | 0 |
| First-class | 180 | 303 | 18 | 10114 | 221* | 35.48 | | 19 | 54 | 107 | 0 |
| List A | 200 | 194 | 11 | 5821 | 110 | 31.80 | 85.54 | 4 | 43 | 69 | 0 |
| Twenty20 | 186 | 185 | 11 | 4258 | 124* | 24.47 | 138.96 | 1 | 23 | 62 | 0 |
| **Bowling** | **Mat** | **Balls** | **Runs** | **Wkts** | **BBI** | **BBM** | **Ave** | **Econ** | **SR** | **5w** | **10** |
| ODIs | 3 | - | - | - | - | - | - | - | - | - | - |
| T20Is | 27 | - | - | - | - | - | - | - | - | - | - |
| First-class | 180 | 330 | 255 | 6 | 2/10 | | 42.50 | 4.63 | 55.0 | 0 | 0 |
| List A | 200 | 12 | 28 | 0 | - | - | - | 14.00 | - | 0 | 0 |
| Twenty20 | 186 | 36 | 65 | 3 | 3/32 | 3/32 | 21.66 | 10.83 | 12.0 | 0 | 0 |

# ADAM LYTH — LHB OB R2 W0 MVP13

YORKSHIRE

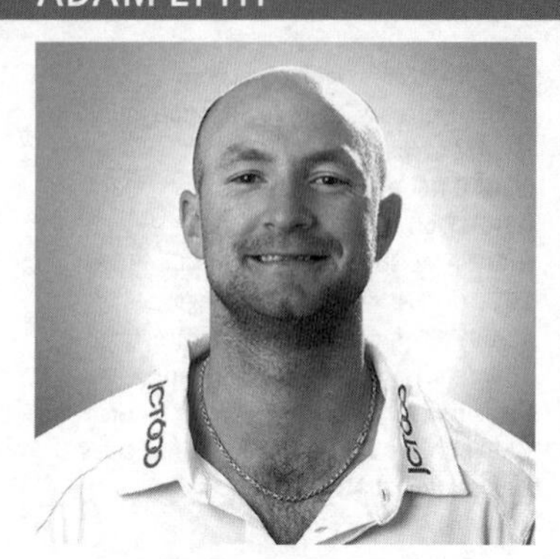

FULL NAME: Adam Lyth
BORN: September 25, 1987, Whitby, Yorkshire
SQUAD NO: 9
HEIGHT: 5ft 9in
NICKNAME: Lythy, Budge
EDUCATION: Caedmon School; Whitby Community School
TEAMS: Yorkshire, England Lions
CAREER: First-class: 2007; List A: 2006; T20: 2008

BEST BATTING: 251 Yorkshire vs Lancashire, Manchester, 2014
BEST BOWLING: 2-15 Yorkshire vs Somerset, Taunton, 2013
COUNTY CAPS: 2010

FAMILY TIES? My brother and dad played for Scarborough and my grandad played for Whitby
CAREER HIGHLIGHTS? Winning the County Championship in 2014, winning the young player award in 2010 and playing for England Lions
BEST PLAYER IN COUNTY CRICKET? Gary Ballance
TIP FOR THE TOP? Mark Wood
CRICKETING HEROES? Graham Thorpe – I just liked the way he batted
IF YOU WEREN'T A CRICKETER? Playing football
DESERT ISLAND DISC? Rod Stewart
FAVOURITE TV? Only Fools And Horses
ACCOMPLISHMENTS? Playing football for Manchester City
FANTASY SLIP CORDON? Keeper: Lee Evans, 1st: David Beckham, 2nd: Tiger Woods, 3rd: Me, Gully: Mila Kunis
TWITTER FEED: @lythy09

| Batting | Mat | Inns | NO | Runs | HS | Ave | SR | 100 | 50 | Ct | St |
|---|---|---|---|---|---|---|---|---|---|---|---|
| First-class | 101 | 160 | 7 | 6505 | 251 | 42.51 | | 14 | 40 | 121 | 0 |
| List A | 85 | 79 | 7 | 2256 | 109* | 31.33 | 87.98 | 1 | 11 | 38 | 0 |
| Twenty20 | 61 | 52 | 2 | 939 | 78 | 18.78 | 123.22 | 0 | 2 | 25 | 0 |
| **Bowling** | **Mat** | **Balls** | **Runs** | **Wkts** | **BBI** | **BBM** | **Ave** | **Econ** | **SR** | **5w** | **10** |
| First-class | 101 | 993 | 639 | 13 | 2/15 | 2/15 | 49.15 | 3.86 | 76.3 | 0 | 0 |
| List A | 85 | 162 | 172 | 2 | 1/6 | 1/6 | 86.00 | 6.37 | 81.0 | 0 | 0 |
| Twenty20 | 61 | 42 | 56 | 3 | 2/5 | 2/5 | 18.66 | 8.00 | 14.0 | 0 | 0 |

# MATT MACHAN LHB OB R0 W0

FULL NAME: Matthew William Machan
BORN: February 15, 1991, Brighton
SQUAD NO: 15
HEIGHT: 5ft 9in
NICKNAME: Meatball, Mach
EDUCATION: Hurstpierpoint College; Brighton College
TEAMS: Scotland, Sussex
CAREER: ODI: 2013; T20I:2013; First-class: 2010; List A: 2010; T20: 2012



BEST BATTING: 119 Sussex vs Loughborough MCCU, Hove, 2014
BEST BOWLING: 1-36 Scotland vs Australia A, Edinburgh, 2013

CAREER HIGHLIGHTS? Playing at the 2015 World Cup and T20 Finals Day in 2012
BEST PLAYER IN COUNTY CRICKET? Ed Joyce, Luke Wright
TIP FOR THE TOP? Sam Billings, Tymal Mills
CRICKETING HEROES? Matt Hayden and Brian Lara – I loved the way they played when I was growing up
NON-CRICKETING HEROES? My mum and dad and also Donald Trump
CRICKET RULE YOU'D CHANGE? Free hits for front-foot no-balls in four-day cricket
IF YOU COULD BE SOMEONE ELSE FOR A DAY? David Beckham
DESERT ISLAND DISC? Every number one of every week from the day the UK chart started
PET HATE? People who make other people feel small in a large group
SURPRISING FACT? I'm a part-owner of a greyhound
TWITTER FEED: @mattmachan

| Batting | Mat | Inns | NO | Runs | HS | Ave | SR | 100 | 50 | Ct | St |
|---|---|---|---|---|---|---|---|---|---|---|---|
| ODIs | 20 | 19 | 0 | 675 | 114 | 35.52 | 76.27 | 1 | 3 | 4 | 0 |
| T20Is | 6 | 6 | 2 | 276 | 67* | 69.00 | 131.42 | 0 | 3 | 2 | 0 |
| First-class | 20 | 30 | 4 | 827 | 119 | 31.80 | 57.43 | 2 | 2 | 9 | 0 |
| List A | 47 | 46 | 5 | 1570 | 126* | 38.29 | 88.30 | 2 | 8 | 15 | 0 |
| Twenty20 | 42 | 42 | 6 | 994 | 90* | 27.61 | 122.56 | 0 | 7 | 21 | 0 |
| **Bowling** | **Mat** | **Balls** | **Runs** | **Wkts** | **BBI** | **BBM** | **Ave** | **Econ** | **SR** | **5w** | **10** |
| ODIs | 20 | 378 | 338 | 8 | 3/31 | 3/31 | 42.25 | 5.36 | 47.2 | 0 | 0 |
| T20Is | 6 | 99 | 108 | 3 | 3/23 | 3/23 | 36.00 | 6.54 | 33.0 | 0 | 0 |
| First-class | 20 | 90 | 72 | 1 | 1/36 | 1/59 | 72.00 | 4.80 | 90.0 | 0 | 0 |
| List A | 47 | 580 | 536 | 11 | 3/31 | 3/31 | 48.72 | 5.54 | 52.7 | 0 | 0 |
| Twenty20 | 42 | 177 | 209 | 5 | 3/23 | 3/23 | 41.80 | 7.08 | 35.4 | 0 | 0 |

# CALUM MACLEOD RHB RMF R0 W0



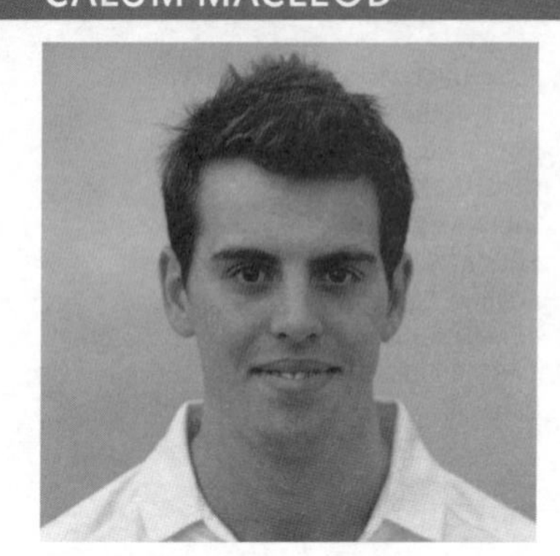

FULL NAME: Calum Scott MacLeod
BORN: November 15, 1988, Glasgow
SQUAD NO: 14
HEIGHT: 6ft 2in
NICKNAME: Cloudy, Highlander, Scot
EDUCATION: Hillpark School
TEAMS: Scotland, Durham, Warwickshire
CAREER: ODI: 2008; T20I: 2009; First-class: 2007; List A: 2008; T20: 2009

BEST BATTING: 84 Durham vs Lancashire, Manchester, 2014
BEST BOWLING: 4-66 Scotland vs Canada, Aberdeen, 2009

CAREER HIGHLIGHTS? My first Scotland cap, opening the bowling in the World T20 and my first century for Scotland
CRICKETING HEROES? Glenn McGrath and Sachin Tendulkar
NON-CRICKETING HEROES? Tiger Woods
IF YOU WEREN'T A CRICKETER? Sports psychologist
DESERT ISLAND DISC? Dire Straits – Brothers In Arms
FAVOURITE TV? Sherlock
SURPRISING FACT? I once presented a Scottish Gaelic TV show called De A Nis
FANTASY SLIP CORDON? Keeper: Tiger Woods, 1st: Sherlock Holmes, 2nd: Me, 3rd: Emma Watson, Gully: Mark Knopfler
TWITTER FEED: @calummacleod640

| Batting | Mat | Inns | NO | Runs | HS | Ave | SR | 100 | 50 | Ct | St |
|---|---|---|---|---|---|---|---|---|---|---|---|
| ODIs | 31 | 29 | 3 | 651 | 175 | 25.03 | 75.08 | 2 | 1 | 9 | 0 |
| T20Is | 15 | 14 | 1 | 289 | 57 | 22.23 | 106.64 | 0 | 3 | 5 | 0 |
| First-class | 14 | 20 | 3 | 419 | 84 | 24.64 | 46.92 | 0 | 3 | 9 | 0 |
| List A | 88 | 81 | 6 | 1651 | 175 | 22.01 | 76.75 | 3 | 5 | 36 | 0 |
| Twenty20 | 43 | 42 | 7 | 1222 | 104* | 34.91 | 125.72 | 1 | 9 | 22 | 0 |
| **Bowling** | **Mat** | **Balls** | **Runs** | **Wkts** | **BBI** | **BBM** | **Ave** | **Econ** | **SR** | **5w** | **10** |
| ODIs | 31 | 372 | 324 | 8 | 2/26 | 2/26 | 40.50 | 5.22 | 46.5 | 0 | 0 |
| T20Is | 15 | 66 | 83 | 2 | 2/17 | 2/17 | 41.50 | 7.54 | 33.0 | 0 | 0 |
| First-class | 14 | 611 | 343 | 15 | 4/66 | 6/102 | 22.86 | 3.36 | 40.7 | 0 | 0 |
| List A | 88 | 878 | 810 | 20 | 3/37 | 3/37 | 40.50 | 5.53 | 43.9 | 0 | 0 |
| Twenty20 | 43 | 84 | 93 | 2 | 2/17 | 2/17 | 46.50 | 6.64 | 42.0 | 0 | 0 |

# WAYNE MADSEN RHB OB R2 W0 MVP38

FULL NAME: Wayne Lee Madsen
BORN: January 2, 1984, Durban , South Africa
SQUAD NO: 77
HEIGHT: 5ft 11in
NICKNAME: Madders, Mads
EDUCATION: Highbury Preparatory School; Kearsney College; University of South Africa
TEAMS: Derbyshire, KwaZulu-Natal
CAREER: First-class: 2004; List A: 2004; T20: 2010



BEST BATTING: 231* Derbyshire vs Northamptonshire, Northampton, 2012
BEST BOWLING: 3-45 KwaZulu-Natal vs Eastern Province, Port Elizabeth, 2008
COUNTY CAPS: 2011

FAMILY TIES? My uncles, Trevor Madsen and Henry Fotheringham, represented South Africa. My other uncle, Mike Madsen, played first class cricket for Natal and so did my cousin Greg Fotheringham. My father Paddy and brother Lloyd both played provincial schools cricket for Natal and KwaZulu-Natal, respectively
CAREER HIGHLIGHTS? Winning the Division Two title with Derbyshire in 2012, winning the Cricket Writers' Club County Championship player of the year and being the first player to 1,000 runs in Division One in 2013, scoring 231* and setting the world's second-highest 9th-wicket partnership of 261 with Tom Poynton
CRICKET RULE YOU'D CHANGE? Free hit for no-balls above the waist
COACHING TIP? Batting: play it late and look to hit it straight! Fielding: energy to the ball creates doubt in the batter's mind and wins games with run-outs!
IF YOU WEREN'T A CRICKETER? Sports coach or game ranger
ACCOMPLISHMENTS? Representing South Africa in 39 hockey test matches, including 2005 Africa Cup (winners), 2006 World Cup and 2006 Commonwealth Games

| Batting | Mat | Inns | NO | Runs | HS | Ave | SR | 100 | 50 | Ct | St |
|---|---|---|---|---|---|---|---|---|---|---|---|
| First-class | 114 | 202 | 13 | 7039 | 231* | 37.24 | 48.44 | 17 | 37 | 100 | 0 |
| List A | 65 | 59 | 11 | 1907 | 138 | 39.72 | 86.01 | 2 | 12 | 44 | 0 |
| Twenty20 | 50 | 49 | 7 | 1062 | 65 | 25.28 | 125.68 | 0 | 5 | 11 | 0 |
| **Bowling** | **Mat** | **Balls** | **Runs** | **Wkts** | **BBI** | **BBM** | **Ave** | **Econ** | **SR** | **5w** | **10** |
| First-class | 114 | 1009 | 530 | 10 | 3/45 | | 53.00 | 3.15 | 100.9 | 0 | 0 |
| List A | 65 | 186 | 137 | 9 | 3/27 | 3/27 | 15.22 | 4.41 | 20.6 | 0 | 0 |
| Twenty20 | 50 | 12 | 12 | 0 | - | - | - | 6.00 | - | 0 | 0 |

# STEVE MAGOFFIN

## LHB RFM R0 W3 MVP35



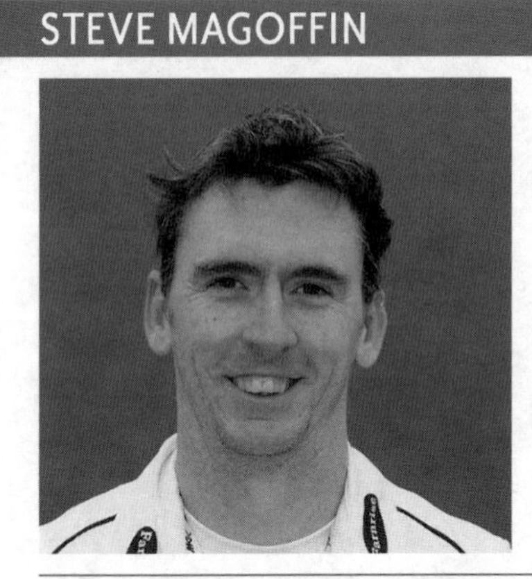

FULL NAME: Steven James Magoffin
BORN: December 17, 1979, Corinda, Australia
SQUAD NO: 64
HEIGHT: 6ft 4in
NICKNAME: Mal
EDUCATION: Indooropilly High School, Curtin University, Perth
TEAMS: Sussex, Queensland, Surrey, Western Australia, Worcestershire
CAREER: First-class: 2004; List A: 2004; T20: 2006

BEST BATTING: 79 Western Australia vs Tasmania, Perth, 2008
BEST BOWLING: 8-20 Sussex vs Somerset, Horsham, 2013

FAMILY TIES? My older brother Chris played grade cricket in Brisbane
CAREER HIGHLIGHTS? Hitting the winning runs in the 2011/12 Sheffield Shield final for the Queensland Bulls. Touring South Africa for the second Test of Australia's tour in 2009 – I didn't play but it was a great experience
MOST MARKED CHARACTERISTIC? Being particularly lanky!
CRICKETING HEROES? Curtly Ambrose, Glenn McGrath, Mike Hussey
NON-CRICKETING HEROES? Tiger Woods, Nathan Buckley (AFL player), Scott Pendlebury (AFL player)
IF YOU WEREN'T A CRICKETER? Not too sure – it's all I've done! But I'd love to be a chef
DESERT ISLAND DISC? Coldplay Live Tour 2012 or The 12th Man Box Set (very popular in Oz!)
FAVOURITE TV? Seinfeld
ACCOMPLISHMENTS? Becoming a father for the first time
FANTASY SLIP CORDON? Keeper: Kramer (from Seinfeld), 1st: Myself, 2nd: John Bishop, 3rd: Michael McIntyre, Gully: James Corden
TWITTER FEED: @magsy64

| Batting | Mat | Inns | NO | Runs | HS | Ave | SR | 100 | 50 | Ct | St |
|---|---|---|---|---|---|---|---|---|---|---|---|
| First-class | 119 | 165 | 45 | 2257 | 79 | 18.80 | 47.81 | 0 | 5 | 29 | 0 |
| List A | 52 | 30 | 20 | 227 | 24* | 22.70 | 77.21 | 0 | 0 | 12 | 0 |
| Twenty20 | 10 | 3 | 1 | 21 | 11* | 10.50 | 116.66 | 0 | 0 | 2 | 0 |
| **Bowling** | **Mat** | **Balls** | **Runs** | **Wkts** | **BBI** | **BBM** | **Ave** | **Econ** | **SR** | **5w** | **10** |
| First-class | 119 | 23682 | 10503 | 441 | 8/20 | | 23.81 | 2.66 | 53.7 | 17 | 2 |
| List A | 52 | 2598 | 2041 | 65 | 4/58 | 4/58 | 31.40 | 4.71 | 39.9 | 0 | 0 |
| Twenty20 | 10 | 204 | 290 | 6 | 2/15 | 2/15 | 48.33 | 8.52 | 34.0 | 0 | 0 |

## SAQIB MAHMOOD RHB RFM R0 W0

FULL NAME: Saqib Mahmood
BORN: February 25, 1997, Birmingham
SQUAD NO: 25
HEIGHT: 6ft 3in
EDUCATION: Matthew Moss High School, Rochdale
TEAMS: Lancashire 2nd XI, England U19
CAREER: Yet to make first-team debut



NOTES: Pace bowler Mahmood joined the Lancashire Academy two years ago and has been rewarded with a full contract. He made his England U19 debut last season, taking 3-12 to help rout South Africa for 77 at Northampton. He was part of the Lancashire U17 side that won the RL Cup and shared the two-day Championship in 2014

# DAWID MALAN

LHB LB R2 W0 MVP17

FULL NAME: Dawid Johannes Malan
BORN: September 3, 1987, Roehampton, Surrey
SQUAD NO: 29
HEIGHT: 6ft
NICKNAME: Mal, Mala
EDUCATION: Paarl Boys' High School; University of South Africa
TEAMS: Middlesex, Boland
CAREER: First-class: 2006; List A: 2006; T20: 2006

BEST BATTING: 156* Middlesex vs CMCCU, Fenner's, 2013
BEST BOWLING: 5-61 Middlesex vs Lancashire, Liverpool, 2012
COUNTY CAPS: 2010

FAMILY TIES? My dad Dawid played for Transvaal B and Western Province B and my brother Charl played for MCCYC and Loughborough MCCU
CAREER HIGHLIGHTS? Scoring 132 on my first-class debut for Middlesex, scoring 103 in the quarter-final of the T20 Cup in 2008 and being named player of the year for Middlesex in 2014
TIP FOR THE TOP? Ravi Patel
CRICKETING HEROES? Gary Kirsten – a fellow left-hander and someone I grew up watching and admiring
NON-CRICKETING HEROES? My dad – he's always there supporting and helping when needed
IF YOU WEREN'T A CRICKETER? I would like to have gone into sports psychology
PET HATE? Answering questionnaires
SURPRISING FACT? I love to go to the cinema by myself
TWITTER FEED: @dmalan29

| Batting | Mat | Inns | NO | Runs | HS | Ave | SR | 100 | 50 | Ct | St |
|---|---|---|---|---|---|---|---|---|---|---|---|
| First-class | 110 | 187 | 13 | 6322 | 156* | 36.33 | 51.94 | 12 | 31 | 138 | 0 |
| List A | 109 | 105 | 16 | 3390 | 134 | 38.08 | 79.13 | 4 | 19 | 39 | 0 |
| Twenty20 | 83 | 79 | 20 | 1961 | 103 | 33.23 | 119.13 | 1 | 7 | 26 | 0 |
| **Bowling** | **Mat** | **Balls** | **Runs** | **Wkts** | **BBI** | **BBM** | **Ave** | **Econ** | **SR** | **5w** | **10** |
| First-class | 110 | 2779 | 1787 | 42 | 5/61 | 5/61 | 42.54 | 3.85 | 66.1 | 1 | 0 |
| List A | 109 | 954 | 894 | 30 | 4/25 | 4/25 | 29.80 | 5.62 | 31.8 | 0 | 0 |
| Twenty20 | 83 | 270 | 321 | 14 | 2/10 | 2/10 | 22.92 | 7.13 | 19.2 | 0 | 0 |

# HAMISH MARSHALL

RHB RM R2 W0

FULL NAME: Hamish John Hamilton Marshall
BORN: February 15, 1979, Warkworth, New Zealand
SQUAD NO: 9
HEIGHT: 5ft 8in
NICKNAME: Marshy
EDUCATION: King's College, Auckland; Mahurangu College
TEAMS: New Zealand, Gloucestershire, Northern Districts, Royal Bengal Tigers
CAREER: Test: 2000; ODI: 2003; T20I: 2005; First-class: 1999; List A: 1998; T20: 2005



BEST BATTING: 170 Northern Districts vs Canterbury, Rangiora, 2010
BEST BOWLING: 4-24 Gloucestershire vs Leicestershire, Leicester, 2009
BENEFIT YEAR: 2015

FAMILY TIES? Twin brother James played cricket for Northern Districts and New Zealand
CAREER HIGHLIGHTS? My first Test century vs Australia
CRICKETING HEROES? Mark Waugh – he made it look so easy
NON-CRICKETING HEROES? Andre Agassi – I always enjoyed watching him play tennis. Also recently I saw a programme on Sam Burgess and thought not only is he a quality athlete at the top of his game but he came across as a top guy and leader
IF YOU COULD BE SOMEONE ELSE FOR A DAY? Rory McIlroy
ACCOMPLISHMENTS? Becoming a dad and cycling 450miles on the PCA Big Bike Ride from Durham to Lord's

| Batting | Mat | Inns | NO | Runs | HS | Ave | SR | 100 | 50 | Ct | St |
|---|---|---|---|---|---|---|---|---|---|---|---|
| Tests | 13 | 19 | 2 | 652 | 160 | 38.35 | 47.31 | 2 | 2 | 1 | 0 |
| ODIs | 66 | 62 | 9 | 1454 | 101* | 27.43 | 73.06 | 1 | 12 | 18 | 0 |
| T20Is | 3 | 3 | 0 | 12 | 8 | 4.00 | 85.71 | 0 | 0 | 1 | 0 |
| First-class | 225 | 374 | 26 | 12652 | 170 | 36.35 | | 26 | 61 | 111 | 0 |
| List A | 286 | 272 | 24 | 6811 | 122 | 27.46 | | 6 | 45 | 105 | 0 |
| Twenty20 | 105 | 99 | 7 | 2329 | 102 | 25.31 | 133.69 | 2 | 9 | 49 | 0 |
| **Bowling** | **Mat** | **Balls** | **Runs** | **Wkts** | **BBI** | **BBM** | **Ave** | **Econ** | **SR** | **5w** | **10** |
| Tests | 13 | 6 | 4 | 0 | - | - | - | 4.00 | - | 0 | 0 |
| ODIs | 66 | - | - | - | - | - | - | - | - | - | - |
| T20Is | 3 | - | - | - | - | - | - | - | - | - | - |
| First-class | 225 | 3649 | 1834 | 39 | 4/24 | | 47.02 | 3.01 | 93.5 | 0 | 0 |
| List A | 286 | 284 | 295 | 4 | 2/21 | 2/21 | 73.75 | 6.23 | 71.0 | 0 | 0 |
| Twenty20 | 105 | 6 | 14 | 0 | - | - | - | 14.00 | - | 0 | 0 |

## DAVID MASTERS RHB RMF R0 W4 MVP88

FULL NAME: David Daniel Masters
BORN: April 22, 1978, Chatham, Kent
SQUAD NO: 9
HEIGHT: 6ft 4in
NICKNAME: Hod, Hoddy
EDUCATION: Fort Luton High
TEAMS: Essex, Kent, Leicestershire
CAREER: First-class: 2000; List A: 2000; T20: 2003

---

BEST BATTING: 119 Leicestershire vs Sussex, Hove, 2003
BEST BOWLING: 8-10 Essex vs Leicestershire, Southend, 2011
COUNTY CAPS: 2007 (Leicestershire); 2008 (Essex); BENEFIT YEAR: 2013 (Essex)

---

FAMILY TIES? My dad Kevin played for Kent and Surrey and my brother Daniel played for Leicestershire
CAREER HIGHLIGHTS? Winning a Lord's final
SUPERSTITIONS? Too many to mention
CRICKETING HEROES? Ian Botham
NON-CRICKETING HEROES? David Beckham and Sir Alex Ferguson
IF YOU WEREN'T A CRICKETER? Builder
DESERT ISLAND DISC? Whitney Houston's Greatest Hits
FAVOURITE TV? Match Of The Day
ACCOMPLISHMENTS? Getting married and having two wonderful children, Alfie and Harrison
FANTASY SLIP CORDON? Keeper: Paul Nixon, 1st: Sir Alex Ferguson, 2nd: Matt Walker, 3rd: David Beckham
TWITTER FEED: @DavehodMasters

| Batting | Mat | Inns | NO | Runs | HS | Ave | SR | 100 | 50 | Ct | St |
|---|---|---|---|---|---|---|---|---|---|---|---|
| First-class | 186 | 226 | 32 | 2639 | 119 | 13.60 | | 1 | 6 | 57 | 0 |
| List A | 161 | 77 | 31 | 542 | 39 | 11.78 | | 0 | 0 | 21 | 0 |
| Twenty20 | 106 | 35 | 17 | 101 | 14 | 5.61 | 69.17 | 0 | 0 | 21 | 0 |
| **Bowling** | **Mat** | **Balls** | **Runs** | **Wkts** | **BBI** | **BBM** | **Ave** | **Econ** | **SR** | **5w** | **10** |
| First-class | 186 | 34491 | 15475 | 612 | 8/10 | | 25.28 | 2.69 | 56.3 | 30 | 0 |
| List A | 161 | 6800 | 5139 | 162 | 5/17 | 5/17 | 31.72 | 4.53 | 41.9 | 2 | 0 |
| Twenty20 | 106 | 2069 | 2546 | 82 | 3/7 | 3/7 | 31.04 | 7.38 | 25.2 | 0 | 0 |

# GLENN MAXWELL

## RHB OB R0 W0

FULL NAME: Glenn James Maxwell
BORN: October 14, 1988, Kew, Melbourne, Australia
SQUAD NO: tbc
HEIGHT: 5ft 11in
NICKNAME: The Big Show
TEAMS: Australia, Yorkshire, Delhi Daredevils, Hampshire, Melbourne Renegades, Mumbai Indians, Victoria
CAREER: Test: 2013; ODI: 2012; T20I: 2012; First-class: 2011; List A: 2010; T20: 2010



BEST BATTING: 155 Australia A vs South Africa A, Pretoria, 2013
BEST BOWLING: 4-42 Victoria vs South Australia, Melbourne, 2012

TWITTER FEED: @Gmaxi_32
NOTES: Yorkshire have signed Australian Maxwell for the T20 Blast. He played for Hampshire in last season's T20 Blast, although he made only 127 runs from 11 innings. He fetched the highest bid at the 2013 IPL auction, with Mumbai Indians paying £637,000 for his services, and went on to play for Surrey in the 2013 Friends Life t20. Made his Test debut during the 2013 series in India and is a regular for his country in limited-overs cricket

| Batting | Mat | Inns | NO | Runs | HS | Ave | SR | 100 | 50 | Ct | St |
|---|---|---|---|---|---|---|---|---|---|---|---|
| Tests | 3 | 6 | 0 | 80 | 37 | 13.33 | 70.17 | 0 | 0 | 2 | 0 |
| ODIs | 45 | 43 | 5 | 1300 | 102 | 34.21 | 125.48 | 1 | 11 | 24 | 0 |
| T20Is | 24 | 20 | 2 | 343 | 74 | 19.05 | 163.33 | 0 | 1 | 12 | 0 |
| First-class | 31 | 51 | 3 | 1939 | 155* | 40.39 | 75.83 | 4 | 12 | 23 | 0 |
| List A | 70 | 66 | 10 | 2095 | 146 | 37.41 | 130.20 | 3 | 15 | 43 | 0 |
| Twenty20 | 112 | 103 | 9 | 2121 | 95 | 22.56 | 157.81 | 0 | 10 | 58 | 0 |
| **Bowling** | **Mat** | **Balls** | **Runs** | **Wkts** | **BBI** | **BBM** | **Ave** | **Econ** | **SR** | **5w** | **10** |
| Tests | 3 | 342 | 271 | 7 | 4/127 | 4/127 | 38.71 | 4.75 | 48.8 | 0 | 0 |
| ODIs | 45 | 1270 | 1161 | 30 | 4/46 | 4/46 | 38.70 | 5.48 | 42.3 | 0 | 0 |
| T20Is | 24 | 318 | 368 | 14 | 3/13 | 3/13 | 26.28 | 6.94 | 22.7 | 0 | 0 |
| First-class | 31 | 2992 | 1778 | 45 | 4/42 | 5/66 | 39.51 | 3.56 | 66.4 | 0 | 0 |
| List A | 70 | 1932 | 1704 | 44 | 4/46 | 4/46 | 38.72 | 5.29 | 43.9 | 0 | 0 |
| Twenty20 | 112 | 897 | 1144 | 32 | 3/13 | 3/13 | 35.75 | 7.65 | 28.0 | 0 | 0 |

# CLINT MCKAY

RHB RFM R0 W0

FULL NAME: Clinton James McKay
BORN: February 20, 1983, Melbourne, Australia
SQUAD NO: tbc
HEIGHT: 6ft 4in
TEAMS: Australia, Leicestershire, Melbourne Stars, Mumbai Indians, Sunrisers Hyderabad, Victoria, Yorkshire
CAREER: Test: 2009; ODI: 2009; T20I: 2010; First-class: 2006; List A: 2006; T20: 2008

BEST BATTING: 65 Victoria vs Western Australia, Melbourne, 2012
BEST BOWLING: 6-40 Victoria vs Tasmania, Melbourne, 2011

TWITTER FEED: @clintmckay27
NOTES: The Australian bowler has joined Leicestershire as their overseas player for 2015. He made his international debut for Australia in November 2009 in an ODI against India at Hyderebad, taking the wicket of Sachin Tendulkar. He made his one and only Test appearance a month later but took just one wicket. While lacking express pace his accuracy has helped him to 59 ODI caps, and he was named Australia's One-Day Cricketer of the Year in 2013

| Batting | Mat | Inns | NO | Runs | HS | Ave | SR | 100 | 50 | Ct | St |
|---|---|---|---|---|---|---|---|---|---|---|---|
| Tests | 1 | 1 | 0 | 10 | 10 | 10.00 | 66.66 | 0 | 0 | 1 | 0 |
| ODIs | 59 | 31 | 10 | 190 | 30 | 9.04 | 56.37 | 0 | 0 | 7 | 0 |
| T20Is | 6 | 4 | 2 | 19 | 7 | 9.50 | 86.36 | 0 | 0 | 0 | 0 |
| First-class | 44 | 60 | 7 | 952 | 65 | 17.96 | 55.90 | 0 | 4 | 14 | 0 |
| List A | 109 | 54 | 13 | 463 | 57 | 11.29 | 67.88 | 0 | 1 | 13 | 0 |
| Twenty20 | 61 | 29 | 14 | 184 | 21* | 12.26 | 126.89 | 0 | 0 | 8 | 0 |
| **Bowling** | **Mat** | **Balls** | **Runs** | **Wkts** | **BBI** | **BBM** | **Ave** | **Econ** | **SR** | **5w** | **10** |
| Tests | 1 | 168 | 101 | 1 | 1/56 | 1/101 | 101.00 | 3.60 | 168.0 | 0 | 0 |
| ODIs | 59 | 2965 | 2364 | 97 | 5/28 | 5/28 | 24.37 | 4.78 | 30.5 | 2 | 0 |
| T20Is | 6 | 136 | 183 | 4 | 2/24 | 2/24 | 45.75 | 8.07 | 34.0 | 0 | 0 |
| First-class | 44 | 8901 | 4097 | 142 | 6/40 | 8/101 | 28.85 | 2.76 | 62.6 | 3 | 0 |
| List A | 109 | 5620 | 4410 | 161 | 5/28 | 5/28 | 27.39 | 4.70 | 34.9 | 2 | 0 |
| Twenty20 | 61 | 1331 | 1824 | 72 | 4/33 | 4/33 | 25.33 | 8.22 | 18.4 | 0 | 0 |

# PETE MCKAY

## LHB WK R0 W0

FULL NAME: Peter John McKay
BORN: October 12, 1994, Staffordshire
SQUAD NO: 18
EDUCATION: Polesworth International Language College, Tamworth
TEAMS: Warwickshire
CAREER: First-class: 2013; List A: 2013; T20: 2013



BEST BATTING: 33 Warwickshire vs Nottinghamshire, Nottingham, 2013

CAREER HIGHLIGHTS? Getting my first contract and representing the Bears
MOST MARKED CHARACTERISTIC? Theatrical reactions
SUPERSTITIONS? Not changing inners too regularly
CRICKETING HEROES? Adam Gilchrist
NON-CRICKETING HEROES? My Aunty Shaz
IF YOU WEREN'T A CRICKETER? Sports media
DESERT ISLAND DISC? You Me At Six – Take Off Your Colours
FAVOURITE TV? Orange Is The New Black
SURPRISING FACT? Head Boy at school

| Batting | Mat | Inns | NO | Runs | HS | Ave | SR | 100 | 50 | Ct | St |
|---|---|---|---|---|---|---|---|---|---|---|---|
| First-class | 3 | 5 | 1 | 73 | 33 | 18.25 | 27.23 | 0 | 0 | 2 | 0 |
| List A | 6 | 5 | 3 | 48 | 22* | 24.00 | 141.17 | 0 | 0 | 5 | 1 |
| Twenty20 | 12 | 4 | 3 | 3 | 2* | 3.00 | 42.85 | 0 | 0 | 6 | 2 |
| **Bowling** | **Mat** | **Balls** | **Runs** | **Wkts** | **BBI** | **BBM** | **Ave** | **Econ** | **SR** | **5w** | **10** |
| First-class | 3 | - | - | - | - | - | - | - | - | - | - |
| List A | 6 | - | - | - | - | - | - | - | - | - | - |
| Twenty20 | 12 | - | - | - | - | - | - | - | - | - | - |

## LEWIS MCMANUS

## RHB WK R0 W0



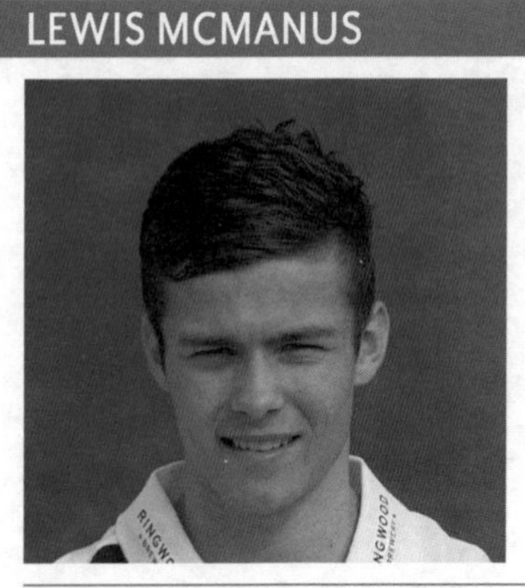


FULL NAME: Lewis David McManus
BORN: October 9, 1994, Poole Hospital
SQUAD NO: 18
HEIGHT: 5ft 10in
NICKNAME: Lewy
EDUCATION: Clayesmore School
TEAMS: Hampshire 2nd XI, England U19
CAREER: Yet to make first-team debut

---

CAREER HIGHLIGHTS? Scoring 105 for Hampshire 2nd XI vs Surrey 2nd XI, playing for England U19 and playing at Lord's aged 14 for MCC
SUPERSTITIONS? Putting kit on in the same order
CRICKETING HEROES? Adam Gilchrist, Andrew Flintoff
NON-CRICKETING HEROES? Floyd Mayweather, Usain Bolt, Rick Ross
CRICKET RULE YOU'D CHANGE? Twelve runs for hitting the ball out of the ground
FAVOURITE TV? Two And A Half Men, A League Of Their Own
FANTASY SLIP CORDON? Keeper: Del Trotter, 1st: Karl Pilkington, 2nd: Usain Bolt, 3rd: Ronnie Corbett, Gully: Trigger
TWITTER FEED: @lewis_mcmanus

# STUART MEAKER RHB RF R0 W1

FULL NAME: Stuart Christopher Meaker
BORN: January 21, 1989, Pietermaritzburg, South Africa
SQUAD NO: 18
HEIGHT: 5ft 11in
NICKNAME: Meakers, Ten Bears
EDUCATION: Cranleigh Senior School
TEAMS: England, Surrey
CAREER: ODI: 2011; T20I: 2012; First-class: 2008; List A: 2008; T20: 2010



BEST BATTING: 94 Surrey vs Bangladeshis, The Oval, 2010
BEST BOWLING: 8-52 Surrey vs Somerset, The Oval, 2012
COUNTY CAPS: 2012 (Surrey

CAREER HIGHLIGHTS? Playing for England
BEST PLAYER IN COUNTY CRICKET? Jason Roy
TIP FOR THE TOP? Rory Burns
CRICKETING HEROES? Allan Donald, Dale Steyn – they bowled fast and were aggressive
NON-CRICKETING HEROES? My grandfather – my original coach!
CRICKET RULE YOU'D CHANGE? Bowlers can have as many fielders as they want on the pitch – it would save me from going for so many runs
IF YOU COULD BE SOMEONE ELSE FOR A DAY? Leonardo DiCaprio
DESERT ISLAND DISC? Bombay Bicycle Club – So Long, See You Tomorrow
PET HATE? People getting on the tube before I've got off. It's just rude
TWITTER FEED: @smeaker18

| Batting | Mat | Inns | NO | Runs | HS | Ave | SR | 100 | 50 | Ct | St |
|---|---|---|---|---|---|---|---|---|---|---|---|
| ODIs | 2 | 2 | 0 | 2 | 1 | 1.00 | 12.50 | 0 | 0 | 0 | 0 |
| T20Is | 2 | - | - | - | - | - | - | - | - | 1 | 0 |
| First-class | 60 | 79 | 13 | 1091 | 94 | 16.53 | 37.94 | 0 | 6 | 8 | 0 |
| List A | 48 | 25 | 10 | 82 | 21* | 5.46 | 52.90 | 0 | 0 | 11 | 0 |
| Twenty20 | 24 | 6 | 4 | 28 | 17 | 14.00 | 147.36 | 0 | 0 | 9 | 0 |
| **Bowling** | **Mat** | **Balls** | **Runs** | **Wkts** | **BBI** | **BBM** | **Ave** | **Econ** | **SR** | **5w** | **10** |
| ODIs | 2 | 114 | 110 | 2 | 1/45 | 1/45 | 55.00 | 5.78 | 57.0 | 0 | 0 |
| T20Is | 2 | 47 | 70 | 2 | 1/28 | 1/28 | 35.00 | 8.93 | 23.5 | 0 | 0 |
| First-class | 60 | 9510 | 5937 | 210 | 8/52 | 11/167 | 28.27 | 3.74 | 45.2 | 11 | 2 |
| List A | 48 | 1778 | 1847 | 48 | 4/47 | 4/47 | 38.47 | 6.23 | 37.0 | 0 | 0 |
| Twenty20 | 24 | 393 | 599 | 20 | 4/30 | 4/30 | 29.95 | 9.14 | 19.6 | 0 | 0 |

# CRAIG MESCHEDE RHB RMF R0 W0

FULL NAME: Craig Anthony Joseph Meschede
BORN: November 21, 1991, Johannesburg, South Africa
SQUAD NO: 26
EDUCATION: King's College, Taunton
TEAMS: Somerset
CAREER: First-class: 2011; List A: 2011; T20: 2011

BEST BATTING: 62 Somerset vs Durham, Chester-le-Street, 2012
BEST BOWLING: 4-43 Somerset vs Surrey, Taunton, 2013

TWITTER FEED: @cmeschy
NOTES: South African-born with a German father, the Somerset allrounder was awarded a senior contract in June 2010. Impressed in the 2011 Caribbean T20, hitting 26 from just 11 balls against Combined Campuses and Colleges. Sachin Tendulkar was his maiden first-class wicket. Scored 53 from just 28 deliveries in a FL t20 victory against Glamorgan in 2011. Claimed nine wickets at 22 in the 2012 CB40, including 4-27 against Scotland, and finished as the joint second-highest wicket-taker in last year's YB40, with 22 wickets at 21.72. Took a career-best match haul of 7-80 in the penultimate County Championship game of 2013, against Surrey. After struggling for a first-team place in 2014, he has joined Glamorgan from Somerset on a season-long loan for 2015

| Batting | Mat | Inns | NO | Runs | HS | Ave | SR | 100 | 50 | Ct | St |
|---|---|---|---|---|---|---|---|---|---|---|---|
| First-class | 28 | 37 | 4 | 657 | 62 | 19.90 | 54.11 | 0 | 4 | 11 | 0 |
| List A | 30 | 17 | 3 | 256 | 40* | 18.28 | 93.43 | 0 | 0 | 7 | 0 |
| Twenty20 | 39 | 30 | 9 | 328 | 53 | 15.61 | 123.30 | 0 | 1 | 7 | 0 |
| **Bowling** | **Mat** | **Balls** | **Runs** | **Wkts** | **BBI** | **BBM** | **Ave** | **Econ** | **SR** | **5w** | **10** |
| First-class | 28 | 2786 | 1693 | 49 | 4/43 | 7/80 | 34.55 | 3.64 | 56.8 | 0 | 0 |
| List A | 30 | 957 | 898 | 37 | 4/5 | 4/5 | 24.27 | 5.63 | 25.8 | 0 | 0 |
| Twenty20 | 39 | 385 | 557 | 21 | 3/9 | 3/9 | 26.52 | 8.68 | 18.3 | 0 | 0 |

# JAIK MICKLEBURGH RHB RMF R0 W0

FULL NAME: Jaik Charles Mickleburgh
BORN: March 30, 1990, Norwich
SQUAD NO: 32
HEIGHT: 5ft 9in
NICKNAME: Juddy
EDUCATION: Bungay High School
TEAMS: Essex, Mid West Rhinos
CAREER: First-class: 2008; List A: 2010; T20: 2010



BEST BATTING: 243 Essex vs Leicestershire, Chelmsford, 2013
COUNTY CAPS: 2013

CAREER HIGHLIGHTS? Representing England U19, first first-class hundred away at Durham, first double-hundred at home to Leicestershire
BEST PLAYER IN COUNTY CRICKET? James Foster
TIP FOR THE TOP? Dan Lawrence, Callum Taylor
SUPERSTITIONS? Chewing gum when batting and always having a spare piece in my pocket
CRICKETING HEROES? Jacques Kallis – he does every skill of the game and very well
NON-CRICKETING HEROES? David Beckham – he's a gun
IF YOU WEREN'T A CRICKETER? Fitness instructor
DESERT ISLAND DISC? Jamie T – Kings and Queens
ACCOMPLISHMENTS? PCA Big Bike Ride
PET HATE? Washing
SURPRISING FACT? I had chocolate-spread rolls everyday of my school life
TWITTER FEED: @jaikm32

| Batting | Mat | Inns | NO | Runs | HS | Ave | SR | 100 | 50 | Ct | St |
|---|---|---|---|---|---|---|---|---|---|---|---|
| First-class | 80 | 140 | 3 | 3897 | 243 | 28.44 | 44.17 | 6 | 18 | 56 | 0 |
| List A | 20 | 16 | 3 | 400 | 73 | 30.76 | 77.36 | 0 | 2 | 8 | 0 |
| Twenty20 | 17 | 12 | 5 | 159 | 47* | 22.71 | 100.63 | 0 | 0 | 8 | 0 |
| **Bowling** | **Mat** | **Balls** | **Runs** | **Wkts** | **BBI** | **BBM** | **Ave** | **Econ** | **SR** | **5w** | **10** |
| First-class | 80 | 78 | 50 | 0 | - | - | - | 3.84 | - | 0 | 0 |
| List A | 20 | - | - | - | - | - | - | - | - | - | - |
| Twenty20 | 17 | - | - | - | - | - | - | - | - | - | - |

# CRAIG MILES

RHB RM R0 W0

FULL NAME: Craig Neil Miles
BORN: July 20, 1994, Swindon
SQUAD NO: 34
HEIGHT: 6ft 4in
NICKNAME: Milo, Miler, Cheese string
EDUCATION: Bradon Forest School; Filton College
TEAMS: Gloucestershire
CAREER: First-class: 2011; List A: 2011; T20: 2013

BEST BATTING: 62* Gloucestershire vs Worcestershire, Cheltenham, 2014
BEST BOWLING: 6-88 Gloucestershire vs Lancashire, Liverpool, 2013
COUNTY CAPS: 2011

FAMILY TIES? My brother Adam played for Cardiff MCCU and has represented Otago A in recent winters
CAREER HIGHLIGHTS? Being the fourth-youngest player to play for Gloucestershire, dismissing Ravi Bopara with my first ball in List A cricket and being selected for ECB Fast Bowling programmes
BEST PLAYER IN COUNTY CRICKET? Jeetan Patel
TIP FOR THE TOP? Gareth Roderick, Olly Stone
CRICKETING HEROES? Andrew Flintoff – Ashes 2005, say no more. Brett Lee – fast!
COACHING TIP? Strong base, full face – no need for an explanation
IF YOU COULD BE SOMEONE ELSE FOR A DAY? Keith Lemon
FAVOURITE TV? Geordie Shore, I'm A Celebrity … Get Me Out Of Here!, Gogglebox
PET HATE? People who eat with their mouth open – disgusting!
SURPRISING FACT? Played for Swindon Town Centre of Excellence from U9-U12
TWITTER FEED: @CMiles34

| Batting | Mat | Inns | NO | Runs | HS | Ave | SR | 100 | 50 | Ct | St |
|---|---|---|---|---|---|---|---|---|---|---|---|
| First-class | 18 | 22 | 2 | 355 | 62* | 17.75 | 49.71 | 0 | 2 | 3 | 0 |
| List A | 14 | 5 | 2 | 29 | 12 | 9.66 | 60.41 | 0 | 0 | 1 | 0 |
| Twenty20 | 2 | 1 | 0 | 2 | 2 | 2.00 | 50.00 | 0 | 0 | 1 | 0 |
| **Bowling** | **Mat** | **Balls** | **Runs** | **Wkts** | **BBI** | **BBM** | **Ave** | **Econ** | **SR** | **5w** | **10** |
| First-class | 18 | 2820 | 1753 | 63 | 6/88 | 7/135 | 27.82 | 3.72 | 44.7 | 4 | 0 |
| List A | 14 | 571 | 565 | 17 | 3/48 | 3/48 | 33.23 | 5.93 | 33.5 | 0 | 0 |
| Twenty20 | 2 | 48 | 78 | 0 | - | - | - | 9.75 | - | 0 | 0 |

# TYMAL MILLS

RHB LF R0 W0

FULL NAME: Tymal Solomon Mills
BORN: August 12, 1992, Dewsbury, Yorkshire
SQUAD NO: 7
HEIGHT: 6ft 2in
NICKNAME: T, Tyrone
EDUCATION: Mildenhall College of Technology; University of East London
TEAMS: Essex, Sussex, England Lions
CAREER: First-class: 2011; List A: 2011; T20: 2012



BEST BATTING: 31* England Lions vs Sri Lanka Emerging Players, Colombo, 2014
BEST BOWLING: 4-25 Essex vs Glamorgan, Cardiff, 2012

CAREER HIGHLIGHTS? Being part of the victorious England Lions tour in Sri Lanka, 2014. Being asked to join the Ashes squad in Australia 2013
MOST MARKED CHARACTERISTIC? Annoying grunt when I bowl!
CRICKETING HEROES? I didn't watch cricket growing up so no real heroes! Enjoy watching Mitchell Johnson bowl now though
NON-CRICKETING HEROES? Denzel Washington – just for being the coolest man alive
CRICKET RULE YOU'D CHANGE? Burn all heavy rollers
COACHING TIP? Don't always try and play it 'by the textbook'. Find your own way
IF YOU COULD BE SOMEONE ELSE FOR A DAY? Any of the One Direction lads – they don't struggle
FAVOURITE TV? Just watched Luther which was top-drawer
PET HATE? People leaving their bedroom light on when they're in the living room!
FANTASY SLIP CORDON? Keeper: Denzel Washington, 1st: Idris Elba, 2nd: Ciara, 3rd: Beyonce, Gully: Myself
TWITTER FEED: @tmills15

| Batting | Mat | Inns | NO | Runs | HS | Ave | SR | 100 | 50 | Ct | St |
|---|---|---|---|---|---|---|---|---|---|---|---|
| First-class | 29 | 34 | 15 | 242 | 31* | 12.73 | 61.57 | 0 | 0 | 9 | 0 |
| List A | 21 | 7 | 4 | 4 | 2* | 1.33 | 23.52 | 0 | 0 | 3 | 0 |
| Twenty20 | 8 | 3 | 2 | 11 | 8* | 11.00 | 91.66 | 0 | 0 | 0 | 0 |
| **Bowling** | **Mat** | **Balls** | **Runs** | **Wkts** | **BBI** | **BBM** | **Ave** | **Econ** | **SR** | **5w** | **10** |
| First-class | 29 | 3240 | 1851 | 52 | 4/25 | 5/79 | 35.59 | 3.42 | 62.3 | 0 | 0 |
| List A | 21 | 688 | 649 | 19 | 3/23 | 3/23 | 34.15 | 5.65 | 36.2 | 0 | 0 |
| Twenty20 | 8 | 102 | 150 | 6 | 3/41 | 3/41 | 25.00 | 8.82 | 17.0 | 0 | 0 |

# TOM MILNES

RHB RFM R0 W0

FULL NAME: Thomas Patrick Milnes
BORN: October 6, 1992, Stourbridge, Worcestershire
SQUAD NO: 8
TEAMS: Warwickshire
CAREER: First-class: 2011; List A: 2013

BEST BATTING: 52* Warwickshire vs Oxford MCCU, Oxford, 2013
BEST BOWLING: 7-39 Warwickshire vs Oxford MCCU, Oxford, 2013

CAREER HIGHLIGHTS? Being part of the 2012 Championship-winning side, making my Championship debut and signing my first professional contract
MOST MARKED CHARACTERISTIC? Being very keen! And ginger
CRICKETING HEROES? Andrew Flintoff, James Anderson, Dale Steyn
IF YOU WEREN'T A CRICKETER? I'd probably be working in a shop
DESERT ISLAND DISC? Oasis – Definitely Maybe
FAVOURITE TV? Alan Partridge
ACCOMPLISHMENTS? Passing my driving test and getting some grades at school
SURPRISING FACT? I used to play football for Aston Villa and I love doing impressions
FANTASY SLIP CORDON? Keeper: Alan Partridge, 1st: Liam Gallagher, 2nd: Andrew Flintoff, 3rd: Myself, Gully: James Corden
TWITTER FEED: @TPMilnes8

| Batting | Mat | Inns | NO | Runs | HS | Ave | SR | 100 | 50 | Ct | St |
|---|---|---|---|---|---|---|---|---|---|---|---|
| First-class | 13 | 13 | 2 | 278 | 52* | 25.27 | 45.57 | 0 | 1 | 3 | 0 |
| List A | 3 | 3 | 1 | 22 | 16 | 11.00 | 64.70 | 0 | 0 | 0 | 0 |
| **Bowling** | **Mat** | **Balls** | **Runs** | **Wkts** | **BBI** | **BBM** | **Ave** | **Econ** | **SR** | **5w** | **10** |
| First-class | 13 | 1135 | 717 | 22 | 7/39 | 9/94 | 32.59 | 3.79 | 51.5 | 1 | 0 |
| List A | 3 | 138 | 177 | 3 | 2/73 | 2/73 | 59.00 | 7.69 | 46.0 | 0 | 0 |

# DARYL MITCHELL

RHB RM R4 W0 MVP11

FULL NAME: Daryl Keith Henry Mitchell
BORN: November 25, 1983, Badsey, nr Evesham
SQUAD NO: 27
HEIGHT: 5ft 10in
NICKNAME: Mitch, Toucan
EDUCATION: Prince Henry's High School; University of Worcester
TEAMS: Worcestershire
CAREER: First-class: 2005; List A: 2005; T20: 2005



BEST BATTING: 298 Worcestershire vs Somerset, Taunton, 2009
BEST BOWLING: 4-49 Worcestershire vs Yorkshire, Leeds, 2009

CAREER HIGHLIGHTS? Winning the Pro40 in 2007, promotion in 2006, 2008, 2010 and 2014, scoring 298 vs Somerset in 2009
MOST MARKED CHARACTERISTIC? My nose
CRICKETING HEROES? Ian Botham, Graeme Hick and Jack Shantry – all legends
NON-CRICKETING HEROES? Paul McGrath – Aston Villa legend. John Carew – he's bigger than me and you, he's gonna score one or two
CRICKET RULE YOU'D CHANGE? Back to five outside circle in one-day cricket. It's too difficult to defend at the death with four
IF YOU WEREN'T A CRICKETER? A darts player
IF YOU COULD BE SOMEONE ELSE FOR A DAY? Rory McIlroy
DESERT ISLAND DISC? Oasis – (What's The Story) Morning Glory?
FAVOURITE TV? Match Of The Day
LEAST FAVOURITE TV? The X Factor
SURPRISING FACT? I played for Aston Villa's School of Excellence as a kid
TWITTER FEED: @mitchwccc

| Batting | Mat | Inns | NO | Runs | HS | Ave | SR | 100 | 50 | Ct | St |
|---|---|---|---|---|---|---|---|---|---|---|---|
| First-class | 131 | 238 | 29 | 8320 | 298 | 39.80 | 44.23 | 19 | 36 | 185 | 0 |
| List A | 100 | 86 | 14 | 2404 | 107 | 33.38 | 82.52 | 2 | 14 | 36 | 0 |
| Twenty20 | 96 | 74 | 19 | 1245 | 68* | 22.63 | 119.02 | 0 | 3 | 44 | 0 |
| **Bowling** | **Mat** | **Balls** | **Runs** | **Wkts** | **BBI** | **BBM** | **Ave** | **Econ** | **SR** | **5w** | **10** |
| First-class | 131 | 1643 | 840 | 19 | 4/49 | | 44.21 | 3.06 | 86.4 | 0 | 0 |
| List A | 100 | 2150 | 1995 | 57 | 4/19 | 4/19 | 35.00 | 5.56 | 37.7 | 0 | 0 |
| Twenty20 | 96 | 1235 | 1649 | 61 | 5/28 | 5/28 | 27.03 | 8.01 | 20.2 | 1 | 0 |

# ROBBIE MONTGOMERY RHB RFM R0 W0

FULL NAME: Robbie Jay Montgomery
BORN: September 22, 1994, Taunton
SQUAD NO: 20
HEIGHT: 5ft 11in
NICKNAME: Monty, Rufio, Cowboy
EDUCATION: Mindarie Senior College
TEAMS: Gloucestershire
CAREER: T20: 2014

---

FAMILY TIES? Grandad trained regularly with West Indies. Ramnaresh Sarwan is a cousin.
CAREER HIGHLIGHTS? Biggest highlight of my career so far is hitting 108 off 66 balls vs Northants 2nd XI. Making T20 debut
BEST PLAYER IN COUNTY CRICKET? Steven Crook, Chris Woakes
TIP FOR THE TOP? Tom Abell, Will Tavaré, Matt Hobden
CRICKETING HEROES? Kevin Pietersen – for his arrogance and his talent. Chris Gayle – for his ability to entertain and strike the ball so big and clean. Alfonso Thomas – for his experience and high-quality death bowling
CRICKET RULE YOU'D CHANGE? Powerplay overs require eight balls as opposed to six, just to maximise the runs per over during the Powerplay
COACHING TIP? Prehab is key! Do correct recovery and stretching and eat the correct foods. If my body's fit I'll perform to my peak
IF YOU COULD BE SOMEONE ELSE FOR A DAY? Eminem – just to feel the worldwide fame, extreme wealth, and the ability to wear baggy clothing and still look good
ACCOMPLISHMENTS? Coming first out of 148 other runners in the U16 cross-country race. Getting qualifications in financial advising through college. Representing Western Australia in age groups
SURPRISING FACT? I actually passed secondary school and have never been punched in the face
FANTASY SLIP CORDON? Keeper: SpongeBob SquarePants, 1st: Homer Simpson, 2nd: My granddad, 3rd: Ed Sheeran, Gully: Postman Pat

| Batting | Mat | Inns | NO | Runs | HS | Ave | SR | 100 | 50 | Ct | St |
|---|---|---|---|---|---|---|---|---|---|---|---|
| Twenty20 | 1 | 1 | 1 | 8 | 8* | - | 200.00 | 0 | 0 | 0 | 0 |
| **Bowling** | **Mat** | **Balls** | **Runs** | **Wkts** | **BBI** | **BBM** | **Ave** | **Econ** | **SR** | **5w** | **10** |
| Twenty20 | 1 | 18 | 50 | 0 | - | - | - | 16.66 | - | 0 | 0 |

# THOMAS MOORE

## RHB RMF R0 W0

FULL NAME: Thomas Cambridge Moore
BORN: March 29, 1992, Basildon, Essex
SQUAD NO: 33
HEIGHT: 6ft 6in
EDUCATION: Brentwood School; St. Martin's School; University of Essex
TEAMS: Essex
CAREER: First-class: 2014; T20: 2014



BEST BATTING: 17 Essex vs Glamorgan, Chelmsford, 2014
BEST BOWLING: 4-78 Essex vs Glamorgan, Chelmsford, 2014

CAREER HIGHLIGHTS? My maiden wicket in front of my family and managing to secure a two-year contract
BEST PLAYER IN COUNTY CRICKET? Jason Roy
TIP FOR THE TOP? Kishen Velani and Harry Podmore
MOST MARKED CHARACTERISTIC? Sense of humour
CRICKETING HEROES? Andrew Flintoff – for his bowling in the 2005 Ashes
CRICKET RULE YOU'D CHANGE? Five fielders outside the ring to hopefully go for fewer runs!
COACHING TIP? Stay low when approaching the ball in the field and throw from a strong steady base
IF YOU COULD BE SOMEONE ELSE FOR A DAY? Marco Corola
FAVOURITE TV? Family Guy
LEAST FAVOURITE TV? Anything reality
PET HATE? Anything being dirty – I like being clean!
SURPRISING FACT? I climbed Kilimanjaro when I was 16
FANTASY SLIP CORDON? Keeper: Russell Brand (would be great to pick his brains), 1st: Carl Cox (to play the music!), 2nd: Freddie Flintoff (because he never drops them!)
TWITTER FEED: @tcm33

| Batting | Mat | Inns | NO | Runs | HS | Ave | SR | 100 | 50 | Ct | St |
|---|---|---|---|---|---|---|---|---|---|---|---|
| First-class | 4 | 4 | 2 | 27 | 17 | 13.50 | 69.23 | 0 | 0 | 1 | 0 |
| Twenty20 | 1 | - | - | - | - | - | - | - | - | 0 | 0 |
| **Bowling** | **Mat** | **Balls** | **Runs** | **Wkts** | **BBI** | **BBM** | **Ave** | **Econ** | **SR** | **5w** | **10** |
| First-class | 4 | 588 | 328 | 8 | 4/78 | 4/105 | 41.00 | 3.34 | 73.5 | 0 | 0 |
| Twenty20 | 1 | 6 | 10 | 0 | - | - | - | 10.00 | - | 0 | 0 |

# EOIN MORGAN LHB RM R1 W0 MVP73

FULL NAME: Eoin Joseph Gerard Morgan
BORN: September 10, 1986, Dublin
SQUAD NO: 7
HEIGHT: 5ft 9in
NICKNAME: Moggie, Morgs
EDUCATION: Catholic University School
TEAMS: England, Ireland, Middlesex, Bangalore Royal Challengers, Kolkata Knight Riders, Sydney Thunder
CAREER: Test: 2010; ODI: 2006; T20I: 2009; First-class: 2004; List A: 2004; T20: 2006

---

BEST BATTING: 209* Ireland vs UAE, Abu Dhabi, 2007
BEST BOWLING: 2-24 Middlesex vs Nottinghamshire, Lord's, 2007
COUNTY CAPS: 2008

---

TWITTER FEED: @Eoin16
NOTES: An Irishman by birth, Morgan switched his allegiance to England in April 2009 after he was named in England's 30-man provisional squad for the 2009 World T20. Made ODI debut for his adopted nation against West Indies in May 2009 at Bristol and his international T20 debut a month later . His Test debut followed against Bangladesh in May 2010. Hit a maiden century in his third Test – 130 vs Pakistan at Trent Bridge. Dropped from England's Test side after the 2012 away series vs Pakistan and has not played a Test since. After a lean 2013, Morgan rediscovered his form in the away ODI series against Australia in January 2014. Was handed the ODI captaincy ahead of the 2015 World Cup

| Batting | Mat | Inns | NO | Runs | HS | Ave | SR | 100 | 50 | Ct | St |
|---|---|---|---|---|---|---|---|---|---|---|---|
| Tests | 16 | 24 | 1 | 700 | 130 | 30.43 | 54.77 | 2 | 3 | 11 | 0 |
| ODIs | 139 | 131 | 21 | 3938 | 124* | 35.80 | 85.05 | 7 | 22 | 59 | 0 |
| T20Is | 50 | 49 | 10 | 1147 | 85* | 29.41 | 131.99 | 0 | 6 | 21 | 0 |
| First-class | 89 | 147 | 16 | 4730 | 209* | 36.10 | 51.40 | 11 | 22 | 70 | 1 |
| List A | 246 | 226 | 34 | 7008 | 161 | 36.50 | 87.19 | 13 | 38 | 94 | 0 |
| Twenty20 | 151 | 140 | 21 | 3147 | 85* | 26.44 | 130.41 | 0 | 14 | 63 | 0 |
| **Bowling** | **Mat** | **Balls** | **Runs** | **Wkts** | **BBI** | **BBM** | **Ave** | **Econ** | **SR** | **5w** | **10** |
| Tests | 16 | - | - | - | - | - | - | - | - | - | - |
| ODIs | 139 | - | - | - | - | - | - | - | - | - | - |
| T20Is | 50 | - | - | - | - | - | - | - | - | - | - |
| First-class | 89 | 102 | 90 | 2 | 2/24 | 2/24 | 45.00 | 5.29 | 51.0 | 0 | 0 |
| List A | 246 | 42 | 49 | 0 | - | - | - | 7.00 | - | 0 | 0 |
| Twenty20 | 151 | - | - | - | - | - | - | - | - | - | - |

## CHARLIE MORRIS RHB RMF R0 W1

FULL NAME: Charles Andrew John Morris
BORN: July 6, 1992, Hereford
SQUAD NO: 31
HEIGHT: 6ft
NICKNAME: Moz, Dug, DGB
EDUCATION: King's College, Taunton; Oxford Brookes University
TEAMS: Worcestershire
CAREER: First-class: 2012; List A: 2013; T20: 2013



BEST BATTING: 33* Oxford MCCU vs Warwickshire, Oxford, 2013
BEST BOWLING: 5-54 Worcestershire vs Derbyshire, Derby, 2014

CAREER HIGHLIGHTS? Signing for Worcestershire, gaining promotion in 2014 to Division One
SUPERSTITIONS? I used to believe in the magpie rhyme and wear the same socks if I'd done well, but not anymore
CRICKETING HEROES? Phil Lewis and Graham Charlesworth – because of their belief in helping me become a professional and hours of coaching. Dale Steyn – because of his ability to bowl quick, aggressive spells and move the ball at pace
CRICKET RULE YOU'D CHANGE? Edges that travel down for four to the third-man boundary don't count
IF YOU WEREN'T A CRICKETER? My aspiration if I wasn't a cricketer would be to become a Royal Marines officer
FAVOURITE TV? Top Gear, Homeland, The Missing
LEAST FAVOURITE TV? Made In Chelsea, The Only Way Is Essex, Geordie Shore, EastEnders
SURPRISING FACT? I'm very OCD with my wardrobe at home and cricket kit
TWITTER FEED: @Morris_9

| Batting | Mat | Inns | NO | Runs | HS | Ave | SR | 100 | 50 | Ct | St |
|---|---|---|---|---|---|---|---|---|---|---|---|
| First-class | 22 | 30 | 17 | 157 | 33* | 12.07 | 29.84 | 0 | 0 | 9 | 0 |
| List A | 11 | 6 | 3 | 31 | 16* | 10.33 | 73.80 | 0 | 0 | 1 | 0 |
| Twenty20 | 3 | 1 | 1 | 2 | 2* | - | 50.00 | 0 | 0 | 1 | 0 |
| **Bowling** | **Mat** | **Balls** | **Runs** | **Wkts** | **BBI** | **BBM** | **Ave** | **Econ** | **SR** | **5w** | **10** |
| First-class | 22 | 4113 | 1945 | 66 | 5/54 | 6/96 | 29.46 | 2.83 | 62.3 | 1 | 0 |
| List A | 11 | 408 | 392 | 10 | 2/25 | 2/25 | 39.20 | 5.76 | 40.8 | 0 | 0 |
| Twenty20 | 3 | 60 | 96 | 2 | 2/44 | 2/44 | 48.00 | 9.60 | 30.0 | 0 | 0 |

## GORDON MUCHALL RHB RM R0 W0

FULL NAME: Gordon James Muchall
BORN: November 2, 1982, Newcastle
SQUAD NO: 24
HEIGHT: 6ft
NICKNAME: Much
EDUCATION: Durham School
TEAMS: Durham
CAREER: First-class: 2002; List A: 2002; T20: 2003

BEST BATTING: 219 Durham vs Kent, Canterbury, 2006
BEST BOWLING: 3-26 Durham vs Yorkshire, Leeds, 2003
COUNTY CAPS: 2005

FAMILY TIES? Granddad Bernard played for Northumberland, brother Paul played at Gloucestershire, brother Matthew played for Northumberland and dad Arthur plays for Durham over 50s
CAREER HIGHLIGHTS? Winning the Championship twice with Durham
CRICKETING HEROES? Mike Hussey, Robin Smith, Dale Benkenstein
NON-CRICKETING HEROES? Jonny Wilkinson
IF YOU WEREN'T A CRICKETER? Coaching or personal trainer
FAVOURITE TV? 24 and Prison Break
SURPRISING FACT? The last game of rugby I ever played was at Twickenham
FANTASY SLIP CORDON? Keeper: Phil Mustard (safe hands, always good for a pearl of wisdom), 1st: James Corden (to make fun out of the rest), 2nd: Andrew Flintoff (able to cover 1st slip), 3rd: Me (I need to fit in somewhere!), Gully: Lee Evans (lots of energy to keep everyone going)
TWITTER FEED: @gmuchall

| Batting | Mat | Inns | NO | Runs | HS | Ave | SR | 100 | 50 | Ct | St |
|---|---|---|---|---|---|---|---|---|---|---|---|
| First-class | 149 | 258 | 15 | 7154 | 219 | 29.44 | 54.37 | 12 | 36 | 104 | 0 |
| List A | 140 | 125 | 27 | 3294 | 101* | 33.61 | | 1 | 20 | 52 | 0 |
| Twenty20 | 89 | 77 | 23 | 1573 | 66* | 29.12 | 114.15 | 0 | 5 | 32 | 0 |
| **Bowling** | **Mat** | **Balls** | **Runs** | **Wkts** | **BBI** | **BBM** | **Ave** | **Econ** | **SR** | **5w** | **10** |
| First-class | 149 | 902 | 626 | 15 | 3/26 | | 41.73 | 4.16 | 60.1 | 0 | 0 |
| List A | 140 | 168 | 144 | 1 | 1/15 | 1/15 | 144.00 | 5.14 | 168.0 | 0 | 0 |
| Twenty20 | 89 | 12 | 8 | 1 | 1/8 | 1/8 | 8.00 | 4.00 | 12.0 | 0 | 0 |

# STEVEN MULLANEY RHB RM R0 W0 MVP82

FULL NAME: Steven John Mullaney
BORN: November 19, 1986, Warrington, Cheshire
SQUAD NO: 5
HEIGHT: 5ft 8in
NICKNAME: Mull, Tev
EDUCATION: St Mary's Catholic High School
TEAMS: Nottinghamshire, Lancashire
CAREER: First-class: 2006; List A: 2006; T20: 2006



BEST BATTING: 165* Lancashire vs Durham UCCE, Durham University, 2007
BEST BOWLING: 4-31 Nottinghamshire vs Essex, Nottingham, 2010

CAREER HIGHLIGHTS? Winning the County Championship in 2010, winning a Lord's final in 2013 and scoring a hundred the first time I played at Lord's
BEST PLAYER IN COUNTY CRICKET? Ed Joyce
TIP FOR THE TOP? Jake Ball, Sam Hain
CRICKETING HEROES? Andrew Flintoff – he made the crowd erupt
NON-CRICKETING HEROES? David Beckham – he's the ultimate role model
CRICKET RULE YOU'D CHANGE? No-balls should be free hits in all cricket
IF YOU COULD BE SOMEONE ELSE FOR A DAY? David Beckham
DESERT ISLAND DISC? Westlife – Greatest Hits
ACCOMPLISHMENTS? I played rugby league for England U15
PET HATE? Back-seat drivers – if you want to drive then get in the drivers' seat. If not, be quiet
FANTASY SLIP CORDON? Keeper: David Beckham, 1st: Liam Neeson, 2nd: Jimmy Bullard, 3rd: James Corden, Gully: Michelle Keegan
TWITTER FEED: @mull05

| Batting | Mat | Inns | NO | Runs | HS | Ave | SR | 100 | 50 | Ct | St |
|---|---|---|---|---|---|---|---|---|---|---|---|
| First-class | 66 | 110 | 6 | 3207 | 165* | 30.83 | 58.21 | 5 | 20 | 48 | 0 |
| List A | 69 | 49 | 8 | 877 | 63* | 21.39 | 95.42 | 0 | 4 | 39 | 0 |
| Twenty20 | 68 | 45 | 16 | 532 | 53 | 18.34 | 135.36 | 0 | 1 | 37 | 0 |
| **Bowling** | **Mat** | **Balls** | **Runs** | **Wkts** | **BBI** | **BBM** | **Ave** | **Econ** | **SR** | **5w** | **10** |
| First-class | 66 | 2807 | 1458 | 34 | 4/31 | 4/48 | 42.88 | 3.11 | 82.5 | 0 | 0 |
| List A | 69 | 2198 | 1764 | 62 | 4/29 | 4/29 | 28.45 | 4.81 | 35.4 | 0 | 0 |
| Twenty20 | 68 | 1140 | 1481 | 47 | 4/19 | 4/19 | 31.51 | 7.79 | 24.2 | 0 | 0 |

## DAVID MURPHY — RHB WK R0 W0

FULL NAME: David Murphy
BORN: June 24, 1989, Welwyn Garden City, Hertfordshire
SQUAD NO: 19
HEIGHT: 6ft 1in
NICKNAME: Murph, Smurf
EDUCATION: Richard Hale School; Loughborough University
TEAMS: Scotland, Northamptonshire
CAREER: First-class: 2009; List A: 2010; T20: 2010

BEST BATTING: 81 Northamptonshire vs Hampshire, Northampton, 2013

CAREER HIGHLIGHTS? Being T20 champions in 2013 and taking the catch to win the game. Getting promoted in 2013 was also a great way to cap off a great year
BEST PLAYER IN COUNTY CRICKET? James Vince
TIP FOR THE TOP? Olly Stone, Ravi Patel, Adam Rossington
CRICKETING HEROES? Steve Waugh – he just epitomised maximum effort at the crease. Jack Russell – as a keeper he was just awesome
CRICKET RULE YOU'D CHANGE? Have a hole that you can hide out in for a while when you drop a catch!
COACHING TIP? Keep your head over the ball when catching as a wicketkeeper
DESERT ISLAND DISC? Elton John – Tumbleweed Connection
SURPRISING FACT? I'm completely deaf in my left ear
FANTASY SLIP CORDON? Keeper: Me, 1st: Stephen Peters (he has always got a good story to tell), 2nd: Micky Flanagan, 3rd: Steve Waugh, Gully: Tony Benn

| Batting | Mat | Inns | NO | Runs | HS | Ave | SR | 100 | 50 | Ct | St |
|---|---|---|---|---|---|---|---|---|---|---|---|
| ODIs | 8 | 7 | 2 | 58 | 20* | 11.60 | 49.15 | 0 | 0 | 8 | 3 |
| T20Is | 4 | 4 | 3 | 35 | 20 | 35.00 | 100.00 | 0 | 0 | 1 | 0 |
| First-class | 53 | 71 | 16 | 1425 | 81 | 25.90 | 42.39 | 0 | 10 | 146 | 13 |
| List A | 39 | 25 | 13 | 272 | 31* | 22.66 | 71.76 | 0 | 0 | 23 | 11 |
| Twenty20 | 39 | 19 | 7 | 129 | 20 | 10.75 | 103.20 | 0 | 0 | 18 | 5 |
| **Bowling** | **Mat** | **Balls** | **Runs** | **Wkts** | **BBI** | **BBM** | **Ave** | **Econ** | **SR** | **5w** | **10** |
| ODIs | 8 | - | - | - | - | - | - | - | - | - | - |
| T20Is | 4 | - | - | - | - | - | - | - | - | - | - |
| First-class | 53 | 6 | 3 | 0 | - | - | - | 3.00 | - | 0 | 0 |
| List A | 39 | - | - | - | - | - | - | - | - | - | - |
| Twenty20 | 39 | - | - | - | - | - | - | - | - | - | - |

# JACK MURPHY

LHB LFM R0 W0

FULL NAME: Jack Roger Murphy
BORN: July 15, 1995, Haverfordwest, Pembrokeshire
SQUAD NO: 7
HEIGHT: 6ft 7in
NICKNAME: Smurf
EDUCATION: Greenhill Secondary School; Cardiff Metropolitan University
TEAMS: Glamorgan 2nd XI
CAREER: Yet to make first-team debut



---

CAREER HIGHLIGHTS? Becoming a professional – that was my mum and dad's dream
BEST PLAYER IN COUNTY CRICKET? Jason Roy
TIP FOR THE TOP? Aneurin Donald
MOST MARKED CHARACTERISTIC? Being so tall – whenever I meet new people or little kids that's always the first thing they say about me!
CRICKETING HEROES? Simon Jones was a star for me – being a Glamorgan player and a fast bowler he was always my idol
NON-CRICKETING HEROES? My mum and dad – if it wasn't for them I would not be where I am now. They always put me or my brother and sister first rather than themselves and I'm very grateful for that
CRICKET RULE YOU'D CHANGE? Lunch is too long and tea is too short – they should both be 30 minutes
IF YOU WEREN'T A CRICKETER? I always wanted to join the RAF
IF YOU COULD BE SOMEONE ELSE FOR A DAY? Dan Bilzerian
DESERT ISLAND DISC? George Ezra
FAVOURITE TV? Friends
LEAST FAVOURITE TV? Big Brother – what a load of rubbish!
ACCOMPLISHMENTS? Managing to get a girlfriend
PET HATE? When you're in bed and someone comes in then leaves the door open when they leave
SURPRISING FACT? My grandad had 16 brothers and sisters
TWITTER FEED: @jmurf95

# TIM MURTAGH LHB RFM R0 W6 MVP49

FULL NAME: Timothy James Murtagh
BORN: August 2, 1981, Lambeth, London
SQUAD NO: 34
HEIGHT: 6ft 2in
NICKNAME: Murts, Jack, Brow
EDUCATION: The John Fisher School
TEAMS: Ireland, Middlesex, Surrey
CAREER: ODI: 2012; T20I: 2012; First-class: 2000; List A: 2000; T20: 2003

BEST BATTING: 74* Surrey vs Middlesex, The Oval, 2004
BEST BOWLING: 7-82 Middlesex vs Derbyshire, Derby, 2009
COUNTY CAPS: 2008 (Middlesex); BENEFIT YEAR: 2015

CAREER HIGHLIGHTS? My first international cap for Ireland, winning the T20 in 2008 and getting capped by Middlesex
MOST MARKED CHARACTERISTIC? Eyebrows
CRICKET RULE YOU'D CHANGE? Five-run penalty for pointless sliding in the field
COACHING TIP? Don't try and bowl too fast
IF YOU WEREN'T A CRICKETER? Spotting trains
IF YOU COULD BE SOMEONE ELSE FOR A DAY? Boris Johnson
ACCOMPLISHMENTS? Getting my wife to accept my wedding proposal while naked on one knee
PET HATE? Filling in long questionnaires
TWITTER FEED: @tjmurtagh

| Batting | Mat | Inns | NO | Runs | HS | Ave | SR | 100 | 50 | Ct | St |
|---|---|---|---|---|---|---|---|---|---|---|---|
| ODIs | 10 | 6 | 2 | 60 | 23* | 15.00 | 75.94 | 0 | 0 | 1 | 0 |
| T20Is | 7 | 2 | 1 | 5 | 3 | 5.00 | 71.42 | 0 | 0 | 1 | 0 |
| First-class | 158 | 212 | 62 | 3171 | 74* | 21.14 | | 0 | 10 | 46 | 0 |
| List A | 152 | 95 | 35 | 691 | 35* | 11.51 | | 0 | 0 | 37 | 0 |
| Twenty20 | 94 | 35 | 12 | 206 | 40* | 8.95 | 105.64 | 0 | 0 | 20 | 0 |
| **Bowling** | **Mat** | **Balls** | **Runs** | **Wkts** | **BBI** | **BBM** | **Ave** | **Econ** | **SR** | **5w** | **10** |
| ODIs | 10 | 438 | 333 | 9 | 3/33 | 3/33 | 37.00 | 4.56 | 48.6 | 0 | 0 |
| T20Is | 7 | 148 | 179 | 7 | 2/24 | 2/24 | 25.57 | 7.25 | 21.1 | 0 | 0 |
| First-class | 158 | 27248 | 14768 | 545 | 7/82 | | 27.09 | 3.25 | 49.9 | 26 | 4 |
| List A | 152 | 6614 | 5756 | 195 | 4/14 | 4/14 | 29.51 | 5.22 | 33.9 | 0 | 0 |
| Twenty20 | 94 | 1852 | 2560 | 100 | 6/24 | 6/24 | 25.60 | 8.29 | 18.5 | 1 | 0 |

# PHIL MUSTARD

## LHB LB WK R0 W0 MVP79

FULL NAME: Philip Mustard
BORN: October 8, 1982, Sunderland, County Durham
SQUAD NO: 19
HEIGHT: 5ft 11in
NICKNAME: Colonel
EDUCATION: Usworth Comprehensive
TEAMS: England, Durham
CAREER: ODI: 2007; T20I: 2008; First-class: 2002; List A: 2000; T20: 2003



BEST BATTING: 130 Durham vs Kent, Canterbury, 2006
BEST BOWLING: 1-9 Durham vs Sussex, Hove, 2013

CAREER HIGHLIGHTS? Making my England debut in Sri Lanka and New Zealand in 2007/08 and playing 10 ODIs. Winning our first trophy for Durham, the FP Trophy, in 2007, and then following up with two Championship victories in 2008 and 2009
SUPERSTITIONS? A little one when I go out to bat: I always look high to my left. Not sure why, but it happens
IF YOU WEREN'T A CRICKETER? Probably selling things, which wouldn't be exciting, but it would be a job
FAVOURITE TV? An Idiot Abroad
ACCOMPLISHMENTS? Bringing up my two boys
TWITTER FEED: @colonel19

| Batting | Mat | Inns | NO | Runs | HS | Ave | SR | 100 | 50 | Ct | St |
|---|---|---|---|---|---|---|---|---|---|---|---|
| ODIs | 10 | 10 | 0 | 233 | 83 | 23.30 | 92.46 | 0 | 1 | 9 | 2 |
| T20Is | 2 | 2 | 0 | 60 | 40 | 30.00 | 162.16 | 0 | 0 | 0 | 0 |
| First-class | 180 | 279 | 34 | 7467 | 130 | 30.47 | 61.47 | 6 | 46 | 601 | 19 |
| List A | 182 | 166 | 9 | 4837 | 143 | 30.80 | | 7 | 30 | 187 | 45 |
| Twenty20 | 152 | 145 | 7 | 3401 | 97* | 24.64 | 124.03 | 0 | 18 | 69 | 33 |

| Bowling | Mat | Balls | Runs | Wkts | BBI | BBM | Ave | Econ | SR | 5w | 10 |
|---|---|---|---|---|---|---|---|---|---|---|---|
| ODIs | 10 | - | - | - | - | - | - | - | - | - | - |
| T20Is | 2 | - | - | - | - | - | - | - | - | - | - |
| First-class | 180 | 7 | 9 | 1 | 1/9 | 1/9 | 9.00 | 7.71 | 7.0 | 0 | 0 |
| List A | 182 | - | - | - | - | - | - | - | - | - | - |
| Twenty20 | 152 | - | - | - | - | - | - | - | - | - | - |

## JOHANN MYBURGH RHB OB R0 W0



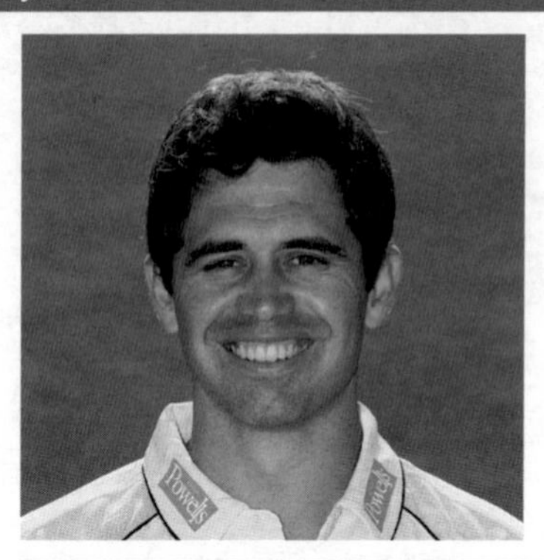


FULL NAME: Johann Gerhardus Myburgh
BORN: October 22, 1980, Pretoria, South Africa
SQUAD NO: 9
TEAMS: Somerset, Auckland, Canterbury, Durham, Hampshire, Northerns, Titans
CAREER: First-class: 1997; List A: 1999; T20: 2005

BEST BATTING: 203 Northerns B vs Easterns, Pretoria, 1998
BEST BOWLING: 4-56 Canterbury vs Northern Districts, Hamilton, 2008

NOTES: Myburgh signed for Somerset ahead of the 2014 season after previous spells in county cricket with Hampshire and, more recently, Durham. He returns for a second season in 2015. The South African allrounder emigrated from his homeland to play cricket in New Zealand, where he represented Canterbury for whom he averages 51.71 in first-class cricket. He broke Graeme Pollock's long-standing record for the youngest scorer of a double-century in South African first-class cricket as a 17-year-old in 1998. He has been living in the UK for a number of years, playing for Sutton CC in the Surrey Championship. His younger brother, Stephan, plays international cricket for the Netherlands

| Batting | Mat | Inns | NO | Runs | HS | Ave | SR | 100 | 50 | Ct | St |
|---|---|---|---|---|---|---|---|---|---|---|---|
| First-class | 93 | 163 | 19 | 6039 | 203 | 41.93 | | 13 | 35 | 55 | 0 |
| List A | 100 | 93 | 9 | 2371 | 112 | 28.22 | | 1 | 14 | 22 | 0 |
| Twenty20 | 49 | 41 | 7 | 969 | 88 | 28.50 | 113.33 | 0 | 4 | 16 | 0 |
| **Bowling** | **Mat** | **Balls** | **Runs** | **Wkts** | **BBI** | **BBM** | **Ave** | **Econ** | **SR** | **5w** | **10** |
| First-class | 93 | 3973 | 1973 | 42 | 4/56 | | 46.97 | 2.97 | 94.5 | 0 | 0 |
| List A | 100 | 1766 | 1493 | 25 | 2/22 | 2/22 | 59.72 | 5.07 | 70.6 | 0 | 0 |
| Twenty20 | 49 | 356 | 441 | 10 | 3/16 | 3/16 | 44.10 | 7.43 | 35.6 | 0 | 0 |

# JIGAR NAIK

RHB OB R0 W0

FULL NAME: Jigar Kumar Hakumatrai Naik
BORN: August 10, 1984, Leicester
SQUAD NO: 22
HEIGHT: 6ft 2in
NICKNAME: Jigs, Jiggles
EDUCATION: Nottingham Trent University; Loughborough University
TEAMS: Leicestershire, Colombo
CAREER: First-class: 2006; List A: 2003; T20: 2008



BEST BATTING: 109* Leicestershire vs Derbyshire, Leicester, 2009
BEST BOWLING: 7-96 Leicestershire vs Surrey, The Oval, 2010

CAREER HIGHLIGHTS? My maiden first-class five-wicket haul, my maiden first-class hundred, getting capped for Leicestershire, topping the national bowling averages in 2010, and being selected for the ECB's Potential Performance Programme in 2011
MOST MARKED CHARACTERISTIC? Long fingers
CRICKETING HEROES? Claude Henderson, Erapalli Prasanna, Sachin Tendulkar
NON-CRICKETING HEROES? Roger Federer, Muhammad Ali
CRICKET RULE YOU'D CHANGE? Revert back to four fielders inside the circle in one-day cricket after the Powerplay
IF YOU WEREN'T A CRICKETER? Systems engineer
DESERT ISLAND DISC? Bollywood Greatest Hits
ACCOMPLISHMENTS? Getting married!
SURPRISING FACT? I play the tabla
TWITTER FEED: @jigarnaik

| Batting | Mat | Inns | NO | Runs | HS | Ave | SR | 100 | 50 | Ct | St |
|---|---|---|---|---|---|---|---|---|---|---|---|
| First-class | 66 | 102 | 24 | 1670 | 109* | 21.41 | 39.00 | 1 | 4 | 39 | 0 |
| List A | 37 | 27 | 10 | 192 | 36* | 11.29 | | 0 | 0 | 5 | 0 |
| Twenty20 | 34 | 13 | 10 | 61 | 16* | 20.33 | 100.00 | 0 | 0 | 9 | 0 |
| **Bowling** | **Mat** | **Balls** | **Runs** | **Wkts** | **BBI** | **BBM** | **Ave** | **Econ** | **SR** | **5w** | **10** |
| First-class | 66 | 10588 | 5820 | 150 | 7/96 | 8/133 | 38.80 | 3.29 | 70.5 | 5 | 0 |
| List A | 37 | 1418 | 1262 | 30 | 3/21 | 3/21 | 42.06 | 5.33 | 47.2 | 0 | 0 |
| Twenty20 | 34 | 639 | 753 | 28 | 3/3 | 3/3 | 26.89 | 7.07 | 22.8 | 0 | 0 |

# GRAHAM NAPIER

## RHB RFM R0 W2 MVP97

FULL NAME: Graham Richard Napier
BORN: January 6, 1980, Colchester
SQUAD NO: 17
HEIGHT: 5ft 9in
NICKNAME: Plank, George, Napes
EDUCATION: Gilberd School, Colchester
TEAMS: Essex, Central Districts, England Lions, Mumbai Indians, Wellington
CAREER: First-class: 1997; List A: 1997; T20: 2003

BEST BATTING: 196 Essex vs Surrey, Whitgift School, 2011
BEST BOWLING: 7-21 Essex vs Cambridge MCCU, Fenner's, 2014
COUNTY CAPS: 2003; BENEFIT YEAR: 2012

CAREER HIGHLIGHTS? Testing myself against the world's best and scoring some runs. Winning the FP Trophy. Scoring 152*, including 16 sixes, in a Twenty20 match. Being included in England's World T20 squad. Playing in the IPL for Mumbai Indians
SUPERSTITIONS? I always like to have lamb the evening before I bat
CRICKETING HEROES? Graham Gooch, Viv Richards, Freddie Flintoff, Alastair Cook
NON-CRICKETING HEROES? Winston Churchill
IF YOU WEREN'T A CRICKETER? A photographer or a chef – potentially both
DESERT ISLAND DISC? Elton John's Greatest Hits
FAVOURITE TV? Africa by David Attenborough, Top Gear
FANTASY SLIP CORDON? Keeper: Russell Crowe, 1st: Winston Churchill, 2nd: Natalie Imbruglia, 3rd: Micky Flanagan, Gully: Elton John
TWITTER FEED: @Graham_Napier

| Batting | Mat | Inns | NO | Runs | HS | Ave | SR | 100 | 50 | Ct | St |
|---|---|---|---|---|---|---|---|---|---|---|---|
| First-class | 151 | 206 | 40 | 5072 | 196 | 30.55 | | 6 | 29 | 55 | 0 |
| List A | 236 | 176 | 21 | 2889 | 79 | 18.63 | | 0 | 14 | 56 | 0 |
| Twenty20 | 111 | 80 | 14 | 1058 | 152* | 16.03 | 145.52 | 1 | 0 | 30 | 0 |
| **Bowling** | **Mat** | **Balls** | **Runs** | **Wkts** | **BBI** | **BBM** | **Ave** | **Econ** | **SR** | **5w** | **10** |
| First-class | 151 | 20704 | 12242 | 386 | 7/21 | | 31.71 | 3.54 | 53.6 | 12 | 0 |
| List A | 236 | 8270 | 7284 | 282 | 7/32 | 7/32 | 25.82 | 5.28 | 29.3 | 4 | 0 |
| Twenty20 | 111 | 2350 | 2998 | 131 | 4/10 | 4/10 | 22.88 | 7.65 | 17.9 | 0 | 0 |

# BRENDAN NASH

LHB LM R1 W0

FULL NAME: Brendan Paul Nash
BORN: December 14, 1977, Attadale, Australia
SQUAD NO: 40
HEIGHT: 5ft 8in
NICKNAME: Bubba, Nashy, Uncle
EDUCATION: Nudgee College, Brisbane
TEAMS: West Indies, Jamaica, Kent, Queensland
CAREER: Test: 2008; ODI: 2008; First-class: 2001; List A: 2001; T20: 2008



BEST BATTING: 207 Jamaica vs Trinidad and Tobago, St Augustine, 2011
BEST BOWLING: 2-7 Jamaica vs Combined Campuses and Colleges, Kingston, 2008

FAMILY TIES? Mum used to love supporting West Indies when she was living there so it was always in my blood
CAREER HIGHLIGHTS? Playing Test cricket – reaching the top of your sport is a great achievement
MOST MARKED CHARACTERISTIC? A fighter who never gives up
CRICKETING HEROES? Allan Border and Curtly Ambrose – Border for his steeliness and Ambrose for the way he could change a game
NON-CRICKETING HEROES? Michael Jordan – because of the way he could win and change a game for his team
IF YOU COULD BE SOMEONE ELSE FOR A DAY? The West Indies' chairman of selectors
DESERT ISLAND DISC? Bob Marley
SURPRISING FACT? I was once ranked No.2 badminton U15 player in Australia

| Batting | Mat | Inns | NO | Runs | HS | Ave | SR | 100 | 50 | Ct | St |
|---|---|---|---|---|---|---|---|---|---|---|---|
| Tests | 21 | 33 | 0 | 1103 | 114 | 33.42 | 43.28 | 2 | 8 | 6 | 0 |
| ODIs | 9 | 7 | 3 | 104 | 39* | 26.00 | 73.75 | 0 | 0 | 1 | 0 |
| First-class | 135 | 221 | 30 | 7523 | 207 | 39.38 | | 18 | 32 | 50 | 0 |
| List A | 88 | 66 | 16 | 1596 | 98* | 31.92 | | 0 | 8 | 28 | 0 |
| Twenty20 | 8 | 6 | 1 | 84 | 26 | 16.80 | 87.50 | 0 | 0 | 1 | 0 |
| **Bowling** | **Mat** | **Balls** | **Runs** | **Wkts** | **BBI** | **BBM** | **Ave** | **Econ** | **SR** | **5w** | **10** |
| Tests | 21 | 492 | 247 | 2 | 1/21 | 1/21 | 123.50 | 3.01 | 246.0 | 0 | 0 |
| ODIs | 9 | 294 | 224 | 5 | 3/56 | 3/56 | 44.80 | 4.57 | 58.8 | 0 | 0 |
| First-class | 135 | 1657 | 801 | 23 | 2/7 | | 34.82 | 2.90 | 72.0 | 0 | 0 |
| List A | 88 | 798 | 562 | 16 | 4/20 | 4/20 | 35.12 | 4.22 | 49.8 | 0 | 0 |
| Twenty20 | 8 | 24 | 40 | 1 | 1/32 | 1/32 | 40.00 | 10.00 | 24.0 | 0 | 0 |

# CHRIS NASH

RHB OB R3 W0 MVP75

FULL NAME: Christopher David Nash
BORN: May 19, 1983, Cuckfield, Sussex
SQUAD NO: 23
HEIGHT: 6ft
NICKNAME: Nashy, Nashdog, Schlong, Knocker
EDUCATION: Collyer's Sixth Form College; Loughborough University
TEAMS: Sussex, Otago, Auckland, England Lions
CAREER: First-class: 2002; List A: 2006; T20: 2006

BEST BATTING: 184 Sussex vs Leicestershire, Leicester, 2010
BEST BOWLING: 4-12 Sussex vs Glamorgan, Cardiff, 2010
COUNTY CAPS: 2008

FAMILY TIES? My brother Mark played for Sussex 2nd XI
CAREER HIGHLIGHTS? Winning the T20 Cup in 2009, the County Championship in 2006 and 2007, being awarded my county cap in 2008, representing England Lions in 2011, being the Pro40 MVP 2011 and getting into the PCA team of the year in 2011 and 2012
BEST PLAYER IN COUNTY CRICKET? Edmund Joyce
MOST MARKED CHARACTERISTIC? My full head of hair
SUPERSTITIONS? Never be nice to Luke Wright
NON-CRICKETING HEROES? Maverick in Top Gun!
CRICKET RULE YOU'D CHANGE? Opening batsmen get double runs for the first 10 overs of County Championship games because it is such a tough job and we deserve all the credit
IF YOU COULD BE SOMEONE ELSE FOR A DAY? Craig Cachopa – just to see what it is like to be so much smaller than everyone else
SURPRISING FACT? Although photos may be deceptive I actually have a full head of hair
TWITTER FEED: @chrisnash23

| Batting | Mat | Inns | NO | Runs | HS | Ave | SR | 100 | 50 | Ct | St |
|---|---|---|---|---|---|---|---|---|---|---|---|
| First-class | 141 | 242 | 17 | 8724 | 184 | 38.77 | 58.94 | 17 | 44 | 67 | 0 |
| List A | 97 | 90 | 3 | 2737 | 124* | 31.45 | 90.09 | 2 | 17 | 24 | 0 |
| Twenty20 | 114 | 108 | 15 | 2124 | 80* | 22.83 | 119.66 | 0 | 9 | 37 | 0 |
| **Bowling** | **Mat** | **Balls** | **Runs** | **Wkts** | **BBI** | **BBM** | **Ave** | **Econ** | **SR** | **5w** | **10** |
| First-class | 141 | 5071 | 2826 | 74 | 4/12 | | 38.18 | 3.34 | 68.5 | 0 | 0 |
| List A | 97 | 1411 | 1278 | 42 | 4/40 | 4/40 | 30.42 | 5.43 | 33.5 | 0 | 0 |
| Twenty20 | 114 | 914 | 1052 | 47 | 4/7 | 4/7 | 22.38 | 6.90 | 19.4 | 0 | 0 |

# ROB NEWTON

RHB LB R0 W0

FULL NAME: Robert Irving Newton
BORN: January 18, 1990, Taunton
SQUAD NO: 21
HEIGHT: 5ft 8in
NICKNAME: Ewok, KOTL
EDUCATION: Framlingham College
TEAMS: Northamptonshire
CAREER: First-class: 2010; List A: 2009; T20: 2010



BEST BATTING: 119* Northamptonshire vs Derbyshire, Northampton, 2012

CAREER HIGHLIGHTS? Scoring a hundred in both innings of a first-class game [against Derbyshire]. Taking the new ball
BEST PLAYER IN COUNTY CRICKET? Darren Stevens
CRICKETING HEROES? Ajaz Akhtar
NON-CRICKETING HEROES? Hank Moody, Vincent Chase
IF YOU WEREN'T A CRICKETER? I'd be drinking the profits at my own bar
DESERT ISLAND DISC? Baha Men – Who Let The Dogs Out?
FAVOURITE TV? Entourage
FANTASY SLIP CORDON? Keeper: Jack Brooks, 1st: Me, 2nd: Ben Howgego, 3rd: Gav Baker
TWITTER FEED: @robbienewts77

| Batting | Mat | Inns | NO | Runs | HS | Ave | SR | 100 | 50 | Ct | St |
|---|---|---|---|---|---|---|---|---|---|---|---|
| First-class | 45 | 77 | 8 | 2310 | 119* | 33.47 | 59.07 | 6 | 7 | 14 | 0 |
| List A | 25 | 23 | 1 | 616 | 88* | 28.00 | 92.21 | 0 | 2 | 3 | 0 |
| Twenty20 | 18 | 16 | 1 | 199 | 38 | 13.26 | 102.57 | 0 | 0 | 0 | 0 |
| **Bowling** | **Mat** | **Balls** | **Runs** | **Wkts** | **BBI** | **BBM** | **Ave** | **Econ** | **SR** | **5w** | **10** |
| First-class | 45 | 13 | 19 | 0 | - | - | - | 8.76 | - | 0 | 0 |
| List A | 25 | - | - | - | - | - | - | - | - | - | - |
| Twenty20 | 18 | - | - | - | - | - | - | - | - | - | - |

# KIERAN NOEMA-BARNETT LHB RM R0 W0

FULL NAME: Kieran Noema-Barnett
BORN: June 4, 1987, Dunedin, New Zealand
SQUAD NO: 11
HEIGHT: 6ft 1in
NICKNAME: Barney, Bear
EDUCATION: Kavanagh College; Massey University
TEAMS: Central Districts, Otago
CAREER: First-class: 2009; List A: 2008; T20: 2007

BEST BATTING: 107 Central Districts vs Auckland, Auckland, 2011
BEST BOWLING: 4-20 Central Districts vs Otago, Dunedin, 2011

CAREER HIGHLIGHTS? I've been involved in winning three championships in New Zealand with the Central Stags. Captaining the side to the four-day title was unreal. Personally a 14-ball fifty in a T20 game would be in there, as well as a first-class hat-trick
SUPERSTITIONS? No breakfast on game days – I need to be hungry
CRICKETING HEROES? Brian Lara – he made it look easy
NON-CRICKETING HEROES? My parents for raising my siblings and me. Manny Pacquiao – he does it all: boxer, congressman, basketball player. His fights are always good to watch
CRICKET RULE YOU'D CHANGE? Getting run out at the non-strikers' end when it's been hit back. It's a tough way to go, a real day-wrecker
IF YOU COULD BE SOMEONE ELSE FOR A DAY? Floyd Mayweather
FAVOURITE TV? Top Cat. He's always scheming
FANTASY SLIP CORDON? Keeper: Manny Pacquiao (he'd create a good atmosphere), 1st: Myself (best seat in the house), 2nd: The Notorious B.I.G. (he's in there to provide a few lyrics), 3rd: Craig Herrick (good friend of mine and he's there for humour and has really poor hands), Gully: Bruce Lee (cat-like reflexes suited to the gully)

| Batting | Mat | Inns | NO | Runs | HS | Ave | SR | 100 | 50 | Ct | St |
|---|---|---|---|---|---|---|---|---|---|---|---|
| First-class | 42 | 65 | 9 | 1703 | 107 | 30.41 | 53.00 | 2 | 10 | 18 | 0 |
| List A | 55 | 44 | 5 | 941 | 67 | 24.12 | 95.53 | 0 | 5 | 25 | 0 |
| Twenty20 | 70 | 65 | 9 | 1001 | 57* | 17.87 | 134.54 | 0 | 3 | 14 | 0 |
| **Bowling** | **Mat** | **Balls** | **Runs** | **Wkts** | **BBI** | **BBM** | **Ave** | **Econ** | **SR** | **5w** | **10** |
| First-class | 42 | 4924 | 2127 | 66 | 4/20 | 6/29 | 32.22 | 2.59 | 74.6 | 0 | 0 |
| List A | 55 | 1854 | 1519 | 37 | 3/42 | 3/42 | 41.05 | 4.91 | 50.1 | 0 | 0 |
| Twenty20 | 70 | 637 | 948 | 26 | 2/13 | 2/13 | 36.46 | 8.92 | 24.5 | 0 | 0 |

# SAM NORTHEAST RHB OB R0 W0 MVP61

FULL NAME: Sam Alexander Northeast
BORN: October 16, 1989, Ashford, Kent
SQUAD NO: 17
HEIGHT: 5ft 11in
NICKNAME: North, Bam, Nick Knight
EDUCATION: Harrow
TEAMS: Kent
CAREER: First-class: 2007; List A: 2007; T20: 2010



BEST BATTING: 176 Kent vs LMCCU, Canterbury, 2011
BEST BOWLING: 1-60 Kent vs Gloucestershire, Cheltenham, 2013
COUNTY CAPS: 2012

TIP FOR THE TOP? Alex Blake
SUPERSTITIONS? I put my right pad on first
CRICKETING HEROES? Graham Thorpe, Steve Waugh
DESERT ISLAND DISC? Starsailor, Snow Patrol, Florence And The Machine
TWITTER FEED: @sanortheast
NOTES: Northeast was hotly tipped from the moment he was selected for the Harrow first team at the age of just 14. He was part of England U19's World Cup squad in 2008. At the end of the 2009 season he scored his maiden first-class hundred but struggled in 2010, averaging 24.57. In 2012 he hit three Championship centuries and finished just short of 1,400 runs in all forms of cricket. He struggled again in 2013 and in 2014 was dropped after scoring only 178 runs in his first 12 innings. He returned to the side at No.5 and went on to make four Championship centuries

| Batting | Mat | Inns | NO | Runs | HS | Ave | SR | 100 | 50 | Ct | St |
|---|---|---|---|---|---|---|---|---|---|---|---|
| First-class | 90 | 157 | 6 | 4905 | 176 | 32.48 | 51.60 | 10 | 28 | 48 | 0 |
| List A | 54 | 48 | 3 | 1479 | 132 | 32.86 | 76.27 | 2 | 8 | 13 | 0 |
| Twenty20 | 48 | 41 | 8 | 834 | 75 | 25.27 | 123.37 | 0 | 5 | 13 | 0 |
| **Bowling** | **Mat** | **Balls** | **Runs** | **Wkts** | **BBI** | **BBM** | **Ave** | **Econ** | **SR** | **5w** | **10** |
| First-class | 90 | 168 | 145 | 1 | 1/60 | 1/60 | 145.00 | 5.17 | 168.0 | 0 | 0 |
| List A | 54 | - | - | - | - | - | - | - | - | - | - |
| Twenty20 | 48 | - | - | - | - | - | - | - | - | - | - |

# LIAM NORWELL

RHB RM R0 W0

FULL NAME: Liam Connor Norwell
BORN: December 27, 1991, Bournemouth, Dorset
SQUAD NO: 24
HEIGHT: 6ft 3in
NICKNAME: Pasty
EDUCATION: Redruth School and Sixth Form
TEAMS: Gloucestershire
CAREER: First-class: 2011; List A: 2012; T20: 2012

---

BEST BATTING: 78 Gloucestershire vs Worcestershire, Cheltenham, 2014
BEST BOWLING: 6-46 Gloucestershire vs Derbyshire, Bristol, 2011
COUNTY CAPS: 2011

---

CAREER HIGHLIGHTS? My six-fer on first-class debut, my record last-wicket partnership for Gloucestershire with Craig Miles at Cheltenham, beating Somerset at Taunton on my T20 debut
CRICKETING HEROES? Andrew Flintoff – the 2005 Ashes is what got me really into cricket and he was the main man at that time!
COACHING TIP? Try not to hold the ball too tightly when running into bowl
IF YOU WEREN'T A CRICKETER? Maybe finishing up at uni or in the armed forces
IF YOU COULD BE SOMEONE ELSE FOR A DAY? Chris Hemsworth
DESERT ISLAND DISC? Metallica – The Black Album
ACCOMPLISHMENTS? Winning the Year 5 80-metre race and scoring the winning try in a Redruth vs Camborne derby
FANTASY SLIP CORDON? Keeper: James Corden, 1st: Kurt Warner, 2nd Slip: Me, 3rd: Thor, Gully: Matthew Corbert
TWITTER FEED: @LCNorwell24

| Batting | Mat | Inns | NO | Runs | HS | Ave | SR | 100 | 50 | Ct | St |
|---|---|---|---|---|---|---|---|---|---|---|---|
| First-class | 28 | 37 | 17 | 294 | 78 | 14.70 | 35.16 | 0 | 1 | 5 | 0 |
| List A | 4 | 1 | 1 | 1 | 1* | - | 33.33 | 0 | 0 | 0 | 0 |
| Twenty20 | 9 | 3 | 3 | 3 | 1* | - | 60.00 | 0 | 0 | 1 | 0 |
| **Bowling** | **Mat** | **Balls** | **Runs** | **Wkts** | **BBI** | **BBM** | **Ave** | **Econ** | **SR** | **5w** | **10** |
| First-class | 28 | 4348 | 2738 | 77 | 6/46 | 8/74 | 35.55 | 3.77 | 56.4 | 2 | 0 |
| List A | 4 | 162 | 177 | 9 | 6/52 | 6/52 | 19.66 | 6.55 | 18.0 | 1 | 0 |
| Twenty20 | 9 | 168 | 239 | 9 | 3/27 | 3/27 | 26.55 | 8.53 | 18.6 | 0 | 0 |

# NIALL O'BRIEN

## LHB LB WK R0 W0 MVP77

FULL NAME: Niall John O'Brien
BORN: November 8, 1981, Dublin
SQUAD NO: 81
HEIGHT: 5ft 8in
NICKNAME: Nobi, Solano, Pebs
EDUCATION: Marian College
TEAMS: Ireland, Kent, Leicestershire, Northamptonshire, Rangpur Riders
CAREER: ODI: 2006; T20I: 2008; First-class: 2004; List A: 2003; T20: 2004



BEST BATTING: 182 Northamptonshire vs Glamorgan, Cardiff, 2012
BEST BOWLING: 1-4 Kent v CUCCE, Fenner's, 2006
COUNTY CAPS: 2011 (Northamptonshire)

FAMILY TIES? My dad Ginger captained Ireland, brother Kevin plays for Ireland, sister Ciara played U23 for Ireland, all three elder brothers played first-team club cricket for Railway Union VV in Dublin
CAREER HIGHLIGHTS? Playing in World Cups for Ireland, getting to play cricket all around the world, getting Man of the Match against Pakistan on St Patrick's Day at the World Cup in 2007, being lucky enough to play county cricket and forge friendships with people
CRICKET RULE YOU'D CHANGE? Longer lunch and tea breaks and shorter session times
ACCOMPLISHMENTS? Coming through a tough passage in life and turning things around when it could have gone downhill very quickly
SURPRISING FACT? I was in a Bollywood movie called Unforgettable
TWITTER FEED: @niallnobiobrien

| Batting | Mat | Inns | NO | Runs | HS | Ave | SR | 100 | 50 | Ct | St |
|---|---|---|---|---|---|---|---|---|---|---|---|
| ODIs | 68 | 67 | 8 | 1761 | 80* | 29.84 | 69.22 | 0 | 13 | 43 | 7 |
| T20Is | 21 | 20 | 1 | 362 | 50 | 19.05 | 98.63 | 0 | 1 | 12 | 8 |
| First-class | 141 | 223 | 23 | 7203 | 182 | 36.01 | 55.76 | 14 | 35 | 372 | 40 |
| List A | 184 | 162 | 20 | 4385 | 121 | 30.88 | 77.58 | 3 | 27 | 144 | 33 |
| Twenty20 | 121 | 104 | 12 | 1906 | 84 | 20.71 | 111.39 | 0 | 5 | 63 | 31 |
| **Bowling** | **Mat** | **Balls** | **Runs** | **Wkts** | **BBI** | **BBM** | **Ave** | **Econ** | **SR** | **5w** | **10** |
| ODIs | 68 | - | - | - | - | - | - | - | - | - | - |
| T20Is | 21 | - | - | - | - | - | - | - | - | - | - |
| First-class | 141 | 18 | 19 | 2 | 1/4 | 1/4 | 9.50 | 6.33 | 9.0 | 0 | 0 |
| List A | 184 | - | - | - | - | - | - | - | - | - | - |
| Twenty20 | 121 | - | - | - | - | - | - | - | - | - | - |

## RICHARD OLIVER LHB RM R0 W0

FULL NAME: Richard Kenneth Oliver
BORN: November 14, 1989, Stoke-on-Trent, Staffordshire
SQUAD NO: 43
HEIGHT: 6ft
NICKNAME: Richie No Runs in Australia...
EDUCATION: Grove High School; Wrekin College
TEAMS: Worcestershire, Shropshire
CAREER: First-class: 2014; List A: 2014; T20: 2014

BEST BATTING: 179 Worcestershire v Gloucestershire, New Road, 2014

CAREER HIGHLIGHTS? Promotion to Division One, my debut Championship century, my T20 highest score of 77 v Northants and being captain of Shropshire
MOST MARKED CHARACTERISTIC? Aggressive batsman. Bowler of pies from the Bakery End
CRICKETING HEROES? Brian Lara, Freddie Flintoff, Shahid Afridi, MS Dhoni
NON-CRICKETING HEROES? Darryn Lyons has been an inspiration to me and done a lot for me. He doesn't follow the crowd and gets things done, he's been hugely successful as a businessman and is now Mayor of Geelong
CRICKET RULE YOU'D CHANGE? No early starts – I need all the sleep I can get!
IF YOU WEREN'T A CRICKETER? Probably selling something out the back of my Del Boy three-wheel van
SURPRISING FACT? I live in a holiday caravan by the river in 'Wooster'
FANTASY SLIP CORDON? Keeper: Rodney Rude (Aussie comedian, he is the funniest guy on the planet) 1st: Kenny Powers from Eastbound and Down (lunatic), 2nd: Kevin Purcell (from Geelong and provider of the worst horse racing tips and worst dad jokes I've ever heard), 3rd: Ashley Sodomaco (my right-hand man at the Geelong City Sharks)
TWITTER FEED: @richieoliva

| Batting | Mat | Inns | NO | Runs | HS | Ave | SR | 100 | 50 | Ct | St |
|---|---|---|---|---|---|---|---|---|---|---|---|
| First-class | 7 | 14 | 0 | 558 | 179 | 39.85 | 83.15 | 1 | 4 | 2 | 0 |
| List A | 5 | 5 | 0 | 34 | 14 | 6.80 | 73.91 | 0 | 0 | 1 | 0 |
| Twenty20 | 13 | 13 | 0 | 279 | 77 | 21.46 | 136.09 | 0 | 1 | 2 | 0 |
| **Bowling** | **Mat** | **Balls** | **Runs** | **Wkts** | **BBI** | **BBM** | **Ave** | **Econ** | **SR** | **5w** | **10** |
| First-class | 7 | - | - | - | - | - | - | - | - | - | - |
| List A | 5 | - | - | - | - | - | - | - | - | - | - |
| Twenty20 | 13 | - | - | - | - | - | - | - | - | - | - |

## GRAHAM ONIONS RHB RFM R0 W5

FULL NAME: Graham Onions
BORN: September 9, 1982, Gateshead
SQUAD NO: 9
HEIGHT: 6ft 2in
NICKNAME: Bunny, Wills
EDUCATION: St Thomas More RC School, Blaydon
TEAMS: England, Durham, Dolphins
CAREER: Test: 2009; ODI: 2009; First-class: 2004; List A: 2003; T20: 2004



BEST BATTING: 41 Durham vs Yorkshire, Leeds, 2007
BEST BOWLING: 9-67 Durham vs Nottinghamshire, Nottingham, 2012
BENEFIT YEAR: 2015

FAMILY TIES? My uncle used to play
CAREER HIGHLIGHTS? My Test debut, taking nine wickets against Notts and the Test match against West Indies in 2012 after my serious back injury
MOST MARKED CHARACTERISTIC? My accent
SUPERSTITIONS? I lick my fingers before I bowl
CRICKETING HEROES? Darren Gough, Dale Steyn
IF YOU WEREN'T A CRICKETER? I'd be struggling! Maybe a PE teacher
DESERT ISLAND DISC? T-Spoon – Sex On The Beach
FANTASY SLIP CORDON? Keeper: Daniel Radcliffe, 1st: Russell Crowe, 2nd: Paul Gascoigne, 3rd: David Beckham, Gully: George Best
TWITTER FEED: @BunnyOnions

| Batting | Mat | Inns | NO | Runs | HS | Ave | SR | 100 | 50 | Ct | St |
|---|---|---|---|---|---|---|---|---|---|---|---|
| Tests | 9 | 10 | 7 | 30 | 17* | 10.00 | 30.92 | 0 | 0 | 0 | 0 |
| ODIs | 4 | 1 | 0 | 1 | 1 | 1.00 | 50.00 | 0 | 0 | 1 | 0 |
| First-class | 126 | 162 | 59 | 1415 | 41 | 13.73 | 51.69 | 0 | 0 | 27 | 0 |
| List A | 85 | 31 | 9 | 130 | 19 | 5.90 | 68.78 | 0 | 0 | 12 | 0 |
| Twenty20 | 44 | 13 | 6 | 61 | 31 | 8.71 | 107.01 | 0 | 0 | 10 | 0 |
| **Bowling** | **Mat** | **Balls** | **Runs** | **Wkts** | **BBI** | **BBM** | **Ave** | **Econ** | **SR** | **5w** | **10** |
| Tests | 9 | 1606 | 957 | 32 | 5/38 | 7/102 | 29.90 | 3.57 | 50.1 | 1 | 0 |
| ODIs | 4 | 204 | 185 | 4 | 2/58 | 2/58 | 46.25 | 5.44 | 51.0 | 0 | 0 |
| First-class | 126 | 21328 | 12088 | 459 | 9/67 | | 26.33 | 3.40 | 46.4 | 21 | 3 |
| List A | 85 | 3508 | 2984 | 98 | 4/45 | 4/45 | 30.44 | 5.10 | 35.7 | 0 | 0 |
| Twenty20 | 44 | 936 | 1034 | 35 | 3/15 | 3/15 | 29.54 | 6.62 | 26.7 | 0 | 0 |

# CRAIG OVERTON RHB RFM R0 W0 MVP89

FULL NAME: Craig Overton
BORN: April 10, 1994, Barnstaple, Devon
SQUAD NO: 12
HEIGHT: 6ft 6in
NICKNAME: Goober
EDUCATION: West Buckland School
TEAMS: Somerset
CAREER: First-class: 2012; List A: 2012; T20L 2014

BEST BATTING: 99 Somerset vs Lancashire, Taunton, 2014
BEST BOWLING: 5-63 Somerset vs Durham, Taunton, 2014

FAMILY TIES? My father played Minor County cricket and my twin brother Jamie also plays for Somerset
CAREER HIGHLIGHTS? My first five-fer for Somerset
BEST PLAYER IN COUNTY CRICKET? Marcus Trescothick
TIP FOR THE TOP? Olly Stone, Craig Miles
CRICKETING HEROES? Andrew Flintoff – because that's what I want to be like
NON-CRICKETING HEROES? Rory McIlroy – due to his dedication to golf!
CRICKET RULE YOU'D CHANGE? Hitting the stumps when you're fielding and it still goes for overthrows. You're punishing good fielding
IF YOU COULD BE SOMEONE ELSE FOR A DAY? David Beckham
DESERT ISLAND DISC? Avicii
FAVOURITE TV? Prison Break
SURPRISING FACT? My brother dropped me on my head while we were wrestling when we were younger!
TWITTER FEED: @craigoverton12

| Batting | Mat | Inns | NO | Runs | HS | Ave | SR | 100 | 50 | Ct | St |
|---|---|---|---|---|---|---|---|---|---|---|---|
| First-class | 21 | 26 | 4 | 514 | 99 | 23.36 | 61.48 | 0 | 4 | 7 | 0 |
| List A | 15 | 12 | 1 | 116 | 36 | 10.54 | 102.65 | 0 | 0 | 6 | 0 |
| Twenty20 | 10 | 5 | 1 | 35 | 15 | 8.75 | 87.50 | 0 | 0 | 5 | 0 |
| **Bowling** | **Mat** | **Balls** | **Runs** | **Wkts** | **BBI** | **BBM** | **Ave** | **Econ** | **SR** | **5w** | **10** |
| First-class | 21 | 2888 | 1628 | 55 | 5/63 | 7/150 | 29.60 | 3.38 | 52.5 | 1 | 0 |
| List A | 15 | 642 | 542 | 10 | 2/30 | 2/30 | 54.20 | 5.06 | 64.2 | 0 | 0 |
| Twenty20 | 10 | 144 | 243 | 4 | 1/23 | 1/23 | 60.75 | 10.12 | 36.0 | 0 | 0 |

# JAMIE OVERTON RHB RFM R0 W0

FULL NAME: Jamie Overton
BORN: April 10, 1994, Barnstaple, Devon
SQUAD NO: 11
HEIGHT: 6ft 5in
NICKNAME: Goober, J
EDUCATION: West Buckland School
TEAMS: Somerset, England Lions
CAREER: First-class: 2012; List A: 2012



BEST BATTING: 56 Somerset vs Warwickshire, Birmingham, 2014
BEST BOWLING: 6-95 Somerset vs Middlesex, Taunton, 2013

FAMILY TIES? My dad played for Devon and my twin brother Craig plays for Somerset too
CAREER HIGHLIGHTS? Getting in the England squad against Australia in 2013
BEST PLAYER IN COUNTY CRICKET? Jeetan Patel
TIP FOR THE TOP? Harry Podmore
MOST MARKED CHARACTERISTIC? Being a twin
CRICKETING HEROES? James Anderson – because growing up I felt we bowled in similar ways
NON-CRICKETING HEROES? Muhammad Ali – because he was just a genius. Rory McIlroy – he makes it look so easy
CRICKET RULE YOU'D CHANGE? Allow more fielders outside the ring in the Powerplay
COACHING TIP? To stay tall at the crease when releasing the ball
IF YOU COULD BE SOMEONE ELSE FOR A DAY? Rory McIlroy
DESERT ISLAND DISC? MKTO
SURPRISING FACT? I was in a film when I was younger
TWITTER FEED: @JamieOverton

| Batting | Mat | Inns | NO | Runs | HS | Ave | SR | 100 | 50 | Ct | St |
|---|---|---|---|---|---|---|---|---|---|---|---|
| First-class | 24 | 33 | 11 | 352 | 56 | 16.00 | 84.61 | 0 | 2 | 1 | 0 |
| List A | 14 | 7 | 4 | 47 | 14 | 15.66 | 95.91 | 0 | 0 | 6 | 0 |
| **Bowling** | **Mat** | **Balls** | **Runs** | **Wkts** | **BBI** | **BBM** | **Ave** | **Econ** | **SR** | **5w** | **10** |
| First-class | 24 | 3269 | 2198 | 52 | 6/95 | 7/134 | 42.26 | 4.03 | 62.8 | 1 | 0 |
| List A | 14 | 516 | 540 | 20 | 4/42 | 4/42 | 27.00 | 6.27 | 25.8 | 0 | 0 |

# WILL OWEN

RHB RFM R0 W0

FULL NAME: William Thomas Owen
BORN: September 2, 1988, St Asaph, Flintshire
SQUAD NO: 34
HEIGHT: 6ft
NICKNAME: Swillo
EDUCATION: Prestatyn High School
TEAMS: Glamorgan
CAREER: First-class: 2007; List A: 2010; T20: 2010

BEST BATTING: 69 Glamorgan vs Derbyshire, Derby, 2011
BEST BOWLING: 5-124 Glamorgan vs Middlesex, Cardiff, 2011

CAREER HIGHLIGHTS? Claiming a five-wicket haul on one-day debut against the Unicorns and scoring my maiden first-class fifty against Derby in 2011
CRICKETING HEROES? Simon Jones, being a Welsh lad growing up watching the 2005 Ashes series
IF YOU WEREN'T A CRICKETER? Policeman
FAVOURITE TV? Eastbound And Down
FANTASY SLIP CORDON? Keeper: Will Bragg, 1st: Ricky Gervais, 2nd: Michael McIntyre, Gully: Darren Hughes
TWITTER FEED: @swillo88

| Batting | Mat | Inns | NO | Runs | HS | Ave | SR | 100 | 50 | Ct | St |
|---|---|---|---|---|---|---|---|---|---|---|---|
| First-class | 24 | 28 | 9 | 363 | 69 | 19.10 | 68.88 | 0 | 1 | 6 | 0 |
| List A | 25 | 13 | 7 | 78 | 13* | 13.00 | 91.76 | 0 | 0 | 6 | 0 |
| Twenty20 | 23 | 1 | 0 | 8 | 8 | 8.00 | 114.28 | 0 | 0 | 2 | 0 |
| **Bowling** | **Mat** | **Balls** | **Runs** | **Wkts** | **BBI** | **BBM** | **Ave** | **Econ** | **SR** | **5w** | **10** |
| First-class | 24 | 3136 | 2241 | 51 | 5/124 | 6/61 | 43.94 | 4.28 | 61.4 | 1 | 0 |
| List A | 25 | 771 | 782 | 37 | 5/49 | 5/49 | 21.13 | 6.08 | 20.8 | 1 | 0 |
| Twenty20 | 23 | 360 | 580 | 17 | 3/21 | 3/21 | 34.11 | 9.66 | 21.1 | 0 | 0 |

# TONY PALLADINO RHB RMF R0 W2 MVP81

FULL NAME: Antonio Paul Palladino
BORN: June 29, 1983, London
SQUAD NO: 28
HEIGHT: 5ft 11in
NICKNAME: Dino, Italian Stallion, Pallas
EDUCATION: Cardinal Pole Sixth Form; Anglia Polytechnic University
TEAMS: Namibia, Derbyshire, Essex
CAREER: First-class: 2003; List A: 2003; T20: 2005



BEST BATTING: 106 Derbyshire vs Australia A, Derby, 2012
BEST BOWLING: 7-53 Derbyshire vs Kent, Derby, 2012
COUNTY CAPS: 2012 (Derbyshire)

CAREER HIGHLIGHTS? Taking a hat-trick vs Leicestershire, my first-class hundred vs Australia A, taking 7-53 vs Kent and winning Division Two of the County Championship with Derbyshire
SUPERSTITIONS? I wear black socks, wear my watch on my right wrist and have a sweatband on the left
CRICKETING HEROES? Ian Botham, Graeme Welch, Mark Turner and Tim Groenwald
CRICKET RULE YOU'D CHANGE? Allow the use of sweets to shine the ball. It's been going on forever but now they've decided to get strict on it
DESERT ISLAND DISC? Edvard Grieg – In The Hall of the Mountain King
FAVOURITE TV? Star Trek
SURPRISING FACT? I have English, Irish, Scottish and Italian heritage
FANTASY SLIP CORDON? Keeper: David Brent (funny), 1st: Patrick Stewart (legend), 2nd: Christian Bale (favourite actor), 3rd: John Terry (hero)
TWITTER FEED: @TonyPalladino28

| Batting | Mat | Inns | NO | Runs | HS | Ave | SR | 100 | 50 | Ct | St |
|---|---|---|---|---|---|---|---|---|---|---|---|
| First-class | 105 | 145 | 31 | 1780 | 106 | 15.61 | 49.15 | 1 | 6 | 30 | 0 |
| List A | 52 | 30 | 7 | 251 | 31 | 10.91 | 90.94 | 0 | 0 | 5 | 0 |
| Twenty20 | 23 | 11 | 5 | 43 | 14* | 7.16 | 79.62 | 0 | 0 | 5 | 0 |
| **Bowling** | **Mat** | **Balls** | **Runs** | **Wkts** | **BBI** | **BBM** | **Ave** | **Econ** | **SR** | **5w** | **10** |
| First-class | 105 | 16713 | 8480 | 290 | 7/53 | | 29.24 | 3.04 | 57.6 | 11 | 0 |
| List A | 52 | 2033 | 1801 | 54 | 5/49 | 5/49 | 33.35 | 5.31 | 37.6 | 1 | 0 |
| Twenty20 | 23 | 418 | 525 | 24 | 4/21 | 4/21 | 21.87 | 7.53 | 17.4 | 0 | 0 |

# MONTY PANESAR LHB SLA R0 W6

FULL NAME: Mudhsuden Singh Panesar
BORN: April 25, 1982, Luton, Bedfordshire
SQUAD NO: 77
HEIGHT: 6ft 1in
EDUCATION: Bedford Modern School, Stopsley High School, Luton, Bedfordshire; Loughborough University
TEAMS: England, Essex, Northamptonshire, Sussex
CAREER: Test: 2006; ODI: 2007; T20I: 2007; First-class: 2001; List A: 2002; T20: 2006

BEST BATTING: 46* Sussex vs Middlesex, Hove, 2010
BEST BOWLING: 7-60 Sussex vs Somerset, Taunton, 2012
COUNTY CAPS: 2006 (Northamptonshire); 2010 (Sussex)

TWITTER FEED: @MontyPanesar
NOTES: Claimed a five-wicket haul in his first Ashes Test, at Perth in 2006. Helped secure an improbable draw in the first Ashes Test at Cardiff in 2009, batting with James Anderson for 37 minutes. Moved to Sussex after 10 years at Northamptonshire ahead of the 2010 season and took 200 first-class wickets at 27.37 in his four years with the club. Took 14 wickets in two matches against Pakistan in UAE on his return to England's Test side in January 2012. A member of the Ashes squad in the winter of 2013/14, he featured in the defeats at Adelaide and Melbourne. Having spent time on loan at Essex in 2013, Panesar signed a two-year deal with the club in October of 2013 but found himself in and out of the side last season

| Batting | Mat | Inns | NO | Runs | HS | Ave | SR | 100 | 50 | Ct | St |
|---|---|---|---|---|---|---|---|---|---|---|---|
| Tests | 50 | 68 | 23 | 220 | 26 | 4.88 | 29.37 | 0 | 0 | 10 | 0 |
| ODIs | 26 | 8 | 3 | 26 | 13 | 5.20 | 28.57 | 0 | 0 | 3 | 0 |
| T20Is | 1 | 1 | 0 | 1 | 1 | 1.00 | 50.00 | 0 | 0 | 0 | 0 |
| First-class | 213 | 263 | 83 | 1484 | 46* | 8.24 | 35.24 | 0 | 0 | 41 | 0 |
| List A | 85 | 29 | 13 | 141 | 17* | 8.81 | 56.17 | 0 | 0 | 15 | 0 |
| Twenty20 | 33 | 7 | 2 | 7 | 3* | 1.40 | 46.66 | 0 | 0 | 3 | 0 |
| **Bowling** | **Mat** | **Balls** | **Runs** | **Wkts** | **BBI** | **BBM** | **Ave** | **Econ** | **SR** | **5w** | **10** |
| Tests | 50 | 12475 | 5797 | 167 | 6/37 | 11/210 | 34.71 | 2.78 | 74.7 | 12 | 2 |
| ODIs | 26 | 1308 | 980 | 24 | 3/25 | 3/25 | 40.83 | 4.49 | 54.5 | 0 | 0 |
| T20Is | 1 | 24 | 40 | 2 | 2/40 | 2/40 | 20.00 | 10.00 | 12.0 | 0 | 0 |
| First-class | 213 | 47070 | 21440 | 697 | 7/60 | | 30.76 | 2.73 | 67.5 | 39 | 6 |
| List A | 85 | 3725 | 2892 | 83 | 5/20 | 5/20 | 34.84 | 4.65 | 44.8 | 1 | 0 |
| Twenty20 | 33 | 648 | 816 | 27 | 3/14 | 3/14 | 30.22 | 7.55 | 24.0 | 0 | 0 |

# MATTHEW PARKINSON RHB LB R0 W0

FULL NAME: Matthew William Parkinson
BORN: October 24, 1996, Bolton, Lancashire
SQUAD NO: 28
HEIGHT: 5ft 9in
NICKNAME: Parky
EDUCATION: Canon Slade; Bolton
TEAMS: Lancashire 2nd XI, Staffordshire
CAREER: Yet to make first-team debut



---

FAMILY TIES? My brother has signed for the academy at Derbyshire CCC and my dad played for the Lancashire Federation U19
CAREER HIGHLIGHTS? Winning the Minor Counties Championship with Staffordshire, representing England U17 and winning Man of the Series against Pakistan
BEST PLAYER IN COUNTY CRICKET? Adil Rashid
TIP FOR THE TOP? Haseeb Hameed of Lancashire and Ryan Davies of Kent
MOST MARKED CHARACTERISTIC? Very loud
CRICKETING HEROES? Shane Warne – obviously his 708 Test wickets is just something else and his presence on the field was immense. Currently I look up to Adil Rashid – the way he contributes with bat and ball
CRICKET RULE YOU'D CHANGE? No free hits for a no-ball
IF YOU COULD BE SOMEONE ELSE FOR A DAY? Gareth Bale – he rips it up at Real Madrid
FAVOURITE TV? Peaky Blinders
LEAST FAVOURITE TV? Antiques Roadshow
PET HATE? Ignorance – it really irks me if someone is blatantly rude
SURPRISING FACT? I have an identical twin who is on the books at Derbyshire
FANTASY SLIP CORDON? Keeper: James Corden (purely for the comedy value he would provide), 1st: Michelle Keegan (absolute worldie!), 2nd: Barack Obama (be interesting to pick his brain), 3rd: myself! Gully: David Beckham (absolute legend)
TWITTER FEED: @mattyparky96

## STEPHEN PARRY

## RHB SLA R0 W0

FULL NAME: Stephen David Parry
BORN: January 12, 1986, Manchester
SQUAD NO: 4
HEIGHT: 6ft
NICKNAME: Pazza
EDUCATION: Audenshaw High School
TEAMS: England, Lancashire
CAREER: ODI: 2014; T20I: 2014; First-class: 2007; List A: 2009; T20: 2009

BEST BATTING: 37 Lancashire vs Durham, Manchester, 2014
BEST BOWLING: 5-23 Lancashire vs DUCCE, Durham University, 2007

CAREER HIGHLIGHTS? Playing for Lancashire and England
CRICKETING HEROES? Shane Warne
NON-CRICKETING HEROES? Muhammad Ali
IF YOU WEREN'T A CRICKETER? Fishing or travelling the world
FAVOURITE TV? Sky Sports News
ACCOMPLISHMENTS? Running a marathon
SURPRISING FACT? Elite table-tennis player
TWITTER FEED: @SDParry86

| Batting | Mat | Inns | NO | Runs | HS | Ave | SR | 100 | 50 | Ct | St |
|---|---|---|---|---|---|---|---|---|---|---|---|
| ODIs | 2 | - | - | - | - | - | - | - | - | 0 | 0 |
| T20Is | 3 | 1 | 0 | 1 | 1 | 1.00 | 100.00 | 0 | 0 | 2 | 0 |
| First-class | 9 | 10 | 1 | 138 | 37 | 15.33 | 50.36 | 0 | 0 | 2 | 0 |
| List A | 65 | 27 | 11 | 223 | 31 | 13.93 | 79.35 | 0 | 0 | 18 | 0 |
| Twenty20 | 76 | 21 | 14 | 72 | 11 | 10.28 | 102.85 | 0 | 0 | 18 | 0 |
| **Bowling** | **Mat** | **Balls** | **Runs** | **Wkts** | **BBI** | **BBM** | **Ave** | **Econ** | **SR** | **5w** | **10** |
| ODIs | 2 | 114 | 92 | 4 | 3/32 | 3/32 | 23.00 | 4.84 | 28.5 | 0 | 0 |
| T20Is | 3 | 48 | 72 | 0 | - | - | - | 9.00 | - | 0 | 0 |
| First-class | 9 | 1276 | 650 | 18 | 5/23 | 5/46 | 36.11 | 3.05 | 70.8 | 1 | 0 |
| List A | 65 | 2794 | 2322 | 83 | 5/17 | 5/17 | 27.97 | 4.98 | 33.6 | 1 | 0 |
| Twenty20 | 76 | 1608 | 1896 | 73 | 4/23 | 4/23 | 25.97 | 7.07 | 22.0 | 0 | 0 |

# JEETAN PATEL RHB OB R0 W3 MVP1

FULL NAME: Jeetan Shashi Patel
BORN: May 7, 1980, Wellington, New Zealand
SQUAD NO: 5
TEAMS: New Zealand, Warwickshire, Wellington
CAREER: Test: 2006; ODI: 2005; T20I: 2005; First-class: 1999; List A: 1999; T20: 2005



BEST BATTING: 120 Warwickshire vs Yorkshire, Birmingham, 2014
BEST BOWLING: 7-75 Warwickshire vs Somerset, Taunton, 2012
COUNTY CAPS: 2012

NOTES: Took 5-145 on debut for Wellington against Auckland in 1999/00. Made New Zealand Test debut in Cape Town against South Africa in April 2006 and took 3-117 in 42 overs, dismissing Graeme Smith, Boeta Dippenaar and AB de Villiers. Took Test-best figures of 5-110 against West Indies in Napier in 2008. This will be his sixth season at Warwickshire. Last season he topped the MVP Rankings and took the most wickets in both the RL Cup and the T20 Blast, with over 100 across all three formats

| Batting | Mat | Inns | NO | Runs | HS | Ave | SR | 100 | 50 | Ct | St |
|---|---|---|---|---|---|---|---|---|---|---|---|
| Tests | 19 | 30 | 7 | 276 | 27* | 12.00 | 46.46 | 0 | 0 | 12 | 0 |
| ODIs | 39 | 13 | 7 | 88 | 34 | 14.66 | 58.66 | 0 | 0 | 12 | 0 |
| T20Is | 11 | 4 | 1 | 9 | 5 | 3.00 | 64.28 | 0 | 0 | 4 | 0 |
| First-class | 181 | 226 | 58 | 3871 | 120 | 23.04 | | 2 | 20 | 86 | 0 |
| List A | 163 | 87 | 29 | 578 | 50 | 9.96 | | 0 | 1 | 63 | 0 |
| Twenty20 | 121 | 41 | 12 | 178 | 34* | 6.13 | 125.35 | 0 | 0 | 38 | 0 |
| **Bowling** | **Mat** | **Balls** | **Runs** | **Wkts** | **BBI** | **BBM** | **Ave** | **Econ** | **SR** | **5w** | **10** |
| Tests | 19 | 4723 | 2520 | 52 | 5/110 | 6/151 | 48.46 | 3.20 | 90.8 | 1 | 0 |
| ODIs | 39 | 1804 | 1513 | 42 | 3/11 | 3/11 | 36.02 | 5.03 | 42.9 | 0 | 0 |
| T20Is | 11 | 199 | 269 | 16 | 3/20 | 3/20 | 16.81 | 8.11 | 12.4 | 0 | 0 |
| First-class | 181 | 36035 | 17735 | 477 | 7/75 | | 37.18 | 2.95 | 75.5 | 16 | 1 |
| List A | 163 | 7744 | 5948 | 191 | 4/16 | 4/16 | 31.14 | 4.60 | 40.5 | 0 | 0 |
| Twenty20 | 121 | 2325 | 2699 | 125 | 4/11 | 4/11 | 21.59 | 6.96 | 18.6 | 0 | 0 |

## RAVI PATEL RHB SLA R0 W0

FULL NAME: Ravi Hasmukh Patel
BORN: August 4, 1991, Harrow, Middlesex
SQUAD NO: 36
HEIGHT: 5ft 9in
NICKNAME: Rav, Ravster
EDUCATION: Merchant Taylors School; Loughborough University
TEAMS: Middlesex, England Lions
CAREER: First-class: 2010; List A: 2010; T20: 2013

BEST BATTING: 26* Middlesex vs Warwickshire, Uxbridge, 2013
BEST BOWLING: 5-69 Middlesex vs CMCCU, Fenner's, 2013

FAMILY TIES? Dad played university cricket in India
CAREER HIGHLIGHTS? Making my debut for England Lions in 2014. Playing against India and getting Virat Kohli out at Lord's in 2014
BEST PLAYER IN COUNTY CRICKET? Sam Robson
TIP FOR THE TOP? Ryan Higgins and Gurjit Sandhu
CRICKETING HEROES? Pragyan Ojha – I love his action and try to bowl like him. Rahul Dravid – I used to love watching him bat
NON-CRICKETING HEROES? Cristiano Ronaldo as he always strives to be the best and I love watching him play football. Also my dad for getting me into cricket when I was young
CRICKET RULE YOU'D CHANGE? Tea changes to 30 minutes from 20. Never long enough
COACHING TIP? Keep it simple. Don't overcomplicate things
IF YOU WEREN'T A CRICKETER? I'd help run my dad's property business
IF YOU COULD BE SOMEONE ELSE FOR A DAY? Kanye West
FAVOURITE TV? Prison Break
TWITTER FEED: @ravi36patel

| Batting | Mat | Inns | NO | Runs | HS | Ave | SR | 100 | 50 | Ct | St |
|---|---|---|---|---|---|---|---|---|---|---|---|
| First-class | 18 | 23 | 11 | 162 | 26* | 13.50 | 39.51 | 0 | 0 | 5 | 0 |
| List A | 10 | 2 | 1 | 0 | 0* | 0.00 | 0.00 | 0 | 0 | 1 | 0 |
| Twenty20 | 22 | 4 | 2 | 3 | 1* | 1.50 | 50.00 | 0 | 0 | 3 | 0 |
| **Bowling** | **Mat** | **Balls** | **Runs** | **Wkts** | **BBI** | **BBM** | **Ave** | **Econ** | **SR** | **5w** | **10** |
| First-class | 18 | 3386 | 1766 | 50 | 5/69 | 8/198 | 35.32 | 3.12 | 67.7 | 1 | 0 |
| List A | 10 | 522 | 489 | 11 | 3/71 | 3/71 | 44.45 | 5.62 | 47.4 | 0 | 0 |
| Twenty20 | 22 | 486 | 522 | 28 | 4/18 | 4/18 | 18.64 | 6.44 | 17.3 | 0 | 0 |

# SAMIT PATEL RHB SLA R3 W0 MVP4

FULL NAME: Samit Rohit Patel
BORN: November 30, 1984, Leicester
SQUAD NO: 21
HEIGHT: 5ft 8in
NICKNAME: Sarnie, Slippery
EDUCATION: Worksop College
TEAMS: England, Nottinghamshire
CAREER: Test: 2012; ODI: 2008; T20I: 2011; First-class: 2002; List A: 2002; T20: 2003



BEST BATTING: 256 Nottinghamshire vs Durham MCCU, Nottingham, 2013
BEST BOWLING: 7-68 Nottinghamshire vs Hampshire, Southampton, 2011
COUNTY CAPS: 2008

FAMILY TIES? My dad played league cricket, my brother Akhil played for Notts for two years
CAREER HIGHLIGHTS? Making my ODI and Test debuts. Taking five wickets against South Africa at The Oval and scoring 70 off 40 balls at Chandigarh against India. Scoring 68 against Sri Lanka in the World T20
SUPERSTITIONS? I always put my right pad on first and always touch the floor before I cross the line as I am walking out to bat
CRICKETING HEROES? Sachin Tendulkar, Stephen Fleming
DESERT ISLAND DISC? Chesney Hawkes – I Am The One And Only
FAVOURITE TV? Fawlty Towers, Only Fools And Horses

| Batting | Mat | Inns | NO | Runs | HS | Ave | SR | 100 | 50 | Ct | St |
|---|---|---|---|---|---|---|---|---|---|---|---|
| Tests | 5 | 7 | 0 | 109 | 33 | 15.57 | 42.41 | 0 | 0 | 2 | 0 |
| ODIs | 36 | 22 | 7 | 482 | 70* | 32.13 | 93.23 | 0 | 1 | 7 | 0 |
| T20Is | 18 | 14 | 2 | 189 | 67 | 15.75 | 109.24 | 0 | 1 | 3 | 0 |
| First-class | 147 | 235 | 14 | 8610 | 256 | 38.95 | 63.88 | 20 | 42 | 98 | 0 |
| List A | 198 | 172 | 27 | 4800 | 129* | 33.10 | 83.59 | 3 | 27 | 58 | 0 |
| Twenty20 | 142 | 127 | 21 | 2667 | 84* | 25.16 | 124.50 | 0 | 17 | 40 | 0 |
| **Bowling** | **Mat** | **Balls** | **Runs** | **Wkts** | **BBI** | **BBM** | **Ave** | **Econ** | **SR** | **5w** | **10** |
| Tests | 5 | 606 | 257 | 4 | 2/27 | 2/36 | 64.25 | 2.54 | 151.5 | 0 | 0 |
| ODIs | 36 | 1187 | 1091 | 24 | 5/41 | 5/41 | 45.45 | 5.51 | 49.4 | 1 | 0 |
| T20Is | 18 | 252 | 321 | 7 | 2/6 | 2/6 | 45.85 | 7.64 | 36.0 | 0 | 0 |
| First-class | 147 | 16672 | 8579 | 208 | 7/68 | | 41.24 | 3.08 | 80.1 | 3 | 1 |
| List A | 198 | 6337 | 5570 | 179 | 6/13 | 6/13 | 31.11 | 5.27 | 35.4 | 2 | 0 |
| Twenty20 | 142 | 2538 | 3071 | 113 | 3/11 | 3/11 | 27.17 | 7.26 | 22.4 | 0 | 0 |

## STEVEN PATTERSON RHB RMF R0 W2 MVP98

FULL NAME: Steven Andrew Patterson
BORN: October 3, 1983, Beverley Westwood Hospital
SQUAD NO: 17
HEIGHT: 6ft 4in
NICKNAME: Dead Man, Patto
EDUCATION: Malet Lambert School; St Mary's Sixth Form College; Leeds University
TEAMS: Yorkshire
CAREER: First-class: 2005; List A: 2003; T20: 2009

---

BEST BATTING: 53 Yorkshire vs Sussex, Hove, 2011
BEST BOWLING: 5-43 Yorkshire vs Nottinghamshire, Nottingham, 2013
COUNTY CAPS: 2012

---

FAMILY TIES? My grandad played for Durham before World War II
CAREER HIGHLIGHTS? Making my Championship debut at Scarborough, receiving my 1st XI cap, playing in the Champions League T20, winning the Championship
CRICKETING HEROES? Glenn McGrath, Shaun Pollock
NON-CRICKETING HEROES? My grandad
CRICKET RULE YOU'D CHANGE? Fewer overs in a day!
IF YOU WEREN'T A CRICKETER? Finance
FAVOURITE TV? Gold Rush
ACCOMPLISHMENTS? Having my son
FANTASY SLIP CORDON? Keeper: Morgan Freeman, 1st: Tiger Woods, 2nd: Me, 3rd: Prince Harry, Gully: Alex Ferguson

| Batting | Mat | Inns | NO | Runs | HS | Ave | SR | 100 | 50 | Ct | St |
|---|---|---|---|---|---|---|---|---|---|---|---|
| First-class | 89 | 97 | 30 | 990 | 53 | 14.77 | 33.51 | 0 | 1 | 14 | 0 |
| List A | 59 | 23 | 16 | 137 | 25* | 19.57 | | 0 | 0 | 8 | 0 |
| Twenty20 | 27 | 5 | 3 | 5 | 3* | 2.50 | 50.00 | 0 | 0 | 4 | 0 |
| **Bowling** | **Mat** | **Balls** | **Runs** | **Wkts** | **BBI** | **BBM** | **Ave** | **Econ** | **SR** | **5w** | **10** |
| First-class | 89 | 13653 | 6510 | 231 | 5/43 | 8/94 | 28.18 | 2.86 | 59.1 | 3 | 0 |
| List A | 59 | 2571 | 2163 | 74 | 6/32 | 6/32 | 29.22 | 5.04 | 34.7 | 1 | 0 |
| Twenty20 | 27 | 563 | 801 | 26 | 4/30 | 4/30 | 30.80 | 8.53 | 21.6 | 0 | 0 |

# DAVID PAYNE

RHB LFM R0 W0

FULL NAME: David Alan Payne
BORN: February 15, 1991, Poole, Dorset
SQUAD NO: 14
HEIGHT: 6ft 2in
NICKNAME: Sid, Payney, Flash Payne
EDUCATION: Lytchett Minster Secondary and Sixth Form
TEAMS: Gloucestershire
CAREER: First-class: 2011; List A: 2009; T20: 2010



BEST BATTING: 62 Gloucestershire vs Glamorgan, Bristol, 2011
BEST BOWLING: 6-26 Gloucestershire vs Leicestershire, Bristol, 2011
COUNTY CAPS: 2011

CAREER HIGHLIGHTS? Holding the record for the best one-day figures at the club of 7-23, taking a six-wicket haul on Championship debut and taking five wickets in quarter-finals of RL Cup
BEST PLAYER IN COUNTY CRICKET? James Taylor
MOST MARKED CHARACTERISTIC? Hole in my chest and flash personality
CRICKETING HEROES? Freddie Flintoff – for his personality in performances. Will Gidman – for being an all-round legend and idol
CRICKET RULE YOU'D CHANGE? Fewer Championship games and a shorter, less congested season
IF YOU WEREN'T A CRICKETER? Something in style or design
ACCOMPLISHMENTS? Being on AFC Bournemouth's academy
PET HATE? Arrogance, don't see a need for it. And it is different to confidence
SURPRISING FACT? I got a Tic Tac stuck up my nose when I was young
TWITTER FEED: @sidpayne7

| Batting | Mat | Inns | NO | Runs | HS | Ave | SR | 100 | 50 | Ct | St |
|---|---|---|---|---|---|---|---|---|---|---|---|
| First-class | 40 | 51 | 16 | 572 | 62 | 16.34 | 44.27 | 0 | 2 | 12 | 0 |
| List A | 44 | 18 | 13 | 70 | 18 | 14.00 | 75.26 | 0 | 0 | 10 | 0 |
| Twenty20 | 32 | 12 | 6 | 30 | 10 | 5.00 | 96.77 | 0 | 0 | 5 | 0 |
| **Bowling** | **Mat** | **Balls** | **Runs** | **Wkts** | **BBI** | **BBM** | **Ave** | **Econ** | **SR** | **5w** | **10** |
| First-class | 40 | 5802 | 3350 | 93 | 6/26 | 9/96 | 36.02 | 3.46 | 62.3 | 2 | 0 |
| List A | 44 | 1754 | 1661 | 81 | 7/29 | 7/29 | 20.50 | 5.68 | 21.6 | 2 | 0 |
| Twenty20 | 32 | 579 | 821 | 35 | 3/17 | 3/17 | 23.45 | 8.50 | 16.5 | 0 | 0 |

## STEPHEN PETERS RHB LB R4 W0

FULL NAME: Stephen David Peters
BORN: December 10, 1978, Harold Wood, Essex
SQUAD NO: 11
HEIGHT: 5ft 11in
NICKNAME: Pedro, Geezer
EDUCATION: The Coopers' Company and Coborn School
TEAMS: Northamptonshire, Essex, Worcestershire
CAREER: First-class: 1996; List A: 1996; T20: 2003

BEST BATTING: 222 Northamptonshire vs Glamorgan, Swansea, 2011
BEST BOWLING: 1-19 Essex vs Oxford UCCE, Chelmsford, 1999
COUNTY CAPS: 2002 (Worcestershire); 2007 (Northamptonshire); BENEFIT YEAR: 2013 (Northamptonshire)

CAREER HIGHLIGHTS? Winning the U19 World Cup with England in 1998, winning the B&H Cup with Essex in 1998, promotion in the Championship and winning the T20 Cup in 2013
BEST PLAYER IN COUNTY CRICKET? Moeen Ali
MOST MARKED CHARACTERISTIC? Banter!
SUPERSTITIONS? Nope – binned them all years ago
NON-CRICKETING HEROES? Paolo Di Canio
COACHING TIP? Get right forward and go right back
IF YOU COULD BE SOMEONE ELSE FOR A DAY? Rory McIlroy
DESERT ISLAND DISC? Nickelback
LEAST FAVOURITE TV? Hollyoaks (shocking acting)
ACCOMPLISHMENTS? Friendships and my lawn!
SURPRISING FACT? I'm a serious chocoholic
TWITTER FEED: @pedropeters222

| Batting | Mat | Inns | NO | Runs | HS | Ave | SR | 100 | 50 | Ct | St |
|---|---|---|---|---|---|---|---|---|---|---|---|
| First-class | 250 | 423 | 32 | 13767 | 222 | 35.20 | | 31 | 67 | 188 | 0 |
| List A | 177 | 163 | 11 | 3444 | 107 | 22.65 | | 2 | 21 | 48 | 0 |
| Twenty20 | 24 | 20 | 3 | 300 | 61* | 17.64 | 98.36 | 0 | 1 | 7 | 0 |
| **Bowling** | **Mat** | **Balls** | **Runs** | **Wkts** | **BBI** | **BBM** | **Ave** | **Econ** | **SR** | **5w** | **10** |
| First-class | 250 | 35 | 31 | 1 | 1/19 | | 31.00 | 5.31 | 35.0 | 0 | 0 |
| List A | 177 | - | - | - | - | - | - | - | - | - | - |
| Twenty20 | 24 | - | - | - | - | - | - | - | - | - | - |

# MARK PETTINI RHB RM R1 W0

FULL NAME: Mark Lewis Pettini
BORN: August 7, 1983, Brighton
SQUAD NO: 24
HEIGHT: 5ft 11in
NICKNAME: Swampy
EDUCATION: Comberton Village College; Hills Road Sixth Form College; Cardiff University
TEAMS: Essex, Mountaineers
CAREER: First-class: 2001; List A: 2001; T20: 2003



BEST BATTING: 208* Essex vs Derbyshire, Chelmsford, 2006
BEST BOWLING: 1-72 Essex vs Leicestershire, Leicester, 2012
COUNTY CAPS: 2006

CAREER HIGHLIGHTS? Winning two Pro40 titles with Essex, being made Essex captain in 2007 and winning the Friends Provident Trophy in 2008
CRICKETING HEROES? Graham Gooch, Andy Flower, Ronnie Irani
DESERT ISLAND DISC? The White Stripes, Foo Fighters, Editors
NOTES: Scored 208* against Derbyshire in 2006. Made England's inaugural 30-man squad for the 2007 World T20, the same month he replaced Ronnie Irani as Essex captain. Led Essex to victory in the 2008 FP Trophy final

| Batting | Mat | Inns | NO | Runs | HS | Ave | SR | 100 | 50 | Ct | St |
|---|---|---|---|---|---|---|---|---|---|---|---|
| First-class | 148 | 248 | 36 | 7532 | 209 | 35.52 | 47.56 | 10 | 45 | 109 | 0 |
| List A | 165 | 153 | 11 | 4039 | 144 | 28.44 | 84.37 | 7 | 25 | 64 | 0 |
| Twenty20 | 110 | 106 | 8 | 2645 | 95* | 26.98 | 128.27 | 0 | 15 | 35 | 0 |
| **Bowling** | **Mat** | **Balls** | **Runs** | **Wkts** | **BBI** | **BBM** | **Ave** | **Econ** | **SR** | **5w** | **10** |
| First-class | 148 | 132 | 263 | 1 | 1/72 | 1/72 | 263.00 | 11.95 | 132.0 | 0 | 0 |
| List A | 165 | - | - | - | - | - | - | - | - | - | - |
| Twenty20 | 110 | - | - | - | - | - | - | - | - | - | - |

# VERNON PHILANDER

RHB RFM R0 W0

FULL NAME: Vernon Darryl Philander
BORN: June 24, 1985, Bellville, South Africa
SQUAD NO: tbc
TEAMS: South Africa, Nottinghamshire, Cape Cobras, Devon, Jamaica Tallawahs, Kent, Middlesex, Somerset
CAREER: Test: 2011; ODI: 2007; T20I: 2007; First-class: 2004; List A: 2004; T20: 2014

BEST BATTING: 168 Western Province vs Griqualand West, Kimberley, 2004
BEST BOWLING: 7-61 Cape Cobras vs Knights, Cape Town, 2012

TWITTER FEED: @VDP_24
NOTES: South Africa's Philander has signed up for six County Championship and three T20 Blast matches this season. He has already had stints in county cricket with Kent, Middlesex and Somerset, taking 33 wickets in the Championship. Philander made his Test debut in 2011, reaching 50 wickets in seven matches – the second-fastest in history. On Test debut he took 5-15 in the second innings against Australia to help bowl South Africa to a win at Cape Town. Philander has two first-class centuries

| Batting | Mat | Inns | NO | Runs | HS | Ave | SR | 100 | 50 | Ct | St |
|---|---|---|---|---|---|---|---|---|---|---|---|
| Tests | 29 | 36 | 10 | 697 | 74 | 26.80 | 43.80 | 0 | 4 | 8 | 0 |
| ODIs | 26 | 16 | 4 | 111 | 23 | 9.25 | 70.25 | 0 | 0 | 6 | 0 |
| T20Is | 7 | 4 | 0 | 14 | 6 | 3.50 | 50.00 | 0 | 0 | 1 | 0 |
| First-class | 112 | 145 | 26 | 3098 | 168 | 26.03 | 46.57 | 2 | 10 | 29 | 0 |
| List A | 116 | 79 | 23 | 1217 | 79* | 21.73 | 73.35 | 0 | 4 | 11 | 0 |
| Twenty20 | 92 | 63 | 33 | 795 | 56* | 26.50 | 134.97 | 0 | 1 | 21 | 0 |
| **Bowling** | **Mat** | **Balls** | **Runs** | **Wkts** | **BBI** | **BBM** | **Ave** | **Econ** | **SR** | **5w** | **10** |
| Tests | 29 | 5717 | 2657 | 121 | 6/44 | 10/102 | 21.95 | 2.78 | 47.2 | 9 | 2 |
| ODIs | 26 | 1084 | 828 | 37 | 4/12 | 4/12 | 22.37 | 4.58 | 29.2 | 0 | 0 |
| T20Is | 7 | 83 | 114 | 4 | 2/23 | 2/23 | 28.50 | 8.24 | 20.7 | 0 | 0 |
| First-class | 112 | 20053 | 8855 | 414 | 7/61 |  | 21.38 | 2.64 | 48.4 | 20 | 2 |
| List A | 116 | 4798 | 3761 | 119 | 4/12 | 4/12 | 31.60 | 4.70 | 40.3 | 0 | 0 |
| Twenty20 | 92 | 1621 | 2123 | 73 | 5/17 | 5/17 | 29.08 | 7.85 | 22.2 | 1 | 0 |

# NEIL PINNER

RHB OB R0 W0

FULL NAME: Neil Douglas Pinner
BORN: September 28, 1990, Wordsley, Stourbridge, Worcestershire
SQUAD NO: 9
HEIGHT: 6ft
NICKNAME: Pins
EDUCATION: RGS Worcester
TEAMS: Worcestershire
CAREER: First-class: 2011; List A: 2011



BEST BATTING: 82 Worcestershire vs Lancashire, Worcester, 2012

CAREER HIGHLIGHTS? First-class and List A debuts
BEST PLAYER IN COUNTY CRICKET? James Vince
TIP FOR THE TOP? Aneesh Kapil and Aadil Ali
SUPERSTITIONS? I tap the boundary rope twice before I walk out to bat
CRICKETING HEROES? Growing up in Worcester I used to watch Graeme Hick and Vikram Solanki batting together at New Road quite a bit. Two very different styles but it was amazing to watch them turn the pressure on to the bowlers so often
CRICKET RULE YOU'D CHANGE? Supersubs in T20. One batsman per team does not have to field. It would mean the biggest names in cricket could extend their careers and continue to entertain and draw big crowds.
COACHING TIP? Keep your head clear when you are batting. Everything will happen naturally if you let it
IF YOU WEREN'T A CRICKETER? I'd probably be travelling the world making cocktails
IF YOU COULD BE SOMEONE ELSE FOR A DAY? Dan Bilzerian
DESERT ISLAND DISC? Royal Blood's debut album is on repeat for me at the moment
FAVOURITE TV? The Walking Dead
LEAST FAVOURITE TV? Miranda
TWITTER FEED: @Neil_Pinner

| Batting | Mat | Inns | NO | Runs | HS | Ave | SR | 100 | 50 | Ct | St |
|---|---|---|---|---|---|---|---|---|---|---|---|
| First-class | 13 | 19 | 0 | 397 | 82 | 20.89 | 39.58 | 0 | 3 | 12 | 0 |
| List A | 17 | 16 | 0 | 227 | 37 | 14.18 | 70.06 | 0 | 0 | 3 | 0 |
| **Bowling** | **Mat** | **Balls** | **Runs** | **Wkts** | **BBI** | **BBM** | **Ave** | **Econ** | **SR** | **5w** | **10** |
| First-class | 13 | 48 | 32 | 0 | - | - | - | 4.00 | - | 0 | 0 |
| List A | 17 | 24 | 27 | 0 | - | - | - | 6.75 | - | 0 | 0 |

# STEFFAN PIOLET

RHB RM R0 W0

FULL NAME: Steffan Andreas Piolet
BORN: August 8, 1988, Redhill, Surrey
SQUAD NO: 21
HEIGHT: 6ft 1in
NICKNAME: Squiff, Jeffs, Pi
EDUCATION: Warden Park School; Central Sussex College
TEAMS: Sussex, Warwickshire
CAREER: First-class: 2009; List A: 2009; T20: 2009

BEST BATTING: 103* Sussex vs Loughborough MCCU, Hove, 2014
BEST BOWLING: 6-17 Warwickshire vs Durham UCCE, Durham, 2009

CAREER HIGHLIGHTS? Winning one-day trophies with Warwickshire
BEST PLAYER IN COUNTY CRICKET? Ed Joyce or Chris Woakes
NON-CRICKETING HEROES? Dave Grohl and Sergio Pizzorno – great musicians
CRICKET RULE YOU'D CHANGE? Toss before warm-ups
COACHING TIP? Fast arm for slower balls
IF YOU WEREN'T A CRICKETER? A lot more relaxed
IF YOU COULD BE SOMEONE ELSE FOR A DAY? Tom Meighan of Kasabian while headlining Glastonbury
DESERT ISLAND DISC? deadmau5 – very relaxing
FAVOURITE TV? Family Guy
PET HATE? Chewing gum – it's filthy!
SURPRISING FACT? I'm half Norwegian
FANTASY SLIP CORDON? Keeper: Tosh.0, 1st: Barack Obama, 2nd: Me, 3rd: Ledley King, Gully: Kevin Bridges
TWITTER FEED: @Spiolet14

| Batting | Mat | Inns | NO | Runs | HS | Ave | SR | 100 | 50 | Ct | St |
|---|---|---|---|---|---|---|---|---|---|---|---|
| First-class | 11 | 19 | 2 | 361 | 103* | 21.23 | 40.60 | 1 | 0 | 8 | 0 |
| List A | 41 | 25 | 6 | 328 | 63* | 17.26 | 96.75 | 0 | 1 | 6 | 0 |
| Twenty20 | 65 | 25 | 9 | 188 | 26* | 11.75 | 109.94 | 0 | 0 | 16 | 0 |
| **Bowling** | **Mat** | **Balls** | **Runs** | **Wkts** | **BBI** | **BBM** | **Ave** | **Econ** | **SR** | **5w** | **10** |
| First-class | 11 | 985 | 570 | 19 | 6/17 | 10/43 | 30.00 | 3.47 | 51.8 | 1 | 1 |
| List A | 41 | 1475 | 1363 | 40 | 4/31 | 4/31 | 34.07 | 5.54 | 36.8 | 0 | 0 |
| Twenty20 | 65 | 1293 | 1525 | 59 | 3/14 | 3/14 | 25.84 | 7.07 | 21.9 | 0 | 0 |

# LIAM PLUNKETT RHB RFM R0 W3

FULL NAME: Liam Edward Plunkett
BORN: April 6, 1985, Middlesbrough, Yorkshire
SQUAD NO: 28
HEIGHT: 6ft 3in
NICKNAME: Pudsy
EDUCATION: Nunthorpe Comprehensive
TEAMS: England, Yorkshire, Dolphins, Durham
CAREER: Test: 2005; ODI: 2005; T20I: 2006; First-class: 2003; List A: 2003; T20: 2003



BEST BATTING: 114 England Lions vs Sri Lanka A, Colombo, 2014
BEST BOWLING: 6-33 Durham vs Leeds/Bradford MCCU, Leeds, 2013

CAREER HIGHLIGHTS? Making my England debut
CRICKETING HEROES? Glenn McGrath
TWITTER FEED: @Liam628
NOTES: After missing almost the entire 2012 season for Durham, Plunkett signed for Yorkshire in October of that year. He claimed 42 first-class wickets in 2013 at 25.35, including a career-best 6-33 against Leeds/Bradford University. In 2014 he played his first Test for England since 2007 and picked up 18 wickets in four Tests before injury ended his summer. He became only the second player to record a five-wicket haul on his Championship debut for Durham, 5-53 vs Yorkshire at Headingley, in 2003. Made his England Test debut in November 2005 vs Pakistan at Lahore

| Batting | Mat | Inns | NO | Runs | HS | Ave | SR | 100 | 50 | Ct | St |
|---|---|---|---|---|---|---|---|---|---|---|---|
| Tests | 13 | 20 | 5 | 238 | 55* | 15.86 | 46.75 | 0 | 1 | 3 | 0 |
| ODIs | 29 | 25 | 10 | 315 | 56 | 21.00 | 83.33 | 0 | 1 | 7 | 0 |
| T20Is | 1 | - | - | - | - | - | - | - | - | 0 | 0 |
| First-class | 138 | 188 | 36 | 3724 | 114 | 24.50 | | 2 | 19 | 79 | 0 |
| List A | 127 | 86 | 31 | 1118 | 72 | 20.32 | 94.34 | 0 | 3 | 29 | 0 |
| Twenty20 | 75 | 45 | 17 | 482 | 41 | 17.21 | 124.54 | 0 | 0 | 16 | 0 |
| **Bowling** | **Mat** | **Balls** | **Runs** | **Wkts** | **BBI** | **BBM** | **Ave** | **Econ** | **SR** | **5w** | **10** |
| Tests | 13 | 2659 | 1536 | 41 | 5/64 | 9/176 | 37.46 | 3.46 | 64.8 | 1 | 0 |
| ODIs | 29 | 1363 | 1321 | 39 | 3/24 | 3/24 | 33.87 | 5.81 | 34.9 | 0 | 0 |
| T20Is | 1 | 24 | 37 | 1 | 1/37 | 1/37 | 37.00 | 9.25 | 24.0 | 0 | 0 |
| First-class | 138 | 21594 | 13010 | 421 | 6/33 | | 30.90 | 3.61 | 51.2 | 11 | 1 |
| List A | 127 | 5270 | 4772 | 151 | 4/15 | 4/15 | 31.60 | 5.43 | 34.9 | 0 | 0 |
| Twenty20 | 75 | 1320 | 1715 | 57 | 5/31 | 5/31 | 30.08 | 7.79 | 23.1 | 1 | 0 |

## HARRY PODMORE

## RHB RMF R0 W0

FULL NAME: Harry William Podmore
BORN: July 23, 1994, Queen Charlotte Hospital, Hammersmith, Middlesex
SQUAD NO: 23
HEIGHT: 6ft 3in
NICKNAME: Podders, Chav
EDUCATION: Twyford Church of England High School
TEAMS: Middlesex
CAREER: List A: 2014, T20: 2014

CAREER HIGHLIGHTS? Playing at Lord's for the first time (on TV!), signing for Middlesex, getting on the England fast bowling programme
BEST PLAYER IN COUNTY CRICKET? Ben Stokes
MOST MARKED CHARACTERISTIC? Good looking
SUPERSTITIONS? Volume has to be on 23 on any electrical device
CRICKETING HEROES? Andrew Flintoff
IF YOU WEREN'T A CRICKETER? UFC fighter
IF YOU COULD BE SOMEONE ELSE FOR A DAY? David Beckham
DESERT ISLAND DISC? Felix Jaehn – Cheerleader
FAVOURITE TV? The Only Way Is Essex
LEAST FAVOURITE TV? Anything to do with wildlife
PET HATE? People playing dumb
SURPRISING FACT? I have my family crest tattooed on my chest
TWITTER FEED: @Harrypod16

| Batting | Mat | Inns | NO | Runs | HS | Ave | SR | 100 | 50 | Ct | St |
|---|---|---|---|---|---|---|---|---|---|---|---|
| List A | 6 | 1 | 1 | 1 | 1* | - | 50.00 | 0 | 0 | 0 | 0 |
| Twenty20 | 7 | 2 | 1 | 10 | 7 | 10.00 | 66.66 | 0 | 0 | 3 | 0 |
| **Bowling** | **Mat** | **Balls** | **Runs** | **Wkts** | **BBI** | **BBM** | **Ave** | **Econ** | **SR** | **5w** | **10** |
| List A | 6 | 236 | 272 | 4 | 2/46 | 2/46 | 68.00 | 6.91 | 59.0 | 0 | 0 |
| Twenty20 | 7 | 133 | 165 | 9 | 3/13 | 3/13 | 18.33 | 7.44 | 14.7 | 0 | 0 |

# JAMES PORTER

RHB RMF R0 W0

FULL NAME: James Alexander Porter
BORN: May 25, 1993, Leytonstone, Essex
SQUAD NO: 44
HEIGHT: 6ft 1in
NICKNAME: Ports
EDUCATION: Oaks Park High School
TEAMS: Essex
CAREER: First-class: 2014



BEST BATTING: 5 Essex vs Worcestershire, Chelmsford, 2014
BEST BOWLING: 3-26 Essex vs Leicestershire, Leicester, 2014

FAMILY TIES? My grandad was the closest thing I had to a tie to cricket as he was in to all sport but I come from a football family and am the first cricketer
CAREER HIGHLIGHTS? Making my first-class debut for Essex
BEST PLAYER IN COUNTY CRICKET? Jesse Ryder
MOST MARKED CHARACTERISTIC? My lack of general knowledge
SUPERSTITIONS? I always pick the closest seat to the door in the dressing room
CRICKETING HEROES? Sir Viv Richards and Andrew Flintoff – they showed how much playing cricket meant to them every time they played
CRICKET RULE YOU'D CHANGE? I would allow ball-tampering. If you're allowed to shine the ball why can't you scratch it?
IF YOU WEREN'T A CRICKETER? Probably working a 9-5 job
IF YOU COULD BE SOMEONE ELSE FOR A DAY? Harry Styles
DESERT ISLAND DISC? Wiz Khalifa – Rolling Papers
FAVOURITE TV? Family Guy
LEAST FAVOURITE TV? Big Brother
PET HATE? Punctuality! I hate it when people are late or make me wait for them
TWITTER FEED: @jamieporter93

| Batting | Mat | Inns | NO | Runs | HS | Ave | SR | 100 | 50 | Ct | St |
|---|---|---|---|---|---|---|---|---|---|---|---|
| First-class | 3 | 3 | 2 | 5 | 5 | 5.00 | 20.00 | 0 | 0 | 1 | 0 |
| **Bowling** | **Mat** | **Balls** | **Runs** | **Wkts** | **BBI** | **BBM** | **Ave** | **Econ** | **SR** | **5w** | **10** |
| First-class | 3 | 187 | 116 | 6 | 3/26 | 3/26 | 19.33 | 3.72 | 31.1 | 0 | 0 |

## WILLIAM PORTERFIELD LHB OB R0 W0 MVP47

FULL NAME: William Thomas Stuart Porterfield
BORN: September 6, 1984, Londonderry
SQUAD NO: 10
EDUCATION: Strabane Grammar School; Leeds Metropolitan University
TEAMS: Ireland, Warwickshire, Gloucestershire
CAREER: ODI: 2006; T20I: 2008; First-class: 2006; List A: 2006; T20: 2008

BEST BATTING: 175 Gloucestershire vs Worcestershire, Cheltenham, 2010
BEST BOWLING: 1-29 Ireland vs Jamaica, Spanish Town, 2010
COUNTY CAPS: 2014

CAREER HIGHLIGHTS? Playing in the World Cup, captaining Ireland
IF YOU WEREN'T A CRICKETER? Maybe a farmer
FAVOURITE TV? Two And A Half Men
FANTASY SLIP CORDON? Keeper: Frankie Boyle, 1st: Jimmy Carr, 2nd: John Bishop, 3rd: Kerry Katona
TWITTER FEED: @purdy34

| Batting | Mat | Inns | NO | Runs | HS | Ave | SR | 100 | 50 | Ct | St |
|---|---|---|---|---|---|---|---|---|---|---|---|
| ODIs | 77 | 76 | 3 | 2238 | 112* | 30.65 | 66.27 | 6 | 10 | 39 | 0 |
| T20Is | 37 | 36 | 4 | 627 | 56* | 19.59 | 114.20 | 0 | 1 | 15 | 0 |
| First-class | 107 | 176 | 7 | 5184 | 175 | 30.67 | 46.43 | 7 | 29 | 116 | 0 |
| List A | 183 | 181 | 6 | 5584 | 112* | 31.90 | 72.12 | 7 | 33 | 90 | 0 |
| Twenty20 | 118 | 117 | 7 | 2773 | 127* | 25.20 | 127.55 | 1 | 14 | 53 | 0 |
| **Bowling** | **Mat** | **Balls** | **Runs** | **Wkts** | **BBI** | **BBM** | **Ave** | **Econ** | **SR** | **5w** | **10** |
| ODIs | 77 | - | - | - | - | - | - | - | - | - | - |
| T20Is | 37 | - | - | - | - | - | - | - | - | - | - |
| First-class | 107 | 108 | 138 | 2 | 1/29 | 1/29 | 69.00 | 7.66 | 54.0 | 0 | 0 |
| List A | 183 | - | - | - | - | - | - | - | - | - | - |
| Twenty20 | 118 | - | - | - | - | - | - | - | - | - | - |

# STUART POYNTER

RHB WK R0 W0

FULL NAME: Stuart William Poynter
BORN: October 18, 1990, Hammersmith, London
SQUAD NO: 90
HEIGHT: 5ft 8in
NICKNAME: Stuey, Points
EDUCATION: Teddington School
TEAMS: Ireland, Durham, Middlesex
CAREER: ODI: 2014; First-class: 2010; List A: 2013



BEST BATTING: 63 Ireland vs Australia A, Stormont, 2013

FAMILY TIES? My uncle Deryck and brother Andrew both played for Ireland
CAREER HIGHLIGHTS? Making my debut for Ireland
BEST PLAYER IN COUNTY CRICKET? James Taylor
TIP FOR THE TOP? Jack Burnham
MOST MARKED CHARACTERISTIC? Ginger hair and beard
CRICKETING HEROES? Jack Russell – just the best keeper I have ever seen and one of the first I saw standing up to pace bowling
NON-CRICKETING HEROES? Rodger Federer – an amazing champion, always so humble and graceful when he is playing
CRICKET RULE YOU'D CHANGE? Can't be out first ball! Just because I have had a lot of that in my life
DESERT ISLAND DISC? Ed Sheeran – X
ACCOMPLISHMENTS? Met the Queen when I was 10 for winning a gold medal for hockey
PET HATE? Loud eaters make me so angry
SURPRISING FACT? I try and play the ukulele
TWITTER FEED: @spoynter_90

| Batting | Mat | Inns | NO | Runs | HS | Ave | SR | 100 | 50 | Ct | St |
|---|---|---|---|---|---|---|---|---|---|---|---|
| ODIs | 3 | 2 | 0 | 15 | 8 | 7.50 | 50.00 | 0 | 0 | 8 | 0 |
| First-class | 8 | 9 | 0 | 201 | 63 | 22.33 | 63.20 | 0 | 1 | 23 | 2 |
| List A | 7 | 6 | 1 | 160 | 109 | 32.00 | 96.38 | 1 | 0 | 13 | 0 |
| **Bowling** | **Mat** | **Balls** | **Runs** | **Wkts** | **BBI** | **BBM** | **Ave** | **Econ** | **SR** | **5w** | **10** |
| ODIs | 3 | - | - | - | - | - | - | - | - | - | - |
| First-class | 8 | - | - | - | - | - | - | - | - | - | - |
| List A | 7 | - | - | - | - | - | - | - | - | - | - |

## TOM POYNTON

## RHB WK R0 W0

FULL NAME: Thomas Poynton
BORN: November 25, 1989, Burton-on-Trent, Staffordshire
SQUAD NO: 23
HEIGHT: 5ft 10in
NICKNAME: TP, Poynts
EDUCATION: John Taylor High School; Repton School
TEAMS: Derbyshire
CAREER: First-class: 2007; List A: 2007; T20: 2007

BEST BATTING: 106 Derbyshire vs Northamptonshire, Northampton, 2012
BEST BOWLING: 2-96 Derbyshire vs Glamorgan, Cardiff, 2010

CAREER HIGHLIGHTS? Winning Division Two with Derbyshire in 2012 and scoring my maiden first-class century against Northamptonshire in the same year
MOST MARKED CHARACTERISTIC? The scar on my left cheek
NON-CRICKETING HEROES? Lisa Lynch. A family friend who sadly lost her battle to cancer a few years ago. The BBC have filmed a one-off special about her story called The C-Word to be aired in the new year. A truly inspiring character who helps put cricket into perspective for me. My father, Keith, who sadly passed away in a road traffic accident in 2014
IF YOU WEREN'T A CRICKETER? I would be working in finance or be an entrepreneur and have my own business
IF YOU COULD BE SOMEONE ELSE FOR A DAY? Winston Churchill – the greatest Briton
SURPRISING FACT? I am a director and shareholder in Yolo Food Company
FANTASY SLIP CORDON? Keeper: Me (for obvious reasons), 1st: Winston Churchill (voted the Greatest Briton to have ever lived), 2nd: Ricky Gervais (my favourite comedian), 3rd: David Beckham (one of the purest blokes around), Gully: Margot Robbie (after her performance in Wolf Of Wall Street, incredible!)

| Batting | Mat | Inns | NO | Runs | HS | Ave | SR | 100 | 50 | Ct | St |
|---|---|---|---|---|---|---|---|---|---|---|---|
| First-class | 33 | 50 | 6 | 941 | 106 | 21.38 | 40.84 | 1 | 5 | 81 | 6 |
| List A | 20 | 13 | 2 | 138 | 40 | 12.54 | 89.61 | 0 | 0 | 11 | 3 |
| Twenty20 | 19 | 12 | 3 | 86 | 19 | 9.55 | 88.65 | 0 | 0 | 12 | 9 |
| **Bowling** | **Mat** | **Balls** | **Runs** | **Wkts** | **BBI** | **BBM** | **Ave** | **Econ** | **SR** | **5w** | **10** |
| First-class | 33 | 48 | 96 | 2 | 2/96 | 2/96 | 48.00 | 12.00 | 24.0 | 0 | 0 |
| List A | 20 | - | - | - | - | - | - | - | - | - | - |
| Twenty20 | 19 | - | - | - | - | - | - | - | - | - | - |

# JOSH POYSDEN

LHB LB R0 W0

FULL NAME: Joshua Edward Poysden
BORN: August 8, 1991, Shoreham-by-Sea, Sussex
SQUAD NO: 14
HEIGHT: 5ft 11in
NICKNAME: Dobby, Bendicii, Mulcher
EDUCATION: Cardinal Newman School; Anglia Ruskin University
TEAMS: Warwickshire
CAREER: First-class: 2011; List A: 2013; T20: 2014



BEST BATTING: 47 Cambridge MCCU vs Surrey, Cambridge, 2011
BEST BOWLING: 3-20 Cambridge MCCU vs Surrey, Cambridge, 2011

FAMILY TIES? My dad used to play club cricket. He once took all 10 wickets in an innings (and never shuts up about it)
CAREER HIGHLIGHTS? My Warwickshire debut and being involved in the T20-winning squad
MOST MARKED CHARACTERISTIC? People often comment on my weird nipples
CRICKETING HEROES? Shane Warne and Mushtaq Ahmed as they are fellow leg twisters
NON-CRICKETING HEROES? I'm a West Ham supporter and my favourite players have been Paolo Di Canio and Carlos Tevez. I'm also an Oasis fan – Noel Gallagher is the man
COACHING TIP? My Cambridge MCCU coach Chris Scott told me to always hit a full toss wide of mid-on, which is a cracking bit of advice
DESERT ISLAND DISC? Tough one between Avicii's True and Oasis' Definitely Maybe
LEAST FAVOURITE TV? Cooking programmes. My dad always watches them at home and I can't stand them!
SURPRISING FACT? I was still playing club 2nd XI cricket at the age of 18
TWITTER FEED: @JoshPoysden14

| Batting | Mat | Inns | NO | Runs | HS | Ave | SR | 100 | 50 | Ct | St |
|---|---|---|---|---|---|---|---|---|---|---|---|
| First-class | 4 | 4 | 0 | 63 | 47 | 15.75 | 43.75 | 0 | 0 | 2 | 0 |
| List A | 10 | 4 | 2 | 15 | 10* | 7.50 | 75.00 | 0 | 0 | 3 | 0 |
| Twenty20 | 1 | - | - | - | - | - | - | - | - | 0 | 0 |
| **Bowling** | **Mat** | **Balls** | **Runs** | **Wkts** | **BBI** | **BBM** | **Ave** | **Econ** | **SR** | **5w** | **10** |
| First-class | 4 | 367 | 264 | 5 | 3/20 | 3/25 | 52.80 | 4.31 | 73.4 | 0 | 0 |
| List A | 10 | 333 | 310 | 9 | 3/33 | 3/33 | 34.44 | 5.58 | 37.0 | 0 | 0 |
| Twenty20 | 1 | 18 | 26 | 0 | - | - | - | 8.66 | - | 0 | 0 |

# ASHWELL PRINCE LHB OB R3 W0 MVP54

FULL NAME: Ashwell Gavin Prince
BORN: May 28, 1977, Port Elizabeth, South Africa
SQUAD NO: 5
HEIGHT: 5ft 9in
NICKNAME: Ash
TEAMS: South Africa, Lancashire, Eastern Province, Mumbai Indians, Nottinghamshire, Warriors, Western Province
CAREER: Test: 2002; ODI: 2002; T20I: 2005; First-class: 1995; List A: 1996; T20: 2004

BEST BATTING: 257* Lancashire vs Northamptonshire, Manchester, 2014
BEST BOWLING: 2-11 South Africans vs Middlesex, Uxbridge, 2008
COUNTY CAPS: 2008 (Nottinghamshire); 2010 (Lancashire)

TWITTER FEED: @ashyp_5
NOTES: The former South Africa batsman signed a two-year deal with the county ahead of the 2013 season after losing his central contract. He topped 1,000 runs in 2012, 2013 and 2014 and hit a career-best 257* against Northamptonshire at Old Trafford last season. He had intended to retire after the 2014 season but reversed his decion and will play on for 2015. In July 2006, he was appointed South Africa's first black captain in the absence of the injured Graeme Smith and he scored 11 centuries in his 66-match Test career, including a series-defining 149 against England at Headingley in 2008

| Batting | Mat | Inns | NO | Runs | HS | Ave | SR | 100 | 50 | Ct | St |
|---|---|---|---|---|---|---|---|---|---|---|---|
| Tests | 66 | 104 | 16 | 3665 | 162* | 41.64 | 43.70 | 11 | 11 | 47 | 0 |
| ODIs | 52 | 41 | 12 | 1018 | 89* | 35.10 | 67.77 | 0 | 3 | 26 | 0 |
| T20Is | 1 | 1 | 0 | 5 | 5 | 5.00 | 83.33 | 0 | 0 | 0 | 0 |
| First-class | 272 | 442 | 48 | 17006 | 257* | 43.16 | | 40 | 85 | 207 | 0 |
| List A | 255 | 225 | 37 | 6079 | 128 | 32.33 | | 3 | 33 | 114 | 0 |
| Twenty20 | 88 | 86 | 7 | 2012 | 74 | 25.46 | 114.31 | 0 | 10 | 44 | 0 |
| **Bowling** | **Mat** | **Balls** | **Runs** | **Wkts** | **BBI** | **BBM** | **Ave** | **Econ** | **SR** | **5w** | **10** |
| Tests | 66 | 96 | 47 | 1 | 1/2 | 1/2 | 47.00 | 2.93 | 96.0 | 0 | 0 |
| ODIs | 52 | 12 | 3 | 0 | - | - | - | 1.50 | - | 0 | 0 |
| T20Is | 1 | - | - | - | - | - | - | - | - | - | - |
| First-class | 272 | 294 | 179 | 4 | 2/11 | | 44.75 | 3.65 | 73.5 | 0 | 0 |
| List A | 255 | 91 | 86 | 0 | - | - | - | 5.67 | - | 0 | 0 |
| Twenty20 | 88 | 4 | 5 | 0 | - | - | - | 7.50 | - | 0 | 0 |

# RYAN PRINGLE RHB OB R0 W0



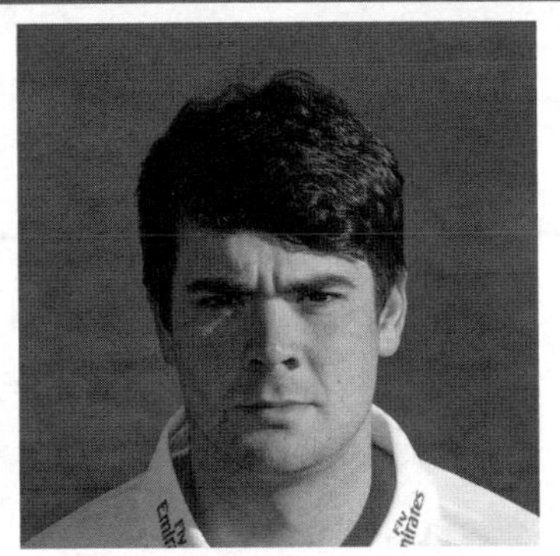

FULL NAME: Ryan David Pringle
BORN: April 17, 1992, Sunderland, County Durham
SQUAD NO: 17
HEIGHT: 6ft 1in
NICKNAME: Rhino
EDUCATION: Hetton Comprehensive; Durham Sixth Form Centre; University of Sunderland
TEAMS: Durham, Northumberland
CAREER: First-class: 2014; List A: 2012; T20: 2013

BEST BATTING: 63* Durham vs Warwickshire, Birmingham, 2014
BEST BOWLING: 2-94 Durham vs Somerset, Taunton, 2014

CAREER HIGHLIGHTS? Maiden first-class 50
BEST PLAYER IN COUNTY CRICKET? Jeetan Patel
TIP FOR THE TOP? Paul Coughlin
SUPERSTITIONS? Left pad first
CRICKETING HEROES? Ricky Ponting – great all-round player and captain. Led from the front
NON-CRICKETING HEROES? My grandad. He's a great bloke who I've always and always will respect and look up to
CRICKET RULE YOU'D CHANGE? All no-balls should result in a free hit
IF YOU WEREN'T A CRICKETER? A real job
IF YOU COULD BE SOMEONE ELSE FOR A DAY? Dan Bilzerian
DESERT ISLAND DISC? Ed Sheeran – X
FAVOURITE TV? Game Of Thrones
PET HATE? When people say "full-fat coke" when they mean to say full sugar
FANTASY SLIP CORDON? Keeper: David Beckham, 1st: Harry Potter, 2nd: Jordan Belfort
TWITTER FEED: @RyanPringle

| Batting | Mat | Inns | NO | Runs | HS | Ave | SR | 100 | 50 | Ct | St |
|---|---|---|---|---|---|---|---|---|---|---|---|
| First-class | 2 | 4 | 1 | 126 | 63* | 42.00 | 56.00 | 0 | 1 | 0 | 0 |
| List A | 12 | 6 | 0 | 48 | 26 | 8.00 | 81.35 | 0 | 0 | 2 | 0 |
| Twenty20 | 20 | 11 | 2 | 56 | 17 | 6.22 | 119.14 | 0 | 0 | 2 | 0 |
| **Bowling** | **Mat** | **Balls** | **Runs** | **Wkts** | **BBI** | **BBM** | **Ave** | **Econ** | **SR** | **5w** | **10** |
| First-class | 2 | 129 | 108 | 2 | 2/94 | 2/95 | 54.00 | 5.02 | 64.5 | 0 | 0 |
| List A | 12 | 231 | 200 | 3 | 1/12 | 1/12 | 66.66 | 5.19 | 77.0 | 0 | 0 |
| Twenty20 | 20 | 246 | 338 | 10 | 2/13 | 2/13 | 33.80 | 8.24 | 24.6 | 0 | 0 |

# MATT PRIOR

## RHB WK R3 W0



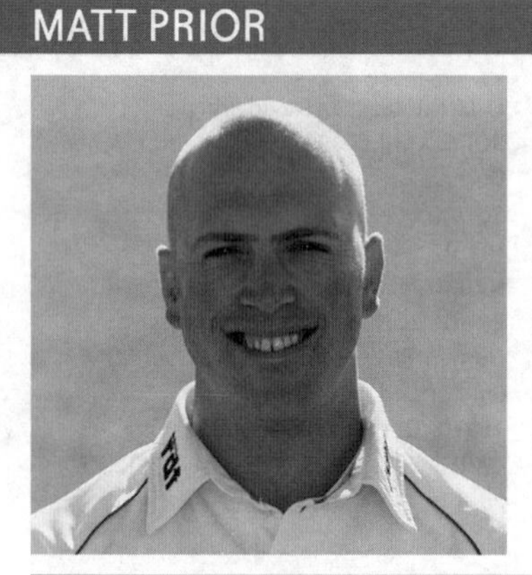

FULL NAME: Matthew James Prior
BORN: February 26, 1982, Johannesburg, South Africa
SQUAD NO: 13
HEIGHT: 5ft 11in
EDUCATION: Brighton College, East Sussex
TEAMS: England, Sussex, Victoria
CAREER: Test: 2007; ODI: 2004; T20I: 2007; First-class: 2001; List A: 2000; T20: 2003

BEST BATTING: 201* Sussex vs LUCCE, Hove, 2004
COUNTY CAPS: 2003; BENEFIT YEAR: 2012

MOST MARKED CHARACTERISTIC? The beard. Is that a characteristic?
DESERT ISLAND DISC? Album: Now That's What I Call Music 21. Song: Mr Bojangles. I love the Robbie Williams version
TWITTER FEED: @MattPrior13
NOTES: After 79 Tests, seven centuries and an average of 40.18, Prior passed the England gloves to Jos Buttler last summer after he required surgery on his Achilles. He made his Sussex debut in 2001 and made his international debut for England three years later, scoring 35 against Zimbabwe in an ODI. He became the first England wicketkeeper to score a century on Test debut, hitting an unbeaten 126 against West Indies at Lord's. He held 23 catches during the 2010-11 Ashes

| Batting | Mat | Inns | NO | Runs | HS | Ave | SR | 100 | 50 | Ct | St |
|---|---|---|---|---|---|---|---|---|---|---|---|
| Tests | 79 | 123 | 21 | 4099 | 131* | 40.18 | 61.66 | 7 | 28 | 243 | 13 |
| ODIs | 68 | 62 | 9 | 1282 | 87 | 24.18 | 76.76 | 0 | 3 | 71 | 8 |
| T20Is | 10 | 8 | 2 | 127 | 32 | 21.16 | 127.00 | 0 | 0 | 6 | 3 |
| First-class | 249 | 381 | 44 | 13228 | 201* | 39.25 | 66.85 | 28 | 75 | 642 | 41 |
| List A | 222 | 204 | 18 | 5072 | 144 | 27.26 | | 4 | 28 | 187 | 31 |
| Twenty20 | 84 | 78 | 5 | 1906 | 117 | 26.10 | 143.63 | 1 | 11 | 46 | 6 |
| **Bowling** | **Mat** | **Balls** | **Runs** | **Wkts** | **BBI** | **BBM** | **Ave** | **Econ** | **SR** | **5w** | **10** |
| Tests | 79 | - | - | - | - | - | - | - | - | - | - |
| ODIs | 68 | - | - | - | - | - | - | - | - | - | - |
| T20Is | 10 | - | - | - | - | - | - | - | - | - | - |
| First-class | 249 | - | - | - | - | - | - | - | - | - | - |
| List A | 222 | - | - | - | - | - | - | - | - | - | - |
| Twenty20 | 84 | - | - | - | - | - | - | - | - | - | - |

# LUKE PROCTER

LHB RMF R0 W0

FULL NAME: Luke Anthony Procter
BORN: June 24, 1988, Oldham, Lancashire
SQUAD NO: 2
HEIGHT: 5ft 11in
EDUCATION: Counthill School, Oldham
TEAMS: Lancashire
CAREER: First-class: 2010; List A: 2009; T20: 2011



BEST BATTING: 106 Lancashire vs Gloucestershire, Bristol, 2013
BEST BOWLING: 7-71 Lancashire vs Surrey, Liverpool, 2012

CAREER HIGHLIGHTS? Winning the County Championship in 2011
SUPERSTITIONS? Putting my right pad on first
CRICKETING HEROES? Marcus Trescothick
IF YOU WEREN'T A CRICKETER? I'd not be doing a lot
FAVOURITE TV? Take Me Out
TWITTER FEED: @vvsprocter

| Batting | Mat | Inns | NO | Runs | HS | Ave | SR | 100 | 50 | Ct | St |
|---|---|---|---|---|---|---|---|---|---|---|---|
| First-class | 46 | 69 | 5 | 1977 | 106 | 30.89 | 42.55 | 1 | 11 | 9 | 0 |
| List A | 20 | 14 | 5 | 252 | 97 | 28.00 | 85.13 | 0 | 2 | 4 | 0 |
| Twenty20 | 19 | 10 | 5 | 85 | 25* | 17.00 | 91.39 | 0 | 0 | 5 | 0 |
| **Bowling** | **Mat** | **Balls** | **Runs** | **Wkts** | **BBI** | **BBM** | **Ave** | **Econ** | **SR** | **5w** | **10** |
| First-class | 46 | 3277 | 1883 | 58 | 7/71 | 8/79 | 32.46 | 3.44 | 56.5 | 2 | 0 |
| List A | 20 | 432 | 451 | 12 | 3/29 | 3/29 | 37.58 | 6.26 | 36.0 | 0 | 0 |
| Twenty20 | 19 | 116 | 176 | 8 | 3/22 | 3/22 | 22.00 | 9.10 | 14.5 | 0 | 0 |

# RICH PYRAH

RHB RM R0 W0

YORKSHIRE

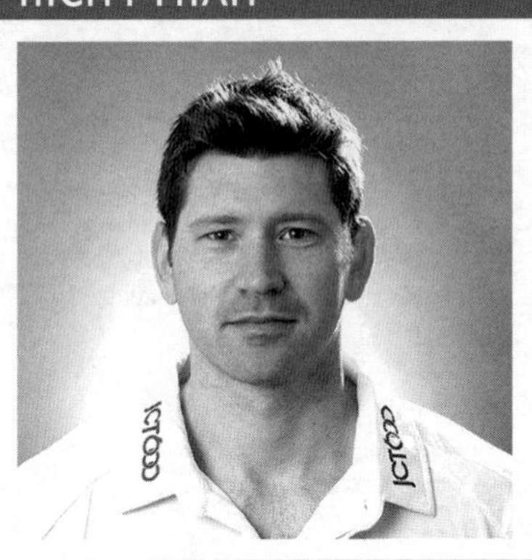


FULL NAME: Richard Michael Pyrah
BORN: November 1, 1982, Dewsbury, Yorkshire
SQUAD NO: 27
HEIGHT: 6 ft 0 in
NICKNAME: RP, Pyro
EDUCATION: Ossett High School
TEAMS: Yorkshire
CAREER: First-class: 2004; List A: 2001; T20: 2005

BEST BATTING: 134* Yorkshire vs Loughborough MCCU, Leeds, 2010
BEST BOWLING: 5-58 Yorkshire vs Nottinghamshire, Leeds, 2011
COUNTY CAPS: 2010; BENEFIT YEAR: 2015

CAREER HIGHLIGHTS? Receiving my 1st XI cap and scoring 117 vs Lancashire after we were 45-8
CRICKETING HEROES? Jacques Kallis, Sachin Tendulkar
NON-CRICKETING HEROES? My family
IF YOU WEREN'T A CRICKETER? I'd be some sort of businessman
FAVOURITE TV? EastEnders, One Born Every Minute
ACCOMPLISHMENTS? Having twins
SURPRISING FACT? I can down a bottle of VK in one second and I played for Sheffield Wednesday as a youngster
FANTASY SLIP CORDON? Keeper: Me, 1st: My dog Charlie, 2nd: Tiger Woods, 3rd: Mila Kunis
TWITTER FEED: @pyrah27

| Batting | Mat | Inns | NO | Runs | HS | Ave | SR | 100 | 50 | Ct | St |
|---|---|---|---|---|---|---|---|---|---|---|---|
| First-class | 48 | 57 | 8 | 1417 | 134* | 28.91 | 56.77 | 3 | 7 | 22 | 0 |
| List A | 114 | 76 | 20 | 1077 | 69 | 19.23 | | 0 | 2 | 36 | 0 |
| Twenty20 | 95 | 65 | 20 | 558 | 42 | 12.40 | 114.11 | 0 | 0 | 35 | 0 |
| **Bowling** | **Mat** | **Balls** | **Runs** | **Wkts** | **BBI** | **BBM** | **Ave** | **Econ** | **SR** | **5w** | **10** |
| First-class | 48 | 4256 | 2454 | 55 | 5/58 | | 44.61 | 3.45 | 77.3 | 1 | 0 |
| List A | 114 | 3788 | 3592 | 140 | 5/50 | 5/50 | 25.65 | 5.68 | 27.0 | 1 | 0 |
| Twenty20 | 95 | 1692 | 2086 | 101 | 5/16 | 5/16 | 20.65 | 7.39 | 16.7 | 1 | 0 |

## IMRAN QAYYUM RHB SLA R0 W0

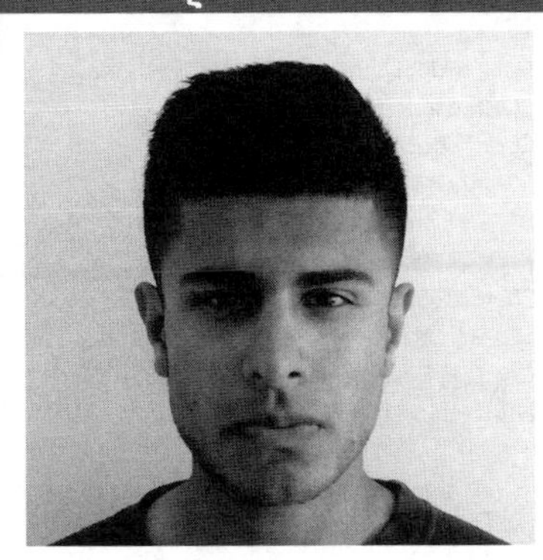

FULL NAME: Imran Qayyum
BORN: May 23, 1993, Ealing, Middlesex
SQUAD NO: 11
HEIGHT: 6ft
NICKNAME: Imy, IQ
EDUCATION: Villiers High School; City University London
TEAMS: Kent 2nd XI, Sussex 2nd XI, Northamptonshire 2nd XI
CAREER: Yet to make first-team debut



---

FAMILY TIES? My father played in Pakistan and my brother plays Minor Counties for Hertfordshire
CAREER HIGHLIGHTS? Signing as a professional at Kent
BEST PLAYER IN COUNTY CRICKET? Samit Patel
TIP FOR THE TOP? Daniel Bell-Drummond
MOST MARKED CHARACTERISTIC? Changing my mind regularly
CRICKETING HEROES? Shahid Afridi – because of the way he plays the game and he's a fan's favourite. Shoaib Akhtar – because he was rapid
CRICKET RULE YOU'D CHANGE? Number of bouncers in an over – I would make it unlimited because the game is too batsman-friendly
IF YOU WEREN'T A CRICKETER? Network marketing
IF YOU COULD BE SOMEONE ELSE FOR A DAY? Steven Gerrard
DESERT ISLAND DISC? 50 Cent – Get Rich Or Die Tryin'
FAVOURITE TV? Friends
ACCOMPLISHMENTS? Graduating in Biomedical Engineering
PET HATE? The song Let It Go – I can't stand it
SURPRISING FACT? I started off as a right-arm seamer
TWITTER FEED: @imranqc

## BEN RAINE

## LHB RFM R0 W0

FULL NAME: Benjamin Alexander Raine
BORN: September 4, 1991, Sunderland, County Durham
SQUAD NO: 44
HEIGHT: 6ft
NICKNAME: The Ranger
EDUCATION: St Aidan's Catholic Academy
TEAMS: Leicestershire, Durham
CAREER: First-class: 2011; List A: 2011; T20: 2014

BEST BATTING: 72 Leicestershire vs Lancashire, Manchester, 2013
BEST BOWLING: 4-98 Leicestershire vs Glamorgan, Swansea, 2013

FAMILY TIES? Dad and grandad both played in the north-east leagues and my brother was a tough competitor in the back yard
CAREER HIGHLIGHTS? The end-of-season PCA dinner
BEST PLAYER IN COUNTY CRICKET? Ben Stokes
TIP FOR THE TOP? Angus Robson
CRICKETING HEROES? Graham Thorpe – serious player, and looks like he enjoyed a slurp off the pitch
IF YOU WEREN'T A CRICKETER? Probably ducking bullets in Afghanistan if my mother would let me go
IF YOU COULD BE SOMEONE ELSE FOR A DAY? Mike Tyson in his prime
FAVOURITE TV? Love a bit of South Park
PET HATE? Slow golfers that don't let you play through
SURPRISING FACT? I was and still am unbeaten on Fight Night Round 3... By human or computer
TWITTER FEED: @benraine88

| Batting | Mat | Inns | NO | Runs | HS | Ave | SR | 100 | 50 | Ct | St |
|---|---|---|---|---|---|---|---|---|---|---|---|
| First-class | 13 | 23 | 2 | 440 | 72 | 20.95 | 39.60 | 0 | 2 | 3 | 0 |
| List A | 4 | 2 | 0 | 50 | 43 | 25.00 | 128.20 | 0 | 0 | 2 | 0 |
| Twenty20 | 11 | 8 | 4 | 61 | 20* | 15.25 | 98.38 | 0 | 0 | 3 | 0 |
| **Bowling** | **Mat** | **Balls** | **Runs** | **Wkts** | **BBI** | **BBM** | **Ave** | **Econ** | **SR** | **5w** | **10** |
| First-class | 13 | 1785 | 1012 | 27 | 4/98 | 4/98 | 37.48 | 3.40 | 66.1 | 0 | 0 |
| List A | 4 | 126 | 158 | 3 | 2/59 | 2/59 | 52.66 | 7.52 | 42.0 | 0 | 0 |
| Twenty20 | 11 | 216 | 269 | 15 | 3/12 | 3/12 | 17.93 | 7.47 | 14.4 | 0 | 0 |

# BOYD RANKIN LHB RFM R0 W1

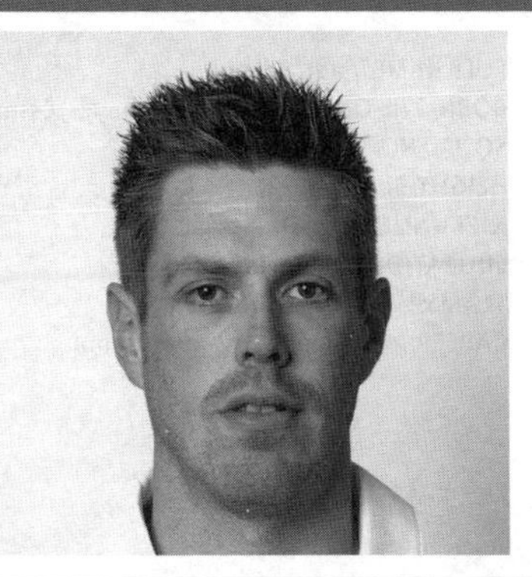

FULL NAME: William Boyd Rankin
BORN: July 5, 1984, Londonderry
SQUAD NO: 30
HEIGHT: 6ft 7in
NICKNAME: Boydo
EDUCATION: Strabane Grammar School; Harper Adams University College
TEAMS: England, Ireland, Warwickshire, Derbyshire
CAREER: Test: 2014; ODI: 2007; T20I: 2009; First-class: 2007; List A: 2006; T20: 2009



BEST BATTING: 43 ICC Combined Associate and Affiliate XI vs England XI, Dubai, 2012
BEST BOWLING: 5-16 Warwickshire vs Essex, Birmingham, 2010
COUNTY CAPS: 2013

FAMILY TIES? My dad played club cricket and my brothers Robert and David have played for Ireland at U19 level, with David also playing for Ireland A. My sister plays club and Ireland development cricket
CRICKETING HEROES? I watched Curtly Ambrose and Glenn McGrath while I was growing up and have tried to emulate them
NON-CRICKETING HEROES? I'm a big fan of George Best
IF YOU WEREN'T A CRICKETER? I would be back home in Ireland on the family farm
FAVOURITE TV? Two And A Half Men
TWITTER FEED: @boydrankin

| Batting | Mat | Inns | NO | Runs | HS | Ave | SR | 100 | 50 | Ct | St |
|---|---|---|---|---|---|---|---|---|---|---|---|
| Tests | 1 | 2 | 0 | 13 | 13 | 6.50 | 54.16 | 0 | 0 | 0 | 0 |
| ODIs | 44 | 18 | 12 | 40 | 7* | 6.66 | 36.36 | 0 | 0 | 6 | 0 |
| T20Is | 17 | 3 | 2 | 13 | 7* | 13.00 | 81.25 | 0 | 0 | 6 | 0 |
| First-class | 75 | 86 | 37 | 396 | 43 | 8.08 | 40.36 | 0 | 0 | 19 | 0 |
| List A | 97 | 33 | 18 | 96 | 18* | 6.40 | 46.37 | 0 | 0 | 17 | 0 |
| Twenty20 | 38 | 9 | 5 | 21 | 7* | 5.25 | 72.41 | 0 | 0 | 9 | 0 |
| **Bowling** | **Mat** | **Balls** | **Runs** | **Wkts** | **BBI** | **BBM** | **Ave** | **Econ** | **SR** | **5w** | **10** |
| Tests | 1 | 125 | 81 | 1 | 1/47 | 1/81 | 81.00 | 3.88 | 125.0 | 0 | 0 |
| ODIs | 44 | 2019 | 1632 | 53 | 4/46 | 4/46 | 30.79 | 4.84 | 38.0 | 0 | 0 |
| T20Is | 17 | 378 | 388 | 18 | 3/20 | 3/20 | 21.55 | 6.15 | 21.0 | 0 | 0 |
| First-class | 75 | 11066 | 6633 | 248 | 5/16 | 8/115 | 26.74 | 3.59 | 44.6 | 6 | 0 |
| List A | 97 | 4052 | 3325 | 116 | 4/34 | 4/34 | 28.66 | 4.92 | 34.9 | 0 | 0 |
| Twenty20 | 38 | 810 | 846 | 47 | 4/9 | 4/9 | 18.00 | 6.26 | 17.2 | 0 | 0 |

## AADIL RASHID

## RHB RFM R0 W0

WORCESTERSHIRE

FULL NAME: Aadil Rashid
BORN: 27th October 1997, Goodmayes, Essex
SQUAD NO: 35
HEIGHT: 5ft 10in
NICKNAME: Rash, Rashman
EDUCATION: Wellington School
TEAMS: Worcestershire 2nd XI
CAREER: Yet to make first-team debut

---

FAMILY TIES? Dad use to play for Warwickshire age groups
CAREER HIGHLIGHTS? Signing a contract at Worcestershire
BEST PLAYER IN COUNTY CRICKET? Adam Lyth
TIP FOR THE TOP? Charlie Morris, Saif Zaib
CRICKETING HEROES? Shoaib Akhtar – his physical presence and confidence has always been something that I look up to
NON-CRICKETING HEROES? Muhammad Ali – his undoubtable self-confidence and belief in his own ability was so great he'd make his opponent believe that he was better
CRICKET RULE YOU'D CHANGE? Drop bowling restrictions for U18s. The more you bowl the more you learn
COACHING TIP? Attack and want every ball to come to you
IF YOU WEREN'T A CRICKETER? A businessman
IF YOU COULD BE SOMEONE ELSE FOR A DAY? Dan Bilzerian
DESERT ISLAND DISC? Nico and Vinz – Black Star Elephant
FAVOURITE TV? Scrubs
ACCOMPLISHMENTS? Being a good older brother
PET HATE? People who whisper in front of me. It's rude
FANTASY SLIP CORDON? Keeper: Lee Evans, 1st: AB de Villiers, 2nd: Steffan Jones, 3rd: Me, Gully: Damian D'Oliveira
TWITTER FEED: @Aadilrashid17

# ADIL RASHID

## RHB LB R1 W2 MVP7

FULL NAME: Adil Usman Rashid
BORN: February 17, 1988, Bradford, Yorkshire
SQUAD NO: 3
HEIGHT: 5ft 8in
NICKNAME: Dilly, Dilo, Rash
EDUCATION: Heaton School, Bradford; Bellevue Sixth Form College, Bradford
TEAMS: England, Yorkshire, South Australia
CAREER: ODI: 2009; T20I: 2009; First-class: 2006; List A: 2006; T20: 2008

BEST BATTING: 180 Yorkshire vs Somerset, Leeds, 2013
BEST BOWLING: 7-107 Yorkshire vs Hampshire, Southampton, 2008
COUNTY CAPS: 2008

CAREER HIGHLIGHTS? Playing for England
CRICKETING HEROES? Sachin Tendulkar, Shane Warne
NON-CRICKETING HEROES? Muhammad Ali
IF YOU WEREN'T A CRICKETER? I'd be a taxi driver
FAVOURITE TV? Friends
TWITTER FEED: @AdilRashid03

| Batting | Mat | Inns | NO | Runs | HS | Ave | SR | 100 | 50 | Ct | St |
|---|---|---|---|---|---|---|---|---|---|---|---|
| ODIs | 5 | 4 | 1 | 60 | 31* | 20.00 | 111.11 | 0 | 0 | 2 | 0 |
| T20Is | 5 | 2 | 1 | 10 | 9* | 10.00 | 52.63 | 0 | 0 | 0 | 0 |
| First-class | 131 | 181 | 33 | 5289 | 180 | 35.73 | | 9 | 29 | 64 | 0 |
| List A | 93 | 66 | 20 | 897 | 71 | 19.50 | 84.78 | 0 | 1 | 29 | 0 |
| Twenty20 | 88 | 52 | 13 | 520 | 36* | 13.33 | 101.76 | 0 | 0 | 22 | 0 |
| **Bowling** | **Mat** | **Balls** | **Runs** | **Wkts** | **BBI** | **BBM** | **Ave** | **Econ** | **SR** | **5w** | **10** |
| ODIs | 5 | 204 | 191 | 3 | 1/16 | 1/16 | 63.66 | 5.61 | 68.0 | 0 | 0 |
| T20Is | 5 | 84 | 120 | 3 | 1/11 | 1/11 | 40.00 | 8.57 | 28.0 | 0 | 0 |
| First-class | 131 | 22177 | 13040 | 375 | 7/107 | 11/114 | 34.77 | 3.52 | 59.1 | 18 | 1 |
| List A | 93 | 3800 | 3259 | 107 | 5/33 | 5/33 | 30.45 | 5.14 | 35.5 | 1 | 0 |
| Twenty20 | 88 | 1727 | 2176 | 95 | 4/20 | 4/20 | 22.90 | 7.55 | 18.1 | 0 | 0 |

# OLLIE RAYNER

## RHB OB R0 W0

FULL NAME: Oliver Philip Rayner
BORN: November 1, 1985, Fallingbostel, Germany
SQUAD NO: 2
HEIGHT: 6ft 5in
NICKNAME: Draynes, Vaynes, Great Raynes
EDUCATION: St Bede's School
TEAMS: Middlesex, Sussex
CAREER: First-class: 2006; List A: 2006; T20: 2006

BEST BATTING: 143* Middlesex vs Nottinghamshire, Nottingham, 2012
BEST BOWLING: 8-46 Middlesex vs Surrey, The Oval, 2013

FAMILY TIES? No family ties – cricket is the only sport not really played in my family, as you can probably tell through watching me!
CAREER HIGHLIGHTS? Winning Division Two of the Championship with Middlesex, both of my hundreds and taking 15 wickets vs Surrey
SUPERSTITIONS? Taking my guard every time I'm back on strike
CRICKETING HEROES? Graeme Swann – I was losing faith in bowling conventional off-spin until he tore up the international scene
NON-CRICKETING HEROES? Jenson Button – he's a king
IF YOU COULD BE SOMEONE ELSE FOR A DAY? Mario Balotelli – I would love to know what's going on in that bloke's mind!
DESERT ISLAND DISC? Chris Isaak – Wicked Games
FAVOURITE TV? Top Gear, Pawn Stars, Storage Wars, Down East Dickering and Duck Dynasty
PET HATE? Wearing sunglasses on a dull day and pinky rings
SURPRISING FACT? I can actually spin a cricket ball!
TWITTER FEED: @ollie2rayner

| Batting | Mat | Inns | NO | Runs | HS | Ave | SR | 100 | 50 | Ct | St |
|---|---|---|---|---|---|---|---|---|---|---|---|
| First-class | 88 | 113 | 20 | 2268 | 143* | 24.38 | 53.46 | 2 | 11 | 106 | 0 |
| List A | 43 | 29 | 15 | 402 | 61 | 28.71 | 97.10 | 0 | 1 | 18 | 0 |
| Twenty20 | 59 | 35 | 13 | 308 | 41* | 14.00 | 103.01 | 0 | 0 | 13 | 0 |
| **Bowling** | **Mat** | **Balls** | **Runs** | **Wkts** | **BBI** | **BBM** | **Ave** | **Econ** | **SR** | **5w** | **10** |
| First-class | 88 | 13243 | 6334 | 179 | 8/46 | 15/118 | 35.38 | 2.86 | 73.9 | 7 | 1 |
| List A | 43 | 1398 | 1259 | 30 | 3/31 | 3/31 | 41.96 | 5.40 | 46.6 | 0 | 0 |
| Twenty20 | 59 | 1061 | 1290 | 33 | 5/18 | 5/18 | 39.09 | 7.29 | 32.1 | 1 | 0 |

# CHRIS READ

## RHB RM WK R3 W0 MVP72

FULL NAME: Christopher Mark Wells Read
BORN: August 10, 1978, Paignton, Devon
SQUAD NO: 7
HEIGHT: 5ft 8in
NICKNAME: Reados, Readie
EDUCATION: Torquay Boys' Grammar School, University of Bath, Loughborough University
TEAMS: England, Nottinghamshire, Gloucestershire
CAREER: Test: 1999; ODI: 2000; T20I: 2006; First-class: 1998; List A: 1995; T20: 2004



BEST BATTING: 240 Nottinghamshire vs Essex, Chelmsford, 2007
COUNTY CAPS: 1999 (Nottinghamshire); BENEFIT YEAR: 2009 (Nottinghamshire)

CAREER HIGHLIGHTS? Winning the County Championship twice
SUPERSTITIONS? Anything to keep the cricketing gods onside!
CRICKETING HEROES? Ian Botham, Ian Healy, Jack Russell
NON-CRICKETING HEROES? Sébastian Loeb
IF YOU WEREN'T A CRICKETER? Racing and road-testing cars or living the dream as a rock star
FAVOURITE TV? Top Gear
ACCOMPLISHMENTS? Running the NYC marathon
FANTASY SLIP CORDON? Keeper: Me, 1st: Natalie Portman, 2nd: Noel Gallagher, 3rd: Will Ferrell, Gully: Jeremy Clarkson

| Batting | Mat | Inns | NO | Runs | HS | Ave | SR | 100 | 50 | Ct | St |
|---|---|---|---|---|---|---|---|---|---|---|---|
| Tests | 15 | 23 | 4 | 360 | 55 | 18.94 | 39.47 | 0 | 1 | 48 | 6 |
| ODIs | 36 | 24 | 7 | 300 | 30* | 17.64 | 73.17 | 0 | 0 | 41 | 2 |
| T20Is | 1 | 1 | 0 | 13 | 13 | 13.00 | 118.18 | 0 | 0 | 1 | 0 |
| First-class | 307 | 462 | 76 | 14191 | 240 | 36.76 | | 21 | 79 | 920 | 48 |
| List A | 308 | 248 | 69 | 5223 | 135 | 29.17 | | 2 | 21 | 289 | 71 |
| Twenty20 | 107 | 91 | 32 | 1341 | 58* | 22.72 | 121.46 | 0 | 1 | 54 | 24 |
| **Bowling** | **Mat** | **Balls** | **Runs** | **Wkts** | **BBI** | **BBM** | **Ave** | **Econ** | **SR** | **5w** | **10** |
| Tests | 15 | - | - | - | - | - | - | - | - | - | - |
| ODIs | 36 | - | - | - | - | - | - | - | - | - | - |
| T20Is | 1 | - | - | - | - | - | - | - | - | - | - |
| First-class | 307 | 96 | 90 | 0 | - | - | - | 5.62 | - | 0 | 0 |
| List A | 308 | - | - | - | - | - | - | - | - | - | - |
| Twenty20 | 107 | - | - | - | - | - | - | - | - | - | - |

## DAN REDFERN

LHB OB R0 W0

FULL NAME: Daniel James Redfern
BORN: April 18, 1990, Shrewsbury, Shropshire
SQUAD NO: 6
HEIGHT: 5ft 10in
NICKNAME: Redders, Reds, Reddog
EDUCATION: Adams' Grammar School
TEAMS: Leicestershire, Derbyshire
CAREER: First-class: 2007; List A: 2006; T20: 2008

BEST BATTING: 133 Derbyshire vs Hampshire, Southampton, 2012
BEST BOWLING: 3-33 Derbyshire vs Durham, Chester-le-Street, 2013
COUNTY CAPS: 2012 (Derbyshire)

CAREER HIGHLIGHTS? My maiden first-class hundred and winning Division Two of the County Championship with Derbyshire in 2012
BEST PLAYER IN COUNTY CRICKET? Ben Stokes
SUPERSTITIONS? No crossing on stairs before going out to bat
CRICKETING HEROES? Brian Lara and Graham Thorpe – two left-handers I grew up watching and admired
NON-CRICKETING HEROES? Stephen Fry – incredibly clever and funny
FAVOURITE TV? The Office is my favourite by far
LEAST FAVOURITE TV? Made In Chelsea – despicable people
FANTASY SLIP CORDON? Keeper: Ricky Gervais (comic genius), 1st: Stephen Fry (for the knowledge he has on so many different subjects), 2nd: Myself, 3rd: Spider-Man (to catch everything so we can just chat), Gully: Megan Fox
TWITTER FEED: @redfern_dan

| Batting | Mat | Inns | NO | Runs | HS | Ave | SR | 100 | 50 | Ct | St |
|---|---|---|---|---|---|---|---|---|---|---|---|
| First-class | 79 | 133 | 8 | 3676 | 133 | 29.40 | 54.91 | 2 | 28 | 39 | 0 |
| List A | 49 | 39 | 1 | 752 | 57* | 19.78 | 73.22 | 0 | 3 | 11 | 0 |
| Twenty20 | 16 | 13 | 0 | 117 | 43 | 9.00 | 100.86 | 0 | 0 | 7 | 0 |
| **Bowling** | **Mat** | **Balls** | **Runs** | **Wkts** | **BBI** | **BBM** | **Ave** | **Econ** | **SR** | **5w** | **10** |
| First-class | 79 | 1129 | 711 | 18 | 3/33 | 3/43 | 39.50 | 3.77 | 62.7 | 0 | 0 |
| List A | 49 | 424 | 351 | 9 | 2/10 | 2/10 | 39.00 | 4.96 | 47.1 | 0 | 0 |
| Twenty20 | 16 | 201 | 246 | 10 | 2/17 | 2/17 | 24.60 | 7.34 | 20.1 | 0 | 0 |

# LUIS REECE LHB LM R0 W0

FULL NAME: Luis Michael Reece
BORN: August 4, 1990, Taunton
SQUAD NO: 21
EDUCATION: St Michael's School; Myerscough College; Leeds Metropolitan University
TEAMS: Lancashire
CAREER: First-class: 2012; List A: 2011



BEST BATTING: 114* Leeds/Bradford MCCU vs Leicestershire, Leicester, 2013
BEST BOWLING: 4-28 Leeds/Bradford MCCU vs Leicestershire, Leicester, 2013

TWITTER FEED: @lreece17
NOTES: Connected to Lancashire since the age of 11, Reece was playing for Lancashire's 2nd XI from the age of 16 but was let go shortly after his 19th birthday. After a spell in Australia he returned to go to Leeds/Bradford University and worked his way back into professional cricket, representing the Unicorns in the CB40 in 2011 and 2012. In May 2012 he scored 164 and took 7-21 – at one stage his figures read 5-0 – for Leeds/Bradford MCCU in a three-day friendly against Sussex. Impressed enough to sign professional terms with Lancashire in September 2012 and he signed off from university by captaining Leeds/Bradford MCCU to a 102-run win over a full-strength Leicestershire side in April 2013, scoring 114* and taking six wickets. Promoted to open the batting for Lancashire in 2013, Reece scored one century and eight half-centuries, seven of which came consecutively, to finish the campaign with an average of 54.81. He found things far tougher last year, averaging just 16.37 from nine matches in the Championship

| Batting | Mat | Inns | NO | Runs | HS | Ave | SR | 100 | 50 | Ct | St |
|---|---|---|---|---|---|---|---|---|---|---|---|
| First-class | 24 | 43 | 5 | 1361 | 114* | 35.81 | 48.29 | 1 | 11 | 16 | 0 |
| List A | 22 | 20 | 4 | 409 | 59 | 25.56 | 84.32 | 0 | 2 | 6 | 0 |
| **Bowling** | **Mat** | **Balls** | **Runs** | **Wkts** | **BBI** | **BBM** | **Ave** | **Econ** | **SR** | **5w** | **10** |
| First-class | 24 | 786 | 445 | 14 | 4/28 | 6/67 | 31.78 | 3.39 | 56.1 | 0 | 0 |
| List A | 22 | 404 | 418 | 6 | 4/35 | 4/35 | 69.66 | 6.20 | 67.3 | 0 | 0 |

# JAMES REGAN

RHB WK R0 W0

FULL NAME: James Alan Regan
BORN: May 30, 1994, Frimley, Surrey
SQUAD NO: 19
HEIGHT: 5ft 10in
NICKNAME: Reags
EDUCATION: King's College, Taunton
TEAMS: Somerset
CAREER: First-class: 2012

FAMILY TIES? My father has played all his life and I've followed him around
CAREER HIGHLIGHTS? Playing against South Africa in the three-day tour match
BEST PLAYER IN COUNTY CRICKET? Jason Roy
TIP FOR THE TOP? Lewis Gregory, Matt Dunn, Alex Lees
CRICKETING HEROES? Kevin Pietersen, AB de Villiers
NON-CRICKETING HEROES? David Beckham – because he's just a great guy. Cristiano Ronaldo – because he's got it all
IF YOU WEREN'T A CRICKETER? Salesman or model
IF YOU COULD BE SOMEONE ELSE FOR A DAY? Cristiano Ronaldo
DESERT ISLAND DISC? Ed Sheeran or Sam Smith
FAVOURITE TV? The Only Way Is Essex
PET HATE? People leaving things in the wrong place. I just don't understand it
FANTASY SLIP CORDON? Keeper: Lee Evans, 1st: David Beckham, 2nd: Cristiano Ronaldo, 3rd: Dan Bilzerian
TWITTER FEED: @reganja23

| Batting | Mat | Inns | NO | Runs | HS | Ave | SR | 100 | 50 | Ct | St |
|---|---|---|---|---|---|---|---|---|---|---|---|
| First-class | 1 | - | - | - | - | - | - | - | - | 0 | 0 |
| **Bowling** | **Mat** | **Balls** | **Runs** | **Wkts** | **BBI** | **BBM** | **Ave** | **Econ** | **SR** | **5w** | **10** |
| First-class | 1 | - | - | - | - | - | - | - | - | - | - |

# ABDUR REHMAN

LHB SLA R0 W0

FULL NAME: Abdur Rehman
BORN: March 1, 1980, Sialkot, Pakistan
SQUAD NO: TBC
TEAMS: Pakistan, Somerset, Gujranwala Cricket Association, Habib Bank Limited, Punjab Stallions, Sialkot, Sialkot Stallions
CAREER: Test: 2007; ODI: 2006; T20I: 2007; First-class: 1997; List A: 1998; T20: 2005

BEST BATTING: 96 Habib Bank Limited vs National Bank Pakistan, Multan, 2006
BEST BOWLING: 9-65 Somerset vs Worcestershire, Taunton, 2012

NOTES: Had to wait until he was 26 for his first international cap, an ODI against the West Indies at Faisalabad. Returned match figures of 8-210 (4-105 in both innings) on Test debut, but played just once more before being dropped for three years. Reached 50 Test wickets in his 11th Test. Claimed 19 wickets in Pakistan's 3-0 series win against England in the UAE in 2012. Took 27 wickets in just four Championship matches in 2012, including a career best 9-65 against Worcestershire. This season will be his second spell at Somerset, after a short stint in 2012

| Batting | Mat | Inns | NO | Runs | HS | Ave | SR | 100 | 50 | Ct | St |
|---|---|---|---|---|---|---|---|---|---|---|---|
| Tests | 22 | 31 | 3 | 395 | 60 | 14.10 | 42.42 | 0 | 2 | 8 | 0 |
| ODIs | 31 | 23 | 6 | 142 | 31 | 8.35 | 53.99 | 0 | 0 | 7 | 0 |
| T20Is | 8 | 5 | 3 | 22 | 7* | 11.00 | 75.86 | 0 | 0 | 6 | 0 |
| First-class | 140 | 190 | 20 | 2996 | 96 | 17.62 | | 0 | 15 | 60 | 0 |
| List A | 146 | 103 | 25 | 1032 | 50 | 13.23 | | 0 | 1 | 33 | 0 |
| Twenty20 | 62 | 26 | 7 | 166 | 21 | 8.73 | 97.64 | 0 | 0 | 28 | 0 |
| **Bowling** | **Mat** | **Balls** | **Runs** | **Wkts** | **BBI** | **BBM** | **Ave** | **Econ** | **SR** | **5w** | **10** |
| Tests | 22 | 6892 | 2910 | 99 | 6/25 | 8/92 | 29.39 | 2.53 | 69.6 | 2 | 0 |
| ODIs | 31 | 1624 | 1142 | 30 | 4/48 | 4/48 | 38.06 | 4.21 | 54.1 | 0 | 0 |
| T20Is | 8 | 156 | 192 | 11 | 2/7 | 2/7 | 17.45 | 7.38 | 14.1 | 0 | 0 |
| First-class | 140 | 31567 | 13835 | 529 | 9/65 | | 26.15 | 2.62 | 59.6 | 25 | 5 |
| List A | 146 | 7708 | 5578 | 209 | 6/16 | 6/16 | 26.68 | 4.34 | 36.8 | 1 | 0 |
| Twenty20 | 62 | 1395 | 1465 | 66 | 3/17 | 3/17 | 22.19 | 6.30 | 21.1 | 0 | 0 |

## GEORGE RHODES

RHB RM R0 W0

FULL NAME: George Harry Rhodes
BORN: October 26, 1993
SQUAD NO: 34
HEIGHT: 5ft 11in
NICKNAME: Rhodesy, Junior Bump
EDUCATION: The Chase High School and Technology College; The University of Worcester
TEAMS: Worcestershire 2nd XI
CAREER: Yet to make first-team debut

---

FAMILY TIES? My father Steve played for England, Worcestershire and Yorkshire and my grandfather Billy played for Nottinghamshire
CAREER HIGHLIGHTS? My 1st XI debut vs Cambridge MCCU
BEST PLAYER IN COUNTY CRICKET? Moeen Ali
TIP FOR THE TOP? Charlie Morris, Tom Kohler-Cadmore, Tom Fell
MOST MARKED CHARACTERISTIC? Big ears, arrow head
NON-CRICKETING HEROES? Nelson Mandela
CRICKET RULE YOU'D CHANGE? Compulsory disco break
COACHING TIP? Do the most you can to be the best you can be
IF YOU WEREN'T A CRICKETER? Join the Royal Marines
IF YOU COULD BE SOMEONE ELSE FOR A DAY? Jordan Belfort (Wolf Of Wall Street)
DESERT ISLAND DISC? Like A Virgin – Madonna
FAVOURITE TV? Hannibal
LEAST FAVOURITE TV? X Factor
ACCOMPLISHMENTS? Skydive!
PET HATE? I don't like turtle pellets
SURPRISING FACT? I have many leather-bound books and my apartment smells of rich mahogany
FANTASY SLIP CORDON? Keeper: Karl Pilkington, 1st: Will Ferrell, 2nd: Johnny Vegas, 3rd: Myself, Gully: David Brent

# WILL RHODES

## LHB RMF R0 W0

FULL NAME: William Michael Harry Rhodes
BORN: March 2, 1995, Nottingham
SQUAD NO: 35
HEIGHT: 6ft 1in
NICKNAME: Codhead
EDUCATION: Cottingham High School
TEAMS: Yorkshire
CAREER: List A: 2013; T20: 2013



---

CAREER HIGHLIGHTS? Making my debut for Yorkshire and captaining England U19 at the World Cup
BEST PLAYER IN COUNTY CRICKET? Adam Lyth
TIP FOR THE TOP? Joe Clarke, Ben Duckett, Dave Sayer, Rob Sayer
MOST MARKED CHARACTERISTIC? My terrible accent
SUPERSTITIONS? I mark the crease 10 times when I first get to the middle
CRICKETING HEROES? Jacques Kallis – absolute gun
NON-CRICKETING HEROES? Jack Chambers, Levi Towell and Jon Dicks – if you've ever been to Space on a Tuesday in Leeds then you'll know why!
CRICKET RULE YOU'D CHANGE? You should get more runs for however big the six is
IF YOU WEREN'T A CRICKETER? I'd probably be a professional footballer
IF YOU COULD BE SOMEONE ELSE FOR A DAY? Hugh Hefner
DESERT ISLAND DISC? 5ive – Invincible
FAVOURITE TV? Midsomer Murders
LEAST FAVOURITE TV? Wouldn't watch it if it was a waste of time!
ACCOMPLISHMENTS? Making it through school. I wasn't the most academic
PET HATE? People who bite their fork when they eat
TWITTER FEED: @will_rhodes152

| Batting | Mat | Inns | NO | Runs | HS | Ave | SR | 100 | 50 | Ct | St |
|---|---|---|---|---|---|---|---|---|---|---|---|
| List A | 7 | 6 | 1 | 53 | 19* | 10.60 | 80.30 | 0 | 0 | 2 | 0 |
| Twenty20 | 2 | 2 | 0 | 13 | 13 | 6.50 | 65.00 | 0 | 0 | 0 | 0 |

| Bowling | Mat | Balls | Runs | Wkts | BBI | BBM | Ave | Econ | SR | 5w | 10 |
|---|---|---|---|---|---|---|---|---|---|---|---|
| List A | 7 | 120 | 133 | 4 | 2/26 | 2/26 | 33.25 | 6.65 | 30.0 | 0 | 0 |
| Twenty20 | 2 | 7 | 14 | 0 | - | - | - | 12.00 | - | 0 | 0 |

# MICHAEL RICHARDSON RHB WK R1 W0

FULL NAME: Michael John Richardson
BORN: October 4, 1986, Port Elizabeth, South Africa
SQUAD NO: 18
HEIGHT: 5ft 10in
NICKNAME: Rory, Chelsea
EDUCATION: Rondebosch Boys High School; Stonyhurst College; University of Nottingham
TEAMS: Durham
CAREER: First-class: 2010; List A: 2012; T20: 2013

BEST BATTING: 146 Durham vs Yorkshire, Chester-le-Street, 2014

FAMILY TIES? My dad David, my granddad John Richardson and my cousin Matthew Richardson all played first-class cricket
CAREER HIGHLIGHTS? Getting my Durham contract, winning the 2013 County Championship and scoring my maiden first-class hundred
BEST PLAYER IN COUNTY CRICKET? Jeetan Patel
TIP FOR THE TOP? Mark Wood
CRICKETING HEROES? Neil McKenzie
NON-CRICKETING HEROES? Jose Mourinho
CRICKET RULE YOU'D CHANGE? Reviews system could be used in county cricket
IF YOU WEREN'T A CRICKETER? Investment manager
IF YOU COULD BE SOMEONE ELSE FOR A DAY? Rafa Nadal or Cristiano Ronaldo
DESERT ISLAND DISC? Kings of Leon – Mechanical Bull
FAVOURITE TV? Suits
SURPRISING FACT? I once cycled from Paris to Geneva
TWITTER FEED: @Richo18howu

| Batting | Mat | Inns | NO | Runs | HS | Ave | SR | 100 | 50 | Ct | St |
|---|---|---|---|---|---|---|---|---|---|---|---|
| First-class | 49 | 81 | 2 | 2347 | 148 | 29.70 | 52.29 | 4 | 12 | 78 | 1 |
| List A | 3 | 2 | 0 | 61 | 45 | 30.50 | 70.93 | 0 | 0 | 2 | 0 |
| Twenty20 | 14 | 8 | 4 | 51 | 19 | 12.75 | 110.86 | 0 | 0 | 6 | 0 |
| **Bowling** | **Mat** | **Balls** | **Runs** | **Wkts** | **BBI** | **BBM** | **Ave** | **Econ** | **SR** | **5w** | **10** |
| First-class | 49 | 24 | 13 | 0 | - | - | - | 3.25 | - | 0 | 0 |
| List A | 3 | - | - | - | - | - | - | - | - | - | - |
| Twenty20 | 14 | - | - | - | - | - | - | - | - | - | - |

# ADAM RILEY RHB OB R0 W1

FULL NAME: Adam Edward Nicholas Riley
BORN: March 23, 1992, Sidcup, Kent
SQUAD NO: 33
HEIGHT: 6ft 2in
NICKNAME: Riles, The General, MadDog, Saggs
EDUCATION: Beths Grammar School; Loughborough University
TEAMS: Kent
CAREER: First-class: 2011; List A: 2011; T20: 2011



BEST BATTING: 23* Kent vs Glamorgan, Cardiff, 2014
BEST BOWLING: 7-150 Kent vs Hampshire, Southampton, 2013

CAREER HIGHLIGHTS? Getting a nine-fer in a Championship win against Surrey and being picked for England Lions
BEST PLAYER IN COUNTY CRICKET? Gary Ballance
TIP FOR THE TOP? Matt Hobden, Toby Lester
CRICKETING HEROES? Shane Warne – I loved watching him bowl
NON-CRICKETING HEROES? Alan Curbishley and Dean Kiely – two Charlton legends when we used to be good!
COACHING TIP? Always fight/compete with the batsmen, never with yourself or your action
IF YOU WEREN'T A CRICKETER? A full-time Charlton fan with a degree in Geography!
ACCOMPLISHMENTS? Completing my degree at Loughborough Uni and getting Charlton promoted on Football Manager on a shoestring budget
SURPRISING FACT? I like my two cats more than my sisters!
FANTASY SLIP CORDON? Keeper: Me, 1st: Alan Curbishley, 2nd: Mr Bean, 3rd: Sir Alex Ferguson, Gully: Shane Warne
TWITTER FEED: @AdamRiley92

| Batting | Mat | Inns | NO | Runs | HS | Ave | SR | 100 | 50 | Ct | St |
|---|---|---|---|---|---|---|---|---|---|---|---|
| First-class | 38 | 48 | 16 | 278 | 23* | 8.68 | 25.62 | 0 | 0 | 20 | 0 |
| List A | 23 | 5 | 3 | 11 | 5* | 5.50 | 47.82 | 0 | 0 | 8 | 0 |
| Twenty20 | 24 | 7 | 4 | 17 | 5* | 5.66 | 85.00 | 0 | 0 | 5 | 0 |
| **Bowling** | **Mat** | **Balls** | **Runs** | **Wkts** | **BBI** | **BBM** | **Ave** | **Econ** | **SR** | **5w** | **10** |
| First-class | 38 | 5468 | 3284 | 99 | 7/150 | 9/123 | 33.17 | 3.60 | 55.2 | 5 | 0 |
| List A | 23 | 828 | 771 | 19 | 2/32 | 2/32 | 40.57 | 5.58 | 43.5 | 0 | 0 |
| Twenty20 | 24 | 454 | 564 | 19 | 4/22 | 4/22 | 29.68 | 7.45 | 23.8 | 0 | 0 |

## ANGUS ROBSON

**RHB LB R1 W0**

FULL NAME: Angus James Robson
BORN: February 19, 1992, Darlinghurst, Sydney, Australia
SQUAD NO: 8
HEIGHT: 5ft 9in
NICKNAME: Gus, Robbo
EDUCATION: Marcellin College; Australian College of Physical Education
TEAMS: Leicestershire
CAREER: First-class: 2013; List A: 2014

BEST BATTING: 115 Leicestershire vs Hampshire, Southampton, 2014

FAMILY TIES? Brother Sam plays for Middlesex and England. Father Jim played 2nd XI for Worcestershire
CAREER HIGHLIGHTS? 1,000 runs in my first season of first-class cricket in 2014 and scoring a century against India in the tour game
BEST PLAYER IN COUNTY CRICKET? Eoin Morgan
TIP FOR THE TOP? Nathan Buck
SUPERSTITIONS? I pick up the grass to check the wind regularly when I bat
CRICKETING HEROES? Ian Bell, Michael Clarke, Mike Atherton
NON-CRICKETING HEROES? Haile Gebrselassie – inspirational runner to people all around the world
CRICKET RULE YOU'D CHANGE? If you take a catch with your hat you get two wickets
IF YOU COULD BE SOMEONE ELSE FOR A DAY? Harry Potter
ACCOMPLISHMENTS? Progressing through a PE teaching degree
SURPRISING FACT? I love all of the Harry Potter films
FANTASY SLIP CORDON? Keeper: Happy Gilmore, 1st: Harry Potter, 2nd: Taylor Swift, 3rd: Myself, Gully: Ryan Gosling
TWITTER FEED: @gusrobson92

| Batting | Mat | Inns | NO | Runs | HS | Ave | SR | 100 | 50 | Ct | St |
|---|---|---|---|---|---|---|---|---|---|---|---|
| First-class | 19 | 34 | 0 | 1145 | 115 | 33.67 | 53.62 | 1 | 9 | 12 | 0 |
| List A | 6 | 6 | 0 | 92 | 28 | 15.33 | 80.00 | 0 | 0 | 1 | 0 |
| **Bowling** | **Mat** | **Balls** | **Runs** | **Wkts** | **BBI** | **BBM** | **Ave** | **Econ** | **SR** | **5w** | **10** |
| First-class | 19 | 105 | 95 | 0 | - | - | - | 5.42 | - | 0 | 0 |
| List A | 6 | - | - | - | - | - | - | - | - | - | - |

# SAM ROBSON

RHB LB R2 W0

FULL NAME: Sam David Robson
BORN: July 1, 1989, Paddington, Sydney, Australia
SQUAD NO: 12
HEIGHT: 6ft
NICKNAME: Robbo, Chum, Jar-counter
TEAMS: England, Middlesex, Australia U19
CAREER: First-class: 2009; List A: 2008; T20: 2011

MIDDLESEX

BEST BATTING: 215* Middlesex vs Warwickshire, Birmingham, 2013
COUNTY CAPS: 2013 (Middlesex)

FAMILY TIES? Brother Angus plays for Leicestershire, father Jim played for Worcester 2nd XI
CAREER HIGHLIGHTS? Being selected to play Test cricket for England, my maiden Test century vs Sri Lanka at Headingley, the Test series win vs India and all other great wins for Middlesex
TIP FOR THE TOP? Tom Helm, Angus Robson
SUPERSTITIONS? Be good to your mother, wear flip-flops in public showers
CRICKETING HEROES? My father
IF YOU WEREN'T A CRICKETER? Maybe a school teacher
IF YOU COULD BE SOMEONE ELSE FOR A DAY? Any big-time actor in Hollywood
DESERT ISLAND DISC? '90s greatest hits
FAVOURITE TV? Seinfeld
PET HATE? Traffic

| Batting | Mat | Inns | NO | Runs | HS | Ave | SR | 100 | 50 | Ct | St |
|---|---|---|---|---|---|---|---|---|---|---|---|
| Tests | 7 | 11 | 0 | 336 | 127 | 30.54 | 44.50 | 1 | 1 | 5 | 0 |
| First-class | 84 | 149 | 13 | 5408 | 215* | 39.76 | 50.68 | 13 | 21 | 86 | 0 |
| List A | 8 | 6 | 0 | 169 | 65 | 28.16 | 74.44 | 0 | 1 | 3 | 0 |
| Twenty20 | 4 | 4 | 2 | 53 | 28* | 26.50 | 103.92 | 0 | 0 | 2 | 0 |
| **Bowling** | **Mat** | **Balls** | **Runs** | **Wkts** | **BBI** | **BBM** | **Ave** | **Econ** | **SR** | **5w** | **10** |
| Tests | 7 | - | - | - | - | - | - | - | - | - | - |
| First-class | 84 | 92 | 72 | 1 | 1/4 | 1/4 | 72.00 | 4.69 | 92.0 | 0 | 0 |
| List A | 8 | - | - | - | - | - | - | - | - | - | - |
| Twenty20 | 4 | - | - | - | - | - | - | - | - | - | - |

## GARETH RODERICK

RHB WK R0 W0

FULL NAME: Gareth Hugh Roderick
BORN: August 29, 1991, Durban, South Africa
SQUAD NO: 27
HEIGHT: 6ft
NICKNAME: Rodgers, The Pear
EDUCATION: Maritzburg College
TEAMS: Gloucestershire, KwaZulu-Natal
CAREER: First-class: 2011; List A: 2011; T20: 2011

BEST BATTING: 171, Gloucestershire vs Leicestershire, Bristol, 2014

CAREER HIGHLIGHTS? Maiden hundred against Kent and my career-best against Leicestershire
BEST PLAYER IN COUNTY CRICKET? Adam Lyth
TIP FOR THE TOP? Craig Miles, Liam Norwell and Jack Taylor
MOST MARKED CHARACTERISTIC? Being a skinny fat lad
CRICKETING HEROES? Steve Waugh – great batsman, captain and leader of men. Herschelle Gibbs – best batsman to watch when on song
IF YOU WEREN'T A CRICKETER? Studying a degree I had no interest in or working back in South Africa with my father
IF YOU COULD BE SOMEONE ELSE FOR A DAY? Justin Bieber. So I could ruin his career
DESERT ISLAND DISC? Michael Bublé
PET HATE? Untidy people. Because I'm not the tidiest, so me plus another untidy person just equals a mess
FANTASY SLIP CORDON? The members of South Park. So I could hear Cartman abuse everything and everyone in sight
TWITTER FEED: @roders369

| Batting | Mat | Inns | NO | Runs | HS | Ave | SR | 100 | 50 | Ct | St |
|---|---|---|---|---|---|---|---|---|---|---|---|
| First-class | 29 | 44 | 9 | 1587 | 171 | 45.34 | 52.28 | 3 | 8 | 67 | 1 |
| List A | 22 | 15 | 3 | 279 | 63 | 23.25 | 81.81 | 0 | 1 | 23 | 2 |
| Twenty20 | 14 | 9 | 2 | 71 | 32 | 10.14 | 93.42 | 0 | 0 | 5 | 0 |
| **Bowling** | **Mat** | **Balls** | **Runs** | **Wkts** | **BBI** | **BBM** | **Ave** | **Econ** | **SR** | **5w** | **10** |
| First-class | 29 | - | - | - | - | - | - | - | - | - | - |
| List A | 22 | - | - | - | - | - | - | - | - | - | - |
| Twenty20 | 14 | - | - | - | - | - | - | - | - | - | - |

# TOBY ROLAND-JONES

## RHB RMF R0 W1 MVP41

FULL NAME: Tobias Skelton Roland-Jones
BORN: January 29, 1988, Ashford, Middlesex
SQUAD NO: 21
HEIGHT: 6ft 4in
NICKNAME: Rojo, TRJ
EDUCATION: Hampton School; Leeds University
TEAMS: Middlesex, England Lions
CAREER: First-class: 2010; List A: 2010; T20: 2011



BEST BATTING: 77 Middlesex vs Somerset, Taunton, 2014
BEST BOWLING: 6-50 Middlesex vs Northamptonshire, Northampton, 2014
COUNTY CAPS: 2012

FAMILY TIES? My older brother Olly played for Middlesex 2nd XI and my dad used to coach age-group cricket
CAREER HIGHLIGHTS? My first five-wicket haul at Lord's vs Surrey, my hat-trick vs Derbyshire and representing England Lions in 2013
MOST MARKED CHARACTERISTIC? Anger when on the cricket pitch and off it; my nose. In our squad only Steven Finn has a bigger one
CRICKETING HEROES? Sir Ian Botham
NON-CRICKETING HEROES? Ricky Gervais, Alan Partridge, Paul Scholes
IF YOU WEREN'T A CRICKETER? I'd be nursing a far larger waist
DESERT ISLAND DISC? Michael Jackson – Thriller
FAVOURITE TV? The Sopranos, The Wire
FANTASY SLIP CORDON? Keeper: David Beckham, 1st: Muhammad Ali, 2nd: Will Ferrell, 3rd: Myself, Gully: Usain Bolt
TWITTER FEED: @tobyrj21

| Batting | Mat | Inns | NO | Runs | HS | Ave | SR | 100 | 50 | Ct | St |
|---|---|---|---|---|---|---|---|---|---|---|---|
| First-class | 53 | 74 | 15 | 1192 | 77 | 20.20 | 55.33 | 0 | 4 | 16 | 0 |
| List A | 38 | 20 | 5 | 171 | 29* | 11.40 | 86.36 | 0 | 0 | 6 | 0 |
| Twenty20 | 18 | 9 | 4 | 70 | 30 | 14.00 | 129.62 | 0 | 0 | 3 | 0 |
| **Bowling** | **Mat** | **Balls** | **Runs** | **Wkts** | **BBI** | **BBM** | **Ave** | **Econ** | **SR** | **5w** | **10** |
| First-class | 53 | 8931 | 4828 | 200 | 6/50 | 12/105 | 24.14 | 3.24 | 44.6 | 11 | 2 |
| List A | 38 | 1663 | 1531 | 64 | 4/42 | 4/42 | 23.92 | 5.52 | 25.9 | 0 | 0 |
| Twenty20 | 18 | 374 | 528 | 19 | 4/25 | 4/25 | 27.78 | 8.47 | 19.6 | 0 | 0 |

# JOE ROOT

## RHB OB R3 W0

FULL NAME: Joseph Edward Root
BORN: December 30, 1990, Sheffield, Yorkshire
SQUAD NO: 5
HEIGHT: 6ft
NICKNAME: Rooty, Roota, Rootfish
EDUCATION: King Ecgbert School; Worksop College
TEAMS: England, Yorkshire
CAREER: Test: 2012; ODI: 2013; T20I: 2012; First-class: 2010; List A: 2009; T20: 2011

BEST BATTING: 236 Yorkshire vs Derbyshire, Leeds, 2013
BEST BOWLING: 3-33 Yorkshire vs Warwickshire, Leeds, 2011
COUNTY CAPS: 2012

FAMILY TIES? My dad played club cricket and represented Nottinghamshire 2nd XI and Colts. My brother Billy has a performance contract at Notts
CAREER HIGHLIGHTS? Winning the Ashes
MOST MARKED CHARACTERISTIC? Bowed legs and baby face
NON-CRICKETING HEROES? Seve Ballesteros, Alan Shearer
DESERT ISLAND DISC? Arctic Monkeys – Whatever People Say I Am, That's What I'm Not
FANTASY SLIP CORDON? Keeper: Jordan Belfort, 1st: Myself, 2nd: Tiger Woods, 3rd: Allan Shearer, Gully: Alex Turner
TWITTER FEED: @joeroot05

| Batting | Mat | Inns | NO | Runs | HS | Ave | SR | 100 | 50 | Ct | St |
|---|---|---|---|---|---|---|---|---|---|---|---|
| Tests | 22 | 40 | 6 | 1732 | 200* | 50.94 | 46.24 | 5 | 7 | 15 | 0 |
| ODIs | 52 | 49 | 5 | 1773 | 121 | 40.29 | 80.88 | 4 | 8 | 21 | 0 |
| T20Is | 9 | 7 | 2 | 183 | 90* | 36.60 | 126.20 | 0 | 1 | 5 | 0 |
| First-class | 69 | 116 | 15 | 4903 | 236 | 48.54 | 51.97 | 12 | 20 | 39 | 0 |
| List A | 81 | 77 | 9 | 2546 | 121 | 37.44 | 80.11 | 5 | 12 | 31 | 0 |
| Twenty20 | 37 | 31 | 6 | 606 | 90* | 24.24 | 117.21 | 0 | 2 | 14 | 0 |
| **Bowling** | **Mat** | **Balls** | **Runs** | **Wkts** | **BBI** | **BBM** | **Ave** | **Econ** | **SR** | **5w** | **10** |
| Tests | 22 | 510 | 225 | 4 | 2/9 | 2/9 | 56.25 | 2.64 | 127.5 | 0 | 0 |
| ODIs | 52 | 774 | 745 | 12 | 2/15 | 2/15 | 62.08 | 5.77 | 64.5 | 0 | 0 |
| T20Is | 9 | 54 | 96 | 4 | 1/13 | 1/13 | 24.00 | 10.66 | 13.5 | 0 | 0 |
| First-class | 69 | 1755 | 914 | 16 | 3/33 | 3/33 | 57.12 | 3.12 | 109.6 | 0 | 0 |
| List A | 81 | 1241 | 1131 | 24 | 2/10 | 2/10 | 47.12 | 5.46 | 51.7 | 0 | 0 |
| Twenty20 | 37 | 204 | 320 | 8 | 1/12 | 1/12 | 40.00 | 9.41 | 25.5 | 0 | 0 |

# ADAM ROSSINGTON RHB WK R0 W0

FULL NAME: Adam Matthew Rossington
BORN: May 5, 1993, Edgware, Middlesex
SQUAD NO: 7
HEIGHT: 6ft
NICKNAME: Rosso, Tug Boat
EDUCATION: Mill Hill School
TEAMS: Northamptonshire, Middlesex
CAREER: First-class: 2010; List A: 2012; T20: 2011



---

BEST BATTING: 103* Middlesex vs CMCCU, Fenner's, 2013

---

CAREER HIGHLIGHTS? Maiden Championship century for Northants and an England U19 hundred
BEST PLAYER IN COUNTY CRICKET? Kumar Sangakkara
TIP FOR THE TOP? Sam Hain, Harry Podmore
CRICKETING HEROES? Paul Weekes – I watched him growing up
NON-CRICKETING HEROES? Phil Taylor and Floyd Mayweather Jr – both top of their sport for a number of years
CRICKET RULE YOU'D CHANGE? All fielders to be inside the circle during the Powerplay, so more boundaries are hit
COACHING TIP? Play the ball late and look where the ball bounces after you hit it
IF YOU COULD BE SOMEONE ELSE FOR A DAY? Dan Bilzerian
ACCOMPLISHMENTS? Buying my first property
PET HATE? Middle-lane drivers – there are three lanes for a reason
SURPRISING FACT? I play golf off six
TWITTER FEED: @rossington17

| Batting | Mat | Inns | NO | Runs | HS | Ave | SR | 100 | 50 | Ct | St |
|---|---|---|---|---|---|---|---|---|---|---|---|
| First-class | 15 | 25 | 2 | 692 | 103* | 30.08 | 69.26 | 2 | 3 | 30 | 4 |
| List A | 16 | 13 | 2 | 419 | 82 | 38.09 | 92.49 | 0 | 3 | 12 | 2 |
| Twenty20 | 29 | 28 | 3 | 435 | 74 | 17.40 | 135.93 | 0 | 2 | 16 | 4 |
| **Bowling** | **Mat** | **Balls** | **Runs** | **Wkts** | **BBI** | **BBM** | **Ave** | **Econ** | **SR** | **5w** | **10** |
| First-class | 15 | - | - | - | - | - | - | - | - | - | - |
| List A | 16 | - | - | - | - | - | - | - | - | - | - |
| Twenty20 | 29 | - | - | - | - | - | - | - | - | - | - |

## TIM ROUSE

RHB OB RO W0

FULL NAME: Timothy David Rouse
BORN: April 9, 1996, Sheffield, Yorkshire
SQUAD NO: 44
EDUCATION: Kingswood School, Bath
TEAMS: Somerset 2nd XI
CAREER: Yet to make first-team debut

NOTES: A top-order batsman and off-spinner, Rouse was offered a scholarship at the end of 2014 after graduating from the Somerset Academy. He will study at university at the same time, and will be available for Somerset from mid June

# JASON ROY

RHB RM R1 W0 MVP30

FULL NAME: Jason Jonathan Roy
BORN: July 21, 1990, Durban, South Africa
SQUAD NO: 20
HEIGHT: 6ft
NICKNAME: Roy The Boy
EDUCATION: Whitgift School
TEAMS: England, Surrey
CAREER: T20I: 2014; First-class: 2010; List A: 2008; T20: 2008



BEST BATTING: 121* Surrey vs Gloucestershire, Bristol, 2014
BEST BOWLING: 3-9 Surrey vs Gloucestershire, Bristol, 2014

CAREER HIGHLIGHTS? My England T20 debut
BEST PLAYER IN COUNTY CRICKET? Moeen Ali
TIP FOR THE TOP? Dominic Sibley, Tom Curran
MOST MARKED CHARACTERISTIC? I am a very approachable person
CRICKETING HEROES? Jacques Kallis – legend
CRICKET RULE YOU'D CHANGE? Free hits in all forms of the game
IF YOU WEREN'T A CRICKETER? Living near the beach
IF YOU COULD BE SOMEONE ELSE FOR A DAY? Barack Obama
DESERT ISLAND DISC? I would take a compilation disc of chilled vibes
FAVOURITE TV? Sons Of Anarchy
FANTASY SLIP CORDON? Keeper: Spider-Man, 1st: Alex Tysoe (Surrey head physio), 2nd: Hulk, 3rd: Me, Gully: Catwoman
TWITTER FEED: @JasonRoy20

| Batting | Mat | Inns | NO | Runs | HS | Ave | SR | 100 | 50 | Ct | St |
|---|---|---|---|---|---|---|---|---|---|---|---|
| T20Is | 1 | 1 | 0 | 8 | 8 | 8.00 | 80.00 | 0 | 0 | 0 | 0 |
| First-class | 50 | 82 | 8 | 2564 | 121* | 34.64 | 81.81 | 4 | 11 | 44 | 0 |
| List A | 60 | 56 | 4 | 1669 | 141 | 32.09 | 107.60 | 5 | 8 | 18 | 0 |
| Twenty20 | 86 | 83 | 4 | 2169 | 101* | 27.45 | 140.93 | 1 | 16 | 40 | 0 |
| **Bowling** | **Mat** | **Balls** | **Runs** | **Wkts** | **BBI** | **BBM** | **Ave** | **Econ** | **SR** | **5w** | **10** |
| T20Is | 1 | - | - | - | - | - | - | - | - | - | - |
| First-class | 50 | 564 | 380 | 11 | 3/9 | 4/47 | 34.54 | 4.04 | 51.2 | 0 | 0 |
| List A | 60 | 6 | 12 | 0 | - | - | - | 12.00 | - | 0 | 0 |
| Twenty20 | 86 | 18 | 39 | 1 | 1/23 | 1/23 | 39.00 | 13.00 | 18.0 | 0 | 0 |

## JACQUES RUDOLPH LHB LB R4 W0 MVP24

FULL NAME: Jacobus Andries Rudolph
BORN: May 4, 1981, Springs, South Africa
SQUAD NO: TBC
HEIGHT: 5ft 10in
EDUCATION: Afrikaanse Hoer Seunskool
TEAMS: South Africa, Glamorgan, Eagles, Jamaica Tallawahs, Northerns, Surrey, Titans, Yorkshire
CAREER: Test: 2003; ODI: 2003; T20I: 2006; First-class: 1997; List A: 2000; T20: 2004

BEST BATTING: 228* Yorkshire vs Durham, Leeds, 2010
BEST BOWLING: 5-80 Eagles vs Cape Cobras, Newlands, 2007
COUNTY CAPS: 2007 (Yorkshire)

CAREER HIGHLIGHTS? Making 222* on my Test debut
CRICKETING HEROES? Justin Langer
DESERT ISLAND DISC? U2, Dire Straits, or The Killers
NOTES: Scored 222* in his debut Test innings, against Bangladesh at Chittagong in 2003, as part of record-breaking unbeaten third-wicket stand of 429 with Boeta Dippenaar. Played for Yorkshire between 2007-2011, passing 1,000 runs in four consecutive seasons (2007-2010). Signed with Glamorgan in September 2013, replacing Marcus North as the club's overseas player. He was the leading run-scorer in the RL Cup last season with 575 runs at 82.14, and also hit the highest score of 169* against Sussex

| Batting | Mat | Inns | NO | Runs | HS | Ave | SR | 100 | 50 | Ct | St |
|---|---|---|---|---|---|---|---|---|---|---|---|
| Tests | 48 | 83 | 9 | 2622 | 222* | 35.43 | 43.81 | 6 | 11 | 29 | 0 |
| ODIs | 45 | 39 | 6 | 1174 | 81 | 35.57 | 68.05 | 0 | 7 | 11 | 0 |
| T20Is | 1 | 1 | 1 | 6 | 6* | - | 85.71 | 0 | 0 | 0 | 0 |
| First-class | 251 | 430 | 26 | 17541 | 228* | 43.41 | | 48 | 82 | 218 | 0 |
| List A | 239 | 227 | 32 | 9665 | 169* | 49.56 | | 17 | 66 | 87 | 0 |
| Twenty20 | 117 | 105 | 17 | 2902 | 83* | 32.97 | 115.80 | 0 | 20 | 34 | 0 |
| **Bowling** | **Mat** | **Balls** | **Runs** | **Wkts** | **BBI** | **BBM** | **Ave** | **Econ** | **SR** | **5w** | **10** |
| Tests | 48 | 664 | 432 | 4 | 1/1 | 1/1 | 108.00 | 3.90 | 166.0 | 0 | 0 |
| ODIs | 45 | 24 | 26 | 0 | - | - | - | 6.50 | - | 0 | 0 |
| T20Is | 1 | - | - | - | - | - | - | - | - | - | - |
| First-class | 251 | 4610 | 2626 | 59 | 5/80 | | 44.50 | 3.41 | 78.1 | 3 | 0 |
| List A | 239 | 464 | 443 | 13 | 4/41 | 4/41 | 34.07 | 5.72 | 35.6 | 0 | 0 |
| Twenty20 | 117 | 235 | 314 | 11 | 3/16 | 3/16 | 28.54 | 8.01 | 21.3 | 0 | 0 |

# CHRIS RUSHWORTH RHB RFM R0 W2 MVP18

FULL NAME: Christopher Rushworth
BORN: July 11, 1986, Sunderland
SQUAD NO: 22
HEIGHT: 6ft 2in
NICKNAME: Rushy, Sponge
EDUCATION: Castle View Comprehensive
TEAMS: Durham
CAREER: First-class: 2010; List A: 2004; T20: 2011



BEST BATTING: 46 Durham vs Somerset, Taunton, 2014
BEST BOWLING: 9-52 Durham vs Northamptonshire, Chester-le-Street, 2014

FAMILY TIES? My father Joe played local cricket, my brother Lee played county age groups and represented England U17 and U19. My cousin Phil Mustard is Durham's wicketkeeper
CAREER HIGHLIGHTS? Winning the County Championship in 2013 and the Royal London One-Day Cup in 2014. Also, taking 15 wickets in a day against Northants in 2014 and breaking the county's record bowling figures
MOST MARKED CHARACTERISTIC? My bald head and 'rotund' figure probably makes me stand out
CRICKETING HEROES? Shaun Pollock and, more recently, Dale Steyn
NON-CRICKETING HEROES? Tiger Woods, Roger Federer, Phil Taylor – for what they've done in their respective sport and took it to a whole new level
IF YOU COULD BE SOMEONE ELSE FOR A DAY? Rory McIlroy
DESERT ISLAND DISC? Stereophonics
FAVOURITE TV? Football, darts, golf – anything on Sky Sports!
PET HATE? People farting in small changing rooms
TWITTER FEED: @rushworth22 (and @cdcoaching116 for my coaching business)

| Batting | Mat | Inns | NO | Runs | HS | Ave | SR | 100 | 50 | Ct | St |
|---|---|---|---|---|---|---|---|---|---|---|---|
| First-class | 55 | 75 | 24 | 641 | 46 | 12.56 | 64.61 | 0 | 0 | 8 | 0 |
| List A | 42 | 17 | 8 | 53 | 12* | 5.88 | 69.73 | 0 | 0 | 8 | 0 |
| Twenty20 | 39 | 8 | 5 | 12 | 5 | 4.00 | 60.00 | 0 | 0 | 5 | 0 |
| **Bowling** | **Mat** | **Balls** | **Runs** | **Wkts** | **BBI** | **BBM** | **Ave** | **Econ** | **SR** | **5w** | **10** |
| First-class | 55 | 8742 | 4621 | 188 | 9/52 | 15/95 | 24.57 | 3.17 | 46.5 | 9 | 2 |
| List A | 42 | 1684 | 1479 | 72 | 5/31 | 5/31 | 20.54 | 5.26 | 23.3 | 2 | 0 |
| Twenty20 | 39 | 741 | 1000 | 37 | 3/19 | 3/19 | 27.02 | 8.09 | 20.0 | 0 | 0 |

# CHRIS RUSSELL RHB RMF R0 W0

FULL NAME: Christopher James Russell
BORN: February 16, 1989, Newport, Isle of Wight
SQUAD NO: 18
HEIGHT: 6ft 1in
NICKNAME: Goobs, Goober
EDUCATION: Medina High School
TEAMS: Worcestershire
CAREER: First-class: 2012; List A: 2010; T20: 2013

BEST BATTING: 22 Worcestershire vs Middlesex, Worcester, 2012
BEST BOWLING: 4-43 Worcestershire vs Warwickshire, Birmingham, 2012

CAREER HIGHLIGHTS? First-class debut, playing against South Africa and Australia
BEST PLAYER IN COUNTY CRICKET? Moeen Ali
TIP FOR THE TOP? Charlie Morris
MOST MARKED CHARACTERISTIC? My topknot
SUPERSTITIONS? I always pad up in a particular order, even though most of the time is doesn't change anything
CRICKETING HEROES? Dale Steyn
CRICKET RULE YOU'D CHANGE? Couldn't be out caught because it would mean I wouldn't get out as often nicking off
IF YOU WEREN'T A CRICKETER? Busking outside Debenhams in town
IF YOU COULD BE SOMEONE ELSE FOR A DAY? Superman
PET HATE? Rudeness
FANTASY SLIP CORDON? Keeper: Micky Flanagan, 1st: Jack Whitehall, 2nd: David Beckham, 3rd: Myself, Gully: James Corden
TWITTER FEED: @Chris18russell

| Batting | Mat | Inns | NO | Runs | HS | Ave | SR | 100 | 50 | Ct | St |
|---|---|---|---|---|---|---|---|---|---|---|---|
| First-class | 18 | 22 | 4 | 129 | 22 | 7.16 | 36.44 | 0 | 0 | 4 | 0 |
| List A | 7 | 2 | 2 | 2 | 1* | - | 50.00 | 0 | 0 | 3 | 0 |
| Twenty20 | 10 | 2 | 2 | 6 | 3* | - | 66.66 | 0 | 0 | 6 | 0 |
| **Bowling** | **Mat** | **Balls** | **Runs** | **Wkts** | **BBI** | **BBM** | **Ave** | **Econ** | **SR** | **5w** | **10** |
| First-class | 18 | 2306 | 1566 | 38 | 4/43 | 6/117 | 41.21 | 4.07 | 60.6 | 0 | 0 |
| List A | 7 | 198 | 205 | 5 | 4/32 | 4/32 | 41.00 | 6.21 | 39.6 | 0 | 0 |
| Twenty20 | 10 | 209 | 342 | 16 | 4/40 | 4/40 | 21.37 | 9.81 | 13.0 | 0 | 0 |

# JESSE RYDER LHB RM R0 W0 MVP8

FULL NAME: Jesse Daniel Ryder
BORN: August 6, 1984, Masterton, Wellington, New Zealand
SQUAD NO: 76
EDUCATION: Napier Boys High
TEAMS: New Zealand, Essex, Central Districts, Otago, Pune Warriors, Royal Challengers Bangalore, Wellington
CAREER: Test: 2008; ODI: 2008; T20I: 2008; First-class: 2002; List A: 2002; T20: 2006



BEST BATTING: 236 Wellington vs Central Districts, Palmerston North, 2014
BEST BOWLING: 5-24 Essex vs Worcestershire, Chelmsford, 2014

NOTES: While off-field problems have stunted Ryder's international appearances, he remains one of the most talented players in county cricket. Has played 18 Tests for New Zealand, with a Test best of 201 against India at Napier in 2009. Has three ODI hundreds, including one off 46 balls against West Indies in January 2014. Was a success for Essex last season, coming eighth in the MVP rankings, taking a surprising 44 Championship wickets and scoring two centuries

| Batting | Mat | Inns | NO | Runs | HS | Ave | SR | 100 | 50 | Ct | St |
|---|---|---|---|---|---|---|---|---|---|---|---|
| Tests | 18 | 33 | 2 | 1269 | 201 | 40.93 | 55.19 | 3 | 6 | 12 | 0 |
| ODIs | 48 | 42 | 1 | 1362 | 107 | 33.21 | 95.31 | 3 | 6 | 15 | 0 |
| T20Is | 22 | 21 | 1 | 457 | 62 | 22.85 | 127.65 | 0 | 3 | 7 | 0 |
| First-class | 95 | 156 | 10 | 6658 | 236 | 45.60 | | 20 | 29 | 92 | 0 |
| List A | 133 | 124 | 8 | 3868 | 115 | 33.34 | 98.27 | 7 | 21 | 43 | 0 |
| Twenty20 | 104 | 101 | 6 | 2546 | 90* | 26.80 | 147.67 | 0 | 19 | 31 | 0 |
| **Bowling** | **Mat** | **Balls** | **Runs** | **Wkts** | **BBI** | **BBM** | **Ave** | **Econ** | **SR** | **5w** | **10** |
| Tests | 18 | 492 | 280 | 5 | 2/7 | 2/15 | 56.00 | 3.41 | 98.4 | 0 | 0 |
| ODIs | 48 | 407 | 412 | 12 | 3/29 | 3/29 | 34.33 | 6.07 | 33.9 | 0 | 0 |
| T20Is | 22 | 60 | 68 | 2 | 1/2 | 1/2 | 34.00 | 6.80 | 30.0 | 0 | 0 |
| First-class | 95 | 6082 | 2874 | 101 | 5/24 | | 28.45 | 2.83 | 60.2 | 4 | 1 |
| List A | 133 | 1613 | 1573 | 44 | 4/39 | 4/39 | 35.75 | 5.85 | 36.6 | 0 | 0 |
| Twenty20 | 104 | 897 | 1172 | 32 | 5/27 | 5/27 | 36.62 | 7.83 | 28.0 | 1 | 0 |

# MATT SALISBURY RHB RMF R0 W0

FULL NAME: Matthew Edward Thomas Salisbury
BORN: April 18, 1993, Chelmsford
SQUAD NO: 18
HEIGHT: 6ft 1in
NICKNAME: Sals
EDUCATION: Shenfield High School; Anglia Ruskin University
TEAMS: Essex
CAREER: First-class: 2012; List A: 2014; T20: 2014

BEST BATTING: 19 Essex vs Worcestershire, Worcester, 2014
BEST BOWLING: 4-50 Essex vs Worcestershire, Worcester, 2014

CAREER HIGHLIGHTS? My first-team debut vs Sri Lanka
BEST PLAYER IN COUNTY CRICKET? Ravi Bopara
TIP FOR THE TOP? Nick Browne
CRICKET RULE YOU'D CHANGE? Hitting the ball out of the ground should be worth 10 runs
IF YOU COULD BE SOMEONE ELSE FOR A DAY? LeBron James
DESERT ISLAND DISC? Kendrick Lamar – Section 80
FAVOURITE TV? Modern Family
PET HATE? Drivers not indicating
FANTASY SLIP CORDON? Keeper: Ricky Gervais, 1st: Kevin Hart, 2nd: Will Ferrell, 3rd: Shaquille O'Neal
TWITTER FEED: @mattsalisbury10

| Batting | Mat | Inns | NO | Runs | HS | Ave | SR | 100 | 50 | Ct | St |
|---|---|---|---|---|---|---|---|---|---|---|---|
| First-class | 8 | 11 | 3 | 60 | 19 | 7.50 | 32.08 | 0 | 0 | 1 | 0 |
| List A | 6 | 1 | 1 | 5 | 5* | - | 27.77 | 0 | 0 | 2 | 0 |
| Twenty20 | 8 | 2 | 2 | 2 | 1* | - | 100.00 | 0 | 0 | 2 | 0 |
| **Bowling** | **Mat** | **Balls** | **Runs** | **Wkts** | **BBI** | **BBM** | **Ave** | **Econ** | **SR** | **5w** | **10** |
| First-class | 8 | 1182 | 739 | 15 | 4/50 | 5/117 | 49.26 | 3.75 | 78.8 | 0 | 0 |
| List A | 6 | 156 | 168 | 5 | 4/55 | 4/55 | 33.60 | 6.46 | 31.2 | 0 | 0 |
| Twenty20 | 8 | 172 | 256 | 10 | 2/19 | 2/19 | 25.60 | 8.93 | 17.2 | 0 | 0 |

# ANDREW SALTER RHB OB R0 W0

FULL NAME: Andrew Graham Salter
BORN: June 1, 1993, Haverfordwest, Pembrokeshire
SQUAD NO: 21
HEIGHT: 5ft 10in
NICKNAME: Salts
EDUCATION: Milford Haven School; Cardiff Metropolitan University
TEAMS: Glamorgan
CAREER: First-class: 2012; List A: 2012; T20: 2014



BEST BATTING: 25 Glamorgan vs Worcestershire, Worcester, 2014
BEST BOWLING: 3-66 Glamorgan vs Leicestershire, Swansea, 2013

FAMILY TIES? My dad played to university standard, inspiring both my brother and myself to play, and my brother represented West Wales at junior level
CAREER HIGHLIGHTS? Reaching the YB40 final at Lord's must be my biggest highlight so far. Taking a wicket with the first ball of my Championship career was also something that I'll never forget
MOST MARKED CHARACTERISTIC? I'd like to think the way I enjoy the game and show enthusiasm would be one of my marked characteristics. Either that or my nose – it gets a lot of attention
CRICKETING HEROES? Robert Croft and Dean Cosker were my childhood cricketing role models. I also always enjoyed watching Graeme Swann 'ripping them' and showing how you can be aggressive with off-spin bowling
ACCOMPLISHMENTS? Playing in a band and playing local gigs was very fun while it lasted
SURPRISING FACT? I play the guitar regularly but try to avoid the Nicki Minaj requests from the Glamorgan boys
TWITTER FEED: @andysalts

| Batting | Mat | Inns | NO | Runs | HS | Ave | SR | 100 | 50 | Ct | St |
|---|---|---|---|---|---|---|---|---|---|---|---|
| First-class | 12 | 17 | 4 | 173 | 25* | 13.30 | 29.37 | 0 | 0 | 4 | 0 |
| List A | 13 | 8 | 5 | 72 | 36* | 24.00 | 107.46 | 0 | 0 | 3 | 0 |
| Twenty20 | 12 | 7 | 6 | 35 | 10 | 35.00 | 112.90 | 0 | 0 | 4 | 0 |
| **Bowling** | **Mat** | **Balls** | **Runs** | **Wkts** | **BBI** | **BBM** | **Ave** | **Econ** | **SR** | **5w** | **10** |
| First-class | 12 | 1562 | 950 | 18 | 3/66 | 5/100 | 52.77 | 3.64 | 86.7 | 0 | 0 |
| List A | 13 | 496 | 400 | 9 | 2/41 | 2/41 | 44.44 | 4.83 | 55.1 | 0 | 0 |
| Twenty20 | 12 | 216 | 280 | 9 | 2/19 | 2/19 | 31.11 | 7.77 | 24.0 | 0 | 0 |

# GURJIT SANDHU

RHB LMF R0 W0

FULL NAME: Gurjit Singh Sandhu
BORN: March 24, 1992, Isleworth, Middlesex
SQUAD NO: 92
HEIGHT: 6ft 4in
NICKNAME: Snip, Gujoun, Surjit
EDUCATION: Isleworth & Syon School; The Heathland School
TEAMS: Middlesex
CAREER: First-class: 2011; List A: 2012; T20: 2013

BEST BATTING: 8 Middlesex vs Sri Lankans, Uxbridge, 2011
BEST BOWLING: 4-49 Middlesex vs CMCCU, Fenner's, 2013

CAREER HIGHLIGHTS? Playing at Lord's and training at Lord's is always a pleasure
BEST PLAYER IN COUNTY CRICKET? Jeetan Patel
TIP FOR THE TOP? Nick Gubbins, Ravi Patel
MOST MARKED CHARACTERISTIC? I look like Mr Potato Head from Toy Story
CRICKETING HEROES? Wasim Akram – as a fellow left-armer I admire his skill and learn from him
CRICKET RULE YOU'D CHANGE? New ball after 50 overs
IF YOU WEREN'T A CRICKETER? A full-time gamer
IF YOU COULD BE SOMEONE ELSE FOR A DAY? Batman – infinite money and secrecy
DESERT ISLAND DISC? J Cole – 2014 Forest Hills Drive
FAVOURITE TV? Homeland
ACCOMPLISHMENTS? Camping in the Australian outback for two nights and coming back alive
FANTASY SLIP CORDON? 1st: Rick Grimes, 2nd: Kobe Bryant, 3rd: Kevin Hart
TWITTER FEED: @Gurjitsandhu92

| Batting | Mat | Inns | NO | Runs | HS | Ave | SR | 100 | 50 | Ct | St |
|---|---|---|---|---|---|---|---|---|---|---|---|
| First-class | 5 | 3 | 2 | 21 | 8 | 21.00 | 42.85 | 0 | 0 | 0 | 0 |
| List A | 2 | 1 | 0 | 0 | 0 | 0.00 | 0.00 | 0 | 0 | 0 | 0 |
| Twenty20 | 6 | 1 | 1 | 2 | 2* | - | 25.00 | 0 | 0 | 1 | 0 |
| **Bowling** | **Mat** | **Balls** | **Runs** | **Wkts** | **BBI** | **BBM** | **Ave** | **Econ** | **SR** | **5w** | **10** |
| First-class | 5 | 558 | 357 | 7 | 4/49 | 4/55 | 51.00 | 3.83 | 79.7 | 0 | 0 |
| List A | 2 | 78 | 48 | 4 | 3/28 | 3/28 | 12.00 | 3.69 | 19.5 | 0 | 0 |
| Twenty20 | 6 | 94 | 168 | 6 | 2/15 | 2/15 | 28.00 | 10.72 | 15.6 | 0 | 0 |

# KUMAR SANGAKKARA LHB OB WK R0 W0

FULL NAME: Kumar Chokshanada Sangakkara
BORN: October 27, 1977, Matale, Sri Lanka
SQUAD NO: 11
TEAMS: Sri Lanka, Central Province, Colombo District Cricket Association, Deccan Chargers, Durham, Jamaica Tallawahs, Kandurata, Kandurata Maroons, Kings XI Punjab, Nondescripts, Sunrisers Hyderabad, Warwickshire
CAREER: Test: 2000; List A: 2000; T20I: 2006; First-class: 1997; List A: 1997; T20: 2004



BEST BATTING: 319 Sri Lanka vs Bangladesh, Chittagong, 2014
BEST BOWLING: 1-13 Sri Lankans vs Zimbabwe A, Harare, 2004

TWITTER FEED: @KumarSanga2
NOTES: This is Sangakkara's third stint in English cricket after spells with Warwickshire and Durham. He retired from ODIs after the World Cup and is set to retire from Tests in July. He is the second batsman to pass 14,000 ODI runs, after Sachin Tendulkar. He is the fifth-highest Test run-scorer of all time, while only three men have scored more than his 38 Test centuries

| Batting | Mat | Inns | NO | Runs | HS | Ave | SR | 100 | 50 | Ct | St |
|---|---|---|---|---|---|---|---|---|---|---|---|
| Tests | 130 | 225 | 17 | 12203 | 319 | 58.66 | 54.25 | 38 | 51 | 178 | 20 |
| ODIs | 402 | 378 | 41 | 14065 | 169 | 41.73 | 78.76 | 24 | 93 | 400 | 99 |
| T20Is | 56 | 53 | 9 | 1382 | 78 | 31.40 | 119.55 | 0 | 8 | 25 | 20 |
| First-class | 223 | 365 | 28 | 17314 | 319 | 51.37 | | 50 | 75 | 344 | 33 |
| List A | 502 | 474 | 51 | 17972 | 169 | 42.48 | | 33 | 114 | 504 | 124 |
| Twenty20 | 155 | 149 | 16 | 3882 | 94 | 29.18 | 123.90 | 0 | 23 | 95 | 41 |
| **Bowling** | **Mat** | **Balls** | **Runs** | **Wkts** | **BBI** | **BBM** | **Ave** | **Econ** | **SR** | **5w** | **10** |
| Tests | 130 | 84 | 49 | 0 | - | - | - | 3.50 | - | 0 | 0 |
| ODIs | 402 | - | - | - | - | - | - | - | - | - | - |
| T20Is | 56 | - | - | - | - | - | - | - | - | - | - |
| First-class | 223 | 246 | 150 | 1 | 1/13 | | 150.00 | 3.65 | 246.0 | 0 | 0 |
| List A | 502 | - | - | - | - | - | - | - | - | - | - |
| Twenty20 | 155 | - | - | - | - | - | - | - | - | - | - |

## ROB SAYER

RHB OB R0 W0

FULL NAME: Robert John Sayer
BORN: January 25, 1995, Huntingdon, Cambridgeshire
SQUAD NO: 12
HEIGHT: 6ft 3in
NICKNAME: Sully, Leo
EDUCATION: Leeds Metropolitan University
TEAMS: Leicestershire 2nd XI, England U19
CAREER: Yet to make first-team debut

---

CAREER HIGHLIGHTS? Playing for England U19 at the World Cup
BEST PLAYER IN COUNTY CRICKET? Adam Lyth
TIP FOR THE TOP? Will Rhodes, Matthew Fisher, Ben Duckett, Dave Sayer
MOST MARKED CHARACTERISTIC? Determination
SUPERSTITIONS? Always right pad and right glove first
CRICKETING HEROES? Graeme Swann and Andrew Flintoff
CRICKET RULE YOU'D CHANGE? If you have scored a hundred or taken a five-fer during the innings then you may have a beer during a drinks break
IF YOU WEREN'T A CRICKETER? Wasting more of my money at uni
IF YOU COULD BE SOMEONE ELSE FOR A DAY? David Beckham
DESERT ISLAND DISC? DJ Russke
FAVOURITE TV? Suits
LEAST FAVOURITE TV? Downton Abbey
PET HATE? People walking slowly in front of me
SURPRISING FACT? I played centre-back for Peterborough Centre of Excellence
FANTASY SLIP CORDON? Keeper: Liam Neeson, 1st: Michelle Keegan, 2nd: Me, 3rd: David Beckham, Gully: Harvey Specter
TWITTER FEED: @Sayer1995

## GEORGE SCOTT RHB RFM R0 W0

FULL NAME: George Frederick Buchan Scott
BORN: November 6, 1995, Hemel Hempstead, Hertfordshire
SQUAD NO: 17
HEIGHT: 6ft 2in
NICKNAME: Scotty
EDUCATION: St Albans School; University of Leeds
TEAMS: Middlesex 2nd XI
CAREER: Yet to make first-team debut



---

FAMILY TIES? Three brothers who play for Hertfordshire CCC
CAREER HIGHLIGHTS? Playing at Lord's for the MCC Schools and Hertfordshire, making my Hertfordshire and Middlesex 2nd XI debuts
TIP FOR THE TOP? Nick Gubbins and Tom Helm
MOST MARKED CHARACTERISTIC? I don't really have any stand-out characteristics
SUPERSTITIONS? No, I try to avoid having any superstitions
CRICKETING HEROES? AB de Villiers – because he seems to be the most talented sportsman in the world
CRICKET RULE YOU'D CHANGE? Free hits for wides (unless I'm bowling)
IF YOU COULD BE SOMEONE ELSE FOR A DAY? Derrick Rose
DESERT ISLAND DISC? Sub Focus mix-tape
FAVOURITE TV? Scrubs
LEAST FAVOURITE TV? Geordie Shore
PET HATE? Footballers diving – it ruins the game!
SURPRISING FACT? I was a music scholar at St Albans School
FANTASY SLIP CORDON? Keeper: Frankie Boyle; 1st: Derrick Rose, 2nd: Myself, 3rd: AB de Villiers, Gully: Dan Carter
TWITTER FEED: @georgefbscott

# AJMAL SHAHZAD

## RHB RFM R0 W0

FULL NAME: Ajmal Shahzad
BORN: July 27, 1985, Huddersfield, Yorkshire
SQUAD NO: 4
HEIGHT: 6ft
NICKNAME: AJ, AJY, Shazza
EDUCATION: Bradford Grammar School; Woodhouse Grove Grammar School; Bradford University; Leeds Metropolitan University
TEAMS: England, Sussex, Nottinghamshire, Lancashire, Yorkshire
CAREER: Test: 2010; ODI: 2010; T20I: 2010; First-class: 2006; List A: 2004; T20: 2006

---

BEST BATTING: 88 Yorkshire vs Sussex, Hove, 2009
BEST BOWLING: 5-51 Yorkshire vs Durham, Chester-le-Street, 2010
COUNTY CAPS: 2010 (Yorkshire)

---

CAREER HIGHLIGHTS? Receiving my Yorkshire cap, representing England across all forms, being part of an Ashes-winning squad and being part of the World T20-winning squad
CRICKET RULE YOU'D CHANGE? Bowl as many bouncers as you want in an over
COACHING TIP? Batting – when in your stance keep your head in line with the middle of middle stump and work in straight lines. Bowling – knee at target when in your jump and have your momentum towards the target. Fielding – catch the bloody thing!
IF YOU WEREN'T A CRICKETER? Pharmacist, accountant or on the front of GQ magazine
SURPRISING FACT? My brain is the size of the average human being
TWITTER FEED: @AJShahzad

| Batting | Mat | Inns | NO | Runs | HS | Ave | SR | 100 | 50 | Ct | St |
|---|---|---|---|---|---|---|---|---|---|---|---|
| Tests | 1 | 1 | 0 | 5 | 5 | 5.00 | 41.66 | 0 | 0 | 2 | 0 |
| ODIs | 11 | 8 | 2 | 39 | 9 | 6.50 | 65.00 | 0 | 0 | 4 | 0 |
| T20Is | 3 | 1 | 1 | 0 | 0* | - | 0.00 | 0 | 0 | 1 | 0 |
| First-class | 80 | 108 | 28 | 1940 | 88 | 24.25 | 42.26 | 0 | 6 | 12 | 0 |
| List A | 76 | 45 | 12 | 449 | 59* | 13.60 | 95.73 | 0 | 1 | 19 | 0 |
| Twenty20 | 45 | 23 | 7 | 165 | 20 | 10.31 | 113.79 | 0 | 0 | 7 | 0 |
| **Bowling** | **Mat** | **Balls** | **Runs** | **Wkts** | **BBI** | **BBM** | **Ave** | **Econ** | **SR** | **5w** | **10** |
| Tests | 1 | 102 | 63 | 4 | 3/45 | 4/63 | 15.75 | 3.70 | 25.5 | 0 | 0 |
| ODIs | 11 | 588 | 490 | 17 | 3/41 | 3/41 | 28.82 | 5.00 | 34.5 | 0 | 0 |
| T20Is | 3 | 66 | 97 | 3 | 2/38 | 2/38 | 32.33 | 8.81 | 22.0 | 0 | 0 |
| First-class | 80 | 12504 | 7140 | 201 | 5/51 | 8/121 | 35.52 | 3.42 | 62.2 | 3 | 0 |
| List A | 76 | 3370 | 3020 | 112 | 5/51 | 5/51 | 26.96 | 5.37 | 30.0 | 1 | 0 |
| Twenty20 | 45 | 924 | 1226 | 37 | 3/30 | 3/30 | 33.13 | 7.96 | 24.9 | 0 | 0 |

# JACK SHANTRY LHB LM R0 W1 MVP31

FULL NAME: Jack David Shantry
BORN: January 29, 1988, Shrewsbury, Shropshire
SQUAD NO: 11
HEIGHT: 6ft 4in
NICKNAME: Shants
EDUCATION: Shrewsbury Sixth Form College; University of Manchester
TEAMS: Worcestershire
CAREER: First-class: 2009; List A: 2009; T20: 2010



BEST BATTING: 101* Worcestershire vs Surrey, Worcester, 2014
BEST BOWLING: 7- 60 Worcestershire vs Oxford MCCU, Oxford, 2013

FAMILY TIES? My father Brian played for Gloucestershire in the late '70s and my brother Adam played for Northamptonshire, Warwickshire and Glamorgan
SUPERSTITIONS? I always pat Joe Leach's belly for luck
CRICKETING HEROES? Wasim Akram – incredibly skilful swing bowler
NON-CRICKETING HEROES? Christopher Hitchens – fearless and intellectual, the most persuasive reasoner I have ever listened to/read
COACHING TIP? When bowling, try and keep a completely blank mind when you're running into bowl. N.B. Chris Russell mastered this technique to such an extent that he has maintained this mindset since 2011
IF YOU COULD BE SOMEONE ELSE FOR A DAY? David Icke – to know if he actually believes what he says he does
ACCOMPLISHMENTS? I once won a game of Connect Four in three moves
SURPRISING FACT? I went to school with Joe Hart and I also played in goal in the same University football team as Matt Smith (Leeds Utd, Fulham, Bristol City)
TWITTER FEED: @JackShantry

| Batting | Mat | Inns | NO | Runs | HS | Ave | SR | 100 | 50 | Ct | St |
|---|---|---|---|---|---|---|---|---|---|---|---|
| First-class | 57 | 75 | 20 | 1070 | 101* | 19.45 | 53.20 | 1 | 2 | 19 | 0 |
| List A | 58 | 25 | 13 | 125 | 18 | 10.41 | 67.20 | 0 | 0 | 14 | 0 |
| Twenty20 | 59 | 14 | 7 | 52 | 12* | 7.42 | 88.13 | 0 | 0 | 14 | 0 |
| **Bowling** | **Mat** | **Balls** | **Runs** | **Wkts** | **BBI** | **BBM** | **Ave** | **Econ** | **SR** | **5w** | **10** |
| First-class | 57 | 10006 | 4903 | 165 | 7/60 | 10/131 | 29.71 | 2.94 | 60.6 | 6 | 1 |
| List A | 58 | 2286 | 2205 | 76 | 4/32 | 4/32 | 29.01 | 5.78 | 30.0 | 0 | 0 |
| Twenty20 | 59 | 1297 | 1661 | 70 | 4/33 | 4/33 | 23.72 | 7.68 | 18.5 | 0 | 0 |

## JOSH SHAW

RHB RMF R0 W0

FULL NAME: Joshua Shaw
BORN: January 3, 1996, Wakefield, Yorkshire
SQUAD NO: 25
HEIGHT: 6ft 1in
NICKNAME: Shawy
EDUCATION: Crofton Academy
TEAMS: Yorkshire 2nd XI, England U19
CAREER: Yet to make first-team debut

---

FAMILY TIES? My father played for Yorkshire.
CAREER HIGHLIGHTS? Taking 10 wickets in a 2nd XI match
BEST PLAYER IN COUNTY CRICKET? Adam Lyth
TIP FOR THE TOP? Dom Sibley
MOST MARKED CHARACTERISTIC? Loving, caring, well-mannered
SUPERSTITIONS? Always put my right socks on first then my right boot. Then when batting my right pad, then my left
CRICKETING HEROES? Ryan Sidebottom, James Anderson, Peter Siddle – they always give 100 per cent in what they are doing and are so passionate about what they do and who they play for
CRICKET RULE YOU'D CHANGE? No field restrictions, so you don't go for many runs in the one-day game
IF YOU WEREN'T A CRICKETER? I would probably be a joiner. Or I would be working for my dad at his embroidery business
IF YOU COULD BE SOMEONE ELSE FOR A DAY? Rory McIlroy
DESERT ISLAND DISC? Arctic Monkeys
FAVOURITE TV? I'm A Celebrity ... Get Me Out Of Here!
LEAST FAVOURITE TV? EastEnders
ACCOMPLISHMENTS? Assisting an orphanage in India
FANTASY SLIP CORDON? Keeper: Peter Kay, 1st: Myself, 2nd: Karl Pilkington, 3rd: David Beckham, Gully: Rory McIlroy
TWITTER FEED: @joshuashaw1

# ATIF SHEIKH

RHB LMF R0 W0

FULL NAME: Atif Sheikh
BORN: February 18, 1991, Nottingham
SQUAD NO: 3
HEIGHT: 6ft 1in
NICKNAME: Sheikhy
EDUCATION: Nottingham Bluecoat Academy
TEAMS: Leicestershire, Derbyshire
CAREER: First-class 2010; T20: 2014



BEST BATTING: 12 Leicestershire vs Essex, Leicester, 2014
BEST BOWLING: 4-97 Leicestershire vs Gloucestershire, Bristol, 2014

FAMILY TIES? Brother Saahd played for Notts U15, brother Faisal played in the Notts leauge, dad just loves to play in the garden!
CAREER HIGHLIGHTS? Taking a hat-trick last season against Gloucestershire in my third first-class game!
BEST PLAYER IN COUNTY CRICKET? Adil Rashid
TIP FOR THE TOP? Aadil Ali, Tom Wells
MOST MARKED CHARACTERISTIC? Boss man
SUPERSTITIONS? Bowling three warm-up balls before my first ball, licking fingers walking back to my mark
CRICKETING HEROES? Wasim Akram – watched him bowl as a kid
CRICKET RULE YOU'D CHANGE? Bowl more than two bouncers in an over, longer tea breaks
COACHING TIP? Bowl as fast as you can!
IF YOU WEREN'T A CRICKETER? Set up my own business or maybe boxing
DESERT ISLAND DISC? Makaveli
PET HATE? Dogs
FANTASY SLIP CORDON? Keeper: Cheryl Cole, 1st: Myself, 2nd: Wasim Akram, 3rd: Muhammad Ali

| Batting | Mat | Inns | NO | Runs | HS | Ave | SR | 100 | 50 | Ct | St |
|---|---|---|---|---|---|---|---|---|---|---|---|
| First-class | 5 | 9 | 2 | 30 | 12 | 4.28 | 42.85 | 0 | 0 | 2 | 0 |
| Twenty20 | 3 | 2 | 0 | 21 | 14 | 10.50 | 105.00 | 0 | 0 | 1 | 0 |
| **Bowling** | **Mat** | **Balls** | **Runs** | **Wkts** | **BBI** | **BBM** | **Ave** | **Econ** | **SR** | **5w** | **10** |
| First-class | 5 | 743 | 596 | 14 | 4/97 | 5/152 | 42.57 | 4.81 | 53.0 | 0 | 0 |
| Twenty20 | 3 | 48 | 43 | 2 | 2/11 | 2/11 | 21.50 | 5.37 | 24.0 | 0 | 0 |

# CHARLIE SHRECK RHB RFM R0 W3 MVP87

FULL NAME: Charles Edward Shreck
BORN: January 6, 1978, Truro, Cornwall
SQUAD NO: 4
HEIGHT: 6ft 7in
NICKNAME: Shrecker, Ogre, Stoat, Chough
EDUCATION: Truro School
TEAMS: Leicestershire, Kent, Nottinghamshire, Wellington
CAREER: First-class: 2003; List A: 1999; T20: 2003

BEST BATTING: 56 Leicestershire vs Surrey, The Oval, 2014
BEST BOWLING: 8-31 Nottinghamshire vs Middlesex, Nottingham, 2006
COUNTY CAPS: 2006 (Nottinghamshire)

CAREER HIGHLIGHTS? Watching Andrew Parkin-Coates get Phil Mustard out after kicking the stumps down the wicket in his delivery stride
CRICKETING HEROES? Viv Richards, Michael Holding, Ian Botham, Rob Key
DESERT ISLAND DISC? Catcha Fire or Black Seeds
PET HATE? Not keeping the kitchen clean!
TWITTER FEED: @Shreck

| Batting | Mat | Inns | NO | Runs | HS | Ave | SR | 100 | 50 | Ct | St |
|---|---|---|---|---|---|---|---|---|---|---|---|
| First-class | 143 | 167 | 90 | 683 | 56 | 8.87 | 37.86 | 0 | 1 | 38 | 0 |
| List A | 59 | 22 | 14 | 47 | 9* | 5.87 | | 0 | 0 | 15 | 0 |
| Twenty20 | 29 | 8 | 5 | 20 | 10 | 6.66 | 68.96 | 0 | 0 | 6 | 0 |
| **Bowling** | **Mat** | **Balls** | **Runs** | **Wkts** | **BBI** | **BBM** | **Ave** | **Econ** | **SR** | **5w** | **10** |
| First-class | 143 | 28337 | 15023 | 474 | 8/31 | | 31.69 | 3.18 | 59.7 | 21 | 2 |
| List A | 59 | 2569 | 2214 | 71 | 5/19 | 5/19 | 31.18 | 5.17 | 36.1 | 2 | 0 |
| Twenty20 | 29 | 598 | 789 | 30 | 4/22 | 4/22 | 26.30 | 7.91 | 19.9 | 0 | 0 |

# DOMINIC SIBLEY

RHB OB R0 W0

FULL NAME: Dominic Peter Sibley
BORN: September 5, 1995, Epsom, Surrey
SQUAD NO: 45
HEIGHT: 6ft 3in
NICKNAME: Frochy
EDUCATION: Whitgift School
TEAMS: Surrey
CAREER: First-class: 2013; List A: 2013



BEST BATTING: 242 Surrey vs Yorkshire, The Oval, 2013

CAREER HIGHLIGHTS? Sharing a dressing room with Ricky Ponting, Hashim Amla, Graeme Smith and Kevin Pietersen
BEST PLAYER IN COUNTY CRICKET? Moeen Ali
TIP FOR THE TOP? Joe Clarke
CRICKETING HEROES? Brian Lara – because he was class
NON-CRICKETING HEROES? Muhammad Ali
IF YOU WEREN'T A CRICKETER? At uni with my mates
IF YOU COULD BE SOMEONE ELSE FOR A DAY? Leonardo DiCaprio
DESERT ISLAND DISC? Kid Ink – Show Me
FAVOURITE TV? Entourage
ACCOMPLISHMENTS? Playing rugby for Harlequins and winning a national football title with my school
PET HATE? People sitting or spilling stuff on my bed – it's where I sleep!
TWITTER FEED: @DomSibley

| Batting | Mat | Inns | NO | Runs | HS | Ave | SR | 100 | 50 | Ct | St |
|---|---|---|---|---|---|---|---|---|---|---|---|
| First-class | 9 | 14 | 0 | 420 | 242 | 30.00 | 39.51 | 1 | 1 | 6 | 0 |
| List A | 3 | 3 | 2 | 43 | 37 | 43.00 | 79.62 | 0 | 0 | 1 | 0 |
| **Bowling** | **Mat** | **Balls** | **Runs** | **Wkts** | **BBI** | **BBM** | **Ave** | **Econ** | **SR** | **5w** | **10** |
| First-class | 9 | 106 | 64 | 1 | 1/41 | 1/42 | 64.00 | 3.62 | 106.0 | 0 | 0 |
| List A | 3 | - | - | - | - | - | - | - | - | - | - |

# PETER SIDDLE

RHB RFM R0 W0

FULL NAME: Peter Matthew Siddle
BORN: November 25, 1984, Traralgon, Australia
SQUAD NO: tbc
HEIGHT: 6ft 1in
NICKNAME: Vicious, Dermie
TEAMS: Australia, Lancashire, Melbourne Renegades, Nottinghamshire, Rest of the World XI, Victoria
CAREER: Test: 2008; ODI: 2009; T20I: 2009; First-class: 2005; List A: 2005; T20: 2006

BEST BATTING: 103* Australia A vs Scotland, Edinburgh, 2013
BEST BOWLING: 8-54 Victoria vs South Australia, Adelaide, 2015

TWITTER FEED: @petersiddle403
NOTES: Lancashire have signed Australian seamer Siddle as their overseas player for the 2015 season, and he will be with them until the end of July. He played 11 Championship matches for Nottinghamshire last season, picking up 37 wickets. He was first called up to the Australian Test squad for the 2008 series against India and made his debut in the second match at Mohali, taking four wickets including that of Sachin Tendulkar. Made his home debut two months later against South Africa, claiming match figures of 8-113 in the third Test at the SCG. He has taken 67 Ashes wickets in 20 Tests, including 16 at an average of 24.12 during the 2013/14 whitewash in Australia

| Batting | Mat | Inns | NO | Runs | HS | Ave | SR | 100 | 50 | Ct | St |
|---|---|---|---|---|---|---|---|---|---|---|---|
| Tests | 56 | 80 | 12 | 973 | 51 | 14.30 | 46.55 | 0 | 2 | 16 | 0 |
| ODIs | 17 | 4 | 2 | 21 | 9* | 10.50 | 116.66 | 0 | 0 | 1 | 0 |
| T20Is | 2 | 1 | 1 | 1 | 1* | - | 100.00 | 0 | 0 | 0 | 0 |
| First-class | 112 | 152 | 28 | 2065 | 103* | 16.65 | 51.06 | 1 | 4 | 40 | 0 |
| List A | 42 | 21 | 8 | 96 | 25* | 7.38 | 81.35 | 0 | 0 | 6 | 0 |
| Twenty20 | 23 | 7 | 5 | 21 | 9* | 10.50 | 80.76 | 0 | 0 | 3 | 0 |
| **Bowling** | **Mat** | **Balls** | **Runs** | **Wkts** | **BBI** | **BBM** | **Ave** | **Econ** | **SR** | **5w** | **10** |
| Tests | 56 | 11887 | 5848 | 192 | 6/54 | 9/104 | 30.45 | 2.95 | 61.9 | 8 | 0 |
| ODIs | 17 | 751 | 581 | 15 | 3/55 | 3/55 | 38.73 | 4.64 | 50.0 | 0 | 0 |
| T20Is | 2 | 48 | 58 | 3 | 2/24 | 2/24 | 19.33 | 7.25 | 16.0 | 0 | 0 |
| First-class | 112 | 21806 | 10934 | 391 | 8/54 | 9/77 | 27.96 | 3.00 | 55.7 | 17 | 0 |
| List A | 42 | 2026 | 1598 | 45 | 4/27 | 4/27 | 35.51 | 4.73 | 45.0 | 0 | 0 |
| Twenty20 | 23 | 503 | 622 | 20 | 4/29 | 4/29 | 31.10 | 7.41 | 25.1 | 0 | 0 |

# RYAN SIDEBOTTOM — LHB LFM R0 W4 MVP69

FULL NAME: Ryan Jay Sidebottom
BORN: January 15, 1978, Huddersfield, Yorkshire
SQUAD NO: 11
HEIGHT: 6ft 4in
NICKNAME: Siddy
EDUCATION: King James' Grammar School, Almondbury
TEAMS: England, Yorkshire, Nottinghamshire
CAREER: Test: 2001; ODI: 2001; T20I: 2007; First-class: 1997; List A: 1997; T20: 2003

---

BEST BATTING: 61 Yorkshire vs Worcestershire, Worcester, 2011
BEST BOWLING: 7-37 Yorkshire vs Somerset, Leeds, 2011
COUNTY CAPS: 2000 (Yorkshire); 2004 (Nottinghamshire); BENEFIT YEAR: 2010 (Nottinghamshire)

---

FAMILY TIES? My father Arnie played for Yorkshire and England
CAREER HIGHLIGHTS? Taking a Test hat-trick against New Zealand and being a World T20 winner in 2010
CRICKETING HEROES? Mark Ealham, Sir Ian Botham, my dad
NON-CRICKETING HEROES? Ryan Giggs, Sam Tomkins, Garreth Carvell
IF YOU WEREN'T A CRICKETER? I'd have been a footballer or maybe a landscape gardener
SURPRISING FACT? I do canvas drawing and I love birdwatching and collecting Steiff bears
TWITTER FEED: @RyanSidebottom

| Batting | Mat | Inns | NO | Runs | HS | Ave | SR | 100 | 50 | Ct | St |
|---|---|---|---|---|---|---|---|---|---|---|---|
| Tests | 22 | 31 | 11 | 313 | 31 | 15.65 | 34.66 | 0 | 0 | 5 | 0 |
| ODIs | 25 | 18 | 8 | 133 | 24 | 13.30 | 68.55 | 0 | 0 | 6 | 0 |
| T20Is | 18 | 1 | 1 | 5 | 5* | - | 125.00 | 0 | 0 | 5 | 0 |
| First-class | 202 | 249 | 69 | 2454 | 61 | 13.63 | | 0 | 3 | 58 | 0 |
| List A | 186 | 89 | 39 | 552 | 32 | 11.04 | | 0 | 0 | 39 | 0 |
| Twenty20 | 85 | 26 | 18 | 140 | 17* | 17.50 | 101.44 | 0 | 0 | 24 | 0 |
| **Bowling** | **Mat** | **Balls** | **Runs** | **Wkts** | **BBI** | **BBM** | **Ave** | **Econ** | **SR** | **5w** | **10** |
| Tests | 22 | 4812 | 2231 | 79 | 7/47 | 10/139 | 28.24 | 2.78 | 60.9 | 5 | 1 |
| ODIs | 25 | 1277 | 1039 | 29 | 3/19 | 3/19 | 35.82 | 4.88 | 44.0 | 0 | 0 |
| T20Is | 18 | 367 | 437 | 23 | 3/16 | 3/16 | 19.00 | 7.14 | 15.9 | 0 | 0 |
| First-class | 202 | 35006 | 16185 | 663 | 7/37 | | 24.41 | 2.77 | 52.7 | 26 | 3 |
| List A | 186 | 8226 | 6134 | 198 | 6/40 | 6/40 | 30.97 | 4.47 | 41.5 | 2 | 0 |
| Twenty20 | 85 | 1797 | 2149 | 93 | 4/25 | 4/25 | 23.10 | 7.17 | 19.3 | 0 | 0 |

## JOHN SIMPSON LHB WK R0 W0 MVP93

FULL NAME: John Andrew Simpson
BORN: July 13, 1988, Bury, Lancashire
SQUAD NO: 20
HEIGHT: 5ft 11in
NICKNAME: Simmo
EDUCATION: St Gabriel's RC High School; Holy Cross College
TEAMS: Middlesex, Lancashire
CAREER: First-class: 2009; List A: 2009; T20: 2009

BEST BATTING: 143 Middlesex vs Surrey, Lord's, 2011
COUNTY CAPS: 2011

FAMILY TIES? Dad played for England Amateurs and Lancashire Cricket Board and holds club and league records in Lancashire/Central Lancashire leagues; grandad, uncle and two cousins play Lancashire age-group and 2nd XI cricket
TIP FOR THE TOP? Tom Helm
CRICKETING HEROES? Jack Russell, Ian Healy, Adam Gilchrist
NON-CRICKETING HEROES? Tiger Woods, Roger Federer, LeBron James, Michael Jordan
CRICKET RULE YOU'D CHANGE? Four byes rule if the keeper dives full stretch and gets nowhere near it
IF YOU WEREN'T A CRICKETER? Golf coach or fashion-brand designer
IF YOU COULD BE SOMEONE ELSE FOR A DAY? Floyd Mayweather
ACCOMPLISHMENTS? Won a few golf tournaments
PET HATE? People who chew food loudly
SURPRISING FACT? Great grandad and grandad played rugby league for Great Britain. Dad played lacrosse for England
TWITTER FEED: @johnsimpson_88

| Batting | Mat | Inns | NO | Runs | HS | Ave | SR | 100 | 50 | Ct | St |
|---|---|---|---|---|---|---|---|---|---|---|---|
| First-class | 82 | 128 | 17 | 3356 | 143 | 30.23 | 48.00 | 4 | 19 | 248 | 16 |
| List A | 50 | 32 | 6 | 623 | 82 | 23.96 | 86.28 | 0 | 3 | 34 | 7 |
| Twenty20 | 41 | 32 | 7 | 433 | 60* | 17.32 | 113.35 | 0 | 1 | 21 | 10 |
| **Bowling** | **Mat** | **Balls** | **Runs** | **Wkts** | **BBI** | **BBM** | **Ave** | **Econ** | **SR** | **5w** | **10** |
| First-class | 82 | - | - | - | - | - | - | - | - | - | - |
| List A | 50 | - | - | - | - | - | - | - | - | - | - |
| Twenty20 | 41 | - | - | - | - | - | - | - | - | - | - |

# BEN SLATER LHB OB R0 W0

FULL NAME: Benjamin Thomas Slater
BORN: August 26, 1991, Chesterfield, Derbyshire
SQUAD NO: 26
HEIGHT: 5ft 10in
NICKNAME: BennySlats, Slats, Slatsy
EDUCATION: Netherthorpe School; Leeds Metropolitan University
TEAMS: Derbyshire
CAREER: First-class: 2012; List A: 2012; T20: 2012



BEST BATTING: 104 Derbyshire vs Leicestershire, Derby, 2014

FAMILY TIES? Both dad and grandad played to a good standard of league cricket. My sister also used to play for Derbyshire Ladies
CAREER HIGHLIGHTS? Making my debut for Derbyshire vs Surrey with Ricky Ponting in the Surrey team, scoring back-to-back hundreds vs Leicestershire in the last game of the 2014 County Championship
BEST PLAYER IN COUNTY CRICKET? Mark Footitt
TIP FOR THE TOP? Harvey Hosein, Tommy Taylor, Ben Cotton
CRICKETING HEROES? Brian Lara and my grandad because they were both left-handed
NON-CRICKETING HEROES? David Beckham
CRICKET RULE YOU'D CHANGE? Longer for tea in Championship matches. It's always rushed and you get no time to put your feet up
DESERT ISLAND DISC? Five – Greatest Hits
LEAST FAVOURITE TV? Anything horror-related
FANTASY SLIP CORDON? Keeper: Richard Johnson, 1st: Greg James, 2nd: Mila Kunis, 3rd: Frankie Sandford, Gully: Me
TWITTER FEED: @BennySlats

| Batting | Mat | Inns | NO | Runs | HS | Ave | SR | 100 | 50 | Ct | St |
|---|---|---|---|---|---|---|---|---|---|---|---|
| First-class | 23 | 43 | 1 | 1230 | 119 | 29.28 | 41.17 | 2 | 7 | 9 | 0 |
| List A | 7 | 6 | 0 | 109 | 46 | 18.16 | 52.65 | 0 | 0 | 1 | 0 |
| Twenty20 | 4 | 4 | 0 | 161 | 57 | 40.25 | 105.22 | 0 | 1 | 0 | 0 |
| **Bowling** | **Mat** | **Balls** | **Runs** | **Wkts** | **BBI** | **BBM** | **Ave** | **Econ** | **SR** | **5w** | **10** |
| First-class | 23 | 9 | 28 | 0 | - | - | - | 18.66 | - | 0 | 0 |
| List A | 7 | - | - | - | - | - | - | - | - | - | - |
| Twenty20 | 4 | - | - | - | - | - | - | - | - | - | - |

# GREG SMITH

## RHB LB R0 W0 MVP68

FULL NAME: Greg Phillip Smith
BORN: November 16, 1988, Leicester
SQUAD NO: tbc
EDUCATION: Oundle School; Durham University
TEAMS: Nottinghashire, Badureliya Sports Club, Kibworth, Lankan Cricket Club, Leicestershire
CAREER: First-class: 2008; List A: 2008; T20: 2012

BEST BATTING: 158* Leicestershire vs Gloucestershire, Leicester, 2010
BEST BOWLING: 1-64 Leicestershire vs Gloucestershire, Leicester, 2008

FAMILY TIES? My step-grandfather played for Sussex
CAREER HIGHLIGHTS? The 2010 T20 campaign with Leicestershire
TIP FOR THE TOP? Rammy Singh
CRICKETING HEROES? Will Jefferson, Justin Langer
NON-CRICKETING HEROES? Dr Peter Greenfield
IF YOU WEREN'T A CRICKETER? An Arctic explorer
DESERT ISLAND DISC? Damien Jurado – Ohio
FAVOURITE TV? Breaking Bad
ACCOMPLISHMENTS? Creating my own breed of apple
TWITTER FEED: @greg_smith14

| Batting | Mat | Inns | NO | Runs | HS | Ave | SR | 100 | 50 | Ct | St |
|---|---|---|---|---|---|---|---|---|---|---|---|
| First-class | 89 | 166 | 8 | 4458 | 158* | 28.21 | 50.45 | 8 | 19 | 72 | 0 |
| List A | 39 | 39 | 5 | 835 | 135* | 24.55 | 78.47 | 1 | 4 | 13 | 0 |
| Twenty20 | 30 | 29 | 2 | 784 | 102 | 29.03 | 124.44 | 1 | 5 | 11 | 0 |
| **Bowling** | **Mat** | **Balls** | **Runs** | **Wkts** | **BBI** | **BBM** | **Ave** | **Econ** | **SR** | **5w** | **10** |
| First-class | 89 | 36 | 73 | 1 | 1/64 | 1/64 | 73.00 | 12.16 | 36.0 | 0 | 0 |
| List A | 39 | - | - | - | - | - | - | - | - | - | - |
| Twenty20 | 30 | - | - | - | - | - | - | - | - | - | - |

# GREG SMITH

## RHB RMF/OB R0 W0

FULL NAME: Gregory Marc Smith
BORN: April 20, 1983, Johannesburg, South Africa
SQUAD NO: 83
HEIGHT: 5ft 9in
NICKNAME: Smithy
EDUCATION: St Stithians College
TEAMS: Essex, Derbyshire, Griqualand West, Mountaineers
CAREER: First-class: 2003; List A: 2003; T20: 2007



BEST BATTING: 177 Essex vs Gloucestershire, Bristol, 2013
BEST BOWLING: 5-42 Essex vs Leicestershire, Chelmsford, 2013
COUNTY CAPS: 2009 (Derbyshire)

FAMILY TIES? My father used to be the financial director of the South African cricket board
CAREER HIGHLIGHTS? Playing in the U19 World Cup final vs Australia and scoring my maiden first-class hundred
BEST PLAYER IN COUNTY CRICKET? Moeen Ali
TIP FOR THE TOP? Matt Dunn, Ben Foakes
CRICKETING HEROES? Jacques Kallis – I always looked up to him for his achievements and also as a fellow allrounder
NON-CRICKETING HEROES? Roger Federer
COACHING TIP? Tennis player
IF YOU WEREN'T A CRICKETER? Superman
FAVOURITE TV? Days Of Our Lives
PET HATE? People eating with their mouth open
SURPRISING FACT? Had to make a decision between tennis and cricket aged 16
TWITTER FEED: @smithyg83

| Batting | Mat | Inns | NO | Runs | HS | Ave | SR | 100 | 50 | Ct | St |
|---|---|---|---|---|---|---|---|---|---|---|---|
| First-class | 120 | 197 | 17 | 5559 | 177 | 30.88 | 58.26 | 7 | 33 | 40 | 0 |
| List A | 108 | 105 | 10 | 2342 | 89 | 24.65 | 81.51 | 0 | 11 | 39 | 0 |
| Twenty20 | 82 | 73 | 3 | 1377 | 100* | 19.67 | 114.36 | 1 | 5 | 32 | 0 |
| **Bowling** | **Mat** | **Balls** | **Runs** | **Wkts** | **BBI** | **BBM** | **Ave** | **Econ** | **SR** | **5w** | **10** |
| First-class | 120 | 12002 | 6392 | 179 | 5/42 | | 35.70 | 3.19 | 67.0 | 4 | 0 |
| List A | 108 | 2839 | 2655 | 72 | 4/53 | 4/53 | 36.87 | 5.61 | 39.4 | 0 | 0 |
| Twenty20 | 82 | 786 | 1069 | 41 | 5/17 | 5/17 | 26.07 | 8.16 | 19.1 | 2 | 0 |

# RUAIDHRI SMITH

## RHB RM R0 W0

FULL NAME: Ruaidhri Alexander James Smith
BORN: August 5, 1994, Glasgow
SQUAD NO: 20
HEIGHT: 6ft 2in
NICKNAME: Trigger
EDUCATION: The Cathedral School, Llandaff; Shrewsbury School; University of Bristol
TEAMS: Scotland, Glamorgan
CAREER: First-class: 2013; List A: 2013; T20: 2014

BEST BATTING: 57* Glamorgan vs Gloucestershire, Bristol, 2014
BEST BOWLING: 3-38 Glamorgan vs Hampshire, Southampton, 2014

FAMILY TIES? My dad used to play club cricket and he introduced me to the game
CAREER HIGHLIGHTS? Taking a wicket with my first ball for Glamorgan
MOST MARKED CHARACTERISTIC? My competitiveness
SUPERSTITIONS? I always put pads etc on in the same order and I never step on crease lines while the ball is dead
CRICKETING HEROES? Andrew Flintoff and Jacques Kallis
NON-CRICKETING HEROES? Jonny Wilkinson
IF YOU WEREN'T A CRICKETER? I'd try to be a rugby player
DESERT ISLAND DISC? I'd take the Harry Potter film series instead
FAVOURITE TV? Sherlock
SURPRISING FACT? I'm a Grade 5 pianist
FANTASY SLIP CORDON? Keeper: Jonny Wilkinson, 1st: Don Bradman, 2nd: Sherlock Holmes, 3rd: Me, Gully: Sir Viv Richards
TWITTER FEED: @RuaidhriSmith

| Batting | Mat | Inns | NO | Runs | HS | Ave | SR | 100 | 50 | Ct | St |
|---|---|---|---|---|---|---|---|---|---|---|---|
| First-class | 11 | 15 | 2 | 205 | 57* | 15.76 | 45.75 | 0 | 1 | 2 | 0 |
| List A | 5 | 3 | 1 | 9 | 7 | 4.50 | 56.25 | 0 | 0 | 2 | 0 |
| Twenty20 | 2 | 1 | 0 | 2 | 2 | 2.00 | 50.00 | 0 | 0 | 0 | 0 |
| **Bowling** | **Mat** | **Balls** | **Runs** | **Wkts** | **BBI** | **BBM** | **Ave** | **Econ** | **SR** | **5w** | **10** |
| First-class | 11 | 1372 | 940 | 22 | 3/38 | 5/87 | 42.72 | 4.11 | 62.3 | 0 | 0 |
| List A | 5 | 90 | 117 | 3 | 3/48 | 3/48 | 39.00 | 7.80 | 30.0 | 0 | 0 |
| Twenty20 | 2 | - | - | - | - | - | - | - | - | - | - |

# TOM SMITH

## LHB RM R0 W1 MVP6

FULL NAME: Thomas Christopher Smith
BORN: December 26, 1985, Liverpool
SQUAD NO: 24
HEIGHT: 6ft 3in
NICKNAME: Smudger
EDUCATION: Parklands High School; Runshaw College
TEAMS: Lancashire, Matabeleland Tuskers, England Lions
CAREER: First-class: 2005; List A: 2005; T20: 2006



BEST BATTING: 128 Lancashire vs Hampshire, Southampton, 2010
BEST BOWLING: 6-46 Lancashire vs Yorkshire, Manchester, 2009
COUNTY CAPS: 2010

FAMILY TIES? My brother played Lancashire age groups
CAREER HIGHLIGHTS? Winning the Championship in 2011 and receiving my Lancashire county cap
BEST PLAYER IN COUNTY CRICKET? Jos Buttler
TIP FOR THE TOP? Haseeb Hameed
CRICKETING HEROES? Andrew Flintoff, Jacques Kallis
NON-CRICKETING HEROES? My parents – they encouraged me to play the game
CRICKET RULE YOU'D CHANGE? No six-run penalty for slow over-rate in T20
DESERT ISLAND DISC? The Courteeners – St. Jude
FAVOURITE TV? James Martin: Home Comforts
LEAST FAVOURITE TV? Coronation Street
FANTASY SLIP CORDON? Keeper: Dave Grohl, 1st: Nicole Scherzinger, 2nd: Tiger Woods, 3rd: David Beckham
TWITTER FEED: @Tcp24

| Batting | Mat | Inns | NO | Runs | HS | Ave | SR | 100 | 50 | Ct | St |
|---|---|---|---|---|---|---|---|---|---|---|---|
| First-class | 98 | 145 | 25 | 3516 | 128 | 29.30 | 46.09 | 3 | 22 | 101 | 0 |
| List A | 67 | 56 | 12 | 1505 | 117 | 34.20 | 88.37 | 2 | 10 | 22 | 0 |
| Twenty20 | 93 | 86 | 12 | 2089 | 92* | 28.22 | 121.38 | 0 | 11 | 41 | 0 |
| **Bowling** | **Mat** | **Balls** | **Runs** | **Wkts** | **BBI** | **BBM** | **Ave** | **Econ** | **SR** | **5w** | **10** |
| First-class | 98 | 12531 | 6434 | 226 | 6/46 | | 28.46 | 3.08 | 55.4 | 6 | 0 |
| List A | 67 | 2490 | 2193 | 77 | 4/48 | 4/48 | 28.48 | 5.28 | 32.3 | 0 | 0 |
| Twenty20 | 93 | 1200 | 1593 | 51 | 3/12 | 3/12 | 31.23 | 7.96 | 23.5 | 0 | 0 |

# TOM SMITH

RHB SLA R0 W0

FULL NAME: Thomas Michael John Smith
BORN: August 29, 1987, Eastbourne, Sussex
SQUAD NO: 6
HEIGHT: 5ft 9in
NICKNAME: Smudge
EDUCATION: Seaford Head Community College
TEAMS: Gloucestershire, Middlesex, Surrey, Sussex
CAREER: First-class: 2007; List A: 2006; T20: 2007

BEST BATTING: 80 Gloucestershire vs Surrey, Bristol, 2014
BEST BOWLING: 4-35 Gloucestershire vs Kent, Canterbury, 2014
COUNTY CAPS: 2006 (Sussex)

CAREER HIGHLIGHTS? Taking five wickets at Lord's in a T20 match for Middlesex against Kent and taking a hat-trick in a CB40 match for Gloucestershire against Somerset
MOST MARKED CHARACTERISTIC? My monotone voice
CRICKETING HEROES? Shane Warne – I loved watching him bowl when I was growing up. James Kirtley – I played at the same league team (Eastbourne CC) and is someone I always looked up to
CRICKET RULE YOU'D CHANGE? LBW – if it pitches outside the stumps and the ball is hitting the stumps, it should still be given out. But, I am a bowler…
IF YOU WEREN'T A CRICKETER? I did an apprenticeship as a plumber, so I guess I would be doing that!
IF YOU COULD BE SOMEONE ELSE FOR A DAY? Shaun Tait – to scare batters with my pace. As a spinner you never get to scare anyone, you just get the pleasure of being whacked into the stands

| Batting | Mat | Inns | NO | Runs | HS | Ave | SR | 100 | 50 | Ct | St |
|---|---|---|---|---|---|---|---|---|---|---|---|
| First-class | 36 | 51 | 9 | 926 | 80 | 22.04 | 39.07 | 0 | 2 | 11 | 0 |
| List A | 43 | 18 | 5 | 204 | 65 | 15.69 | 75.00 | 0 | 1 | 20 | 0 |
| Twenty20 | 65 | 30 | 21 | 220 | 36* | 24.44 | 118.91 | 0 | 0 | 21 | 0 |
| **Bowling** | **Mat** | **Balls** | **Runs** | **Wkts** | **BBI** | **BBM** | **Ave** | **Econ** | **SR** | **5w** | **10** |
| First-class | 36 | 5421 | 3049 | 62 | 4/35 | 5/92 | 49.17 | 3.37 | 87.4 | 0 | 0 |
| List A | 43 | 1426 | 1339 | 33 | 3/26 | 3/26 | 40.57 | 5.63 | 43.2 | 0 | 0 |
| Twenty20 | 65 | 1223 | 1490 | 61 | 5/24 | 5/24 | 24.42 | 7.30 | 20.0 | 1 | 0 |

# WILL SMITH RHB OB R1 W0 MVP32

FULL NAME: William Rew Smith
BORN: September 28, 1982, Luton, Bedfordshire
SQUAD NO: 2
HEIGHT: 5ft 9in
NICKNAME: Smudger, Jiggy
EDUCATION: Bedford School; Durham University
TEAMS: Hampshire, Durham, Nottinghamshire
CAREER: First-class: 2002; List A: 2002; T20: 2003



BEST BATTING: 201* Durham vs Surrey, Guildford, 2008
BEST BOWLING: 3-34 DUCCE vs Leicestershire, Leicester, 2005

FAMILY TIES? Brother, Ben, played Northamptonshire U19
CAREER HIGHLIGHTS? Winning four Championships (Division One) and helping to win Division Two in my first year while at Hampshire
BEST PLAYER IN COUNTY CRICKET? A cross between Ed Joyce, Darren Stevens, Peter Trego and Steve Magoffin
TIP FOR THE TOP? Tom Alsop
MOST MARKED CHARACTERISTIC? My (lack of) height
CRICKETING HEROES? Graeme Fowler – taught me a lot about a lot! Dale Benkenstein and Michael Di Venuto – two great men to play with and talk to about the game
IF YOU WEREN'T A CRICKETER? Horse racing media pundit
IF YOU COULD BE SOMEONE ELSE FOR A DAY? Patrick Veitch. Google him...
FAVOURITE TV? QI
FANTASY SLIP CORDON? Keeper: Myself, 1st: Stephen Fry, 2nd: AP McCoy, 3rd: Ross Noble, Gully: Jonty Rhodes
TWITTER FEED: @WillSmith_2

| Batting | Mat | Inns | NO | Runs | HS | Ave | SR | 100 | 50 | Ct | St |
|---|---|---|---|---|---|---|---|---|---|---|---|
| First-class | 138 | 231 | 16 | 7191 | 201* | 33.44 | 43.77 | 16 | 25 | 79 | 0 |
| List A | 96 | 82 | 7 | 2108 | 120* | 28.10 | 74.22 | 2 | 15 | 32 | 0 |
| Twenty20 | 85 | 68 | 17 | 905 | 55 | 17.74 | 120.34 | 0 | 3 | 39 | 0 |
| **Bowling** | **Mat** | **Balls** | **Runs** | **Wkts** | **BBI** | **BBM** | **Ave** | **Econ** | **SR** | **5w** | **10** |
| First-class | 138 | 1340 | 882 | 20 | 3/34 | | 44.10 | 3.94 | 67.0 | 0 | 0 |
| List A | 96 | 293 | 273 | 11 | 2/19 | 2/19 | 24.81 | 5.59 | 26.6 | 0 | 0 |
| Twenty20 | 85 | 551 | 635 | 27 | 3/15 | 3/15 | 23.51 | 6.91 | 20.4 | 0 | 0 |

# VIKRAM SOLANKI

RHB OB R6 W0

FULL NAME: Vikram Singh Solanki
BORN: April 1, 1976, Udaipur, India
SQUAD NO: 42
HEIGHT: 6ft
NICKNAME: Vik
EDUCATION: Regis School Wolverhampton; Open University
TEAMS: England, Surrey, Worcestershire, Rajasthan
CAREER: ODI: 2000; T20I: 2005; First-class: 1995; List A: 1993; T20: 2004

---

BEST BATTING: 270 Worcestershire vs Gloucestershire, Cheltenham, 2008
BEST BOWLING: 5-40 Worcestershire vs Middlesex, Lord's, 2004
COUNTY CAPS: 1998 (Worcestershire); BENEFIT YEAR: 2007 (Worcestershire)

---

FAMILY TIES? My father and brother both played
CAREER HIGHLIGHTS? Playing for England
BEST PLAYER IN COUNTY CRICKET? Moeen Ali
TIP FOR THE TOP? Jason Roy, Rory Burns, Zafar Ansari, Matthew Dunn, Tom Curran, Dominic Sibley, Aneesh Kapil
MOST MARKED CHARACTERISTIC? I'm fairly boring!
CRICKETING HEROES? Graeme Hick and Tom Moody – for their guidance in my younger years. Ricky Ponting – in order to appreciate what it takes to be the best
IF YOU WEREN'T A CRICKETER? My only other childhood ambition was to be a pilot
ACCOMPLISHMENTS? I'm most proud of my sons Aditya and Arya

| Batting | Mat | Inns | NO | Runs | HS | Ave | SR | 100 | 50 | Ct | St |
|---|---|---|---|---|---|---|---|---|---|---|---|
| ODIs | 51 | 46 | 5 | 1097 | 106 | 26.75 | 72.93 | 2 | 5 | 16 | 0 |
| T20Is | 3 | 3 | 0 | 76 | 43 | 25.33 | 124.59 | 0 | 0 | 3 | 0 |
| First-class | 324 | 544 | 33 | 18325 | 270 | 35.86 | | 34 | 98 | 348 | 0 |
| List A | 401 | 371 | 31 | 11041 | 164* | 32.47 | | 16 | 64 | 162 | 0 |
| Twenty20 | 77 | 75 | 2 | 1708 | 100 | 23.39 | 121.04 | 1 | 9 | 39 | 0 |
| **Bowling** | **Mat** | **Balls** | **Runs** | **Wkts** | **BBI** | **BBM** | **Ave** | **Econ** | **SR** | **5w** | **10** |
| ODIs | 51 | 111 | 105 | 1 | 1/17 | 1/17 | 105.00 | 5.67 | 111.0 | 0 | 0 |
| T20Is | 3 | - | - | - | - | - | - | - | - | - | - |
| First-class | 324 | 7238 | 4230 | 90 | 5/40 | | 47.00 | 3.50 | 80.4 | 4 | 1 |
| List A | 401 | 1122 | 987 | 28 | 4/14 | 4/14 | 35.25 | 5.27 | 40.0 | 0 | 0 |
| Twenty20 | 77 | 96 | 145 | 5 | 1/6 | 1/6 | 29.00 | 9.06 | 19.2 | 0 | 0 |

# CAMERON STEEL

RHB LB R0 W0

FULL NAME: Cameron Tate Steel
BORN: September 13, 1995, Greenbrae, California, USA
SQUAD NO: 22
HEIGHT: 5ft 10in
NICKNAME: Lex, Lexington, Steely
EDUCATION: Scotch College, Perth; Durham University
TEAMS: Middlesex 2nd XI, Somerset 2nd XI, Durham MCCU
CAREER: First-class: 2014



BEST BATTING: 68 Durham MCCU vs Durham, Chester-le-Street, 2014
BEST BOWLING: 1-39 Durham MCCU vs Durham, Chester-le-Street, 2014

FAMILY TIES? My dad and grandad played a little bit. My sister played for Western Australia until U18 level
BEST PLAYER IN COUNTY CRICKET? James Taylor
TIP FOR THE TOP? Tom Abell, Nick Gubbins, Ryan Higgins
MOST MARKED CHARACTERISTIC? My terrible chat
CRICKETING HEROES? Mike Hussey – just everything about the way he plays his cricket
NON-CRICKETING HEROES? Usain Bolt, Andy Murray, Rafael Nadal
CRICKET RULE YOU'D CHANGE? All wides and no-balls would be followed by a free hit
IF YOU WEREN'T A CRICKETER? Studying more than I do at the moment
IF YOU COULD BE SOMEONE ELSE FOR A DAY? Charlie Sheen
DESERT ISLAND DISC? Ben Howard – Every Kingdom
FAVOURITE TV? Friday Night Lights
ACCOMPLISHMENTS? West of England U9 chess champion
PET HATE? Grammar and spelling errors in texts, tweets and articles. It just really annoys me
SURPRISING FACT? I have three passports. American, British and Australian
FANTASY SLIP CORDON? Keeper: Charlie Sheen, 1st: Frankie Boyle, 2nd: Coach Taylor from Friday Night Lights, 3rd: Me, Gully: Beyoncé
TWITTER FEED: @cameronsteel2

| Batting | Mat | Inns | NO | Runs | HS | Ave | SR | 100 | 50 | Ct | St |
|---|---|---|---|---|---|---|---|---|---|---|---|
| First-class | 2 | 3 | 0 | 121 | 68 | 40.33 | 34.08 | 0 | 1 | 2 | 0 |
| **Bowling** | **Mat** | **Balls** | **Runs** | **Wkts** | **BBI** | **BBM** | **Ave** | **Econ** | **SR** | **5w** | **10** |
| First-class | 2 | 54 | 39 | 1 | 1/39 | 1/39 | 39.00 | 4.33 | 54.0 | 0 | 0 |

## DARREN STEVENS

RHB RM R3 W1 MVP2

FULL NAME: Darren Ian Stevens
BORN: April 30, 1976, Leicester
SQUAD NO: 3
HEIGHT: 5ft 11in
NICKNAME: Stevo
EDUCATION: John Cleveland College; Charles Keene College
TEAMS: Kent, Leicestershire, Dhaka Gladiators, Otago
CAREER: First-class: 1997; List A: 1997; T20: 2003

BEST BATTING: 208 Kent vs Middlesex, Canterbury, 2009
BEST BOWLING: 7-21 Kent vs Surrey, Canterbury, 2011
COUNTY CAPS: 2002 (Leicestershire); 2005 (Kent)

BEST PLAYER IN COUNTY CRICKET? Moeen Ali
TIP FOR THE TOP? Sam Billings, Adam Riley, Jason Roy, Matt Dunn, Craig Miles
CRICKETING HEROES? Sir Vivian Richards
COACHING TIP? Eyes level and watch the ball closely
IF YOU WEREN'T A CRICKETER? Golfer
IF YOU COULD BE SOMEONE ELSE FOR A DAY? Rory McIlroy
DESERT ISLAND DISC? Ed Sheeran
FAVOURITE TV? Game Of Thrones
LEAST FAVOURITE TV? EastEnders
PET HATE? Bad manners. It's not difficult to say please or thank you
TWITTER FEED: @Stevo208

| Batting | Mat | Inns | NO | Runs | HS | Ave | SR | 100 | 50 | Ct | St |
|---|---|---|---|---|---|---|---|---|---|---|---|
| First-class | 235 | 376 | 23 | 12482 | 208 | 35.35 | | 29 | 59 | 177 | 0 |
| List A | 270 | 251 | 28 | 6681 | 133 | 29.95 | | 5 | 43 | 109 | 0 |
| Twenty20 | 163 | 153 | 38 | 3470 | 77 | 30.17 | 136.93 | 0 | 16 | 58 | 0 |
| **Bowling** | **Mat** | **Balls** | **Runs** | **Wkts** | **BBI** | **BBM** | **Ave** | **Econ** | **SR** | **5w** | **10** |
| First-class | 235 | 15925 | 7713 | 258 | 7/21 | | 29.89 | 2.90 | 61.7 | 10 | 1 |
| List A | 270 | 4189 | 3463 | 108 | 5/32 | 5/32 | 32.06 | 4.96 | 38.7 | 2 | 0 |
| Twenty20 | 163 | 1542 | 1953 | 82 | 4/14 | 4/14 | 23.81 | 7.59 | 18.8 | 0 | 0 |

# PAUL STIRLING RHB OB R0 W0

FULL NAME: Paul Robert Stirling
BORN: September 3, 1990, Ireland
SQUAD NO: 39
HEIGHT: 5ft 10in
NICKNAME: Stirlo
EDUCATION: Belfast High School
TEAMS: Ireland, Middlesex
CAREER: ODI: 2008; T20I: 2009; First-class: 2008; List A: 2008; T20: 2008



BEST BATTING: 115 Ireland vs Australia A, Belfast, 2013
BEST BOWLING: 2-43 Ireland vs Jamaica, Spanish Town, 2010

FAMILY TIES? Brother Richard has played in an U19 World Cup in Sri Lanka
CAREER HIGHLIGHTS? Century at Lord's vs Lancashire
BEST PLAYER IN COUNTY CRICKET? Ed Joyce
CRICKETING HEROES? Ricky Ponting – watching him score all those runs in the Ashes down under throughout the years
NON-CRICKETING HEROES? Brian O'Driscoll
CRICKET RULE YOU'D CHANGE? Only two fielders allowed outside of the fielding restrictions for the entire T20 innings
IF YOU COULD BE SOMEONE ELSE FOR A DAY? Rory McIlroy
DESERT ISLAND DISC? Les Misérables soundtrack
SURPRISING FACT? My dad Brian was an international rugby referee back in the day
TWITTER FEED: @stirlo90

| Batting | Mat | Inns | NO | Runs | HS | Ave | SR | 100 | 50 | Ct | St |
|---|---|---|---|---|---|---|---|---|---|---|---|
| ODIs | 55 | 54 | 1 | 1840 | 177 | 34.71 | 95.63 | 5 | 7 | 25 | 0 |
| T20Is | 26 | 26 | 4 | 584 | 79 | 26.54 | 128.35 | 0 | 5 | 7 | 0 |
| First-class | 26 | 42 | 2 | 1282 | 115 | 32.05 | 61.39 | 3 | 9 | 13 | 0 |
| List A | 115 | 111 | 5 | 3425 | 177 | 32.31 | 96.97 | 8 | 12 | 49 | 0 |
| Twenty20 | 94 | 94 | 7 | 2160 | 82* | 24.82 | 136.96 | 0 | 15 | 26 | 0 |
| **Bowling** | **Mat** | **Balls** | **Runs** | **Wkts** | **BBI** | **BBM** | **Ave** | **Econ** | **SR** | **5w** | **10** |
| ODIs | 55 | 1549 | 1159 | 29 | 4/11 | 4/11 | 39.96 | 4.48 | 53.4 | 0 | 0 |
| T20Is | 26 | 300 | 346 | 12 | 3/21 | 3/21 | 28.83 | 6.92 | 25.0 | 0 | 0 |
| First-class | 26 | 753 | 394 | 7 | 2/43 | 3/92 | 56.28 | 3.13 | 107.5 | 0 | 0 |
| List A | 115 | 2201 | 1732 | 49 | 4/11 | 4/11 | 35.34 | 4.72 | 44.9 | 0 | 0 |
| Twenty20 | 94 | 820 | 899 | 40 | 4/10 | 4/10 | 22.47 | 6.57 | 20.5 | 0 | 0 |

## BEN STOKES

## LHB RM R0 W0 MVP39

FULL NAME: Benjamin Andrew Stokes
BORN: June 4, 1991, Christchurch, New Zealand
SQUAD NO: 38
HEIGHT: 6ft 2in
NICKNAME: Stokesy, Benji, Stoker
EDUCATION: Cockermouth School
TEAMS: England, Durham
CAREER: Test: 2013; ODI: 2011; T20I: 2011; First-class: 2010; List A: 2009; T20: 2010

BEST BATTING: 185 Durham vs Lancashire, Chester-le-Street, 2011
BEST BOWLING: 7-67 Durham vs Sussex, Chester-le-Street, 2014

CAREER HIGHLIGHTS? Making my Test debut
SUPERSTITIONS? Swiping my bat across the crease at the end of every over
CRICKETING HEROES? Herschelle Gibbs
CRICKET RULE YOU'D CHANGE? You don't have to play if it's under 15 degrees
IF YOU WEREN'T A CRICKETER? I'd be on the dole
SURPRISING FACT? My father played one Test match for New Zealand at rugby league and I was a right-handed batsman when I was younger
FANTASY SLIP CORDON? 1st: Michael McIntyre, 2nd: Jordan Belfort, 3rd: Alan from The Hangover, Gully: Bane from Batman
TWITTER FEED: @benstokes38

| Batting | Mat | Inns | NO | Runs | HS | Ave | SR | 100 | 50 | Ct | St |
|---|---|---|---|---|---|---|---|---|---|---|---|
| Tests | 6 | 11 | 0 | 279 | 120 | 25.36 | 49.38 | 1 | 0 | 2 | 0 |
| ODIs | 24 | 19 | 1 | 282 | 70 | 15.66 | 75.80 | 0 | 1 | 9 | 0 |
| T20Is | 7 | 5 | 1 | 49 | 31 | 12.25 | 128.94 | 0 | 0 | 0 | 0 |
| First-class | 72 | 118 | 7 | 3765 | 185 | 33.91 | | 9 | 16 | 39 | 0 |
| List A | 89 | 78 | 10 | 2086 | 164 | 30.67 | 96.61 | 4 | 7 | 35 | 0 |
| Twenty20 | 54 | 48 | 8 | 979 | 77 | 24.47 | 131.40 | 0 | 4 | 20 | 0 |
| **Bowling** | **Mat** | **Balls** | **Runs** | **Wkts** | **BBI** | **BBM** | **Ave** | **Econ** | **SR** | **5w** | **10** |
| Tests | 6 | 1228 | 724 | 22 | 6/99 | 8/161 | 32.90 | 3.53 | 55.8 | 1 | 0 |
| ODIs | 24 | 690 | 713 | 20 | 5/61 | 5/61 | 35.65 | 6.20 | 34.5 | 1 | 0 |
| T20Is | 7 | 48 | 92 | 0 | - | - | - | 11.50 | - | 0 | 0 |
| First-class | 72 | 7420 | 4587 | 162 | 7/67 | 10/121 | 28.31 | 3.70 | 45.8 | 3 | 1 |
| List A | 89 | 2126 | 1961 | 77 | 5/61 | 5/61 | 25.46 | 5.53 | 27.6 | 1 | 0 |
| Twenty20 | 54 | 508 | 706 | 22 | 2/14 | 2/14 | 32.09 | 8.33 | 23.0 | 0 | 0 |

# OLLY STONE

## RHB RFM R0 W0

FULL NAME: Oliver Peter Stone
BORN: October 9, 1993, Norwich
SQUAD NO: 9
HEIGHT: 6ft 2in
NICKNAME: Stoney
EDUCATION: Thorpe St Andrew High School; Moulton College
TEAMS: Northamptonshire
CAREER: First-class: 2012; List A: 2012; T20: 2011



BEST BATTING: 26* Northamptonshire vs Yorkshire, Northampton, 2012
BEST BOWLING: 5-48 Northamptonshire vs Sussex, Northampton, 2014

CAREER HIGHLIGHTS? My first five-wicket haul, making my first-class debut and playing and captaining England U19
BEST PLAYER IN COUNTY CRICKET? Joe Root
MOST MARKED CHARACTERISTIC? A terrible haircut
SUPERSTITIONS? Sleeping in my bowling boots
CRICKETING HEROES? Andrew Flintoff, Paul Bradshaw
NON-CRICKETING HEROES? My brothers because they made me look good
IF YOU WEREN'T A CRICKETER? I'd be in my local pub or on a farm
FAVOURITE TV? I love a bit of QI
ACCOMPLISHMENTS? Catching my biggest carp
PET HATE? Stephen Peters, because of his terrible gags
SURPRISING FACT? My great-grandfather invented the garlic crusher
FANTASY SLIP CORDON? Keeper: Lee Evans, 1st: James Middlebrook, 2nd: Delia Smith, 3rd: Myself, Gully: Jay Cartwright
TWITTER FEED: @ollystone2

| Batting | Mat | Inns | NO | Runs | HS | Ave | SR | 100 | 50 | Ct | St |
|---|---|---|---|---|---|---|---|---|---|---|---|
| First-class | 8 | 12 | 3 | 93 | 26* | 10.33 | 32.97 | 0 | 0 | 5 | 0 |
| List A | 11 | 7 | 3 | 31 | 21 | 7.75 | 40.78 | 0 | 0 | 3 | 0 |
| Twenty20 | 16 | 8 | 4 | 15 | 6* | 3.75 | 78.94 | 0 | 0 | 3 | 0 |
| **Bowling** | **Mat** | **Balls** | **Runs** | **Wkts** | **BBI** | **BBM** | **Ave** | **Econ** | **SR** | **5w** | **10** |
| First-class | 8 | 1311 | 705 | 24 | 5/48 | 6/90 | 29.37 | 3.22 | 54.6 | 1 | 0 |
| List A | 11 | 304 | 304 | 2 | 1/12 | 1/12 | 152.00 | 6.00 | 152.0 | 0 | 0 |
| Twenty20 | 16 | 247 | 344 | 10 | 2/18 | 2/18 | 34.40 | 8.35 | 24.7 | 0 | 0 |

# MARK STONEMAN

## LHB R2 W0 MVP43

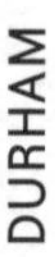

FULL NAME: Mark Daniel Stoneman
BORN: June 26, 1987, Newcastle
SQUAD NO: 26
HEIGHT: 5ft 10in
NICKNAME: Rocky
EDUCATION: Whickham Comprehensive School
TEAMS: Durham
CAREER: First-class: 2007; List A: 2008; T20: 2010

BEST BATTING: 187 Durham vs Middlesex, Chester-le-Street, 2014

FAMILY TIES? My grandfather played and was later a local league umpire. My father played many years as a local league professional
CAREER HIGHLIGHTS? Being part of three County Championship-winning sides. Captaining Durham
MOST MARKED CHARACTERISTIC? Passion
CRICKETING HEROES? My dad, Brian Lara, Michael Di Venuto, Dale Benkenstein
NON-CRICKETING HEROES? Mark Wahlberg, Georges St-Pierre
IF YOU WEREN'T A CRICKETER? I'd be a PE teacher
DESERT ISLAND DISC? ABBA – Greatest Hits
FAVOURITE TV? Game Of Thrones
TWITTER FEED: @mark23stone

| Batting | Mat | Inns | NO | Runs | HS | Ave | SR | 100 | 50 | Ct | St |
|---|---|---|---|---|---|---|---|---|---|---|---|
| First-class | 101 | 175 | 5 | 5211 | 187 | 30.65 | 54.83 | 11 | 26 | 55 | 0 |
| List A | 44 | 42 | 4 | 1523 | 136* | 40.07 | 91.80 | 4 | 9 | 14 | 0 |
| Twenty20 | 27 | 27 | 2 | 387 | 51 | 15.48 | 101.84 | 0 | 1 | 12 | 0 |
| **Bowling** | **Mat** | **Balls** | **Runs** | **Wkts** | **BBI** | **BBM** | **Ave** | **Econ** | **SR** | **5w** | **10** |
| First-class | 101 | 138 | 85 | 0 | - | - | - | 3.69 | - | 0 | 0 |
| List A | 44 | - | - | - | - | - | - | - | - | - | - |
| Twenty20 | 27 | - | - | - | - | - | - | - | - | - | - |

# JAMES SYKES

LHB SLA R0 W0

FULL NAME: James Stuart Sykes
BORN: April 26, 1992, Huntingdon
SQUAD NO: 80
HEIGHT: 6ft 2in
NICKNAME: Sykesy
EDUCATION: St Ivo School
TEAMS: Leicestershire
CAREER: First-class: 2013; List A: 2012; T20: 2012



BEST BATTING: 34 Leicestershire vs Lancashire, Manchester, 2013
BEST BOWLING: 4-176 Leicestershire vs Essex, Chelmsford, 2013

FAMILY TIES? Making my debut and playing at Lord's
BEST PLAYER IN COUNTY CRICKET? James Vince
TIP FOR THE TOP? Tom Kohler-Cadmore, Lewis Hill
SUPERSTITIONS? Putting shoes and pads on in a certain order
CRICKETING HEROES? Shane Warne – because he was the king of spin
NON-CRICKETING HEROES? David Beckham – just an absolute hero
CRICKET RULE YOU'D CHANGE? No reverse-stroke shots
IF YOU WEREN'T A CRICKETER? Trying to cut people's hair
IF YOU COULD BE SOMEONE ELSE FOR A DAY? Scott Disick
DESERT ISLAND DISC? Kanye West – The College Dropout
SURPRISING FACT? Planning on becoming a barber after cricket
FANTASY SLIP CORDON? Keeper: Micky Flanagan, 1st: Kanye West, 2nd: Scott Disick, 3rd: David Beckham, 4th: Myself
TWITTER FEED: @Sykesy20

| Batting | Mat | Inns | NO | Runs | HS | Ave | SR | 100 | 50 | Ct | St |
|---|---|---|---|---|---|---|---|---|---|---|---|
| First-class | 10 | 18 | 3 | 174 | 34 | 11.60 | 35.95 | 0 | 0 | 5 | 0 |
| List A | 17 | 8 | 3 | 41 | 15 | 8.20 | 75.92 | 0 | 0 | 3 | 0 |
| Twenty20 | 3 | 1 | 1 | 2 | 2* | - | 50.00 | 0 | 0 | 0 | 0 |
| **Bowling** | **Mat** | **Balls** | **Runs** | **Wkts** | **BBI** | **BBM** | **Ave** | **Econ** | **SR** | **5w** | **10** |
| First-class | 10 | 1857 | 1114 | 20 | 4/176 | 5/180 | 55.70 | 3.59 | 92.8 | 0 | 0 |
| List A | 17 | 600 | 540 | 15 | 3/34 | 3/34 | 36.00 | 5.40 | 40.0 | 0 | 0 |
| Twenty20 | 3 | 54 | 65 | 2 | 2/24 | 2/24 | 32.50 | 7.22 | 27.0 | 0 | 0 |

# JONATHAN TATTERSALL

## RHB LB R0 W0

FULL NAME: Jonathan Andrew Tattersall
BORN: December 15, 1994, Harrogate, Yorkshire
SQUAD NO: 12
HEIGHT: 5ft 8in
NICKNAME: Tatts, Bone man
EDUCATION: King James's Secondary School
TEAMS: Yorkshire
CAREER: List A: 2013

---

FAMILY TIES? My dad played for my local cricket club Knaresborough and my brother James also played for Yorkshire 2nd XI
CAREER HIGHLIGHTS? Scoring my first hundred for the 2nd XI at Bristol, being selected for numerous tours with England U19 and playing in the U19 World Cup. Also, being 12th man for England at Headingley on two occasions vs New Zealand and Sri Lanka
BEST PLAYER IN COUNTY CRICKET? Adam Lyth
TIP FOR THE TOP? Matthew Fisher, Ben Duckett
CRICKETING HEROES? Michael Vaughan and Ian Bell – for technical aspects of their game and leadership on the pitch
CRICKET RULE YOU'D CHANGE? Leg-side wides on turning pitches should be more lenient
IF YOU COULD BE SOMEONE ELSE FOR A DAY? Alan Partridge
DESERT ISLAND DISC? Lighthouse Family – Ocean Drive
FAVOURITE TV? The Thick Of It
FANTASY SLIP CORDON? Keeper: Chandler from Friends, 1st: Peter Kay, 2nd: Myself, 3rd: Mila Kunis, Gully: Lee Mack
TWITTER FEED: @JonnyTatts

| Batting | Mat | Inns | NO | Runs | HS | Ave | SR | 100 | 50 | Ct | St |
|---|---|---|---|---|---|---|---|---|---|---|---|
| List A | 1 | 1 | 0 | 0 | 0 | 0.00 | 0.00 | 0 | 0 | 0 | 0 |
| **Bowling** | **Mat** | **Balls** | **Runs** | **Wkts** | **BBI** | **BBM** | **Ave** | **Econ** | **SR** | **5w** | **10** |
| List A | 1 | - | - | - | - | - | - | - | - | - | - |

# WILLIAM TAVARÉ

RHB RMF R1 W0

FULL NAME: William Andrew Tavaré
BORN: January 1, 1990, Bristol
SQUAD NO: 4
HEIGHT: 6ft
NICKNAME: Tav, Beak, Mezut, Zuckers, Postman Pat, Screach
EDUCATION: Bristol Grammar School
TEAMS: Gloucestershire, Tamil Union Cricket and Athletic Club
CAREER: First-class: 2010; List A: 2014



BEST BATTING: 139 Gloucestershire vs Hampshire, Bristol, 2014

FAMILY TIES? My uncle Chris played for England, my dad Jeremy played for Gloucestershire 2nd XI and my grandad was a keen cricketer
CAREER HIGHLIGHTS? My debut hundred vs Hampshire
BEST PLAYER IN COUNTY CRICKET? Chris Dent, Sam Billings
MOST MARKED CHARACTERISTIC? My beak
CRICKETING HEROES? Being family, uncle Chris was a big inspiration
NON-CRICKETING HEROES? Jonny Wilkinson for his work ethic and commitment and for being such a down-to-earth bloke
CRICKET RULE YOU'D CHANGE? Can't be caught down the leg-side as it's a horrible way to get out
COACHING TIP? Back yourself
DESERT ISLAND DISC? Bombay Bicycle Club – A Different Kind Of Fix
PET HATE? People not thanking me when I let them through on the road
SURPRISING FACT? When I was four weeks old I moved to Dallas for a year
FANTASY SLIP CORDON? Keeper: Jonny Wilkinson, 1st: Rachel Stevens, 2nd: Myself, 3rd: Michael Jordan
TWITTER FEED: @wtav90

| Batting | Mat | Inns | NO | Runs | HS | Ave | SR | 100 | 50 | Ct | St |
|---|---|---|---|---|---|---|---|---|---|---|---|
| First-class | 21 | 37 | 3 | 1276 | 139 | 37.52 | 46.70 | 4 | 6 | 12 | 0 |
| List A | 5 | 5 | 0 | 139 | 77 | 27.80 | 68.13 | 0 | 1 | 0 | 0 |
| **Bowling** | **Mat** | **Balls** | **Runs** | **Wkts** | **BBI** | **BBM** | **Ave** | **Econ** | **SR** | **5w** | **10** |
| First-class | 21 | - | - | - | - | - | - | - | - | - | - |
| List A | 5 | - | - | - | - | - | - | - | - | - | - |

## BRAD TAYLOR RHB OB R0 W0

FULL NAME: Bradley Jacob Taylor
BORN: March 14, 1997, Winchester, Hampshire
SQUAD NO: 93
HEIGHT: 6ft
NICKNAME: Bradders
EDUCATION: Alton College
TEAMS: Hampshire
CAREER: First-class: 2013; List A: 2013; T20: 2014

BEST BATTING: 20 Hampshire vs Lancashire, Southport, 2013
BEST BOWLING: 4-64 Hampshire vs Lancashire, Southport, 2013

FAMILY TIES? My dad is a Level 3 coach
CAREER HIGHLIGHTS? Taking four wickets on my first-class debut, getting Simon Katich on one-day debut and being Man of the Match for England U19 against South Africa U19 on TV
BEST PLAYER IN COUNTY CRICKET? James Vince
MOST MARKED CHARACTERISTIC? Long-sleeve shirt with sleeves rolled up
CRICKETING HEROES? Daniel Vettori, Graeme Swann
NON-CRICKETING HEROES? LeBron James – he works hard and is always motivated to become better even though he is the best in the world at his sport
COACHING TIP? When bowling spin try to spin every ball as much as you can
FAVOURITE TV? Friday Night Dinner
LEAST FAVOURITE TV? The X Factor
ACCOMPLISHMENTS? I was part of Southampton's football academy as a goalkeeper
SURPRISING FACT? I'm a massive Southampton fan and go to every single home game where possible
TWITTER FEED: @bradtay93

| Batting | Mat | Inns | NO | Runs | HS | Ave | SR | 100 | 50 | Ct | St |
|---|---|---|---|---|---|---|---|---|---|---|---|
| First-class | 2 | 3 | 1 | 21 | 20 | 10.50 | 42.85 | 0 | 0 | 2 | 0 |
| List A | 2 | 1 | 1 | 2 | 2* | - | 50.00 | 0 | 0 | 0 | 0 |
| Twenty20 | 1 | - | - | - | - | - | - | - | - | 1 | 0 |
| **Bowling** | **Mat** | **Balls** | **Runs** | **Wkts** | **BBI** | **BBM** | **Ave** | **Econ** | **SR** | **5w** | **10** |
| First-class | 2 | 246 | 180 | 5 | 4/64 | 4/106 | 36.00 | 4.39 | 49.2 | 0 | 0 |
| List A | 2 | 90 | 73 | 4 | 2/23 | 2/23 | 18.25 | 4.86 | 22.5 | 0 | 0 |
| Twenty20 | 1 | 6 | 16 | 0 | - | - | - | 16.00 | - | 0 | 0 |

## CALLUM TAYLOR

## RHB RM R0 W0

FULL NAME: Callum John Taylor
BORN: June 26, 1997, Norwich
SQUAD NO: 12
TEAMS: England U15, Norfolk
CAREER: Yet to make first-team debut



NOTES: Allrounder Taylor made his Minor Counties debut for Norfolk aged just 16 in 2013, hitting a matchwinning 48 from 33 balls. Scored a half-century in the 2nd XI Championship final against Leicestershire last season. Was awarded a two-year contract at the end of 2014

# JACK TAYLOR

## RHB OB R0 W0

FULL NAME: Jack Martin Robert Taylor
BORN: November 12, 1991, Banbury, Oxfordshire
SQUAD NO: 10
HEIGHT: 6ft
NICKNAME: Schild, J-Swag, Fivehead
EDUCATION: Chipping Norton School
TEAMS: Gloucestershire
CAREER: First-class: 2010; List A: 2011; T20: 2011

BEST BATTING: 63 Gloucestershire vs Glamorgan, Swansea, 2012
BEST BOWLING: 4-125 Gloucestershire vs Essex, Chelmsford, 2014
COUNTY CAPS: 2010

FAMILY TIES? Father and grandfather played Minor Counties for Oxfordshire. My brother, Matt, also plays for Gloucestershire
CAREER HIGHLIGHTS? T20 debut vs Somerset at Bristol and getting Man of the Match for taking 4-16 and scoring 38, reaching the 50-over quarter-finals in 2014, overcoming bowling ban to then play for the first team the year after
MOST MARKED CHARACTERISTIC? Loud voice, always winding up teammates (mainly Gareth 'The Pear' Roderick)
CRICKETING HEROES? Dan Vettori – gun finger spinner. Shane Warne – always up for the battle
NON-CRICKETING HEROES? Justin Timberlake – he's got it all. He can sing, dance, act and can probably rotate the strike too!
COACHING TIP? Bowling – always try to spin the ball hard
SURPRISING FACT? I am a god in the kitchen
TWITTER FEED: @jacktaylor141

| Batting | Mat | Inns | NO | Runs | HS | Ave | SR | 100 | 50 | Ct | St |
|---|---|---|---|---|---|---|---|---|---|---|---|
| First-class | 15 | 24 | 2 | 527 | 63 | 23.95 | 72.09 | 0 | 2 | 8 | 0 |
| List A | 14 | 9 | 3 | 170 | 53 | 28.33 | 125.00 | 0 | 1 | 2 | 0 |
| Twenty20 | 21 | 18 | 5 | 120 | 38 | 9.23 | 118.81 | 0 | 0 | 4 | 0 |
| **Bowling** | **Mat** | **Balls** | **Runs** | **Wkts** | **BBI** | **BBM** | **Ave** | **Econ** | **SR** | **5w** | **10** |
| First-class | 15 | 2030 | 1193 | 29 | 4/125 | 4/103 | 41.13 | 3.52 | 70.0 | 0 | 0 |
| List A | 14 | 514 | 427 | 18 | 4/38 | 4/38 | 23.72 | 4.98 | 28.5 | 0 | 0 |
| Twenty20 | 21 | 311 | 401 | 17 | 4/16 | 4/16 | 23.58 | 7.73 | 18.2 | 0 | 0 |

# JAMES TAYLOR RHB LB R4 W0 MVP42

FULL NAME: James William Arthur Taylor
BORN: January 6, 1990, Nottingham
SQUAD NO: 4
HEIGHT: 5ft 6in
NICKNAME: Jimmy, Titch
EDUCATION: Shrewsbury School
TEAMS: England, Nottinghamshire, Leicestershire
CAREER: Test: 2012; ODI: 2011; First-class: 2008; List A: 2008; T20: 2008



BEST BATTING: 242* England Lions vs Sri Lanka A, Dambulla, 2014
COUNTY CAPS: 2009 (Leicestershire); 2012 (Nottinghamshire)

CRICKETING HEROES? Sachin Tendulkar
TWITTER FEED: TWITTER FEED: @jamestaylor20
NOTES: Taylor made his England Test debut against South Africa at Headingley in 2012. Captained the winter tour of England Lions to Australia in 2012/13, having led them several times before. Made his ODI debut against Ireland in 2011. Cricket Writers' Young Player of the Year 2009. Joined Nottinghamshire for 2012 after four successful seasons with Leicestershire and topped 1,000 first-class runs for the season in 2013, averaging 49.04. Enjoyed a successful tour of Sri Lanka with England Lions in early 2014, hitting 242* against Sri Lanka A in Dambulla. Became a mainstay in England's ODI side in late 2014 after hitting 444 runs in the Royal London Cup. Graduated from Minor Counties cricket with Shropshire and the academy at Worcestershire to the playing staff at Leicestershire. Represented England in the 2008 U19 World Cup

| Batting | Mat | Inns | NO | Runs | HS | Ave | SR | 100 | 50 | Ct | St |
|---|---|---|---|---|---|---|---|---|---|---|---|
| Tests | 2 | 3 | 0 | 48 | 34 | 16.00 | 31.57 | 0 | 0 | 2 | 0 |
| ODIs | 16 | 16 | 2 | 484 | 98* | 34.57 | 76.58 | 0 | 5 | 5 | 0 |
| First-class | 119 | 196 | 26 | 7939 | 242* | 46.70 | | 18 | 39 | 78 | 0 |
| List A | 115 | 111 | 24 | 4445 | 146* | 51.09 | 83.11 | 12 | 25 | 24 | 0 |
| Twenty20 | 79 | 71 | 22 | 1719 | 62* | 35.08 | 116.14 | 0 | 8 | 26 | 0 |
| **Bowling** | **Mat** | **Balls** | **Runs** | **Wkts** | **BBI** | **BBM** | **Ave** | **Econ** | **SR** | **5w** | **10** |
| Tests | 2 | - | - | - | - | - | - | - | - | - | - |
| ODIs | 16 | - | - | - | - | - | - | - | - | - | - |
| First-class | 119 | 228 | 176 | 0 | - | - | - | 4.63 | - | 0 | 0 |
| List A | 115 | 138 | 170 | 5 | 4/61 | 4/61 | 34.00 | 7.39 | 27.6 | 0 | 0 |
| Twenty20 | 79 | 74 | 100 | 2 | 1/10 | 1/10 | 50.00 | 8.10 | 37.0 | 0 | 0 |

# MATT TAYLOR

RHB LMF R0 W0

FULL NAME: Matthew David Taylor
BORN: July 8, 1994, Banbury, Oxfordshire
SQUAD NO: 36
HEIGHT: 6ft 2in
NICKNAME: Melon, Swede, Balloon
EDUCATION: Chipping Norton Secondary School
TEAMS: Gloucestershire
CAREER: First-class: 2013; List A: 2011

BEST BATTING: 32* Gloucestershire vs Essex, Chelmsford, 2014
BEST BOWLING: 5-75 Gloucestershire vs Hampshire, Bristol, 2014

FAMILY TIES? Grandfather and father played for Oxfordshire, and Oxfordshire 50+. My brother Jack also plays for Gloucestershire
CAREER HIGHLIGHTS? Making my Pro40 debut in 2011, making my County Championship debut in 2013, also me and my brother playing our first Championship game together in 2014
BEST PLAYER IN COUNTY CRICKET? Jeetan Patel
TIP FOR THE TOP? Craig Miles, Jordan Garrett
MOST MARKED CHARACTERISTIC? Very small head
CRICKETING HEROES? Darren Gough – great attitude towards the game
NON-CRICKETING HEROES? Ronaldo – for the confidence in his own ability
COACHING TIP? Load and explode
IF YOU COULD BE SOMEONE ELSE FOR A DAY? Leonardo DiCaprio
DESERT ISLAND DISC? Ed Sheeran – X
FAVOURITE TV? Criminal Minds
FANTASY SLIP CORDON? Keeper: Michelle Keegan, 1st: Ed Sheeran, 2nd: Me, 3rd: Kendall Jenner, Gully: Cara Delevingne
TWITTER FEED: matt_taylor94

| Batting | Mat | Inns | NO | Runs | HS | Ave | SR | 100 | 50 | Ct | St |
|---|---|---|---|---|---|---|---|---|---|---|---|
| First-class | 13 | 15 | 7 | 149 | 32* | 18.62 | 41.85 | 0 | 0 | 2 | 0 |
| List A | 2 | 1 | 1 | 7 | 7* | - | 140.00 | 0 | 0 | 1 | 0 |
| **Bowling** | **Mat** | **Balls** | **Runs** | **Wkts** | **BBI** | **BBM** | **Ave** | **Econ** | **SR** | **5w** | **10** |
| First-class | 13 | 1844 | 1209 | 26 | 5/75 | 6/101 | 46.50 | 3.93 | 70.9 | 1 | 0 |
| List A | 2 | 83 | 89 | 4 | 2/43 | 2/43 | 22.25 | 6.43 | 20.7 | 0 | 0 |

# ROB TAYLOR

## LHB LM R0 W0



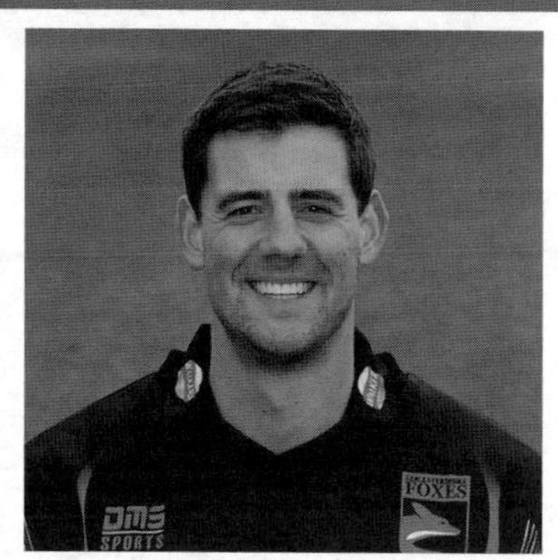


FULL NAME: Robert Meadows Lombe Taylor
BORN: December 21, 1989, Northampton
SQUAD NO: 42
HEIGHT: 6ft 3in
NICKNAME: Tayls, T, Bobby, Meadows
EDUCATION: Harrow School; Loughborough University
TEAMS: Scotland, Leicestershire
CAREER: ODI: 2013; T20I: 2013; First-class: 2010; List A: 2012; T20: 2012

BEST BATTING: 101* LMCCU vs Leicestershire, Leicester, 2011
BEST BOWLING: 5-55 Leicestershire vs Gloucestershire, Leicester, 2014

CAREER HIGHLIGHTS? Making my first-class debut for Leicestershire, scoring my first first-class hundred, making my debut for Scotland and qualifying for the 2015 World Cup
MOST MARKED CHARACTERISTIC? Broken nose. Red cheeks
CRICKETING HEROES? Mitchell Johnson because he bowls rockets and swings it! Matt Hayden because he whacked it!
CRICKET RULE YOU'D CHANGE? You should be allowed to bowl with a sidearm
IF YOU WEREN'T A CRICKETER? Full-time social golfer
FAVOURITE TV? Top Gear
PET HATE? People who don't look you in the eye when you shake hands
FANTASY SLIP CORDON? Keeper: Jonny Wilkinson, 1st: Myself, 2nd: Batman, 3rd: Matthew Hayden, Gully: Gerard Butler
TWITTER FEED: @robtaylor1989

| Batting | Mat | Inns | NO | Runs | HS | Ave | SR | 100 | 50 | Ct | St |
|---|---|---|---|---|---|---|---|---|---|---|---|
| ODIs | 12 | 11 | 3 | 133 | 46* | 16.62 | 94.32 | 0 | 0 | 6 | 0 |
| T20Is | 4 | 4 | 2 | 71 | 41* | 35.50 | 154.34 | 0 | 0 | 4 | 0 |
| First-class | 31 | 53 | 3 | 1055 | 101* | 21.10 | 62.31 | 1 | 5 | 15 | 0 |
| List A | 38 | 35 | 10 | 444 | 48* | 17.76 | 101.36 | 0 | 0 | 16 | 0 |
| Twenty20 | 35 | 26 | 8 | 277 | 41* | 15.38 | 139.19 | 0 | 0 | 19 | 0 |
| **Bowling** | **Mat** | **Balls** | **Runs** | **Wkts** | **BBI** | **BBM** | **Ave** | **Econ** | **SR** | **5w** | **10** |
| ODIs | 12 | 575 | 504 | 16 | 3/39 | 3/39 | 31.50 | 5.25 | 35.9 | 0 | 0 |
| T20Is | 4 | 60 | 83 | 1 | 1/16 | 1/16 | 83.00 | 8.30 | 60.0 | 0 | 0 |
| First-class | 31 | 4040 | 2639 | 66 | 5/55 | 6/120 | 39.98 | 3.91 | 61.2 | 3 | 0 |
| List A | 38 | 1627 | 1524 | 51 | 3/39 | 3/39 | 29.88 | 5.62 | 31.9 | 0 | 0 |
| Twenty20 | 35 | 556 | 745 | 30 | 4/11 | 4/11 | 24.83 | 8.03 | 18.5 | 0 | 0 |

## TOM TAYLOR

RHB RMF R0 W0

FULL NAME: Thomas Alex Ian Taylor
BORN: December 21, 1994, Stoke-on-Trent, Staffordshire
SQUAD NO: 15
HEIGHT: 6ft 3in
NICKNAME: Audi, Anne Robinson
EDUCATION: Trentham High School; Newcastle-under-Lyme College; Leeds Metropolitan University
TEAMS: Derbyshire
CAREER: First-class: 2014; List A: 2014

BEST BATTING: 40 Derbyshire vs Leicestershire, Leicester, 2014
BEST BOWLING: 5-58 Derbyshire vs Gloucestershire, Cheltenham, 2014

FAMILY TIES? Father, cousins, uncles all play cricket; other family members used to run my home club
CAREER HIGHLIGHTS? Making my first-class debut, first first-class wicket was Hashim Amla, first first-class five-wicket haul, first professional contract with Derbyshire
BEST PLAYER IN COUNTY CRICKET? Mark Footitt
TIP FOR THE TOP? Ben Slater
CRICKETING HEROES? Shane Warne – enjoyable to watch bowl, Brian Lara – enjoyable to watch bat
CRICKET RULE YOU'D CHANGE? Use technology instead of umpires
IF YOU COULD BE SOMEONE ELSE FOR A DAY? Tom Cruise
DESERT ISLAND DISC? Arctic Monkeys – AM
PET HATE? Teeth grinding while asleep – hate the noise
SURPRISING FACT? I'm a Port Vale fan
FANTASY SLIP CORDON? Keeper: Tom Cruise, 1st: Barack Obama, 2nd: LeBron James, 3rd: Ronaldo, 4th: Jennifer Lawrence, Gully: Cameron Diaz
TWITTER FEED: @TomTaylor43

| Batting | Mat | Inns | NO | Runs | HS | Ave | SR | 100 | 50 | Ct | St |
|---|---|---|---|---|---|---|---|---|---|---|---|
| First-class | 6 | 9 | 2 | 115 | 40 | 16.42 | 36.27 | 0 | 0 | 1 | 0 |
| List A | 4 | - | - | - | - | - | - | - | - | 0 | 0 |
| **Bowling** | **Mat** | **Balls** | **Runs** | **Wkts** | **BBI** | **BBM** | **Ave** | **Econ** | **SR** | **5w** | **10** |
| First-class | 6 | 852 | 451 | 15 | 5/58 | 6/86 | 30.06 | 3.17 | 56.8 | 1 | 0 |
| List A | 4 | 176 | 174 | 5 | 3/48 | 3/48 | 34.80 | 5.93 | 35.2 | 0 | 0 |

# RYAN TEN DOESCHATE

## RHB RMF R0 W0

FULL NAME: Ryan Neil ten Doeschate
BORN: June 30, 1980, Port Elizabeth, South Africa
SQUAD NO: 27
HEIGHT: 5ft 11in
NICKNAME: Tendo
TEAMS: Netherlands, Essex, Adelaide Strikers, Canterbury, Chittagong Kings, Impi, Kolkata Knight Riders, Mashonaland Eagles, Otago, Tasmania, Western Province
CAREER: ODI: 2006; T20I: 2008; First-class: 2003; List A: 2003; T20: 2003



BEST BATTING: 259* Netherlands vs Canada, Pretoria, 2006
BEST BOWLING: 6-20 Netherlands vs Canada, Pretoria, 2006
COUNTY CAPS: 2006

CRICKETING HEROES? Jacques Kallis, Kepler Wessels
DESERT ISLAND DISC? Phil Collins
TWITTER FEED: @rtendo27
NOTES: Netherlands international who won the inaugural ICC Associate ODI Player of the Year in 2007 and the ICC Affiliate Player of the Year award in 2010. Scored 686 runs at an average of 228.66 in the ICC Intercontinental Cup in 2006, recording four consecutive hundreds, including a competition record 259* vs Canada in Pretoria. Made a century (119) against England at Nagpur in the 2011 World Cup, becoming the first batsman from the Netherlands to make a hundred in the World Cup finals, and scored a second century against Ireland at Kolkata

| Batting | Mat | Inns | NO | Runs | HS | Ave | SR | 100 | 50 | Ct | St |
|---|---|---|---|---|---|---|---|---|---|---|---|
| ODIs | 33 | 32 | 9 | 1541 | 119 | 67.00 | 87.70 | 5 | 9 | 13 | 0 |
| T20Is | 9 | 9 | 4 | 214 | 56 | 42.80 | 128.91 | 0 | 1 | 3 | 0 |
| First-class | 115 | 169 | 24 | 6709 | 259* | 46.26 | | 21 | 26 | 67 | 0 |
| List A | 177 | 147 | 42 | 4804 | 180 | 45.75 | | 9 | 26 | 52 | 0 |
| Twenty20 | 240 | 211 | 47 | 4931 | 121* | 30.06 | 138.27 | 2 | 21 | 88 | 0 |
| **Bowling** | **Mat** | **Balls** | **Runs** | **Wkts** | **BBI** | **BBM** | **Ave** | **Econ** | **SR** | **5w** | **10** |
| ODIs | 33 | 1580 | 1327 | 55 | 4/31 | 4/31 | 24.12 | 5.03 | 28.7 | 0 | 0 |
| T20Is | 9 | 204 | 241 | 12 | 3/23 | 3/23 | 20.08 | 7.08 | 17.0 | 0 | 0 |
| First-class | 115 | 9583 | 6347 | 186 | 6/20 | | 34.12 | 3.97 | 51.5 | 7 | 0 |
| List A | 177 | 4806 | 4581 | 153 | 5/50 | 5/50 | 29.94 | 5.71 | 31.4 | 1 | 0 |
| Twenty20 | 240 | 1844 | 2475 | 94 | 4/24 | 4/24 | 26.32 | 8.05 | 19.6 | 0 | 0 |

## SEAN TERRY

RHB OB R0 W0

FULL NAME: Sean Paul Terry
BORN: August 1, 1991, Southampton
SQUAD NO: 10
HEIGHT: 5ft 11in
NICKNAME: ST
EDUCATION: Aquinas College; Notre Dame University
TEAMS: Hampshire
CAREER: First-class: 2012; List A: 2012

BEST BATTING: 59* Hampshire vs LMCCU, Southampton, 2012

FAMILY TIES? My dad Paul played for Hampshire and England
CAREER HIGHLIGHTS? Anytime I've played in the 1st XI for Hampshire
BEST PLAYER IN COUNTY CRICKET? James Vince
TIP FOR THE TOP? Lewis McManus, Tom Alsop and Stevie Eskinazi
MOST MARKED CHARACTERISTIC? Known for my large head and sweaty hands
CRICKETING HEROES? Dad (heard he was half-decent); other heroes are Michael Clarke and Sachin Tendulkar
NON-CRICKETING HEROES? Mum – all-round legend
CRICKET RULE YOU'D CHANGE? Openers shouldn't have to bat for any less then 10 overs before the end of play
IF YOU COULD BE SOMEONE ELSE FOR A DAY? Barack Obama
DESERT ISLAND DISC? Anything by the Red Hot Chili Peppers
PET HATE? People who walk slowly in front of you, especially in airports
SURPRISING FACT? Have three passports (pretty sure it's legal)
FANTASY SLIP CORDON? Keeper: Denzel Washington, 1st: Myself, 2nd: Jay Z, 3rd: Michael Clarke, Gully: Mila Kunis
TWITTER FEED: @sterry91

| Batting | Mat | Inns | NO | Runs | HS | Ave | SR | 100 | 50 | Ct | St |
|---|---|---|---|---|---|---|---|---|---|---|---|
| First-class | 6 | 7 | 1 | 208 | 59* | 34.66 | 46.95 | 0 | 3 | 5 | 0 |
| List A | 8 | 6 | 1 | 161 | 63 | 32.20 | 84.29 | 0 | 2 | 1 | 0 |
| **Bowling** | **Mat** | **Balls** | **Runs** | **Wkts** | **BBI** | **BBM** | **Ave** | **Econ** | **SR** | **5w** | **10** |
| First-class | 6 | - | - | - | - | - | - | - | - | - | - |
| List A | 8 | - | - | - | - | - | - | - | - | - | - |

# SHIV THAKOR

RHB RM R0 W0

FULL NAME: Shivsinh Jaysinh Thakor
BORN: October 22, 1993, Leicester
SQUAD NO: 57
HEIGHT: 5ft 11in
NICKNAME: Shiva, Shivy, Shivametimbers
EDUCATION: Uppingham School
TEAMS: Derbyshire, Leicestershire
CAREER: First-class: 2011; List A: 2011; T20: 2013



BEST BATTING: 134 Leicestershire vs Loughborough MCCU, 2011
BEST BOWLING: 3-37 Leicestershire vs Surrey, Leicester, 2011

CAREER HIGHLIGHTS? Captaining England U19, becoming the youngest centurion for Leicestershire, and scoring 134 on my first-class debut
BEST PLAYER IN COUNTY CRICKET? Mark Footitt
TIP FOR THE TOP? Tom Taylor, Harvey Hosein, Greg Cork, Will Davies, Ben Cotton
CRICKETING HEROES? Sachin Tendulkar has always been a hero of mine for his achievements both on and off the field for 20 years. Jacques Kallis – because he is undoubtedly one of the greatest allrounders in the game
IF YOU COULD BE SOMEONE ELSE FOR A DAY? Cristiano Ronaldo
FAVOURITE TV? Suits and White Collar
ACCOMPLISHMENTS? Meeting the Prime Minister at Downing Street
SURPRISING FACT? I can't swim
FANTASY SLIP CORDON? Keeper: Paul Chowdhry, 1st: Jessica Alba, 2nd: Myself, 3rd: Cristiano Ronaldo, Gully: Leonardo DiCaprio
TWITTER FEED: @thakor57

| Batting | Mat | Inns | NO | Runs | HS | Ave | SR | 100 | 50 | Ct | St |
|---|---|---|---|---|---|---|---|---|---|---|---|
| First-class | 24 | 39 | 6 | 1288 | 134 | 39.03 | 46.87 | 2 | 9 | 6 | 0 |
| List A | 24 | 22 | 3 | 356 | 83* | 18.73 | 78.76 | 0 | 3 | 5 | 0 |
| Twenty20 | 8 | 6 | 1 | 62 | 42 | 12.40 | 98.41 | 0 | 0 | 2 | 0 |
| **Bowling** | **Mat** | **Balls** | **Runs** | **Wkts** | **BBI** | **BBM** | **Ave** | **Econ** | **SR** | **5w** | **10** |
| First-class | 24 | 1141 | 796 | 16 | 3/57 | 3/57 | 49.75 | 4.18 | 71.3 | 0 | 0 |
| List A | 24 | 487 | 577 | 17 | 4/49 | 4/49 | 33.94 | 7.10 | 28.6 | 0 | 0 |
| Twenty20 | 8 | 78 | 109 | 6 | 3/30 | 3/30 | 18.16 | 8.38 | 13.0 | 0 | 0 |

# ALFONSO THOMAS RHB RFM R0 W1 MVP19

FULL NAME: Alfonso Clive Thomas
BORN: February 9, 1977, Cape Town, South Africa
SQUAD NO: 8
EDUCATION: Ravensmead Secondary School; Parrow High School, Cape Town
TEAMS: South Africa, Somerset, Adelaide Strikers, Dhaka Gladiators, Dolphins, North West, Northerns, Pune Warriors, Titans, Warwickshire, Western Province
CAREER: T20I: 2007; First-class: 1998; List A: 2000; T20: 2004

BEST BATTING: 119* North West vs Northerns, Centurion, 2002
BEST BOWLING: 7-54 Titans vs Cape Cobras, Newlands, 2005
COUNTY CAPS: 2008 (Somerset)

TWITTER FEED: @alfonsothomas
NOTES: First emerged in the 2003/04 South African season, claiming 36 wickets in eight SuperSport Series matches for Titans. He was drafted in to replace the injured Andre Nel in South Africa's Test squad that toured India in 2004. Made his international debut aged 30 in 2007, but signed with Somerset as a Kolpak player the following year and has not played for South Africa since. Leading wicket-taker in the 2010 FP t20 with 33 wickets, and took 109 wickets in all competitions that year. Claimed 42 first-class wickets at 25.64 in 2013 for Somerset. Last season he took 53 Championship wickets

| Batting | Mat | Inns | NO | Runs | HS | Ave | SR | 100 | 50 | Ct | St |
|---|---|---|---|---|---|---|---|---|---|---|---|
| T20Is | 1 | - | - | - | - | - | - | - | - | 0 | 0 |
| First-class | 157 | 218 | 45 | 4051 | 119* | 23.41 | | 2 | 14 | 37 | 0 |
| List A | 164 | 80 | 38 | 673 | 49* | 16.02 | | 0 | 0 | 35 | 0 |
| Twenty20 | 214 | 68 | 34 | 407 | 30* | 11.97 | 106.82 | 0 | 0 | 64 | 0 |
| **Bowling** | **Mat** | **Balls** | **Runs** | **Wkts** | **BBI** | **BBM** | **Ave** | **Econ** | **SR** | **5w** | **10** |
| T20Is | 1 | 24 | 25 | 3 | 3/25 | 3/25 | 8.33 | 6.25 | 8.0 | 0 | 0 |
| First-class | 157 | 28364 | 13677 | 518 | 7/54 | | 26.40 | 2.89 | 54.7 | 24 | 2 |
| List A | 164 | 6961 | 6041 | 216 | 4/18 | 4/18 | 27.96 | 5.20 | 32.2 | 0 | 0 |
| Twenty20 | 214 | 4328 | 5347 | 248 | 5/24 | 5/24 | 21.56 | 7.41 | 17.4 | 1 | 0 |

# IVAN THOMAS

RHB RMF R0 W0

FULL NAME: Ivan Alfred Astley Thomas
BORN: September 25, 1991, Greenwich, London
SQUAD NO: 5
HEIGHT: 6ft 4in
NICKNAME: Blade, Big Iv, Backpacker
EDUCATION: The John Roan School; University of Leeds
TEAMS: Kent
CAREER: First-class: 2012; List A: 2014



BEST BATTING: 11 LBMCCU vs Yorkshire, Leeds, 2012
BEST BOWLING: 3-39 LBMCCU vs Somerset, Taunton, 2014

CAREER HIGHLIGHTS? Playing against South Africa
BEST PLAYER IN COUNTY CRICKET? Marcus Trescothick
TIP FOR THE TOP? Nick Gubbins
MOST MARKED CHARACTERISTIC? My ginger locks
SUPERSTITIONS? If the sun rises in the west I can't play that day
CRICKETING HEROES? Andrew Flintoff
CRICKET RULE YOU'D CHANGE? If a batsman gets dropped, the runs he gets after he is dropped are halved until he gets out
IF YOU WEREN'T A CRICKETER? Travelling the world
IF YOU COULD BE SOMEONE ELSE FOR A DAY? Dan Bilzerian
DESERT ISLAND DISC? Wu-Tang Clan – 36 Chambers
FAVOURITE TV? The Wire
LEAST FAVOURITE TV? Loose Women
SURPRISING FACT? I'm a quarter Jamaican
FANTASY SLIP CORDON? Keeper: David Brent, 1st: Alan Partridge, 2nd: Neil deGrasse Tyson, 3rd: Mark Corrigan, Gully: Jeremy Usborne
TWITTER FEED: @ivanthomas_5

| Batting | Mat | Inns | NO | Runs | HS | Ave | SR | 100 | 50 | Ct | St |
|---|---|---|---|---|---|---|---|---|---|---|---|
| First-class | 8 | 12 | 6 | 57 | 11 | 9.50 | 30.00 | 0 | 0 | 2 | 0 |
| List A | 1 | 1 | 0 | 1 | 1 | 1.00 | 8.33 | 0 | 0 | 0 | 0 |
| **Bowling** | **Mat** | **Balls** | **Runs** | **Wkts** | **BBI** | **BBM** | **Ave** | **Econ** | **SR** | **5w** | **10** |
| First-class | 8 | 1113 | 467 | 16 | 3/39 | 3/45 | 29.18 | 2.51 | 69.5 | 0 | 0 |
| List A | 1 | 54 | 47 | 0 | - | - | - | 5.22 | - | 0 | 0 |

# AARON THOMASON RHB RFM R0 W0

FULL NAME: Aaron Dean Thomason
BORN: June 26, 1997, Birmingham
SQUAD NO: 26
HEIGHT: 5ft 11in
NICKNAME: Thomo
EDUCATION: Barr Beacon School
TEAMS: Warwickshire
CAREER: List A: 2014

---

FAMILY TIES? My brother Lee played for Unicorns
CAREER HIGHLIGHTS? Making my first-team debut at Lord's
BEST PLAYER IN COUNTY CRICKET? Jeetan Patel
TIP FOR THE TOP? Sam Hain
MOST MARKED CHARACTERISTIC? Fiery and committed
CRICKETING HEROES? Freddie Flintoff – he can bat, bowl, field and enjoys life. Ian Bell – the perfect pro
NON-CRICKETING HEROES? My brother – he's better than me at cricket
CRICKET RULE YOU'D CHANGE? Get on the pitch quicker after rain – the public deserve as much cricket as possible for their money
IF YOU WEREN'T A CRICKETER? Working at McDonald's
IF YOU COULD BE SOMEONE ELSE FOR A DAY? Michelle Keegan's partner
DESERT ISLAND DISC? Ed Sheeran – Thinking Out Loud
FAVOURITE TV? The Office
LEAST FAVOURITE TV? Big Brother
ACCOMPLISHMENTS? Scoring a hat-trick in a cup final for my school football team
PET HATE? Queues and people who smoke
SURPRISING FACT? I went to the same school as Chris Woakes
FANTASY SLIP CORDON? Keeper: Karl Pilkinton, 1st: Ricky Gervais, 2nd: Myself, 3rd: David Jason, Gully: Freddie Flintoff (not a dull moment in the day!)

| Batting | Mat | Inns | NO | Runs | HS | Ave | SR | 100 | 50 | Ct | St |
|---|---|---|---|---|---|---|---|---|---|---|---|
| List A | 1 | 1 | 1 | 0 | 0* | - | - | 0 | 0 | 0 | 0 |
| **Bowling** | **Mat** | **Balls** | **Runs** | **Wkts** | **BBI** | **BBM** | **Ave** | **Econ** | **SR** | **5w** | **10** |
| List A | 1 | 24 | 23 | 0 | - | - | - | 5.75 | - | 0 | 0 |

# JAMES TOMLINSON

## LHB LMF R0 W2

FULL NAME: James Andrew Tomlinson
BORN: June 12, 1982, Winchester, Hampshire
SQUAD NO: 21
HEIGHT: 6ft 1in
NICKNAME: Tommo, Bird, Dangerous Dave
EDUCATION: Crickdale College; Cardiff University
TEAMS: Hampshire
CAREER: First-class: 2002; List A: 2000; T20: 2006



BEST BATTING: 51 Hampshire vs Gloucestershire, Southampton, 2014
BEST BOWLING: 8-46 Hampshire vs Somerset, Taunton, 2008
COUNTY CAPS: 2008

FAMILY TIES? Both brothers Hugh and Ralph played league cricket. Grandfather played a bit up north and watched cricket regularly at Scarborough
CAREER HIGHLIGHTS? Staying up in Division One in 2010 – Jimmy Adams taking a fine catch at deep short-leg off me with two minutes to go! Winning the Division Two title in 2014 – what a relief. Growing a beard. Playing under Shane Warne. Being coached by Bruce Reid and Wasim Akram
SUPERSTITIONS? I claim not to. But I do
CRICKETING HEROES? All the left-arm overs who were around in the '90s. Wasim Akram, Mark Ilott, Bruce Reid etc
NON-CRICKETING HEROES? Chris Packham – I love wildlife and he is currently standing up for birds in particular
IF YOU COULD BE SOMEONE ELSE FOR A DAY? A nature reserve designer
DESERT ISLAND DISC? Not a clue but I would take my binoculars
FAVOURITE TV? Only Connect is an excellent programme. Many others are not

| Batting | Mat | Inns | NO | Runs | HS | Ave | SR | 100 | 50 | Ct | St |
|---|---|---|---|---|---|---|---|---|---|---|---|
| First-class | 114 | 140 | 66 | 818 | 51 | 11.05 | 30.16 | 0 | 1 | 24 | 0 |
| List A | 36 | 21 | 11 | 53 | 14 | 5.30 |  | 0 | 0 | 3 | 0 |
| Twenty20 | 2 | 1 | 0 | 5 | 5 | 5.00 | 125.00 | 0 | 0 | 0 | 0 |
| **Bowling** | **Mat** | **Balls** | **Runs** | **Wkts** | **BBI** | **BBM** | **Ave** | **Econ** | **SR** | **5w** | **10** |
| First-class | 114 | 19900 | 10935 | 348 | 8/46 |  | 31.42 | 3.29 | 57.1 | 12 | 1 |
| List A | 36 | 1319 | 1150 | 39 | 4/47 | 4/47 | 29.48 | 5.23 | 33.8 | 0 | 0 |
| Twenty20 | 2 | 42 | 48 | 1 | 1/20 | 1/20 | 48.00 | 6.85 | 42.0 | 0 | 0 |

# REECE TOPLEY RHB LFM R0 W0

FULL NAME: Reece James William Topley
BORN: February 21, 1994, Ipswich
SQUAD NO: 6
HEIGHT: 6ft 5in
NICKNAME: Toppers, Smash, Neil
EDUCATION: Royal Hospital School
TEAMS: England Lions, Essex
CAREER: First-class: 2011; List A: 2011; T20: 2012

BEST BATTING: 9 Essex vs Hampshire, Southampton, 2014
BEST BOWLING: 6-29 Essex vs Worcestershire, Chelmsford, 2013
COUNTY CAPS: 2013

FAMILY TIES? My father Don played for Essex and Surrey and my uncle Peter played for Kent
CAREER HIGHLIGHTS? Touring with the England Lions and taking two 10-wicket hauls
BEST PLAYER IN COUNTY CRICKET? James Taylor
TIP FOR THE TOP? Sebastián Pedley
SUPERSTITIONS? I wear the same whites if I have bowled well the day before
CRICKETING HEROES? Wasim Akram – best left-arm bowler ever in my opinion
NON-CRICKETING HEROES? David Beckham – absolute legend. Johnny Knoxville
CRICKET RULE YOU'D CHANGE? No run-ups and throwing allowed
IF YOU WEREN'T A CRICKETER? Acting
ACCOMPLISHMENTS? Speak Spanish to a very good standard
PET HATE? Batsmen
FANTASY SLIP CORDON? Keeper: Jimmy Hendrix, 1st: David Beckham, 2nd: James Dean, 3rd: Marilyn Monroe, 4th: Elvis, Gully: Me
TWITTER FEED: @reece_topley

| Batting | Mat | Inns | NO | Runs | HS | Ave | SR | 100 | 50 | Ct | St |
|---|---|---|---|---|---|---|---|---|---|---|---|
| First-class | 29 | 34 | 16 | 52 | 12 | 2.88 | 16.93 | 0 | 0 | 7 | 0 |
| List A | 21 | 6 | 2 | 25 | 19 | 6.25 | 55.55 | 0 | 0 | 4 | 0 |
| Twenty20 | 32 | 4 | 3 | 6 | 4* | 6.00 | 46.15 | 0 | 0 | 8 | 0 |
| **Bowling** | **Mat** | **Balls** | **Runs** | **Wkts** | **BBI** | **BBM** | **Ave** | **Econ** | **SR** | **5w** | **10** |
| First-class | 29 | 5382 | 3017 | 118 | 6/29 | 11/85 | 25.56 | 3.36 | 45.6 | 7 | 2 |
| List A | 21 | 858 | 830 | 30 | 4/26 | 4/26 | 27.66 | 5.80 | 28.6 | 0 | 0 |
| Twenty20 | 32 | 672 | 910 | 47 | 4/26 | 4/26 | 19.36 | 8.12 | 14.2 | 0 | 0 |

# JAMES TREDWELL

LHB OB R0 W1

FULL NAME: James Cullum Tredwell
BORN: February 27, 1982, Ashford, Kent
SQUAD NO: 15
HEIGHT: 5ft 11in
NICKNAME: Tredders, Pingu, Tricky
EDUCATION: Southlands Community Comprehensive
TEAMS: England, Kent, Sussex
CAREER: Test: 2010; ODI: 2010; T20I: 2012; First-class: 2001; List A: 2000; T20: 2003



BEST BATTING: 123* Kent vs New Zealanders, Canterbury, 2008
BEST BOWLING: 8-66 Kent vs Glamorgan, Canterbury, 2009
COUNTY CAPS: 2007 (Kent)

FAMILY TIES? My father played a good level of club cricket in Kent
CAREER HIGHLIGHTS? Having the opportunity to represent my country
MOST MARKED CHARACTERISTIC? Stubbornness
COACHING TIP? Make sure you want to do it then enjoy every minute and give it your all
FAVOURITE TV? All of the old-school British comedy sitcoms like Porridge and Only Fools And Horses
ACCOMPLISHMENTS? My family
PET HATE? Lateness – because it's rude

| Batting | Mat | Inns | NO | Runs | HS | Ave | SR | 100 | 50 | Ct | St |
|---|---|---|---|---|---|---|---|---|---|---|---|
| Tests | 1 | 1 | 0 | 37 | 37 | 37.00 | 58.73 | 0 | 0 | 1 | 0 |
| ODIs | 44 | 25 | 11 | 163 | 30 | 11.64 | 67.35 | 0 | 0 | 13 | 0 |
| T20Is | 17 | 6 | 3 | 32 | 22 | 10.66 | 160.00 | 0 | 0 | 2 | 0 |
| First-class | 149 | 212 | 25 | 4136 | 123* | 22.11 | 44.27 | 3 | 15 | 161 | 0 |
| List A | 237 | 155 | 56 | 1712 | 88 | 17.29 | | 0 | 4 | 98 | 0 |
| Twenty20 | 135 | 59 | 20 | 431 | 34* | 11.05 | 108.83 | 0 | 0 | 38 | 0 |
| **Bowling** | **Mat** | **Balls** | **Runs** | **Wkts** | **BBI** | **BBM** | **Ave** | **Econ** | **SR** | **5w** | **10** |
| Tests | 1 | 390 | 181 | 6 | 4/82 | 6/181 | 30.16 | 2.78 | 65.0 | 0 | 0 |
| ODIs | 44 | 2062 | 1641 | 59 | 4/41 | 4/41 | 27.81 | 4.77 | 34.9 | 0 | 0 |
| T20Is | 17 | 317 | 416 | 7 | 1/16 | 1/16 | 59.42 | 7.87 | 45.2 | 0 | 0 |
| First-class | 149 | 26471 | 13530 | 375 | 8/66 | | 36.08 | 3.06 | 70.5 | 12 | 3 |
| List A | 237 | 9998 | 7821 | 252 | 6/27 | 6/27 | 31.03 | 4.69 | 39.6 | 1 | 0 |
| Twenty20 | 135 | 2582 | 3091 | 109 | 4/21 | 4/21 | 28.35 | 7.18 | 23.6 | 0 | 0 |

## PETER TREGO

## RHB RM R0 W1 MVP5

FULL NAME: Peter David Trego
BORN: June 12, 1981, Weston-super-Mare, Somerset
SQUAD NO: 7
HEIGHT: 6ft
NICKNAME: Tregs, Pirate, Big Tone
EDUCATION: Wyvern School
TEAMS: Somerset, Central Districts, England Lions, Kent, Mashonaland Eagles, Middlesex
CAREER: First-class: 2000; List A: 1999; T20: 2003

BEST BATTING: 141 Central Districts vs Auckland, Auckland, 2013
BEST BOWLING: 7-84 Somerset vs Yorkshire, Leeds, 2014
COUNTY CAPS: 2007 (Somerset); BENEFIT YEAR: 2015

CAREER HIGHLIGHTS? Winning the PCA MVP award, all of my England Lions appearances and playing in the Hong Kong Sixes
MOST MARKED CHARACTERISTIC? I would guess my tattoos but I'd like to think my calves…
CRICKETING HEROES? Graham Rose, Sir Ian Botham, Justin Langer
CRICKET RULE YOU'D CHANGE? Duckworth Lewis – it's a shambles for modern one-day cricket!
IF YOU WEREN'T A CRICKETER? Something manual and dominating Sunday football
IF YOU COULD BE SOMEONE ELSE FOR A DAY? Iron Man or Wolverine
DESERT ISLAND DISC? Green Day – Dookie
FAVOURITE TV? Family Guy
PET HATE? Pets! My house is like a bloody zoo and it drives me crackers!
FANTASY SLIP CORDON? Keeper: Tiger Woods, 1st: John Cleese, 2nd: Myself, 3rd: Iron Man, 4th: Wolverine, Gully: Spider-Man
TWITTER FEED: @tregs140

| Batting | Mat | Inns | NO | Runs | HS | Ave | SR | 100 | 50 | Ct | St |
|---|---|---|---|---|---|---|---|---|---|---|---|
| First-class | 172 | 251 | 32 | 7224 | 141 | 32.98 | | 11 | 42 | 72 | 0 |
| List A | 153 | 131 | 22 | 3329 | 147 | 30.54 | | 6 | 15 | 47 | 0 |
| Twenty20 | 146 | 133 | 17 | 2849 | 94* | 24.56 | 122.74 | 0 | 14 | 39 | 0 |
| **Bowling** | **Mat** | **Balls** | **Runs** | **Wkts** | **BBI** | **BBM** | **Ave** | **Econ** | **SR** | **5w** | **10** |
| First-class | 172 | 20828 | 12054 | 339 | 7/84 | | 35.55 | 3.47 | 61.4 | 4 | 1 |
| List A | 153 | 5142 | 4812 | 146 | 5/40 | 5/40 | 32.95 | 5.61 | 35.2 | 2 | 0 |
| Twenty20 | 146 | 1662 | 2336 | 75 | 4/27 | 4/27 | 31.14 | 8.43 | 22.1 | 0 | 0 |

# CHRIS TREMLETT RHB RFM R0 W0

FULL NAME: Christopher Timothy Tremlett
BORN: September 2, 1981, Southampton
SQUAD NO: 33
HEIGHT: 6ft 8in
NICKNAME: Goober, Trem
EDUCATION: Thornden School
TEAMS: England, Surrey, Hampshire
CAREER: Test: 2007; ODI: 2005; T20I: 2007; First-class: 2000; List A: 2000; T20: 2004



BEST BATTING: 90 Surrey vs Leicestershire, The Oval, 2014
BEST BOWLING: 8-96 Surrey vs Durham, Chester-le-Street, 2013
COUNTY CAPS: 2004 (Hampshire)

FAMILY TIES? My dad Tim played for Hampshire and England A and my grandfather Maurice played for Somerset and England
CAREER HIGHLIGHTS? Playing for England and winning the Ashes
NON-CRICKETING HEROES? Michael Jordan – the best-ever sportsman
CRICKET RULE YOU'D CHANGE? Back to five men outside the circle. It's too batsman-friendly
IF YOU WEREN'T A CRICKETER? A plasterer
IF YOU COULD BE SOMEONE ELSE FOR A DAY? Hugh Hefner
SURPRISING FACT? I can fit a tennis ball in my mouth
TWITTER FEED: @ChrisTremlett33

| Batting | Mat | Inns | NO | Runs | HS | Ave | SR | 100 | 50 | Ct | St |
|---|---|---|---|---|---|---|---|---|---|---|---|
| Tests | 12 | 15 | 4 | 113 | 25* | 10.27 | 37.79 | 0 | 0 | 4 | 0 |
| ODIs | 15 | 11 | 4 | 50 | 19* | 7.14 | 56.17 | 0 | 0 | 4 | 0 |
| T20Is | 1 | - | - | - | - | - | - | - | - | 0 | 0 |
| First-class | 143 | 178 | 44 | 2377 | 90 | 17.73 | | 0 | 10 | 37 | 0 |
| List A | 133 | 83 | 27 | 563 | 38* | 10.05 | | 0 | 0 | 27 | 0 |
| Twenty20 | 59 | 22 | 11 | 100 | 13 | 9.09 | 105.26 | 0 | 0 | 5 | 0 |
| **Bowling** | **Mat** | **Balls** | **Runs** | **Wkts** | **BBI** | **BBM** | **Ave** | **Econ** | **SR** | **5w** | **10** |
| Tests | 12 | 2902 | 1431 | 53 | 6/48 | 8/150 | 27.00 | 2.95 | 54.7 | 2 | 0 |
| ODIs | 15 | 784 | 705 | 15 | 4/32 | 4/32 | 47.00 | 5.39 | 52.2 | 0 | 0 |
| T20Is | 1 | 24 | 45 | 2 | 2/45 | 2/45 | 22.50 | 11.25 | 12.0 | 0 | 0 |
| First-class | 143 | 24746 | 12939 | 453 | 8/96 | | 28.56 | 3.13 | 54.6 | 13 | 0 |
| List A | 133 | 6129 | 5002 | 180 | 4/25 | 4/25 | 27.78 | 4.89 | 34.0 | 0 | 0 |
| Twenty20 | 59 | 1187 | 1452 | 75 | 4/16 | 4/16 | 19.36 | 7.33 | 15.8 | 0 | 0 |

## MARCUS TRESCOTHICK LHB RM R6 W0 MVP67

FULL NAME: Marcus Edward Trescothick
BORN: December 25, 1975, Keynsham, Somerset
SQUAD NO: 2
HEIGHT: 6ft 3in
NICKNAME: Banger, Tresco
EDUCATION: Sir Bernard Lovell School
TEAMS: England, Somerset
CAREER: Test: 2000; ODI: 2000; T20I: 2005; First-class: 1993; List A: 1993; T20: 2004

BEST BATTING: 284 Somerset vs Northamptonshire, Northampton, 2007
BEST BOWLING: 4-36 Somerset vs Young Australia, Taunton, 1995
COUNTY CAPS: 1999; BENEFIT YEAR: 2008

TWITTER FEED: @Trescricket
NOTES: His maiden Test appearance came against West Indies at Old Trafford in 2000. His highest Test score was 219 against South Africa in a decisive nine-wicket victory at The Oval. Played his last Test against Pakistan at the same ground in 2006. Wisden Cricketer of the Year in 2005 and PCA Player of the Year in 2000, 2009 and 2011. Has the English record for ODI hundreds, scoring 12. Passed 1,000 runs five years in a row between 2007 and 2011, with 1,673 runs in 2011 alone. After a rare blip in 2013, he returned to form in 2014 and once against passed 1,000 Championship runs

| Batting | Mat | Inns | NO | Runs | HS | Ave | SR | 100 | 50 | Ct | St |
|---|---|---|---|---|---|---|---|---|---|---|---|
| Tests | 76 | 143 | 10 | 5825 | 219 | 43.79 | 54.51 | 14 | 29 | 95 | 0 |
| ODIs | 123 | 122 | 6 | 4335 | 137 | 37.37 | 85.21 | 12 | 21 | 49 | 0 |
| T20Is | 3 | 3 | 0 | 166 | 72 | 55.33 | 126.71 | 0 | 2 | 2 | 0 |
| First-class | 327 | 561 | 30 | 22220 | 284 | 41.84 | | 55 | 110 | 450 | 0 |
| List A | 372 | 357 | 29 | 12229 | 184 | 37.28 | | 28 | 63 | 149 | 0 |
| Twenty20 | 84 | 82 | 5 | 2318 | 108* | 30.10 | 152.50 | 2 | 17 | 29 | 0 |
| **Bowling** | **Mat** | **Balls** | **Runs** | **Wkts** | **BBI** | **BBM** | **Ave** | **Econ** | **SR** | **5w** | **10** |
| Tests | 76 | 300 | 155 | 1 | 1/34 | 1/34 | 155.00 | 3.10 | 300.0 | 0 | 0 |
| ODIs | 123 | 232 | 219 | 4 | 2/7 | 2/7 | 54.75 | 5.66 | 58.0 | 0 | 0 |
| T20Is | 3 | - | - | - | - | - | - | - | - | - | - |
| First-class | 327 | 2704 | 1551 | 36 | 4/36 | | 43.08 | 3.44 | 75.1 | 0 | 0 |
| List A | 372 | 2010 | 1644 | 57 | 4/50 | 4/50 | 28.84 | 4.90 | 35.2 | 0 | 0 |
| Twenty20 | 84 | - | - | - | - | - | - | - | - | - | - |

# JONATHAN TROTT — RHB RM R6 W0

FULL NAME: Ian Jonathan Leonard Trott
BORN: April 22, 1981, Cape Town, South Africa
SQUAD NO: 9
HEIGHT: 6ft
NICKNAME: Booger, Trotters
EDUCATION: Stellenbosch University
TEAMS: England, Warwickshire, Boland, Otago, Western Province
CAREER: Test: 2009; List A: 2009; T20I: 2007; First-class: 2000; List A: 2000; T20: 2003



BEST BATTING: 226 England vs Bangladesh, Lord's, 2010
BEST BOWLING: 7-39 Warwickshire vs Kent, Canterbury, 2003
COUNTY CAPS: 2005

CRICKETING HEROES? Sachin Tendulkar, Adam Hollioake, Steve Waugh, Jacques Kallis
SURPRISING FACT? I'm a San Francisco 49ers fan
TWITTER FEED: @Trotty
NOTES: Represented South Africa A. Scored 245 on debut for Warwickshire 2nd XI. Hit 134 on County Championship debut for Warwickshire vs Sussex at Edgbaston in 2003. Made 119 on Test debut for England in the deciding match of the 2009 Ashes at The Oval. One of the four Wisden Cricketers of the Year for 2011. ICC Cricketer of the Year for 2011. Finished the 2013 ICC Champions Trophy as the tournament's second-highest run-scorer, with 229 runs at 57.25

| Batting | Mat | Inns | NO | Runs | HS | Ave | SR | 100 | 50 | Ct | St |
|---|---|---|---|---|---|---|---|---|---|---|---|
| Tests | 49 | 87 | 6 | 3763 | 226 | 46.45 | 47.39 | 9 | 18 | 29 | 0 |
| ODIs | 68 | 65 | 10 | 2819 | 137 | 51.25 | 77.06 | 4 | 22 | 14 | 0 |
| T20Is | 7 | 7 | 1 | 138 | 51 | 23.00 | 95.83 | 0 | 1 | 0 | 0 |
| First-class | 220 | 367 | 40 | 14945 | 226 | 45.70 | | 37 | 72 | 192 | 0 |
| List A | 244 | 228 | 41 | 8834 | 137 | 47.24 | | 17 | 60 | 70 | 0 |
| Twenty20 | 79 | 74 | 16 | 2122 | 86* | 36.58 | 114.27 | 0 | 13 | 18 | 0 |
| **Bowling** | **Mat** | **Balls** | **Runs** | **Wkts** | **BBI** | **BBM** | **Ave** | **Econ** | **SR** | **5w** | **10** |
| Tests | 49 | 702 | 398 | 5 | 1/5 | 1/5 | 79.60 | 3.40 | 140.4 | 0 | 0 |
| ODIs | 68 | 183 | 166 | 2 | 2/31 | 2/31 | 83.00 | 5.44 | 91.5 | 0 | 0 |
| T20Is | 7 | - | - | - | - | - | - | - | - | - | - |
| First-class | 220 | 5414 | 3050 | 64 | 7/39 | | 47.65 | 3.38 | 84.5 | 1 | 0 |
| List A | 244 | 1648 | 1531 | 54 | 4/55 | 4/55 | 28.35 | 5.57 | 30.5 | 0 | 0 |
| Twenty20 | 79 | 144 | 234 | 8 | 2/19 | 2/19 | 29.25 | 9.75 | 18.0 | 0 | 0 |

## ANDY UMEED RHB LB R0 W0

FULL NAME: Andrew Robert Isaac Umeed
BORN: April 19, 1996, Glasgow
SQUAD NO: 23
TEAMS: Warwickshire 2nd XI
CAREER: Yet to make first-team debut

---

NOTES: Batsman Umeed has come through the Warwickshire Academy. He is a regular for Scotland U19 and played in the 2012 and 2014 U19 World Cups. He was Scotland U19's leading run-scorer in the 2013 season with 565 runs at an average of 47.08

# FREDDIE VAN DEN BERGH RHB SLA R0 W0

FULL NAME: Freddie Oliver Edward van den Bergh
BORN: June 14, 1992, Bickley, Kent
SQUAD NO: 5
HEIGHT: 6ft 3in
NICKNAME: Vanders
EDUCATION: Whitgift School; Durham University
TEAMS: Surrey
CAREER: First-class: 2011; List A: 2014



BEST BATTING: 34 Surrey vs Nottinghamshire, Nottingham, 2013
BEST BOWLING: 4-48 Surrey vs Nottinghamshire, Nottingham, 2013

CAREER HIGHLIGHTS? Making my first-class debut for Surrey when Kevin Pietersen was captaining, and making my List A debut last year at Guildford
BEST PLAYER IN COUNTY CRICKET? Jeetan Patel
TIP FOR THE TOP? Matthew Dunn
CRICKETING HEROES? Freddie Flintoff –watching him in the 2005 Ashes was incredible. Also Dan Vettori – as a fellow left-arm spinner watching him bowl was great to learn from
NON-CRICKETING HEROES? Dan Carter – for the way he conducts himself on and off the pitch
CRICKET RULE YOU'D CHANGE? Have five men allowed out during the middle overs in one-day cricket
IF YOU WEREN'T A CRICKETER? Looking for a job or travelling on a year out
IF YOU COULD BE SOMEONE ELSE FOR A DAY? Barack Obama
DESERT ISLAND DISC? Brother & Bones – For All We Know
FAVOURITE TV? Suits
PET HATE? People biting their nails – it looks horrible
SURPRISING FACT? I used to play the oboe when I was younger
TWITTER FEED: @freddievdb15

| Batting | Mat | Inns | NO | Runs | HS | Ave | SR | 100 | 50 | Ct | St |
|---|---|---|---|---|---|---|---|---|---|---|---|
| First-class | 6 | 8 | 1 | 57 | 34 | 8.14 | 54.80 | 0 | 0 | 1 | 0 |
| List A | 3 | 1 | 1 | 29 | 29* | - | 107.40 | 0 | 0 | 0 | 0 |
| **Bowling** | **Mat** | **Balls** | **Runs** | **Wkts** | **BBI** | **BBM** | **Ave** | **Econ** | **SR** | **5w** | **10** |
| First-class | 6 | 817 | 522 | 11 | 4/84 | 5/145 | 47.45 | 3.83 | 74.2 | 0 | 0 |
| List A | 3 | 156 | 122 | 0 | - | - | - | 4.69 | - | 0 | 0 |

# KISHEN VELANI

RHB RM R0 W0

FULL NAME: Kishen Shailesh Velani
BORN: September 2, 1994, Newham, London
SQUAD NO: 8
NICKNAME: Joggy, Bruno
EDUCATION: Brentwood School
TEAMS: Essex
CAREER: First-class: 2013; List A: 2014; T20: 2014

BEST BATTING: 29 Essex vs Kent, Chelmsford, 2014

CAREER HIGHLIGHTS? Playing for England U19 and making my first-class debut
BEST PLAYER IN COUNTY CRICKET? Moeen Ali
MOST MARKED CHARACTERISTIC? Shyness
CRICKETING HEROES? Sachin Tendulkar
NON-CRICKETING HEROES? Kobe Bryant
CRICKET RULE YOU'D CHANGE? Free hit every time a wide is bowled
IF YOU WEREN'T A CRICKETER? Golfer
DESERT ISLAND DISC? Drake – Take Care
FAVOURITE TV? Arrow
ACCOMPLISHMENTS? Winning the Independent Schools final in football when I was 15
FANTASY SLIP CORDON? Keeper: Sachin Tendulkar, 1st: Kobe Bryant, 2nd: James Corden, 3rd: Drake, Gully: Me
TWITTER FEED: @kishenvelani8

| Batting | Mat | Inns | NO | Runs | HS | Ave | SR | 100 | 50 | Ct | St |
|---|---|---|---|---|---|---|---|---|---|---|---|
| First-class | 5 | 7 | 1 | 120 | 29 | 20.00 | 49.18 | 0 | 0 | 0 | 0 |
| List A | 5 | 4 | 0 | 61 | 27 | 15.25 | 107.01 | 0 | 0 | 2 | 0 |
| Twenty20 | 3 | 2 | 0 | 36 | 34 | 18.00 | 138.46 | 0 | 0 | 0 | 0 |
| **Bowling** | **Mat** | **Balls** | **Runs** | **Wkts** | **BBI** | **BBM** | **Ave** | **Econ** | **SR** | **5w** | **10** |
| First-class | 5 | 39 | 21 | 0 | - | - | - | 3.23 | - | 0 | 0 |
| List A | 5 | - | - | - | - | - | - | - | - | - | - |
| Twenty20 | 3 | - | - | - | - | - | - | - | - | - | - |

# JAMES VINCE

## RHB RM R2 W0 MVP20

FULL NAME: James Michael Vince
BORN: March 14, 1991, Cuckfield, Sussex
SQUAD NO: 14
HEIGHT: 6ft 2in
NICKNAME: Vincey
EDUCATION: Warminster School
TEAMS: Hampshire, England Lions
CAREER: First-class: 2009; List A: 2009; T20: 2010



BEST BATTING: 240 Hampshire vs Essex, Southampton, 2014
BEST BOWLING: 5-41 Hampshire vs LMCCU, Southampton, 2013
COUNTY CAPS: 2013

FAMILY TIES? My old man couldn't have been any worse
CAREER HIGHLIGHTS? Winning the T20 and scoring my first hundred for Hampshire
SUPERSTITIONS? I put my kit on in the same order
CRICKETING HEROES? Stephen Parry, Jimmy Adams, Neil McKenzie
FAVOURITE TV? The Only Way Is Essex
TWITTER FEED: @vincey14

| Batting | Mat | Inns | NO | Runs | HS | Ave | SR | 100 | 50 | Ct | St |
|---|---|---|---|---|---|---|---|---|---|---|---|
| First-class | 89 | 144 | 16 | 5496 | 240 | 42.93 | 64.50 | 15 | 21 | 76 | 0 |
| List A | 80 | 78 | 6 | 2574 | 131 | 35.75 | 93.80 | 3 | 13 | 27 | 0 |
| Twenty20 | 79 | 75 | 8 | 1856 | 93* | 27.70 | 131.35 | 0 | 13 | 48 | 0 |
| **Bowling** | **Mat** | **Balls** | **Runs** | **Wkts** | **BBI** | **BBM** | **Ave** | **Econ** | **SR** | **5w** | **10** |
| First-class | 89 | 1308 | 786 | 18 | 5/41 | 6/56 | 43.66 | 3.60 | 72.6 | 1 | 0 |
| List A | 80 | 84 | 84 | 1 | 1/18 | 1/18 | 84.00 | 6.00 | 84.0 | 0 | 0 |
| Twenty20 | 79 | 48 | 49 | 2 | 1/5 | 1/5 | 24.50 | 6.12 | 24.0 | 0 | 0 |

# ADAM VOGES

RHB SLA R0 W0

FULL NAME: Adam Charles Voges
BORN: October 4, 1979, Subiaco, Australia
SQUAD NO: 32
HEIGHT: 6ft 1in
NICKNAME: V, Vogesy, Happy
TEAMS: Australia, Middlesex, Hampshire, Melbourne Stars, Nottinghamshire, Perth Scorchers, Rajasthan Royals, Western Australia
CAREER: ODI: 2007; T20I: 2007; First-class: 2002; List A: 2004; T20: 2006

---

BEST BATTING: 235* Western Australia vs Queensland, Perth, 2013
BEST BOWLING: 249 Western Australia vs South Australia, Adelaide, 2015

---

FAMILY TIES? My dad played and umpired
CAREER HIGHLIGHTS? My maiden international ODI hundred, winning the Matador Cup with Western Australia, winning the Championship with Nottinghamshire and scoring a hundred on debut for Middlesex
MOST MARKED CHARACTERISTIC? Sticking my tongue out when concentrating
CRICKETING HEROES? I loved watching Dean Jones bat. I thought he revolutionised one-day cricket in Australia
IF YOU COULD BE SOMEONE ELSE FOR A DAY? Mark Webber
DESERT ISLAND DISC? Pearl Jam – Elderly Woman Behind The Counter In A Small Town
FAVOURITE TV? The Simpsons and Family Guy
LEAST FAVOURITE TV? All reality TV
TWITTER FEED: @acvoges

| Batting | Mat | Inns | NO | Runs | HS | Ave | SR | 100 | 50 | Ct | St |
|---|---|---|---|---|---|---|---|---|---|---|---|
| ODIs | 31 | 28 | 9 | 870 | 112* | 45.78 | 87.17 | 1 | 4 | 7 | 0 |
| T20Is | 7 | 5 | 2 | 139 | 51 | 46.33 | 121.92 | 0 | 1 | 3 | 0 |
| First-class | 153 | 263 | 36 | 10105 | 249 | 44.51 | 50.67 | 23 | 53 | 210 | 0 |
| List A | 171 | 163 | 38 | 5449 | 112* | 43.59 | 79.33 | 5 | 41 | 67 | 0 |
| Twenty20 | 152 | 141 | 26 | 3440 | 82* | 29.91 | 126.70 | 0 | 14 | 63 | 0 |
| **Bowling** | **Mat** | **Balls** | **Runs** | **Wkts** | **BBI** | **BBM** | **Ave** | **Econ** | **SR** | **5w** | **10** |
| ODIs | 31 | 301 | 276 | 6 | 1/3 | 1/3 | 46.00 | 5.50 | 50.1 | 0 | 0 |
| T20Is | 7 | 12 | 5 | 2 | 2/5 | 2/5 | 2.50 | 2.50 | 6.0 | 0 | 0 |
| First-class | 153 | 2998 | 1566 | 45 | 4/92 | | 34.80 | 3.13 | 66.6 | 0 | 0 |
| List A | 171 | 1755 | 1518 | 33 | 3/25 | 3/25 | 46.00 | 5.18 | 53.1 | 0 | 0 |
| Twenty20 | 152 | 536 | 711 | 26 | 2/4 | 2/4 | 27.34 | 7.95 | 20.6 | 0 | 0 |

# GRAHAM WAGG

RHB LM R0 W2 MVP51

FULL NAME: Graham Grant Wagg
BORN: April 28, 1983, Rugby, Warwickshire
SQUAD NO: 8
HEIGHT: 6ft
NICKNAME: Waggy
EDUCATION: Ashlawn School, Rugby
TEAMS: Glamorgan, Derbyshire, Warwickshire
CAREER: First-class: 2002; List A: 2000; T20: 2003



BEST BATTING: 116* Glamorgan vs Kent, Canterbury, 2014
BEST BOWLING: 6-29 Glamorgan vs Surrey, The Oval, 2014
COUNTY CAPS: 2007 (Derbyshire)

FAMILY TIES? My dad played 2nd XI cricket, Minor Counties and a good standard of Premier League – he could bowl a heavy ball and hit a long ball. My little man Brayden Wagg is just learning, so watch out for his name
CAREER HIGHLIGHTS? Getting my first contract at Warwickshire and playing for England Schools in all the age-groups
CRICKETING HEROES? Ian Botham, Allan Donald, Viv Richards
IF YOU WEREN'T A CRICKETER? Full-time dad I suppose
FAVOURITE TV? Banged Up Abroad
SURPRISING FACT? I'm a dark horse on the snooker table
TWITTER FEED: @GGWagg

| Batting | Mat | Inns | NO | Runs | HS | Ave | SR | 100 | 50 | Ct | St |
|---|---|---|---|---|---|---|---|---|---|---|---|
| First-class | 113 | 163 | 18 | 3613 | 116* | 24.91 | 65.78 | 2 | 22 | 36 | 0 |
| List A | 112 | 93 | 14 | 1411 | 54 | 17.86 | | 0 | 1 | 35 | 0 |
| Twenty20 | 75 | 58 | 14 | 681 | 62 | 15.47 | 123.59 | 0 | 1 | 21 | 0 |
| **Bowling** | **Mat** | **Balls** | **Runs** | **Wkts** | **BBI** | **BBM** | **Ave** | **Econ** | **SR** | **5w** | **10** |
| First-class | 113 | 19474 | 11404 | 340 | 6/29 | | 33.54 | 3.51 | 57.2 | 10 | 1 |
| List A | 112 | 4291 | 4234 | 125 | 4/35 | 4/35 | 33.87 | 5.92 | 34.3 | 0 | 0 |
| Twenty20 | 75 | 1297 | 1704 | 72 | 5/14 | 5/14 | 23.66 | 7.88 | 18.0 | 1 | 0 |

## JAMES WAINMAN RHB LM R0 W0

FULL NAME: James Charles Wainman
BORN: January 25, 1993, Harrogate, Yorkshire
SQUAD NO: 15
HEIGHT: 6ft 4in
NICKNAME: Wainers
EDUCATION: Leeds Grammar School
TEAMS: Yorkshire
CAREER: List A: 2014

---

FAMILY TIES? My dad played good standard club cricket and coached me as a junior
CAREER HIGHLIGHTS? My first List A game against Sri Lanka A, taking 3 for 51 and scoring 33 runs
MOST MARKED CHARACTERISTIC? Consistency
SUPERSTITIONS? Left sock and left boot always go on first
CRICKETING HEROES? Glenn McGrath
COACHING TIP? Do the simple things well
IF YOU COULD BE SOMEONE ELSE FOR A DAY? Leonardo DiCaprio
FAVOURITE TV? Entourage
TWITTER FEED: @jcwainman

| Batting | Mat | Inns | NO | Runs | HS | Ave | SR | 100 | 50 | Ct | St |
|---|---|---|---|---|---|---|---|---|---|---|---|
| List A | 1 | 1 | 0 | 33 | 33 | 33.00 | 122.22 | 0 | 0 | 1 | 0 |
| **Bowling** | **Mat** | **Balls** | **Runs** | **Wkts** | **BBI** | **BBM** | **Ave** | **Econ** | **SR** | **5w** | **10** |
| List A | 1 | 48 | 51 | 3 | 3/51 | 3/51 | 17.00 | 6.37 | 16.0 | 0 | 0 |

# DAVID WAINWRIGHT LHB SLA R0 W1

FULL NAME: David John Wainwright
BORN: March 21, 1985, Pontefract, Yorkshire
SQUAD NO: 21
HEIGHT: 5ft 9in
NICKNAME: Wainers
EDUCATION: Hemsworth High School; Hemsworth Arts and Community College; Loughborough University
TEAMS: Derbyshire, Yorkshire, England Lions
CAREER: First-class: 2004; List A: 2005; T20: 2007



BEST BATTING: 109 Derbyshire vs Leicestershire, Leicester, 2014
BEST BOWLING: 6-33 Derbyshire vs Northamptonshire, Derby, 2012
COUNTY CAPS: 2010 (Yorkshire); 2012 (Derbyshire)

FAMILY TIES? Grandfather played for Yorkshire Schoolboys, father played league cricket
CAREER HIGHLIGHTS? Promotion with Derbyshire in 2012, playing for England Lions, century at Scarborough for Yorkshire
BEST PLAYER IN COUNTY CRICKET? Jeetan Patel
TIP FOR THE TOP? Harvey Hosein, Tommy Taylor
MOST MARKED CHARACTERISTIC? Mysterious birthmark
CRICKETING HEROES? Daniel Vettori, Brian Charles Lara
NON-CRICKETING HEROES? Steven Gerrard, Will Smith
CRICKET RULE YOU'D CHANGE? Play everyone twice in the T20
IF YOU WEREN'T A CRICKETER? Plumbing
IF YOU COULD BE SOMEONE ELSE FOR A DAY? Will Smith
FAVOURITE TV? Family Guy
LEAST FAVOURITE TV? Heartbeat
SURPRISING FACT? Former world number one at Super Stickman Golf

| Batting | Mat | Inns | NO | Runs | HS | Ave | SR | 100 | 50 | Ct | St |
|---|---|---|---|---|---|---|---|---|---|---|---|
| First-class | 77 | 108 | 25 | 2173 | 109 | 26.18 | 45.88 | 3 | 9 | 28 | 0 |
| List A | 77 | 38 | 20 | 354 | 41 | 19.66 | 79.72 | 0 | 0 | 23 | 0 |
| Twenty20 | 45 | 19 | 13 | 107 | 20* | 17.83 | 93.85 | 0 | 0 | 10 | 0 |
| **Bowling** | **Mat** | **Balls** | **Runs** | **Wkts** | **BBI** | **BBM** | **Ave** | **Econ** | **SR** | **5w** | **10** |
| First-class | 77 | 12771 | 6691 | 178 | 6/33 | | 37.58 | 3.14 | 71.7 | 6 | 0 |
| List A | 77 | 2840 | 2327 | 66 | 4/11 | 4/11 | 35.25 | 4.91 | 43.0 | 0 | 0 |
| Twenty20 | 45 | 829 | 1005 | 36 | 3/6 | 3/6 | 27.91 | 7.27 | 23.0 | 0 | 0 |

# ALEX WAKELY

RHB RM R0 W0

FULL NAME: Alex George Wakely
BORN: November 3, 1988, London
SQUAD NO: 8
HEIGHT: 6ft 2in
EDUCATION: Bedford School
TEAMS: Northamptonshire
CAREER: First-class: 2007; List A: 2005; T20: 2009

BEST BATTING: 113* Northamptonshire vs Glamorgan, Cardiff, 2009
BEST BOWLING: 2-62 Northamptonshire vs Somerset, Taunton, 2007
COUNTY CAPS: 2012

FAMILY TIES? My dad played Minor Counties cricket
CAREER HIGHLIGHTS? Winning the T20 competition and scoring a hundred at Lord's
MOST MARKED CHARACTERISTIC? Being relaxed and smiley
CRICKETING HEROES? David Sales, Matthew Hayden, Mike Hussey, Ian Harvey
NON-CRICKETING HEROES? Michael Jordan, Bruce Wayne, Bill Gates, my grandad
IF YOU WEREN'T A CRICKETER? I would love to play golf but realistically I would work in the city or in marketing
DESERT ISLAND DISC? Fort Minor – Remember The Name
FAVOURITE TV? The Walking Dead, The Blacklist
ACCOMPLISHMENTS? Getting married and achieving 3 A-Levels
SURPRISING FACT? I play the piano and love the City Index
FANTASY SLIP CORDON? Keeper: My grandad, 1st: Christian Bale, 2nd: Me, 3rd: Adam Sandler, Gully: Gandalf
TWITTER FEED: @AlexWakely1

| Batting | Mat | Inns | NO | Runs | HS | Ave | SR | 100 | 50 | Ct | St |
|---|---|---|---|---|---|---|---|---|---|---|---|
| First-class | 79 | 122 | 5 | 3387 | 113* | 28.94 | 45.93 | 2 | 21 | 43 | 0 |
| List A | 52 | 50 | 6 | 1364 | 102 | 31.00 | 85.62 | 1 | 9 | 16 | 0 |
| Twenty20 | 59 | 58 | 9 | 1247 | 62 | 25.44 | 117.86 | 0 | 7 | 20 | 0 |
| **Bowling** | **Mat** | **Balls** | **Runs** | **Wkts** | **BBI** | **BBM** | **Ave** | **Econ** | **SR** | **5w** | **10** |
| First-class | 79 | 399 | 322 | 6 | 2/62 | 2/62 | 53.66 | 4.84 | 66.5 | 0 | 0 |
| List A | 52 | 132 | 107 | 5 | 2/14 | 2/14 | 21.40 | 4.86 | 26.4 | 0 | 0 |
| Twenty20 | 59 | 12 | 29 | 0 | - | - | - | 14.50 | - | 0 | 0 |

# MARK WALLACE LHB WK R1 W0 MVP99

FULL NAME: Mark Alexander Wallace
BORN: November 19, 1981, Abergavenny, Monmouthshire
SQUAD NO: 18
HEIGHT: 5ft 9in
NICKNAME: Gromit
EDUCATION: Crickhowell High School
TEAMS: Glamorgan
CAREER: First-class: 1999; List A: 1999; T20: 2003



BEST BATTING: 139 Glamorgan vs Surrey, The Oval, 2009
COUNTY CAPS: 2003; BENEFIT YEAR: 2013

FAMILY TIES? My father still plays club cricket for Abergavenny and turns out for Wales Over 50s and 60s
CAREER HIGHLIGHTS? Winning one-day trophies and captaining Glamorgan
CRICKETING HEROES? Ian Healy, Alec Stewart, Steve James, Brendon McCullum, Justin Langer
NON-CRICKETING HEROES? Rory McIlroy, Harry Potter
IF YOU WEREN'T A CRICKETER? Journalist, student
FAVOURITE TV? Spooks, EastEnders
ACCOMPLISHMENTS? My family: wife and two kids (Harry and Ioan)
SURPRISING FACT? I work as a rugby writer in the winter for Media Wales. Single handicap golfer
TWITTER FEED: @MarkWallace18

| Batting | Mat | Inns | NO | Runs | HS | Ave | SR | 100 | 50 | Ct | St |
|---|---|---|---|---|---|---|---|---|---|---|---|
| First-class | 233 | 371 | 29 | 9968 | 139 | 29.14 | | 15 | 46 | 611 | 52 |
| List A | 197 | 161 | 32 | 2684 | 118* | 20.80 | | 2 | 7 | 177 | 44 |
| Twenty20 | 114 | 89 | 22 | 1227 | 69* | 18.31 | 127.94 | 0 | 1 | 45 | 27 |
| **Bowling** | **Mat** | **Balls** | **Runs** | **Wkts** | **BBI** | **BBM** | **Ave** | **Econ** | **SR** | **5w** | **10** |
| First-class | 233 | 6 | 3 | 0 | - | - | - | 3.00 | - | 0 | 0 |
| List A | 197 | - | - | - | - | - | - | - | - | - | - |
| Twenty20 | 114 | - | - | - | - | - | - | - | - | - | - |

# MAX WALLER

RHB LB R0 W0

SOMERSET

FULL NAME: Max Thomas Charles Waller
BORN: March 3, 1988, Salisbury, Wiltshire
SQUAD NO: 10
HEIGHT: 6ft
NICKNAME: Goose, Maxy
EDUCATION: Millfield School; Bournemouth University
TEAMS: Somerset
CAREER: First-class: 2009; List A: 2009; T20: 2009

BEST BATTING: 28 Somerset vs Hampshire, Southampton, 2009
BEST BOWLING: 3-33 Somerset vs CMCCU, Taunton, 2012

CAREER HIGHLIGHTS? Playing in the Champions League twice, playing at T20 Finals Day and my first-class debut
BEST PLAYER IN COUNTY CRICKET? Steve Magoffin
TIP FOR THE TOP? Sam Billings, Lewis Gregory
CRICKETING HEROES? Shane Warne – because he's the best bowler to have ever played the game. Jonty Rhodes – best fielder ever
NON-CRICKETING HEROES? Thierry Henry – Arsenal legend. Floyd Mayweather – talks it up, backs it up! Seve Ballesteros – golfing genius, made it look easy
IF YOU WEREN'T A CRICKETER? I'd be an artist – drawing or painting
IF YOU COULD BE SOMEONE ELSE FOR A DAY? Leonardo DiCaprio
FAVOURITE TV? Million Dollar Listing New York
LEAST FAVOURITE TV? Coronation Street
ACCOMPLISHMENTS? Selling paintings in an art shop
SURPRISING FACT? I 'used' to collect rocks and gemstones
TWITTER FEED: @MaxTCWaller

| Batting | Mat | Inns | NO | Runs | HS | Ave | SR | 100 | 50 | Ct | St |
|---|---|---|---|---|---|---|---|---|---|---|---|
| First-class | 8 | 9 | 1 | 91 | 28 | 11.37 | 42.92 | 0 | 0 | 5 | 0 |
| List A | 39 | 14 | 10 | 71 | 25* | 17.75 | 73.95 | 0 | 0 | 15 | 0 |
| Twenty20 | 57 | 12 | 6 | 10 | 3 | 1.66 | 38.46 | 0 | 0 | 26 | 0 |
| **Bowling** | **Mat** | **Balls** | **Runs** | **Wkts** | **BBI** | **BBM** | **Ave** | **Econ** | **SR** | **5w** | **10** |
| First-class | 8 | 840 | 493 | 10 | 3/33 | 3/57 | 49.30 | 3.52 | 84.0 | 0 | 0 |
| List A | 39 | 1192 | 1126 | 28 | 3/39 | 3/39 | 40.21 | 5.66 | 42.5 | 0 | 0 |
| Twenty20 | 57 | 1032 | 1238 | 58 | 4/16 | 4/16 | 21.34 | 7.19 | 17.7 | 0 | 0 |

# JONATHON WEBB

## RHB RM R0 W0

FULL NAME: Jonathon Patrick Webb
BORN: January 12, 1992, Solihull, Warwickshire
SQUAD NO: 12
HEIGHT: 6ft
NICKNAME: Webby, Lil John
EDUCATION: Bromsgrove School; University of Leeds
TEAMS: Warwickshire
CAREER: First-class: 2012; T20: 2014



BEST BATTING: 38 Leeds/Bradford MCCU vs Surrey, The Oval, 2012

CAREER HIGHLIGHTS? Winning the T20 Blast in 2014
BEST PLAYER IN COUNTY CRICKET? Jeetan Patel
TIP FOR THE TOP? Josh Poysden, Freddie Coleman, Ben Cox
NON-CRICKETING HEROES? John Mayer, Austin Powers – both dominate their field!
IF YOU WEREN'T A CRICKETER? A graphic designer
IF YOU COULD BE SOMEONE ELSE FOR A DAY? Austin Powers
DESERT ISLAND DISC? John Mayer – Live in LA
FAVOURITE TV? House Of Cards
ACCOMPLISHMENTS? Getting a 2:1 from Leeds Uni
PET HATE? Rude people with no manners
SURPRISING FACT? I can play the harmonica!
TWITTER FEED: @jpwebby

| Batting | Mat | Inns | NO | Runs | HS | Ave | SR | 100 | 50 | Ct | St |
|---|---|---|---|---|---|---|---|---|---|---|---|
| First-class | 4 | 8 | 0 | 77 | 38 | 9.62 | 39.28 | 0 | 0 | 3 | 0 |
| Twenty20 | 11 | 11 | 0 | 154 | 50 | 14.00 | 110.00 | 0 | 1 | 3 | 0 |
| **Bowling** | **Mat** | **Balls** | **Runs** | **Wkts** | **BBI** | **BBM** | **Ave** | **Econ** | **SR** | **5w** | **10** |
| First-class | 4 | - | - | - | - | - | - | - | - | - | - |
| Twenty20 | 11 | - | - | - | - | - | - | - | - | - | - |

## SAM WELLER

## RHB RF R0 W0

FULL NAME: Sam David Weller
BORN: November 21, 1994, Chiselhurst, Kent
SQUAD NO: 19
HEIGHT: 6ft 2in
NICKNAME: Sammy, Wells, Wimble
EDUCATION: Millfield School; Oxford Brookes University
TEAMS: Kent 2nd XI, Oxford MCCU
CAREER: First-class: 2014

BEST BATTING: 18 Oxford MCCU vs Warwickshire, Oxford, 2014
BEST BOWLING: 3-66 Oxford MCCU vs Warwickshire, Oxford, 2014

FAMILY TIES? Grandfather played cricket and has been a life-long Kent supporter. Father played some cricket and loves to watch it
CAREER HIGHLIGHTS? Receiving my professional contract at Kent, taking my first first-class wicket and taking the wicket of Jonathon Trott in a MCCU first-class game
BEST PLAYER IN COUNTY CRICKET? Darren Stevens
TIP FOR THE TOP? Ben Duckett, Saif Zaib, Tom Abell
SUPERSTITIONS? Don't like touching the popping crease when walking back to my mark. Bat wearing a jumper
CRICKETING HEROES? Freddie Flintoff – loved the way he played cricket and that he was so pumped/aggressive during playing. James Anderson – his pure skill when bowling and his ability to set up batsmen so easily
COACHING TIP? When bowling, the load-up arm should be straight at the side of the body with the wrist behind the ball
FAVOURITE TV? Breaking Bad
LEAST FAVOURITE TV? Loose Women
ACCOMPLISHMENTS? Scholarship to Millfield School. Head of house for my boarding house
SURPRISING FACT? I lived in Singapore for three years from the ages of 10 to 13
TWITTER FEED: @sweller94

| Batting | Mat | Inns | NO | Runs | HS | Ave | SR | 100 | 50 | Ct | St |
|---|---|---|---|---|---|---|---|---|---|---|---|
| First-class | 2 | 3 | 1 | 33 | 18* | 16.50 | 30.00 | 0 | 0 | 0 | 0 |
| **Bowling** | **Mat** | **Balls** | **Runs** | **Wkts** | **BBI** | **BBM** | **Ave** | **Econ** | **SR** | **5w** | **10** |
| First-class | 2 | 276 | 126 | 6 | 3/66 | 3/60 | 21.00 | 2.73 | 46.0 | 0 | 0 |

# LUKE WELLS

## LHB OB R1 W0

FULL NAME: Luke William Peter Wells
BORN: December 29, 1990, Eastbourne, Sussex
SQUAD NO: 31
EDUCATION: St Bede's Sch, Upper Dicker
TEAMS: Sussex, Colombo Cricket Club, England Lions
CAREER: First-class: 2010; List A: 2010; T20: 2011



BEST BATTING: 208 Sussex vs Surrey, The Oval, 2013
BEST BOWLING: 3-38 Sussex vs Yorkshire, Scarborough, 2014

FAMILY TIES? Father Alan played for Sussex, Kent and England and my uncle Colin played for Sussex, Derbyshire and England
CAREER HIGHLIGHTS? Definitely scoring my first double-hundred at The Oval. Representing the England Lions vs Australia
MOST MARKED CHARACTERISTIC? Resilience
SUPERSTITIONS? One – I only ever bat in the same pair of whites
CRICKETING HEROES? Father Alan, Sachin Tendulkar, Brian Lara and Matthew Hayden
NON-CRICKETING HEROES? Cristiano Ronaldo
IF YOU WEREN'T A CRICKETER? Probably teaching
DESERT ISLAND DISC? Bastille – Bad Blood
FAVOURITE TV? Family Guy for comedy but also love a bit of Criminal Minds now and then
ACCOMPLISHMENTS? I was deputy head boy at school. Flappy Bird score of 100!
FANTASY SLIP CORDON? Keeper: Stewie Griffin, 1st: Ricky Gervais, 2nd: Sachin Tendulkar, 3rd: Myself, Gully: Gandalf
TWITTER FEED: @luke_wells07

| Batting | Mat | Inns | NO | Runs | HS | Ave | SR | 100 | 50 | Ct | St |
|---|---|---|---|---|---|---|---|---|---|---|---|
| First-class | 67 | 115 | 8 | 3674 | 208 | 34.33 | 43.76 | 8 | 16 | 38 | 0 |
| List A | 13 | 9 | 0 | 80 | 23 | 8.88 | 58.39 | 0 | 0 | 1 | 0 |
| Twenty20 | 5 | 5 | 0 | 18 | 11 | 3.60 | 66.66 | 0 | 0 | 1 | 0 |
| **Bowling** | **Mat** | **Balls** | **Runs** | **Wkts** | **BBI** | **BBM** | **Ave** | **Econ** | **SR** | **5w** | **10** |
| First-class | 67 | 1216 | 733 | 14 | 3/38 | 3/40 | 52.35 | 3.61 | 86.8 | 0 | 0 |
| List A | 13 | 77 | 61 | 3 | 3/19 | 3/19 | 20.33 | 4.75 | 25.6 | 0 | 0 |
| Twenty20 | 5 | 1 | 4 | 0 | - | - | - | 24.00 | - | 0 | 0 |

## TOM WELLS

## RHB RFM R0 W0

FULL NAME: Thomas Joshua Wells
BORN: March 15, 1993, Grantham, Lincolnshire
SQUAD NO: 7
HEIGHT: 6ft 2in
NICKNAME: Wellsy
EDUCATION: Beauchamp College
TEAMS: Leicestershire
CAREER: First-class: 2013; List A: 2012; T20: 2013

BEST BATTING: 82 Leicestershire vs Hampshire, Leicester, 2013
BEST BOWLING: 1-36 Leicestershire vs Lancashire, Leicester, 2013

CAREER HIGHLIGHTS? Being part of any winning Leicestershire side
BEST PLAYER IN COUNTY CRICKET? Angus Robson
TIP FOR THE TOP? Zak Chappell, Aadil Ali
CRICKETING HEROES? Paul Nixon – next-door neighbour and got me into the game
CRICKET RULE YOU'D CHANGE? You should be able to score a 12 if you hit it far enough
COACHING TIP? Watch the ball very hard!
IF YOU WEREN'T A CRICKETER? An ice-road trucker!
IF YOU COULD BE SOMEONE ELSE FOR A DAY? Cristiano Ronaldo – he's doing pretty well for himself
DESERT ISLAND DISC? Any One Direction makes the trip!
FAVOURITE TV? Arrow and Suits
ACCOMPLISHMENTS? My cooking
SURPRISING FACT? I can in fact juggle with five balls
TWITTER FEED: @t_wells15

| Batting | Mat | Inns | NO | Runs | HS | Ave | SR | 100 | 50 | Ct | St |
|---|---|---|---|---|---|---|---|---|---|---|---|
| First-class | 6 | 10 | 0 | 205 | 82 | 20.50 | 61.74 | 0 | 1 | 3 | 0 |
| List A | 10 | 9 | 4 | 152 | 32* | 30.40 | 98.06 | 0 | 0 | 4 | 0 |
| Twenty20 | 16 | 14 | 5 | 207 | 51 | 23.00 | 125.45 | 0 | 1 | 3 | 0 |
| **Bowling** | **Mat** | **Balls** | **Runs** | **Wkts** | **BBI** | **BBM** | **Ave** | **Econ** | **SR** | **5w** | **10** |
| First-class | 6 | 252 | 163 | 1 | 1/36 | 1/36 | 163.00 | 3.88 | 252.0 | 0 | 0 |
| List A | 10 | 36 | 39 | 0 | - | - | - | 6.50 | - | 0 | 0 |
| Twenty20 | 16 | - | - | - | - | - | - | - | - | - | - |

# RIKI WESSELS

RHB WK R1 W0 MVP23

FULL NAME: Mattheus Hendrik Wessels
BORN: November 12, 1985, Australia
SQUAD NO: 9
HEIGHT: 5ft 11in
NICKNAME: Blood, Weasel, Riki Bobby
EDUCATION: Woodridge College, Port Elizabeth; University of Northampton
TEAMS: Nottinghamshire, Abahani Limited, Khulna Royal Bengals, Mid West Rhinos, Nondescripts, Northamptonshire, Sydney Sixers
CAREER: First-class: 2004; List A: 2005; T20: 2005



BEST BATTING: 199 Nottinghamshire vs Sussex, Hove, 2012
BEST BOWLING: 1-10 Mid West Rhinos vs Matabeleland Tuskers, Bulawayo, 2009

CAREER HIGHLIGHTS? That has to be my first first-class hundred, and also the finals I've taken part in
CRICKETING HEROES? Michael Slater, Justin Langer
NON-CRICKETING HEROES? All the soldiers fighting currently, having lost a few friends to the war myself
IF YOU WEREN'T A CRICKETER? I'd probably be in the army on the front line
FAVOURITE TV? Dr Who
ACCOMPLISHMENTS? Helping Macmillan Cancer UK raise money and helping people who need it more than myself
SURPRISING FACT? I've bungee-jumped at Victoria Falls, I lived in Colombo for six months and I love hunting
TWITTER FEED: @rikiwessels

| Batting | Mat | Inns | NO | Runs | HS | Ave | SR | 100 | 50 | Ct | St |
|---|---|---|---|---|---|---|---|---|---|---|---|
| First-class | 140 | 232 | 20 | 7534 | 199 | 35.53 | 63.87 | 15 | 38 | 233 | 14 |
| List A | 133 | 124 | 13 | 3028 | 100 | 27.27 | 99.31 | 1 | 16 | 95 | 0 |
| Twenty20 | 127 | 115 | 18 | 2695 | 95* | 27.78 | 134.95 | 0 | 13 | 41 | 15 |
| **Bowling** | **Mat** | **Balls** | **Runs** | **Wkts** | **BBI** | **BBM** | **Ave** | **Econ** | **SR** | **5w** | **10** |
| First-class | 140 | 210 | 115 | 3 | 1/10 | 1/10 | 38.33 | 3.28 | 70.0 | 0 | 0 |
| List A | 133 | 49 | 48 | 1 | 1/0 | 1/0 | 48.00 | 5.87 | 49.0 | 0 | 0 |
| Twenty20 | 127 | - | - | - | - | - | - | - | - | - | - |

# TOM WESTLEY RHB OB R0 W0 MVP28

FULL NAME: Thomas Westley
BORN: March 13, 1989, Cambridge
SQUAD NO: 21
HEIGHT: 6ft 2in
NICKNAME: Westie, Shellsy, Wezzo
EDUCATION: Linton Valley College; Hills Road Sixth Form College; University of Durham
TEAMS: Essex
CAREER: First-class: 2007; List A: 2006; T20: 2010

BEST BATTING: 185 Essex vs Glamorgan, Colchester, 2012
BEST BOWLING: 4-55 DMCCU vs Durham, Durham University, 2010
COUNTY CAPS: 2013

FAMILY TIES? My dad, uncle and brother all play for Weston Colville CC. My dad also harbours ambitions to play for England Over-60s. Currently plays for Cambs Over-50s. Doing well
CAREER HIGHLIGHTS? Captaining England U19, receiving my Essex county cap and beinfg named Essex Player of the Year in 2014
BEST PLAYER IN COUNTY CRICKET? Ravi Bopara
TIP FOR THE TOP? Callum Taylor and Dan Lawrence
SUPERSTITIONS? Left pad goes on first
CRICKETING HEROES? Jacques Kallis
FAVOURITE TV? Game Of Thrones
PET HATE? Jaik Mickleburgh never washing up
SURPRISING FACT? I was part of the first ever group of students to study Harry Potter academically
TWITTER FEED: @Westley21

| Batting | Mat | Inns | NO | Runs | HS | Ave | SR | 100 | 50 | Ct | St |
|---|---|---|---|---|---|---|---|---|---|---|---|
| First-class | 96 | 164 | 14 | 4688 | 185 | 31.25 | 50.31 | 8 | 23 | 67 | 0 |
| List A | 40 | 36 | 3 | 1132 | 111* | 34.30 | 86.61 | 1 | 10 | 5 | 0 |
| Twenty20 | 23 | 18 | 4 | 553 | 109* | 39.50 | 148.25 | 2 | 1 | 2 | 0 |
| **Bowling** | **Mat** | **Balls** | **Runs** | **Wkts** | **BBI** | **BBM** | **Ave** | **Econ** | **SR** | **5w** | **10** |
| First-class | 96 | 3205 | 1673 | 38 | 4/55 | 4/34 | 44.02 | 3.13 | 84.3 | 0 | 0 |
| List A | 40 | 520 | 423 | 13 | 4/60 | 4/60 | 32.53 | 4.88 | 40.0 | 0 | 0 |
| Twenty20 | 23 | 48 | 61 | 1 | 1/7 | 1/7 | 61.00 | 7.62 | 48.0 | 0 | 0 |

# IAN WESTWOOD

LHB OB R0 W0

FULL NAME: Ian James Westwood
BORN: July 13, 1982, Birmingham
SQUAD NO: 22
HEIGHT: 5ft 7in
NICKNAME: Westy
EDUCATION: Solihull Sixth Form College
TEAMS: Warwickshire
CAREER: First-class: 2003; List A: 2001; T20: 2005



BEST BATTING: 178 Warwickshire vs West Indies A, Birmingham, 2006
BEST BOWLING: 2-39 Warwickshire vs Hampshire, Southampton, 2009
COUNTY CAPS: 2008; BENEFIT YEAR: 2015

FAMILY TIES? My grandad was a member at Warwickshire and my brother played Warwickshire junior cricket
CAREER HIGHLIGHTS? Getting my county cap and being named club captain
BEST PLAYER IN COUNTY CRICKET? Marcus Trescothick
CRICKETING HEROES? Stuart Eustace, Phil Stephenson, Vanraaj Padhaal
IF YOU WEREN'T A CRICKETER? No idea!
FAVOURITE TV? House
SURPRISING FACT? I'm a Birmingham City FC fan

| Batting | Mat | Inns | NO | Runs | HS | Ave | SR | 100 | 50 | Ct | St |
|---|---|---|---|---|---|---|---|---|---|---|---|
| First-class | 130 | 217 | 20 | 6526 | 178 | 33.12 | 44.92 | 13 | 35 | 73 | 0 |
| List A | 60 | 50 | 9 | 940 | 65 | 22.92 | | 0 | 3 | 7 | 0 |
| Twenty20 | 38 | 27 | 12 | 342 | 49* | 22.80 | 114.00 | 0 | 0 | 5 | 0 |
| **Bowling** | **Mat** | **Balls** | **Runs** | **Wkts** | **BBI** | **BBM** | **Ave** | **Econ** | **SR** | **5w** | **10** |
| First-class | 130 | 538 | 300 | 7 | 2/39 | | 42.85 | 3.34 | 76.8 | 0 | 0 |
| List A | 60 | 264 | 227 | 3 | 1/28 | 1/28 | 75.66 | 5.15 | 88.0 | 0 | 0 |
| Twenty20 | 38 | 54 | 91 | 5 | 3/29 | 3/29 | 18.20 | 10.11 | 10.8 | 0 | 0 |

## ADAM WHEATCROFT — RHB RMF R0 W0



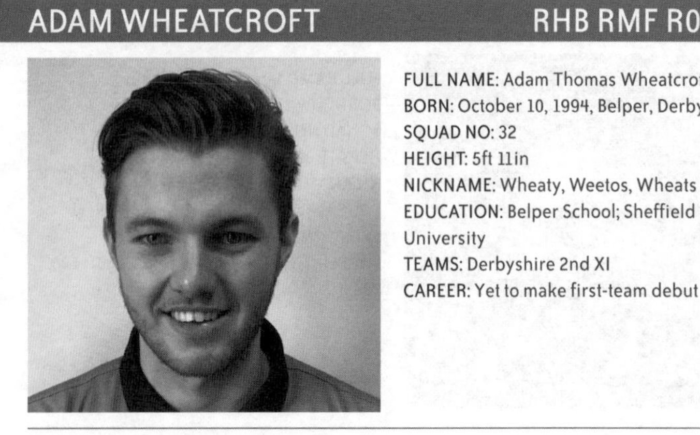

FULL NAME: Adam Thomas Wheatcroft
BORN: October 10, 1994, Belper, Derbyshire
SQUAD NO: 32
HEIGHT: 5ft 11in
NICKNAME: Wheaty, Weetos, Wheats
EDUCATION: Belper School; Sheffield Hallam University
TEAMS: Derbyshire 2nd XI
CAREER: Yet to make first-team debut

---

CAREER HIGHLIGHTS? Signing my first professional contract with Derbyshire
BEST PLAYER IN COUNTY CRICKET? Mark Footitt
TIP FOR THE TOP? Myself
CRICKETING HEROES? Brett Lee – because of the amount of work on and off the field he did and the atmosphere he created when he came on to bowl
CRICKET RULE YOU'D CHANGE? I've been thinking for 30 minutes and I still can't decide on anything
COACHING TIP? Having a strong base to bowl from – put the hard work in in the gym to develop strong legs and core and your bowling will be 100 times better
IF YOU COULD BE SOMEONE ELSE FOR A DAY? James Anderson – because that's where I aim to be
DESERT ISLAND DISC? Pharrell Williams – Happy
FAVOURITE TV? Broadchurch
LEAST FAVOURITE TV? Emmerdale – because I can't bare to watch it with my grandparents
PET HATE? Public spitting
SURPRISING FACT? I self-taught myself to play guitar and am a qualified lifeguard
FANTASY SLIP CORDON? Keeper: Will Smith, 1st: Del Boy, 2nd: Myself, 3rd: Pixie Lott
TWITTER FEED: @AdamWheatcroft

# ADAM WHEATER RHB WK R0 W0

FULL NAME: Adam Jack Aubrey Wheater
BORN: February 13, 1990, Whipps Cross Hospital, London
SQUAD NO: 31
TEAMS: Hampshire, Essex, Matabeleland Tuskers
CAREER: First-class: 2008; List A: 2010; T20: 2009



BEST BATTING: 164 Essex vs Northamptonshire, Chelmsford, 2011
BEST BOWLING: 1-86 Essex vs Leicestershire, Leicester, 2012

CAREER HIGHLIGHTS? My career-best score of 164 against Northants and having the opportunity to see the world through cricket
MOST MARKED CHARACTERISTIC? I'm argumentative
CRICKETING HEROES? Alec Stewart, Nasser Hussain, Adam Gilchrist
IF YOU WEREN'T A CRICKETER? I'd find myself a very wealthy girlfriend I could sponge off
DESERT ISLAND DISC? Snow Patrol – Greatest Hits
FAVOURITE TV? Jamie Oliver's cooking shows
ACCOMPLISHMENTS? I won a bottle of vodka at my local pub quiz
FANTASY SLIP CORDON? Keeper: Spider-Man (he's taking everyone's catches), 1st: Anthony Kiedis (he would have some stories to tell), 2nd: Micky Flanagan (just in case you had a long time in the field), 3rd: Shakira (to teach me Spanish)

| Batting | Mat | Inns | NO | Runs | HS | Ave | SR | 100 | 50 | Ct | St |
|---|---|---|---|---|---|---|---|---|---|---|---|
| First-class | 78 | 112 | 14 | 3760 | 164 | 38.36 | 71.02 | 7 | 21 | 115 | 5 |
| List A | 53 | 40 | 5 | 842 | 135 | 24.05 | 103.05 | 1 | 3 | 19 | 4 |
| Twenty20 | 55 | 37 | 10 | 363 | 34 | 13.44 | 100.27 | 0 | 0 | 16 | 11 |
| **Bowling** | **Mat** | **Balls** | **Runs** | **Wkts** | **BBI** | **BBM** | **Ave** | **Econ** | **SR** | **5w** | **10** |
| First-class | 78 | 24 | 86 | 1 | 1/86 | 1/86 | 86.00 | 21.50 | 24.0 | 0 | 0 |
| List A | 53 | - | - | - | - | - | - | - | - | - | - |
| Twenty20 | 55 | - | - | - | - | - | - | - | - | - | - |

## GRAEME WHILES LHB RMF R0 W0

FULL NAME: Graeme Philip Whiles
BORN: December 14, 1993, Harrogate, Yorkshire
SQUAD NO: 36
HEIGHT: 6ft 3in
NICKNAME: Kenny, Whilesy, Uni lad
EDUCATION: King James's School, Knaresborough; University of Worcester
TEAMS: Worcestershire 2nd XI, Yorkshire 2nd XI
CAREER: Yet to make first-team debut

---

BEST PLAYER IN COUNTY CRICKET? James Taylor or James Vince
TIP FOR THE TOP? Charlie Morris
MOST MARKED CHARACTERISTIC? Questions. I drive a lot of lads insane; I think it's my journalism side coming out but I always have at least one question every couple of minutes
CRICKETING HEROES? Brett Lee is my all-time favourite. There are probably guys who have been faster and guys who have taken more wickets but he is right up there with both
NON-CRICKETING HEROES? Rosa Parks – anyone who is willing to stand up for what is right and what they believe in impresses me
CRICKET RULE YOU'D CHANGE? More bouncers per over!
COACHING TIP? A huge one that has helped me with pushing out my front arm towards the batsman is holding a cricket ball in my non-bowling arm when I bowl. Then when you are in your bound, imagine you are punching the batsman with the ball and you will extend more
IF YOU WEREN'T A CRICKETER? I actually did some work experience at All Out Cricket and loved it so I would definitely look into some cricket magazine work
IF YOU COULD BE SOMEONE ELSE FOR A DAY? It would have to be a musician like Paolo Nutini. Guys like him are so talented with songwriting, musical instruments and singing. I think it would be great to have that ability to move people with music
PET HATE? I hate it when someone uses something of yours without asking
SURPRISING FACT? I collect records. I have only started recently so I only have around 20 but it is definitely something I want to pursue further
TWITTER FEED: @GraemeWhiles

# GRAEME WHITE

RHB SLA R0 W0

FULL NAME: Graeme Geoffrey White
BORN: April 18, 1987, Milton Keynes, Buckinghamshire
SQUAD NO: 87
HEIGHT: 5ft 10in
NICKNAME: Whitey, G
EDUCATION: Stowe School
TEAMS: Northamptonshire, Nottinghamshire
CAREER: First-class: 2006; List A: 2007; T20: 2007



BEST BATTING: 65 Northamptonshire vs Glamorgan, Colwyn Bay, 2007
BEST BOWLING: 4-72 Nottinghamshire vs Durham, Nottingham, 2011

FAMILY TIES? My dad played club cricket, my sister played England Women's age groups and my brother played county age groups
BEST PLAYER IN COUNTY CRICKET? Ben Stokes
CRICKETING HEROES? James Middlebrook, Paul Franks, Stephen Peters – all fantastic role models
CRICKET RULE YOU'D CHANGE? Bigger boundaries – less chance of me getting hit for six!
IF YOU WEREN'T A CRICKETER? A model
IF YOU COULD BE SOMEONE ELSE FOR A DAY? Cristiano Ronaldo
DESERT ISLAND DISC? Akon – Lonely
FAVOURITE TV? Suits – has to be the best programme ever!
PET HATE? David Murphy – everything he does!
FANTASY SLIP CORDON? Keeper: David Brent, 1st: Mark Nelson, 2nd: Myself, 3rd: Stephen Fry, Gully: Jack Whitehall

| Batting | Mat | Inns | NO | Runs | HS | Ave | SR | 100 | 50 | Ct | St |
|---|---|---|---|---|---|---|---|---|---|---|---|
| First-class | 27 | 40 | 5 | 455 | 65 | 13.00 | 44.00 | 0 | 2 | 8 | 0 |
| List A | 49 | 26 | 10 | 214 | 39* | 13.37 | 85.25 | 0 | 0 | 20 | 0 |
| Twenty20 | 53 | 21 | 9 | 142 | 34 | 11.83 | 146.39 | 0 | 0 | 19 | 0 |
| **Bowling** | **Mat** | **Balls** | **Runs** | **Wkts** | **BBI** | **BBM** | **Ave** | **Econ** | **SR** | **5w** | **10** |
| First-class | 27 | 3206 | 1868 | 39 | 4/72 | 7/89 | 47.89 | 3.49 | 82.2 | 0 | 0 |
| List A | 49 | 1533 | 1374 | 45 | 5/35 | 5/35 | 30.53 | 5.37 | 34.0 | 1 | 0 |
| Twenty20 | 53 | 785 | 1028 | 44 | 5/22 | 5/22 | 23.36 | 7.85 | 17.8 | 1 | 0 |

## HARRY WHITE RHB LMF R0 W0

FULL NAME: Harry White
BORN: February 19, 1995, Derby
SQUAD NO: 19
HEIGHT: 6ft 4in
NICKNAME: Chalky, Bambi
EDUCATION: John Port School; Repton School
TEAMS: Derbyshire 2nd XI
CAREER: Yet to make first-team debut

---

FAMILY TIES? My brother Wayne also plays for Derbyshire
CAREER HIGHLIGHTS? Being selected for the Bunbury Festival and achieving a place on the Derbyshire staff
BEST PLAYER IN COUNTY CRICKET? Mark Footitt
TIP FOR THE TOP? Harvey Hosein, Ben Duckett
MOST MARKED CHARACTERISTIC? Being the best at Call Of Duty in the squad
SUPERSTITIONS? I always have to buy a lucozade before each game
CRICKETING HEROES? Unfortunately I have to say my brother Wayne White – he has been there from garden cricket to where I am today in my progress. Jimmy Anderson – definitely up there for me as he defines swing bowling
NON-CRICKETING HEROES? Steven Gerrard – being a Liverpool fan growing up he has always been my idol
IF YOU WEREN'T A CRICKETER? Probably still doing my previous job which was setting up for events at Derbyshire. I'm sure the lads will miss abusing me and telling me to sweep the indoor school for them
IF YOU COULD BE SOMEONE ELSE FOR A DAY? Lee Evans – purely to see what goes through his mind on a daily basis
FAVOURITE TV? Top Gear
LEAST FAVOURITE TV? Emmerdale
ACCOMPLISHMENTS? Passing my driving test after the 600th time
PET HATE? Having dirty shoes of any kind. They have to be spotless for any occasion
TWITTER FEED: @harrywhite_95

## ROBBIE WHITE RHB RFM R0 W0

FULL NAME: Robbie White
BORN: September 15, 1995, Ealing, London
SQUAD NO: 14
HEIGHT: 5ft 9in
NICKNAME: Whitey
EDUCATION: Harrow School; Loughborough University
TEAMS: Middlesex 2nd XI
CAREER: Yet to make first-team debut



---

CAREER HIGHLIGHTS? Playing at Lord's (Eton vs Harrow) and my 2nd XI debut at Hove
BEST PLAYER IN COUNTY CRICKET? James Vince
TIP FOR THE TOP? Nick Gubbins
SUPERSTITIONS? Pad up in same order every game
CRICKETING HEROES? Matt Prior – hard-working, determined and leader of the team
NON-CRICKETING HEROES? Tiger Woods – always performed under pressure and created a legacy. Roger Federer – top bloke despite dominating
CRICKET RULE YOU'D CHANGE? In limited-overs cricket, there should be an over of free hits nominated by the batting side at any point
COACHING TIP? Watch the middle of the ball, rather than just the whole ball
IF YOU WEREN'T A CRICKETER? Working in the City
IF YOU COULD BE SOMEONE ELSE FOR A DAY? Rory McIlroy
DESERT ISLAND DISC? KC And The Sunshine Band – Give It Up
FAVOURITE TV? Gogglebox
LEAST FAVOURITE TV? How I Met Your Mother
ACCOMPLISHMENTS? Playing football for Chelsea when I was seven
PET HATE? Lorries overtaking lorries on the motorway. Should be illegal
SURPRISING FACT? I've never eaten a mushroom
FANTASY SLIP CORDON? Keeper: Nelson Mandela, 1st: Me, 2nd: James Corden, 3rd: Winston Churchill, Gully: Hugh Grant
TWITTER FEED: @Rwhitey15

# WAYNE WHITE

## RHB RMF R0 W0

FULL NAME: Wayne Andrew White
BORN: April 22, 1985, Derby
SQUAD NO: 35
HEIGHT: 6ft 3in
NICKNAME: Chalky, Sticks, Waz
EDUCATION: John Port School, Derby; Nottingham Trent University
TEAMS: Derbyshire, Lancashire, Leicestershire
CAREER: First-class: 2005; List A: 2006; T20: 2009

BEST BATTING: 101* Leicestershire vs Derbyshire, Derby, 2010
BEST BOWLING: 5-54 Leicestershire vs Derbyshire, Derby, 2012
COUNTY CAPS: 2012 (Leicestershire)

FAMILY TIES? My brother Harry also plays for Derbyshire
CAREER HIGHLIGHTS? Winning the T20 Cup and scoring my first hundred
CRICKETING HEROES? Mike Hendrick, Dominic Cork
IF YOU WEREN'T A CRICKETER? I'd be trying to be a footballer
FAVOURITE TV? 90210
ACCOMPLISHMENTS? Playing in the FA Cup
SURPRISING FACT? I can DJ
TWITTER FEED: @wayneAwhite

| Batting | Mat | Inns | NO | Runs | HS | Ave | SR | 100 | 50 | Ct | St |
|---|---|---|---|---|---|---|---|---|---|---|---|
| First-class | 76 | 121 | 17 | 2511 | 101* | 24.14 | 51.86 | 1 | 13 | 24 | 0 |
| List A | 68 | 55 | 15 | 755 | 46* | 18.87 | 84.73 | 0 | 0 | 15 | 0 |
| Twenty20 | 52 | 40 | 16 | 370 | 26 | 15.41 | 113.84 | 0 | 0 | 27 | 0 |
| **Bowling** | **Mat** | **Balls** | **Runs** | **Wkts** | **BBI** | **BBM** | **Ave** | **Econ** | **SR** | **5w** | **10** |
| First-class | 76 | 9382 | 6015 | 166 | 5/54 | | 36.23 | 3.84 | 56.5 | 4 | 0 |
| List A | 68 | 2257 | 2426 | 66 | 6/29 | 6/29 | 36.75 | 6.44 | 34.1 | 1 | 0 |
| Twenty20 | 52 | 657 | 1051 | 25 | 3/27 | 3/27 | 42.04 | 9.59 | 26.2 | 0 | 0 |

# ROSS WHITELEY

LHB LM R0 W0

FULL NAME: Ross Andrew Whiteley
BORN: September 13, 1988, Sheffield, Yorkshire
SQUAD NO: 44
HEIGHT: 6ft 2in
NICKNAME: Rossco, Pico, Shaggy
EDUCATION: Repton School; Leeds Metropolitan University
TEAMS: Worcestershire, Derbyshire
CAREER: First-class: 2008; List A: 2008; T20: 2011



BEST BATTING: 130* Derbyshire vs Kent, Derby, 2011
BEST BOWLING: 2-6 Derbyshire vs Hampshire, Derby, 2012

FAMILY TIES? My brother Adam played Derbyshire age groups, academy and in a handful of 2nd XI games
CAREER HIGHLIGHTS? Being champions of Division Two in the Championship in 2012, promotion from Division Two in 2014 and selection for Hong Kong Sixes in 2012
SUPERSTITIONS? I scratch my mark three times every time I get on strike
CRICKETING HEROES? Matthew Hayden – becasue of his ability to bully a bowling attack
NON-CRICKETING HEROES? Dan Bilzerian – his Instagram says it all
CRICKET RULE YOU'D CHANGE? An enforced break half-way through the season to freshen up – it could potentially help injuries
COACHING TIP? If you're going to try and hit a six, don't just try and hit it over the rope, try and hit it out of the ground because failure to do that will still get it over the rope
IF YOU COULD BE SOMEONE ELSE FOR A DAY? Dan Bilzerian
PET HATE? People changing plans at the last minute
TWITTER FEED: @rosswhiteley44

| Batting | Mat | Inns | NO | Runs | HS | Ave | SR | 100 | 50 | Ct | St |
|---|---|---|---|---|---|---|---|---|---|---|---|
| First-class | 44 | 69 | 7 | 1601 | 130* | 25.82 | 44.55 | 2 | 6 | 22 | 0 |
| List A | 33 | 28 | 3 | 473 | 53 | 18.92 | 77.28 | 0 | 2 | 10 | 0 |
| Twenty20 | 32 | 30 | 11 | 558 | 84* | 29.36 | 138.80 | 0 | 1 | 7 | 0 |
| **Bowling** | **Mat** | **Balls** | **Runs** | **Wkts** | **BBI** | **BBM** | **Ave** | **Econ** | **SR** | **5w** | **10** |
| First-class | 44 | 1993 | 1392 | 28 | 2/6 | 4/43 | 49.71 | 4.19 | 71.1 | 0 | 0 |
| List A | 33 | 309 | 340 | 6 | 1/17 | 1/17 | 56.66 | 6.60 | 51.5 | 0 | 0 |
| Twenty20 | 32 | 54 | 87 | 2 | 1/12 | 1/12 | 43.50 | 9.66 | 27.0 | 0 | 0 |

# DAVID WILLEY

## LHB LFM R0 W0 MVP66

FULL NAME: David Jonathan Willey
BORN: February 28, 1990, Northampton
SQUAD NO: 15
HEIGHT: 6ft 1in
NICKNAME: Willow, Will
EDUCATION: Northampton School For Boys
TEAMS: Northamptonshire
CAREER: First-class: 2009; List A: 2009; T20: 2009

BEST BATTING: 81 Northamptonshire vs Glamorgan, Northampton, 2013
BEST BOWLING: 5-29 Northamptonshire vs Gloucestershire, Northampton, 2011

FAMILY TIES? My dad used to play a bit [Peter Willey played for England, Northamptonshire and Leicestershire]
CAREER HIGHLIGHTS? Being T20 champions with Northants and Man of the Match in the final
BEST PLAYER IN COUNTY CRICKET? Jeetan Patel
TIP FOR THE TOP? Saif Zaib
MOST MARKED CHARACTERISTIC? Inconsistent and extreme
SUPERSTITIONS? Left pad on first and turn right before starting my run-up
IF YOU WEREN'T A CRICKETER? Probably travelling the world
DESERT ISLAND DISC? Acoustic Lounge
FAVOURITE TV? An Idiot Abroad
FANTASY SLIP CORDON? Keeper: Karl Pilkington (I'd like to hear his opinions on everything!), 1st: Peter Willey (he'd probably bounce off Pilkington and be sour together), 2nd: Myself, 3rd: Michael McIntyre
TWITTER FEED: @david_willey

| Batting | Mat | Inns | NO | Runs | HS | Ave | SR | 100 | 50 | Ct | St |
|---|---|---|---|---|---|---|---|---|---|---|---|
| First-class | 52 | 72 | 9 | 1614 | 81 | 25.61 | 59.75 | 0 | 12 | 11 | 0 |
| List A | 53 | 41 | 5 | 846 | 167 | 23.50 | 100.23 | 2 | 2 | 19 | 0 |
| Twenty20 | 73 | 50 | 14 | 772 | 95 | 21.44 | 128.88 | 0 | 2 | 27 | 0 |
| **Bowling** | **Mat** | **Balls** | **Runs** | **Wkts** | **BBI** | **BBM** | **Ave** | **Econ** | **SR** | **5w** | **10** |
| First-class | 52 | 7018 | 3854 | 133 | 5/29 | 10/75 | 28.97 | 3.29 | 52.7 | 5 | 1 |
| List A | 53 | 1612 | 1518 | 47 | 5/62 | 5/62 | 32.29 | 5.65 | 34.2 | 1 | 0 |
| Twenty20 | 73 | 932 | 1165 | 58 | 4/9 | 4/9 | 20.08 | 7.50 | 16.0 | 0 | 0 |

# GARY WILSON

## RHB WK R0 W0 MVP76

FULL NAME: Gary Craig Wilson
BORN: February 5, 1986, Dundonald, Northern Ireland
SQUAD NO: 14
HEIGHT: 5 ft 10 in
NICKNAME: Gaz, Wils
EDUCATION: Methodist College, Belfast
TEAMS: Ireland, Surrey
CAREER: ODI: 2007; T20I: 2008; First-class: 2005; List A: 2006; T20: 2008



BEST BATTING: 160* Surrey vs Leicestershire, The Oval, 2014

CAREER HIGHLIGHTS? Playing in the World Cup and beating England, plus my maiden Championship and ODI hundreds
SUPERSTITIONS? I put my left pad on first
CRICKETING HEROES? Alec Stewart
NON-CRICKETING HEROES? David Beckham, Sir Alex Ferguson
IF YOU WEREN'T A CRICKETER? Probably a fireman or policeman
FAVOURITE TV? Spooks, The Apprentice, TOWIE
SURPRISING FACT? I have the biggest head in the changing room in terms of volume and I played Ulster Schools rugby
FANTASY SLIP CORDON? Keeper: David Beckham, 1st: Myself, 2nd: Sir Alex Ferguson, 3rd: Michael McIntyre, Gully: Tiger Woods
TWITTER FEED: @gwilson14

| Batting | Mat | Inns | NO | Runs | HS | Ave | SR | 100 | 50 | Ct | St |
|---|---|---|---|---|---|---|---|---|---|---|---|
| ODIs | 56 | 54 | 5 | 1235 | 113 | 25.20 | 74.53 | 1 | 8 | 46 | 9 |
| T20Is | 34 | 29 | 4 | 511 | 41* | 20.44 | 91.08 | 0 | 0 | 18 | 3 |
| First-class | 60 | 88 | 13 | 2553 | 160* | 34.04 | | 3 | 14 | 103 | 3 |
| List A | 138 | 123 | 11 | 2558 | 113 | 22.83 | 69.85 | 1 | 16 | 100 | 22 |
| Twenty20 | 108 | 92 | 22 | 1841 | 63* | 26.30 | 112.18 | 0 | 6 | 53 | 16 |
| **Bowling** | **Mat** | **Balls** | **Runs** | **Wkts** | **BBI** | **BBM** | **Ave** | **Econ** | **SR** | **5w** | **10** |
| ODIs | 56 | - | - | - | - | - | - | - | - | - | - |
| T20Is | 34 | - | - | - | - | - | - | - | - | - | - |
| First-class | 60 | 108 | 89 | 0 | - | - | - | 4.94 | - | 0 | 0 |
| List A | 138 | - | - | - | - | - | - | - | - | - | - |
| Twenty20 | 108 | - | - | - | - | - | - | - | - | - | - |

# CHRIS WOAKES

## RHB RFM R0 W2 MVP95

WARWICKSHIRE

FULL NAME: Christopher Roger Woakes
BORN: March 2, 1989, Birmingham
SQUAD NO: 19
HEIGHT: 6ft 2in
NICKNAME: Woaksy, Woako, Wiz, GB
TEAMS: England, Warwickshire, Sydney Thunder, Wellington
CAREER: Test: 2013; ODI: 2011; T20I: 2011; First-class: 2006; List A: 2007; T20: 2008

BEST BATTING: 152* Warwickshire vs Derbyshire, Derby, 2013
BEST BOWLING: 7-20 Warwickshire vs Hampshire, Birmingham, 2011
COUNTY CAPS: 2009

CAREER HIGHLIGHTS? Winning the CB40 in 2010 with Warwickshire and making my debut for England in Australia in January 2011
CRICKETING HEROES? Jacques Kallis
NON-CRICKETING HEROES? Paul 'God' McGrath
IF YOU WEREN'T A CRICKETER? Struggling to find a job!
FAVOURITE TV? An Idiot Abroad or A League Of Their Own
FANTASY SLIP CORDON? Keeper: Shay Given, 1st: Myself, 2nd: Angelina Jolie, 3rd: Karl Pilkington, Gully: David Beckham
TWITTER FEED: @crwoakes19

| Batting | Mat | Inns | NO | Runs | HS | Ave | SR | 100 | 50 | Ct | St |
|---|---|---|---|---|---|---|---|---|---|---|---|
| Tests | 4 | 5 | 3 | 75 | 26* | 37.50 | 54.74 | 0 | 0 | 2 | 0 |
| ODIs | 33 | 27 | 6 | 358 | 41 | 17.04 | 75.68 | 0 | 0 | 16 | 0 |
| T20Is | 6 | 5 | 3 | 39 | 19* | 19.50 | 121.87 | 0 | 0 | 1 | 0 |
| First-class | 102 | 143 | 37 | 4015 | 152* | 37.87 | | 8 | 16 | 45 | 0 |
| List A | 102 | 69 | 19 | 870 | 49* | 17.40 | 83.01 | 0 | 0 | 28 | 0 |
| Twenty20 | 77 | 46 | 26 | 519 | 55* | 25.95 | 134.80 | 0 | 1 | 31 | 0 |
| **Bowling** | **Mat** | **Balls** | **Runs** | **Wkts** | **BBI** | **BBM** | **Ave** | **Econ** | **SR** | **5w** | **10** |
| Tests | 4 | 570 | 313 | 6 | 3/30 | 4/54 | 52.16 | 3.29 | 95.0 | 0 | 0 |
| ODIs | 33 | 1560 | 1546 | 47 | 6/45 | 6/45 | 32.89 | 5.94 | 33.1 | 2 | 0 |
| T20Is | 6 | 114 | 187 | 4 | 1/29 | 1/29 | 46.75 | 9.84 | 28.5 | 0 | 0 |
| First-class | 102 | 17274 | 8833 | 346 | 7/20 | 11/97 | 25.52 | 3.06 | 49.9 | 15 | 3 |
| List A | 102 | 4156 | 3901 | 114 | 6/45 | 6/45 | 34.21 | 5.63 | 36.4 | 2 | 0 |
| Twenty20 | 77 | 1470 | 2003 | 77 | 4/21 | 4/21 | 26.01 | 8.17 | 19.0 | 0 | 0 |

# CHRIS WOOD

RHB LMF R0 W0

FULL NAME: Christopher Philip Wood
BORN: June 27, 1990, Basingstoke, Hampshire
SQUAD NO: 25
HEIGHT: 6ft 3in
NICKNAME: Woody, Nuts
EDUCATION: Amery Hill School; Alton College
TEAMS: Hampshire
CAREER: First-class: 2010; List A: 2010; T20: 2010



BEST BATTING: 105* Hampshire vs Leicestershire, Leicester, 2012
BEST BOWLING: 5-39 Hampshire vs Kent, Canterbury, 2014

CAREER HIGHLIGHTS? Winning the T20 Cup in 2010 and 2012 and winning the CB40 in 2012
BEST PLAYER IN COUNTY CRICKET? Ben Stokes
TIP FOR THE TOP? Mark Wood, Brad Taylor
CRICKETING HEROES? Andrew Flintoff, Dimitri Mascarenhas
CRICKET RULE YOU'D CHANGE? No-balls – free hits in Championship cricket
DESERT ISLAND DISC? Family Guy
PET HATE? Losing games!
SURPRISING FACT? I have played semi-pro football
TWITTER FEED: @CWoody27

| Batting | Mat | Inns | NO | Runs | HS | Ave | SR | 100 | 50 | Ct | St |
|---|---|---|---|---|---|---|---|---|---|---|---|
| First-class | 34 | 48 | 4 | 1039 | 105* | 23.61 | 65.30 | 1 | 5 | 12 | 0 |
| List A | 54 | 30 | 8 | 245 | 41 | 11.13 | 90.07 | 0 | 0 | 19 | 0 |
| Twenty20 | 71 | 21 | 8 | 135 | 27 | 10.38 | 106.29 | 0 | 0 | 21 | 0 |
| **Bowling** | **Mat** | **Balls** | **Runs** | **Wkts** | **BBI** | **BBM** | **Ave** | **Econ** | **SR** | **5w** | **10** |
| First-class | 34 | 5113 | 2554 | 93 | 5/39 | 7/49 | 27.46 | 2.99 | 54.9 | 3 | 0 |
| List A | 54 | 2153 | 1983 | 79 | 5/22 | 5/22 | 25.10 | 5.52 | 27.2 | 1 | 0 |
| Twenty20 | 71 | 1437 | 1974 | 71 | 4/24 | 4/24 | 27.80 | 8.24 | 20.2 | 0 | 0 |

## LUKE WOOD

## LHB LM R0 W0

FULL NAME: Luke Wood
BORN: August 2, 1995, Sheffield, Yorkshire
SQUAD NO: tbc
EDUCATION: Portland Comprehensive School, Worksop
TEAMS: Nottinghamshire
CAREER: First-class: 2014

BEST BATTING: 12 Nottinghamshire vs Sussex, Nottingham, 2014
BEST BOWLING: 2-87 Nottinghamshire vs Sussex, Nottingham, 2014

TWITTER FEED: @lwood_95
NOTES: Young seamer Wood has signed a two-year professional contract at Notts after impressing in the 2nd XI last season. He helped England U19 beat South Africa U19 in the one-day series last August. He played club cricket for Cuckney CC before joining the Notts academy in 2009. He caught the eye of Notts coach Mick Newell on a pre-season tour to Barbados ahead of the 2014 season

| Batting | Mat | Inns | NO | Runs | HS | Ave | SR | 100 | 50 | Ct | St |
|---|---|---|---|---|---|---|---|---|---|---|---|
| First-class | 1 | 2 | 1 | 17 | 12 | 17.00 | 43.58 | 0 | 0 | 0 | 0 |
| **Bowling** | **Mat** | **Balls** | **Runs** | **Wkts** | **BBI** | **BBM** | **Ave** | **Econ** | **SR** | **5w** | **10** |
| First-class | 1 | 234 | 180 | 3 | 2/87 | 3/180 | 60.00 | 4.61 | 78.0 | 0 | 0 |

# MARK WOOD

RHB RFM R0 W0

FULL NAME: Mark Andrew Wood
BORN: January 11, 1990, Ashington, Northumberland
SQUAD NO: 33
HEIGHT: 6ft
NICKNAME: Woody
EDUCATION: Ashington High School
TEAMS: Durham
CAREER: First-class: 2011; List A: 2011; T20: 2013



BEST BATTING: 58* Durham vs Nottinghamshire, Nottingham, 2013
BEST BOWLING: 5-32 England Lions vs Sri Lanka A Emerging Players, Colombo, 2014

FAMILY TIES? My dad Derek and uncle Neil Wood played 1st XI cricket for Ashington CC and Minor Counties cricket for Northumberland
CAREER HIGHLIGHTS? Making my debut vs Durham University, my first first-class five-fer against Nottinghamshire at Trent Bridge, winning the County Championship, being selected for the England Lions and taking five-fer against Sri Lanka A for England Lions in Colombo
MOST MARKED CHARACTERISTIC? I step back like a sprinter at the start of my run-up
CRICKETING HEROES? Graham Onions, Stephen Harmison, Ben Harmison, Michael Holding, Ian Botham
NON-CRICKETING HEROES? Lennox Lewis, David Beckham, Jonny Wilkinson
SURPRISING FACT? I was in the Newcastle United FC Academy
FANTASY SLIP CORDON? Keeper: Denis Cyplenkov (Russian wrestler with the biggest hands in the world), 1st: Sanka Coffie (from Cool Runnings – because he'd be a top sledger), 2nd: Leslie Nielsen (to keep morale up in the field), 3rd: Vinnie Jones (famous for getting his hands around balls) Gully: Jason Bourne (because he lived on the edge!)
TWITTER FEED: @MAWood33

| Batting | Mat | Inns | NO | Runs | HS | Ave | SR | 100 | 50 | Ct | St |
|---|---|---|---|---|---|---|---|---|---|---|---|
| First-class | 23 | 35 | 7 | 554 | 58* | 19.78 | 48.85 | 0 | 1 | 7 | 0 |
| List A | 18 | 8 | 3 | 28 | 15* | 5.60 | 80.00 | 0 | 0 | 5 | 0 |
| Twenty20 | 9 | 4 | 1 | 24 | 12 | 8.00 | 92.30 | 0 | 0 | 1 | 0 |
| **Bowling** | **Mat** | **Balls** | **Runs** | **Wkts** | **BBI** | **BBM** | **Ave** | **Econ** | **SR** | **5w** | **10** |
| First-class | 23 | 3399 | 1936 | 74 | 5/32 | 6/47 | 26.16 | 3.41 | 45.9 | 5 | 0 |
| List A | 18 | 642 | 562 | 21 | 3/23 | 3/23 | 26.76 | 5.25 | 30.5 | 0 | 0 |
| Twenty20 | 9 | 144 | 229 | 3 | 1/9 | 1/9 | 76.33 | 9.54 | 48.0 | 0 | 0 |

## SAM WOOD

## LHB OB R0 W0

FULL NAME: Samuel Kenneth William Wood
BORN: April 3, 1993, Nottingham
SQUAD NO: 23
HEIGHT: 6ft
NICKNAME: Woody
EDUCATION: Colonel Frank Seely School
TEAMS: Nottinghamshire
CAREER: First-class: 2011; List A: 2011; T20: 2014

BEST BATTING: 45 Nottinghamshire vs Surrey, The Oval, 2012
BEST BOWLING: 3-64 Nottinghamshire vs Surrey, The Oval, 2012

FAMILY TIES? My dad played league cricket
CAREER HIGHLIGHTS? Playing in the U19 World Cup in Australia and making my first-class debut
MOST MARKED CHARACTERISTIC? Not saying much
SUPERSTITIONS? I push my pads down before every ball
CRICKETING HEROES? Brian Lara
NON-CRICKETING HEROES? Muhammad Ali
CRICKET RULE YOU'D CHANGE? An extra half-hour for the lunch break
DESERT ISLAND DISC? Time To Say Goodbye
FAVOURITE TV? Coronation Street
SURPRISING FACT? I've got an obsession with Coronation Street
FANTASY SLIP CORDON? Keeper: Me, 1st: Lee Evans, 2nd: Peter Kay, 3rd: Ricky Gervais, Gully: Kevin Bridges
TWITTER FEED: @SamWood33

| Batting | Mat | Inns | NO | Runs | HS | Ave | SR | 100 | 50 | Ct | St |
|---|---|---|---|---|---|---|---|---|---|---|---|
| First-class | 3 | 4 | 1 | 77 | 45 | 25.66 | 40.10 | 0 | 0 | 0 | 0 |
| List A | 9 | 6 | 0 | 63 | 32 | 10.50 | 66.31 | 0 | 0 | 3 | 0 |
| Twenty20 | 10 | 5 | 2 | 30 | 13* | 10.00 | 136.36 | 0 | 0 | 1 | 0 |
| **Bowling** | **Mat** | **Balls** | **Runs** | **Wkts** | **BBI** | **BBM** | **Ave** | **Econ** | **SR** | **5w** | **10** |
| First-class | 3 | 192 | 92 | 3 | 3/64 | 3/84 | 30.66 | 2.87 | 64.0 | 0 | 0 |
| List A | 9 | 180 | 163 | 5 | 2/24 | 2/24 | 32.60 | 5.43 | 36.0 | 0 | 0 |
| Twenty20 | 10 | 72 | 117 | 3 | 2/21 | 2/21 | 39.00 | 9.75 | 24.0 | 0 | 0 |

# BEN WRIGHT

RHB RM R0 W0

FULL NAME: Ben James Wright
BORN: December 5, 1987, Preston, Lancashire
SQUAD NO: 29
HEIGHT: 5ft 11in
NICKNAME: Bej, Keller
EDUCATION: Cowbridge Comprehensive
TEAMS: Glamorgan
CAREER: First-class: 2006; List A: 2006; T20: 2007



BEST BATTING: 172 Glamorgan vs Gloucestershire, Cardiff, 2007
BEST BOWLING: 1-14 Glamorgan vs Essex, Chelmsford, 2007
COUNTY CAPS: 2011

CAREER HIGHLIGHTS? Scoring a hundred vs Middlesex at Lord's
CRICKETING HEROES? Andrew Flintoff, Matthew Maynard
NON-CRICKETING HEROES? Jonny Wilkinson
IF YOU WEREN'T A CRICKETER? Fitness trainer
FAVOURITE TV? Eastbound And Down
ACCOMPLISHMENTS? Playing rugby for Wales at U16 level
TWITTER FEED: @bej29w

| Batting | Mat | Inns | NO | Runs | HS | Ave | SR | 100 | 50 | Ct | St |
|---|---|---|---|---|---|---|---|---|---|---|---|
| First-class | 84 | 139 | 10 | 3506 | 172 | 27.17 | 50.48 | 6 | 14 | 44 | 0 |
| List A | 73 | 66 | 12 | 1332 | 79 | 24.66 | 75.55 | 0 | 7 | 16 | 0 |
| Twenty20 | 54 | 43 | 13 | 529 | 55* | 17.63 | 104.33 | 0 | 1 | 14 | 0 |
| **Bowling** | **Mat** | **Balls** | **Runs** | **Wkts** | **BBI** | **BBM** | **Ave** | **Econ** | **SR** | **5w** | **10** |
| First-class | 84 | 276 | 174 | 2 | 1/14 | 1/14 | 87.00 | 3.78 | 138.0 | 0 | 0 |
| List A | 73 | 132 | 126 | 1 | 1/19 | 1/19 | 126.00 | 5.72 | 132.0 | 0 | 0 |
| Twenty20 | 54 | 24 | 22 | 1 | 1/16 | 1/16 | 22.00 | 5.50 | 24.0 | 0 | 0 |

# CHRIS WRIGHT

RHB RFM R0 W1



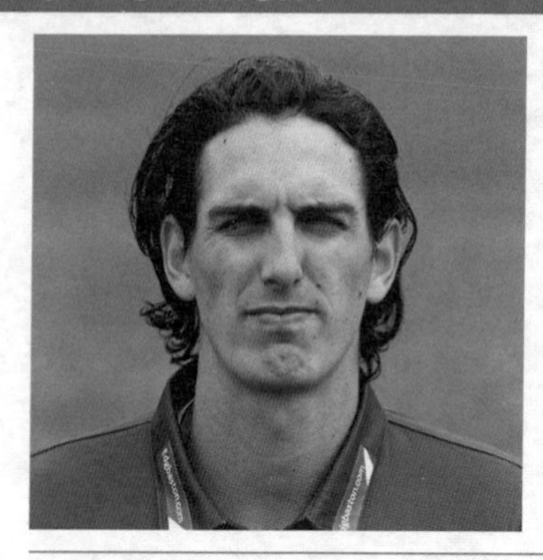

FULL NAME: Christopher Julian Clement Wright
BORN: July 14, 1985, Chipping Norton, Oxfordshire
SQUAD NO: 31
HEIGHT: 6ft 3in
NICKNAME: Wrighty, The Baron
EDUCATION: Eggars Grammar School, Alton
TEAMS: Warwickshire, Essex, Middlesex, Tamil Union Cricket and Athletic Club
CAREER: First-class: 2004; List A: 2004; T20: 2004

---

BEST BATTING: 77 Essex vs CMCCU, Fenner's, 2011
BEST BOWLING: 6-22 Essex vs Leicestershire, Leicester, 2008

---

CAREER HIGHLIGHTS? Winning the County Championship in 2012 and the FP Trophy in 2008
MOST MARKED CHARACTERISTIC? My awesome lid!
DESERT ISLAND DISC? Linkin Park – Hybrid Theory
ACCOMPLISHMENTS? Two lovely children
FANTASY SLIP CORDON? Keeper: Me, 1st: Phil Edwards, 2nd: Tony Palladino, 3rd: Gareth James, Gully: Matt Hooper
TWITTER FEED: @ChrisWright1985

| Batting | Mat | Inns | NO | Runs | HS | Ave | SR | 100 | 50 | Ct | St |
|---|---|---|---|---|---|---|---|---|---|---|---|
| First-class | 101 | 122 | 29 | 1609 | 77 | 17.30 | 52.37 | 0 | 7 | 16 | 0 |
| List A | 90 | 38 | 17 | 219 | 42 | 10.42 | 78.49 | 0 | 0 | 16 | 0 |
| Twenty20 | 55 | 14 | 9 | 28 | 6* | 5.60 | 103.70 | 0 | 0 | 12 | 0 |
| **Bowling** | **Mat** | **Balls** | **Runs** | **Wkts** | **BBI** | **BBM** | **Ave** | **Econ** | **SR** | **5w** | **10** |
| First-class | 101 | 16201 | 9693 | 284 | 6/22 | | 34.13 | 3.58 | 57.0 | 8 | 0 |
| List A | 90 | 3455 | 3217 | 91 | 4/20 | 4/20 | 35.35 | 5.58 | 37.9 | 0 | 0 |
| Twenty20 | 55 | 1119 | 1657 | 50 | 4/24 | 4/24 | 33.14 | 8.88 | 22.3 | 0 | 0 |

# LUKE WRIGHT

## RHB RMF R0 W0 MVP12

FULL NAME: Luke James Wright
BORN: March 7, 1985, Grantham, Lincolnshire
SQUAD NO: 10
HEIGHT: 5ft 11in
NICKNAME: Bammers
EDUCATION: Ratcliffe College; Loughborough University
TEAMS: England, Sussex, Dhaka Gladiators, Impi, Leicestershire, Melbourne Stars, Pune Warriors
CAREER: ODI: 2007; T20I: 2007; First-class: 2003; List A 2002; T20: 2004



BEST BATTING: 189 Sussex vs Durham, Hove, 2014
BEST BOWLING: 5-65 Sussex vs Derbyshire, Derby, 2010
COUNTY CAPS: 2007; BENEFIT YEAR: 2015

FAMILY TIES? My father Keith was a very keen village cricketer and my brother Ashley was a pro at Leicestershire
CAREER HIGHLIGHTS? Winning the World T20 with England in the West Indies, being selected in the team of the tournament for the World T20 in Sri Lanka, having the highest T20 score in English domestic cricket and every trophy we have won at Sussex
CRICKETING HEROES? My brother Ashley and Jacques Kallis
COACHING TIP? Play with a smile on your face and always take the positive option
DESERT ISLAND DISC? Elton John
SURPRISING FACT? I help stick Chris Nash's wig on before each match
TWITTER FEED: @lukewright204

| Batting | Mat | Inns | NO | Runs | HS | Ave | SR | 100 | 50 | Ct | St |
|---|---|---|---|---|---|---|---|---|---|---|---|
| ODIs | 50 | 39 | 4 | 707 | 52 | 20.20 | 86.21 | 0 | 2 | 18 | 0 |
| T20Is | 51 | 45 | 5 | 759 | 99* | 18.97 | 137.00 | 0 | 4 | 14 | 0 |
| First-class | 98 | 147 | 19 | 5069 | 189 | 39.60 | 65.52 | 14 | 23 | 39 | 0 |
| List A | 178 | 144 | 21 | 3768 | 143* | 30.63 | | 9 | 10 | 56 | 0 |
| Twenty20 | 214 | 195 | 18 | 4724 | 153* | 26.68 | 146.11 | 4 | 22 | 70 | 0 |
| **Bowling** | **Mat** | **Balls** | **Runs** | **Wkts** | **BBI** | **BBM** | **Ave** | **Econ** | **SR** | **5w** | **10** |
| ODIs | 50 | 1038 | 884 | 15 | 2/34 | 2/34 | 58.93 | 5.10 | 69.2 | 0 | 0 |
| T20Is | 51 | 330 | 465 | 18 | 2/24 | 2/24 | 25.83 | 8.45 | 18.3 | 0 | 0 |
| First-class | 98 | 8210 | 4823 | 120 | 5/65 | | 40.19 | 3.52 | 68.4 | 3 | 0 |
| List A | 178 | 4752 | 4231 | 111 | 4/12 | 4/12 | 38.11 | 5.34 | 42.8 | 0 | 0 |
| Twenty20 | 214 | 1799 | 2563 | 79 | 3/17 | 3/17 | 32.44 | 8.54 | 22.7 | 0 | 0 |

# ALEX WYATT

RHB RFM R0 W0

LEICESTERSHIRE

FULL NAME: Alexander Charles Frederick Wyatt
BORN: July 23, 1990, Roehampton, London
SQUAD NO: 16
HEIGHT: 6ft 7in
NICKNAME: Waz, Dirty Old Waz
EDUCATION: Oakham School; Open University
TEAMS: Leicestershire
CAREER: First-class: 2009; List A: 2009; T20: 2009

BEST BATTING: 32 Leicestershire vs Hampshire, Southampton, 2014
BEST BOWLING: 3-35 Leicestershire vs Hampshire, Leicester, 2012

CAREER HIGHLIGHTS? Taking 3-14 on T20 debut against Durham in 2009
TIP FOR THE TOP? Aadil Ali, Zak Chappell, Neil Pinner
MOST MARKED CHARACTERISTIC? My height at 6ft 7in makes me stand out from the crowd alongside fellow giant Charlie Shreck
CRICKETING HEROES? Glenn McGrath was the one I watched most on the TV as a young boy. With his pinpoint accuracy and incredible skill he is a bowling legend
COACHING TIP? Play in the V until 33
IF YOU COULD BE SOMEONE ELSE FOR A DAY? Bruce Almighty
DESERT ISLAND DISC? The High Kings – Memory Lane
FAVOURITE TV? The Walking Dead or Game Of Thrones
LEAST FAVOURITE TV? Something down the line of Keeping Up With The Kardashians or Housewives of various cities
FANTASY SLIP CORDON? Keeper: Will Ferrell, 1st: Alice Eve, 2nd: Steve Carell, 3rd: Margot Robbie, Gully: Will Smith
TWITTER FEED: @acfwyatt

| Batting | Mat | Inns | NO | Runs | HS | Ave | SR | 100 | 50 | Ct | St |
|---|---|---|---|---|---|---|---|---|---|---|---|
| First-class | 26 | 35 | 12 | 204 | 32 | 8.86 | 50.62 | 0 | 0 | 3 | 0 |
| List A | 14 | 7 | 3 | 13 | 9* | 3.25 | 68.42 | 0 | 0 | 2 | 0 |
| Twenty20 | 5 | 1 | 1 | 0 | 0* | - | - | 0 | 0 | 1 | 0 |
| **Bowling** | **Mat** | **Balls** | **Runs** | **Wkts** | **BBI** | **BBM** | **Ave** | **Econ** | **SR** | **5w** | **10** |
| First-class | 26 | 3865 | 2075 | 57 | 3/35 | 6/115 | 36.40 | 3.22 | 67.8 | 0 | 0 |
| List A | 14 | 452 | 478 | 11 | 2/36 | 2/36 | 43.45 | 6.34 | 41.0 | 0 | 0 |
| Twenty20 | 5 | 96 | 115 | 3 | 3/14 | 3/14 | 38.33 | 7.18 | 32.0 | 0 | 0 |

## MICHAEL YARDY LHB SLA R2 W0

FULL NAME: Michael Howard Yardy
BORN: November 27, 1980, Pembury, Kent
SQUAD NO: 20
HEIGHT: 6ft
NICKNAME: Yards, Paolo
EDUCATION: William Parker School, Hastings
TEAMS: England, Sussex, Central Districts
CAREER: ODI: 2006; T20I: 2006; First-class: 2000; List A: 1999; T20: 2004



BEST BATTING: 257 Sussex vs Bangladeshis, Hove, 2005
BEST BOWLING: 5-83 Sussex vs Bangladeshis, Hove, 2005
COUNTY CAPS: 2005; BENEFIT YEAR: 2014

CAREER HIGHLIGHTS? The successes with Sussex. Winning the World T20 in 2010
BEST PLAYER IN COUNTY CRICKET? Marcus Trescothick
CRICKETING HEROES? Graham Gooch, Michael Atherton, Alec Stewart, Graham Thorpe
NON-CRICKETING HEROES? Paolo Di Canio, Paul Gascoigne
IF YOU WEREN'T A CRICKETER? Doing a proper job
FAVOURITE TV? Outnumbered

| Batting | Mat | Inns | NO | Runs | HS | Ave | SR | 100 | 50 | Ct | St |
|---|---|---|---|---|---|---|---|---|---|---|---|
| ODIs | 28 | 24 | 8 | 326 | 60* | 20.37 | 69.06 | 0 | 2 | 10 | 0 |
| T20Is | 14 | 8 | 5 | 96 | 35* | 32.00 | 133.33 | 0 | 0 | 8 | 0 |
| First-class | 182 | 302 | 27 | 9999 | 257 | 36.36 | | 21 | 46 | 170 | 0 |
| List A | 205 | 175 | 31 | 3639 | 98* | 25.27 | | 0 | 23 | 75 | 0 |
| Twenty20 | 113 | 88 | 30 | 1218 | 76* | 21.00 | 102.43 | 0 | 2 | 38 | 0 |
| **Bowling** | **Mat** | **Balls** | **Runs** | **Wkts** | **BBI** | **BBM** | **Ave** | **Econ** | **SR** | **5w** | **10** |
| ODIs | 28 | 1332 | 1075 | 21 | 3/24 | 3/24 | 51.19 | 4.84 | 63.4 | 0 | 0 |
| T20Is | 14 | 276 | 299 | 11 | 2/19 | 2/19 | 27.18 | 6.50 | 25.0 | 0 | 0 |
| First-class | 182 | 3591 | 2119 | 28 | 5/83 | | 75.67 | 3.54 | 128.2 | 1 | 0 |
| List A | 205 | 6287 | 5336 | 138 | 6/27 | 6/27 | 38.66 | 5.09 | 45.5 | 1 | 0 |
| Twenty20 | 113 | 2139 | 2333 | 91 | 3/21 | 3/21 | 25.63 | 6.54 | 23.5 | 0 | 0 |

## SAIF ZAIB

## LHB SLA R0 W0

FULL NAME: Saif Ali Zaib
BORN: May 22, 1998, High Wycombe, Buckinghamshire
SQUAD NO: 5
EDUCATION: Royal Grammar School
TEAMS: Northamptonshire
CAREER: List A: 2014

TWITTER FEED:@zaib_05
NOTES: The talented batsman was handed a three-year deal last October aged just 16. He made his Northants debut last season against New Zealand A and has impressed for the 2nd XI. He went to school at RGS Wycombe, where his innings of 230 remains a school record. In 2013 he chose to join the Northants academy, who beat off competition from Sussex and Gloucestershire

| Batting | Mat | Inns | NO | Runs | HS | Ave | SR | 100 | 50 | Ct | St |
|---|---|---|---|---|---|---|---|---|---|---|---|
| List A | 1 | - | - | - | - | - | - | - | - | 0 | 0 |

| Bowling | Mat | Balls | Runs | Wkts | BBI | BBM | Ave | Econ | SR | 5w | 10 |
|---|---|---|---|---|---|---|---|---|---|---|---|
| List A | 1 | 18 | 30 | 0 | - | - | - | 10.00 | - | 0 | 0 |

## ASHAR ZAIDI LHB SLA R0 W0

FULL NAME: Syed Ashar Ahmed Zaidi
BORN: July 13, 1981, Karachi, Pakistan
SQUAD NO: 1
HEIGHT: 5ft 7in
TEAMS: Sussex, Islamabad, Gazi Tank Cricketers
CAREER: First-class: 1999; List-A:1999; T20:2006



BEST BATTING: 202 Islamabad vs Sialkot, Sialkot, 2009
BEST BOWLING: 4-50 Islamabad vs Hyderabad, Hyderabad, 2009

CAREER HIGHLIGHTS? There have been many, including representing Pakistan U19 and A and playing county cricket in England
BEST PLAYER IN COUNTY CRICKET? Ed Joyce, Steve Magoffin
TIP FOR THE TOP? Harry Finch, Haseeb Hameed
MOST MARKED CHARACTERISTIC? Gutsy
CRICKETING HEROES? Saeed Anwar, Brian Lara
CRICKET RULE YOU'D CHANGE? No bouncers
COACHING TIP? Keep a still head and watch the ball all the way
IF YOU WEREN'T A CRICKETER? Air-force pilot
FAVOURITE TV? Friends
ACCOMPLISHMENTS? Having a lovely family
PET HATE? No pets allowed
TWITTER FEED: @Asharzaidi1981

| Batting | Mat | Inns | NO | Runs | HS | Ave | SR | 100 | 50 | Ct | St |
|---|---|---|---|---|---|---|---|---|---|---|---|
| First-class | 100 | 162 | 12 | 5512 | 202 | 36.74 | | 11 | 28 | 79 | 0 |
| List A | 77 | 73 | 8 | 2349 | 141 | 36.13 | | 4 | 11 | 28 | 0 |
| Twenty20 | 15 | 14 | 3 | 215 | 42* | 19.54 | 122.15 | 0 | 0 | 4 | 0 |
| **Bowling** | **Mat** | **Balls** | **Runs** | **Wkts** | **BBI** | **BBM** | **Ave** | **Econ** | **SR** | **5w** | **10** |
| First-class | 100 | 4625 | 2238 | 78 | 4/50 | | 28.69 | 2.90 | 59.2 | 0 | 0 |
| List A | 77 | 2459 | 1706 | 59 | 4/39 | 4/39 | 28.91 | 4.16 | 41.6 | 0 | 0 |
| Twenty20 | 15 | 192 | 275 | 7 | 3/32 | 3/32 | 39.28 | 8.59 | 27.4 | 0 | 0 |

The World's Best Cricket Magazin

# ALLOUTCRICKET

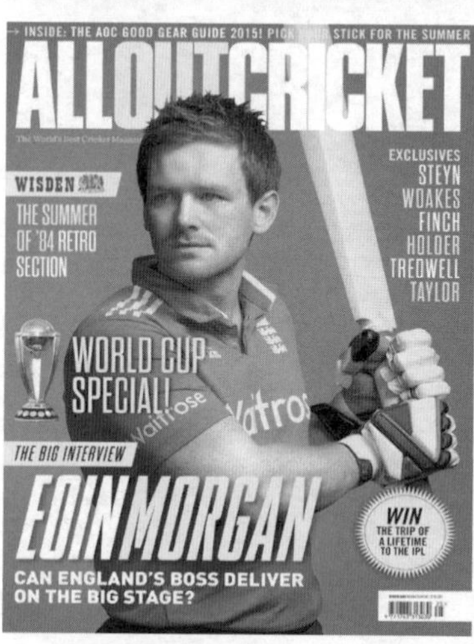


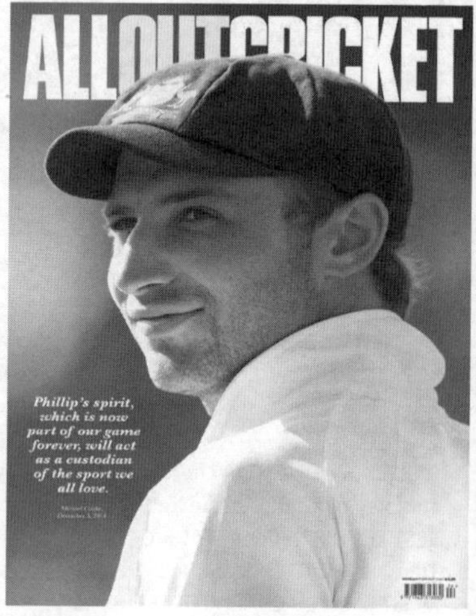

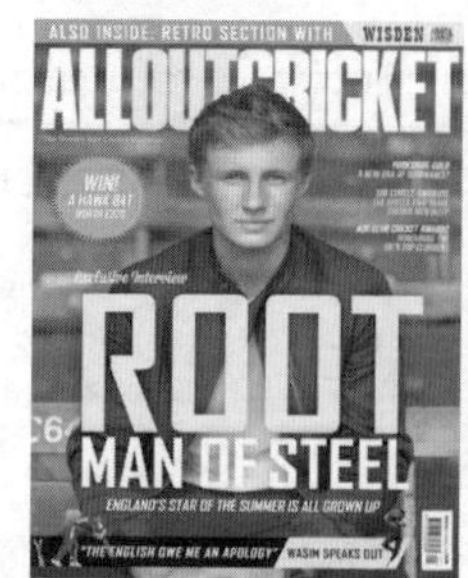


*Now includes bespoke Wisden section every month*

**GOLDEN SUMMERS**

*in association with*

**WISDEN**

Visit **www.aocsubs.com**

England
Women

# ENGLAND WOMEN

CAPTAIN: Charlotte Edwards
HEAD OF PERFORMANCE: Paul Shaw

## 2015 SUMMER FIXTURES

July 21
England Women vs Australia Women
1st Royal London ODI
Taunton

July 23
England Women vs Australia Women
2nd Royal London ODI
Bristol

July 26
England Women vs Australia Women
3rd Royal London ODI
Worcester

August 11-14
England Women vs Australia Women
Kia Test
Canterbury

August 26
England Women vs Australia Women
1st NatWest International T20
Chelmsford

August 28
England Women vs Australia Women
2nd NatWest International T20
Hove

August 31
England Women vs Australia Women
3rd NatWest International T20
Cardiff

# TAMMY BEAUMONT RHB WK

FULL NAME: Tamsin Tilley Beaumont
BORN: March 11, 1991, Dover, Kent
SQUAD NO: 12
HEIGHT: 5ft 3in
NICKNAME: Tambo
EDUCATION: Sir Roger Manwood's School; Loughborough University
TEAMS: England Women, Kent Women
CAREER: Test: 2013; ODI: 2009; T20I: 2009



BEST ODI BATTING: 44 England vs India, Taunton, 2012

FAMILY TIES? My father and brother played at our local cricket club, Sandwich Town
CAREER HIGHLIGHTS? Making my England debut, winning the Ashes in 2013, and being Player of the Match vs New Zealand in Barbados, 2013
BEST PLAYER IN COUNTY CRICKET? Charlotte Edwards
CRICKETING HEROES? Ricky Ponting – classy batter with a lot of fight. AB de Villiers – serious ability and exciting to watch
NON-CRICKETING HEROES? Tanni Grey-Thompson – am incredible athlete and inspiratio
CRICKET RULE YOU'D CHANGE? No balls should be free hits in Test matches too
IF YOU WEREN'T A CRICKETER? Ski instructor or rep in Whistler, Canada
IF YOU COULD BE SOMEONE ELSE FOR A DAY? The President of the United States
DESERT ISLAND DISC? James Bay – Hold Back The River
FAVOURITE TV? Grey's Anatomy or Game Of Thrones
LEAST FAVOURITE TV? EastEnders, Hollyoaks or any soap
PET HATE? People who don't try but make excuses when there's no change
SURPRISING FACT? I was National Schools Gymnastics Champion as a girl
TWITTER FEED: @Tammy_Beaumont

| Batting | Mat | Inns | NO | Runs | HS | Ave | SR | 100 | 50 | Ct | St |
|---|---|---|---|---|---|---|---|---|---|---|---|
| Tests | 2 | 3 | 0 | 25 | 12 | 8.33 | 35.71 | 0 | 0 | 1 | 0 |
| ODIs | 23 | 16 | 4 | 207 | 44 | 17.25 | 42.24 | 0 | 0 | 6 | 4 |
| T20Is | 33 | 19 | 3 | 133 | 29* | 8.31 | 66.16 | 0 | 0 | 7 | 4 |
| **Bowling** | **Mat** | **Balls** | **Runs** | **Wkts** | **BBI** | **BBM** | **Ave** | **Econ** | **SR** | **5w** | **10** |
| Tests | 2 | - | - | - | - | - | - | - | - | - | - |
| ODIs | 23 | - | - | - | - | - | - | - | - | - | - |
| T20Is | 33 | - | - | - | - | - | - | - | - | - | - |

## KATHERINE BRUNT RHB RFM

FULL NAME: Katherine Helen Brunt
BORN: July 2, 1985, Barnsley, Yorkshire
SQUAD NO: 26
HEIGHT: 5ft 5in
NICKNAME: Brunty, Nunny
EDUCATION: Penistone Grammar School
TEAMS: England Women, Yorkshire Women
CAREER: Test: 2004; ODI: 2005; T20I: 2005

BEST ODI BATTING: 26 England vs New Zealand, Mount Maunganui, 2015
BEST ODI BOWLING: 5-18 England vs Australia, Wormsley, 2011

CAREER HIGHLIGHTS? There are too many! Winning the Ashes in 2005 was probably my favourite, and also the whole of 2009 as we won everything including an Ashes and both the ODI and T20 world cups
MOST MARKED CHARACTERISTIC? My aggression during games! I'm not like that off the pitch though
CRICKETING HEROES? Curtly Ambrose and Darren Gough. Darren is who I modelled my action on and Curtly was very cool
NON-CRICKETING HEROES? My dad. He worked 25 years down the pit and ran marathons regularly for fun. He used to run to the pit and back every day which was about 11 miles!
IF YOU WEREN'T A CRICKETER? I'd be a UFC cage fighter!
DESERT ISLAND DISC? The Notorious B.I.G – Greatest Hits
SURPRISING FACT? I'm a softy at heart
FANTASY SLIP CORDON? Keeper: The Notorious B.I.G, 1st: Me, 2nd: Curtly Ambrose, 3rd: Sandra Bullock, Gully: Beyoncé
TWITTER FEED: @KBrunt26

| Batting | Mat | Inns | NO | Runs | HS | Ave | SR | 100 | 50 | Ct | St |
|---|---|---|---|---|---|---|---|---|---|---|---|
| Tests | 9 | 11 | 4 | 110 | 52 | 15.71 | 26.50 | 0 | 1 | 2 | 0 |
| ODIs | 79 | 35 | 10 | 277 | 26 | 11.08 | 78.02 | 0 | 0 | 19 | 0 |
| T20Is | 47 | 19 | 11 | 105 | 35 | 13.12 | 99.05 | 0 | 0 | 11 | 0 |
| **Bowling** | **Mat** | **Balls** | **Runs** | **Wkts** | **BBI** | **BBM** | **Ave** | **Econ** | **SR** | **5w** | **10** |
| Tests | 9 | 1722 | 707 | 34 | 6/69 | 9/111 | 20.79 | 2.46 | 50.6 | 2 | 0 |
| ODIs | 79 | 3916 | 2175 | 96 | 5/18 | 5/18 | 22.65 | 3.33 | 40.7 | 3 | 0 |
| T20Is | 47 | 1026 | 828 | 46 | 3/6 | 3/6 | 18.00 | 4.84 | 22.3 | 0 | 0 |

# KATE CROSS RHB RMF

FULL NAME: Kathryn Laura Cross
BORN: October 3, 1991, Manchester
SQUAD NO: 26
HEIGHT: 5ft 8in
NICKNAME: Crossy, Sunny
EDUCATION: Bury Grammar School; University of Leeds
TEAMS: England Women, Lancashire Women
CAREER: Test: 2014; ODI:2013; T20I 2013

BEST ODI BATTING: 4* England vs India, Scarborough, 2014
BEST ODI BOWLING: 5-24 England vs New Zealand, Lincoln, 2015

FAMILY TIES? My brother Bobby was a professional cricketer for a season at Lancashire. My sister Jennifer also played cricket for Lancashire for a few seasons
MOST MARKED CHARACTERISTIC? My sarcasm or my poor sense of humour. And of course my beaming smile – I am a northerner after all
SUPERSTITIONS? I have to leave my bat in the crease until the umpire says 'over'. And I can't turn right at the top of my run-up, it has to be left
NON-CRICKETING HEROES? My dad – as a former professional footballer himself he is on hand with advice and knowledge for me whenever I need it
CRICKET RULE YOU'D CHANGE? It cannot be played in less than 15 degrees. And there should be an equivalent of a 'free hit' for bowlers. Not sure how that would work though
IF YOU WEREN'T A CRICKETER? Forensic psychologist, or primary school teacher
ACCOMPLISHMENTS? I still hold the record for longest tennis ball throw in my school
PET HATE? I hate it when plugs are switched on and nothing is plugged in
SURPRISING FACT? I can make a three-leaf clover with my tongue
TWITTER FEED: @katecross16

| Batting | Mat | Inns | NO | Runs | HS | Ave | SR | 100 | 50 | Ct | St |
|---|---|---|---|---|---|---|---|---|---|---|---|
| Tests | 2 | 4 | 1 | 9 | 4 | 3.00 | 16.07 | 0 | 0 | 0 | 0 |
| ODIs | 9 | 3 | 2 | 5 | 4* | 5.00 | 35.71 | 0 | 0 | 2 | 0 |
| T20Is | 4 | - | - | - | - | - | - | - | - | 0 | 0 |
| **Bowling** | **Mat** | **Balls** | **Runs** | **Wkts** | **BBI** | **BBM** | **Ave** | **Econ** | **SR** | **5w** | **10** |
| Tests | 2 | 422 | 141 | 12 | 3/29 | 6/70 | 11.75 | 2.00 | 35.1 | 0 | 0 |
| ODIs | 9 | 414 | 301 | 13 | 5/24 | 5/24 | 23.15 | 4.36 | 31.8 | 1 | 0 |
| T20Is | 4 | 72 | 83 | 3 | 2/27 | 2/27 | 27.66 | 6.91 | 24.0 | 0 | 0 |

## JODIE DIBBLE RHB LMF

FULL NAME: Jodie Marie Dibble
BORN: September 17, 1994, Exeter, Devon
SQUAD NO: TBC
HEIGHT: 5ft 10in
NICKNAME: Dibbs
EDUCATION: St John's School; Taunton School
TEAMS: England Women, Berkshire Women, Devon Women
CAREER: T20I: 2014

---

FAMILY TIES? My brother Adam plays for Somerset
CAREER HIGHLIGHTS? The World T20 final in Bangladesh, 2014
TIP FOR THE TOP? Alli Kelly
SUPERSTITIONS? Left pad before right pad. And I have lucky pants!
NON-CRICKETING HEROES? Jonny Wilkinson, Davina McCall, David Walliams
CRICKET RULE YOU'D CHANGE? If the ball would have hit the stumps then it should be out, no matter where it pitches
COACHING TIP? Fielding – find a ready position that works for you. And visualise picking the ball up and hitting the stumps
IF YOU WEREN'T A CRICKETER? A police officer – Officer Dibble!
IF YOU COULD BE SOMEONE ELSE FOR A DAY? Duchess of Cambridge
DESERT ISLAND DISC? Brandon Flowers – Flamingo
FAVOURITE TV? Gavin And Stacey
SURPRISING FACT? I can tap dance
FANTASY SLIP CORDON? Keeper: Michael McIntyre, 1st: Prince Harry; 2nd: Davina McCall, 3rd: Eddie Redmayne, Gully: Miranda Hart
TWITTER FEED: @jodiedibble48

| Batting | Mat | Inns | NO | Runs | HS | Ave | SR | 100 | 50 | Ct | St |
|---|---|---|---|---|---|---|---|---|---|---|---|
| T20Is | 1 | 1 | 0 | 0 | 0 | 0.00 | 0.00 | 0 | 0 | 0 | 0 |
| **Bowling** | **Mat** | **Balls** | **Runs** | **Wkts** | **BBI** | **BBM** | **Ave** | **Econ** | **SR** | **5w** | **10** |
| T20Is | 1 | 12 | 21 | 0 | - | - | - | 10.50 | - | 0 | 0 |

# CHARLOTTE EDWARDS RHB LB

FULL NAME: Charlotte Marie Edwards
BORN: December 17, 1979, Huntingdon
SQUAD NO: 23
HEIGHT: 5ft 9in
NICKNAME: Lottie
EDUCATION: Abbey College
TEAMS: England Women, Kent Women
CAREER: Test: 1996; ODI: 1997; T20I: 2004



BEST ODI BATTING: 173* England vs Ireland, Pune, 1997
BEST ODI BOWLING: 4-30 England vs Sri Lanka, Colombo, 2010

FAMILY TIES? My dad Clive played Minor Counties for Huntingdonshire
CAREER HIGHLIGHTS? The two World Cup wins in 2009 and the Ashes win 2013-14
MOST MARKED CHARACTERISTIC? My unique running style
CRICKETING HEROES? Steve Waugh – successful captain who always led from the front
NON-CRICKETING HEROES? Steffi Graf was my first female role model when growing up
IF YOU COULD BE SOMEONE ELSE FOR A DAY? The Queen
DESERT ISLAND DISC? Take That – Greatest Hits
FAVOURITE TV? Homes Under The Hammer
ACCOMPLISHMENTS? Winning Ready Steady Cook against Mike Gatting
PET HATE? Laziness is something I really get frustrated
SURPRISING FACT? I played in the school brass band!
FANTASY SLIP CORDON? Keeper: Clare Balding, 1st: Dawn French (both very funny and would keep me entertained), 3rd: Steve Waugh (to pick his brains) 4th: Gary Barlow (to maybe sing a few tunes!)
TWITTER FEED: @Lottie2323

| Batting | Mat | Inns | NO | Runs | HS | Ave | SR | 100 | 50 | Ct | St |
|---|---|---|---|---|---|---|---|---|---|---|---|
| Tests | 22 | 41 | 5 | 1645 | 117 | 45.69 | | 4 | 9 | 10 | 0 |
| ODIs | 185 | 174 | 23 | 5812 | 173* | 38.49 | | 9 | 45 | 50 | 0 |
| T20Is | 84 | 82 | 13 | 2299 | 92* | 33.31 | 106.68 | 0 | 10 | 14 | 0 |
| **Bowling** | **Mat** | **Balls** | **Runs** | **Wkts** | **BBI** | **BBM** | **Ave** | **Econ** | **SR** | **5w** | **10** |
| Tests | 22 | 1118 | 577 | 12 | 2/28 | 2/54 | 48.08 | 3.09 | 93.1 | 0 | 0 |
| ODIs | 185 | 1627 | 1174 | 54 | 4/30 | 4/30 | 21.74 | 4.32 | 30.1 | 0 | 0 |
| T20Is | 84 | 303 | 330 | 9 | 3/21 | 3/21 | 36.66 | 6.53 | 33.6 | 0 | 0 |

## GEORGIA ELWISS RHB RMF

FULL NAME: Georgia Amanda Elwiss
BORN: May 31, 1991, Wolverhampton
SQUAD NO: 34
HEIGHT: 5ft 8in
NICKNAME: GG, Gelwiss
EDUCATION: Wolverhampton Girls High School; Loughborough University
TEAMS: England Women, Sussex Women, Staffordshire Women
CAREER: ODI: 2011; T20I: 2011

BEST ODI BATTING: 10 England vs India, Taunton, 2012
BEST ODI BOWLING: 3-17 England vs India, Wormsley, 2012

CAREER HIGHLIGHTS? Winning the Player of the Series award in 2012 and retaining the Ashes in 2014
BEST PLAYER IN COUNTY CRICKET? Sarah Taylor or Charlotte Edwards
TIP FOR THE TOP? Georgia Adams, Georgia Hennessy, Nat Sciver
MOST MARKED CHARACTERISTIC? My never-ending smile!
SUPERSTITIONS? I have to put my left pad and left glove on before my right ones
CRICKETING HEROES? Allan Donald – because he ran in and bowled fast. AB de Villiers – because he can win games from any situation
CRICKET RULE YOU'D CHANGE? You can't be out first ball!
COACHING TIP? Relax, enjoy it ... and imagine the batter to be 2ft tall when you're bowling!
IF YOU WEREN'T A CRICKETER? An astronaut on the moon!
IF YOU COULD BE SOMEONE ELSE FOR A DAY? Cheryl Cole
PET HATE? Traffic lights!
FANTASY SLIP CORDON? Keeper: Sarah Taylor (because she would catch everything and because she's my best mate), 1st: Me, 2nd: Jenny Gunn (for her bants), 3rd: Robert Downey Jr (for his comedy), Gully: George W Bush (I'd like a chat...)
TWITTER FEED: @gelwiss

| Batting | Mat | Inns | NO | Runs | HS | Ave | SR | 100 | 50 | Ct | St |
|---|---|---|---|---|---|---|---|---|---|---|---|
| ODIs | 10 | 2 | 1 | 12 | 10 | 12.00 | 50.00 | 0 | 0 | 2 | 0 |
| T20Is | 8 | - | - | - | - | - | - | - | - | 0 | 0 |
| **Bowling** | **Mat** | **Balls** | **Runs** | **Wkts** | **BBI** | **BBM** | **Ave** | **Econ** | **SR** | **5w** | **10** |
| ODIs | 10 | 504 | 277 | 11 | 3/17 | 3/17 | 25.18 | 3.29 | 45.8 | 0 | 0 |
| T20Is | 8 | 115 | 106 | 5 | 2/30 | 2/30 | 21.20 | 5.53 | 23.0 | 0 | 0 |

# TASH FARRANT LHB LM

FULL NAME: Natasha Eleni Farrant
BORN: May 29, 1996
SQUAD NO: 53
HEIGHT: 5ft 6in
NICKNAME: Faz
EDUCATION: Sevenoaks School
TEAMS: England Women, Kent Women
CAREER: ODI: 2013; T20I: 2013



BEST ODI BATTING: 1* England vs West Indies, Port of Spain, 2013
BEST ODI BOWLING: 1-14 England vs West Indies, Port of Spain, 2013

CAREER HIGHLIGHTS? My England debut two summers ago against Pakistan, winning back-to-back Ashes, being part of the team that won the T20 game in Hobart to retain the Ashes!
BEST PLAYER IN COUNTY CRICKET? Still has got to be Charlotte Edwards!
TIP FOR THE TOP? Grace Gibbs
MOST MARKED CHARACTERISTIC? My outrageously loud laugh
SUPERSTITIONS? I have to touch the ground at the crease on the way back to my mark – I wouldn't be able to bowl if I didn't do it!
CRICKETING HEROES? Wasim Akram – the best lefty ever!
CRICKET RULE YOU'D CHANGE? All of the rules that favour the batsmen!
COACHING TIP? If you want to bowl an outswinger bowl it at 100 per cent, an inswinger-bowl at 90 per cent of your full pace (for lefties only)
IF YOU COULD BE SOMEONE ELSE FOR A DAY? Danni Wyatt – I'd love to know what's going on in her head...
SURPRISING FACT? I have my Grade 6 singing. No idea how though!
FANTASY SLIP CORDON? Keeper: Jack Whitehall, 1st: Fearne Cotton, 2nd: Thierry Henry, 3rd and Gully: My brothers
TWITTER FEED: @tashfarrant

| Batting | Mat | Inns | NO | Runs | HS | Ave | SR | 100 | 50 | Ct | St |
|---|---|---|---|---|---|---|---|---|---|---|---|
| ODIs | 1 | 1 | 1 | 1 | 1* | - | 12.50 | 0 | 0 | 0 | 0 |
| T20Is | 7 | 1 | 1 | 1 | 1* | - | 100.00 | 0 | 0 | 0 | 0 |
| **Bowling** | **Mat** | **Balls** | **Runs** | **Wkts** | **BBI** | **BBM** | **Ave** | **Econ** | **SR** | **5w** | **10** |
| ODIs | 1 | 42 | 14 | 1 | 1/14 | 1/14 | 14.00 | 2.00 | 42.0 | 0 | 0 |
| T20Is | 7 | 161 | 138 | 4 | 2/15 | 2/15 | 34.50 | 5.14 | 40.2 | 0 | 0 |

## LYDIA GREENWAY LHB OB

FULL NAME: Lydia Sophie Greenway
BORN: August 6, 1985, Farnborough, Kent
SQUAD NO: 20
HEIGHT: 5ft 9in
EDUCATION: Hayes School; Loughborough College
TEAMS: England Women, Kent Women
CAREER: Test: 2003; ODI: 2003; T20I: 2004

BEST ODI BATTING: 125* England vs South Africa, Potchefstroom, 2011

CAREER HIGHLIGHTS? Winning the two World Cups in 2009 and Ashes wins
BEST PLAYER IN COUNTY CRICKET? Sarah Bartlett
TIP FOR THE TOP? Emma Lamb
MOST MARKED CHARACTERISTIC? I've got a birthmark on my toe
CRICKETING HEROES? Adam Gilchrist and Marcus Trecothick – I used to love watching how freely they played
NON-CRICKETING HEROES? My family
CRICKET RULE YOU'D CHANGE? Free hits for all no-balls
IF YOU WEREN'T A CRICKETER? Maybe a PE teacher
IF YOU COULD BE SOMEONE ELSE FOR A DAY? The Queen – just to have a nose around the palace!
DESERT ISLAND DISC? Hits of the '80s
FAVOURITE TV? Friends
ACCOMPLISHMENTS? Cycling to Paris for charity
PET HATE? Rudeness and bad manners
TWITTER FEED: @lydiagreenway

| Batting | Mat | Inns | NO | Runs | HS | Ave | SR | 100 | 50 | Ct | St |
|---|---|---|---|---|---|---|---|---|---|---|---|
| Tests | 13 | 22 | 1 | 324 | 70 | 15.42 | 30.56 | 0 | 2 | 14 | 0 |
| ODIs | 121 | 107 | 26 | 2413 | 125* | 29.79 | 62.43 | 1 | 11 | 51 | 0 |
| T20Is | 77 | 67 | 21 | 1141 | 80* | 24.80 | 97.60 | 0 | 2 | 47 | 0 |
| **Bowling** | **Mat** | **Balls** | **Runs** | **Wkts** | **BBI** | **BBM** | **Ave** | **Econ** | **SR** | **5w** | **10** |
| Tests | 13 | - | - | - | - | - | - | - | - | - | - |
| ODIs | 121 | - | - | - | - | - | - | - | - | - | - |
| T20Is | 77 | - | - | - | - | - | - | - | - | - | - |

## REBECCA GRUNDY LHB SLA

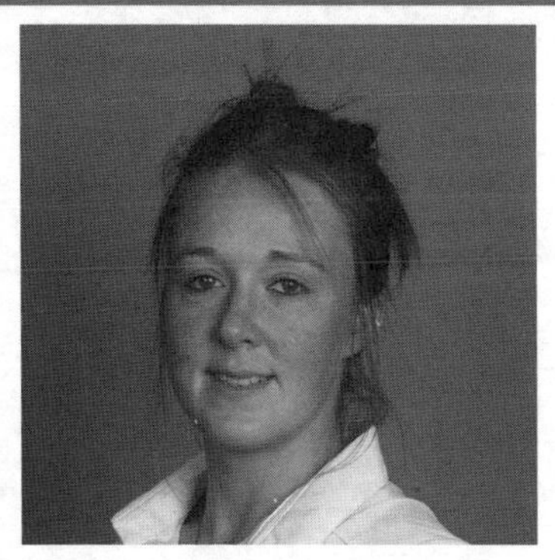

FULL NAME: Rebecca Louise Grundy
BORN: July 12, 1990, Solihull, Warwickshire
SQUAD NO: tbc
HEIGHT: 5ft 6in
NICKNAME: Grunners, Carol
EDUCATION: The Sixth Form College, Solihull; Loughborough College
TEAMS: England Women, Warwickshire Women
CAREER: T20I: 2014



BEST ODI BATTING: 1* England vs New Zealand, Mount Maunganui, 2015
BEST ODI BOWLING: 3-36 England vs New Zealand, Lincoln, 2015

FAMILY TIES? None, full of armchair cricketers!
CAREER HIGHLIGHTS? Making my debut in the 2014 World T20
BEST PLAYER IN COUNTY CRICKET? Charlotte Edwards
TIP FOR THE TOP? Emma Lamb, Hannah Jones, Bryony Smith
MOST MARKED CHARACTERISTIC? Finding cow corner
IF YOU WEREN'T A CRICKETER? Campervan and the open road
IF YOU COULD BE SOMEONE ELSE FOR A DAY? David Attenborough
ACCOMPLISHMENTS? Conquering what was the world's highest commercial bungee jump in South Africa
PET HATE? Lateness. Who likes to be sat on the phone pretending like you're Miss Popular while everyone else is missing! No, this has never happened to me… ever
SURPRISING FACT? I can speak relatively fluent Afrikaans
FANTASY SLIP CORDON? Keeper: Mr Tickle (long arms), 1st: Jenny Gunn, 2nd: Georgia Elwiss, 3rd: Me(1-3 slip for conversation), 4th: Channing Tatum (just because), Gully: Shaquille O'Neal
TWITTER FEED: @grundy_becky

| Batting | Mat | Inns | NO | Runs | HS | Ave | SR | 100 | 50 | Ct | St |
|---|---|---|---|---|---|---|---|---|---|---|---|
| ODIs | 4 | 2 | 2 | 2 | 1* | - | 50.00 | 0 | 0 | 0 | 0 |
| T20Is | 6 | 1 | 1 | 1 | 1* | - | 100.00 | 0 | 0 | 2 | 0 |
| **Bowling** | **Mat** | **Balls** | **Runs** | **Wkts** | **BBI** | **BBM** | **Ave** | **Econ** | **SR** | **5w** | **10** |
| ODIs | 4 | 240 | 138 | 7 | 3/36 | 3/36 | 19.71 | 3.45 | 34.2 | 0 | 0 |
| T20Is | 6 | 144 | 105 | 6 | 2/13 | 2/13 | 17.50 | 4.37 | 24.0 | 0 | 0 |

## JENNY GUNN RHB RMF

FULL NAME: Jennifer Louise Gunn
BORN: May 9, 1986, Nottingham
SQUAD NO: 24
HEIGHT: 5ft 10in
NICKNAME: Chuckie
EDUCATION: Rushcliffe School
TEAMS: England Women, Nottinghamshire Women, South Australia Women
CAREER: Test: 2004; ODI: 2004; T20I: 2004

BEST ODI BATTING: 73 England vs New Zealand, Taunton, 2007
BEST ODI BOWLING: 5-22 England vs Pakistan, Louth, 2013

FAMILY TIES? I would like to say I'm related to the great Gunns of Nottinghamshire cricket but I'm not
CAREER HIGHLIGHTS? Winning two World Cups and five Ashes
MOST MARKED CHARACTERISTIC? That I look like I throw the ball when I bowl
SUPERSTITIONS? Right pad on first and I walk round the ground before an England game with Dani Hazell
CRICKETING HEROES? Andrew Symonds – he could bat, bowl and field. Exciting player to watch and he's from the mighty Midlands
NON-CRICKETING HEROES? My dad – he played for Nottingham Forest in the European Cup days and always taught me to push myself, be competitive but have fun all the way
IF YOU WEREN'T A CRICKETER? Singing and dancing in the West End, or a chef
IF YOU COULD BE SOMEONE ELSE FOR A DAY? Any racing driver
LEAST FAVOURITE TV? I hate The Only Way Is Essex and Big Brother
ACCOMPLISHMENTS? 25m swimming badge
PET HATE? Rude people. Manners cost nothing

| Batting | Mat | Inns | NO | Runs | HS | Ave | SR | 100 | 50 | Ct | St |
|---|---|---|---|---|---|---|---|---|---|---|---|
| Tests | 11 | 19 | 2 | 391 | 62* | 23.00 | 30.38 | 0 | 1 | 6 | 0 |
| ODIs | 125 | 96 | 24 | 1435 | 73 | 19.93 | 56.16 | 0 | 5 | 43 | 0 |
| T20Is | 83 | 55 | 14 | 638 | 69 | 15.56 | 101.26 | 0 | 1 | 50 | 0 |
| **Bowling** | **Mat** | **Balls** | **Runs** | **Wkts** | **BBI** | **BBM** | **Ave** | **Econ** | **SR** | **5w** | **10** |
| Tests | 11 | 2189 | 645 | 29 | 5/19 | 5/59 | 22.24 | 1.76 | 75.4 | 1 | 0 |
| ODIs | 125 | 5082 | 3181 | 115 | 5/22 | 5/22 | 27.66 | 3.75 | 44.1 | 2 | 0 |
| T20Is | 83 | 965 | 1010 | 55 | 5/18 | 5/18 | 18.36 | 6.27 | 17.5 | 1 | 0 |

# DANIELLE HAZELL RHB OB

FULL NAME: Danielle Hazell
BORN: May 13, 1988, Durham
SQUAD NO: 17
HEIGHT: 5ft 3in
NICKNAME: Pet
EDUCATION: Deerness Valley School
TEAMS: England Women, Yorkshire Women
CAREER: Test: 2011; ODI: 2009; T20I: 2009



BEST ODI BATTING: 24* England vs Ireland, Kibworth, 2010
BEST ODI BOWLING: 3-22 England vs Sri Lanka, Colombo, 2010

CAREER HIGHLIGHTS? My England debut in 2009 in the West Indies
MOST MARKED CHARACTERISTIC? Northern accent
CRICKETING HEROES? Ricky Ponting
NON-CRICKETING HEROES? Alan Shearer
IF YOU WEREN'T A CRICKETER? Property tycoon
DESERT ISLAND DISC? Maria McKee – Show Me Heaven
FAVOURITE TV? Neighbours
FANTASY SLIP CORDON? Keeper: Me, 1st: Peter Andre, 2nd: Gavin Henson, 3rd: Alan Shearer, Gully: My mam
TWITTER FEED: @dani1788

| Batting | Mat | Inns | NO | Runs | HS | Ave | SR | 100 | 50 | Ct | St |
|---|---|---|---|---|---|---|---|---|---|---|---|
| Tests | 3 | 5 | 1 | 28 | 15 | 7.00 | 17.17 | 0 | 0 | 1 | 0 |
| ODIs | 39 | 20 | 4 | 215 | 24* | 13.43 | 84.98 | 0 | 0 | 6 | 0 |
| T20Is | 60 | 24 | 8 | 160 | 18* | 10.00 | 86.48 | 0 | 0 | 8 | 0 |
| **Bowling** | **Mat** | **Balls** | **Runs** | **Wkts** | **BBI** | **BBM** | **Ave** | **Econ** | **SR** | **5w** | **10** |
| Tests | 3 | 390 | 204 | 2 | 2/32 | 2/52 | 102.00 | 3.13 | 195.0 | 0 | 0 |
| ODIs | 39 | 1820 | 1187 | 35 | 3/22 | 3/22 | 33.91 | 3.91 | 52.0 | 0 | 0 |
| T20Is | 60 | 1368 | 1170 | 65 | 4/12 | 4/12 | 18.00 | 5.13 | 21.0 | 0 | 0 |

## AMY JONES RHB WK

FULL NAME: Amy Ellen Jones
BORN: June 13, 1993, Solihull, Warwickshire
SQUAD NO: 40
HEIGHT: 5ft 9in
NICKNAME: Jonesy
EDUCATION: John Willmott School; Loughborough College
TEAMS: England Women, Warwickshire Women
CAREER: ODI: 2013; T20I:2013

BEST ODI BATTING: 41 England vs Sri Lanka, Mumbai, 2013

FAMILY TIES? My younger sister played for Warwickshire U13
CAREER HIGHLIGHTS? Making my debut in the 2012 World Cup in India and scoring 41 and being a part of the Ashes-winning team in Australia last year!
BEST PLAYER IN COUNTY CRICKET? Charlotte Edwards – hits centuries for fun!
MOST MARKED CHARACTERISTIC? I'm well known for sleeping a lot, mainly when travelling. I think some of my teammates get a little jealous
CRICKETING HEROES? I have always enjoyed watching wicketkeeper/batsmen like AB de Villiers and Brendon McCullum because they are the type of players that draw people to the game – aggressive and exciting
NON-CRICKETING HEROES? Paula Radcliffe –incredible determination and commitment to her sport
IF YOU WEREN'T A CRICKETER? I would probably be trying to make it as a footballer. I played for Aston villa when I was younger but chose to concentrate on cricket
IF YOU COULD BE SOMEONE ELSE FOR A DAY? Beyoncé – I'd love to be able to sing and sell out arenas
DESERT ISLAND DISC? Ed Sheeran – X
TWITTER FEED: @amyjones313

| Batting | Mat | Inns | NO | Runs | HS | Ave | SR | 100 | 50 | Ct | St |
|---|---|---|---|---|---|---|---|---|---|---|---|
| ODIs | 4 | 2 | 0 | 45 | 41 | 22.50 | 70.31 | 0 | 0 | 1 | 0 |
| T20Is | 9 | 5 | 0 | 33 | 14 | 6.60 | 71.73 | 0 | 0 | 3 | 0 |
| **Bowling** | **Mat** | **Balls** | **Runs** | **Wkts** | **BBI** | **BBM** | **Ave** | **Econ** | **SR** | **5w** | **10** |
| ODIs | 4 | - | - | - | - | - | - | - | - | - | - |
| T20Is | 9 | - | - | - | - | - | - | - | - | - | - |

# HEATHER KNIGHT RHB RM/OB

FULL NAME: Heather Clare Knight
BORN: December 26, 1990, Plymouth
SQUAD NO: 5
HEIGHT: 5ft 7in
NICKNAME: Trev
EDUCATION: Plymstock School; Cardiff University
TEAMS: England Women, Berkshire Women
CAREER: Test: 2011; ODI: 2010; T20I: 2010

BEST ODI BATTING: 79 England vs New Zealand, Mount Maunganui, 2015
BEST ODI BOWLING: 4-47 England vs New Zealand, Mount Maunganui, 2015

FAMILY TIES? My brother played county age-group cricket for Devon and I played with him for Plymstock 1st XI
CAREER HIGHLIGHTS? Winning the Ashes and being Player of the Series in 2013
MOST MARKED CHARACTERISTIC? My webbed feet
CRICKETING HEROES? Mike Atherton – I loved his humility and the way he gritted out innings
NON-CRICKETING HEROES? Denise Lewis – she always had a smile on her face when she was competing
IF YOU COULD BE SOMEONE ELSE FOR A DAY? The Queen
DESERT ISLAND DISC? The Verve – Urban Hymns
FAVOURITE TV? Dexter
ACCOMPLISHMENTS? Getting a degree in Biomedical Sciences
FANTASY SLIP CORDON? Keeper: Miranda Hart, 1st: Me, 2nd: Tom Hardy, 3rd: Albus Dumbledore
TWITTER FEED: @heatherknight55

| Batting | Mat | Inns | NO | Runs | HS | Ave | SR | 100 | 50 | Ct | St |
|---|---|---|---|---|---|---|---|---|---|---|---|
| Tests | 4 | 8 | 0 | 198 | 157 | 24.75 | 41.86 | 1 | 0 | 4 | 0 |
| ODIs | 49 | 45 | 9 | 1012 | 79 | 28.11 | 62.12 | 0 | 7 | 12 | 0 |
| T20Is | 23 | 19 | 4 | 224 | 30 | 14.93 | 104.18 | 0 | 0 | 8 | 0 |
| **Bowling** | **Mat** | **Balls** | **Runs** | **Wkts** | **BBI** | **BBM** | **Ave** | **Econ** | **SR** | **5w** | **10** |
| Tests | 4 | 42 | 19 | 1 | 1/7 | 1/7 | 19.00 | 2.71 | 42.0 | 0 | 0 |
| ODIs | 49 | 402 | 267 | 14 | 4/47 | 4/47 | 19.07 | 3.98 | 28.7 | 0 | 0 |
| T20Is | 23 | 129 | 80 | 7 | 3/10 | 3/10 | 11.42 | 3.72 | 18.4 | 0 | 0 |

## BETH LANGSTON

## RHB RM

FULL NAME: Bethany Alicia Langston
BORN: September 6, 1992, Harold Wood, Essex
SQUAD NO: 42
HEIGHT: 5ft 7in
NICKNAME: Langers
EDUCATION: Hall Mead School; Coopers' Company and Coborn School; Loughborough University
TEAMS: England Women, Essex Women
CAREER: T20I: 2013

---

CAREER HIGHLIGHTS? Making my England debut in the West Indies in 2013 and taking a wicket
BEST PLAYER IN COUNTY CRICKET? Charlotte Edwards
TIP FOR THE TOP? Cordelia Griffith
MOST MARKED CHARACTERISTIC? Wearing glasses – I've worn them for as long as I can remember and I'm really quite blind without them!
CRICKETING HEROES? Dale Steyn – always great to watch as he bowls so quick but he also has lots of other tricks up his sleeve
NON-CRICKETING HEROES? Jo Pavey – I really admire her perseverance and dedication to her sport to win a European gold medal just ten months after giving birth
CRICKET RULE YOU'D CHANGE? One person gets to bowl their allocated overs with a Sidearm
IF YOU WEREN'T A CRICKETER? I wouldn't mind being a zookeeper as I love animals
IF YOU COULD BE SOMEONE ELSE FOR A DAY? Kate Middleton – it would be cool being a princess for the day and hanging out with the Windsors
DESERT ISLAND DISC? Red Hot Chili Peppers – Greatest Hits
ACCOMPLISHMENTS? Being selected for my primary school quiz team
SURPRISING FACT? I once got mistaken for actually playing bass guitar in a rock band
TWITTER FEED: @B_Langers92

| Batting | Mat | Inns | NO | Runs | HS | Ave | SR | 100 | 50 | Ct | St |
|---|---|---|---|---|---|---|---|---|---|---|---|
| T20Is | 2 | - | - | - | - | - | - | - | - | 1 | 0 |
| **Bowling** | **Mat** | **Balls** | **Runs** | **Wkts** | **BBI** | **BBM** | **Ave** | **Econ** | **SR** | **5w** | **10** |
| T20Is | 2 | 48 | 44 | 1 | 1/16 | 1/16 | 44.00 | 5.50 | 48.0 | 0 | 0 |

## LAURA MARSH RHB OB

FULL NAME: Laura Alexandra Marsh
BORN: December 5, 1986, Pembury, Kent
SQUAD NO: 7
HEIGHT: 5ft 5in
NICKNAME: Boggy
EDUCATION: Brighton College; Loughborough University
TEAMS: England Women; Kent Women
CAREER: Test: 2006; ODI: 2006; T20I: 2007



BEST ODI BATTING: 67 England vs Ireland, Kibworth, 2010
BEST ODI BOWLING: 5-15 England vs Pakistan, Sydney, 2009

CAREER HIGHLIGHTS? Winning the ODI and T20I World Cups in 2009 and winning the Ashes in 2008 and 2013
BEST PLAYER IN COUNTY CRICKET? Charlotte Edwards
TIP FOR THE TOP? Georgia Hennessy
MOST MARKED CHARACTERISTIC? My pin-head
CRICKETING HEROES? Jonty Rhodes – I loved his athleticism and ability in the field. AB de Villiers – there isn't anything he can't do!
NON-CRICKETING HEROES? Andy Murray, Jessica Ennis, Rory McIlroy – I enjoy watching all of them in action
CRICKET RULE YOU'D CHANGE? I would make free hits a rule across all formats of the game, for both front-foot no-balls and balls over waist height
IF YOU WEREN'T A CRICKETER? Trying to become a professional golfer
PET HATE? People who make lots of noise and don't close their mouths when they eat!
SURPRISING FACT? I was once national javelin champion
TWITTER FEED: @lauramarsh7

| Batting | Mat | Inns | NO | Runs | HS | Ave | SR | 100 | 50 | Ct | St |
|---|---|---|---|---|---|---|---|---|---|---|---|
| Tests | 6 | 8 | 0 | 110 | 55 | 13.75 | 21.91 | 0 | 1 | 4 | 0 |
| ODIs | 71 | 42 | 7 | 491 | 67 | 14.02 | 66.26 | 0 | 1 | 15 | 0 |
| T20Is | 58 | 51 | 6 | 729 | 54 | 16.20 | 99.31 | 0 | 1 | 6 | 0 |
| Bowling | Mat | Balls | Runs | Wkts | BBI | BBM | Ave | Econ | SR | 5w | 10 |
| Tests | 6 | 1289 | 475 | 14 | 3/44 | 4/83 | 33.92 | 2.21 | 92.0 | 0 | 0 |
| ODIs | 71 | 3624 | 2346 | 85 | 5/15 | 5/15 | 27.60 | 3.88 | 42.6 | 1 | 0 |
| T20Is | 58 | 1299 | 1139 | 56 | 3/17 | 3/17 | 20.33 | 5.26 | 23.1 | 0 | 0 |

## SONIA ODEDRA RHB RMF

FULL NAME: Sonia Balu Odedra
BORN: June 3, 1988, Isleworth, Middlesex
SQUAD NO: tbc
HEIGHT: 5ft 5in
NICKNAME: Son, Sonny
EDUCATION: City of Leicester School; Birmingham University
TEAMS: England Women; Nottinghamshire Women
CAREER: Test: 2014

CAREER HIGHLIGHTS? Getting my first Test cap and taking my first international wicket
BEST PLAYER IN COUNTY CRICKET? Charlotte Edwards
TIP FOR THE TOP? Georgie Boyce
CRICKETING HEROES? Freddie Flintoff – loved watching him play with a lot of passion! MS Dhoni – I like the way he is always very calm and collected
COACHING TIP? Work on getting a strong wrist for better control and swing – simply toss the ball up making sure the seam stays up and repeat more than 1,000 times
IF YOU WEREN'T A CRICKETER? Thinking about why I was not able to be a cricketer
IF YOU COULD BE SOMEONE ELSE FOR A DAY? Sachin Tendulkar
FAVOURITE TV? EastEnders
LEAST FAVOURITE TV? Coronation Street
PET HATE? Being ignored – I find it very rude
SURPRISING FACT? I got my first coaching aged 20 – I'd never had any coaching before that
FANTASY SLIP CORDON? Keeper: Batman, 1st: Bart Simpson, 2nd: Danni Wyatt, Gully: Me
TWITTER FEED: @soniaodedra

| Batting | Mat | Inns | NO | Runs | HS | Ave | SR | 100 | 50 | Ct | St |
|---|---|---|---|---|---|---|---|---|---|---|---|
| Tests | 1 | 2 | 0 | 2 | 1 | 1.00 | 5.88 | 0 | 0 | 0 | 0 |
| **Bowling** | **Mat** | **Balls** | **Runs** | **Wkts** | **BBI** | **BBM** | **Ave** | **Econ** | **SR** | **5w** | **10** |
| Tests | 1 | 162 | 50 | 1 | 1/25 | 1/50 | 50.00 | 1.85 | 162.0 | 0 | 0 |

## NATALIE SCIVER RHB RM

FULL NAME: Natalie Ruth Sciver
BORN: August 20, 1992, Tokyo, Japan
SQUAD NO: 39
HEIGHT: 5ft 10in
NICKNAME: Seive
EDUCATION: Epsom College; Loughborough University
TEAMS: England Women, Surrey Women
CAREER: Test: 2014; ODI: 2013; T20I: 2013

BEST ODI BATTING: 65* England vs New Zealand, Lincoln, 2015
BEST ODI BOWLING: 3-19 England vs West Indies, Port of Spain, 2013

CAREER HIGHLIGHTS? Winning back the Ashes in 2013 and then regaining them in Australia the following winter
CRICKETING HEROES? Freddie Flintoff – he could bat, bowl and field
NON-CRICKETING HEROES? David Beckham – I used to support Manchester United because of him. Such a gentleman
CRICKET RULE YOU'D CHANGE? No leg-side wides! The day I don't bowl a leg-side wide in a game will be a good one!
IF YOU WEREN'T A CRICKETER? I'd love to be a dancer, maybe a backing dancer
ACCOMPLISHMENTS? I got into a youth team at Chelsea FC, and did pretty well at slalom snowboarding when I lived in Poland
PET HATE? People eating with their mouth open. My brother used to do it all the time
SURPRISING FACT? I was born in Japan
FANTASY SLIP CORDON? Keeper: Roger Federer, 1st: Beyoncé, 2nd: Rebel Wilson, 3rd: Me, Gully: Chris Brown
TWITTER FEED: @natsciver

| Batting | Mat | Inns | NO | Runs | HS | Ave | SR | 100 | 50 | Ct | St |
|---|---|---|---|---|---|---|---|---|---|---|---|
| Tests | 2 | 4 | 0 | 85 | 49 | 21.25 | 31.13 | 0 | 0 | 1 | 0 |
| ODIs | 17 | 11 | 4 | 271 | 65* | 38.71 | 97.13 | 0 | 2 | 6 | 0 |
| T20Is | 25 | 22 | 5 | 283 | 37* | 16.64 | 89.27 | 0 | 0 | 14 | 0 |
| **Bowling** | **Mat** | **Balls** | **Runs** | **Wkts** | **BBI** | **BBM** | **Ave** | **Econ** | **SR** | **5w** | **10** |
| Tests | 2 | 143 | 61 | 1 | 1/30 | 1/30 | 61.00 | 2.55 | 143.0 | 0 | 0 |
| ODIs | 17 | 310 | 228 | 11 | 3/19 | 3/19 | 20.72 | 4.41 | 28.1 | 0 | 0 |
| T20Is | 25 | 329 | 348 | 19 | 4/21 | 4/21 | 18.31 | 6.34 | 17.3 | 0 | 0 |

# ANYA SHRUBSOLE RHB RFM

ENGLAND WOMEN

FULL NAME: Anya Shrubsole
BORN: December 7, 1991, Bath
SQUAD NO: 41
HEIGHT: 5ft 10in
NICKNAME: Hoof
EDUCATION: Hayesfield School; Loughborough University
TEAMS: England Women, Somerset Women
CAREER: Test: 2013; ODI: 2008; T20I: 2008

BEST ODI BATTING: 29 England vs New Zealand, Mount Maunganui, 2015
BEST ODI BOWLING: 5-17 England vs South Africa, Cuttack, 2013

FAMILY TIES? Dad played Minor Counties cricket
CAREER HIGHLIGHTS? Making my international debut, winning the 2009 World Cup in Australia, back- to-back Ashes series wins
MOST MARKED CHARACTERISTIC? Using my feet to field the ball when bowling
CRICKETING HEROES? Michael Holding (or any of the West Indian quicks)! I'm not sure a seam attack of this quality and pace will ever be seen again
NON-CRICKETING HEROES? Sir Steve Redgrave – overcame a lot to achieve what he has in an immensely tough sport
IF YOU COULD BE SOMEONE ELSE FOR A DAY? The Queen
DESERT ISLAND DISC? Stevie Wonder – Songs In The Key Of Life
PET HATE? Lack of manners – they cost nothing
SURPRISING FACT? I can play the flute pretty well
FANTASY SLIP CORDON? Keeper: Michael McIntyre, 1st: Usain Bolt, 2nd: Myself, 3rd: Ryan Gosling, Gully: Michael Holding
TWITTER FEED: @Anya_Shrubsole

| Batting | Mat | Inns | NO | Runs | HS | Ave | SR | 100 | 50 | Ct | St |
|---|---|---|---|---|---|---|---|---|---|---|---|
| Tests | 3 | 5 | 0 | 30 | 14 | 6.00 | 28.03 | 0 | 0 | 1 | 0 |
| ODIs | 28 | 9 | 4 | 89 | 29 | 17.80 | 97.80 | 0 | 0 | 9 | 0 |
| T20Is | 36 | 6 | 3 | 13 | 10 | 4.33 | 108.33 | 0 | 0 | 10 | 0 |
| **Bowling** | **Mat** | **Balls** | **Runs** | **Wkts** | **BBI** | **BBM** | **Ave** | **Econ** | **SR** | **5w** | **10** |
| Tests | 3 | 708 | 269 | 11 | 4/51 | 7/99 | 24.45 | 2.27 | 64.3 | 0 | 0 |
| ODIs | 28 | 1279 | 930 | 34 | 5/17 | 5/17 | 27.35 | 4.36 | 37.6 | 1 | 0 |
| T20Is | 36 | 712 | 661 | 49 | 5/11 | 5/11 | 13.48 | 5.57 | 14.5 | 1 | 0 |

# SARAH TAYLOR

RHB WK

FULL NAME: Sarah Jane Taylor
BORN: May 20, 1989, London Hospital, Whitechapel, London
SQUAD NO: 30
HEIGHT: 5ft 9in
NICKNAME: Squirt, Dave
EDUCATION: St Bede's School; Brighton College
TEAMS: England Women; Sussex Women
CAREER: Test: 2006; ODI: 2006; T20I: 2006



BEST ODI BATTING: 129 England vs South Africa, Lord's, 2008

CAREER HIGHLIGHTS? Winning the World T20 at Lord's in 2009, being part of a 268-run opening partnership and winning the Ashes down under in 2014
BEST PLAYER IN COUNTY CRICKET? Charlotte Edwards – who else?!
TIP FOR THE TOP? Georgia Hennessy
CRICKETING HEROES? Rebecca Rolls – brilliant batter/keeper
NON-CRICKETING HEROES? Steffi Graf – a great player and lovely person. Also have to pay a mention to my family!
IF YOU WEREN'T A CRICKETER? I wanted to be an archeologist
IF YOU COULD BE SOMEONE ELSE FOR A DAY? The Queen
FAVOURITE TV? Gilmore Girls
LEAST FAVOURITE TV? I'm A Celebrity ... Get Me Out Of Here!
PET HATE? The wrong use of their, there and they're! It's not hard people!
SURPRISING FACT? I have a teddy bear called Bephy that comes with me on every tour
FANTASY SLIP CORDON? Keeper: Me, 1st: Fat Amy (Rebel Wilson), 2nd: Michael Clarke, 3rd: Prince Phillip, Gully: David Attenborough
TWITTER FEED: @Sarah_taylor30

| Batting | Mat | Inns | NO | Runs | HS | Ave | SR | 100 | 50 | Ct | St |
|---|---|---|---|---|---|---|---|---|---|---|---|
| Tests | 7 | 13 | 1 | 266 | 40 | 22.16 | 50.18 | 0 | 0 | 14 | 2 |
| ODIs | 95 | 88 | 11 | 3144 | 129 | 40.83 | 79.61 | 5 | 16 | 72 | 38 |
| T20Is | 70 | 68 | 10 | 1744 | 77 | 30.06 | 108.18 | 0 | 11 | 20 | 42 |
| **Bowling** | **Mat** | **Balls** | **Runs** | **Wkts** | **BBI** | **BBM** | **Ave** | **Econ** | **SR** | **5w** | **10** |
| Tests | 7 | - | - | - | - | - | - | - | - | - | - |
| ODIs | 95 | - | - | - | - | - | - | - | - | - | - |
| T20Is | 70 | - | - | - | - | - | - | - | - | - | - |

# FRAN WILSON

RHB OB

FULL NAME: Frances Claire Wilson
BORN: November 7, 1991, Farnham, Surrey
SQUAD NO: 35
HEIGHT: 5ft 4in
EDUCATION: University of Bath; Loughborough University
TEAMS: England Women, Middlesex Women, Somerset Women
CAREER: ODI: 2010; T20I: 2010

CAREER HIGHLIGHTS? My England debut in 2010 and captaining England A vs India in 2014
BEST PLAYER IN COUNTY CRICKET? Charlotte Edwards
MOST MARKED CHARACTERISTIC? Being happy
CRICKET RULE YOU'D CHANGE? You can't be out first ball
COACHING TIP? Working out what works for you and having the confidence to stick with it regardless of what others are doing
IF YOU WEREN'T A CRICKETER? Playing another sport and travelling
IF YOU COULD BE SOMEONE ELSE FOR A DAY? Danni Wyatt – cricketer and Lady of Leisure
DESERT ISLAND DISC? Ed Sheeran
FAVOURITE TV? Made In Chelsea
LEAST FAVOURITE TV? Top Gear
ACCOMPLISHMENTS? Graduating from University of Bath and having the best four years there
PET HATE? Moaning!
TWITTER FEED: @fwilson07

| Batting | Mat | Inns | NO | Runs | HS | Ave | SR | 100 | 50 | Ct | St |
|---|---|---|---|---|---|---|---|---|---|---|---|
| ODIs | 2 | 1 | 0 | 0 | 0 | 0.00 | 0.00 | 0 | 0 | 2 | 0 |
| T20Is | 5 | 4 | 1 | 33 | 17 | 11.00 | 86.84 | 0 | 0 | 1 | 0 |
| **Bowling** | **Mat** | **Balls** | **Runs** | **Wkts** | **BBI** | **BBM** | **Ave** | **Econ** | **SR** | **5w** | **10** |
| ODIs | 2 | - | - | - | - | - | - | - | - | - | - |
| T20Is | 5 | - | - | - | - | - | - | - | - | - | - |

# LAUREN WINFIELD

RHB WK

FULL NAME: Lauren Winfield
BORN: August 16, 1990, York
SQUAD NO: 58
HEIGHT: 5ft 6in
NICKNAME: Loz
EDUCATION: Lougborough University
TEAMS: England Women, Yorkshire Women
CAREER: Tests: 2014; ODI: 2013; T20I: 2013

BEST ODI BATTING: 31 England vs Wesy Indies, Port of Spain, 2013

FAMILY TIES? My dad plays and my brother played representative cricket before going to uni. Mum watches most games and makes a good picnic
CAREER HIGHLIGHTS? Winning back-to-back Ashes, making my Test debut and my first Player of the Match
TIP FOR THE TOP? Georgia Hennessy, Hollie Armitage
MOST MARKED CHARACTERISTIC? My big pineapple hair bun
CRICKETING HEROES? Graham Dilley and AB de Villiers. Dils was a fantastic coach and inspiring guy. AB is unique, a genius and world-class
CRICKET RULE YOU'D CHANGE? Fewer fielders outside the ring
IF YOU COULD BE SOMEONE ELSE FOR A DAY? Richard Branson
DESERT ISLAND DISC? Lighthouse Family
PET HATE? Bad manners and eating with your mouth open
SURPRISING FACT? I used to play football for Leeds United
FANTASY SLIP CORDON? Keeper: Muhammad Ali, 1st: David Beckham, 2nd: Myself, 3rd: Beyoncé, Gully: Will Smith
TWITTER FEED: @lozwinfield

| Batting | Mat | Inns | NO | Runs | HS | Ave | SR | 100 | 50 | Ct | St |
|---|---|---|---|---|---|---|---|---|---|---|---|
| Tests | 1 | 2 | 0 | 43 | 35 | 21.50 | 35.83 | 0 | 0 | 0 | 0 |
| ODIs | 10 | 10 | 2 | 138 | 31 | 17.25 | 52.27 | 0 | 0 | 2 | 0 |
| T20Is | 13 | 13 | 1 | 236 | 74 | 19.66 | 94.77 | 0 | 1 | 6 | 0 |
| **Bowling** | **Mat** | **Balls** | **Runs** | **Wkts** | **BBI** | **BBM** | **Ave** | **Econ** | **SR** | **5w** | **10** |
| Tests | 1 | - | - | - | - | - | - | - | - | - | - |
| ODIs | 10 | - | - | - | - | - | - | - | - | - | - |
| T20Is | 13 | - | - | - | - | - | - | - | - | - | - |

# DANIELLE WYATT RHB OB

FULL NAME: Danielle Nicole Wyatt
BORN: April 22, 1991, Stoke-on-Trent, Staffordshire
SQUAD NO: 28
HEIGHT: 5ft 4in
NICKNAME: Waggy
EDUCATION: St Peter's High School; Stoke-On-Trent Sixth Form College
TEAMS: England, Nottinghamshire
CAREER: ODI: 2010; T20I: 2010

BEST ODI BATTING: 40 England vs West Indies, Mumbai, 2013
BEST ODI BOWLING: 3-7 England vs South Africa, Cuttack, 2013

CAREER HIGHLIGHTS? Winning two Ashes and winning the National T20 with Notts Ladies
MOST MARKED CHARACTERISTIC? Well, it was my black mole on my bum cheek, but that recently got removed so now I'd say my massive forehead!
SUPERSTITIONS? If I got runs one game I would wear the same socks the next game!
NON-CRICKETING HEROES? David Beckham. I'm lucky enough to have met him. He's an iconic sportsman who I admire a lot. I want to meet him again, for dinner next time. He smelt so nice! And my grandad Ray – he's such an inspiration to me
CRICKET RULE YOU'D CHANGE? The lbw rule and then I'd just swing from across my stumps
IF YOU WEREN'T A CRICKETER? Probably a window cleaner. I love cleaning. Or a WAG. Not sure who to though
PET HATE? When lads walk into the gym with their singlet hanging off there nipples!
SURPRISING FACT? I fell out of a tree and broke my wrist and foot when I was 10 thinking I was Tarzan
FANTASY SLIP CORDON? Keeper: David Beckham, 1st: Cristiano Ronaldo (because I want to chill with both of them all day), 2nd: Myself, 3rd: Rihanna, 4th: Nana Baggaley (because she would say the funniest things)
TWITTER FEED: @danni_wyatt

| Batting | Mat | Inns | NO | Runs | HS | Ave | SR | 100 | 50 | Ct | St |
|---|---|---|---|---|---|---|---|---|---|---|---|
| ODIs | 33 | 26 | 3 | 378 | 40 | 16.43 | 66.19 | 0 | 0 | 5 | 0 |
| T20Is | 56 | 36 | 6 | 395 | 41 | 13.16 | 101.80 | 0 | 0 | 8 | 0 |
| **Bowling** | **Mat** | **Balls** | **Runs** | **Wkts** | **BBI** | **BBM** | **Ave** | **Econ** | **SR** | **5w** | **10** |
| ODIs | 33 | 800 | 660 | 25 | 3/7 | 3/7 | 26.40 | 4.95 | 32.0 | 0 | 0 |
| T20Is | 56 | 711 | 671 | 46 | 4/11 | 4/11 | 14.58 | 5.66 | 15.4 | 0 | 0 |

★ RATE AND REVIEW THE LATEST KIT

★ VIDEOS AND ADVICE

★ OFFERS AND COMPETITIONS

ALLOUTCRICKET

THE INDEPENDENT GEAR GUIDE

gear.alloutcricket.com

NatWest
T20
BLAST

YOUR
WEEKEND
STARTS HERE

V NORTHAMPTONSHIRE STEELBACKS
FRIDAY MAY 15

V YORKSHIRE VIKINGS
FRIDAY MAY 29

V BIRMINGHAM BEARS
SATURDAY JUNE 06

V WORCESTERSHIRE RAPIDS
FRIDAY JUNE 12

V LANCASHIRE LIGHTN
THURSDAY JUNE 25

V LEICESTERSHIRE FOX
FRIDAY JULY 03

V NOTTS OUTLAWS
FRIDAY JULY 17

DURHAM JETS

Emirates Durham

BOOK NOW AT WWW.DURHAMCCC.CO.UK
OR TEL: 0844 499 4466

*The*
Umpires

# ROB BAILEY

**NAME:** Robert John Bailey
**BORN:** October 28, 1963, Biddulph, Staffordshire
**HEIGHT:** 6ft 3in
**APPOINTED TO FIRST-CLASS LIST:** 2006
**INTERNATIONAL PANEL:** 2011-
**ELITE PANEL:** 2014
**ODIS UMPIRED:** 9 (plus 4 as TV umpire)
**T20IS UMPIRED:** 11 (plus 4 as TV umpire)
**COUNTIES AS PLAYER:** Northamptonshire, Derbyshire
**ROLE:** Right-hand bat; off-spin bowler
**COUNTY DEBUT:** 1982 (Northants), 2000 (Derbys)
**TEST DEBUT:** 1988
**ODI DEBUT:** 1985

---

**NOTES:** A talented batsman, Bailey was perhaps unfortunate to play all four of his Tests against the fearsome West Indies pace attack of the late 1980s and early 1990s. In 1990 he struck 1,987 runs in the season for Northamptonshire. Has umpired at every T20 Finals Day since 2008

| Batting | Mat | Inns | NO | Runs | HS | Ave | SR | 100 | 50 | Ct | St |
|---|---|---|---|---|---|---|---|---|---|---|---|
| Tests | 4 | 8 | 0 | 119 | 43 | 14.87 | 36.50 | 0 | 0 | 0 | 0 |
| ODIs | 4 | 4 | 2 | 137 | 43* | 68.50 | 69.89 | 0 | 0 | 1 | 0 |
| First-class | 374 | 628 | 89 | 21844 | 224* | 40.52 | | 47 | 111 | 272 | 0 |
| List A | 396 | 376 | 65 | 12076 | 153* | 38.82 | | 10 | 79 | 111 | 0 |
| **Bowling** | **Mat** | **Balls** | **Runs** | **Wkts** | **BBI** | **BBM** | **Ave** | **Econ** | **SR** | **5w** | **10** |
| Tests | 4 | - | - | - | - | - | - | - | - | - | |
| ODIs | 4 | 36 | 25 | 0 | - | - | - | 4.16 | 0 | 0 | 0 |
| First-class | 374 | 9713 | 5144 | 121 | 5/54 | | 42.51 | 3.17 | 80.2 | 2 | 0 |
| List A | 396 | 3092 | 2564 | 72 | 5/45 | 5/45 | 35.61 | 4.97 | 42.9 | 1 | 0 |

# NEIL BAINTON

NAME: Neil Laurence Bainton
BORN: October 2, 1970, Romford, Essex
HEIGHT: 5ft 8in
APPOINTED TO FIRST-CLASS LIST: 2006



WHAT HAS BEEN YOUR CAREER HIGHLIGHT AS AN UMPIRE? Being appointed to the first-class list and being fourth umpire in two Test matches
WHAT'S YOUR FAVOURITE COUNTY GROUND? Colwyn Bay. Always an enjoyable week
WHAT WAS THE HIGHLIGHT OF YOUR PLAYING CAREER? I played for South of England U15 at England Schools Festival in 1986
WHAT ARE YOUR FAVOURITE PASTIMES OUTSIDE OF CRICKET? Playing golf badly
CAN YOU TELL US A SURPRISING FACT ABOUT YOURSELF? I still work as a postman during the winter months

# PAUL BALDWIN

NAME: Paul Kerr Baldwin
BORN: July 18, 1973, Epsom, Surrey
APPOINTED TO FIRST-CLASS LIST: 2015
ODIS UMPIRED: 18
T20IS UMPIRED: 9

---

DO YOU HAVE ANY RITUALS, QUIRKS OR SUPERSTITIONS AS AN UMPIRE? I count the over with coins in a certain order, ranked by size, largest on the bottom, smallest on the top
WHAT'S BEEN YOUR MOST MEMORABLE DISMISSAL? In my first County Championship match Kyle Hogg was bowling to Dominic Cork, Dom was plumb in front and he walked on me before I even had the chance to give him out LBW
WHAT WAS THE HIGHLIGHT OF YOUR PLAYING CAREER? Being selected to captain RAF Brüggen, my club side in Germany in 1996, which I captained for the next four years
WHAT ARE YOUR FAVOURITE PASTIMES OUTSIDE OF CRICKET? Equestrian Photography - mostly when our horses compete
CAN YOU TELL US A SURPRISING FACT ABOUT YOURSELF? I appeared as an extra in two films in Germany, one as an RAF pilot and the other as an American military policeman protecting Lyndon B. Johnson!

# MARK BENSON

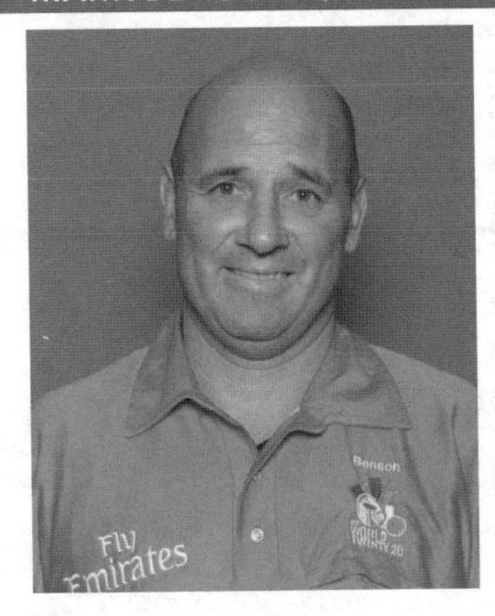


NAME: Mark Richard Benson
BORN: July 6, 1958, Shoreham, Sussex
NICKNAME: Benny
APPOINTED TO FIRST-CLASS LIST: 2000
INTERNATIONAL PANEL: 2004-2006
ELITE PANEL: 2006-2010
TESTS UMPIRED: 27 (plus 9 as TV umpire)
ODIS UMPIRED: 72 (plus 25 as TV umpire)
T20IS UMPIRED: 19 (plus 6 as TV umpire)
COUNTY AS PLAYER: Kent
ROLE: Left-hand bat; off-spin bowler
COUNTY DEBUT: 1980
TEST DEBUT: 1986
ODI DEBUT: 1986

---

DO YOU HAVE ANY RITUALS, QUIRKS OR SUPERSTITIONS AS AN UMPIRE? I change my footwear every session
WHAT HAS BEEN YOUR CAREER HIGHLIGHT AS AN UMPIRE? Being appointed to the ECB umpiring panel
WHAT'S YOUR FAVOURITE COUNTY GROUND? The old Southampton ground
WHAT'S BEEN YOUR MOST MEMORABLE DISMISSAL? I gave Mark Boucher out LBW in an ODI, although it had pitched outside leg, was too high and he hit it!
WHAT WAS THE HIGHLIGHT OF YOUR PLAYING CAREER? Winning the Sunday League when captain of Kent
WHAT ARE YOUR FAVOURITE PASTIMES OUTSIDE OF CRICKET? Playing bridge
CAN YOU TELL US A SURPRISING FACT ABOUT YOURSELF? I have dual nationality with Seychelles

| Batting | Mat | Inns | NO | Runs | HS | Ave | SR | 100 | 50 | Ct | St |
|---|---|---|---|---|---|---|---|---|---|---|---|
| Tests | 1 | 2 | 0 | 51 | 30 | 25.50 | 31.48 | 0 | 0 | 0 | 0 |
| ODIs | 1 | 1 | 0 | 24 | 24 | 24.00 | 41.37 | 0 | 0 | 0 | 0 |
| First-class | 292 | 491 | 34 | 18387 | 257 | 40.23 | | 48 | 99 | 140 | 0 |
| List A | 269 | 257 | 11 | 7838 | 119 | 31.86 | | 5 | 53 | 68 | 0 |
| **Bowling** | **Mat** | **Balls** | **Runs** | **Wkts** | **BBI** | **BBM** | **Ave** | **Econ** | **SR** | **5w** | **10** |
| Tests | 1 | - | - | - | - | - | - | - | - | - | |
| ODIs | 1 | - | - | - | - | - | - | - | - | - | |
| First-class | 292 | 467 | 493 | 5 | 2/55 | | 98.60 | 6.33 | | 0 | 0 |
| List A | 269 | - | - | - | - | - | - | - | - | - | |

# MARTIN BODENHAM

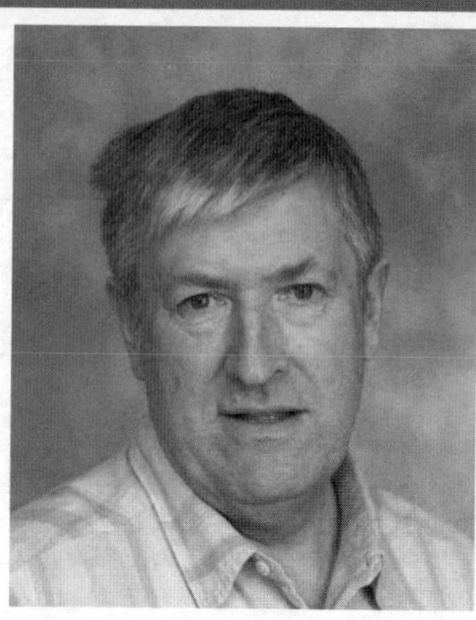

NAME: Martin John Dale Bodenham
BORN: April 23, 1950, Brighton
HEIGHT: 6ft 1in
APPOINTED TO FIRST-CLASS LIST: 2009
COUNTY AS PLAYER: Sussex 2nd XI
ROLE: Right-hand bat; wicketkeeper

---

NOTES: Bodenham is the first person to both referee in football's Premier League and umpire in first-class cricket. As a referee he took charge of three FA Cup semi-finals and the League Cup final in 1997, as well as being fourth official for the 1994 European Cup final between AC Milan and Barcelona. He once sent off Wimbledon's Vinnie Jones for threatening to break an opponent's legs and gave Roy Keane a yellow card while he was going off on a stretcher

# NICK COOK

NAME: Nicholas Grant Billson Cook
BORN: June 17, 1956, Leicester
HEIGHT: 6ft
NICKNAME: Beast
APPOINTED TO FIRST-CLASS LIST: 2009
COUNTIES AS PLAYER: Leicestershire, Northamptonshire
ROLE: Right-hand bat; slow left-arm bowler
COUNTY DEBUT: 1978 (Leics), 1986 (Northants)
TEST DEBUT: 1983
ODI DEBUT: 1984



DO YOU HAVE ANY RITUALS, QUIRKS OR SUPERSTITIONS AS AN UMPIRE? I like to walk out to the left of my colleague
SOMETHING WE DIDN'T KNOW ABOUT YOU: I have two Siamese cats
NOTES: Officiated as TV umpire in the CB40 final at Lord's in 2011. Reserve umpire in two Tests, including the 2013 Ashes Test at Old Trafford. As a player he took 5-35 on Test debut, against New Zealand at Lord's

| Batting | Mat | Inns | NO | Runs | HS | Ave | SR | 100 | 50 | Ct | St |
|---|---|---|---|---|---|---|---|---|---|---|---|
| Tests | 15 | 25 | 4 | 179 | 31 | 8.52 | 23.58 | 0 | 0 | 5 | 0 |
| ODIs | 3 | - | - | - | - | - | - | - | - | 2 | 0 |
| First-class | 356 | 365 | 96 | 3137 | 75 | 11.66 | | 0 | 4 | 197 | 0 |
| List A | 223 | 89 | 36 | 491 | 23 | 9.26 | | 0 | 0 | 74 | 0 |
| **Bowling** | **Mat** | **Balls** | **Runs** | **Wkts** | **BBI** | **BBM** | **Ave** | **Econ** | **SR** | **5w** | **10** |
| Tests | 15 | 4174 | 1689 | 52 | 6/65 | 11/83 | 32.48 | 2.42 | 80.2 | 4 | 1 |
| ODIs | 3 | 144 | 95 | 5 | 2/18 | 2/18 | 19.00 | 3.95 | 28.8 | 0 | 0 |
| First-class | 356 | 64460 | 25507 | 879 | 7/34 | | 29.01 | 2.37 | 73.3 | 31 | 4 |
| List A | 223 | 10077 | 6812 | 200 | 4/22 | 4/22 | 34.06 | 4.05 | 50.3 | 0 | 0 |

# NIGEL COWLEY

NAME: Nigel Geoffrey Charles Cowlrey
BORN: March 1, 1953, Shaftesbury, Dorset
HEIGHT: 5ft 7in
NICKNAME: Dougall
APPOINTED TO FIRST-CLASS LIST: 2000
COUNTIES AS PLAYER: Hampshire, Glamorgan
ROLE: Right-hand bat; off-spin bowler
COUNTY DEBUT: 1974 (Hants), 1990 (Glam)

NOTES: Has stood as a reserve umpire in four Tests and three ODIs, as well as officiating in one women's ODI and one women's T20I. As a player he was an allrounder, passing 1,000 runs and taking 56 wickets in 1984 for Hampshire. In 1988 he took 1-17 from his 11 overs to help Hampshire win the B&H Cup against Derbyshire

| Batting | Mat | Inns | NO | Runs | HS | Ave | SR | 100 | 50 | Ct | St |
|---|---|---|---|---|---|---|---|---|---|---|---|
| First-class | 271 | 375 | 62 | 7309 | 109* | 23.35 | - | 2 | 36 | 105 | 0 |
| List A | 305 | 226 | 45 | 3022 | 74 | 16.69 | - | 0 | 5 | 69 | 0 |
| **Bowling** | **Mat** | **Balls** | **Runs** | **Wkts** | **BBI** | **BBM** | **Ave** | **Econ** | **SR** | **5w** | **10** |
| First-class | 271 | 32662 | 14879 | 437 | 6/48 | - | 34.04 | 2.73 | 74.7 | 5 | 0 |
| List A | 305 | 11704 | 8038 | 248 | 5/24 | 5/24 | 32.41 | 4.12 | 47.1 | 1 | 0 |

# JEFF EVANS

NAME: Jeffrey Howard Evans
BORN: August 7, 1954, Llanelli, Carmarthenshire
HEIGHT: 5ft 8in
APPOINTED TO FIRST-CLASS LIST: 2001



---

**WHAT'S YOUR FAVOURITE COUNTY GROUND?** That has to be Lord's for obvious reasons
**WHAT'S BEEN YOUR MOST MEMORABLE DISMISSAL?** Giving Brian Lara out first ball in the Indian Cricket League
**WHAT'S THE FUNNIEST MOMENT YOU'VE EVER EXPERIENCED ON A CRICKET FIELD?**
Watching the band of the Royal Gurkha Regiment march towards the boundary in Canterbury, only for them to immediately turn around and march towards the pitch. At this point my colleague Vanburn Holder called "play" with the band situated at mid-off
**IF YOU COULD CHANGE ONE RULE ABOUT CRICKET, WHAT WOULD IT BE?**
That either umpire could adjudicate on decisions. There are occasions where the umpire at the striker's end is in a better position to make a decision which protocol dictates is the jurisdiction of the bowler's end official
**CAN YOU TELL US A SURPRISING FACT ABOUT YOURSELF?**
I hold a PCV driving licence (Passenger Carrying Vehicle) and regularly drive ski groups out to the Alps in the winter so that I can indulge my passion for skiing

# RUSSELL EVANS

NAME: Russell John Evans
BORN: October 1, 1965, Calverton, Nottinghamshire
APPOINTED TO FIRST-CLASS LIST: 2015
COUNTIES AS A PLAYER: Nottinghamshire
ROLE: Right-hand bat, Right-arm medium bowler
COUNTY DEBUT: 1987 (Notts)

---

DO YOU HAVE ANY RITUALS, QUIRKS OR SUPERSTITIONS AS AN UMPIRE? Routines are important in umpiring but I would not like to go down the superstitions route. I like to be early at the ground, sometimes beating the ground officials...
WHAT HAS BEEN YOUR CAREER HIGHLIGHT AS AN UMPIRE? Getting on the first-class list for 2015. It is a great system and you have to prove your worth
WHAT'S YOUR FAVOURITE COUNTY GROUND? There are many grounds I like visiting. Generally you are welcomed by ground staff, dressing-room attendants and players so I enjoy umpiring at pretty much all grounds. Trent Bridge is special and obviously Lord's as the home of cricket
WHAT'S THE FUNNIEST MOMENT YOU'VE EVER EXPERIENCED ON A CRICKET FIELD? A colleague at Notts who bowled one past second slip's right hand and the third man couldn't stop it going for four for laughing. I won't name names...
WHAT WAS THE HIGHLIGHT OF YOUR PLAYING CAREER? Making my first-class debut or scoring 209* in New Zealand
CAN YOU TELL US A SURPRISING FACT ABOUT YOURSELF? Not exactly surprising, but 'can't cook, won't cook'

| Batting | Mat | Inns | NO | Runs | HS | Ave | SR | 100 | 50 | Ct | St |
|---|---|---|---|---|---|---|---|---|---|---|---|
| First-class | 7 | 11 | 3 | 201 | 59 | 25.12 | - | 0 | 2 | 5 | 0 |
| List A | 16 | 14 | 1 | 211 | 56 | 16.23 | - | 0 | 1 | 1 | 0 |
| **Bowling** | **Mat** | **Balls** | **Runs** | **Wkts** | **BBI** | **BBM** | **Ave** | **Econ** | **SR** | **5w** | **10** |
| First-class | 7 | 198 | 97 | 3 | 3/40 | - | 32.33 | 2.93 | 66.0 | 0 | 0 |
| List A | 16 | - | - | - | - | - | - | - | - | - | |

# STEVE GALE

NAME: Stephen Clifford Gale
BORN: June 3, 1952, Shrewsbury, Shropshire
APPOINTED TO FIRST-CLASS LIST: 2001
COUNTIES AS A PLAYER: Shropshire
ROLE: Right-hand bat; leg-spin bowler



---

DO YOU HAVE ANY RITUALS, QUIRKS OR SUPERSTITIONS AS AN UMPIRE? I use six pound coins to count the number of deliveries
WHAT HAS BEEN YOUR CAREER HIGHLIGHT AS AN UMPIRE? England Lions vs Australia
WHAT'S YOUR FAVOURITE COUNTY GROUND? Durham is a top venue
WHAT'S THE FUNNIEST MOMENT YOU'VE EVER EXPERIENCED ON A CRICKET FIELD? During the Lions vs Australia match, a bail flew about 50 yards and as a fielder went to pick it up a large seagull picked it up and sat on the pavilion for about five minutes with the bail in its beak
WHAT WAS THE HIGHLIGHT OF YOUR PLAYING CAREER? Captaining my club Shrewsbury to success at Lord's
WHAT ARE YOUR FAVOURITE PASTIMES OUTSIDE OF CRICKET? Playing golf and taking coastal walks in Cornwall
CAN YOU TELL US A SURPRISING FACT ABOUT YOURSELF? I'm the first person from Shropshire to become a first-class umpire

## STEVE GARRATT

NAME: Steven Arthur Garratt
BORN: July 5, 1953, Nottingham
HEIGHT: 6ft 2in
NICKNAME: Trigger
APPOINTED TO FIRST-CLASS LIST: 2008

---

WHAT HAS BEEN YOUR CAREER HIGHLIGHT AS AN UMPIRE? My appointment to the Full first-class umpires list in 2008
WHAT'S YOUR FAVOURITE COUNTY GROUND? It has to be Lord's because of the history of the place, the way you are treated and of course the food!
WHAT'S THE FUNNIEST MOMENT YOU'VE EVER EXPERIENCED ON A CRICKET FIELD? At Canterbury in 2011 during the England Lions match against Australia an England batsman was bowled and one of the bails spiralled into the outfield. Before it could be retrieved a seagull flew down and picked it up and flew off
IF YOU COULD CHANGE ONE RULE ABOUT CRICKET, WHAT WOULD IT BE? The third umpire in televised matches should be able to rectify (overrule) any decision where the evidence is clear and conclusive
CAN YOU TELL US A SURPRISING FACT ABOUT YOURSELF? In 1980 I played rugby union at Murrayfield in the National Police Knockout Cup Final

# MICHAEL GOUGH

NAME: Michael Andrew Gough
BORN: December 18, 1978, Hartlepool
HEIGHT: 6ft 5in
NICKNAME: Goughy
APPOINTED TO FIRST-CLASS LIST: 2009
INTERNATIONAL PANEL: 2013-
ELITE PANEL: 2014
ODIS UMPIRED: 14 (3 as TV umpire)
T20IS UMPIRED: 4 (3 as TV umpire)
COUNTIES AS PLAYER: Durham
ROLE: Right-hand bat; off-spin bowler
COUNTY DEBUT: 1998

---

SOMETHING WE DON'T KNOW ABOUT YOU: I'm a qualified football referee and a season-ticket holder at Hartlepool United
FAVOURITE GROUND: Worcester
RITUALS AND QUIRKS: I step onto the pitch with my left foot first and my left foot is also the first off the pitch
NOTES: Gough started umpiring in 2005 after retiring from the first-class game and was appointed to the ECB reserve list in 2006. He is believed to be the youngest first-class umpire in the history of the game. In 2011 he officiated at T20 Finals Day at Edgbaston and was named PCA Umpire of the Year. He has been reserve umpire in four Tests and umpired during the 2015 World Cup

| Batting | Mat | Inns | NO | Runs | HS | Ave | SR | 100 | 50 | Ct | St |
|---|---|---|---|---|---|---|---|---|---|---|---|
| First-class | 67 | 119 | 3 | 2952 | 123 | 25.44 | | 2 | 15 | 57 | 0 |
| List A | 49 | 45 | 4 | 974 | 132 | 23.75 | | 1 | 3 | 14 | 0 |
| **Bowling** | **Mat** | **Balls** | **Runs** | **Wkts** | **BBI** | **BBM** | **Ave** | **Econ** | **SR** | **5w** | **10** |
| First-class | 67 | 2486 | 1350 | 5/66 | | 45.00 | 45.00 | 3.25 | 82.8 | 1 | 0 |
| List A | 49 | 1136 | 947 | 21 | 3/26 | 45.09 | 45.09 | 5.00 | 54.0 | 0 | 0 |

# IAN GOULD

**NAME:** Ian James Gould
**BORN:** August 19, 1957, Taplow, Buckinghamshire
**HEIGHT:** 5ft 7in
**NICKNAME:** Gunner
**APPOINTED TO FIRST-CLASS LIST:** 2002
**INTERNATIONAL PANEL:** 2006-
**ELITE PANEL:** 2010-
**TESTS UMPIRED:** 43 (15 as TV umpire)
**ODIS UMPIRED:** 100 (29 as TV umpire)
**T20IS UMPIRED:** 29 (15 as TV umpire)
**COUNTIES AS PLAYER:** Middlesex, Sussex
**ROLE:** Left-hand bat; wicketkeeper
**COUNTY DEBUT:** 1975 (Middx), 1981 (Sus)
**ODI DEBUT:** 1983

---

**NOTES:** PCA Umpire of the Year in 2005 and 2007. Umpired at the 2007, 2011 and 2015 World Cups and the 2009, 2010, 2012 and 2014 World T20s. As a player he kept wicket for England at the 1983 World Cup and captained Sussex to victory in the 1986 NatWest Trophy

| Batting | Mat | Inns | NO | Runs | HS | Ave | SR | 100 | 50 | Ct | St |
|---|---|---|---|---|---|---|---|---|---|---|---|
| ODIs | 18 | 14 | 2 | 155 | 42 | 12.91 | 63.78 | 0 | 0 | 15 | 3 |
| First-class | 298 | 399 | 63 | 8756 | 128 | 26.05 | | 4 | 47 | 536 | 67 |
| List A | 315 | 270 | 41 | 4377 | 88 | 19.11 | | 0 | 20 | 242 | 37 |
| **Bowling** | **Mat** | **Balls** | **Runs** | **Wkts** | **BBI** | **BBM** | **Ave** | **Econ** | **SR** | **5w** | **10** |
| ODIs | 18 | - | - | - | - | - | - | - | - | - | - |
| First-class | 298 | 478 | 365 | 7 | 3/10 | - | 52.14 | 4.58 | 68.2 | 0 | 0 |
| List A | 315 | 20 | 16 | 1 | 1/0 | 1/0 | 16.00 | 4.80 | 20.0 | 0 | 0 |

# PETER HARTLEY

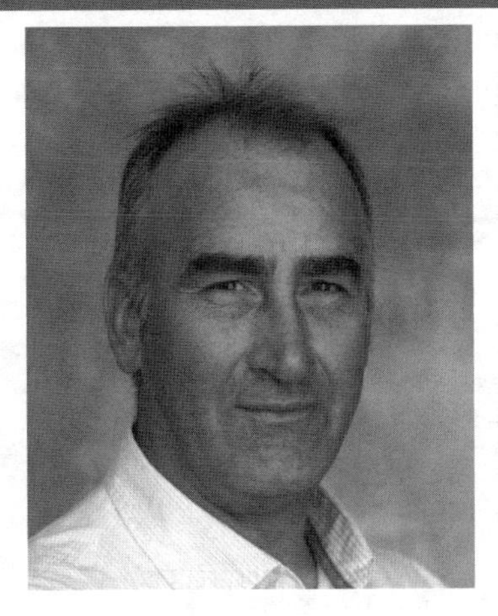

NAME: Peter John Hartley
BORN: April 18, 1960, Keighley, Yorkshire
HEIGHT: 6ft
NICKNAME: Jack
APPOINTED TO FIRST-CLASS LIST: 2003
INTERNATIONAL PANEL: 2006-2009
ODIS UMPIRED: 6 (plus 10 as TV umpire)
T20IS UMPIRED: 3 (plus 4 as TV umpire)
COUNTIES AS PLAYER: Warwickshire, Yorkshire, Hampshire
ROLE: Right-hand bat; right-arm fast-medium bowler
COUNTY DEBUT: 1982 (Warks), 1985 (Yorks), 1998 (Hants)



---

WHAT HAS BEEN YOUR CAREER HIGHLIGHT AS AN UMPIRE? Standing in one-day finals days
WHAT'S YOUR FAVOURITE COUNTY GROUND? Lord's
WHAT WAS THE HIGHLIGHT OF YOUR PLAYING CAREER? Playing with and against many very good players
WHAT ARE YOU FAVOURITE PASTIMES OUTSIDE OF CRICKET? Playing golf and skiing
IF YOU COULD CHANGE ONE RULE ABOUT CRICKET, WHAT WOULD IT BE? Any ball that passes above the height of the stumps (without bouncing) should be a no-ball

| Batting | Mat | Inns | NO | Runs | HS | Ave | SR | 100 | 50 | Ct | St |
|---|---|---|---|---|---|---|---|---|---|---|---|
| First-class | 232 | 283 | 66 | 4321 | 127* | 19.91 | | 2 | 14 | 68 | 0 |
| List A | 269 | 170 | 62 | 1765 | 83 | 16.34 | | 0 | 4 | 46 | 0 |
| **Bowling** | **Mat** | **Balls** | **Runs** | **Wkts** | **BBI** | **BBM** | **Ave** | **Econ** | **SR** | **5w** | **10** |
| First-class | 232 | 37108 | 20635 | 683 | 9/41 | - | 30.21 | 3.33 | 54.3 | 23 | 0 |
| List A | 269 | 12636 | 9069 | 356 | 5/20 | 5/20 | 25.47 | 4.30 | 35.4 | 5 | 0 |

# RICHARD ILLINGWORTH

NAME: Richard Keith Illingworth
BORN: August 23, 1963, Bradford
HEIGHT: 5ft 11in
NICKNAME: Harry, Lucy
APPOINTED TO FIRST-CLASS LIST: 2006
INTERNATIONAL PANEL: 2009 –
ELITE PANEL: 2013 –
TESTS UMPIRED: 14 (5 as TV umpire)
ODIS UMPIRED: 36 (23 as TV umpire)
T20IS UMPIRED: 11 (3 as TV umpire)
COUNTIES AS A PLAYER: Worcestershire, Derbyshire
ROLE: Right-hand bat; slow left-arm bowler
COUNTY DEBUT: 1982 (Worcs), 2001 (Derbys)
TEST DEBUT: 1991 ODI DEBUT: 1991

---

DO YOU HAVE ANY RITUALS, QUIRKS OR SUPERSTITIONS AS AN UMPIRE? I use old penny coins (dated 1967) to count balls in the over
WHAT HAS BEEN YOUR CAREER HIGHLIGHT AS AN UMPIRE? I guess the Test series between South Africa and Australia in February 2014. Fantastic tussle between the top two teams in the world at the time
WHAT'S YOUR FAVOURITE COUNTY GROUND? New Road, Worcester – not only is it a beautiful place to play but the area is a great place to live. It has so many great memories
WHAT'S BEEN YOUR MOST MEMORABLE DISMISSAL? As a player, bowling Phil Simmons with my first ball in Test cricket. I guess that is up there!
WHAT WAS THE HIGHLIGHT OF YOUR PLAYING CAREER? Being fortunate enough to realise a childhood dream of playing for England and winning trophies with Worcestershire
CAN YOU TELL US A SURPRISING FACT ABOUT YOURSELF? I do actually possess a sense of humour

| Batting | Mat | Inns | NO | Runs | HS | Ave | SR | 100 | 50 | Ct | St |
|---|---|---|---|---|---|---|---|---|---|---|---|
| Tests | 9 | 14 | 7 | 128 | 28 | 18.28 | 32.08 | 0 | 0 | 5 | 0 |
| ODIs | 25 | 11 | 5 | 68 | 14 | 11.33 | 57.14 | 0 | 0 | 8 | 0 |
| First-class | 376 | 435 | 122 | 7027 | 120* | 22.45 | | 4 | 21 | 161 | 0 |
| List A | 381 | 185 | 87 | 1458 | 53* | 14.87 | | 0 | 1 | 93 | 0 |
| **Bowling** | **Mat** | **Balls** | **Runs** | **Wkts** | **BBI** | **BBM** | **Ave** | **Econ** | **SR** | **5w** | **10** |
| Tests | 9 | 1485 | 615 | 19 | 4/96 | 6/150 | 32.36 | 2.48 | 78.1 | 0 | 0 |
| ODIs | 25 | 1501 | 1059 | 30 | 3/33 | 3/33 | 35.30 | 4.23 | 50.0 | 0 | 0 |
| First-class | 376 | 65868 | 26213 | 831 | 7/50 | | 31.54 | 2.38 | 79.2 | 27 | 6 |
| List A | 381 | 16918 | 11157 | 412 | 5/24 | 5/24 | 27.08 | 3.95 | 41.0 | 2 | 0 |

# RICHARD KETTLEBOROUGH

NAME: Richard Allan Kettleborough
BORN: March 15, 1973, Sheffield
HEIGHT: 5ft 10in
NICKNAME: Ketts
APPOINTED TO FIRST-CLASS LIST: 2006
INTERNATIONAL PANEL: 2008-
ELITE PANEL: 2011-
TESTS UMPIRED: 26 (11 as TV umpire)
ODIS UMPIRED: 53 (24 as TV umpire)
T20IS UMPIRED: 17 (7 as TV umpire)
COUNTIES AS PLAYER: Yorkshire, Middlesex
ROLE: Left-hand bat; right-arm medium bowler
COUNTY DEBUT: 1994 (Yorks), 1998 (Middx)



---

DO YOU HAVE ANY RITUALS, QUIRKS OR SUPERSTITIONS AS AN UMPIRE? I always take a picture of my children out to the middle with me
CAREER HIGHLIGHTS AS AN UMPIRE: Officiating in my first Test match between Sri Lanka and West Indies in Galle in 2010 and being appointed to the ICC Elite Panel
FAVOURITE GROUND: Trent Bridge and Scarborough

| Batting | Mat | Inns | NO | Runs | HS | Ave | SR | 100 | 50 | Ct | St |
|---|---|---|---|---|---|---|---|---|---|---|---|
| First-class | 33 | 56 | 6 | 1258 | 108 | 25.16 | | 1 | 7 | 20 | 0 |
| List A | 21 | 16 | 4 | 290 | 58 | 24.16 | | 0 | 1 | 6 | 0 |
| **Bowling** | **Mat** | **Balls** | **Runs** | **Wkts** | **BBI** | **BBM** | **Ave** | **Econ** | **SR** | **5w** | **10** |
| First-class | 33 | 378 | 243 | 3 | 2/26 | | 81.00 | 3.85 | 126.0 | 0 | 0 |
| List A | 21 | 270 | 230 | 6 | 2/43 | 2/43 | 38.33 | 5.11 | 45.0 | 0 | 0 |

# NIGEL LLONG

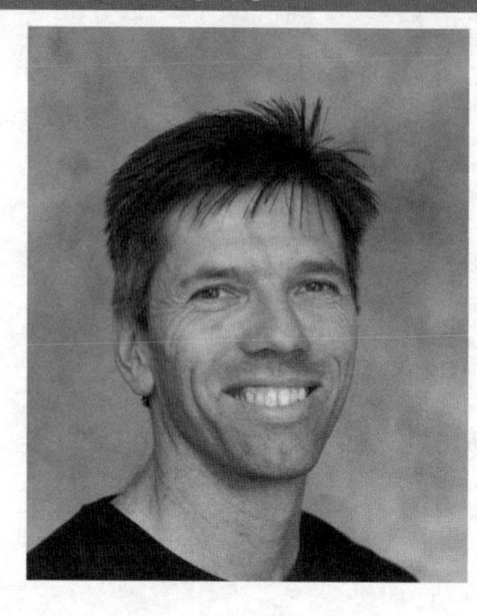

NAME: Nigel James Llong
BORN: February 11, 1969, Ashford, Kent
HEIGHT: 6ft
NICKNAME: Nidge
APPOINTED TO FIRST-CLASS LIST: 2002
INTERNATIONAL PANEL: 2004-06 as TV umpire, 2006-present as full member
ELITE PANEL: 2012-
TESTS UMPIRED: 26
ODIS UMPIRED: 91 (47 as TV umpire)
T20IS UMPIRED: 20 (10 as TV umpire)
COUNTY AS PLAYER: Kent
ROLE: Left-hand bat; off-spin bowler
COUNTY DEBUT: 1990

---

NOTES: Umpired at the 2007, 2009 and 2012 World T20s and the 2011 and 2015 World Cup. Officiated at the 2004, 2007, 2009 and 2010 T20 Finals Day. As a player his best season was in 1994, when he made 943 runs at 42.86 for Kent

| Batting | Mat | Inns | NO | Runs | HS | Ave | SR | 100 | 50 | Ct | St |
|---|---|---|---|---|---|---|---|---|---|---|---|
| First-class | 68 | 108 | 11 | 3024 | 130 | 31.17 | | 6 | 16 | 59 | 0 |
| List A | 136 | 115 | 24 | 2302 | 123 | 25.29 | | 2 | 8 | 41 | 0 |
| **Bowling** | **Mat** | **Balls** | **Runs** | **Wkts** | **BBI** | **BBM** | **Ave** | **Econ** | **SR** | **5w** | **10** |
| First-class | 68 | 2273 | 1259 | 35 | 5/21 | | 35.97 | 3.32 | 64.9 | 2 | 0 |
| List A | 136 | 1317 | 1210 | 40 | 4/24 | 4/24 | 30.25 | 5.51 | 32.9 | 0 | 0 |

# GRAHAM LLOYD

NAME: Graham David Lloyd
BORN: July 1, 1969, Accrington, Lancashire
APPOINTED TO FIRST-CLASS LIST: 2014
COUNTY AS PLAYER: Lancashire
ROLE: Right-hand bat, right-arm medium bowler
COUNTY DEBUT: 1988
ODI DEBUT: 1996

UMPIRES

CAREER HIGHLIGHT AS AN UMPIRE: Umpiring the Somerset vs India tour match a couple of years ago
FAVOURITE GROUND: Worcester
FUNNIEST MOMENT ON A CRICKET FIELD: Ian Austin doing his Bob Willis impression and losing his footing in his delivery stride, resulting in him rolling uncontrollably down the wicket
BEST TEA ON THE COUNTY CIRCUIT: Lord's
FAVOURITE PASTIMES OUTSIDE OF CRICKET? Horse-racing and football
CAN YOU TELL US A SURPRISING FACT ABOUT YOURSEL?: As a teenager I represented Lancashire and North of England at tennis

| Batting | Mat | Inns | NO | Runs | HS | Ave | SR | 100 | 50 | Ct | St |
|---|---|---|---|---|---|---|---|---|---|---|---|
| ODIs | 6 | 5 | 1 | 39 | 22 | 9.75 | 48.75 | 0 | 0 | 2 | 0 |
| First-class | 203 | 323 | 28 | 11279 | 241 | 38.23 | | 24 | 64 | 140 | 0 |
| List A | 295 | 258 | 48 | 6117 | 134 | 29.12 | | 4 | 29 | 67 | 0 |
| **Bowling** | **Mat** | **Balls** | **Runs** | **Wkts** | **BBI** | **BBM** | **Ave** | **Econ** | **SR** | **5w** | **10** |
| ODIs | 6 | - | - | - | - | - | - | - | - | - | - |
| First-class | 203 | 339 | 440 | 2 | 1/4 | | 220.00 | 7.78 | 169.5 | 0 | 0 |
| List A | 295 | 72 | 103 | 1 | 1/23 | 1/23 | 103.00 | 8.58 | 72.0 | 0 | 0 |

# JEREMY LLOYDS

**NAME:** Jeremy William Lloyds
**BORN:** November 17, 1954, Penang, Malaysia
**HEIGHT:** 5ft 11in
**NICKNAME:** Jerry
**APPOINTED TO FIRST-CLASS LIST:** 1998
**INTERNATIONAL PANEL:** 2002-2004 as TV umpire; 2004-2006 as full member
**TESTS UMPIRED:** 5 (plus 10 as TV umpire)
**ODIS UMPIRED:** 18 (plus 22 as TV umpire)
**T20IS UMPIRED:** 1
**COUNTIES AS PLAYER:** Somerset, Gloucestershire
**ROLE:** Left-hand bat; off-spin bowler
**COUNTY DEBUT:** 1979 (Som), 1985 (Gloucs)

---

**NOTES:** An allrounder when a player, Lloyds passed 1,000 runs three times for Gloucestershire. As an umpire he has stood in the C&G final in 2006 and officiated at the T20 Finals Day in 2007, 2008 and 2012

| Batting | Mat | Inns | NO | Runs | HS | Ave | SR | 100 | 50 | Ct | St |
|---|---|---|---|---|---|---|---|---|---|---|---|
| First-class | 267 | 408 | 64 | 10679 | 132* | 31.04 | | 10 | 62 | 229 | 0 |
| List A | 177 | 150 | 26 | 1982 | 73* | 15.98 | | 0 | 5 | 58 | 0 |
| **Bowling** | **Mat** | **Balls** | **Runs** | **Wkts** | **BBI** | **BBM** | **Ave** | **Econ** | **SR** | **5w** | **10** |
| First-class | 267 | 24175 | 12943 | 333 | 7/88 | | 38.86 | 3.21 | 72.5 | 13 | 1 |
| List A | 177 | 1522 | 1129 | 26 | 3/14 | 3/14 | 43.42 | 4.45 | 58.5 | 0 | 0 |

# NEIL MALLENDER

NAME: Neil Alan Mallender
BORN: August 13, 1961, Kirk Sandall, Yorkshire
HEIGHT: 6ft
NICKNAME: Ghostie
APPOINTED TO FIRST-CLASS LIST: 1999
INTERNATIONAL PANEL: 2002-2004
TESTS UMPIRED: 3 (plus 5 as TV umpire)
ODIS UMPIRED: 22 (plus 10 as TV umpire)
COUNTIES AS PLAYER: Northamptonshire, Somerset
ROLE: Right-hand bat; right-arm fast-medium bowler
COUNTY DEBUT: 1980 (Northants), 1987 (Som)
TEST DEBUT: 1992



---

DO YOU HAVE ANY RITUALS, QUIRKS OR SUPERSTITIONS AS AN UMPIRE? I will never pick an end. I always toss up or flick a bail up to decide the end
WHAT HAS BEEN YOUR CAREER HIGHLIGHT AS AN UMPIRE? Umpiring at the 2003 World Cup
WHAT'S YOUR FAVOURITE COUNTY GROUND? I love Taunton and Chester-le-Street
WHAT'S BEEN YOUR MOST MEMORABLE DISMISSAL? Giving Sachin Tendulkar out LBW to Ronnie Irani in an ODI at Lord's
WHAT'S THE FUNNIEST MOMENT YOU'VE EVER EXPERIENCED ON A CRICKET FIELD? Watching Mark Davies of Durham face Andrew Flintoff as nightwatchman in a game at Old Trafford
WHAT WAS THE HIGHLIGHT OF YOUR PLAYING CAREER? My Test debut at Headingley
WHAT ARE YOUR FAVOURITE PASTIMES OUTSIDE OF CRICKET? Playing golf
CAN YOU TELL US A SURPRISING FACT ABOUT YOURSELF? I enjoy rock/metal music. My favourite group is a Dutch group called Within Temptation – highly recommended!

| Batting | Mat | Inns | NO | Runs | HS | Ave | SR | 100 | 50 | Ct | St |
|---|---|---|---|---|---|---|---|---|---|---|---|
| Tests | 2 | 3 | 0 | 8 | 4 | 2.66 | 36.36 | 0 | 0 | 0 | 0 |
| First-class | 345 | 396 | 122 | 4709 | 100* | 17.18 | | 1 | 10 | 111 | 0 |
| List A | 325 | 163 | 75 | 1146 | 38* | 13.02 | | 0 | 0 | 60 | 0 |
| **Bowling** | **Mat** | **Balls** | **Runs** | **Wkts** | **BBI** | **BBM** | **Ave** | **Econ** | **SR** | **5w** | **10** |
| Tests | 2 | 449 | 215 | 10 | 5/50 | 8/122 | 21.50 | 2.87 | 44.9 | 1 | 0 |
| First-class | 345 | 53215 | 24654 | 937 | 7/27 | | 26.31 | 2.77 | 56.7 | 36 | 5 |
| List A | 325 | 15488 | 9849 | 387 | 7/37 | 7/37 | 25.44 | 3.81 | 40.0 | 3 | 0 |

# DAVID MILLNS

NAME: David James Millns
BORN: February 7, 1965, Clipstone, Nottinghamshire
HEIGHT: 6ft 3in
NICKNAME: Rocket Man
APPOINTED TO FIRST-CLASS LIST: 2009
COUNTIES AS A PLAYER: Nottinghamshire, Leicestershire
ROLE: Left-hand bat, right-arm fast bowler
COUNTY DEBUT: 1988 (Notts), 1990 (Leics)

---

DO YOU HAVE ANY RITUALS, QUIRKS OR SUPERSTITIONS AS AN UMPIRE? I get changed into my umpiring gear as soon as I arrive at a ground
WHAT HAS BEEN YOUR CAREER HIGHLIGHT AS AN UMPIRE? Fetching David Boon away from his Lord's lunch to inspect a damaged pitch during the India Test last year
WHAT'S YOUR FAVOURITE COUNTY GROUND? Lord's – the place is special
WHAT'S BEEN YOUR MOST MEMORABLE DISMISSAL? As a player nicking off on 99 against Warwickshire still grinds the stomach sometimes
WHAT'S THE FUNNIEST MOMENT YOU'VE EVER EXPERIENCED ON A CRICKET FIELD? Any time I had to watch from the non-striker's end when Alan Mullally tried to bat
WHAT ARE YOUR FAVOURITE PASTIMES OUTSIDE OF CRICKET? Mountain biking is the favourite at the moment
IF YOU COULD CHANGE ONE RULE ABOUT CRICKET, WHAT WOULD IT BE? Tea would be 30 minutes for Championship matches
CAN YOU TELL US A SURPRISING FACT ABOUT YOURSELF? I'm a qualified Advanced Scuba Diver

| Batting | Mat | Inns | NO | Runs | HS | Ave | SR | 100 | 50 | Ct | St |
|---|---|---|---|---|---|---|---|---|---|---|---|
| First-class | 171 | 203 | 63 | 3082 | 121 | 22.01 | | 3 | 8 | 76 | 0 |
| List A | 91 | 49 | 26 | 338 | 39* | 14.69 | | 0 | 0 | 18 | 0 |
| **Bowling** | **Mat** | **Balls** | **Runs** | **Wkts** | **BBI** | **BBM** | **Ave** | **Econ** | **SR** | **5w** | **10** |
| First-class | 171 | 26571 | 15129 | 553 | 9/37 | | 27.35 | 3.41 | 48.0 | 23 | 4 |
| List A | 91 | 3931 | 3144 | 83 | 4/26 | 4/26 | 37.87 | 4.79 | 47.3 | 0 | 0 |

# STEVE O'SHAUGHNESSY

NAME: Steven Joseph O'Shaughnessy
BORN: September 9, 1961, Bury, Lancashire
APPOINTED TO FIRST-CLASS LIST: 2011
COUNTIES AS PLAYER: Lancashire, Worcestershire
ROLE: Right-hand bat; right-arm medium bowler
COUNTY DEBUT: 1980 (Lancs), 1988 (Worcs)



NOTES: O'Shaughnessy started umpiring in 2007 and was appointed to the full list for the 2011 season. He has officiated in four women's ODIs, including in the 2013 Ashes series

| Batting | Mat | Inns | NO | Runs | HS | Ave | SR | 100 | 50 | Ct | St |
|---|---|---|---|---|---|---|---|---|---|---|---|
| First-class | 112 | 181 | 28 | 3720 | 159* | 24.31 | | 5 | 16 | 57 | 0 |
| List A | 176 | 151 | 23 | 2999 | 101* | 23.42 | | 1 | 15 | 44 | 0 |
| **Bowling** | **Mat** | **Balls** | **Runs** | **Wkts** | **BBI** | **BBM** | **Ave** | **Econ** | **SR** | **5w** | **10** |
| First-class | 112 | 7179 | 4108 | 114 | 4/66 | | 36.03 | 3.43 | 62.9 | 0 | 0 |
| List A | 176 | 5389 | 4184 | 115 | 4/17 | 4/17 | 36.38 | 4.65 | 46.8 | 0 | 0 |

# TIM ROBINSON

NAME: Robert Timothy Robinson
BORN: November 21, 1958, Sutton-in-Ashfield, Nottinghamshire
HEIGHT: 6ft
NICKNAME: Robbo, Chop
APPOINTED TO FIRST-CLASS LIST: 2007
ODIS UMPIRED: 4 (plus 1 as TV umpire)
T20IS UMPIRED: 3 (plus 4 as TV umpire)
COUNTY AS PLAYER: Nottinghamshire
ROLE: Right-hand bat; right-arm medium bowler
COUNTY DEBUT: 1978
TEST DEBUT: 1984
ODI DEBUT: 1984

---

DO YOU HAVE ANY RITUALS, QUIRKS OR SUPERSTITIONS AS AN UMPIRE? I try and walk out on the left-hand side
WHAT HAS BEEN YOUR CAREER HIGHLIGHT AS AN UMPIRE? Standing in the England v Australia T20I when Aaron Finch hit the world-record score at Southampton
WHAT'S YOUR FAVOURITE COUNTY GROUND? Trent Bridge
WHAT'S BEEN YOUR MOST MEMORABLE DISMISSAL? Giving Alastair Cook out LBW second ball in my international debut which proved correct after he reviewed it!
WHAT'S THE FUNNIEST MOMENT YOU'VE EVER EXPERIENCED ON A CRICKET FIELD? Paul Johnson's bat handle breaking and getting covered in sawdust which the batmakers had packed the handle with
WHAT WAS THE HIGHLIGHT OF YOUR PLAYING CAREER? Scoring 175 in the Ashes at Leeds
IF YOU COULD CHANGE ONE RULE ABOUT CRICKET, WHAT WOULD IT BE? Lengthen the tea interval to half an hour

| Batting | Mat | Inns | NO | Runs | HS | Ave | SR | 100 | 50 | Ct | St |
|---|---|---|---|---|---|---|---|---|---|---|---|
| Tests | 29 | 49 | 5 | 1601 | 175 | 36.38 | 41.62 | 4 | 6 | 8 | 0 |
| ODIs | 26 | 26 | 0 | 597 | 83 | 22.96 | 58.18 | 0 | 3 | 6 | 0 |
| First-class | 425 | 739 | 85 | 27571 | 220* | 42.15 | | 63 | 141 | 257 | 0 |
| List A | 397 | 386 | 40 | 11879 | 139 | 34.33 | | 9 | 75 | 120 | 0 |
| **Bowling** | **Mat** | **Balls** | **Runs** | **Wkts** | **BBI** | **BBM** | **Ave** | **Econ** | **SR** | **5w** | **10** |
| Tests | 29 | 6 | 0 | 0 | - | - | - | 0.00 | - | 0 | 0 |
| ODIs | 26 | - | - | - | - | - | - | - | - | - | |
| First-class | 425 | 259 | 289 | 4 | 1/22 | | 72.25 | 6.69 | 64.7 | 0 | 0 |
| List A | 397 | - | - | - | - | - | - | - | - | - | - |

# MARTIN SAGGERS

NAME: Martin John Saggers
BORN: May 23, 1972, King's Lynn, Norfolk
HEIGHT: 6ft 2in
NICKNAME: Saggs
APPOINTED TO FIRST-CLASS LIST: 2012
COUNTIES AS PLAYER: Durham, Kent
ROLE: Right-hand bat; right-arm fast-medium bowler
COUNTY DEBUT: 1996 (Dur), 1999 (Kent)
TEST DEBUT: 2003



WHAT HAS BEEN YOUR CAREER HIGHLIGHT AS AN UMPIRE? I don't have any specific highlights, but just having the opportunity to watch some fantastic games of cricket, right where the action is happening
WHAT'S BEEN YOUR MOST MEMORABLE DISMISSAL? Giving my former room-mate and friend out, Jon Batty, when he was playing for Gloucestershire. He told me that he wasn't going to walk
WHAT WAS THE HIGHLIGHT OF YOUR PLAYING CAREER? Getting a wicket with my very first delivery in my debut home Test
WHAT ARE YOU FAVOURITE PASTIMES OUTSIDE OF CRICKET? I dabble a little bit in wildlife photography and often travel to South Africa and go on safari
CAN YOU TELL US A SURPRISING FACT ABOUT YOURSELF? I once filmed a television advert in 1997 with Hansie Cronje in South Africa for Standard Bank

| Batting | Mat | Inns | NO | Runs | HS | Ave | SR | 100 | 50 | Ct | St |
|---|---|---|---|---|---|---|---|---|---|---|---|
| Tests | 3 | 3 | 0 | 1 | 1 | 0.33 | 3.33 | 0 | 0 | 1 | 0 |
| First-class | 119 | 147 | 43 | 1165 | 64 | 11.20 | | 0 | 2 | 27 | 0 |
| List A | 124 | 68 | 34 | 313 | 34* | 9.20 | | 0 | 0 | 23 | 0 |
| Twenty20 | 10 | 1 | 0 | 5 | 5 | 5.00 | 62.50 | 0 | 0 | 2 | 0 |
| **Bowling** | **Mat** | **Balls** | **Runs** | **Wkts** | **BBI** | **BBM** | **Ave** | **Econ** | **SR** | **5w** | **10** |
| Tests | 3 | 493 | 247 | 7 | 2/29 | 3/62 | 35.28 | 3.00 | 70.4 | 0 | 0 |
| First-class | 119 | 20676 | 10513 | 415 | 7/79 | | 25.33 | 3.05 | 49.8 | 18 | 0 |
| List A | 124 | 5622 | 4229 | 166 | 5/22 | 5/22 | 25.47 | 4.51 | 33.8 | 2 | 0 |
| Twenty20 | 9 | 186 | 256 | 6 | 2/14 | 2/14 | 42.66 | 8.25 | 31.0 | 0 | 0 |

# ALEX WHARF

NAME: Alexander George Wharf
BORN: June 4, 1975, Bradford, Yorkshire
HEIGHT: 6ft 4in
NICKNAME: Gangster
APPOINTED TO FIRST-CLASS LIST: 2014
COUNTIES AS PLAYER: Yorkshire, Nottinghamshire, Glamorgan
ROLE: Right-hand bat; right-arm medium fast bowler
COUNTY DEBUT: 1994 (Yorks), 1998 (Notts), 2000 (Glam)
ODI DEBUT: 2004

---

NOTES: As a player Wharf was called up to the England ODI side in 2004 after impressing for Glamorgan. He took a wicket with his fifth ball, removing India's Sourav Ganguly at Trent Bridge. He retired in 2009 because of a knee injury and moved into umpiring four years ago

| Batting | Mat | Inns | NO | Runs | HS | Ave | SR | 100 | 50 | Ct | St |
|---|---|---|---|---|---|---|---|---|---|---|---|
| ODIs | 13 | 5 | 3 | 19 | 9 | 9.50 | 67.85 | 0 | 0 | 1 | 0 |
| First-class | 121 | 184 | 29 | 3570 | 128* | 23.03 | | 6 | 14 | 63 | 0 |
| List A | 155 | 109 | 22 | 1411 | 72 | 16.21 | | 0 | 1 | 42 | 0 |
| Twenty20 | 34 | 20 | 7 | 157 | 19 | 12.07 | 120,76 | 0 | 0 | 5 | 0 |
| **Bowling** | **Mat** | **Balls** | **Runs** | **Wkts** | **BBI** | **BBM** | **Ave** | **Econ** | **SR** | **5w** | **10** |
| ODIs | 13 | 584 | 428 | 18 | 4/24 | 4/24 | 23.77 | 4.39 | 32.4 | 0 | 0 |
| First-class | 121 | 16825 | 10941 | 293 | 6/59 | | 37.34 | 3.90 | 57.4 | 5 | 0 |
| List A | 155 | 6497 | 5552 | 192 | 6/5 | 6/5 | 28.91 | 5.12 | 33.8 | 1 | 0 |
| Twenty20 | 32 | 644 | 1028 | 39 | 4/39 | 4/39 | 26.35 | 9.57 | 16.5 | 0 | 0 |

# PAD UP

## THE WORLD'S BEST CRICKET MAGAZINE JUST GOT BETTER

ADDITIONAL CONTENT - INTERACTIVE - AVAILABLE ON ALL MAJOR DEVICES

ALLOUTCRICKET.COM/SUBSCRIBE

## REAL PEOPLE, REAL NEEDS

The pressure is on, and the whole world feels like it's against you... only this time it's not a game. Sometimes the greatest challenges cricketers face are not on the pitch. This is when they need our support more than ever. With your help, the PCA Benevolent fund safeguards our players against illness or at a time of crisis, while we provide the care and support that's always been at the heart of the game.

For more information, or to get involved
Jason Ratcliffe, *Assistant CEO* **jratcliffe@thepca.co.uk**
Emily Lewis, *Head of Events & Fundraising* **elewis@thepca.co.uk** 020 7449 4225

thepca.co.uk/benevolent_fund
www.twitter.com/pcabenevolent

Roll *of*
Honour

## LV= COUNTY CHAMPIONSHIP TABLES



### Division One

| Team | Mat | Won | Lost | Tied | Draw | Aban | Pts |
|---|---|---|---|---|---|---|---|
| Yorkshire | 16 | 8 | 1 | 0 | 7 | 0 | 255 |
| Warwickshire | 16 | 8 | 4 | 0 | 4 | 0 | 238 |
| Sussex | 16 | 6 | 4 | 0 | 5 | 1 | 210 |
| Notts | 16 | 6 | 6 | 0 | 4 | 0 | 206 |
| Durham | 16 | 5 | 4 | 0 | 7 | 0 | 199 |
| Somerset | 16 | 4 | 2 | 0 | 10 | 0 | 198 |
| Middlesex | 16 | 4 | 5 | 0 | 6 | 1 | 170 |
| Lancashire | 16 | 3 | 6 | 0 | 7 | 0 | 154 |
| Northants | 16 | 0 | 12 | 0 | 4 | 0 | 79 |

### Division Two

| Team | Mat | Won | Lost | Tied | Draw | Aban | Pts |
|---|---|---|---|---|---|---|---|
| Hampshire | 16 | 7 | 1 | 0 | 8 | 0 | 240 |
| Worcs | 16 | 8 | 3 | 0 | 5 | 0 | 237 |
| Essex | 16 | 7 | 2 | 0 | 7 | 0 | 229 |
| Derbyshire | 16 | 6 | 5 | 0 | 5 | 0 | 188 |
| Surrey | 16 | 4 | 5 | 0 | 7 | 0 | 183 |
| Kent | 16 | 4 | 6 | 0 | 6 | 0 | 171 |
| Gloucs | 16 | 4 | 5 | 0 | 7 | 0 | 163 |
| Glamorgan | 16 | 3 | 6 | 0 | 7 | 0 | 153 |
| Leics | 16 | 0 | 10 | 0 | 6 | 0 | 108 |

WENSLYDALE
CREA ERY

# ROYAL LONDON ONE-DAY CUP 2014

## Group A

| Team | Mat | Won | Lost | Tied | N/R | Pts | Net RR |
|---|---|---|---|---|---|---|---|
| Yorkshire | 8 | 6 | 2 | 0 | 0 | 12 | +1.040 |
| Essex | 8 | 5 | 1 | 0 | 2 | 12 | +0.387 |
| Gloucs | 8 | 4 | 2 | 0 | 2 | 10 | -0.016 |
| Derbyshire | 8 | 4 | 2 | 0 | 2 | 8 | +0.045 |
| Leics | 8 | 3 | 4 | 0 | 1 | 7 | -0.393 |
| Northants | 8 | 2 | 4 | 0 | 2 | 6 | -0.277 |
| Worcs | 8 | 2 | 4 | 0 | 2 | 6 | -0.328 |
| Lancashire | 8 | 2 | 5 | 0 | 1 | 5 | -0.279 |
| Hampshire | 8 | 1 | 5 | 0 | 2 | 4 | -0.569 |

## Group B

| Team | Mat | Won | Lost | Tied | N/R | Pts | Net RR |
|---|---|---|---|---|---|---|---|
| Notts | 8 | 4 | 1 | 1 | 2 | 11 | +0.364 |
| Kent | 8 | 4 | 1 | 1 | 2 | 11 | +0.245 |
| Warwickshire | 8 | 4 | 3 | 0 | 1 | 9 | +0.343 |
| Durham | 8 | 4 | 3 | 0 | 1 | 9 | +0.212 |
| Glamorgan | 8 | 4 | 4 | 0 | 0 | 8 | +0.230 |
| Somerset | 8 | 3 | 4 | 1 | 0 | 7 | +0.067 |
| Middlesex | 8 | 3 | 4 | 0 | 1 | 7 | -0.280 |
| Sussex | 8 | 3 | 5 | 0 | 0 | 6 | -0.501 |
| Surrey | 8 | 1 | 5 | 1 | 1 | 4 | -0.643 |

QUARTER-FINALS

Nottinghamshire vs Derbyshire at Nottingham, Aug 26 *Notts won by 85 runs*
Nottinghamshire 313-5 (50/50 ov); Hampshire 228 (44.5/50 ov)

Yorkshire vs Durham at Leeds, Aug 28 *Dur won by 31 runs*
Durham 237 (48.4/50 ov); Yorkshire 206 (48.1/50 ov)

Essex vs Warwickshire at Chelmsford, Aug 28 *War won by 67 runs*
Warwickshire 271-7 (50/50 ov); Essex 204 (42.4/50 ov)

Kent vs Gloucestershire at Canterbury, Aug 29 *Kent won by 24 runs*
Kent 242 (48.3/50 ov); Gloucestershire 218 (47.3/50 ov)

SEMI-FINAL

Warwickshire vs Kent at Birmingham, Sep 4 *Warks won by 6 wickets*
Kent 215-8 (50/50 ov); Warwickshire 219-4 (46.3/50 ov)

Durham vs Nottinghamshire at Chester-le-Street, Sep 6 *Dur won by 83 runs*
Durham 353-8 (50/50 ov); Nottinghamshire 270 (46.1/50 ov)

FINAL

Durham vs Warwickshire at Lord's, Sep 20 *Dur won by 3 wickets*
Warwickshire 165 (47/50 ov); Durham 166-7 (40.2/50 ov)

TYNE
DURHAM
ROYAL LONDON
ONE-DAY CUP
2014 FINALISTS
PORT
TYNE
ROYAL
LONDON

# NATWEST T20 BLAST

## North Division

| Team | Mat | Won | Lost | Tied | N/R | Pts | Net RR |
|---|---|---|---|---|---|---|---|
| Lancashire | 14 | 10 | 2 | 0 | 2 | 22 | +0.846 |
| Notts | 14 | 9 | 3 | 0 | 2 | 20 | +0.642 |
| Worcs | 14 | 8 | 4 | 0 | 2 | 18 | +0.480 |
| Warwickshire | 14 | 7 | 5 | 0 | 2 | 16 | +0.235 |
| Yorkshire | 14 | 6 | 5 | 0 | 3 | 15 | +0.588 |
| Durham | 14 | 5 | 7 | 0 | 2 | 12 | +0.106 |
| Northants | 14 | 4 | 7 | 0 | 3 | 11 | -0.899 |
| Leics | 14 | 4 | 9 | 0 | 1 | 9 | -0.552 |
| Derbyshire | 14 | 1 | 12 | 0 | 1 | 3 | -1.406 |

## South Division

| Team | Mat | Won | Lost | Tied | N/R | Pts | Net RR |
|---|---|---|---|---|---|---|---|
| Essex | 14 | 10 | 4 | 0 | 0 | 20 | +0.401 |
| Surrey | 14 | 9 | 5 | 0 | 0 | 18 | +0.426 |
| Hampshire | 14 | 9 | 5 | 0 | 0 | 18 | +0.136 |
| Glamorgan | 14 | 6 | 5 | 1 | 2 | 15 | +0.145 |
| Somerset | 14 | 6 | 7 | 0 | 1 | 13 | -0.107 |
| Kent | 14 | 6 | 7 | 1 | 0 | 13 | -0.229 |
| Sussex | 14 | 6 | 8 | 0 | 0 | 12 | -0.022 |
| Gloucs | 14 | 5 | 7 | 0 | 2 | 10 | -0.362 |
| Middlesex | 14 | 2 | 11 | 0 | 1 | 5 | -0.457 |

QUARTER-FINALS

Lancashire vs Glamorgan at Manchester, Aug 1-2 *Lancs won by 1 run*
Lancashire 137-8 (20/20 ov); Glamorgan 136-7 (20/20)

Surrey vs Worcestershire at The Oval, Aug 2 *Surrey won by 3 wickets*
Worcestershire 141-9 (20/20 ov); Surrey 144-7 (16.3/20 ov)

Essex vs Warwickshire at Chelmsford, Aug 2 *Warks won by 19 runs*
Warwickshire 197-2 (20/20 ov); Essex 178-5 (20/20 ov)

Nottinghamshire vs Hampshire at Nottingham, Aug 3 *Hants won by 5 wickets*
Nottinghamshire 197-2 (20/20 ov); Hampshire 198-5 (19/20 ov)

SEMI-FINALS

Surrey vs Warwickshire at Birmingham, Aug 23 *Warks won by 16 runs*
Warwickshire 194-4 (20/20 ov); Surrey 178-7 (20/20 ov)

Hampshire vs Lancashire at Birmingham, Aug 23 *Lancs won by 41 runs (D/L)*
Lancashire 160-5 (19/19 ov); Hampshire 101 (14.1/16 ov; target 143)

FINAL

Warwickshire vs Lancashire at Birmingham, Aug 23 *Warks won by 4 runs*
Warwickshire 181-5 (20/20 ov); Lancashire 177-8 (20/20 ov)

## FIRST-CLASS BATTING AVERAGES *Minimum of 20 innings*

| Name | Mat | Inns | NO | Runs | HS | Ave | BF | SR | 100 | 50 | 0 | 4s | 6s |
|---|---|---|---|---|---|---|---|---|---|---|---|---|---|
| A Lyth | 17 | 24 | 1 | 1619 | 251 | 70.39 | 3068 | 52.77 | 7 | 6 | 2 | 208 | 7 |
| JM Vince | 16 | 28 | 3 | 1525 | 240 | 61.00 | 1984 | 76.86 | 4 | 7 | 1 | 225 | 4 |
| EC Joyce | 15 | 24 | 2 | 1501 | 164* | 68.22 | 2485 | 60.40 | 8 | 3 | 3 | 192 | 8 |
| GS Ballance | 14 | 21 | 1 | 1390 | 174 | 69.50 | 2486 | 55.91 | 6 | 6 | 1 | 178 | 12 |
| DKH Mitchell | 16 | 27 | 4 | 1334 | 172* | 58.00 | 2763 | 48.28 | 5 | 4 | 2 | 163 | 3 |
| CJL Rogers | 15 | 28 | 4 | 1333 | 241* | 55.54 | 2140 | 62.28 | 4 | 4 | 1 | 197 | 2 |
| APR Gidman | 17 | 30 | 2 | 1278 | 264 | 45.64 | 1919 | 66.59 | 4 | 3 | 2 | 178 | 7 |
| JHK Adams | 16 | 29 | 1 | 1215 | 231 | 43.39 | 2537 | 47.89 | 1 | 8 | 2 | 163 | 7 |
| MH Wessels | 17 | 31 | 4 | 1213 | 158 | 44.92 | 1962 | 61.82 | 1 | 8 | 1 | 152 | 22 |
| WR Smith | 16 | 27 | 4 | 1187 | 151* | 51.60 | 2442 | 48.60 | 2 | 6 | 0 | 144 | 1 |
| SG Borthwick | 16 | 28 | 1 | 1187 | 216 | 43.96 | 2197 | 54.02 | 3 | 5 | 3 | 159 | 4 |
| AG Prince | 16 | 28 | 1 | 1160 | 257* | 42.96 | 2146 | 54.05 | 3 | 3 | 2 | 121 | 5 |
| ME Trescothick | 17 | 27 | 0 | 1156 | 133 | 42.81 | 2142 | 53.96 | 4 | 6 | 2 | 183 | 9 |
| DJ Malan | 15 | 26 | 1 | 1137 | 154* | 45.48 | 2258 | 50.35 | 2 | 4 | 2 | 182 | 1 |
| SR Patel | 17 | 32 | 0 | 1125 | 156 | 35.15 | 1666 | 67.52 | 2 | 6 | 5 | 169 | 3 |
| WL Madsen | 17 | 30 | 2 | 1088 | 111* | 38.85 | 2242 | 48.52 | 1 | 8 | 0 | 138 | 1 |
| AJ Robson | 16 | 30 | 0 | 1086 | 115 | 36.20 | 1985 | 54.71 | 1 | 9 | 4 | 161 | 0 |
| JJ Roy | 18 | 25 | 4 | 1078 | 121* | 51.33 | 1283 | 84.02 | 3 | 5 | 0 | 136 | 19 |
| DJ Bell-Drummond | 17 | 29 | 3 | 1058 | 153 | 40.69 | 2547 | 41.53 | 3 | 6 | 3 | 137 | 1 |
| RJ Burns | 18 | 32 | 4 | 1055 | 199 | 37.67 | 2248 | 46.93 | 2 | 5 | 4 | 144 | 1 |
| JE Root | 11 | 17 | 3 | 1052 | 200* | 75.14 | 1723 | 61.05 | 3 | 6 | 1 | 117 | 3 |
| SM Davies | 17 | 25 | 1 | 1040 | 174 | 43.33 | 1625 | 64.00 | 3 | 5 | 1 | 144 | 0 |
| NRD Compton | 17 | 27 | 3 | 1034 | 156 | 43.08 | 2334 | 44.30 | 2 | 5 | 2 | 120 | 6 |
| AD Hales | 12 | 22 | 1 | 1032 | 183 | 49.14 | 1454 | 70.97 | 3 | 5 | 2 | 146 | 12 |
| ZS Ansari | 18 | 30 | 7 | 1029 | 112 | 44.73 | 2856 | 36.02 | 2 | 6 | 2 | 120 | 0 |
| MJ Richardson | 17 | 29 | 0 | 1025 | 148 | 35.34 | 2101 | 48.78 | 2 | 5 | 0 | 125 | 5 |
| MD Stoneman | 17 | 29 | 0 | 1021 | 187 | 35.20 | 1595 | 64.01 | 3 | 4 | 2 | 135 | 5 |
| AZ Lees | 16 | 23 | 0 | 1018 | 138 | 44.26 | 2098 | 48.52 | 2 | 5 | 1 | 135 | 7 |
| LWP Wells | 16 | 29 | 1 | 1016 | 162 | 36.28 | 2256 | 45.03 | 1 | 7 | 2 | 139 | 4 |
| WA Tavaré | 16 | 28 | 2 | 1014 | 139 | 39.00 | 2165 | 46.83 | 4 | 3 | 4 | 145 | 5 |
| SD Robson | 18 | 31 | 3 | 1010 | 163 | 36.07 | 1975 | 51.13 | 2 | 5 | 0 | 137 | 1 |
| WD Bragg | 17 | 31 | 3 | 1008 | 100* | 36.00 | 2344 | 43.00 | 1 | 6 | 1 | 127 | 1 |
| JWA Taylor | 15 | 28 | 2 | 992 | 126 | 38.15 | 1951 | 50.84 | 1 | 8 | 3 | 133 | 3 |
| JS Foster | 17 | 25 | 3 | 976 | 132 | 44.36 | 1752 | 55.70 | 2 | 5 | 3 | 131 | 6 |
| NJ O'Brien | 15 | 28 | 3 | 971 | 133 | 38.84 | 1616 | 60.08 | 2 | 5 | 4 | 125 | 8 |
| J Allenby | 17 | 29 | 2 | 969 | 100 | 35.88 | 1566 | 61.87 | 1 | 5 | 2 | 127 | 13 |
| PD Collingwood | 17 | 29 | 5 | 966 | 102 | 40.25 | 1753 | 55.10 | 3 | 5 | 2 | 101 | 12 |
| MM Ali | 15 | 21 | 1 | 962 | 162 | 48.10 | 1789 | 53.77 | 2 | 6 | 1 | 119 | 16 |
| CMW Read | 17 | 27 | 5 | 952 | 96 | 43.27 | 1628 | 58.47 | 0 | 6 | 0 | 132 | 5 |
| IR Bell | 11 | 19 | 1 | 940 | 189* | 52.22 | 1552 | 60.56 | 3 | 5 | 1 | 110 | 12 |
| LJ Wright | 12 | 21 | 3 | 933 | 189 | 51.83 | 1417 | 65.84 | 3 | 3 | 0 | 128 | 7 |
| BP Nash | 16 | 26 | 2 | 926 | 126 | 38.58 | 1500 | 61.73 | 1 | 5 | 2 | 122 | 7 |
| SA Northeast | 15 | 25 | 1 | 905 | 128 | 37.70 | 1714 | 52.80 | 4 | 4 | 3 | 109 | 3 |
| DI Stevens | 17 | 27 | 2 | 904 | 105 | 36.16 | 1243 | 72.72 | 1 | 4 | 0 | 122 | 19 |
| PA Jaques | 11 | 20 | 2 | 894 | 150* | 49.66 | 1432 | 62.43 | 2 | 6 | 1 | 134 | 1 |
| PJ Horton | 16 | 30 | 2 | 891 | 140 | 31.82 | 2058 | 43.29 | 2 | 3 | 5 | 107 | 0 |
| EJG Morgan | 11 | 20 | 1 | 871 | 191 | 45.84 | 1655 | 52.62 | 2 | 4 | 3 | 118 | 6 |
| CB Cooke | 13 | 21 | 1 | 870 | 171 | 43.50 | 1600 | 54.37 | 1 | 8 | 3 | 100 | 1 |
| CD Nash | 12 | 22 | 0 | 867 | 178 | 39.40 | 1379 | 62.87 | 1 | 6 | 0 | 135 | 0 |
| RS Bopara | 13 | 20 | 1 | 863 | 162 | 45.42 | 1905 | 45.30 | 2 | 2 | 1 | 93 | 7 |

GM
MAZA

# FIRST-CLASS BOWLING AVERAGES *Minimum of 2000 balls*

| Player | Mat | Inns | Overs | Mdns | Runs | Wkts | BBI | BBM | Ave | Econ | SR | 5 | 10 |
|---|---|---|---|---|---|---|---|---|---|---|---|---|---|
| MHA Footitt | 17 | 31 | 489.2 | 103 | 1612 | 84 | 6/48 | 9/122 | 19.19 | 3.29 | 34.9 | 6 | 0 |
| SJ Magoffin | 15 | 27 | 539.0 | 144 | 1405 | 72 | 6/60 | 8/40 | 19.51 | 2.60 | 44.9 | 4 | 0 |
| JA Brooks | 17 | 33 | 540.2 | 113 | 1941 | 71 | 5/36 | 8/112 | 27.33 | 3.59 | 45.6 | 2 | 0 |
| C Rushworth | 17 | 27 | 501.1 | 105 | 1611 | 65 | 9/52 | 15/95 | 24.78 | 3.21 | 46.2 | 3 | 1 |
| Saeed Ajmal | 9 | 17 | 417.3 | 116 | 1038 | 63 | 7/19 | 13/94 | 16.47 | 2.48 | 39.7 | 6 | 2 |
| MG Hogan | 13 | 23 | 444.5 | 106 | 1232 | 63 | 5/58 | 10/125 | 19.55 | 2.76 | 42.3 | 3 | 1 |
| JS Patel | 16 | 27 | 536.2 | 136 | 1553 | 59 | 5/49 | 8/145 | 26.32 | 2.89 | 54.5 | 1 | 0 |
| ME Claydon | 16 | 28 | 525.1 | 93 | 1761 | 59 | 5/61 | 9/151 | 29.84 | 3.35 | 53.4 | 3 | 0 |
| JM Anderson | 11 | 22 | 460.4 | 135 | 1205 | 58 | 5/41 | 10/89 | 20.77 | 2.61 | 47.6 | 4 | 1 |
| TJ Murtagh | 14 | 24 | 527.4 | 116 | 1646 | 58 | 6/60 | 10/192 | 28.37 | 3.11 | 54.5 | 5 | 1 |
| AC Thomas | 15 | 27 | 486.3 | 129 | 1365 | 57 | 5/40 | 8/107 | 23.94 | 2.80 | 51.2 | 3 | 0 |
| AEN Riley | 17 | 27 | 529.4 | 89 | 1755 | 57 | 5/62 | 9/123 | 30.78 | 3.31 | 55.7 | 3 | 0 |
| JD Shantry | 16 | 29 | 497.0 | 124 | 1336 | 56 | 6/53 | 10/131 | 23.85 | 2.68 | 53.2 | 2 | 1 |
| CAJ Morris | 17 | 31 | 528.4 | 141 | 1450 | 56 | 5/54 | 6/96 | 25.89 | 2.74 | 56.6 | 1 | 0 |
| DI Stevens | 17 | 29 | 526.4 | 123 | 1553 | 56 | 6/64 | 9/89 | 27.73 | 2.94 | 56.4 | 6 | 0 |
| TC Smith | 15 | 22 | 365.3 | 83 | 1105 | 54 | 5/42 | 8/132 | 20.46 | 3.02 | 40.6 | 4 | 0 |
| J Allenby | 17 | 27 | 451.4 | 123 | 1119 | 54 | 6/54 | 10/128 | 20.72 | 2.47 | 50.1 | 2 | 1 |
| GR Napier | 12 | 21 | 252.0 | 49 | 813 | 52 | 7/21 | 9/32 | 15.63 | 3.22 | 29.0 | 2 | 0 |
| KHD Barker | 16 | 27 | 456.5 | 96 | 1412 | 51 | 6/46 | 8/66 | 27.68 | 3.09 | 53.7 | 2 | 0 |
| RJ Sidebottom | 13 | 24 | 367.1 | 91 | 905 | 49 | 7/44 | 9/65 | 18.46 | 2.46 | 44.9 | 2 | 0 |
| AU Rashid | 15 | 26 | 379.4 | 73 | 1216 | 49 | 5/117 | 8/194 | 24.81 | 3.20 | 46.4 | 1 | 0 |
| PD Trego | 15 | 28 | 442.4 | 92 | 1391 | 49 | 7/84 | 11/153 | 28.38 | 3.14 | 54.2 | 1 | 1 |
| ST Finn | 11 | 19 | 393.1 | 58 | 1475 | 48 | 6/80 | 9/173 | 30.72 | 3.75 | 49.1 | 2 | 0 |
| JA Tomlinson | 16 | 26 | 416.5 | 103 | 1215 | 47 | 6/48 | 7/86 | 25.85 | 2.91 | 53.2 | 1 | 0 |
| MP Dunn | 14 | 23 | 399.4 | 76 | 1547 | 47 | 5/48 | 6/84 | 32.91 | 3.87 | 51.0 | 2 | 0 |
| MS Panesar | 15 | 24 | 403.2 | 114 | 1144 | 46 | 6/111 | 11/168 | 24.86 | 2.83 | 52.6 | 4 | 1 |
| Azharullah | 14 | 22 | 462.1 | 92 | 1504 | 46 | 7/76 | 10/158 | 32.69 | 3.25 | 60.2 | 1 | 1 |
| CR Woakes | 12 | 22 | 354.1 | 89 | 1129 | 45 | 5/35 | 8/140 | 25.08 | 3.18 | 47.2 | 2 | 0 |
| L Gregory | 10 | 19 | 342.5 | 75 | 1160 | 45 | 6/47 | 11/122 | 25.77 | 3.38 | 45.7 | 3 | 1 |
| JD Ryder | 12 | 22 | 289.5 | 76 | 796 | 44 | 5/24 | 10/110 | 18.09 | 2.74 | 39.5 | 4 | 1 |
| LE Plunkett | 12 | 23 | 372.5 | 59 | 1283 | 44 | 5/64 | 9/176 | 29.15 | 3.44 | 50.8 | 1 | 0 |
| SC Kerrigan | 16 | 27 | 530.0 | 99 | 1556 | 44 | 4/38 | 8/147 | 35.36 | 2.93 | 72.2 | 0 | 0 |
| TS Roland-Jones | 13 | 21 | 406.1 | 87 | 1337 | 43 | 6/50 | 12/105 | 31.09 | 3.29 | 56.6 | 3 | 1 |
| AP Palladino | 15 | 26 | 431.4 | 133 | 1032 | 42 | 5/62 | 5/62 | 24.57 | 2.39 | 61.6 | 1 | 0 |
| DA Cosker | 17 | 29 | 425.4 | 115 | 1183 | 42 | 5/39 | 9/133 | 28.16 | 2.77 | 60.8 | 3 | 0 |
| C Overton | 13 | 22 | 345.1 | 67 | 1198 | 42 | 5/63 | 7/150 | 28.52 | 3.47 | 49.3 | 1 | 0 |
| NL Buck | 9 | 17 | 327.1 | 54 | 1290 | 42 | 5/76 | 7/140 | 30.71 | 3.94 | 46.7 | 3 | 0 |
| CE Shreck | 15 | 26 | 560.0 | 135 | 1759 | 42 | 3/44 | 4/102 | 41.88 | 3.14 | 80.0 | 0 | 0 |
| SC Meaker | 9 | 16 | 293.4 | 42 | 1072 | 41 | 7/90 | 11/196 | 26.14 | 3.65 | 42.9 | 2 | 1 |
| LJ Fletcher | 12 | 22 | 358.1 | 83 | 1103 | 41 | 4/76 | 6/120 | 26.90 | 3.07 | 52.4 | 0 | 0 |
| MT Coles | 15 | 23 | 353.3 | 80 | 1165 | 41 | 4/84 | 7/175 | 28.41 | 3.29 | 51.7 | 0 | 0 |
| GG Wagg | 12 | 21 | 367.4 | 77 | 1258 | 41 | 6/29 | 8/172 | 30.68 | 3.42 | 53.8 | 1 | 0 |
| HF Gurney | 11 | 21 | 353.3 | 65 | 1277 | 41 | 4/22 | 6/71 | 31.14 | 3.61 | 51.7 | 0 | 0 |
| WRS Gidman | 14 | 21 | 374.3 | 103 | 968 | 40 | 6/50 | 9/84 | 24.20 | 2.58 | 56.1 | 2 | 0 |
| CJ Jordan | 10 | 19 | 347.0 | 74 | 1164 | 40 | 5/76 | 7/50 | 29.10 | 3.35 | 52.0 | 1 | 0 |
| DD Masters | 10 | 19 | 299.3 | 94 | 746 | 39 | 6/46 | 7/83 | 19.12 | 2.49 | 46.0 | 2 | 0 |
| GJ Batty | 12 | 16 | 400.3 | 113 | 915 | 39 | 8/68 | 8/68 | 23.46 | 2.28 | 61.6 | 1 | 0 |
| SA Patterson | 16 | 29 | 423.4 | 139 | 1041 | 39 | 4/54 | 5/69 | 26.69 | 2.45 | 65.1 | 0 | 0 |
| G Chapple | 15 | 24 | 500.4 | 99 | 1415 | 39 | 5/51 | 7/132 | 36.28 | 2.82 | 77.0 | 1 | 0 |

OLD SPECKLED HEN
SAMURAI
ROYAL LONDON

## FIRST-CLASS WICKETKEEPING *Minimum of 30 dismissals*

| Name | Mat | Inns | Dis | Ct | St | Max Dis Mat | Dis/Inn |
|---|---|---|---|---|---|---|---|
| MA Wallace | 17 | 32 | 71 | 68 | 3 | 5 (5ct 0st) | 2.218 |
| TR Ambrose | 16 | 28 | 63 | 58 | 5 | 6 (6ct 0st) | 2.250 |
| JS Foster | 17 | 31 | 60 | 57 | 3 | 6 (6ct 0st) | 1.935 |
| SW Billings | 17 | 30 | 59 | 53 | 6 | 6 (6ct 0st) | 1.966 |
| CMW Read | 17 | 31 | 58 | 57 | 1 | 4 (4ct 0st) | 1.870 |
| BC Brown | 16 | 27 | 57 | 53 | 4 | 6 (6ct 0st) | 2.111 |
| P Mustard | 14 | 22 | 47 | 46 | 1 | 5 (5ct 0st) | 2.136 |
| NJ O'Brien | 15 | 27 | 47 | 43 | 4 | 4 (4ct 0st) | 1.740 |
| JM Bairstow | 14 | 26 | 45 | 41 | 4 | 6 (6ct 0st) | 1.730 |
| C Kieswetter | 14 | 27 | 43 | 39 | 4 | 4 (4ct 0st) | 1.592 |
| JC Buttler | 13 | 25 | 39 | 39 | 0 | 4 (4ct 0st) | 1.560 |
| JA Simpson | 15 | 25 | 39 | 36 | 3 | 4 (4ct 0st) | 1.560 |
| GC Wilson | 17 | 21 | 35 | 33 | 2 | 4 (4ct 0st) | 1.666 |
| OB Cox | 16 | 30 | 35 | 32 | 3 | 4 (4ct 0st) | 1.166 |
| GD Cross | 11 | 20 | 34 | 30 | 4 | 5 (3ct 2st) | 1.700 |
| MJ Prior | 7 | 10 | 30 | 30 | 0 | 4 (4ct 0st) | 3.000 |

# FIRST-CLASS FIELDING *Minimum of 17 catches*

| Name | Mat | Inns | Ct | Max | Ct/Inn |
|---|---|---|---|---|---|
| A Lyth | 17 | 33 | 36 | 4 | 1.090 |
| SG Borthwick | 16 | 26 | 30 | 3 | 1.153 |
| DKH Mitchell | 16 | 30 | 28 | 3 | 0.933 |
| MH Wessels | 17 | 31 | 24 | 3 | 0.774 |
| JM Vince | 16 | 26 | 22 | 3 | 0.846 |
| ME Trescothick | 17 | 32 | 22 | 2 | 0.687 |
| DJ Malan | 15 | 25 | 21 | 2 | 0.840 |
| WL Madsen | 17 | 31 | 21 | 3 | 0.677 |
| T Westley | 17 | 31 | 21 | 3 | 0.677 |
| JC Hildreth | 16 | 30 | 19 | 2 | 0.633 |
| SR Patel | 17 | 31 | 19 | 2 | 0.612 |
| JJ Roy | 18 | 32 | 19 | 3 | 0.593 |
| CJ Jordan | 10 | 19 | 18 | 3 | 0.947 |
| IR Bell | 11 | 21 | 18 | 3 | 0.857 |
| AN Cook | 11 | 21 | 18 | 3 | 0.857 |
| R Clarke | 13 | 22 | 18 | 3 | 0.818 |
| WTS Porterfield | 14 | 24 | 18 | 3 | 0.750 |
| RJ Burns | 18 | 30 | 18 | 2 | 0.600 |
| V Chopra | 17 | 29 | 17 | 4 | 0.586 |
| SD Robson | 18 | 31 | 17 | 3 | 0.548 |

# MVP TOP 100

| # | Name | County | Batting | Bowling | Field | Capt. | Wins | Pld | Pts | Average |
|---|---|---|---|---|---|---|---|---|---|---|
| 1 | Patel, Jeetan | Warks | 104.09 | 478.32 | 18 | 0 | 24.0 | 41 | 624 | 15.23 |
| 2 | Stevens, Darren | Kent | 228.52 | 352.60 | 24 | 0 | 15.0 | 39 | 620 | 15.91 |
| 3 | Allenby, Jim | Glamorgan | 294.84 | 245.12 | 22 | 6 | 12.0 | 37 | 580 | 15.67 |
| 4 | Patel, Samit | Notts | 306.05 | 179.47 | 22 | 0 | 20.0 | 38 | 528 | 13.88 |
| 5 | Trego, Peter | Somerset | 247.32 | 246.65 | 11 | 0 | 13.0 | 36 | 518 | 14.39 |
| 6 | Smith, Tom | Lancs | 202.24 | 272.35 | 19 | 0 | 15.0 | 30 | 509 | 16.95 |
| 7 | Rashid, Adil | Yorks | 130.95 | 298.03 | 14 | 0 | 19.0 | 34 | 462 | 13.59 |
| 8 | Ryder, Jesse | Essex | 243.44 | 185.97 | 12 | 0 | 20.0 | 33 | 462 | 13.99 |
| 9 | Collingwood, Paul | Durham | 245.78 | 173.87 | 15 | 5 | 16.0 | 38 | 456 | 11.99 |
| 10 | Chopra, Varun | Warks | 370.26 | 0.00 | 34 | 22 | 24.0 | 40 | 450 | 11.26 |
| 11 | Mitchell, Daryl | Worcs | 328.43 | 36.29 | 34 | 18 | 18.0 | 37 | 435 | 11.76 |
| 12 | Wright, Luke | Sussex | 395.42 | 10.48 | 13 | 0 | 13.0 | 32 | 432 | 13.50 |
| 13 | Lyth, Adam | Yorks | 333.14 | 27.63 | 51 | 0 | 20.0 | 35 | 432 | 12.34 |
| 14 | Joyce, Ed | Sussex | 393.41 | 0.00 | 16 | 11 | 11.0 | 29 | 431 | 14.88 |
| 15 | Hogan, Michael | Glamorgan | 27.71 | 372.10 | 15 | 0 | 11.0 | 33 | 425 | 12.89 |
| 16 | Gidman, Will | Gloucs | 174.05 | 233.20 | 5 | 0 | 8.0 | 26 | 420 | 16.16 |
| 17 | Malan, Dawid | Middx | 336.38 | 38.11 | 35 | 0 | 9.0 | 37 | 418 | 11.31 |
| 18 | Rushworth, Chris | Durham | 37.41 | 362.26 | 2 | 0 | 13.0 | 33 | 415 | 12.57 |
| 19 | Thomas, Alfonso | Somerset | 45.33 | 343.20 | 8 | 2 | 13.0 | 34 | 412 | 12.10 |
| 20 | Vince, James | Hants | 349.45 | 7.48 | 27 | 9 | 18.0 | 36 | 411 | 11.40 |
| 21 | Footitt, Mark | Derbyshire | 23.27 | 363.33 | 5 | 0 | 10.0 | 29 | 402 | 13.86 |
| 22 | Hastings, John | Durham | 109.52 | 272.64 | 6 | 0 | 13.0 | 26 | 401 | 15.43 |
| 23 | Wessels, Riki | Notts | 340.26 | -1.20 | 39 | 0 | 20.0 | 38 | 398 | 10.48 |
| 24 | Rudolph, Jacques | Glamorgan | 365.86 | 4.58 | 15 | 0 | 12.0 | 37 | 398 | 10.75 |
| 25 | Hales, Alex | Notts | 353.83 | -0.20 | 24 | 0 | 19.0 | 30 | 396 | 13.21 |
| 26 | Bresnan, Tim | Yorks | 95.26 | 261.83 | 17 | 0 | 16.0 | 29 | 390 | 13.45 |
| 27 | Clarke, Rikki | Warks | 139.14 | 202.90 | 28 | 0 | 19.0 | 34 | 389 | 11.44 |
| 28 | Westley, Tom | Essex | 303.22 | 47.06 | 16 | 0 | 21.0 | 38 | 387 | 10.19 |
| 29 | Brooks, Jack | Yorks | 21.18 | 341.45 | 9 | 0 | 15.0 | 27 | 387 | 14.32 |
| 30 | Roy, Jason | Surrey | 334.82 | 15.61 | 19 | 0 | 15.0 | 33 | 385 | 11.66 |
| 31 | Shantry, Jack | Worcs | 69.07 | 284.49 | 12 | 0 | 17.0 | 35 | 382 | 10.92 |
| 32 | Smith, Will | Hants | 224.64 | 123.81 | 15 | 0 | 18.0 | 39 | 381 | 9.77 |
| 33 | Gregory, Lewis | Somerset | 103.80 | 257.68 | 12 | 0 | 7.0 | 22 | 380 | 17.29 |
| 34 | Croft, Steven | Lancs | 211.79 | 121.62 | 30 | 0 | 16.0 | 34 | 379 | 11.16 |
| 35 | Magoffin, Steve | Sussex | 34.12 | 336.53 | 1 | 0 | 7.0 | 18 | 379 | 21.04 |
| 36 | Adams, Jimmy | Hants | 328.63 | 0.00 | 17 | 9 | 18.0 | 40 | 373 | 9.33 |
| 37 | Borthwick, Scott | Durham | 228.11 | 82.74 | 44 | 0 | 15.0 | 36 | 370 | 10.27 |
| 38 | Madsen, Wayne | Derbyshire | 321.10 | -0.90 | 24 | 11 | 11.0 | 37 | 366 | 9.89 |
| 39 | Stokes, Ben | Durham | 158.98 | 183.59 | 12 | 0 | 11.0 | 21 | 366 | 17.41 |
| 40 | Claydon, Mitchell | Kent | 38.98 | 297.38 | 6 | 0 | 13.0 | 36 | 355 | 9.86 |
| 41 | Roland-Jones, Toby | Middx | 99.38 | 244.32 | 6 | 0 | 4.0 | 25 | 354 | 14.15 |
| 42 | Taylor, James | Notts | 300.55 | 0.00 | 18 | 14 | 19.0 | 35 | 352 | 10.04 |
| 43 | Stoneman, Mark | Durham | 306.19 | -1.36 | 14 | 12 | 17.0 | 40 | 348 | 8.70 |
| 44 | Coles, Matt | Hants | 81.54 | 238.75 | 10 | 0 | 17.0 | 38 | 347 | 9.13 |
| 45 | Durston, Wes | Derbyshire | 215.15 | 101.14 | 16 | 0 | 10.0 | 29 | 342 | 11.80 |
| 46 | Ambrose, Tim | Warks | 169.82 | 0.00 | 150 | 0 | 22.0 | 37 | 342 | 9.24 |
| 47 | Porterfield, William | Warks | 281.71 | 0.00 | 36 | 0 | 23.0 | 39 | 341 | 8.74 |
| 48 | Middlebrook, James | Northants | 148.13 | 170.14 | 18 | 0 | 3.0 | 29 | 339 | 11.70 |
| 49 | Murtagh, Tim | Middx | 41.06 | 287.97 | 4 | 0 | 6.0 | 20 | 339 | 16.95 |
| 50 | Lees, Alex | Yorks | 302.82 | 0.00 | 16 | 0 | 19.0 | 34 | 338 | 9.94 |

| # | Name | County | Batting | Bowling | Field | Capt. | Wins | Pld | Pts | Average |
|---|---|---|---|---|---|---|---|---|---|---|
| 51 | Wagg, Graham | Glamorgan | 96.42 | 220.68 | 10 | 0 | 10.0 | 28 | 337 | 12.05 |
| 52 | Rogers, Chris | Middx | 311.00 | -0.20 | 14 | 4 | 7.0 | 23 | 336 | 14.60 |
| 53 | Howell, Benny | Gloucs | 123.92 | 184.26 | 14 | 0 | 13.0 | 33 | 335 | 10.16 |
| 54 | Prince, Ashwell | Lancs | 300.88 | 0.00 | 19 | 0 | 12.0 | 30 | 332 | 11.06 |
| 55 | Ajmal, Saeed | Worcs | 23.68 | 291.35 | 5 | 0 | 11.0 | 19 | 331 | 17.42 |
| 56 | Billings, Sam | Kent | 215.14 | -1.92 | 99 | 0 | 15.0 | 39 | 327 | 8.39 |
| 57 | Bairstow, Jonny | Yorks | 210.92 | -0.10 | 96 | 0 | 15.0 | 28 | 322 | 11.49 |
| 58 | Fletcher, Luke | Notts | 44.20 | 254.87 | 6 | 0 | 15.0 | 29 | 320 | 11.04 |
| 59 | Barker, Keith | Warks | 66.90 | 233.94 | 8 | 0 | 9.0 | 18 | 318 | 17.66 |
| 60 | Horton, Paul | Lancs | 256.27 | 0.00 | 29 | 14 | 17.0 | 38 | 316 | 8.32 |
| 61 | Northeast, Sam | Kent | 287.40 | -0.32 | 11 | 3 | 14.0 | 37 | 315 | 8.51 |
| 62 | Cosker, Dean | Glamorgan | 37.19 | 246.91 | 17 | 0 | 13.0 | 38 | 314 | 8.26 |
| 63 | Azharullah, Mohammad | Northants | 24.34 | 277.74 | 5 | 0 | 6.0 | 32 | 313 | 9.78 |
| 64 | Ansari, Zafar | Surrey | 150.36 | 131.68 | 16 | 0 | 15.0 | 35 | 313 | 8.94 |
| 65 | Bopara, Ravi | Essex | 221.52 | 63.04 | 8 | 0 | 19.0 | 30 | 312 | 10.40 |
| 66 | Willey, David | Northants | 141.65 | 151.29 | 12 | 0 | 5.0 | 24 | 310 | 12.91 |
| 67 | Trescothick, Marcus | Somerset | 254.85 | 0.00 | 35 | 9 | 10.0 | 33 | 309 | 9.36 |
| 68 | Smith, Greg | Leics | 281.36 | 0.00 | 20 | 0 | 7.0 | 36 | 309 | 8.57 |
| 69 | Sidebottom, Ryan | Yorks | 14.80 | 279.16 | 4 | 0 | 9.0 | 20 | 307 | 15.35 |
| 70 | Foster, James | Essex | 173.40 | 0.00 | 102 | 7 | 22.0 | 39 | 305 | 7.82 |
| 71 | Hall, Andrew | Northants | 115.57 | 170.11 | 16 | 0 | 0.0 | 20 | 302 | 15.08 |
| 72 | Read, Chris | Notts | 174.47 | 0.00 | 101 | 6 | 20.0 | 38 | 301 | 7.93 |
| 73 | Morgan, Eoin | Middx | 272.37 | -0.84 | 14 | 5 | 8.0 | 30 | 299 | 9.95 |
| 74 | Finn, Steven | Middx | 34.92 | 250.69 | 7 | 0 | 4.0 | 18 | 297 | 16.48 |
| 75 | Nash, Chris | Sussex | 229.05 | 35.43 | 13 | 4 | 12.0 | 32 | 293 | 9.17 |
| 76 | Wilson, Gary | Surrey | 177.38 | 0.00 | 86 | 13 | 15.0 | 38 | 291 | 7.66 |
| 77 | O'Brien, Niall | Leics | 197.57 | 0.00 | 85 | 0 | 6.0 | 34 | 289 | 8.50 |
| 78 | Crook, Steven | Northants | 131.58 | 141.02 | 11 | 0 | 5.0 | 23 | 289 | 12.55 |
| 79 | Mustard, Phil | Durham | 176.31 | 0.00 | 97 | 0 | 15.0 | 37 | 288 | 7.79 |
| 80 | Gidman, Alex | Gloucs | 253.53 | 0.00 | 19 | 4 | 10.0 | 34 | 287 | 8.43 |
| 81 | Palladino, Tony | Derbyshire | 54.93 | 214.82 | 6 | 0 | 10.0 | 29 | 286 | 9.86 |
| 82 | Mullaney, Steven | Notts | 126.92 | 114.29 | 25 | 0 | 18.0 | 33 | 284 | 8.61 |
| 83 | Carberry, Michael | Hants | 263.28 | -0.92 | 7 | 0 | 13.0 | 32 | 282 | 8.82 |
| 84 | Cobb, Josh | Leics | 198.03 | 56.83 | 17 | 4 | 4.0 | 30 | 280 | 9.34 |
| 85 | Ervine, Sean | Hants | 185.08 | 60.22 | 15 | 0 | 18.0 | 39 | 279 | 7.14 |
| 86 | Kieswetter, Craig | Somerset | 198.80 | 0.00 | 69 | 0 | 9.0 | 23 | 277 | 12.03 |
| 87 | Shreck, Charlie | Leics | 47.50 | 213.88 | 7 | 0 | 5.0 | 28 | 274 | 9.77 |
| 88 | Masters, David | Essex | 11.16 | 244.79 | 4 | 0 | 14.0 | 24 | 274 | 11.40 |
| 89 | Overton, Craig | Somerset | 74.22 | 180.26 | 11 | 0 | 8.0 | 26 | 273 | 10.52 |
| 90 | Leach, Joseph | Worcs | 96.63 | 162.23 | 5 | 0 | 10.0 | 23 | 273 | 11.89 |
| 91 | Hildreth, James | Somerset | 225.00 | 3.33 | 29 | 2 | 13.0 | 36 | 272 | 7.56 |
| 92 | Batty, Gareth | Surrey | 24.71 | 226.10 | 9 | 0 | 12.0 | 29 | 272 | 9.37 |
| 93 | Simpson, John | Middx | 148.93 | 0.00 | 109 | 0 | 9.0 | 37 | 267 | 7.21 |
| 94 | Bollinger, Dougie | Kent | 15.22 | 234.43 | 7 | 0 | 10.0 | 24 | 267 | 11.12 |
| 95 | Woakes, Chris | Warks | 57.69 | 195.83 | 5 | 0 | 8.0 | 16 | 267 | 16.66 |
| 96 | Gurney, Harry | Notts | 7.38 | 234.18 | 7 | 0 | 17.0 | 26 | 266 | 10.21 |
| 97 | Napier, Graham | Essex | 33.26 | 207.86 | 6 | 0 | 16.0 | 27 | 263 | 9.75 |
| 98 | Patterson, Steve | Yorks | 23.82 | 220.39 | 1 | 0 | 13.0 | 23 | 258 | 11.23 |
| 99 | Wallace, Mark | Glamorgan | 131.98 | 0.00 | 106 | 7 | 13.0 | 38 | 258 | 6.78 |
| 100 | Chapple, Glen | Lancs | 82.25 | 163.83 | 5 | 3 | 3.0 | 15 | 257 | 17.14 |

Notes

# NOTES

# NOTES

# NOTES

# NOTES

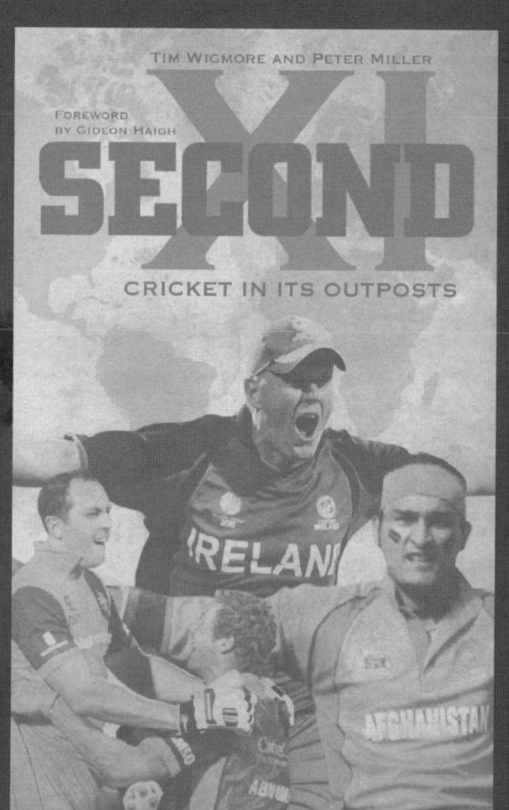


amazon.co

W
Waterstones

WHSmit

Available in paperb
from all good stoc
priced £12.99

**_The Second XI_ tells the captivating tale of cricket's journey in ten nations beyond the Test world: a vibrant game fighting for more recognition.**

With a foreword from Gideon Haigh, *The Second XI* shows how cricket resonates far beyond sport, touching on war, sectarianism and women's rights. This book asks what it would take for America and China to embrace the game. It explains how Kenya reached the World Cup semi-finals and what happened next; why an Emirati faced Allan Donald armed only with a sunhat; and how cricket in the Netherlands almost collapsed after two bad days.

**Tim Wigmore and Peter Miller**
**Foreword by Gideon Haigh**

See the rest of the Pitch Publishing sports titles at **www.pitchpublishing.co.uk**